Statue of Liberty—Ellis Island Centennial Series

Books in the Statue of Liberty—Ellis Island Centennial Series

The Immigrant World of Ybor City: Italians and Their Latin Neighbors
in Tampa, 1885–1985
Gary R. Mormino and George E. Pozzetta

The Butte Irish: Class and Ethnicity in an American Mining Town,
1875–1925
David M. Emmons

THE BUTTE IRISH

THE BUTTE IRISH

Class and Ethnicity in an American Mining Town

1875–1925

David M. Emmons

UNIVERSITY OF ILLINOIS PRESS
Urbana and Chicago

Publication of this work was made possible in part by a grant
from the Statue of Liberty—Ellis Island Foundation.

First paperback edition, 1990

Library of Congress Cataloging-in-Publication Data
Emmons, David M.
The Butte Irish : class and ethnicity in an American mining town,
1875–1925 / David M. Emmons.
p.   cm.—(Statue of Liberty—Ellis Island Centennial Series)
Bibliography: p.
Includes index.
ISBN 0-252-06155-1 (paper: alk. paper)
ISBN 978-0-252-06155-4 (paper: alk. paper)
1. Irish Americans—Montana—Butte—History.
2. Ethnicity—Montana—Butte.
3. Butte (Mont.)—History.
4. Butte (Mont.)—History.
I. Title II. Series
F739.B8E48 1989   88-23231
978.6'68—dc 19   CIP

To all the children

John Winnie, Jr. and Ann Elizabeth,
Mari Kathleen, and Michael Joseph Emmons

Contents

Preface

This book began in 1982 when Catherine Dowling, a graduate student from Dublin, burst into my office with the news that she had found some Clan-na-Gael records at the World Museum of Mining in Butte. She used a part of those records to prepare her M.A. thesis. Later that year Michael Garrity uncovered some more "Irish stuff" at the museum, incorporating it into his senior honors paper.

By then my own interest in this growing body of materials was such that a personal inspection seemed in order. I found records everywhere—in boxes, on shelves, as "studio props" in some of the museum's permanent displays; in all over seventy bound volumes and many hundreds of pages of loose material. Every major Irish-American organization in Butte was represented: the Robert Emmet Literary Association, the Butte camp of the revolutionary Clan-na-Gael; the three divisions of the Ancient Order of Hibernians; the Irish Volunteers; the Friends of Irish Freedom; and the American Association for the Recognition of the Irish Republic. Among the bound volumes were membership and financial records, reports and proceedings, day books and minute books. The loose material ranged from correspondence to canceled checks.

In an act of extraordinary generosity, Al Hooper and the other directors of the World Museum of Mining let me bring this material to the University of Montana for microfilming. Two full carloads and twelve reels later the original records were returned to Butte and the Irish Collection was in place. It may be the largest and richest collection of primary materials on an Irish-American community to be found anywhere.

And it told a remarkable story. Professor Charles Tilly has written that social history is the account of how ordinary people "live the big changes." It represents an effort "to recapture an ethos, an outlook, a rhythm of everyday life." It provides "sketches of an age, of a city, of a social class."* For Tilly the big changes were the development of capitalism and the growth of national states. My focus was necessarily narrower, but the big changes were big enough: the movement from one part of the world to another and different part; the consolidation of capital; and the social and ethnic differences that divided an otherwise aggressive and self-conscious working class.

More specifically, the story of Butte's Irish provided a revealing look at such significant issues as class formation and immigrant assimilation (and the relationship between the two); the sources and uses of social power; community building; immigrant selectivity; intergenerational differences within ethnic working-class communities; and the formation of a set of cultural values at variance with those of an acquisitive and individualistic capitalism. This is the stuff of social history. But more conventional historical themes also emerged: Irish-American nationalism; the industrialization process in the American West; and worker protest.

Community studies, whether social or narrative, or—as I think of this one—a combination of both, are based on the assumption that whether the community was typical or unique the specific informs our understanding of the general. In some respects, Butte's Irish world was similar to those of other immigrant workers in industrializing America; in other respects, it was strikingly dissimilar. In either role, it offers instructive lessons.

One final remark: I use the phrase "a fair living" throughout this study to make a number of important and related points. Fair can mean adequate, as in an adequate wage. It can also mean decent or just, or most fundamentally, the acknowledgment of the dignity of both work and worker. Living sends similarly mixed but related messages. It has an economic sense—literally making a living. But it carries as well a social connotation—it can mean life, the qualitative standards of living. A fair living, in other words, is both found and made; you form it and it forms you.

I have incurred a number of debts in the preparation of this book. Professor Kerby Miller of the University of Missouri loaned me important source material, then read and critiqued the entire manuscript. His suggestions saved me from a number of errors and strengthened

*Charles Tilly, "Retrieving European Lives," in *Reliving the Past: The Worlds of Social History*, ed. Olivier Zunz (Chapel Hill: University of North Carolina Press, 1985), pp. 11, 13.

the book considerably. Professor Linda Frey, my friend and colleague at the University of Montana, also read the entire manuscript and offered invaluable criticism and support. Chapters 5 and 7 are better for the detailed readings given them by Professors Ralph Mann of the University of Colorado and Richard Drake of the University of Montana.

My debt to Al Hooper and the World Museum of Mining has been noted. Thanks are also due to Professor H. D. Hampton and the Hammond Committee at the University of Montana for the grants necessary to film the Irish Collection and to travel to other libraries, and to the University of Montana for the sabbatical that permitted me to begin my research. Three articles resulted from that research; portions of them—much revised—appear in various chapters of this book and are reprinted with permission: "Immigrant Workers and Industrial Hazards: The Irish Miners of Butte, 1880–1919," *Journal of American Ethnic History*, 5 (Fall, 1985), 41–64; "The Orange and the Green in Montana: A Reconsideration of the Clark-Daly Feud," *Arizona and the West*, 28 (Autumn, 1986), 225–45; and "An Aristocracy of Labor: The Irish Miners of Butte, 1878–1914," *Labor History*, 28 (Summer, 1987), 275–306.

Teresa Cox took my hundreds of pages of manuscript census data and made sense of them with an SPSSx program, the workings of which remain mysterious—and wondrous—to me. Susan Driscoll Matule prepared the final manuscript copy. True to her Butte Irish background, she was uncommonly generous with her time, her labor, and her skills. Richard Wentworth of the University of Illinois Press liked the project from the beginning; the Board of Editors of the Statue of Liberty/Ellis Island Series, chaired by Professor Roger Daniels of the University of Cincinnati, liked it at the end. I am grateful for the encouragement of both.

Thanks, too, to my handball partners for reasons all handball players—and no one else—will understand; to Don Leary and Bill Farr for their photographs and good conversation; to Father Sarsfield O'Sullivan for sharing with me his time and his special knowledge of and feelings for Butte and its Irish; and to Dave Walter, Dale Johnson, Mary Murphy, Sara McClernan, and Ed Nolan—archivists and friends who helped in a variety of ways.

Finally, I offer special thanks to my wife Caroline. This project was like an uninvited, often ill-behaved house guest that came for the weekend and stayed five years. She not only tolerated this boorish intruder, she made it feel welcome and then listened patiently and with understanding as I jabbered on about its hidden—for many months, deeply hidden—virtues.

Introduction: Out of Ireland

No study of the Irish in the United States can begin without some reference to the famine years of 1845–49. This is more than mere courtesy—it always is when the reference is to a time when nearly a million people died of starvation and disease. But the emigration out of Ireland during and immediately after the Great Hunger needs also to be noted. It established standards against which the later Irish and even non-Irish immigration would be judged. In terms of numbers, percentages of whole populations, selectivity by class, and preparation for American conditions, the immigration of the Famine and post-Famine years is the norm. And so let it be noted that in 1847, two years after the potato blight destroyed the crop on which the Irish poor relied, almost 106,000 Irish immigrated to the United States. In the next seven years, from 1848 to 1854, 1.1 million more left Ireland and joined them.[1]

In addition to the numbers, there was the fact that these Famine immigrants were 40 percent of the whole American immigration for those years. They came to a nation unprepared for massive infusions of people, particularly people poor beyond the normal powers of description and embracing a religion and a culture different from what the host society knew and clearly preferred. Emigrant pushes are always selective, and the Famine selected those Irish least equipped to handle the demands of the industrializing American cities they entered. They were typically rural, Catholic, Irish-speaking, unskilled, tied to family and community, and impoverished. To this must be added the fact that the Famine immigrants had little in the way of advance Irish presence, few established Irish communities to contain and comfort them. These Irish-Americans had to construct a world on hostile ground and with scant resources.[2]

Historians of the Irish in America have concentrated on this first great wave of Irish immigration, for understandable reasons. The Famine struck Ireland with cataclysmic effect. There is tragedy in every chapter of Ireland's past, but the years from 1845 to 1849 serve as a kind of historical ideogram, the graphic symbol of a suffering people. No other group experienced so awful an emigrant push. The Irish Famine was unique and there is drama and historical significance in the study of it. It involved huge numbers of people and it profoundly affected both Ireland and the United States.[3]

The Famine, however, was not only a discrete historical event; it was part of an ongoing historical process. Had the "Irish Problem" been something as simple as potato blights and an imbalance in some abstract man-land ratio, the emigrants and those who died would have served as demographic correctives, mechanical adjustments preventing any recurrence. But the problems were not that simple. So let it also be noted that in 1883, a year marked by no apocalyptic event, 81,000 Irish left for America; this is a greater percentage of the Irish population than immigrated in 1846. In 1905, almost 53,000 made their way to the United States. In all, between 1856 and 1921, long after most of the physical effects of the Great Famine had faded, more than 3.7 million Irish men, women, and children left Ireland for what they hoped would be less-unforgiving lands. Of that total, just under 3.1 million came to the United States. By the early 1900s there was a sense in Ireland that the emigration would never end, that the Irish would wander forever.[4]

This post-Famine immigration seems distinctly different from that of the Famine, if for no other reason than that starving times cannot explain it. Too much, however, should not be made of discontinuities. In the first place, the Famine was a symptom, not the cause of Ireland's miseries; to be sure, it accentuated those miseries, making obvious even to the most obtuse that Ireland was a sick society, unable to provide a decent living for a high percentage of its people. Thus, the Famine increased dramatically the size of the Irish exodus. But there would have been a sizeable emigration in the late 1840s without it; there remained a sizeable emigration after the 1840s despite it. In this connection it is worth noting that the emigrations of 1842, 1846, 1885, and 1905 were almost identical—and identically large. The forces producing those totals were different—though often the differences were of degree not of kind—but they were still selective of the same regions and of similar classes.[5]

In another sense, the Irish emigration of 1856-1921 was part of a general as well as a continuing Irish phenomenon; it was one of the largest and most significant of the many human migrations of the late nineteenth and early twentieth centuries. Like those others, the Irish emigration was both cause and consequence of the European and American process of industrialization and, later, the interdependent Atlantic economy that developed out of it. Ireland's role in that process was subordinate if not actually subservient; other nations supplied credit or resources or new technologies. Ireland, in the historian Kerby Miller's phrase, was basically "a fountain of emigrants." Its principal responsibility was to provide workers—men and women, most of them unskilled—who did the heavy work of industrializing societies.[6]

But even in this context there were pressures peculiar to Ireland, as well as those common to other European and Asian nations but felt with greater force in Ireland. Those 3.7 million emigrants were driven out—or at least encouraged to leave—by a variety of interrelated processes. Miller discusses six of them: the continuing deindustrialization of southern Ireland resulting from the dumping of American and English goods on the Irish market (the growth in the production of those goods created the demand for Irish workers); the mechanization and contraction of northern Ireland's textile industry; the commercialization of Irish agriculture, accompanied by falling prices and rising debts; the ravaging effect of the above three developments on the west of Ireland, the most economically vulnerable part of the island; new marriage and inheritance patterns that "consigned most farmers' children to emigrant ships"; and, most important, the switch from tillage to pasturage and the increasing use of machines rather than men on Ireland's farms. In sum, there were no jobs, no inheritances, no dowries, no access to the land, no promise—or even faint hope—of a secure future.[7]

These were powerful forces, less dramatic than potato blight and starvation but as irresistible and as selective in their effects. They were also either under way before the Famine or nascent in one form or another with or without the Famine. They neither slowed the emigration nor narrowed its geographical and social base. America continued to receive the least skilled of rural Ireland's surplus population and it continued to receive them in substantial numbers. Those of the second, post-Famine wave of immigration were more politicized than the first— more aware of their rights both as Irish and as workers—and they were surely more devout in their Catholicism. The later emigrants were usually less reluctant to leave Ireland, though no less homesick having left it. But these were relatively minor differences. More significant were the continuities. The values of the later immigrants reflected cultural traditions that had barely changed in centuries. The Irish were still a social people, garrulous and communal. They needed their society; they took their identities from it. The last to leave, moreover, were no less poor than the first, no less frightened by the uncertainties of industrial worlds, and, until about 1905, only marginally better prepared to enter them. The description applied to the first Irish immigrants applied to all of them; they only know how to dig.[8]

The differences at the other end of their emigration were as minor. Obviously, the later the emigration, the more earlier-arriving Irish were in place to provide a measure of cultural continuity. Too much should not be made of this difference either. Later Irish immigrants did not find a socially homogenous Irish-American world, nor did they always find themselves clasped immediately to the bosom of ethnic solidarity. A great deal of social differentiation had taken place in Irish-America, but that did not mean that the last Irish to arrive necessarily benefited from the successes of the first. Irish immigrants continued to do the heavy work. This was true in 1850; it was true in 1910. In Miller's phrase, at the turn of the century they were "still rooted firmly in proletarian conditions."[9]

Social differentiation, of course, was a part of the history of every immigrant group, but only the Irish immigration was so continuous an affair. It ran almost without interruption for eighty years and it must have seemed to the established Irish, of whatever class, that there was always another boatload of impoverished immigrants pulling into port. The newcomers were offered jobs; indeed, they often immigrated upon the promise of one. But economic power, as in Ireland, resided where it always had—with the economically secure—and power remained a more important determinant of social position than ethnic affinity and neighborliness.

The fact that many Irish-Americans, of whatever generation, acted the role of political exile affected this social reality only slightly. Exiles thought of themselves as driven from Ireland by English treachery as surely as by economic misfortune; indeed, the misfortune was a consequence of the treachery. There was less a sense of exile with the later-arriving Irish, many of whom evinced an unseemly eagerness to be rid of Ireland, regardless of what or who was responsible for Ireland's economic miseries. And at all times and for all Irish, the potency of the exile image was as much a function of their ability to accommodate to American industrial society as of their Irish past, or even their memories of that past. The poorer Irish internalized the exile motif more than the successful, though settled and solvent immigrants may have been more vocal in their expression of it. Exile, however, was a part of the self-image of all classes. The resulting Anglophobia, as central to the Irish community as the Catholic Church, served to mend some—but never all—of the social and economic differences between them.[10]

More obvious, then, than any discontinuities in the Irish emigrant experience is that economics was always the pull and always the push, and that the later-arriving Irish, though aided by the presence of those who had come before them, still faced a difficult adjustment. But the hard truth was that at no time between 1845 and 1921 could Ireland provide the Irish with steady work and the measure of security that steady work gave. Only the industrializing nations of the world, particularly the United States, could provide even a chance at that kind of security. How good a chance depended not on ethnic connections and preferment—that could be counted on only to supply the first job— but on how well the Irish worker took care of that job and on the whimsy of the industrial cycle. But America did offer a chance to work, if not the promise of steady work. That was a great deal more than Ireland could offer. Thus, by the middle of the nineteenth century the possibility of emigration to the United States had become part of the social and economic calculus involved in the coming of age in Ireland. It affected every decision from when, whether, and whom to marry to schooling, careers, and clerical vocations.[11]

And so Ireland assumed its role in the industrialization of America. The Irish had not sought the part; sending "excess" sons and daughters to work in other peoples' factories was at best dispiriting. But, though unsought, it was a vital role. Economically superfluous in Ireland, the emigrants were economically indispensible in Boston or Wilkes-Barre, Chicago or San Francisco. And they knew it. The Irish were a literate people with a well-developed communications and transportation system. American agents took advantage of both, promising reduced fares on steamships and railroads, good jobs and housing at immigrant destinations. These promises were too self-serving to be taken seriously, but they did indicate where the jobs could be found and they cannot have been entirely discounted.[12]

There were, however, other and far more important sources of information. The Irish already in America were steady correspondents. They belonged to their families as their families, to a certain extent, belonged to Ireland. Immigrant letters kept both associations intact. The letters were seldom effusive or even positive; they spoke of jobs, but they spoke more eloquently of how dangerous many of those jobs were and how easily they could be lost. The result of injury or idleness was destitution and, according to one letter, "destitution in America made life unbearable." Anyone, another immigrant cautioned, who could make a "fair living at home are better stay theire."[13]

But for every warning—indeed, often accompanying the warning—there was a letter with remittance money in it. Some of the money financed a relative's emigration; some of it provided dowries or debt relief and thus prevented an emigration. The point was the same regardless of how the recipients used the money—it was a fair living the Irish sought. Should Ireland not be able to provide it, they would look in America, guided usually by family members who had emigrated before them. The new immigrants would then take their turn in this chain immigration, using part of their wages to provide others of their family with that same chance at security and dignity. Most of Ireland's poor made that living in one of America's industrial cities; they sustained the connection with family and Ireland by fixing themselves to the city's Irish community and fulfilling their responsibilities from that new social base.[14]

Unhappily for the Irish, the search for stable work and a decent living was seldom as easy as moving to Boston or New York. They encountered a hostile middle and upper class as well as an entrenched and, initially at least, anti-Irish working class. In addition, there *was* a whimsy to industrial cycles; economic instability shoved them around in this country as surely as it had in Ireland. The Irish had wandered to America; they would wander in it, a part of a floating proletariat. They developed in the process what the historian John Bodnar calls a close "familiarity with transiency," but in the case of the Irish familiarity literally bred contempt. In their migrancy they were a little like the other migrant workers who entered the United States in the late nineteenth and early twentieth centuries. But these other migrants, mostly southeastern Europeans, roamed America so that they might return to Europe. Their repatriation rates—up to 80 percent—indicate that their familiarity with transiency served well the interests of solvency, security, and the enjoyment of both at home. But Ireland was no more capable of absorbing the returning emigrant in 1910 than it had been in 1850; the Irish repatriation rate was nearer 10 percent.[15]

If the Irish were to feel at home it would have to be by bringing a measure of home with them and constructing from it American Irishtowns, ethnic communities that could serve as facsimiles or at least replicas of Irish society. At the heart of those Irishtowns were the ethnic/nationalist associations, which served a variety of functions. Like membership in the Catholic Church, with which some of them were affiliated, belonging to one of the Irish clubs was a badge of ethnicity; it identified one as a protector of Ireland—and of the Irish, wherever found. Members were both the avengers, however rhetorical and indirect, of ancient wrongs against Ireland and the Irish people as well as the guardians of their members' rights as Irishmen and workers.[16]

These associational functions sound more radical than they were. The language of Irish-American nationalism was threatening but there was little the Irish could do about liberating the homeland from three or four thousand miles away. Indeed, given the disagreements within Irish-America on the means and ends of that liberation there would have been little enough they could have done had they all gone home. The fact that those disagreements mirrored class distinctions—that they arose in part as expressions of the social differentiation within the Irish communities—made them as intractable and unyielding as the similar divisions in Ireland. It is possible, in fact, that the greater and more rapid differentiation in America made them more intractable than in Ireland. That point can be debated. What cannot is that U.S. policy toward Ireland's enemy (for which read England) and Ireland's friends (for which read any enemy of England) severely restricted the Irish-Americans' ability to work for radical solutions to the Irish Question—even had they wished to. The fact that American policy toward England moved between 1850 and 1920 from hostility to cordiality to open alliance destroyed what few options Irish-American nationalists had left.[17]

As for their defense of worker rights, these were avowedly ethnic associations, regardless of how overwhelmingly working-class their memberships. Working-class issues belonged properly to working-class (as opposed to ethnic) associations. The problem was that Irish laborers dominated the Irish associations and Irishmen often dominated the labor associations. It was never impossible to embrace the cause of both Ireland and worker but neither was it ever easy. The Irish clubs defended only Irish worker claims. Dependent as most Irish were on daily wages, that meant that the associations had to try to insure that the days worked were sufficient to satisfy the Irish hunger for economic stability. The Irish associations had to find their members work, if not locally then by referring them to other intact communities of workers; they had to do what they could to see that the work was safe and steady; and they had to take care of the victims when it proved to be neither. More often than not, finding the work involved direct appeals to those more powerful Irish who had the jobs to give. This required interclass cooperation.[18]

Keeping the work was even trickier. That required a control of the work force in the interests of ethnic job preference, in other words, the exclusion—where possible—of non-Irish rivals for the jobs necessary to sustain the Irish associations and the Irish community of which they were part. Even the unions divided their attention; holding off management with one hand, protecting the rights and privileges of established workers from the threats posed by the New Immigration with the other. It is true that hostility to English exploitation of Ireland and the Irish gave Irish-Americans a unique perspective on all exploiters, capitalists included. These were workers as well as exiled Irish warriors. It is also true that the lessons of protest on one front could be applied to protest on several. There was even an ideological seam, a line where the rights of Ireland and the rights of all workers were joined, and there were times when ethnic nationalism and working-class protest reinforced one another. But there was a far tighter seam that marked the place where the rights of Ireland were joined only with the rights of *Irish* workers and there were more times when that ethnic exclusivity was used against rather than in defense of the rights of all workers.[19]

No reproach is intended by these comments. The Irish communities and the associations that kept them intact were indispensible if the Irish workers were not to wander endlessly and if they and Ireland were to be avenged. Both objects required the steady jobs the associations had been instrumental in finding and the community indispensible in providing. Finding them required cooperation with more powerful Irish; providing them required a quick course in American values; keeping them required the exclusion of powerless non-Irish. No one of those was a shortcut to radicalism anymore than eyeing American policy through the prism of Ireland's interests was a shortcut to full involvement in American life. In both instances, however, the Irish behaved as their history had taught them to behave. To expect differently of them is pointless.

Obviously, these Irish associations did far more than just ease emigrant homesickness and give expression to Irish rage. They were central to the Irish workers' search for steady employment and social stability. A mutually dependent relationship between work, Irish nationalism, associational life, and community survival was one consequence. Another was that the Irish had a kind of bifurcated immigrant experience. At any given moment during the years of the post-1856 Irish transatlantic relocation and in any of the American industrial cities where they lived and worked, there would exist two classes of Irish workers, the settled immigrants and the as-yet-unsettled migrants. The latter were not excluded from the ethnic community and its associations; indeed, their transiency was often sponsored by what was essentially a system of linked worker enclaves. The wanderers were a conspicuous part of the Irish-American world.[20]

They became a hazard to that world only when their itineracy jumped the system's tracks and took place outside the community's institutions or in defiance of its values. When that happened, the Irish working-class divided three ways: some were settled, some were about to be, some would never be. The result was considerable intraethnic tension. Migrants, in sum, were expected to become immigrants; those a part of the drifting working-class enclave were expected to attach themselves to one of its fixed and self-sufficient parts. The Irish had limited options. Emigration was one of them; transiency was another. But the option of emigration, once exercised, was lost, and transiency ended when a fair living was found. The Irish simply could not wander forever; to do so was to risk the social equivalent of falling off the edge of the earth.

Among the effects of this Irish emigrant selection was a wider geographical dispersal of the Irish worker than historicans have previously thought. True, the Irish were concentrated in the industrial cities and towns of the East and Midwest, but any place with jobs and an Irish presence was a potential destination. They were too social to tolerate for long the isolation of a prairie homestead; they may also have been too poor and too unprepared to file on one. But they were as suited to western cities as to eastern cities; as attracted to western industrial jobs as to eastern. The Irish were preoccupied with making a fair living; they were mobile, unable to go home, and deficient in work skills. All combined to put them on the road; many would take it as far as it ran. They avoided the South and they limited themselves—or were limited by that same want of refined skills—to western mining camps or towns with an abundance of unskilled jobs. Many of the men did know only how to dig, many of the women only how to wash. But there were digging and washing jobs from coast to coast and the Irish were a determined and purposeful people.[21]

Contributing to the historical neglect of these westering Irishmen has been the assumption that the American West was the exclusive province of native-born Protestants who wished to farm or graze their cattle on it. Farmers and cattlemen there were, but there was also an urban West, filled with miners and smeltermen, loggers, railroad workers, longshoremen, and industrial tradesmen of every sort. Many were Irish. They were found in commercial and industrial cities like Denver and San Francisco or, and in significant numbers, as skilled diggers deep in the copper mines of Michigan or the quartz mines of California,

Nevada, and Colorado. The Irish did not flock to these places, but then neither did anyone else in those years, immigrant or native.[22]

These western cities and mining camps suited them. They provided work, and the host society—assuming there was one—was reasonably tolerant of an Irish Catholic work force. In this more fluid social environment, the Irish communities flourished—their life expectancy and influence limited only by the safety and stability of the jobs on which they depended. Too often the jobs were hazardous and evanescent but that was true wherever the Irish went. Those who were able to settle into one of these western communities, to marry and have children, were luckier than most. They had job and family, the friendship of their mates, the fraternal companionship of their associations, the comfort of their Church, and a chance to act out in relative peace their image of themselves as exiled patriots—not a bad definition of a fair living, and nearer to it than that provided by any other place they had ever known.

NOTES

1. For the Famine and Famine emigration see particularly Miller, *Emigrants*, pp. 280–344; Woodham-Smith, *Great Hunger*, pp. 206–38; Gallager, *Paddy's Lament*, pp. 115–234; Kennedy, *The Irish*, pp. 40–43, 86–109; Taylor, *Distant Magnet*, pp. 35–37; Donnelly, *Land and People*, pp. 75–83, 98–113; McDonagh, "Irish Famine Emigration," pp. 357–446; Ó Gráda, "Irish Emigration," pp. 93–104. The statistics are from Miller, *Emigrants*, pp. 569–71, 576–78, 582; *Statistical History*, pp. 56–57; Vaughn and Fitzpatrick, *Irish Statistics*, pp. 344–53.

2. Miller, *Emigrants*, pp. 280–344. On anti-Irish sentiments see George Potter, *Golden Door*, pp. 241–315; Billington, *Protestant Crusade*, David Potter, *Impending Crisis*, pp. 243–46, 251, 254. On emigrant selectivity see Bodnar, *Transplanted*, pp. 1–38; Blessing, "Irish Emigration," pp. 11–38, esp. pp. 11, 18, 24.

3. For historians' preoccupation with the Famine emigration see Miller, "Assimilation," p. 87.

4. Miller, *Emigrants*, p. 569; *Statistical History*, pp. 56–57.

5. Miller, *Emigrants*, pp. 346–47, 361–421; Joseph Lee, *Modernisation*, pp. 1–9; Diner, *Erin's Daughters*, pp. 3–5, 8–10; Kennedy, *The Irish*, pp. 2–3, 27; Miller, "Assimilation," p. 88; Blessing, "Irish Emigration," pp. 13–21; *Statistical History*, pp. 56–57.

6. Miller, *Emigrants*, p. 362; quote from p. 11. Golab, *Immigrant Destinations*, pp. 43–66.

7. Miller, *Emigrants*, p. 363. On dowries, see also Diner, *Erin's Daughters*, p. 33.

8. Miller, *Emigrants*, pp. 133, 326–27, 428–31, 521–22, 582; Miller, "Assimilation," pp. 88, 92, 107–8; Blessing, "Irish Emigration," pp. 19, 21; Golab,

Immigrant Destinations, pp. 121–22. For more on the Irish immigrants' preparation for industrial conditions, see Thompson, *English Working Class,* pp. 429–40; Erickson, *American Industry,* p. 24; Davitt, *Fall of Feudalism,* p. 100.

9. Blessing, "Irish Emigration," p. 15. The quote is from Miller, "Assimilation," p. 87; see also p. 92; Ó Gráda, "Irish Emigration," pp. 97–98. On social differentiation in the Irish-American community see Miller, *Emigrants,* pp. 494–95; Foner, "Land League," pp. 151–53, 160–63, 168–79. Irish immigrant occupations are given in Commissioner General of Immigration, *Annual Report,* 1903, pp. 24–26. On social differentiation generally among all immigrant groups, see Bodnar, *Transplanted,* pp. 117–43, 169–84.

10. Miller, *Emigrants,* passim, particularly pp. 364, 412, 556; Miller, "Assimilation," pp. 102–8. See also Foner, "Land League," pp. 161, 167–68, 172–79.

11. Miller, *Emigrants,* p. 345; Miller, "Assimilation," p. 88; Ó Gráda, "Irish Emigration," pp. 98–99; Golab, *Immigrant Destinations,* p. 48; Connell, "Catholicism and Marriage," p. 135; Schrier, *Ireland,* pp. 15–17; Kennedy, *The Irish,* pp. 163, 195.

12. Miller, *Emigrants,* pp. 353–58; Ó Gráda, "Irish Emigration," p. 101; Joseph Lee, *Modernisation,* p. 13; Donnelly, *Land and People,* p. 249.

13. Miller, *Emigrants,* pp. 4–7, 272–73, 357–59, 425–26, 510–20; Miller, "Assimilation," pp. 93–95; Donnelly, *Land and People,* pp. 159–232.

14. Miller, *Emigrants,* pp. 271–73, 292–95, 483–90; Diner, *Erin's Daughters,* pp. 11–12; Schrier, *American Emigration,* pp. 24–38, 105–11.

15. The "familiarity with transiency" quote is from Bodnar, *Transplanted,* p. 43. See also Bodnar, *Workers' World,* pp. 13–14, 63–66; Brody, "Workers," pp. 147–48. Golab cites repatriation rates for the Irish and the migrant workers in *Immigrant Destinations,* p. 48. The literature on Irish mobility—geographic and social—is vast. See, for example, Thernstrom, "Working Class Mobility," pp. 24–25; Thernstrom, *Poverty and Progress,* pp. 22, 99–102, 109–11, 155–57, 200; Thernstrom, *Other Bostonians,* pp. 186–94; Thernstrom and Knights, "Men in Motion," pp. 27–31; Hirsch, *Roots,* pp. 47–50; Gitelman, *Workingmen of Waltham,* pp. 60–64; Walkowitz, *Worker City,* pp. 29–30; Dennis Clark, *Irish in Philadelphia,* pp. 65–80; Funchion, "Irish Chicago," pp. 26–29, 35.

16. Golab refers to these associations as part of the "institutional infrastructure" of immigrant communities (*Immigrant Destinations,* p. 142). The various Irish-American associations—nationalist, fraternal, social, revolutionary, benevolent, and religious—are conveniently sketched in Funchion, *Organizations.*

17. Miller, *Emigrants,* pp. 336–44, 440–42, 532–36; Foner, "Land League," pp. 150–79; Thomas N. Brown, *Irish-American Nationalism,* pp. 49–56, 178–79. For a useful summary of the enormously complex relationship between Irish nationalism and class divisions see Rumpf and Hepburn, *Nationalism and Socialism,* pp. 1–27. Perkins, *Great Rapprochement.*

18. On the disproportionate Irish involvement in American labor see Montgomery, "Irish"; Montgomery, *Beyond Equality,* pp. 120–26; Doyle, "Irish" and Wilentz, "Industrializing America." Shaw, *Making of an Immigrant City,* makes clear how difficult it was for Irish workers to balance their ethnic and class

responsibilities. In "Land League," Foner argues that Irish-American nationalism and worker protest were symbiotic movements.

19. On job exclusivity see Hobsbawm, "Aristocracy," pp. 229, 234–36, 239, 250–51. The use of labor unions to protect Irish jobs is noted in Miller, "Assimilation," p. 95; Walkowitz discusses the transfer of protest methods in *Worker City*, pp. 166–70; Foner, "Land League."

20. Bodnar, *Workers' World*, pp. 63–66; Golab, *Immigrant Destinations*, p. 148.

21. Vedder and Gallaway, "Geographical Distribution," pp. 26–29, 34. For direct expressions of Irish immigrant destinations, see Commissioner General of Immigrations, *Annual Report*, 1903, pp. 7, 20–21; Immigration Commission, *Reports*, III:363–65. (This is the well-known Dellingham Report.) The standard histories of the Irish in America concentrate almost exclusively on the Irish in the eastern cities. William Shannon, *American Irish*, and McCaffrey, *Irish Diaspora*, are good examples. Golab discusses the "imperative of clustering" as a dominant part of the southeastern European immigrants' culture. This imperative left them unprepared for the isolation of settling America's farms. The same points could be made regarding the Irish (*Immigrant Destinations*, pp. 120–22).

22. For the Irish in the West, see Burchell, *San Francisco Irish;* Walsh, "Irish"; Blessing, "West among Strangers"; Brundage, "Making of Working-class Radicalism," pp. 50–88; Ralph Mann, *After the Gold Rush*, pp. 86–94, 120–25, 142–46; Lingenfelter, *Hardrock Miners*, pp. 6–7, 103–4; Ronald C. Brown, *Hard-Rock Miners*, pp. 8–10; Wyman, *Hardrock Epic*, pp. 41, 45–47, 145, 158.

CHAPTER 1

From Ireland to Butte

I

Nowhere do all of the factors involved in the development of an Irish working class in the West converge as they do in the copper-mining center of Butte, Montana. Butte was the only one of the western mining camps that became an industrial city. In population, production, and size of work force it had no rivals among mining cities anywhere in the world. All of this is known and often recounted. Less well known is that Butte was one of the most overwhelmingly Irish cities in the United States. (Irish for these purposes, and following accepted practice, includes both the immigrant and the second generation.) By 1900 there were approximately 12,000 such in a total Silver Bow County (Butte) population of 47,635. Thus, 25 percent of the residents of Silver Bow County, 2,500 miles from the nearest eastern port, were either Irish-born or the children of Irish-born. For Butte City the numbers were 8,026 Irish in a total population of 30,470, or 26 percent. This is a higher percentage of Irish than in any other American city at the turn of the century. Boston may at one time have been more Irish, but it had lost that distinction by 1900.[1]

The men in this total were overwhelmingly miners. In 1894, in the Anaconda Mine alone, there were 1,250 Irish-born miners. Of 5,369 working-class Irishmen in 1900, both first and second generation, 3,589 (two of every three) worked in the deep mines. Approximately 1,200 more worked for the mining companies as hoisting engineers, carpenters, pumpmen, blacksmiths, or in any of a variety of other trades. This increased the percentage of Irish who worked in the mines to a remarkable 90 percent of the whole. The place and its mines must have seemed even more Irish than they were. One of Butte's copper kings

counted 7,000 Irishmen in the mines in 1902, and an Irish-American
nationalist was sure that 39,000 were living in Butte in 1915. Both
figures were inflated but both spoke to indisputable facts. A significant
number of Irish miners lived in Butte and they made their presence
felt.[2]

Obviously, these were post-Famine immigrants. Of the 3,454 Irish-
born in Butte in 1900, only 16 percent had emigrated before 1870; 19
percent came to the United States in the 1870s; 37 percent in the 1880s,
and 28 percent in the 1890s. The majority of Irishmen who emigrated
during those years had been farmers or farm laborers. This may not
have been the case with the Butte Irish. Many, of course, arrived as
children, and many of those who came as adults passed through American mining towns on their way to Butte. Moreover, as will be seen,
a sizeable percentage of Butte's Irishmen came from mining regions in
Ireland. This does not mean that their emigration was less a consequence of the uncertainties of their class or of their inability to move
out of it. It does mean that the work they undertook in Butte was less
mysterious to them than was ordinarily the case with the Irish in
America.[3]

Most of the Irish men and Irish women who came to Butte were
under thirty, and a significant percentage were unmarried at the time
of their emigration. Marriage, particularly to another Irish Catholic,
was a significant part of the process of settling into Butte's Irish community; but marriage, like the general process of which it was a part,
was postponed until the town and its work opportunities had proven
themselves. That took time, and an analysis of the housing arrangements and marital status of Butte's working Irish indicates that an
appreciable percentage of them had not had time enough. According
to the Manuscript Census of 1900, 2,803 of Butte's Irish were single
residents of the city's scores of working-class boardinghouses. In 1910
the figure was still 2,285, indicating that this pattern was not a consequence of "frontier" conditions but a feature of industrializing Butte
and of the enormous worker turnover that was part of that industrializing process.[4]

It cannot be known with any certainty from where in Ireland these
immigrants came. In Butte, Irish county distinctions had no meaning
to the non-Irish. They knew them as "savages," "harps," "cannibals,"
"maneaters," or "flannelmouths." A miners' song, however, identified
"two of them from Mizen Head, / Two more of them from Clare, /
Two of them from Dingle Town, the place of great renown." Another
contained lyrics describing "hoboes from Kerry, and hoboes from Cork."
More specific, if only slightly more exact or scientific, data on the Irish

county of origin can be had by determining Butte's most common Irish surnames and tracing them to the county with which those names are most commonly associated. This method assumes a close association of name and place, but in the case of Ireland this is a relatively safe assumption. More conventional data furnish checks on the whole proceedings. It is known, for example, that six of Ireland's thirty-two counties accounted for almost 48 percent of the total immigration to 1900. Those six, Cork, Kerry, Tipperary, Limerick, Galway, and Mayo, all in the West, should be well represented in Butte. Occupational considerations and the relative number of men and women emigrating from different counties provide additional corroboration.[5]

According to city directories for six representative years (1886, 1892, 1897, 1902, 1908, and 1914), the six most common Irish surnames in Butte were Sullivan, Harrington, Murphy, Kelly, Shea, and O'Neill. With the exception of Kelly, which is ubiquitous in Ireland, the half-dozen are closely associated with County Cork. When the list is expanded to include such contending surnames as Holland, Crowley, Lynch, and McCarthy, all more commonly encountered in Cork than any other county in Ireland and all in Butte's first fifteen Irish surnames, the dominance of Cork becomes more obvious. County Donegal was well represented by Shovlins, Peoples, Gallaghers, and McGees; Clare by McLaughlins and Shannons; Tipperary by Meaghers (or Mahers). There were, in addition, Ryans, Hogans, Kennedys, and Moriaritys; indeed, there can have been few areas of Catholic Ireland without some representation in Butte. But assuming even a measure of accuracy to the name-place association, County Cork in southwestern Ireland supplied a hugely disproportionate share of Butte's Irish population.[6]

A recently published genealogy gives a more complete picture of this Cork connection. Riobard O'Dwyer traced the family histories of over 6,000 men and women from one parish, Eyeries, in one township, Castletownbere, in the westernmost section of County Cork. Over 1,700 people from that tiny corner of Ireland emigrated to the United States between 1870 and 1915; of that total, 1,138 (707 men and 431 women) made their way to Butte. The predominance of Sullivan among Butte surnames—there were over 1,200 of them in 1908—is more easily understood when it is noted that members of seventy-seven different Sullivan (or O'Sullivan) families left Castletownbere for Butte. As late as 1917 Father Patrick Brosnan, a Butte priest from County Limerick, wrote back to his father that "Everyone here is from Castletownbere . . . Butte is a great city. We have seven fine Catholic parishes, all Irish."[7]

Some of these West Corkmen were landless farm laborers whose complaints were the same as those of others of that class wherever found in the West of Ireland in the nineteenth century. The pattern of eviction and emigration, as rhythmic as the seasons, was as much a part of West Cork's history as of County Mayo's or County Donegal's. What distinguishes West Cork from Mayo or, indeed, from the rest of Cork, and what explains the dominance of West Corkmen among the Irish of Butte, was the presence of the Puxley family's copper mines at Hungry Hill near Berehaven.

There is no history of those mines, although Daphne du Maurier based her novel *Hungry Hill*, with the Puxley-like Brodericks as the mine-owning family, on an authorized use of family records. The novel is an accurate enough retelling of the story of these mines to serve present purposes. Local Irish and imported Cornish miners worked Hungry Hill from its establishment during the Napoleonic Wars until competition from Michigan and Montana mines forced it to suspend copper operations and begin the less-profitable and far less labor-extensive mining of tin in the late 1880s. Soon after the conversion to tin, the Puxleys sold the mines to absentee owners in London. The new owners plundered the mines, then closed them, throwing 1,700 men out of work. Some of the Berehaven miners emigrated before the transfer of ownership, but the closure speeded that emigration appreciably and, seeking like work in the United States, the veterans of Hungry Hill made their way to the copper mines of Michigan's Upper Peninsula or to the even larger mines of Butte.[8]

The other great suppliers of Irish immigration to Butte were those same Michigan copper mines, the anthracite coalfields of Pennsylvania, and the gold and silver quartz mines of California, Nevada, Utah, and Colorado. There was an abundance of Irishmen in each. They were the most numerous immigrant group in the four coal-mining counties of Luzerne, Schuylkill, Carbon, and Columbia, Pennsylvania, between 1870 and 1890. They occupied the same position in the copper-mining counties of Houghton and Marquette, Michigan, in 1870, and, among European immigrants, in the quartz-mining counties of Lake in Colorado, Storey and White Pine in Nevada, Placer, Sierra, El Dorado, Amador, Calaveras, and Mono in California. In none of the major mining regions of any of those states did the Irish ever rank lower than third among European immigrant groups. Obviously, there was a large pool of experienced Irish mine laborers from which Butte could draw its work force.[9]

Unfortunately, more precise information on previous residency is not available. The United States Census Bureau did not begin to ask about prior residency until 1940—a remarkable oversight for a nation of wanderers. Some help is provided by analyzing the place of birth of the children of Butte's Irish-born. The problem with this method, however, is implied by its statement: The unmarried and hence childless were the most mobile, but their routes to Butte cannot be traced. Still, and with this bias in mind, the results from 1900 and 1910 tell an instructive story. Michigan was the most common state of previous residence; Pennsylvania was second; the western mining states were next, followed by the industrial states of the Midwest and the East. A small percentage of Irish had spent some time as adults in England. An analysis of the birthplace of Butte's second-generation Irish tells a similar story. Again, Michigan leads the list, followed by Pennsylvania, New York, Nevada, Wisconsin, and California.[10]

Another and smaller sample can be found using the membership records of the Butte divisions of the Ancient Order of Hibernians (AOH), an Irish nationalist organization. In some cases, new or transfer members were asked their previous place of residence. One hundred ninety-three such cases have been found from two separate periods, 1884–92 and 1905–12. During the earlier period, the most frequently mentioned states were, in order of reference, Michigan, Pennsylvania, Colorado, and California. During the later years, Utah led the list (mines had closed in Park City and Eureka) followed by Pennsylvania, California, and Nevada. Another of the Butte Irish associations, the Robert Emmet Literary Association (RELA), was alerted by its national headquarters of the closing of the mines in Park City and told to initiate the members of the disbanded Park City chapter "whenever they appear among [you]." The Emmets also received by transfer members from Ishpeming, Michigan; Aspen and Leadville, Colorado; Bisbee and Tombstone, Arizona; Avoca, Pennsylvania; and Eureka, Utah.[11]

Even when other mines were operating, a considerable number of Irishmen were always on the move. They were part of a naturally roving work force, a vagabond proletariat that required little in the way of conventionally defined push and pull factors to put on the road again. When Seán Ruiséal, the Irish poet and self-styled Spailpin Fanach (itinerant laborer) complained of "wandering like a helpless cripple / Without a woman to love me," he was in one of the mining districts of the West. There were thousands of others, some even with women to love them, whose laments were similar. These roaming Irishmen brought to Butte news of events and conditions in the different camps, often speaking before the Irish organizations to which they also belonged. These clubs served as clearinghouses of employment and related information for a significant percentage of the transient Irish work force. It was possible for members to transfer from one chapter to another with relative ease, and since most of the western camps had one or more Irish clubs, the exchange of members and information was constant. Before affiliating in Butte, however, the transfer had to explain why he left his previous chapter. Explanations ranged from "leaving the land and coming to America" in the case of one who transferred from Ireland, to "got out of work, had to leave" for a miner from Pennsylvania, to "out in the hills, lost track of business" for a Nevada placer miner. All three were Irish-born. Obviously, the route from Ireland to Butte was seldom a direct one.[12]

In sum, the Irish-born among Butte's thousands of Irishmen were principally drawn from the idled copper miners of West Cork and from the landless farm laborers and small farmers of the West of Ireland. Many of them, as well as many of the second generation, had made intermediate stops in the industrial cities of England or the United States, and many more had had some experience in mining either in the coalfields of the United States or the hard-rock mines of Michigan and the American West. They moved for the same reasons that prompted the relocation of others of their class. The mines in which they had been working played out, putting them once again on the road. This explains the immigration out of the copper mines of West Cork in Ireland, but it explains as well the migration from Virginia City, Nevada; or from Cripple Creek and Aspen, Colorado; Park City, Utah; Wood River Idaho; and, though they had not really been exhausted, the mines of Houghton, Calumet, and Hancock, Michigan.

Stephan Thernstrom has argued that no American industry had a stable work force in the 1880s and 1890s, but a case can be made that the Irishmen of the western mining regions constituted the most surpassingly mobile working class in America. In this sense, Butte built its labor force by being at the end of a sequential if totally unsystematic immigration. There are some revealing individual stories of this Irish working-class mobility. The *Manuscript Census* of 1910 includes the entry for John Hale, a forty-two-year-old Irish-born miner who had emigrated with his parents in 1875. His wife of twenty-one years, born in England of Irish parents, had had nine children—a twenty-year-old had been born in Montana, an eighteen-year-old in Utah, a seventeen- and a sixteen-year-old in Colorado, a thirteen-year-old in Utah, and a ten-, an eight-, a six-, and a three-year-old in Montana. Of Dan and Mary O'Leary's five children, the first was born in Michigan, the next two in Colorado, the fourth in Utah, and the last, two-year-old Patrick, in Montana. Dan and Johanna Harrington's first child was born in Utah; the next two in Montana; the next pair in New Mexico; the sixth in Utah; and the seventh and last in Montana. At that, these would probably have appeared remarkably settled lives to forty-seven-year-old

William O'Brien, who testified in 1913 that he left County Cork when he was seventeen and spent the next thirty years mining in Africa, Australia, New Zealand, Tasmania, Canada, Alaska, Mexico, and South America. It must also be pointed out that these stories are from 1910; the census of 1900, when Butte was newer and even less stable, shows a much higher percentage of children born in widely scattered parts of the world.[13]

II

The Irish who migrated to Butte came to fill jobs in the copper mines, and it was in this capacity that they formed an immigrant working class. But before Butte's industrialization, the town had had a brief and unpromising placer gold-mining period and a longer and considerably more profitable experience as a silver-mining district. As such it was one of the stops for America's migrant hard-rock men—many of them Irish. Irishmen named the town, the creek from which the county takes its name, and what became its largest mine—the Anaconda. Another Irishman began the first mining company; yet another opened the first saloon. The *Manuscript Census* of 1870 lists a scattering of Irish placer miners and a few others who worked in the flume and hydraulic operations of other owners. In 1878 a list of contract miners included Pat and Frank Shovlin, William Larkin, Pat Monahan, John Hanifan, and two Michaels, Denis, Daniel, and Eugene Sullivan. By 1880 the Irish population had grown considerably, numbering over six hundred in Butte City and over nine hundred in the county.[14]

These early Irish arrivals would undoubtedly have attracted a few hundred more, but one of their number, the Irish-born Marcus Daly, clearly influenced the migration of a few thousand. Daly came to Butte in 1876. His career until then was not strikingly different from that of hundreds of other Irish immigrants. Born in Ballyjamesduff in the Ulster county of Cavan in 1841, Daly left Ireland for New York in 1856. His way may have been paid from remittance money sent from his sister in San Francisco. After five years in New York, the twenty-one-year-old Daly joined his sister in California and then moved on to Virginia City, Nevada, where he worked in the silver mines of the Comstock. He was a skilled and hardworking miner, and he advanced quickly to a supervisory position. Leaving the Comstock, he took a job in Salt Lake City with the Walker Brothers' mining company. In 1876 the Walkers sent him to the struggling silver camp of Butte to investigate the commercial potential of the Alice Mine. Daly was favorably impressed with the property and recommended its purchase. He joined

$5,000 of his own money to the Walkers' $25,000 and, with his new bride, went to Butte to manage the Walkers' new mine. Daly made a great deal of money on the Alice and in 1880 used some of it to buy the Anaconda Mine, another silver producer, from an Irishman, Edward Hickey.[15]

Thus began one of the most remarkable careers in the history of American mining. The story of Butte and Marcus Daly has been told often. It is a good story, revealing much of the history of American mining and finance. Daly converted the Anaconda Mine from silver to copper, bought other mines, built a smelter and city to support it in nearby Anaconda, Montana, and amassed an enormous fortune from the whole operation. But the point is not this one Irishman's visible and substantial wealth. At issue is his influence on the immigration of thousands of considerably more modest and anonymous Irishmen who helped him get it.

Until the early 1880s the Irish miners drifted into Butte as they had drifted in and out of other mining camps in the West. As Daly began to develop the Anaconda properties, however, the lure of Butte began to appear brighter because of Daly's presence, and the Irish movement into the city became noticeable. There are some who assign to Daly a very direct role in that Irish immigration. An early source, for example, states that Daly "imported Irish miners," indeed, that he "brought in shiploads of [them] to work his properties." A recent history adds that Daly "even encouraged immigration directly from Ireland itself." That last point exaggerates his role. There is no evidence that Daly actively recruited Irish miners, though such recruitment was not unknown in the Pennsylvania mines. No deals for reduced fares for incoming miners appear to have been struck between Daly and the railroads that served Butte; there is no indication that Daly took out advertisements in Irish newspapers—including those of West Cork—or sent agents into Ireland to blazon Butte's opportunities.[16]

Still, there can be no question that Daly was the single most important reason for the massive Irish immigration into Butte in the 1880s and 1890s. The Montana Writers' Project history of Butte says that thousands of Irish "followed . . . Daly to the town." Father Brosnan made clear why. As he explained in a letter to his father, "Marcus Daly was the man that made Butte an Irish town. . . . He did not care for any man but an Irishman and . . . did not give a job to anyone else." Brosnan overstated the case—but only slightly. That knowledge among the itinerant Irish may have been recruitment enough. Daly, for example, had lived in Virginia City, Storey County, Nevada. In 1870 there were almost 2,200 Irish immigrants and untold second-generation

Irish in Storey County. O'Dwyer reports that more than one hundred miners from West Cork alone helped build Virginia City's Catholic church. As the mines of that region played out, knowledge of Daly's success and his willingness to share a part of it with other Irishmen would have been a powerful draw.[17]

Daly's devotion to Ireland and things Irish was also a conspicuous part of his personality. He was supposed to have sprung from a family of rebels and his own reading material may have included Patrick Ford's Irish nationalist newspaper, the *Irish World and American Industrial Liberator*. The first point cannot be supported. If the second is true, Daly received a large dose of radical economics along with his Irish patriotism. But whatever the source of his inspiration, Daly was a consistent and generous patron of the Irish cause. He was a member of both the Butte and Anaconda divisions of the Irish Catholic Ancient Order of Hibernians. He was proposed for membership in the Robert Emmet Literary Society, the avowedly revolutionary Butte camp of the secretive Clan-na-Gael, and, although he was apparently never initiated, his nomination attests to his sympathy with its goals. He also supported the Clan in a number of ways, including hosting the 1886 visit of the Irish nationalist Michael Davitt. In addition to these political activities, Daly was the honorary chairman of the Thomas Francis Meagher Memorial Association, a group of Butte and Anaconda Irishmen who were responsible for the Meagher statue on the capitol grounds in Helena, and was a generous benefactor of the Catholic Church in Butte, Anaconda, and Minneapolis and St. Paul.[18]

All of this must have endeared Daly to the Irish in Butte and to those who considered moving there. But it was his promise of jobs, not his political and religious advocacy, that kept their allegiance. This promise was not solely the result of his ethnocentrism. Daly needed skilled miners, and he must have been impressed with what he had seen of the Irishmen in the camps of California, Nevada, and Utah. The result was the same regardless of Daly's motive. Irishmen of whatever level of skill and experience who knew of the hiring practices of Daly's Anaconda Company made their way to Butte.[19]

III

But even the magic of Daly's Irishness would have been inadequate had the promised job not been a good one, had Butte not been accessible, had there not been satisfactory housing. Moreover, for those Irish who knew nothing of Daly or Butte—and that was probably a good percentage of those outside the mountain West—Butte's advantages would have to be publicized. Fortunately, Daly had powerful allies in promoting Butte, and the city's job opportunities compared well with those available anywhere else in America.

Ironically, Butte's rapid industrialization created a problem for the early promoters eager to tell the story of the American West to prospective immigrants. The image of the West, including Montana, was of a pastural and agricultural alternative to the less-lovely aspects of the East. Butte—the name fit the place, short, squat, and hard—did some considerable violence to the image. It was, by all accounts, one of America's ugliest cities. Father Brosnan wrote to his mother that "there is not a tree nor a shrub nor a blade of grass up here but all the wealth is underground." This in 1917, forty years after Daly had begun the industrial mining of copper. Gertrude Atherton, in one of her Butte novels, wrote of the "appalling surface barrenness of the place," "the sulphur and arsenic fumes of ore roasted in the open or belching from the smelters." It looked "like a gigantic ship wreck." Clyde Murphy, another Butte novelist, said it resembled "a black and yellow jungle of smelters, roasting ovens, cranes and stacks which breathed out yellow, acrid smoke." Its "recreational" opportunities were equally industrial. By 1905 Butte's red light district was reported to be the second largest in the United States, behind only New Orleans's infamous Corduroy Road. In appearance and population Butte was the antithesis of rural and Protestant America.[20]

This gave pause to even the most sanguine promoters of western settlement. Linus Brockett, for example, wrote in 1882 that Butte was inhabited by a "rougher class," and that "infidel clubs . . . gambling and drinking saloons and brothels, [were] very numerous. . . . The only remedy . . . [was] for moral, and especially Christian people to put down . . . Sabbath-breaking, gambling and drinking." He allowed that "the struggle [would] be severe at first" but the prosperity of the community required that the stable element assert its control. Butte's "stabilization" was nearer completion by 1887 when William Thayer wrote his *Marvels of the New West*. Thayer called Butte "clean, enterprising" (it was certainly that), with "schools, churches, and law-abiding" citizens. Sundays, he went on, were spent in church. But there was a hint that these social amenities were more in the process of becoming than the present circumstance, and more than just a hint that they had not always been the case. "The Anglo-Saxon race finally asserts itself in the mining camp, to control its boistrous elements." Butte was witnessing, Thayer maintained, an application of "Herbert Spencer's theories of Anglo-Saxon superiority." It would soon be a proper place for civilized habitation.[21]

It is doubtful that many Irish were deterred by Brockett's faint praise or by Thayer's references to Anglo-Saxon superiority. Butte's attractions would never fit the image of a paradisiacal West, but earthly paradise was hardly on the Irish mind. What Butte promised was a fair living. There was no disputing that, and no shortage of agents eager to relay the message. The Union Pacific Railroad, completed to Butte by spur line in 1881, spoke of its mines as the "best in the world." Production values had jumped from $1,200,000 in 1881 to more than $27,000,000 in 1890, providing "employment to more men, at better wages, than those of any other mining camp in the world." Since that wage was the standard for the entire western region—$3.50 per day for underground work—Butte's claim to better wages was based on its mine owners' ability to offer steady employment, not on their willingness to pay more for a day's work. By 1891 the average wage for the 4,800 men working its mines was $100 per month; by 1899 the Anaconda Company alone paid more wages than all the mills of Fall River and Lowell combined, "more than Kansas pays those who reap its wheat or Louisiana those who pick its cotton." In fact, wages for all classes and trades were high enough that all "can, at least, very soon own a home."[22]

State and local agencies made similar promises. The state's inspector of mines referred to high monthly wages, as did Montana's delegate to the National Mining Congress held in Helena in 1892. The Butte Chamber of Commerce repeated the claim in 1895. Again, the theme was stability. Butte, said the chamber, was a copper town, not a silver camp. Copper demanded a major capital investment and a stable work force. As a result, although the boom was barely begun, the bust would never come. And the evidence was convincing. By 1895 Butte produced more than one-quarter of the world's copper; its 6,400 miners took home $640,000 every month.[23]

What made the chamber's promotion so impressive—and so unusual—was its accuracy. When Thomas Edison turned on the Pearl Street Station in 1882, he not only lit up the streets of New York City, he created Butte. Copper was the ideal medium for electricity, and Butte was underlaid with it. By 1887 two of Butte's mines placed first and third in the world in the production of copper; this while the district was still second nationally in silver production. Little wonder that by 1890 Montana led the nation in percentage of total male population employed; by 1900 it was first in the nation in per capita income, reflecting its first place in wages paid. An 1889 study of the nation's 250,000 railroad workers indicated that 155,000 of them made less than $300 per year; only 5,000 made the $1,000 per year that was the average wage among twice that many Butte miners. Nationwide in the 1880s, industrial workers made less than $600 per year, with an average working day of eleven hours.[24]

Butte's miners made $3.50 for a nine-, later eight-, hour shift. That was double the daily wage of most industrial workers. More to the point, every day was a workday. The Butte Miners' Union, for example, adamantly opposed any Sunday mine closing because many of the men wanted the option of working six or seven shifts a week. They seem also to have had the option of working fifty to fifty-two weeks a year. The censuses of 1900 and 1910 asked each wage earner how many weeks or months he had been idle in the calendar year preceding the census. Eighteen ninety-nine and most of 1909 were relatively prosperous times in Butte, but the data indicate steady employment particularly for the younger men, and the older miners, many of them home owners, seem not to have been laid off but to have taken four to six weeks' vacation time. One Butte Irishman put the matter in a way all Irish could understand: "The average working man," said Dan Lynch, "could get as much in Ireland as in America, outside of Montana." The claim that by 1905 Butte's payroll was the highest per capita in the world was probably true.[25]

And getting there was easy. Between 1881 and 1908, four transcontinental rail lines entered Butte, guaranteeing access from almost every direction and every port of entry. Fares from New York City to Butte remained almost unchanged from the mid-1880s until 1914. An individual, traveling "immigrant colonist" class, paid $48.00 for through service to Butte; this was less than the fare charged individual immigrants and considerably less than that charged "regular domestic" traffic. From Chicago or the Twin Cities, the fare to Butte was about $25.00. Few Irish, particularly those with remittance money, could have been priced out of Butte.[26]

The same point can be made regarding housing upon arrival. Marcus Daly had built the Florence Hotel—the Big Ship as it was known—expressly for newly arrived miners. Praised by its manager as "the zenith of service for working men in America," the Florence had a library, gymnasium, billiard room, lobby, reading room, bath room and "dry"—a change room for miners. It was built near the Anaconda Mine, and the ethnicity of its employees and its residents reflected the preferences of its owner. According to one of its managers, himself Irish-born, "all the help were Irish, mostly born in Ireland, many of them spoke Gaelic." Over six hundred men could live in the Big Ship. According to the *Manuscript Census,* 202 of the 377 residents in 1900 were first- or second-generation Irish. Other Irish, particularly those from

West Cork, stayed at the Mullen House; only slightly smaller than the Florence, it was run by Nonie O'Sullivan Harrington primarily for the miners from her native village in West County Cork. In 1900, 199 of its 267 boarders were Irishmen. Cost for room and board was about $35.00 per month.[27]

Everything was in place for a large Irish immigration. There were some Butte Irish who discouraged further immigration because it might deflate wages; others who viewed every immigrant as a lost patriot warrior; a few who saw the addition of more poor and unsophisticated Irish as a hindrance to the further advance of those who were neither. Generally, however, the story out of Butte was altogether encouraging to further Irish immigration, promising preferential treatment for steady jobs at good wages. The population figures reflect how strong that tug was.[28]

IV

Sooner or later a resident immigrant population was itself enough to insure the steady arrival of others of the same group. When that point was reached, and it appears to have been reached in Butte by 1895, letters to Ireland became more important than any other pull. By 1895 the Irish immigration into Butte had become self-sustaining—Irish following Irish. Hugh O'Daly, for example, visited other western mining towns but settled on Butte because many of the other towns were insufficiently Irish and/or had no Catholic church. As with O'Daly, the process was initiated by personal correspondence. Butte's Irishness and its employment opportunities—they were rapidly becoming the same thing—had to have been recounted in thousands of letters.[29]

But these were not the only objective sources of information. The repatriation of a Butte Irishman, or the receipt of money from Butte for whatever cause, spoke as persuasively of the prosperity of the town and of the Irish share in that prosperity. There is, of course, irony in some of this. Among the rewards of living in Butte was the opportunity to leave it. O'Daly "had the one idea of returning to Ireland when [he] had a stake." And a miners' song concluded with a

> Hurrah for Old Ireland, the land of good miners
>   The dear little isle I see in my dreams.
> I'll go back to Old Ireland
>   to the girl who waits for me;
> To hell with your mines and your mining machines.[30]

To hell with them perhaps—but they made possible the exile's return. The *Butte Bystander* estimated that 40 percent of the Irish who came to Butte between 1880 and 1890 went back to Ireland within the decade. Only 8 percent of the Germans returned; only 10 percent of the Scandinavians. In fact, the Irish rate rivaled that of the notoriously homesick Italians. The *Bystander*'s estimate is considerably higher than the actual percentage of repatriates. O'Dwyer lists 124 West Corkmen who returned from Butte of the 707 who emigrated, and even this 18 percent figure is greater than that assumed for the Irish nationally. What the *Bystander* story probably reflected was the number of Irishmen who talked about going home.[31]

As important as the number returning was the relatively prosperous condition in which they returned. Almost all of them went back with enough money to "settle down," that is, to buy a small farm, or to "return to the home place." John Murphy, to cite only one example, immigrated to Butte, worked the mines for about ten years, returned to his native Cahirkeem, bought two farms, married a local girl, and fathered twelve children. The lesson cannot have been lost on many. Neither can that implied by the many Butte Irishmen who returned only for visits. Hugh O'Daly, despite his professed intention to return permanently, instead made six tourist trips to Ireland.[32]

Those trips can only have impressed his countrymen with O'Daly's, as well as Butte's, solvency. Those who sent money made the same point, if not quite as directly. Financial support for Irish nationalism will be discussed in later chapters, but Ireland's needs went beyond the expulsion of England. In the late 1870s, the *Irish World* was filled with stories of hunger and suffering in the old country. Any response from Butte had three effects: it took some of the edge off the hard times; it convinced a grateful Ireland that Butte's Irish were doing well; and it called attention to Butte as a possible immigrant destination.[33]

The effects were regularly felt. In 1890, John Brondel, Catholic bishop of Montana, returned from a trip to Ireland and reported crop failures throughout the western Irish counties. He instructed the priests in the Montana diocese to take up collections at Mass and send the money to Archbishop Walsh in Dublin. Butte's Ancient Order of Hibernians also responded to the economic distress in the West of Ireland in the late 1890s. It sent five hundred dollars in April of 1898; "an entertainment" by the Ladies' Auxiliary of the Hibernians raised $250.00 more "to relieve the suffering." There were also routine requests for aid in the construction or repair of Irish churches. Two hundred and fifty dollars, for example, was sent by the AOH to "Father McFadden for the Cathedral to St. Columbkill" in County Donegal.[34]

The most interesting, however, and in some ways the most instructive of these requests came from the Sisters of Charity in Ballahgaderin, County Mayo. The sisters complained of their "sickness at heart seeing our young people compelled by the grip of poverty and utter dearth of all employment to go off in hundreds every Spring, to face the exile's hard lot . . . , alone [and] friendless." This was not an uncommon complaint but the sisters noted that these exiles were also "very ignorant of house work." The loneliness they could do nothing about, but if the young women of their area were to find employment in the United States, they had to have the requisite skills. The Sisters of Charity thus set about training them as domestics in what was essentially a preparatory school for immigrant Irish maids. It was to continue their work that the sisters sought the assistance of Montana's Irish, an instance of push and pull factors operating simultaneously.[35]

Some of Butte's Irish returned to Ireland; more returned money. But the largest share of them brought as much of Ireland as they could to Butte. The Irish, according to one historian, had a "unique reputation for the efforts they made . . . to reunite their families." Here was another immigrant lure. When the men left Ireland, it was with the idea of returning to, or paying for the emigration of, the families they had left behind. The Butte newspapers, for example, periodically posted notices warning of emigration restriction laws that could prevent "husbands and fathers already located (in Butte) from sending for their wives and children." There are no data indicating how many Irishmen did, in fact, send for their families. The *Manuscript Census*, however, lists 159 married Irishmen whose wives were not with them in Butte in 1900, 106 in 1910. Wives and children were widely scattered. Con Lowney, for example, left a wife and two children in Hancock, Michigan. This was in 1896 and Lowney had been working in Butte's mines for four years. John McVeigh's situation was similar. Like Lowney, he was a miner and had been in Butte since 1892. His wife and four children, however, were still in Ireland.[36]

There was another element to McVeigh's residency in Butte that was a part of the general Irish immigration. He was preceded to Butte by a brother and a sister, and his own immigration was at their urging. There is no evidence where and with whom he lived in Butte, but the well-established pattern was for the most recent arrival to join those who had already established themselves. Only if the immigrants stayed with their host kin for any length of time could these arrangements be called extended or stem families. Otherwise, they were simply nuclear families helping out—and being helped by the presence, however temporary, of other wage earners. Extended families influenced both the rate of immigration and the destination of the immigrants, but so did nuclear families willing to serve as temporary hosts. On this point the *Manuscript Census*, by listing all occupants and their relationship to the head of the household, tells an important story about the elasticity and durability of the Irish family network. In 1900, 389 Irish wage earners lived with in-laws, siblings, or uncles and/or aunts. In 1910 the figure was 392. It seems reasonable that the overwhelming majority of these migrants came not only to live with their relatives but in response to promises made in advance of their immigration.[37]

Irish emigration, marriage, and family habits insured a large and constant supply of these host kin. The pattern was for only one or two members of large nuclear families to stay in Ireland, marry, and have large families of their own. The siblings of these childbearing Irish either remained celibate or emigrated. One result was that the Irish children of any given generation had an abundance of aunts and uncles or older brothers and sisters, or both, from whom they received news of America and to whom they could go upon their own immigration. If the host kin had married after his or her own immigration, the number of candidates for assisted emigration and later support would have approximately doubled.[38]

There are literally thousands of examples of the workings of this system. Two, one each from the 1900 and the 1910 census, will suffice. In 1888 Patrick Cronin emigrated to the United States. He married Maggie Driscoll, probably in Butte, in 1894, the year of Maggie's immigration. In 1896, James Driscoll, Cronin's brother-in-law, joined the household, both men working in the mines. Since both Driscoll and Cronin are West Cork names, there was likely an Irish courtship, an enforced absence, and a joyful reunion followed by the prearranged arrival of the bride's brother and, in 1899, the predictable arrival of the Cronins' first child.[39]

The four-member Cronin/Driscoll family cannot have seriously stretched available living space. There were other instances, however, when "extended" family might have meant extended into the street. In 1910 the house at 241 E. Granite Street held nine related members of the Barry/Mulholland family. They ranged in age from one year to fifty-one, two of the nine were born in Ireland, four in England, two in Michigan and one, the infant, in Montana. There were three male wage earners. Two of these three were miners: Thomas Barry, the head of the household, and his fifty-one-year-old father-in-law, Richard Mulholland. The third, twenty-two-year-old Michael Mulholland, Barry's brother-in-law, was a blacksmith, more than likely employed in the mines. Charge of the home was left in the hands of twenty-four-year-old Mary Mulholland Barry. There were four separate years of immigration for the six family members not born in the United States. That their immigrations were related seems obvious.[40]

These family arrangements were commonplace, but there may have been as many who immigrated in response to friends or more distant relatives whose exact relationship was obscured by a different name. Here the records of the Butte Irish associations provide useful data. Both the Ancient Order of Hibernians and the Robert Emmet Literary Association had rules requiring that new members be known by the person proposing them for membership for at least three years. There were probably some interested Butte Irishmen who had to wait the requisite three years before seeking membership, but there cannot have been many. The records are filled with references like "known for 22 years" or "knew him in the old country." It cannot be shown that knowing someone meant assisting in or even influencing that person's immigration to Butte, but the cumulative weight of the references to previous knowledge together with the tight weave of Irish society offer powerful circumstantial evidence that it did.[41]

The assistance of family and friends in jobs and housing must have been a powerful stimulus to immigration. But there is some reason to believe that the assistance was not always directed from America to Ireland; there were times, in other words, when Irish emigrated not necessarily to benefit themselves but to offer support to kin who had emigrated earlier. Anna Hanley O'Brien, for example, came to the United States in 1902 when she was twenty years old. She married (probably in Butte) and had three children born in Butte between 1905 and 1908. Her husband died in 1908 or 1909, leaving her with three children under four years of age, a mortgage on a home, and no visible means of support. In 1909 her twenty-four-year-old Irish-born brother, Michael Hanley, joined her in the overwhelmingly Irish Dublin Gulch section of Butte, got a job in the Anaconda Mine and, presumably, paid the bills.[42]

Michael Hanley was one of thousands of Irish and Irish-Americans who made their way, often with intermediate stops, to the mines of Butte. Few of these thousands came as strangers. They were part of a group migration, even when the members of the group emigrated at different times. One story had it that when "Pat" wrote to "Mike" he told him, "Don't stop in the United States; come right on out to Butte." Another insisted that Irishmen arrived with signs that said simply "To Butte" still pinned to their jackets. There must have been many in the rural areas of the West of Ireland who knew more about Butte than they did about Dublin, and emigration to it was always an option for them. Pushed out of Ireland, pulled into Butte, they took the path of their friends and kin, establishing, according to one twentieth-century source, a standard route: "Skibereen to Queenstown; Queenstown to Boston; Boston to Butte and the Mountain Con Mine" where Jim Brennan was the foreman and known to favor fellow Irish job applicants.[43]

But the pull was stronger and its sources more diverse than is implied by the Skibereen to Mountain Con story. There was more to the attraction than jobs. There was a palpable Irish presence in Butte, and that presence was known from Waterford through Cork to Donegal. David Brody has argued that "the movement of immigrants into American industry . . . was not random, but—rather—flowed through well-defined networks based on family and village ties." The road from Ireland to Butte provides as telling and persuasive an example of Brody's thesis as can be found anywhere in industrializing America.[44]

NOTES

1. Butte's story was most recently told in Malone, *Battle for Butte*, pp. 3–56. Bureau of Census, *Twelfth Census, Population,* part 1, pp. clxxvi–clxxix, 768, 798, 875. Figures for second-generation Irish residing in Silver Bow County are not given. The 25 percent figure is obtained by using the ratio of Irish-born to the second generation in the county in 1910, applying that ratio to 1900. Bureau of Census, *13th Census,* pp. 592, 594.

2. Occupational statistics are from Bureau of Census, *MS Census,* 1900. Anaconda Copper Mining Company, "General Office Records," Subject File 522, Anaconda Company Papers. Montana, Dept. of Labor, *First Biennial Report,* p. 206. The copper king was F. Augustus Heinze. His remarks are found in the newspaper he owned, the *Reveille* (Butte), Sept. 20, 1902; John Connolly, 1915. AOH D3, MB, Oct. 2, 1915.

3. Bureau of Census, *MS Census,* 1900; Vaughn and Fitzpatrick, *Irish Statistics,* pp. 299–339. Miller, *Emigrants,* p. 582. The substance and significance of the Irish background is discussed in Wilentz's excellent review essay, "Industrializing America," p. 586. See also Foner, "Land League," pp. 150–200.

4. Bureau of Census, *MS Census,* 1900, 1910; Kennedy, *The Irish,* 71–73, 81–82, 149–58.

5. Hand, "Folklore," p. 177n64; Hand et al. "Songs," pp. 10, 11, 23, 32. On name/place association see McLysaght, *Irish Families,* pp. 16–17, 28–37. On the counties supplying the immigrants, see Schrier, *Ireland,* p. 41; Vaughn and Fitzpatrick, *Irish Statistics,* pp. 269–343; Miller, *Emigrants,* pp. 570–71.

6. Crofutt, *Butte City Directory;* Polk, *Butte City Directory,* 1891–92, 1897, 1902, 1908, 1914. McLysaght, *Irish Families,* passim; Shannon interview.

7. Riobard O'Dwyer, *My Ancestors,* passim. A hand count was made of those who went directly or indirectly to Butte. *Polk, City Directory,* 1908. Father

Patrick Brosnan to his father, Feb. 18, 1917, Brosnan Letters. I am indebted to Professor Kerby Miller for sending me a copy of these letters.

8. Du Maurier, *Hungry Hill,* pp. 337, 343, 361; Riobard O'Dwyer, *My Ancestors,* pp. vi, vii. For very brief discussions of copper mining in Ireland see *Copper Handbook,* V:140; Joseph Lee, *Modernisation,* p. 119; Liam O'Dwyer, *Beara,* p. 34. O'Daly, Life (hereafter with hand-counted page in brackets). Once again, my thanks to Kerby Miller for sharing this autobiography with me.

9. Bureau of the Census, *Ninth Census,* pp. 346–47, 359, 364, 369–70; *Tenth Census,* pp. 491–92, 512, 520, 527; *Eleventh Census,* pp. 615–16, 640, 653, 663–64. For the Irish in western quartz mining see Ralph Mann, *After the Gold Rush,* pp. 86–94, 120–25, 142–46; Lingenfelter, *Hardrock Miners,* pp. 6–7, 103–4; Wyman, *Hardrock Epic,* pp. 45–47, 145, 158. For the Irish in Pennsylvania coal mining see Broehl, *Molly Maguires* and Lewis, *Lament for the Molly Maguires.* For Michigan see Riobard O'Dwyer, *My Ancestors,* and Erickson, *American Industry,* pp. 6–7, 43–44.

10. Bureau of Census, *MS Census,* 1900, 1910.

11. AOH, Membership and Dues Ledger, Apr., 1882–Mar. 1987, and 1889–92; AOH, Memberships. The alert from national headquarters to the RELA is found in RELA, MB, Sept. 20, 1906. The references to transfer members are from RELA, MB, Jan. 13, 1887; June 13, 1889; Feb. 11, 1897; Dec. 22, 1898; Dec. 13, 1900; July 1, 1904; Apr. 6, 1905; Jan. 11, 1906.

12. See, for example, Devoy, *Post Bag,* I:255. Seán Ruiséal's lament is from Miller, *Emigrants,* p. 513. See also *Miller,* "Assimilation," pp. 101–2 RELA, MB, May 31, 1888; Aug. 21, 1890; Feb. 18, 1897. AOH, Membership and Dues Ledgers, 1882–1887.

13. Thernstrom, "Working Class Mobility," pp. 24–25. On this same point of worker transiency see also Malone, *Battle for Butte,* pp. 5–8, 57, 58; Ronald C. Brown, *Hard-Rock Miners,* pp. 3–7, 10, 161–66; Lingenfelter, *Hardrock Miners,* pp. 3–4; Wyman, *Hardrock Epic,* pp. 58–59, 252–53; Dubofsky, "Origins," p. 380; Vernon Jensen, *Heritage of Conflict,* pp. 10–18. O'Brien's wanderings are recounted in pp. 3778–79. Industrial Commission, *Mining at Butte,* 1915, pp. 3778–79. (The year, either 1911 or 1915, that the testimony was taken will be included in citations.) Some of the 1915 report consists of testimony taken by the State of Montana in 1911 under the heading Montana, Joint Committee . . . of the Twelfth Legislative Assembly . . . to Investigate the Sanitary Conditions and the Conditions of Ventilation of the Mines . . . of Butte, *Proceedings,* 1911.

14. Malone, *Battle for Butte,* pp. 3–34. WPA, *Copper Camp,* pp. 16–17. AOH D1, MB, Feb., 22; Mar. 1, 1899. Bureau of Census, *MS Census,* 1870; William Read to Walker Brothers, July 19, 1878, Alice Mining Co. Records, Letter Press Books. Bureau of Census, *MS Census,* 1880; Bureau of Census, *Tenth Census,* 1880, *Compendium,* part I, p. 518.

15. This account of Daly's early career is taken from Malone, *Battle for Butte,* pp. 6, 17–20; Toole, "Marcus Daley"; Daly, *Biography of Marcus Daly* (Butte, 1934). Hugh Daly is the same man who wrote his autobiography using the

name O'Daly. Marcosson, *Anaconda*, pp. 42–45; Shoebotham, *Anaconda*, pp. 1–62.

16. Glasscock, *War of the Copper Kings*, pp. 74, 104; Malone, *Battle for Butte*, p. 64. Norma Smith also said the Irish "followed" Daly to Butte ("Rise and Fall," p. 10). Erickson, *American Industry*, pp. 107, 109. Daly and the railroad developer J. J. Hill were good friends but the pooling agreement of 1886 made it unlikely—and maybe illegal—for any kind of arrangement to be made between the two. Johnson and Huebner, *Railroad Rates*, I:120. Riobard O'Dwyer found no evidence that Daly actively recruited in West Cork. Remarks to Professor David Taylor, University of Montana, Aug. 26, 1986.

17. WPA, *Copper Camp*, p. 245; Brosnan to his father, Feb. 18, 1917, Brosnan Letters; Bureau of Census, *Ninth Census*, p. 364. Riobard O'Dwyer, *My Ancestors*, p. 228. See also O'Daly, Life, [9, 11, 130–31, 155].

18. Daly, *Biography of Marcus Daly*, pp. 2–3; Shoebotham, *Anaconda*, p. 40. For the politics of the *Irish World* see Foner, "Land League," pp. 169–70; Thomas N. Brown, *Irish-American Nationalism*, pp. 49–56, 178–79; Rodechko, "Patrick Ford." For Daly's Irishness see Remarks of J. J. Lynch in AOH, *Proceedings*, 1906. For Daly's affiliation with the AOH see AOH D1, MB, Nov. 14, 28, 1900. For RELA membership proposal see MB, July 29, Aug. 5, 1886. Davitt's visit and Daly's involvement are discussed in RELA, MB, Oct. 14, 1886; AOH D1, MB, July 7, 1886. Hugh O'Daly said Marcus Daly was a close friend of Davitt and Charles Stewart Parnell (Daly, *Biography of Marcus Daly*, p. 10). See also on this point Lindsay, *Amazing Experiences*, pp. 67, 72, 81–82. For Daly's involvement with the Thomas Francis Meagher Memorial Association see the *Montana Catholic* (Butte), July 15, 1899, and RELA and Phil Sheridan Club (Anaconda), Proceedings of a Joint Meeting . . . for a Monument to Thomas Francis Meagher, Butte, Jan. 1, 1898, Reports. Bishop John Brondel acknowledged Daly's generosity to the Catholic Diocese of Montana in a letter to his brother, the Rev. Charles Brondel, Jan., 25, 1902, Brondel Papers. See also Franchi, "History of the Catholic Schools of Butte," and the anonymous "History of St. Lawrence O'Toole Parish." Rev. Francis Xavier Batens commented on Daly's generosity with the Catholic parishes of Anaconda in *Anaconda Standard*, Mar. 12, 1922. Daly's contributions to Archbishop John Ireland's seminary in St. Paul are noted in J. J. Hill to Daly, Mar. 6, 1896; John Ireland to J. J. Hill, Mar. 13, Dec. 11, 1896, and Jan. 25, 1897, in J. J. Hill Papers. I am indebted to Tom White for bringing this material to my attention and for allowing me to use it.

19. Lindsay, *Amazing Experiences*, pp. 81–82; WPA, *Copper Camp*, pp. vii–viii, 3, 8, 209, 210; Malone, *Battle for Butte*, pp. 18–19; Marcosson, *Anaconda*, p. 61; Bishop John Brondel to the *Catholic Sentinel* (Helena), Oct. 3, 1888, in Brondel Papers. *Helena Independent*, Feb. 20, 1889. The *Examiner* (Butte), Sept. 3, 1896, Apr. 19, 1896. Daly also "imported" Welsh and Cornish workers for certain skilled jobs (Daly, *Biography of Marcus Daly*, p. 7; Marcosson, *Anaconda*, p. 66). See also the remarks regarding ethnicity in the mines in William Read to Walker Brothers, July 18, 1878, Alice Mining Co. Records, Letter Press Books.

20. For an overview of the Edenic myth and its significance to western land promoters, see Emmons, *Garden*. For descriptions of Butte, see WPA, *Copper Camp*, p. 291; Malone, *Battle for Butte*, pp. 57–64; Brosnan to mother, Nov. 20, 1917, Brosnan Letters; Atherton, *Perch of the Devil*, p. 57; Clyde Murphy, *Glittering Hill*, pp. 12–13.

21. Brockett, *Our Western Empire*, p. 1003; Thayer, *Marvels*, pp. 341–44, 521, 714. See also Slotkin, *Fatal Environment*.

22. Union Pacific Railroad, *Resources . . . 1890*, pp. 78–79; Union Pacific Railroad . . . 1891, pp. 47, 51, 54–55. O'Farrell, *Butte*, pp. 8–9.

23. Montana Territory had an immigration society as early as 1872. Taylor, *Distant Magnet*, p. 72. Montana, Mine Inspector, *Report . . . 1889*, p. 75; McKnight, *Mines of Montana*, pp. 21–22; Montana World's Fair Committee, *Montana*, pp. 69–76; Butte Chamber of Commerce, *Resources*, pp. 7–10.

24. Marcosson, *Anaconda*, pp. 5, 48–49; WPA, *Copper Camp*, p. 20; *Engineering and Mining Journal*, Jan. 7, 1888; Malone, *Battle for Butte*, pp. 52–54; E. S. Lee et al. *Population Redistribution*, pp. 587, 753; Bureau of the Census, *Twelfth Census*, Manufactures, part 2, pp. 500, 504, 505; Taylor, *Distant Magnet*, pp. 188, 201; Long, *Wages and Earnings*, pp. 121–66; Wyman, *Hardrock Epic*, pp. 35–37, 67–68; Ronald C. Brown, *Hard-Rock Miners*, p. 102.

25. Con F. Kelley, in Industrial Commission, *Mining at Butte*, 1915, p. 3712. Bureau of Census, *MS Census*, 1900, asked for "months not employed." *MS Census*, 1910 asked for "weeks out of work in 1909." Dan Lynch made the remark about wages in Ireland and America. AOH D3, MB, July 15, 1907. WPA, *Copper Camp*, p. 291. Father Brosnan also reported that Butte paid "the highest wages in the world" (to father, n.d., 1917, Brosnan Letters).

26. Johnson and Huebner, *Railroad Rates*, II:119, 120, 124; Taylor, *Distant Magnet*, p. 96; Great Northern Railway, "Harvest Excursions."

27. Daly, *Biography of Marcus Daly*, pp. 7–8; Riobard O'Dwyer, *My Ancestors*, p. 101; O'Daly, *Life*, [35]; Wyman, *Hardrock Epic*, pp. 65, 67. Bureau of Census, *MS Census*, 1900; The *Butte Bystander* had a story on living and working conditions in which the average monthly cost of room and board was given as $31.35 (Mar. 17, 1894).

28. The mining companies wanted a labor surplus; the unions preferred a labor shortage. William Read to Walker Brothers, June 30, 1878, Alice Mining Co. Records, Letter Press Books; Ronald E. Brown, *Hard-Rock Miners*, pp. 5–6; Burchell, *San Francisco Irish*, pp. 38, 68. The workers' response is discussed in *Butte Bystander*, Feb. 10, 1894, and Feb. 4, 1896; WFM, Executive Board, Report, pp. 418–20. Western History Collection, University of Colorado, Boulder; hereafter cited as WHC; Remarks of Joseph Shannon in Industrial Commission, *Mining at Butte*, 1915, p. 3853. For the argument that every emigrant was a lost patriot, see Schrier, *Ireland*, p. 59: RELA, MB, Oct. 3, 1907; Sept. 1, 1910. The possibility that well-off Irish were embarrassed by the immigration of poorer Irish is suggested in Funchion, "Irish Chicago," p. 28. See also Kennedy, *The Irish*, p. 23.

29. O'Daly, *Life*, [3, 6, 7, 11].

30. Ibid., [6]; Hand et al., "Songs," 32; Shannon interview.

31. *Butte Bystander*, Dec. 30, 1893; Riobard O'Dwyer, *My Ancestors*, passim; Golab, *Immigrant Destinations*, p. 58.

32. Riobard O'Dwyer, *My Ancestors*, passim. Murphy's repatriation is found on p. 256. O'Daly, Life, [95]. See also Miller, *Emigrants*, p. 426.

33. For an account of the paper's popularity in the West, see the letter from Colonel Edward Daniels in the issue of Nov. 22, 1879. Almost any issue from 1878 to 1883 contained at least one story of conditions in Ireland. There were some explicit requests for relief money. Local Butte papers also reported on famine conditions in Ireland. See, for example, *Butte Bystander*, Jan. 19, 1895, and Sept. 11, 1897.

34. Brondel to the priests of the diocese, Dec. 4, 1890, Brondel Papers; AOH D1, MB, Aug. 25, 1897; Apr. 13, June 1, July 6, 1898.

35. Sisters of Charity to Andrew O'Connell, Apr. 17, 1886, O'Connell Papers. See also the letter from the Sisters to the AOH, in AOH D1, MB, Mar. 3, 1897. The *Butte Bystander* had a story on immigrant ships filled with young Irish women (May 18, 1897).

36. Taylor, *Distant Magnet*, p. 101. See, for example, the notice published in the *Butte Bystander* by W. M. Tuohy (or Twohey), the general agent of the Northern Pacific Railroad and a prominent Butte Irishman (Feb. 18, 1893). Bureau of Census, *MS Census*, 1900 and 1910. *Butte Bystander*, Apr. 14, 1896. The story on Lowney and McVeigh was an account of a mine explosion that had taken their lives and those of four other Irishmen.

37. Bureau of Census, *MS Census*, 1900 and 1910; Kennedy, *The Irish*, p. 13.

38. Kennedy, *The Irish*, p. 13.

39. Bureau of Census, *MS Census*, 1900; McLysaght, *Irish Families*, pp. 343, 346.

40. Bureau of Census, *MS Census*, 1910.

41. AOH, *Constitution, 1886*; AOH, *Ritual and Manual, 1901*; AOH, Membership and Dues Ledgers; AOH D1 and 3, MB; RELA, MB.

42. Bureau of Census, *MS Census*, 1910.

43. Hand, "Folklore," p. 177; Curtin interview; WPA, *Copper Camp*, p. 173.

44. Brody, "Workers," pp. 147–48.

CHAPTER 2

Remembered Pasts

I

Like every immigrant group, the Irish who came to Butte brought with them an assortment of memories. As they concerned England and English policy, this remembered past bound many of the Irish to ancient and atavistic hatreds. The emigrants, however unconscious they may have been of the fact, were the products of Irish history. That history had never been kind, and for many Irish the store of memories had now to include among its cruelties his or her own emigration. But the Irish who came to the United States were more than just exiled warriors temporarily assigned to America's cities. They were also immigrant laborers, usually the lowest placed and least skilled, whose work experiences in Ireland would in part determine their response to the worlds of industrializing America. They were, in other words, both Irish patriots and contributing members of an emerging working class. It is important to recognize that these were separate roles; but it is even more important to understand that they were related. Often they were mutually reinforcing; occasionally they were mutually incompatible. The point is that one role was very seldom played out in the absence of the other; each was, in fact, a test of the other.

Adam Smith once wrote that "a man is of all sorts of luggage the most difficult to be transported." He was not speaking necessarily of the Irish but he certainly had in mind the ability of old patterns and habits, old fears, loves, and hates to confound the immigrants' adjustment to the felt realities of new worlds. The Irish response to these new realities was not predetermined by these experiences. They were conditioned by their past, not programmed by it. But that conditioning is important because unless it is understood, at least in its most general

expression, the Irish worker/Irish nationalist response to Butte is un-
intelligible and whatever lessons are to be learned from that response
are lost. When it is recalled that the Irish of Butte had taken vastly
different routes to the place and had accumulated in the process vastly
different memories, the importance of knowing something more about
who these Irish were—and, within the obvious limits, what their experiences had been—becomes even clearer.[1]

Some of the Irish, whether miners from Berehaven or landless farm
laborers from Donegal, went directly to Butte, many of them assisted
by the remittance money of the Irish who had gone before them. Others,
regardless of the year of their emigration, made their way to Butte only
after a number of intervening stops. The significant point is that two-
thirds of them ended up working in Butte's mines, forming a large and
ethnically homogenous working class. Their work backgrounds, however, differed dramatically. The twenty-year-old who emigrated from
West Cork in 1898 cannot have been personally familiar with the work
rhythms and discipline of underground mining, though it is likely he
had heard of its demands from his father or grandfather. This gave
him an advantage over the immigrant farm laborer from Donegal, for
whom Butte must have seemed as strange and remote as the nether
side of the moon. But neither can have possessed the industrial wisdom
of the West Irish spalpeen, or migrant laborer, who had worked in the
mills of the English midlands, or the immigrant to the factories of the
industrial northeastern part of the United States. And these seasoned
industrial workers could doubtless have learned much from the Berehaven immigrant of 1882. But the most work-wise of the Butte Irish
were drawn from yet another source: the experienced hard-rock miners
who came from the copper mines of Michigan or the gold and silver
quartz mines of California, Nevada, Utah, and Colorado.

Butte's Irish came from these five relatively distinct sources, ranked
on the basis of the difficulty of their adjustment to conditions in Butte.
Even the last listed, the older hands who had worked in other western
mining districts, had had no experience with industrialized mining on
a scale as huge as Butte's was to become. There were substantial differences between Eureka, Utah, or Austin, Nevada, and Butte, Montana. But it is also true that the population of Irish miners in Butte
contained many thousands who knew what the world of hard-rock
mining demanded of a worker and what the worker might reasonably
demand of it. At issue in these speculations regarding prior residency
is the important question of the extent of Irish preparation for the work
discipline and social demands of Butte. The available evidence suggests
that most of the city's Irish working class brought with it a fair un-

derstanding of the form and substance of the industrial world. Marcus Daly knew that, and Irish workers were doubly attractive to him because of it. This was not, of course, the common pattern among Irish workers in America, where the unprepared Irish were seldom recruited and often resented.

Many of the emigrants to Butte also brought with them the exile's mentality, the perception that England had denied them fundamental rights because they were Irish or because they were poor. But this only made keener their appreciation of the uses to which Irish and working-class organizations could be put in the effort to recover rights denied them for whatever reason. Even those who came to Butte directly from rural West Ireland had learned that lesson. If nothing else, the West Irish peasant of 1880 was far less likely to assume that famines were God's doing; God brought the blight but government made the famine. God could only be prayed to; governments could be brought down. Whatever heading such a lesson comes under, it was an important one to learn.[2]

As always, it seems, there was an irony, almost a capriciousness, in the way history played tricks on the Irish. Butte's Irish immigrants were part of the second great wave of immigration, unaffected in any direct way by the Famine or its consequences. Indeed, they left an Ireland in a way made stronger and more prosperous by the deaths and emigration of the Famine years. But only Englishmen, and the most cold-blooded of them at that, contended that famine was an acceptable shortcut to economic progress. Still, there was progress of sorts in the post-Famine years: Literacy rates rose, so did bank deposits; diets improved; new farming methods were introduced. But the beneficiaries of these changes did not emigrate; they stayed to form what passed for a middle class. The creation of this Irish "bourgeoisie," however, served principally to remind the Irish poor who did leave that not all of their enemies were clothed in English red or Scots-Irish orange. The middling Irish farmer was as likely as the British to drive the laborers off the land; the changes in Irish society included the social fragmentation of its uniquely Irish Catholic component. Economic changes not only did not prevent emigration, they promoted it.[3]

Problems arose in Ireland when America was not able to receive all those whom Ireland sent, as between 1873 and 1879 when industrial depression in the U.S. closed off a number of immigrant job opportunities. One consequence of this American depression was a net increase in the already sizeable number of discontented and rebellious Irish in Ireland. This is obviously not the place for an extended discussion of the causes or the course of Irish rural discontent. The important consideration is that the rural West Irishman—and not for the first time—counted rebellion, not submission or starvation, as an alternative to leaving Ireland.[4]

This reawakening of the West of Ireland had profound implications for the history of Ireland, but it was of more than casual significance to the history of the United States. The Irish immigrant was no more disposed to docility in the face of American industrialization than he had been in the face of landlordism. Occupationally, he may still have known only how to dig, how to "throw mud with a crooked stick," as one fictional Irishman put it. But politically he was the product of a society in which many of the traces of the deferential pattern of the early nineteenth century had been erased. The Irish may well have been the most politically aware of all the European peasantry, as well as the first of that class to become politically aware. Both the timing and the extent of that politicization—again the irony—were the consequence of the Famine, or more specifically of the knowledge that men and their governments caused famines and that men could be made to yield.[5]

The Butte Irish retained that simple lesson. It is even possible that those most likely to demand change were the first to book passage on the immigrant ships and the first to board America's westbound trains. It is important, however, to reemphasize that the changes were not necessarily radical, particularly as radical is defined in theoretical or ideological terms. Even their sympathy for "revolutionary" measures arose first because they were Irish, not because they were workers. Later, as those two roles became more nearly related aspects of a single role, some Irish workers would broaden their definition of resistance and extend their list of targets to include capitalists as well as Englishmen. But even then resistance was not revolution; worker as well as Irish protest—even at its most riotous—was not inherently radical. It was only Irish and working-class. As the English historian Eric Hobsbawm writes, it is "wrong to suppose that any class is revolutionary per se," and the Irish working class, when it demanded its rights, was as likely to appeal to precapitalist communalism as to postcapitalist communism. America would get the most disaffected of the Irish Catholics, but their disaffection was directed toward nothing more—and nothing less—than demands for job stability and an acknowledgment by capital of the workers' personal dignity. Seldom, in fact, was it directed toward anything else.[6]

As likely to be retained by these immigrants as the possibility of change were the specific means of affecting it. Again, the tactics of the Irish rebels, whether Fenians, Land Leaguers, Home Rulers, or Republicans, need only be understood in broadest outline, beginning with an awareness of the twin objects of the modern Irish resistance. The rebels wanted a free Ireland, an Ireland rid of English parliamentary control; but this essentially political object would be of little value without a revolution in the control and ownership of Irish lands. The effort to pair those two goals was a dominant aspect of the rest of Irish as well as Irish-American history. There were certain tactics, however, which served both causes and these the Irish brought to state of the art. The tactics ranged from the civilly disobedient—boycotts and hunger strikes, for example—to the uncivilly terroristic—dynamiting and assassination. Each required a careful attention to organization, a subordination of means to ends—or at least an eye to the main chance—an alliance of Ireland's different factions and classes, and a polite but firm independence from the Catholic Church and its hierarchy. The Irish record in each of these areas was not one of unmixed success. The interclass alliance lasted only until the many Irish who were poor began to make demands upon the few Irish who were not; and even the most radical and/or non-Catholic of the Irish reformers made the obligatory bows to the Church.[7]

The important consideration, however, is that the Irish immigrant had been schooled in the various forms of political and economic resistance and that those forms were a part of the recollected past. Each of those forms, it must be noted, required either a communal response or at least community support—what one historian has called "remarkable self discipline and total communal participation." Moreover, although there were many instances of Irish political protest before the Famine, those that came after it reflected the growing social differentiation within the Irish Catholic population. The communities, in other words, would not be of all Irishmen, and these protests were thus better preparation for industrial worlds. As a consequence of this post-Famine reformism, though they might be unfamiliar with the pace and dynamics of industrialization the Irish in America were as ready as most, native or immigrant, to lay claim to their rights and, in the words of another English historian, E. P. Thompson, to "locate [themselves] in history and society."[8]

The issues, of course, changed from old worlds to new. In Ireland the demands were for land reform and some degree of political independence, not necessarily in that order. American society forced the Irish to reconcile these "Irish questions" with new and mostly working-class issues. The ability to resist, however, served their needs in both countries. And so Eric Foner can argue that the Irish in the 1860s and 1870s "brought cultural and political traditions that merged into . . .

expressions of . . . native American radicalism." These traditions, of course, need not have been radical to have merged into movements that were. Similarly, Daniel Walkowitz in his study of the industrial workers of Troy, New York, finds that the Irish among them "came mainly from southern and western Ireland . . . and carried with them traditions of organized . . . resistance." Again, resistance was not necessarily radicalism, and what radicalism there was would give way to ethnic exclusiveness and working-class pragmatism. Irish traditions, however, including those of resistance and protest, retained their applicability to American conditions.[9]

II

In the case of Butte, the usefulness of the remembered past went beyond a generalized ability to organize associations for mutual benefit. This was because of the Irishness of the place and because Butte was one of the few cities in America where many of the Irish workers knew how to do the work, where their skill and experience counted for as much as their muscle. Butte's industrial growth, coincident with its development generally, occurred in the 1880s and 1890s. Many of its Irish had had time to learn the requisite skills. Moreover, the West Cork connection, the disproportionately large immigration to Butte from the copper mines near Berehaven, meant that many of them had mastered those skills, or at least had known those who had, long before Butte required them. The same might be said of those who had passed through other mining regions in the United States. But the emphasis is rightly on the mines of West Cork; it is hard to think of another part of Ireland that sent its young men directly to an American city ready to do that city's work.

As has been noted, little is known about the details of the operation of the copper mines of West Cork. What follows is pieced together from diverse sources. There were six mines in the Allihies district, and they appear to have been relatively deep; those at Kealogue, for example, went down more than a quarter-mile, a depth Butte's mines would not reach until the 1890s. Thus, machinery was necessary to sink the mines and engines were used to hoist the copper ore. Daphne du Maurier writes of the miners descending into the mine shafts by long and narrow ladders. That may have been the case in the very early years on Hungry Hill, but by the mid-nineteenth century the men were lowered into the mines in buckets using a transom and winch.[10]

That was not the extent of the mechanization. Because of their location on Bantry Bay, the mines reached far below the level of the sea, and du Maurier wrote of the "engine houses with great pumps" to remove the water and of periodic flooding when the pumps failed. In addition, the rock in which the copper ore was embedded was granite, not "chalk" as was the case in Cornwall where the miners merely "shovel and wheel out ore as fast as they can put it in a barrow." At the Puxley mines they blasted the ore out, first with gunpowder, later with dynamite, and shoveled it into cars. The blasting was dangerous and specialized work and the Irish paid, as they were to pay later in Butte, in lost limbs and lost lives. As for the man with the shovel, he was known, both in Ireland and in the western United States, as a mucker, an appropriate name derived from *muc*, the Irish word for pig.[11]

There were other features that introduced the Irish to some of the less-lovely aspects of industrialization. Women and young children were commonly used in the dressing sheds, washing the ore. Wages for the children, some as young as nine, were two shillings per week. The 1,700 men working the mines in the 1870s averaged about two pounds sterling per week for a ten-hour shift. The mines operated twenty-four hours a day, seven days a week. The workers lived in company-owned "cottages," often located miles from the mine. A loud bell announced their shift in time for the walk to work. Their meals were usually carried to them by their wives. The mine captains, almost always Cornishmen who lived in the "Big Houses" nearer the mines and separate from the Irish quarters, had complete carge of hiring.[12]

What resentments the workers felt were seldom expressed. Du Maurier has one of the wives of the Puxleys/Brodericks complain of the "crowd of wretched devils working underground . . . glad of the employment to keep themselves from starving, and cursing the master who gave it to them, all in the same breath." Occasionally, however, this "strange, impotent resentment" took more substantial form, as in 1882 when farmer and miner agitation forced a 29 percent reduction in the Puxleys' rents, or later in the 1880s when "fences were broken, chicken and pigs stolen, orchards robbed and a spirit of terrorism began to spread abroad." Clearly, not all the violence in Ireland was the work of farmers and farm laborers; the "wretched devils working underground" were also in a rebellious mood.[13]

It appears that the mines of West Cork were adequate training grounds for those of the United States. There were, however, some differences. The Butte mines were considerably larger than the Irish. Five thousand men were employed in Butte's three hundred mines as early as 1884. There would be more than ten thousand men working underground by 1910. In 1887 just short of 80 million pounds of copper, worth more than $16 million, was shipped out of Butte. By 1890 both figures had almost doubled, and by 1910 production had risen to 4.7 million tons. There were, in addition, a few uniquely Irish features to the operations on Hungry Hill. Puxley, for example, was also the owner of a 7,300-acre estate, small parcels of which he leased to tenants. Some of these tenants also worked in his mines and used their wages to pay the rent. Butte provided nothing comparable. More to the political point were the restrictions on the importation of gunpowder and dynamite during periods of "local disturbance," restrictions which caused expensive delays in operation. But these relatively minor variations did not count for much when the West Corkman went underground in Butte. He even encountered, as he had in Ireland, "little pixies who burrowed underground and bewitched the miners." The drifts and stopes in the mines, the hoists that lowered them, and the feel of copper ore were all part of a remembered past.[14]

The story so far is of an Irish immigrant population well prepared to meet the workday demands of industrializing Butte. And the many for whom Butte's mines were altogether new were eased into them by the sizeable core of experienced men. This is not quite the same as saying they were not "uprooted" by their immigration, because clearly they were. It is to say that they were not without resources, psychological as well as social, as they confronted Butte and its mines. Ireland had taught them well enough, and there were good teachers for what still needed to be learned. The similarities between Ireland and Butte are as important in understanding these Irish as the differences.[15]

III

This point applies equally, however, to those aspects of late nineteenth-century Irish culture which were less ameliorative in their influence. The reference is not to vestigial remnants of a peasant and preindustrial world. Much of what survived of that world was easily fitted into the new world they encountered. Call these aspects simply the negative legacy of the Famine and the changes in Irish society which followed it.[16]

One of them was alcoholism. Some of the Irish did drink to excess, or at least spend an "excessive" amount of time in places where drink was served. But to concentrate solely on the amount drunk without an investigation of the role of the *shebeen* (*sibín*, unlicensed pub) and the working-class saloon in Irish and Irish-American culture is misleading. If they provided nothing more than a place to sing—and they provided quite a lot more—their usefulness would be assured. The Irish

rebellion was one of several in history set to music, and the shebeen
and the saloon were the places where the songs of rebellion could be
safely sung. Emigration did not affect that, though it sometimes changed
the target of the rebelliousness. The Irish modified the lyrics accordingly. This is not to dismiss the problem of the Irish and drink. It is
only to suggest that the issue be investigated with greater imagination
and sensitivity than has so far been shown.[17]

There were other and related demons in the collective Irish past.
Mental illness did increase after the Famine. Whether this was a consequence of the sufferings of those years or of better social bookkeeping
by the English is uncertain. There may have been some self-hate as
the Irish contemplated their dead and the failure of any to avenge
them. It is even possible that delayed marriage or permanent bache-
lorhood created a subculture of socially inadequate and sexually frustrated "boyos" and barroom patriots. Celibacy has seldom been asked
to bear a heavier responsibility. The immigrants did not necessarily
bring these allegedly dysfunctional characteristics with them; but they
were the products of a society where the characteristics were known.[18]

The one undeniable reality of late nineteenth-century Irish life is not,
however, to be found in any of the above. No Irishman or Irishwoman,
mad or sane, drunk or sober, celibate or sexually profligate, could
escape the reality of an out-migration that almost depopulated entire
regions. The population of County Cork, by way of obvious example,
fell from 650,000 in 1851 to 392,000 in 1911—this during years when
birth rates exceeded death rates in Ireland by six per thousand. In other
words, more than half a million Corkonians, many with strong ties to
the place, left between those years. This was the part of the remembered past that seems most relevant, Irish leaving and Irish planning
to leave. For over a century no generation of Irish children came of
age certain of Ireland's ability to provide a permanent home. The effect
of this uncertainty on both those who stayed and those who left was
profound if ultimately incalculable. Whether, on balance, its lessons
served the immigrant well or poorly is less important than the understanding that they were ineradicable.[19]

As with all peoples', the Irish memory was sometimes selective and
self-serving, and nowhere more so than when the Old Land was recalled. Ireland was frozen in time for those who left it, and frozen in
contorted aspect. English policy was not solely responsible for the
migration, but the Irish may be excused if they tended to ignore the
subtleties of economic analysis for the heartier fare of political rage.
Particularly was this the case when an individual's own emigration

was involved. Here was direct evidence of England's last and cruelest crime.[20]

But the reaction cannot have been much different for those who stayed. Statistics in this instance are inadequate but they do indicate the dimensions of the issue. The following are from the one parish of Eyeries, West Cork, and are drawn only from those families that sent at least one member to Butte. There were 378 of those families; 3,089 children were born to them and 1,707 of those children emigrated, considerably more than half. As noted, of that total, 1,138, a remarkable two in every three, went to Butte. On every page of Riobard O'Dwyer's genealogy is evidence of the wrenching impact of this emigration. Jack and Kate Healy had five children; all emigrated to Butte. Of John and Ellen Murphy's ten children, seven emigrated, five to Butte. Jack and Mary McCarthy had a family of eight children, the six who emigrated all went to Butte. Of Tade and Nora Sheehan's seven children, only one stayed in Ireland, the others, with twelve years separating them in age, went to Butte.[21]

A number of general conclusions can be drawn from these figures. At least one member of every family stayed in West Cork, usually to marry and have children—a fair percentage of whom would have to emigrate. Equally clear was that brothers and sisters who emigrated tried to stay together. They left Ireland but they did not leave the family, a point of obvious significance in determining immigrant destinations. There must have been some comfort in this for the parents watching their children leave. There was comfort, too, for the emigrants, knowing that part of West Cork was waiting in Butte. But it is difficult to know what to make of the history of two generations of Harringtons. Their story begins in 1818 and ends in 1918, nicely bracketing the 19th century. Twenty-two children were born to the families, eleven to each generation. Five of the twenty-two entered religious orders, fourteen emigrated, seven of those, one from the first generation, six from the second, to Butte. Of the Butte immigrants, three from the second generation, Daniel, Denis, and Timothy, were killed in mining accidents.[22]

It would be a mistake to assume from these examples that the memories of West Cork, any more than the lives spent there, were unrelentingly tragic. It would, however, be equally mistaken to assume that these and the countless other instances of family dislocation did not somehow influence the perceptions—social, cultural, political, and economic—of the people of the West of Ireland and of the people driven from there. It cannot have been easy watching "the pick and flower of the land," as one Corkman put it, emigrating to the United States.

The playwright John Millington Synge reported from West Kerry that "a ragged ballad-singer" boarded a train and "sang a long ballad about the sorrows of mothers who see all their children going away from them to America."[23]

The reaction of the emigrating children was doubtless more ambivalent, but their leave-taking and the conditions that forced it cannot have softened their feelings of resentment. Breeding children for the export trade soured the mood of both parent and child, and it was not coincidental that it was from the West and South of Ireland, and most particularly from County Cork, that a great share of Irish rebelliousness came. It was this almost-congenital sense of rebellion in Catholic Ireland that the conspicuously non-Catholic William Butler Yeats meant when he wrote that "Great hatred, little room, / Maimed us at the start. / I carry from my mother's womb / A fanatic heart."[24]

IV

Fanatic the Irish heart may have been, but it was also a divided heart—and this was the most destructive aspect of the remembered Irish past. In both Ireland and the United States, bitter divisions marked the reform and nationalist movements. Some of the splits in the Irish nationalist movement were organizational feuds, the consequence of personal animosities. Others arose because of differences of opinion over tactics, or over the eventual form that an Irish nation was to take. The choice of tactics ran from polite, even deferential, parliamentary obstruction to dynamiting and other forms of "physical force." By the 1880s the options available to a free Ireland, however that freedom might be won, ranged from Home Rule, a kind of British protectorate with symbolic and legislative ties to crown and Parliament, to an independent workers' republic owing no allegiance to anyone or anything outside Ireland.[25]

Irish-American nationalism reflected these divisions. The Fenians, for example, the largest and most radical of the Irish-American nationalist groups of the 1850s and 1860s were divided into three rival organizations, which attempted to unify in 1865 by forming the Clan-na-Gael. The Irish-American counterpart of the revolutionary Irish Republican Brotherhood succeeded only until the Clan itself began to split apart. The same fate befell the Irish Confederation and the United Irish League, both formed as checks on Irish-American factionalism. The immigrants did learn that the clan and county rivalries of Ireland were irrelevant in the United States, where such fine distinctions were lost on the often anti-Irish natives, and the Irish-American ranks may have been less riddled with spies and informers than the Irish. But with these exceptions, the nationalism of Irish-America was as fractious as that of Ireland. By 1886 John Boyle O'Reilly, leader of the Irish-American "conservatives," complained to the "radical" John Devoy that he was "sick to death of the deadly bitterness of these fights." O'Reilly was not the last to be afflicted.[26]

The nationalist movements could probably have finessed the managerial problems. Less easily handled were the deeper divisions which underlay Irish and Irish-American society. They could be patched, but, based as they were on ineradicable differences of class, they could never be eliminated. In Ireland the problem surfaced during the first heady days of agrarian rebellion in the late 1870s. Led finally by the Irish Land League, this resistance to the control of Irish lands by English landlords, many of them absentee, represented one of the first steps in the political reawakening of the Irish tenant farmer. Unfortunately for the cause of Irish unity, it did little at first to relieve the no-less-demeaning dependence of the Irish farm laborer upon that same Irish tenant. The tenants began to move toward "peasant proprietorship"; the farm laborers began to move toward the United States. The agrarian reformers of whatever vintage tried to resolve this inter-Irish dispute, and with some success. Wages for farm laborers more than doubled between 1845 and 1914, but at that there were almost 12,000 Irish laborers and fewer than 500 Irish farmers who entered through Ellis Island in 1902.[27]

It would be remarkable if this disproportionate immigration of poor farm laborers was not reflected in differences in immigrant attitudes. It would be even more remarkable if those differences could be shown. One possibility, however, suggests itself. The farm laborers were more nearly pushed than pulled out of Ireland. The changes in Irish society, including much higher wages for their labor, elevated their expectations without providing any real opportunity for the realization of those expectations. Thus, the nature and intensity of both the Irish and the Irish-American nationalist movements were affected by this process of immigrant selection and the greater commitment of the exiled Irish farm laborers.[28]

There were other related divisions. Irish-Americans, particularly the children of Famine immigrants, were often more radical in their nationalism, though not necessarily in their reformism, than those Irish-born whose memories of Ireland did not include the Famine. This differentiation was as much a function of age as of origin, a generational gap of sorts. And that gap affected almost every aspect of Irish immigrant life. The date as well as the place of birth was a partial determinant of job skills, intent to repatriate, degree of assimilation, and occupational mobility. In other words, the Irish-American community was no more homogenous or united in its Irish nationalism than in anything else. The divisions within that community were partly owing to the simple matter of the timing of ethnic memories.[29]

More serious rifts arose between the Irish in Ireland and those in the United States, whatever their age or place of birth. The very fact of residence in New York, or Boston, or Butte diminished in subtle but significant ways the authority of the immigrant Irish. This may explain the Irish-Americans' emphasis on "depopulation" as chief among England's sins. Two conclusions were implied by this emphasis. One was that those who were forced to emigrate were more aggrieved than those lucky enough to be able to stay. The second, following logically from the first, was that emigration was draining Ireland of its source of revolutionary strength and inspiration. Neither attitude was conspicuously popular in Ireland.[30]

The same can be said of the tendency of some Irish-Americans—fewer than was once thought—to equate a free Ireland with their own social and economic status. Shame attached to descent from an "enslaved" people, and for many Irish-Americans involvement in Irish nationalist movements was more an exercise in ethnic self-congratulation than an expression of undying devotion to the homeland or to the reform of its social and economic systems. For them, an independent Ireland was a prerequisite to their own liberation, and a certain confusion of means and ends was one consequence of this ethnic defensiveness.[31]

Less-substantial differences between the Irish and the Irish-Americans arose because of the latter's earlier involvement as industrial workers and their drift into associations reflecting class and occupational distinction. This involvement began in the 1840s, coincident with their immigration. In Ireland, though not among Irishmen in industrial England, the industrial worker/nationalist did not arise until the early 1900s; until then Irishmen worked on farms, not in factories. Thus, the methods and language of class protest were not the same in Ireland and Irish-America.

The immigrants brought to their worker organizations these traditions of resistance and struggle; Ireland had taught them how to fight. America would partly redefine the enemy, but the basic challenge in both places was the same: The Irish had to avoid a diffusion of energy or conflict of purpose. As Daniel Walkowitz notes in his discussion of the Irish in Troy, ethnic traditions of resistance and struggle could "feed labor militancy, but . . . they could also drain working-class solidarity into exclusively inter-class ethnic concerns in later years." By later years, Walkowitz means after Troy's Irish had become used to a world based on class as well as ethnic and national distinctions.[32]

Walkowitz's point could be applied to Ireland as well; on that point, in fact, rests a major share of the history of the Irish and Irish-American worker. The issue is not the multiple uses to which Irish militancy could be put, but rather the fact that a division between economic reform and political nationalism was as much a part of the Irish movement as of the Irish-American. Most of the Irish were poor; all of Ireland was unfree. The poor could be helped only by fundamental economic reform; Ireland only by political liberation. These were separate issues and separate causes; different constituencies arose around each of them. The nationalists of whatever class had to convince the poor that a free Ireland would be an economically and socially different and better Ireland. The poor were not always convinced. The reformers in their turn had to convince the nationalists that economic and social changes would hasten, not retard, Irish independence. They, too, had a mixed record of success. This was the deepest division in that fanatic Irish heart and the most important political aspect of the collective Irish memory.

But as important as the division was the effort to heal it, to reconcile necessary social and economic reforms with political independence, and to reconcile both with a suspicious but not innately hostile Catholic hierarchy. The effort absorbed the better part of Irish energies for half a century. There were a few times when the issue was one of chronology and priority. Was land reform a prerequisite to independence or must reform await that day of political deliverance? There were more times when the job of reconciling goals proved more difficult than the mere ordering of them, as when English-sponsored land reform, by providing a measure of economic relief, blunted the nationalism of Irish rural poor, or when the reformers demanded of an otherwise conservative group of nationalists and churchmen changes that seemed to edge perilously toward revolution or that diverted attention from the nationalist cause.

Further complicating the effort were the splits within both the reform and the nationalist movements. Land reform, in the Irish context, could mean anything from peasant proprietorship to land nationalization to a primitive communism. And the land system was not the only aspect of the Irish economy needing reform. By 1900, as Irish industrialization proceeded, the urban workers, led by James Connolly and James Larkin, began to press their demands, as their counterparts in America and England had earlier. The split between the urban and the rural reform movements was not irreconcilable but it did complicate the matter of drafting a reform agenda. The nationalists for their part were no more united than the reformers. There were Repealers, Home Rulers, Free Staters, and Republicans. The specifics of their demands are not important in this context—what is was that each had a different idea of what a free Ireland would look like. Those options, moreover, represented only the constitutional mechanics of independence. The nationalists were also divided on the best means to achieve that independence. If this were not enough, cultural nationalists turned Ireland into an ideological battleground of conflicting claims. There were spokesmen for a Catholic Ireland and a nonsectarian Ireland; Gaelic speakers and English speakers; Sinn Feiners and Irish Irelanders. Irish games, songs, literature, and clothes were represented by some as vital to the national effort, by others as superfluous. There were some who were pro-Irish and others, particularly among the Irish-Americans, unaware of the changes since their own emigration, who were simply anti-English.[33]

Finally, there was the implied division between the theorists and politicians, the intellectuals broadly defined, and the farmer/laborer groups. This division was more obvious in the United States, where non-Irish intellectual reformers tended often toward anti-Catholicism. Since most of these reformers were Republicans, a good percentage of the Irish-Americans did the obvious and fixed themselves to the Democratic party. In certain areas the local party was converted into another Irish club competing for the allegiance of the Irish worker. In Ireland, though anti-clericalism occasionally crept into the debates, the "intellectuals" were either Irish and Catholic or willing to tolerate the idiosyncrasies of both.[34]

Tolerance, however, did not necessarily mean understanding. The peasant and working classes resented their poverty; the intellectuals resented England's arrogant assumption that Ireland could not rule itself. One consequence of this deep division was that the former tended toward reform, the latter toward nationalism. But this particular problem may not have ended there. The Irish historian F. S. L. Lyons has suggested that the reform sought by the peasants, whether Irish or immigrant, was severely limited. And how could it have been otherwise? The demographics of post-Famine Ireland, "late marriages, large families, and many unmarried sons and daughters . . . was a recipe for conservatism, and the Irish peasant . . . was a very conservative person indeed." The nationalists and the theoreticians constantly had to take this into account. Peasant discontent could be put to "radical" use, but only if considerable care was taken.[35]

V

Healing these rifts—mending that fanatic and divided heart—would not be easy. The hope in Ireland was to bring as many of these diverse and occasionally divisive elements as possible into working coalitions, literally to unite economic reform with political freedom by grafting the one onto the other. The graft line, the seam, would always be visible; but through luck, or grace, or force of will, it would hold. The alliance was known first as the New Departure, a coalition of Home Rulers and land reformers. To effect it and the other coalitions that came after it, landless agricultural laborers and urban industrial workers had to be persuaded that an all-Irish parliament, not to mention such abstractions as Gaelic cultural nationalism, were as important as a chance to make a better living. It meant persuading middle-class shopkeepers and intellectuals that a redistribution of land, as well as other forms of property, was the price—and the dividend—of Irish independence. And finally, it meant trying to persuade the Irish Catholic hierarchy that reform and nationalism were not antithetical to the teachings and future prospects of the Church. This last was not an impossible calling; the hierarchy, particularly toward the bottom, was drawn from the same classes that produced the resistance, and a significant number of rebel priests and bishops spoke the language of both reform and nationalism. Still, to call the task of building coalitions formidable is to understate.[36]

The stakes were different and more complicated in America—though they may not have been as high. If nothing else, the cause of economic reform necessarily involved those Irish-Americans on the class side of the seam with non-Irish if not anti-Irish workers, in effect creating a third category of activists and a second graft line. In Irish-America, including Butte, there were Irish champions of Ireland, of the Irish workers, and of the working class. The last of these causes required a near-total subordination of ethnicity to class; the first a near-total subordination of class to ethnicity. The struggle was for the political soul of the man in the middle, the Irish worker. The claimants were the familiar ones: ethnic nationalists and class-conscious reformers. All sides sought an American version of the New Departure, an alliance that would permit the enemies of Ireland and the enemies of the Irish to be fought simultaneously.

In preindustrial Ireland, this meant that the West Irish tenant farmer had to be shown that nationalism was a prerequisite to reform. In the industrializing United States the issues were less clear. A commitment to reform was a function of the Irish-American's level of satisfaction with his own social and economic status and of his willingness to join hands with an American reform tradition that had, on more than one occasion, shown an unmistakable and quite illiberal hostility to his nation and his religion. When levels of satisfaction were low, that is, when the promises of American life were not kept, the Irish worker diverted some of his attention from English landlords to American plutocrats. Such, in fact, became "a new Irish passion" during the hard times of the 1870s. Similarly, when the reformers treated the Irish as victims rather than agents of injustice, as Wendell Phillips, James Redpath, and, temporarily, Henry George did, the Irish allied themselves with the wider world of reform. At those moments, the seam was almost invisible.[37]

The most instructive example of this Irish-American political hybridization occurred in the title and the content of the newspaper published by the Irish-born Patrick Ford. The *Irish World and American Industrial Liberator* was headquartered in New York but read wherever the Irish were to be found in the United States. Ford's paper was the conscience of the Irish-American working class, and it spoke along the seam. Ireland free meant nothing unless the Irish were free—all the Irish, farm laborers, tenants, workers, shopkeepers, whether in Ireland or the United States. Implied by this was that America was not a "larger and more benevolent Ireland." Land was as monopolized here as in Ireland; the worker as exploited here as in Ireland, and "idle-owned lands with idle-starving people [was] murder" here as in Ireland.[38]

Clearly, reform was more important to Ford than nationalism. He had not lost sight of a free Ireland; he only insisted that it had also and first to be humane. There would be disappointments. Like Marx, Ford thought the English industrial working class would support Home Rule for Ireland as a prerequisite to their own liberation. They did not, though one suspects Ford was less surprised by this than Marx. He tried to convert the Irish-American working class to his own definitions of Irish and worker but with only occasional success. But he never stopped speaking to the complexities of the Irish and Irish-American world. His journalistic and ideological rivals in the United States embraced simpler, almost self-indulgent theories.[39]

This is particularly true of the intense and single-minded nationalism of John Devoy and his newspaper, the *Gaelic American*. For Devoy there was only one issue: Ireland had to be rid of England and of things English, and physical force was to be the weapon of its liberation. There is radicalism in this. Thomas Brown writes that Devoy was "Lenin-like" in his intensity, but his vision barely extended beyond an independent Ireland. It is inconceivable that he would have understood

Ford's comment that "the cause of the poor in Donegal is the cause of the [Irish-American] factory slave in Fall River." Michael Davitt's comment to a group of Irish miners in Virginia City, Nevada, would have been only slightly more comprehensible to Devoy. "We can afford to put away the harp," Davitt said in reference to Irish independence, "until we have abolished poverty, mud cabins, and social degradation." But those were precisely the problems the patriots, including Devoy, tended to ignore in their recitals of Celtic glories and Saxon crimes. For Davitt and Ford this rhetorical patriotism—"sunburstery," Davitt called it—detracted from the larger object of reform. Devoy simply reversed the order. We must put away concern for poverty, wherever found, until the harp again in Tara's halls was heard.[40]

Few were as one-dimensional in their reformism as Devoy. John Boyle O'Reilly of the *Boston Pilot*, for example, was aware of the strange contradictions implied by the generic label Irish Catholic worker. He knew that each of the categories required its own expression of allegiance, if not devotion, and that each meant something slightly different in the American and Irish contexts. To acknowledge the problem, however, was not to attempt its solution.[41]

Perhaps there was no solution. The rival claimants were, after all, appealing to different parts of the whole. The cause of Ireland could, theoretically, be made the cause of the working class, but only by risking the alienation of the middle class and those who aspired to it both in Ireland and in the United States. Workers rebelled and rebels worked, and some, like Patrick Ford and James Connolly, attempted to respond to the needs of both. But Ford's success was limited and Connolly, the Irish socialist, was executed following the Rising of 1916, the fate of those who chose Ireland over socialism. Connolly knew that his participation in this rebellion of nationalists would seem incomprehensible to his socialist allies. "They will never understand," he said. "They will all forget I am an Irishman."[42]

Ford, however, remains the key figure in understanding what Foner calls the "complex interplay of class, ethnicity, and radicalism in industrializing America." No one worked harder to see that the seam between Irish and worker held. In the process, Ford gave as complete expression as it was ever to have to "grass roots Irish-American radicalism." He "reflected and helped to shape a developing labor consciousness." If Marcus Daly did, in fact, read the *Irish World*, and if he was influenced by its pages, he must be counted among the most uncommon of America's industrial barons. His perceptions would certainly not have been the same as those others, and his understanding of the Irishhmen who worked his mines would have been significantly improved.[43]

The *Irish World* and its battle at the seam of Irish and worker was the single most important element in the remembered past of the Butte Irish. If they had not read it in Ireland, they probably encountered it in America, and there seems to have been no escaping it in the western mining regions. According to a government geologist in 1879, the paper was seen everywhere in the mountain states—"its keen blade of the finest temper dealing powerful blows upon the mailed heads of hoary wrongs." Ford obviously inspired a certain fervor. Evidence of other areas where the paper was commonly found is provided by the list of local branches of the American Land League that were in general sympathy with the *Irish World*. These branches reported to Ford's paper and routed their contributions to the Irish Land League through it. In 1881 the contributions were tabulated by state. The anthracite coal regions of Pennsylvania were well represented, as were the adjacent industrial towns of Scranton and Wilkes-Barre. Contributions were also received from Bisbee and Tombstone, Arizona; Bodie and Eureka, California; Alma, Breckenridge, Leadville, and Golden City, Colorado; Lead City, Dakota Territory; Cherry Creek, Eureka, and Virginia City, Nevada; and Beartown and Butte City, Montana. These areas had much in common, beyond their obvious concentrations of Irish. Each was in or near a major mining region, each was to supply a considerable Irish population to Butte, and, most significantly, each had established a tradition of Irish and/or working-class militancy.[44]

In Pennsylvania this resistance was in the violent form of Molly Maguire terrorism. The Molly Maguires, offspring of the local divisions of the Ancient Order of Hibernians, fought a twenty-year duel with Pennsylvania mine owners and their predominantly Welsh and Cornish foremen and superintendents. This is not to suggest that the *Irish World* was responsible for Molly Maguire terrorism; the Mollies were born before Patrick Ford began his newspaper, and they continued their resistance without any encouragement from it. What is clear is that few Irishmen can have come from that part of Pennsylvania without a solid background in the methods and principles of Irish worker protest.[45]

The western mining regions were only a little less violent than the anthracite fields, and even this relative calm is best explained by reference to the greater success enjoyed by the early western miners' unions. At every stop on the mining frontier, workers—many of them Irish—formed a miners' union. In his history of this labor movement, a history which ends in 1893 before many of the Irish had arrived in

the United States, Richard Lingenfelter lists over forty men with unmistakably Irish names in positions of leadership in the western unions.
Here too, then, a combination of ethnic traditions of resistance, industrialization, and—though it would be difficult to assess its influence
with any precision—the *Irish World*, produced an Irish working class
aware of its rights and confident of its ability to protect them.[46]

But, as the amount of money they sent to the Irish Land Leagues
would attest, these Pennsylvania coal miners and western hard-rock
men had not forgotten the needs of the Old Land. The Land League
program of forcing a radical change in English law on land tenure
obviously appealed to the landless immigrants. At issue was the ability
to give equal time and energy to both reform and nationalist causes.
In 1876 a Berehaven emigrant, identified only as "Ballaghaslane Beara,"
wrote from Virginia City, Nevada, to the *Irish World*. It was a remarkable letter, expressing as well as it can be expressed the strength of
the seam at which Irish was grafted to worker. "We are slaves in the
United States," he began, "and . . . the reason for such a state of things
is plain: Because we haven't an Irish nation. England defrauded us of
the means by which, when leaving Ireland for America, we could afford
to settle down on a western farm; and we are therefore chained down
. . . in the mire of the cities." "Beara" went on to complain of Anglo-
American reluctance to hire Irish, a point which an alert Marcus Daly,
a former resident of Virginia City, might well have noted. No one
identified the seam as clearly and as unselfconsciously as "Ballaghaslane Beara." It cannot be known if he followed Daly to Butte. He
may well have, but even if he did not, thousands who shared his ideas
and experiences did.[47]

And whatever their place of origin, they brought to Butte well-established traditions of support for both Irish nationalism and working-
class reform. Bodie, California, for example, had both the strongest
miners' union in the state and the most generous Land League chapter.
But this point is true not just of the Molly Maguires or the western
miners' union men. Witness the O'Dwyers of Caolrua, Eyeries, West
Cork. Mike had been an active Fenian and Land League organizer;
imprisoned in the 1880s, he emigrated to Butte upon his release. His
brother, William, was an author, teacher, and Gaelic scholar. He was,
as well, the first secretary of the local Land League and an avowed
revolutionary. Three other brothers, Denis, Patrick, and John were miners; Denis and Patrick were imprisoned for Land League activities; John
had four sons who were active rebels. Of these three, Denis and Patrick
emigrated after their release from the Fermoy prison; Pat was killed
in a mine shaft accident in Calumet, Michigan.[48]

VI

These were the lessons learned, the memories retained by the Irish emigrants to Butte. Most of those emigrants were convinced of England's treachery; almost as many that England's crimes against Ireland and capital's crimes against Irish workers were related, though not quite synonymous. Many of them had had some experience in hard-rock mining. Whether from Ireland or the United States, their level of preparedness for industrialization was higher than that of most Irish emigrants, regardless of the timing of their emigration. By preparedness is meant a knowledge of the work regimen and of the methods available to the working class to protect its rights within it.

If the above may be considered a composite of the Butte Irish miner, let the career of John Daly speak for its individual parts. Daly was Irish-born, probably, if his surname is any indication, in County Cavan or Westmeath in central Ireland. He was a member of both of Butte's Irish nationalist associations, attesting to his "patriotism," an officer in the Butte Miners' Union, evidence, theoretically at least, of his working-class consciousness. He was also what was known as a "practical" miner, an important distinction meaning he had learned the trade by practicing it—in Daly's case for nineteen of his thirty-one years. Mining the way Daly did was a skilled trade. But "practical" meant more than just being able to find and dig ore. As Daly put it, "I worked in England when I was a boy; that is where I was first broke in." He had started work when he was twelve years old; he understood work—its pace and its mood. He knew what to expect of it and what it expected of him. Butte's mines can still have held surprises for him, but clearly Daly was no industrial naif. Not all of Butte's Irish workers were broken in; indeed, few can have been as experienced in the demands of an industrial world as John Daly. And even those who were could nonetheless have felt, as Daly did, the melancholia and disorientation that accompanied the relocation from one part of the world to another. But the central point remains: A significant percentage of Butte's Irish workers were acquainted with the requirements of their world and with their rights within it.[49]

NOTES

1. Adam Smith is quoted in Vedder and Gallaway, "Geographical Distribution," p. 23.

2. The best discussion of this point is in Foner, "Land League."

3. Joseph Lee, *Modernisation*, pp. 1–3, 8, 10, 13, 14–20, 27, 31, 38, 88–89, 92–97, 102–4, 108–9, 111, 122; Miller, *Emigrants*, pp. 360–63. On literacy see

also Donnelly, *Land and People*, pp. 232, 249, 251–54; Commissioner General of Immigration, *Annual Report, 1903*, p. 11; and Lyons, *Culture and Anarchy*, p. 9. The increase in resident landownership is discussed in Rumpf and Hepburn, *Nationalism and Socialism*, pp. 4, 54, 227; Kennedy, *The Irish*, p. 30; Clark and Donnelly, "Introduction," in *Irish Peasants*, p. 280. See, too, the remarks of J. J. Lynch, RELA, MB, Aug. 26, 1909. Thomas N. Brown discusses the growing sense of Irish nationalism that accompanied these advances in *Irish-American Nationalism*, pp. 3–6. For some English responses to the Famine, see Gallagher, *Paddy's Lament*, pp. 85, 142–48, and Woodham-Smith, *Great Hunger*, pp. 105, 366, 373–76, 379.

4. Joseph Lee, *Modernisation*, pp. 10, 82; Donnelly, *Land and People*, pp. 251–57; Kennedy, *The Irish*, p. 78; Vaughn and Fitzpatrick, *Irish Statistics*, pp. 299–338; *Statistical History*, pp. 55–56.

5. Joseph Lee, *Modernisation*, pp. 89–106, 163–64, and passim. The "crooked stick" reference is quoted in Thomas N. Brown, *Irish-American Nationalism*, p. 63. On the emigration of the disaffected see Kennedy, *The Irish*, pp. 192–94.

6. Hobsbawm, "Debating Labor Aristocracy," p. 222, and "Aristocracy," pp. 245, 247. See also Kennedy, *The Irish*, pp. 192–94; Walkowitz, *Worker City*, p. 115; Thompson, *English Working Class*, pp. 436–44; Blessing, "Irish Emigration," p. 24.

7. Thomas N. Brown, *Irish-American Nationalism*, pp. 85–100; Joseph Lee, *Modernisation*, pp. 42–48, 65–88, 97–105; Palmer, *Land League Crisis*, pp. 108–31. On the use of the boycott see Gordon, "Labor Boycott."

8. The reference to the importance of discipline and community in boycotting is from Joseph Lee, *Modernisation*, p. 94. The ability to "locate . . . in history and society" is from Thompson, *English Working Class*, p. 194. See also Cantor, "Introduction," p. 10.

9. Foner, "Land League," p. 180; Walkowitz, *Worker City*, pp. 166–67.

10. *Copper Handbook*, V:140; Malone, *Battle for Butte*, p. 62; Riobard O'Dwyer, *My Ancestors*, pp. v–vii, 167, 241; du Maurier, *Hungry Hill*, pp. 2–4, 29. Leary interview—Leary was born in Butte and has visited the West Cork mining regions on a number of occasions.

11. Du Maurier, *Hungry Hill*, pp. 38, 268, 328, 351; Riobard O'Dwyer, *My Ancestors*. pp. vi, 80, 211, 241. The origin of *mucker* was related by Father Sarsfield O'Sullivan (interview). Father O'Sullivan is the son of Berehaven emigrants.

12. Riobard O'Dwyer, *My Ancestors*, pp. v, 242–43; Lyons, *Culture and Anarchy*, p. 23; du Maurier, *Hungry Hill*, pp. 2–4, 13–14, 23, 26, 238, 351–52; O'Sullivan interview.

13. Du Maurier, *Hungry Hill*, pp. 12–13, 237, 366–67; Donnelly, *Land and People*, p. 298.

14. WPA, *Copper Camp*, p. 20; *Engineering and Mining Journal*, Jan. 7, 1888; Union Pacific Railroad, *Resources . . . 1891*, p. 47; Malone, *Battle for Butte*, pp. 53–54. For the 1910 production figures, see the remarks of Con Kelley to the Industrial Commission, *Mining at Butte*, 1915, p. 3687. Donnelly, *Land and*

People, p. 165n, 298; du Maurier, *Hungry Hill*, pp. 17, 61, 76, 384; Hand, "Folklore," pp. 1–6.

15. At issue is the argument between the "breakdown-assimilation" school of immigration studies best represented by Oscar Handlin and a new and far more convincing interpretation based on immigrant resourcefulness and cultural integrity. Handlin's views are best expressed in *Boston's Immigrants* and in *The Uprooted*. For a discussion of this and related points see Wilentz, "Industrializing America." Valuable material is also included in Rabinowitz, "Race, Ethnicity"; Brody, "Workers"; and Hays, "Politics."

16. For a discussion of the compatibility of preindustrial and industrial values see Walkowitz, *Worker City*, p. 130; Thompson, *English Working Class*, pp. 429–36; Cantor, "Introduction," p. 9.

17. Wilentz, "Industrializing America," p. 583; Glassie, *Passing the Time*, pp. 80–85, 247–57; Devoy, *Recollections*, p. 286; Lyons, *Culture and Anarchy*, pp. 9–10; Stivers, *Hair of the Dog*, pp. 15–33, 136–63; Rorabaugh, *Alcoholic Republic*, pp. 10–11, 143–44, 263–64; Finnane, *Insanity*, pp. 146–49; Scheper-Hughes, *Saints, Scholars, and Schizophrenics*. Michael Davitt stated that political songs were the mark of the Land League movement in the West of Ireland (*Fall of Feudalism*, pp. 166–67). For the way some of these songs were adjusted see Hand et al. "Songs."

18. Thomas N. Brown, *Irish-American Nationalism*, p. 20; Donnelly, *Land and People*, p. 250; Finnane, *Insanity*, pp. 129–74; Scheper-Hughes, "Inheritance," esp. pp. 50–51; Joseph Lee, *Modernisation*, pp. 3–6; Kennedy, *The Irish*, pp. 151, 163.

19. Donnelly, *Land and People*, pp. 159, 221, 226, 232; Vaughn and Fitzpatrick, *Irish Statistics*, p. 9; Joseph Lee, *Modernisation*, p. 6; Scheper-Hughes, "Inheritance," p. 50; Synge, *In Wicklow*, pp. 106, 150; Joseph Lee, *Modernisation*, p. 2.

20. Miller, *Emigrants*, 4–10, 428–29, 545–53; Thomas N. Brown, *Irish-American Nationalism*, p. 21; Joseph Lee, *Modernisation*, p. 94; Funchion, "Irish Chicago," pp. 18–19.

21. Riobard O'Dwyer, *My Ancestors*, passim. The Healys' story is on p. 2, the Murphys' on p. 9, the McCarthys' on p. 115, and the Sheehans' on p. 251.

22. Ibid., pp. 200–201.

23. Donnelly, *Land and People*, p. 229; Synge, *In Wicklow*, p. 106.

24. Rumpf and Hepburn, *Nationalism and Socialism*, p. 5, 40, 44; Joseph Lee, *Modernisation*, p. 58; Riobard O'Dwyer, *My Ancestors*, pp. 122–23; Donnelly, *Land and People*, pp. 327, 330ff. The quote from Yeats is from "Remorse for Intemperate Speech."

25. The story of the feuding within the Irish nationalist movement is a long and complicated one. The following very incomplete list of sources indicates the outlines of the issue as it related to both means and ends. Devoy, *Post Bag*, I:141, 457, 463, 501–2; II:32–33, 63, 79, 142, 358; O'Brien, *Parnell*, I:197–204; II:15, 29–31; Devoy, *Recollections*, p. 351; Short, *Dynamite War*, treats the extremist wing of the movement.

26. Devoy, *Post Bag*, I:2, 5, 26, 47; II:280, 287; O'Reilly's complaint is found in a letter to Devoy, May 3, 1886, *Post Bag*, II:280. Devoy, *Recollections*, pp. 268–71, 275, 344–45, 354; Thomas N. Brown, *Irish-American Nationalism*, pp. 7–8, 21, 38–41, 68–74; Funchion, "Irish Chicago," pp. 21, 33–34, 350n; Tansill, *America and the Fight*, pp. 41, 77–78, 120; Carroll, *American Opinion*, pp. 6, 156–59; Alan J. Ward, *Ireland and Anglo-American Relations*, pp. 8–9; Davitt, *Fall of Feudalism*, pp. 257–58; Foner, "Land League," pp. 162–66.

27. Joseph Lee, *Modernisation*, pp. 1–3, 10, 38, 82, 92–93, 121, 122; Lee also notes that spraying and the use of blight-resistant potatoes had "taken the potato out of politics" by 1885; farmers did not have to worry about crop failures. Miller, *Emigrants*, pp. 466–69, 481; Donnelly, *Land and People*, pp. 159, 226–30, 251–57; Vaughn and Fitzpatrick, *Irish Statistics*, pp. 9–14, 33–41; du Maurier, *Hungry Hill*, pp. 4, 7. For occupations see Commissioner General of Immigration, *Annual Report*, 1903, pp. 24, 26; and Kennedy, *The Irish*, p. 76.

28. Joseph Lee, *Modernisation*, p. 66. See also Kennedy, *The Irish*, pp. 192, 193, 194; Taylor, *Distant Magnet*, pp. 91, 97.

29. Thomas N. Brown, *Irish-American Nationalism*, pp. 21–22; Funchion, "Irish Chicago," pp. 31–33; Walkowitz, *Worker City*, p. 115; Hays, "Politics," pp. 170–71; Burchell, *San Francisco Irish*, pp. 38, 100; Arthur Mann, *One and Many*; Rabinowitz, "Race, Ethnicity."

30. Thomas N. Brown, *Irish-American Nationalism*, pp. 17–24; Lyons, *Culture and Anarchy*, p. 15; Foner, "Land League," p. 156. There was an understandable tendency among the Irish to expect money, not advice, from Irish-Americans; there was an equally understandable tendency among Irish-Americans to presume that their money, if not their greater wisdom, earned for them the right to influence policy. Since neither side could afford to alienate the other, these tendencies were usually muted. See for example, Tansill, *America and the Fight*, pp. 361–64, 383–96; Carroll, *American Opinion*, pp. 4, 6–9, 156–59; Ward, *Ireland*, pp. 1–22 passim. For references to "depopulation" see *Montana Catholic* (Butte), Oct. 14, 1899; *Helena Daily Independent*, May 9, 1901; remarks of John Finerty in *Anaconda Standard*, July 5, 1905; AOH D3, MB, Dec. 10, 1906; RELA, MB, Oct. 3, 1907; Sept. 1, 1910; Friends of Irish Freedom, *Resolutions*; FOIF, "Ireland's Case for Independence," p. 10; FOIF, "Are You a Member?"

31. Thomas N. Brown, *Irish-American Nationalism*, pp. 23–28 and passim. See also Montgomery, *Beyond Equality*, pp. 132–34.

32. Walkowitz, *Worker City*, pp. 136–38, 143, 168–69. Taylor writes that working-class Irish-Americans "were bound to be pursuing several objectives at the same time . . . and . . . enthusiastic pursuit of one . . . might have unfavorable repercussions on another" (*Distant Magnet*, p. 233). See also Cantor, "Introduction," pp. 3, 9, 15; Rumpf and Hepburn, *Nationalism and Socialism*, p. 11.

33. The literature on these topics is enormous. Solid, interpretive accounts include Joseph Lee, *Modernisation*; Lyons, *Ireland*; Mansergh, *Irish Question*; Hachey, *Britain and Irish Separatism*; and O'Farrell, *England's Irish Question*. The Irish-American involvement is detailed in the two volumes of John Devoy's

Post Bag, which contain much of the voluminous correspondence among the leaders both in Ireland and the United States.

34. On the Republican reformers and nativism see David Potter, *Impending Crisis,* pp. 243–46, 251–54; Foner, *Free Soil,* pp. 226–60; George Potter, *Golden Door,* pp. 371–86; Cross, "The Irish," pp. 179–80; Kleppner, *Cross of Culture,* pp. 31–32, 53–56, 76–79; Richard Jensen, *Winning,* pp. 73–76; Thomas N. Brown, *Irish-American Nationalism,* pp. 133–37; Foner, "Land League," pp. 163–65, 177–78, 199; Montgomery, *Beyond Equality,* pp. 129–34; Martin and Byrne, *Scholar Revolutionary;* O'Brien, *Parnell,* I:192; Davitt, *Fall of Feudalism,* p. 42.

35. The point that the poor resented their poverty more than they resented England was made by Father O'Sullivan (interview). The Lyons quote is from *Culture and Anarchy,* p. 52. See also Joseph Lee, *Modernisation,* pp. 3–5, 72; Kennedy, *The Irish,* pp. 149, 151, 163.

36. On the role of the Catholic Church see Emmet Larkin's three volumes, *Church and Creation; Church and Plan of Campaign;* and *Church and Fall of Parnell.* On the class origins of the clergy see Connell, "Catholicism and Marriage," p. 122; Kennedy, *The Irish,* pp. 36–38; Joseph Lee, *Modernisation,* pp. 91, 114–22. The coalition ultimately splintered. See Thomas N. Brown, *Irish-American Nationalism,* p. 178; Clark and Donnelly, *Irish Peasants,* p. 280.

37. The point regarding levels of satisfaction is made in Walkowitz, *Worker City,* pp. 128, 254–55; Foner, "Land League," pp. 152–53, 167; Thomas N. Brown, *Irish-American Nationalism,* pp. 19, 56–57, 63; the quote is from p. 63; Davitt, *Fall of Feudalism,* p. 252. Miller, *Emigrants,* pp. 364, 412; and "Assimilation," pp. 102–8. Phillips, Redpath, and George are discussed in Foner, "Land League," pp. 150–51, 160, 162, 181, 184–86, 189–91, 193–95, 197–99; Thomas N. Brown, *Irish-American Nationalism,* pp. 118–19, 123–24, 148–50; Devoy, *Post Bag,* I:545–46; II:103; Davitt, *Fall of Feudalism,* pp. 224, 268, 274. See also George, *Irish Land Question.*

38. For the paper's popularity on both sides of the Atlantic see O'Brien, *Parnell,* I:244; Foner, "Land League," p. 161; Thomas N. Brown, *Irish-American Nationalism,* p. 106; *Irish World and American Industrial Liberator,* Nov. 8, 1879. Ford had a "Spread the Light Fund" to support subscriptions in Ireland. See, for example, *Irish World,* Oct. 23, 1880. The reference to the United States as a greater and more benevolent Ireland is from Thomas N. Brown, *Irish-American Nationalism,* p. 19. Michael Davitt called the U.S. "freer and happier" (*Fall of Feudalism,* p. 252). See also Walkowitz, *Worker City,* pp. 128, 154–255; Burchell, *San Francisco Irish,* p. 114. The quote from *Irish World* is from July 12, 1879.

39. A glance at almost any of the weekly issues from the late 1870s on will indicate the range of Ford's vision; a closer reading will reveal the intensity of his commitments. See also Rodechko, "Patrick Ford"; Foner, "Land League," pp. 166–67, 197; Thomas N. Brown, *Irish-American Nationalism,* pp. 78, 167; Montgomery, *Beyond Equality,* p. 133; Mansergh, *Irish Question,* pp. 103–32; du Maurier, *Hungry Hill,* p. 246; O'Brien, *Parnell,* I:242–43.

40. Foner, "Land League," pp. 162–68; Thomas N. Brown, *Irish-American Nationalism*, pp. 30, 90–91, 108, 110, 123. The reference to Lenin is on p. 123; the Fall River comparison on p. 108. Davitt, *Fall of Feudalism*, pp. 257–58; *Irish World*, Oct. 23, 1880.

41. Foner, "Land League," pp. 162–63, 167; Thomas N. Brown, *Irish-American Nationalism*, pp. 52–53, 181; Davitt, *Fall of Feudalism*, pp. 257–59.

42. Connolly's remarks are from Lyons, *Culture and Anarchy*, p. 97. For Connolly's blend of nationalism and socialism (and Catholicism) see Joseph Lee, *Modernisation*, pp. 140–41, 149–52; Rumpf and Hepburn, *Nationalism and Socialism*, p. 11.

43. Foner, "Land League," pp. 151, 169–70.

44. *Irish World*, Nov. 22, 1879, and Sept. 24, 1881; Foner, "Land League," pp. 168–74. For evidence of Irish nationalist as distinct from Irish reform activity in those regions see Devoy, *Post Bag*, I:48–49, 149, 153, 183, 217, 239, 343, 486, 500, 518, 551, 554, 555; II:12, 13, 290–91; Lingenfelter, *Hardrock Miners*, pp. 53, 133. See also the data on previous residency in AOH, Membership and Dues Ledgers.

45. Broehl, *Molly Maguires*. For the *Irish World* accounts of Molly activities see June 10, 1876; June 30, 1877. The Irish were also well represented among the railroad strikers of 1877. Thomas N. Brown, *Irish-American Nationalism*, pp. 46–47.

46. Lingenfelter, *Hardrock Miners*, passim; Wyman, *Hardrock Epic*, pp. 46, 161–62, 165–66; Burchell, *San Francisco Irish*, pp. 106–7; Vernon Jensen, *Heritage of Conflict*, pp. 17–21. Richard Peterson argues that relative peace prevailed because the mine owners understood and met the needs of their workers (*Bonanza Kings*, pp. 66–86). For a discussion of the Irish and unions generally, see Thomas N. Brown, *Irish-American Nationalism*, pp. 23–24; Montgomery, *Beyond Equality*, pp. 120–34, and "Irish," pp. 205–18.

47. *Irish World*, Jan. 1, 1876, in Thomas N. Brown, *Irish-American Nationalism*, p. 63. See also the remarks of Michael Davitt in that same city reported in the *Irish World*, Oct. 23, 1880.

48. Lingenfelter, *Hardrock Miners*, p. 131; *Irish World*, Sept. 18, 1881; Riobard O'Dwyer, *My Ancestors*, pp. 122–23, 237. See also the account of John Harrington, in ibid., p. 118.

49. Industrial Commission, *Mining at Butte*, 1911, p. 3947.

CHAPTER 3

Butte, America: Building an Irish Commmunity

I

There was a parodox in the Irish presence in Butte. Almost simultaneous with their entry into America's eastern cities, there began a movement to send the Irish to America's western farms. Clergy and laity, politicians and labor leaders took turns in warning the Irish of the baneful influences of urban and industrial worlds. In Ireland their priests spoke of the loss of innocence and the loss of faith that were bound to result from any extended residence in America's cities. Curiously, many in those same cities agreed and began preparations to relocate the Irish in the West.[1]

Montana was not the first choice of most of those who sought to colonize the Irish on western farms; Minnesota and Nebraska seemed to offer better prospects. Their climates were thought to be more moderate, and they were undoubtedly easier to reach. But Montana had its spokesmen as well. It was the ambition of Thomas Francis Meagher, exiled Irish revolutionary and first governor of the territory, "to be the representative and champion of the Irish Race in the wild great mountains." He hoped to settle a large number of Irish in Montana and had even begun preliminary discussions with Bishop Thomas Grace and Father John Ireland, both of St. Paul and both sympathetic, regarding the establishment of a vicarate in the territorial capital of Helena. Meagher died before his plan could be implemented, but John Ireland, when he succeeded to the bishopric, continued to press for the settlement of unclaimed western lands with landless Irish workers.[2]

There were some Irish and clerical opponents of these relocation schemes. Bishop John Hughes of New York, for example, though he understood how the promise of western lands tugged on Irish workers, doubted that the Irish had the requisite pioneering qualities—including the ability to live without benefit of a resident priest—to make good on the promise. The West was a place of doubtful advantage for a people unused to its isolation and peculiar hardships. There was plenty of time for the Irish to develop the necessary skills, or for the United States to grow to the point where those kinds of talents would not be needed. Until then Hughes preferred that the Irish affinity for America's cities be strengthened, not contested. John Hughes died in 1864, just before Meagher was appointed territorial governor of Montana and almost two decades before Marcus Daly had begun to develop Butte's enormous deposits of high-grade copper. But had Bishop Hughes lived to see the Butte of 1900 there is reason to believe he would have approved of the place; certainly he would have found it recognizable.[3]

Butte was Western only in its geographic location. Joseph Kinsey Howard called it the "black heart of Montana, feared and distrusted," a kind of industrial island surrounded by mountains, trees, and grass. Ivan Doig in his recent novel of a rural Montana boyhood is more specific. It was literally marvelous, "in all this wide Montana landscape, [to find] a city where shifts of men tunneled like gophers." At best, it seemed an unlikely way to make a living. But the truth, Doig's young Jick McCaskill adds, "may have been that parts of Montana like ours were apprehensive, actually a little scared, of Butte. There seemed to be something spooky about a place that lived by eating its own guts . . . Butte I would surely have to see someday."[4]

It did not become less spooky upon closer inspection. No other of America's industrial cities sat in quite so unlikely a place. There was no congruity between the city and the state, little sense of a common past and even less anticipation of a shared future. In the things that counted, Butte, within little more than a decade of its founding, had begun to reveal what most presumed to be uniquely eastern characteristics. It was eastern in its industrialization, its Catholicism, its immigrant population, its politics. The Irish, of course, were a part of the esoterica. They worked the mines, they went to the Catholic Mass, they exhibited what to many seemed a witless fidelity to the Democratic party. And, if the story is true, it was they who detached the city from the state by insisting on calling it Butte, America.[5]

Only in its weather and in its newness did Butte resemble Montana. The former required a considerable adjustment. South Butte, on the "flats," is at an elevation of 5,400 feet above sea level; the Butte "suburb" of Walkerville, on the hill just north of the city, is more than 1,000 feet higher than that. It was and is a severe place—stark, seemingly barren, and uncommonly cold. For a people many of whom were still more used to that soft Irish mist, learning to live with the physical environment of Butte cannot have been a simple matter of bundling up. Like the South Italians who migrated to Buffalo, New York, Butte's Irish had to adjust their work and leisure routines to the merciless demands of a climate vastly different from what they had known. Some, the "snowbirds" they were called, left Butte in the winter to work the mines of Arizona and Mexico; others, usually the married and more stable element in the Irish working class, hung on grimly and waited for spring.[6]

Also like the state, Butte had had a short history. In very important ways this benefited the Irish. As was true everywhere—from Boston and New York to Denver and San Francisco—Butte was the property of those who got there first. Unlike those other cities, however, in Butte these "natives" were Irish. Not only did they encounter no hostile and entrenched society upon their arrival, they encountered no society at all. There seems little question that the Irish fared best where the resident non-Irish population was least well entrenched and where industrial job opportunities were most numerous. Detroit in 1850, with its resident Catholic population, was an infinitely friendlier place than Philadelphia, which was itself more gracious in its welcome to the Irish than New York. And even Butte's weather cannot have required as difficult an adjustment as Boston's society.[7]

The Irish, of course, did not have the place entirely to themselves. Butte was one of the most ethnically mixed towns in the United States. In the early years, the Irish shared it with the English—Cornish, mostly— who actually outnumbered them until about 1901–3. Later, other immigrant groups contested the Irish dominance. By 1910 there were just under 3,000 "Austrians" in Silver Bow County, over 2,500 Germans, nearly 1,600 Italians, and at least 1,500 Finns. But there were still more than 10,000 Irish, many of them settled, some of them extremely well placed. More important, in fact, than mere numbers in explaining the Irish flavor of Butte was their early arrival and their continuous presence.[8]

In this context, Butte had advantages no other American city could match. It belonged to the Irish in almost the same way Salt Lake City belonged to the Mormons. They could build an Irish community to their own specifications. But more was involved in this proprietorship than the timing of the Irish arrival. Not only was Butte new, it was born industrial, or at least industrializing. There was no clumsy and halting transition from preindustrial village to industrial town. There was scarcely any social dislocation at all as it moved from gold and silver camp to mining town. The Irish, moreover, were a part of what little dislocation there was, and they adjusted to it as quickly as the few others in Butte at the time. Similarly, the first Irish in Butte encountered none of the hostility that usually resulted when inexperienced immigrant workers moved into an area with an established native work force.[9]

There are other general points to raise. Butte's Irish world was larger, proportionate to the whole city, than those of other Irish immigrants. The Irish of Butte were not a beleaguered urban minority clinging to faint traces of an Irish past. Butte was their town, and not only because there were so many of them. They got there first, and theirs was the dominant culture. They were the host society, as responsible for Butte as it was for them. It remains an interesting question whether the Irish assimilated the values of the rest of Butte or forced an assimilation of their own. They had still, on occasion, to face the world outside of Butte. They had few claims on the state and none at all on the nation. With the exception of Anaconda, only twenty-six miles west, there was no Irish community of any size within 350 miles of the place. The Irishman's reference to Butte as "Butte, America" reflected the striking incongruity between the city and the state and region.

Later Irish immigrants, those who came after the initial sorting-out process, were in a somewhat different position. The opportunities for quick access to the middle class were almost gone, taken by the Irish who arrived before them. To be sure, the "entrenched aristocracy" was itself Irish and Catholic and what social ordering took place did not reflect religious and ethnic prejudices as well. In addition, the early arrivals were no less Anglophobic than the later ones. This would not be enough to prevent class divisions from arising, but it did mean that there would be more interethnic harmony for the Irish than for other immigrant groups. Still, those who came after about 1895 filled the lower ranks of Irish society and, like Irish-American communities everywhere, Butte, America, became fragmented and pluralistic. Since class and ethnic identities were extensions of one another, this social differentiation had significant consequences for Irish/worker protest.

There were, however, four factors in Butte that mitigated that fragmentation and set Butte slightly apart from other American Irishtowns. First, community and family ties, though present everywhere in Irish-America, may have been stronger in Butte, particularly for the West Corkmen. Those ties insured a friendly reception and continued support. Second, miners, because of the enormous risks they assumed, were a special breed of worker. They were paid more, and they were accorded a greater degree of respect by the middle class. Third, and related to the point above, the Irish in Butte were associated with mining in the same way, though without the pejorative implications, that the Chinese were associated with laundering. It was more than what they did; it was what they were. Nine of every ten men were involved directly in the digging and recovery of copper ore; even the most imperious of lace-curtain Irish would find it hazardous to affront so huge a percentage of the Irish world. Finally, the exponential growth of Butte's copper industry together with the turnover in the work force guaranteed a steady supply of new jobs, muting, at least until 1907–8, almost any inter-Irish conflict between older, settled miners and younger, as-yet-unsettled job seekers. Until then, whatever the timing of their arrival and their place in the social and economic order, the Irish were welcome in Butte.[10]

These were important distinctions, but they only lessened the effects of social differentiation in Butte's Irish community; they did not eliminate it. Indeed, because they got there first, many of Butte's earliest Irish arrivals moved more rapidly than was ordinarily the case with the Irish into the middle and managerial classes. This placed more social distance between the first arrivals and the Irish who followed them; in other words, the class differentiation which became a part of every ethnic community came sooner to Butte simply because an Irish middle class arose sooner. Butte's working Irish did not lose sight of their Irishness and align themselves only around the banners of class and occupation. It was an Irish town they were determined to build, and only as that ethnicity contributed to class awareness would it resemble a worker city. But it is also true that the established Irish of whatever class, many of whom were themselves settled into a place for the first time in their lives, had to manufacture a community from socially disparate elements.

Stephan Thernstrom was one of the first to point out that the history of America's cities, as well as the history of the immigrant workers who entered them, involves more than just the story of metropolitan centers like New York or Chicago. There were significant differences between the history of the Irish in Newburyport, Massachusetts, and those in Boston. But there were equally important differences between the Irish experience in Newburyport and that in Butte. The differences are not attributable to the size or economic function of the towns. Like Butte, Newburyport was middle-sized and industrial. The big difference lay in the fact that in Butte the Irish bore the primary responsibility for insuring social order and community. They did not respond to Butte so much as Butte responded to them.[11]

These unique features of Butte's Irish world also meant that it would be different, at least in its origins, from the ethno-occupational enclaves described by John Bodnar. These enclaves, most of them immigrant East European, were more than communities. They were "complex social phenomena" that "grew up around such bases as race, ethnicity, [job] skill, or shared economic status." The nature of the enclave varied for different people, places, and times, but all enclaves had a "tendency to be circumscribed," to be isolated socially and politically from the higher social classes, and from those of the same class where work and ethnic origins were different. As might be expected from their numbers, Butte's Irish miners were not politically or socially circumscribed, at least in the early years. That is an important exception, one with obvious consequences for the workers' awareness of their status and their rights. It is not, however, one that had much effect on capital's conceptualization of social power, or on the uses to which capital put that power. When the Irish workers began to understand that, to realize that power relationships in Irish Butte were not appreciably different from those in less-congenial settings, their world became much like that of Bodnar's enclaves. Social differentiation—though always to a lesser extent than Bodnar describes—did cut the workers off from Irish of higher rank; their status as Irish miners did divide them from other workers and from non-Irish miners. These are characteristics they shared with other enclaves. Certainly Butte's Irish community acted like an enclave, and that may be more important than the fact that its origins and the political context in which it functioned were different from Bodnar's examples.[12]

Whether what they were building is called an enclave or a community, the very fact that the Irish were building anything may have alarmed even them. It was an unaccustomed role and not one in which they can have felt very comfortable. They were universally characterized as a source of instability, as wreckers of existing communities, not builders of new ones. Little else but wreckage could be expected from a people whom the English had dismissed as barbarians, "white chimpanzees," "squalid apes," or "human swinery." Daphne du Maurier used words like "idle," "feckless," and "good-for-nothing" to convey the Puxleys' contempt for the Irish character. But the Puxleys' harshest criticism was reserved for the alleged Irish and Catholic regressiveness. They seemed not to be of the nineteenth century, rather they lived "in the past of two hundred years ago," and had to "be made to fit in with progress and the general scheme of things." The Irish, naturally, resented these unflattering caricatures and offered up countless examples of Celtic heroism by way of refutation. But even the most careful chron-

iclers of Irish glories could not make up for the obvious: the Irish had
had little experience with what the late nineteenth century considered
progress, including urban living.[13]

Social disparity and inexperience, moreover, were not the last of
their problems. Irish community builders had also to deal with a high
degree of population turnover. By whatever name—out-migration,
transiency, geographical mobility—the movement of people into and
out of America's cities is recognized as one of the most important
aspects of modern American history, affecting everything from community stability to working class radicalism. The populations of western cities were particularly nomadic but those of eastern industrial
towns, of whatever size, were only scarcely less so. Butte was both
western and industrial and its turnover rate reflects it.[14]

As noted previously, Butte's Irish were drawn from among the most
transient of America's workers. Many of these Irish were able to settle
in but more were not. Based on persistence between census periods,
only 17 percent, approximately 1,000 out of almost 6,000 nondependent Irish and Irish-Americans remained in Butte between 1900 and
1910. The figures for Irish miners are comparable. There were 3,197
of them in 1900 who had a reasonable actuarial chance of living ten
more years. Only 478, or 15 percent of these, were still in Butte in
1910. Using five years rather than ten as the determinant of persistence
changes the percentage significantly, suggesting that the Irish community was perhaps beginning to settle in between 1905 and 1910. At
that, however, only 23 percent of Butte's Irish in 1910 were residents
in 1905.[15]

These figures are about what one would expect from a place like
Butte in the first decade of the twentieth century. It was an industrializing town with a strong Irish working-class component and it went
through major industrial shutdowns in 1903 and 1907–8. Also at issue
were the stages and diversions in the Irish immigrant experience. At
any moment the Irish-American world consisted of three parts: the
settled of whatever class; the unsettled workers who moved along paths
laid out by the ethnic communities and who hoped one day to settle
and enter one of them; and the transient workers who either could not
or would not fix themselves. The second of these groups was always
the largest—as Butte's persistence rate indicates. That that rate was not
uncommonly low, however, would have been of little comfort to the
significant number of Irish who did persist and whose responsibility
it was to bring a semblance of order to a disordered Irish world.

Almost symbolic of the population turnover were the residents of
Butte's boardinghouses. Almost half of Butte's Irishmen in 1900 and

1910 lodged and/or ate in one of the many miners' homes. The boardinghouse/saloon culture that resulted was not the stuff of which stable communities were usually made. Many of the boardinghouse Irish probably intended to stay in the city, and their temporary residence in what were essentially the urban equivalents of lumber camps did not interfere with the establishment of a stable Irish community. Others, the young ones new to Butte, lived in them because they were affordable and close to the mines. As a first home they had obvious advantages, particularly when they were run for and by countrymen. As early as 1889 there were sixteen Butte boardinghouses owned or managed by Irish. Most of these were in the overwhelmingly Irish Dublin Gulch section. For some the boardinghouses were clearly a part of the emerging Irish community.[16]

But there were a great many more Irish for whom the boardinghouse was the last stop in Butte, not the first. When they left the house, they left the town. The problem is determining which and how many Irish fit each category. The censuses provide sketchy and incomplete information—in part because intent is not easily measured. The data indicate that the Irish boardinghouse residents were usually single men who worked in the mines, probably had not been in Butte long, but were no less likely to have applied for or received their citizenship papers than the overall Irish-born male population. This does not show much. More revealing is the analysis of the Irish residents of the Florence Hotel in 1900. Located within walking distance of many of the mines, it was home for hundreds of Irish miners. In 1900, 202 of its 377 tenants were immigrant or second-generation Irishmen. Of the 202, 180 were miners and another ten were unskilled mine laborers; 192 were unmarried and the ten married men had not, obviously, brought their wives with them. It was an older group than might have been expected. The average age was a little over thirty-three years; no one was under twenty-one, sixty-six of the total were more than thirty-six. This is an important consideration. There can have been very few young, summertime adventurers among these 202. Some of them may have been willing transients, but even for them, as for the rest, the business of work was a serious one.[17]

The turnover rate for these 202 would indicate, however, that though Butte was an ideal place to find jobs, few kept them. Census linkage between 1900 and 1910 turned up exactly four men who lived in the Florence Hotel in 1900 and were still in Butte in 1910. A check against the *City Directory* of 1905 indicates that only twenty-six of the 137 whose names were uncommon enough to permit of reasonable accuracy persisted for five years. Clearly the boardinghouses were tem-

porary residences; in fact, if boardinghouse residents are subtracted
from the total of Irish miners, the persistence rate almost doubles from
15 to 29 percent. There may be some errors in these figures. Census
enumerators were unusually casual in compiling information on boardinghouses. For example, in 1900, twenty-nine men with Irish surnames boarded at 30 West Quartz. Only their ages were recorded; every
other category was marked "unknown." It seems probable that the
enumerators decided to speed the counting process by skipping over
those who, because of their wandering natures, literally did not count.
But this only confirms the point.[18]

Along with other evidence of Irish working-class turnover, the above
figures indicate that the persistence rate among the Irish working class
of Butte was slightly lower than among other American workers. There
were many hundreds every year who wandered into Butte, and as
many others who wandered out. The task of building a community
was more difficult as a result. Only the persistent got married, voted,
went to church, supported the schools, bought homes, joined clubs,
participated in their unions. By definition, however, those who persisted were always enough. Once the families, political parties, schools,
churches, clubs, and unions were in place, they, and the beliefs and
values that founded and sustained them, provided the social and political adhesive that held the Irish community together. The Irish population could turn over yearly; Irishtown would still survive.[19]

There is another important consideration. Economically, the itinerants were almost as valued as the settled. Butte's grocers, saloonkeepers, clothiers, and other merchants, the principal sources of stability
in every American new town, seem to have understood this. They
needed a stable work force less than they needed operating mines
paying good wages to men who spent those wages in town. Since
many of the men did not figure to be in town long, little of this trade
was done on credit, but it was the size of the paycheck, not the long-
range plans of its recipient, that was at issue. The Butte Chamber of
Commerce, in its effort to attract more business to the "Mining City,"
made precisely that point. Wages in the mines were good and the
workers spent their money locally. As for the work force, it was constantly changing, but it was also constantly growing. Irish merchants
were among the beneficiaries of this growth, and to the extent that the
Irish middle class prospered, so did the Irish community.[20]

On the question of wages, then, there existed an alliance between
the working and the middle classes. But the alliance broke and the
sense of ethnic community suffered when the workers decided to save
rather than spend—and many had reason to save, to live in Butte as

cheaply as possible. Some of these hoarders may have been saving to bring a wife and family to join them. This was a tolerable interruption in the spending cycle. But others saved that they might more quickly leave. The Cornish, for example, were thought to be highly skilled workers but, unfortunately, workers whose wages went back to Cornwall—back home, the Cornish said. The latter point was also made about the later immigrants from Southern Europe. In a revealing letter from Leadville, Colorado, a merchant bemoaned the fact that of a $100,000 mine payroll, $65,000 "goes to the old countries . . . not much left for poor old Leadville." Most of this money went to support families in Europe. But some of it, particularly Irish money, went to support various nationalist causes from Home Rule to violent Irish republicanism. The Leadville merchant, himself Irish, admitted that "quite a bunch goes to help out the . . . cause in Ireland."[21]

A frugal, or "patriotic," or homesick working class was an obstacle to community prosperity and hence community stability. And each of the deterrents to a free-spending mine work force operated in Butte. In the 1880s and 1890s the mine owners did what they could to minimize the problem by paying their workers every Friday. Weekly paydays just before a weekend had a predictable effect on workers' spending habits. Even when monthly paydays were the rule, they were staggered so that every Friday was payday for at least a half-dozen mines. Some of the miners frustrated the tactic by working seven shifts, but generally the Butte payroll seems to have been spent in Butte and that part of it that was Irish spent with Irish merchants.[22]

There was also in Butte the related and touchy question of company stores. In other mining towns, the mining companies owned boardinghouses, homes, and stores, and required their employees to live in and shop at company-owned properties. This was one method the companies used to recover a percentage of the workers' wages. In addition to the potential for gouging, the ownership of stores by large corporations (many of them absentee) worked an undoubted hardship on the resident merchant and middle class. Any sense of community, ethnic or general, required a kind of interclass reciprocity. Neither the merchant nor the working class could perform its expected community function if the latter was effectively removed as an economic participant.[23]

There remained other obstacles to a fully realized Butte, America. It was one of the few Irish areas in the United States where more men than women had immigrated. The transiency of its work force was not the only—or even the best—explanation. Emigrating Irish women were not in tow to Irish men. They had escaped that "extreme degree of male dominance" they had known in rural Ireland; jobs in English or American cities provided them with a degree of economic and social independence unimaginable in their homeland. Butte, however, was not a likely destination for them; monoindustrial towns seldom were. There were too few jobs for women, too few opportunities—however opportunity was defined. The result was that in 1900 there were over 5,200 Irish men and slightly fewer than 2,400 Irish women; the numbers for 1910—just over 4,900 men and 2,900 women—indicate some change as Butte's economy became more diversified and its Irish community developed and matured. In fact, however, assuming that women are a steadier influence than men and that married men are more stable than unmarried, both census years suggest that the demographics of Butte represented a kind of formula for disorder.[24]

The initial imbalance between men and women was only partially offset as the actuarial realities of working in Butte's mines began to make themselves felt. The mines created more Irish widows—fifty to one hundred per year from accidents alone—than Irish fortunes. Census statistics tell a part of the story. In 1900 there were 135 Irish widows under fifty years of age with a combined total of 392 children living at home; in 1910, the figures were 434 and 1,117. A closer look at what these numbers meant can be had by considering the 100 block of East La Platta Street in 1910. There were ten homes on the block, eight of them occupied by Irish widows. The women ranged in age from thirty-two to fifty-five; six had been born in Ireland, two in Michigan of Irish parents. Four of them rented rooms to single miners; three had working children; one sold milk and eggs; and two were without any visible means of support. A combined total of forty-eight children had been born to the eight, thirty-four of them were still living, and thirty-two of those, ranging in age from two years to twenty-four, were living at home. Lest this story seem unreservedly bleak, it should also be noted that seven of the eight owned their homes. The basic point, however, is the same—single, transient men, widows, and one-parent children are not the usual elements of a stable social order.[25]

II

As partial cause, consequence, and symptom of all of the above, Butte was among the most rowdy and dangerous towns in the United States. This was not, of course, solely attributable to the Irish presence, but neither was it something the Irish could ignore. Butte's restricted red-light district has been noted. The city's almost three hundred saloons, far more than any other city in the state, were open twenty-four hours a day, seven days a week. There was wide-open gambling. Silver Bow County provided almost half the state's penitentiary population and more than half its inmates in the state hospital. Its ethnically mixed population included, in addition to pimps and prostitutes, such exotic specimens as "Turkish peddlars," "palmists" and "fortune tellers," "hurdygurdy" men, Hungarian opera singers, countless musicians, artists, and "theatrical" people, "circus acrobats," a German feather dyer, gamblers and faro dealers, "bushelmen," scavengers and vagrants, and at least one "duelist."[26]

So picturesque a population posed certain hazards. Mortuary records for 1906–7 list scores of deaths from acute alchoholism, drug addiction, syphilis, suicide (usually from carbolic acid), and stabbing and gunshot wounds. Add to these typhoid fever and, as additions to the enormous toll among the miners, the deaths of children in falls down abandoned and unmarked mine shafts. Butte managed to combine the presumed chaos of the frontier with the confusion of industrialization. These were not, of course, features unique to the Irish in Butte or to Butte among America's industrializing cities. Still, they obviously contributed to the apparent disorder of the place.[27]

In addition to these hazards, there was the constant threat of tuberculosis and related respiratory diseases. Between 1911 and 1916 Butte's death rate for all forms of TB was 237.45 per 100,000, more than twice the national average. During these years, Butte was a deadlier place than New York City; Newark and Paterson, New Jersey; Gary, Indiana; Portsmouth, Ohio; and Bethlehem, Carlisle, and Carnegie, Pennsylvania. Residence in no other Montana town was remotely as lethal. Butte's mortality rate for all respiratory disease was 513.8 per 100,000; in Missoula, only 120 miles to the west, the rate was 207.7.[28]

Unlike the other hazards, however, here was one that did seem peculiarly and tragically Irish, in both origin and target. In 1912 the County Board of Health, in an effort to explain "the high death rate from Tuberculosis in Silver Bow County," investigated the sanitary conditions in the mines as well as those "under which the miners live on the surface." The unpublished report, accompanied by 133 photographs, provides a remarkably graphic look at conditions below and above ground in the world's greatest mining city. What gives it special significance here, however, is the fact that the board began its investigation knowing that a majority of those who died from tuberculosis between 1908 and 1912 were born in Ireland.[29]

More precisely, 270 of 465 tuberculosis victims from Silver Bow County were immigrant Irish men. This was 58 percent of the whole

number of deaths but it was drawn from about 10 percent of the population. There were almost as many English immigrants in Butte as
Irish, but more than three times as many Irish as English died of TB.
The Irish death rate was twenty-five times that of the Italians, twenty
times that of the Germans. These were smaller populations but certainly not proportionately smaller. Great numbers of all the ethnic
groups in Butte worked in the mines and, though work underground
increased the chance of TB, it cannot be used as an explanation for the
susceptibility of the Irish, a susceptibility that set them apart as surely
as their brogues.[30]

It followed that the incidence of tuberculosis would be highest in
the Irish neighborhoods. The board said the area of greatest concentration of TB victims described "an irregular Maltese cross." The board
members were being polite. It described Dublin Gulch, Corktown, and
the Irish neighborhoods of Centerville. The statistics are remarkable.
In the overwhelmingly Irish L-shaped area bounded by East Park on
the south, North Main on the west, Warren Avenue on the east, La
Platta on the north, with Ohio Street and Summit Road forming the
crook of the L, there were 144 deaths from tuberculosis. In the much
larger and much less Irish area to the northeast of this L, there were
fourteen.[31]

Explaining the phenomenon proved more difficult than defining it.
The board pointed out that sanitation and ventiliation were wholly
inadequate in the affected area. The board inspected 438 houses, with
a total of 1,418 rooms; 2,949 people occupied those rooms. The average
resident had only 335 cubic feet of inside air. "Living and sleeping in
such restricted air space," they could not "expect to maintain health."
The sanitation facilities could be charitably called primitive. One house
on East Daly Street, in an Irish neighborhood, was described as a
"[v]ery dirty and filthy place, bad odor, woman very unclean, had
running sores on her hips, her face and hands were covered with
pimples, no garbage can and slops etc. thrown into street." This was
not an isolated case; whole Irish neighborhoods were condemned. The
700 block on North Wyoming Street was described as "very dirty, many
people keep hogs and cows, slops and refuse thrown into alley." Ridgely
Avenue "would require a boat to get through." The houses fronting
on Mullin Street had "piles of decayed meat in the alley; manure is
very much in evidence." There was "so much refuse in the alley [behind
East La Platta] that it is almost impossible to drive through. People
also have pigs." Even the Florence Hotel, Marcus Daly's "zenith of
service for the working man," had only eight toilets, all in the base-

ment, and was reported to be "very dark and dirty . . . slops thrown into shed in the rear."[32]

This was not the first time such reports had been made. As early as 1888 a writer for *Harper's New Monthly Magazine* described the life of Butte miners as "modern slavery;" their cabins were "perched on rocky ledges, crowded into narrow gulches, unpainted, blackened by smoke, unrelieved by tree or shrub or grass-plot, they . . . were like hovels—untidy, neglected, and oppressive." In 1893 conditions in the Dublin Gulch section were described as in a "horrible state" with kitchen refuse, piles of manure, and stagnant water "everywhere." Two years earlier, the *Butte Intermountain*, in a brief, very matter-of-fact story on conditions in the city's Third Ward, provided more detail. In 1890 there were 141 houses in this Irish and working-class ward; 1,134 people lived in them. By 1891 the number of houses had increased to 152, the number of people had decreased to 937. In this entire area there was no new vegetation between 1890 and 1891: "There was still only one tree and one yard with grass." The story went on to note the "bad condition" of the privies, the number of horses, cows, and domestic fowl sharing the neighborhood, and the need for more cesspools.[33]

The above, plus the references to inadequate refuse disposal in the board's report, indicates that the Irish areas of the city may have been less tidy than others in Butte. Certainly they were more crowded. These are important considerations. Remarkably, however, the board offered no evidence to support a charge that ill-kept neighborhoods and carelessly managed Irish boardinghouses were the cause of the incidence of tuberculosis. The Irish acknowledged only that their working-class neighborhoods were older than the others and denied, with some heat, that they were less well kept. More convincing was their point that large sections of Dublin Gulch and Corktown were found to be as clean and well maintained as any parts of the city. Neither side to this dispute, however, could explain how 10 percent of the population could account for 58 percent of the fatal tuberculosis.[34]

More recent investigations offer instructive clues. Tuberculosis is a malady of urban and industrial worlds, or more precisely of unprotected preindustrial people forced into industrial environments. Sephardic and Ashkenazic Jewish immigrants to the United States, genetically "sheltered" by generations spent in crowded ghettos, had a relatively low rate of TB. Yemenite Jews, on the other hand, immigrants from agricultural regions where the disease was almost unknown, had a significantly higher incidence. Each of Butte's other ethnic groups had had some earlier genetic contact with the disease. Only the Irish were unprotected. The result was that Irish immigrants to industrial cities died at an earlier age and had a higher overall death rate than had been the case in Ireland even during the famine of the mid-1840s. As the sociologist Robert Kennedy noted, emigration promised certain advantages but escape from an early death was clearly not one of them. Nowhere was that more true than in Butte.[35]

III

It was in this place, then, and from these elements that the persistent Irish had to provide the continuity of belief and organizations that would build and sustain their town. The obstacles to community were enormous; a shifting, largely male population with too many temptations and too few commitments, a mysterious susceptibility to tuberculosis, and an inordinate number of widows and single-parent children. Even the alliance of working and middle class was fragile. Community would have to come from the fact that they were all Irish and most of them made their living in the mines. In this instance, as in others, the phrase "making a living" should be taken and used literally. Their Irishness and the nature of their work saturated and defined their lives. Community building would be made easier as a consequence.

The fact that they had settled the place also helped. The earliest labels attached to the place reflected an Irish presence. The mines bore such names as Exile of Erin, Michael Davitt, Druid, and Hibernia. The Irish changed the name of Town Gulch to Dublin Gulch after discovering that almost all who lived there were Irish-born. At that, the adjacent areas of Hungry Hill and Corktown more accurately reflected old-world origins. Their first two churches had as their patrons St. Patrick and St. Lawrence O'Toole.[36]

But the Irish had also to give substance to these largely ceremonial legacies. According to observers, they brought to the task certain inherited skills. Town building was thought beyond their understanding and capabilities but the idea of commonwealth, however primitive, assuredly was not. Indeed, the Irish were thought to be an innately social people; Horace Plunkett, the Anglo-Irish reformer, wrote in the late nineteenth century that what "the Irishman is really attached to . . . is not a home but a social order: the pleasant amenities, the courtesies, the leisureliness, the associations of religion and the friendly faces of neighbors." The Irishman, said another Anglo-Irish, is "a communist socially." This may have been what the Irishwoman meant when she complained that the English-imposed land system in Ireland led to a pattern of isolated tenant farms and only weekly opportunities to gather in villages for talk and diversion. She much preferred the French and Italian systems where farm families lived in the village and walked out to their farms.[37]

She might have found Butte more congenial than rural Ireland—the women often did. This, obviously, was less an inherited than an acquired skill, but once learned the women became another and powerful source of community strength. As free to emigrate as the men and, if anything, even more disillusioned with Ireland, women, whether single or married, were vital to the formation and defense of the Irish enclave. In Butte, as in the rest of Irish-America, the single women were as narrowly placed occupationally as the Irish men. Ninety percent of them worked as maids, domestics, kitchen helpers, seamstresses, or launderers. The remaining 10 percent included teachers, nuns, shopkeepers, and boardinghouse managers. The result of this occupational grouping was an ethnic, gender, and occupational community separate from that of the working-class Irish men but as closely knit. The entire enclave was made more cohesive as a result.

Married Irish women were equally important. Ireland had little appeal for them; constant wandering in America even less. As with the men, the ethnic enclave was their preferred alternative to either—but only because it required a far greater degree of female participation than had the Irish world they had left. Let the Irish community become too similar to rural Ireland and the women would spurn it as surely as they had Ireland. In Butte, at least, they had little to fear. Butte, America, was quintessentially urban and married Irish women were central to its safekeeping. Like the unmarried women, they occupied spheres separate from those of Irish men, but they participated fully in a shared community. They cared for the children—many of them as the sole parent; they contributed to the family's economic stability by taking in boarders, sustained the Catholic churches, raised money for Ireland and the Irish. Mostly, they stayed put, whether merely resigned to Butte or genuinely fond of the place is beside the point; they were determined to make a home of it.[38]

There were other features of living and working in Butte that eased the task of community building. The Irish neighborhoods were organized around the Irish mines, a considerable improvement over West Cork where Irish miners were segregated from the mines in which they worked. In Butte the men walked to work and, given the steepness of its hills and the rigors of its climate, few wanted to walk any farther than was necessary. Marcus Daly gave them jobs, so they lived as near Daly's properties as they could; the ethnicity of his mines was a function of Irish proximity to them and vice versa. The completion of the city's street-railway system in 1887 seems to have changed neighborhood patterns only slightly. The Irish still lived near the mines and near each other.[39]

The working class can have had only minimal contact with the non-Irish. Their neighborhoods were almost totally Irish and, as a consequence, so were their churches and schools, their saloons, their funeral houses, their clubs and fraternities. Particularly for the men, knowledge of the larger Butte had to have been limited. The miners' union hall was the one exception, and it only a partial one, to a world as Irish and Catholic as the ones they had left. What understanding the Irish had of the lives and affairs of the men and women outside the Gulch came either from the single Irish women who worked as maids—as often as not in the homes of "lace curtain" Irish on the West Side—or from Irish women married to miners and bound to the non-Irish wives of miners in ways their husbands would scarcely understand. Particularly on the borders of ethnic neighborhoods or in the stores that served more than one ethnic community, they exchanged recipes, child-raising stories, and the fears common to all miners' wives. These were anything but trivial encounters. Wives of Irish miners knew more of the non-Irish world than did their husbands and, more significantly, were far more tolerant of that world and more appreciative of how much of it they shared. And they taught the children.[40]

Still, it was an insular world the Butte Irish inhabited, and the men in particular seldom left it. They seldom had to. Dublin Gulch and Corktown provided most of what they needed—their jobs, their church, their companions, their meeting places. It provided as well the informal network of mutual aid that allowed struggling Irish to survive the hard times. Here too, Irish women were vital parts of the social process. Daniel Walkowitz discusses the emotional and material support the Irish of Troy's Limerick Alley gave to one another "during long winters of unemployment," ranging from shared food and housing to day care. This was a traditional part of Irish sociability dating back to the Famine—the poor helping the poor. Butte's Irish, many of them bound by family and county ties, honored the tradition. Father Sarsfield O'Sullivan, who grew up in Dublin Gulch, remembers his mother telling him that Father Michael Hannan routinely made a show of helping the needy in the Gulch as a way of reminding the others of their manners—and of their obligation to help those in the neighborhood who were temporarily short. There were, in addition, benefit dances for blind miners, collections and raffles for widows, weekly checks for the families of men out of work or on the road looking for it. The number of widows with no visible income who owned homes without encumbrance would even suggest that mortgages were paid off. As will be seen, Irish mine foremen "pensioned" men too old to work underground by giving them topside jobs as watchmen; certain political jobs were reserved, by long-standing tradition, for the blind or otherwise disabled. There was even a kind of missing Irishmen's bureau conducted through the pages of Butte's Irish and Catholic newspapers.[41]

IV

As the numbers indicate, this was a working-class Irishtown. In both census years fewer than 600 of more than 6,000 nondependent Irish, men and women, first and second generation, were self-employed or had white collar or professional jobs. The whole question of social differentiation is influenced if not determined by the fact that Irish workers had plenty of company. It cannot be known if their status made them unhappy, a subject of obvious significance in building a working-class community. That any workers wanted to be socially mobile, that they identified with and embraced the values implied by that mobility, must not be assumed. This is particularly true when dealing with Irish immigrant workers, for whom security of position was often more important than opportunity for advancement. What Ireland could not provide was predictability. Fixity of tenure and fair rents were two of the three Fs demanded by the Land League agitators of the 1880s, and the third, free sale, could suggest entrepreneurial restlessness only in an open and expanding economy, which Ireland, most assuredly, was not.[42]

At issue is the culture of Irish Catholicism, an elusive if not ultimately indefineable concept. Kerby Miller, however, has captured a sense of it, and his ideas deserve a close and attentive reading. The worldview the Irish brought with them from Ireland to America emphasized communalism rather than individualism; custom rather than innovation; conformity over initiative. The Irish were fatalistic, not optimistic; passive rather than active; dependent instead of independent; nonresponsible rather than responsible. Miller applies these attitudes and values to emigration, but assuming even a reasonable continuity of outlook, they would be equally useful in explaining the Irish response to other social phenomena, including social differentiation and worker protest. If that is true, job security would have been more important, because more comprehensible, than either social mobility or the various forms of worker radicalism. The Irish immigrant, initially at least, would be looking for a fair living—a home, neighbors of like mind and heart, good health for his children, and, most particularly, the steady job necessary to each of the above. These would be far more important than the chance to move upward socially or to contest the capitalists.[43]

Butte can have altered their expectations only slightly. In the early years nothing was fixed and many Irishmen took advantage of the opportunities provided to make a very great deal of money. Irishtown, however, did not march to their drumbeat. The wealth of a Marcus Daly or a D. J. Hennessy served as neither inspiration nor goad to the majority of the Irish who worked in the mines of the one or shopped in the store of the other. There was, of course, no scarcity of Irish who, as surely as Daly, had taken advantage of Butte's newness to move quickly into the merchant and middle classes. By 1900 these Irish were only marginally unlike the entrenched middle classes of whatever ethnic background in America's older industrial cities. Their success, however—partly because less grand than Daly's and less grandly displayed—was more important as an expression of the openness and fluidity of the Irish world of Butte than as a source of interethnic jealousy.[44]

It cannot, then, be assumed that the working-class Irish envied the lives of the West Side Irish aristocracy, or even accepted the values those lives reflected. In fact, since success, conventionally defined, took these middle- and upper-class Irish out of the Irish neighborhoods and away from family and community, the far more immediate and compelling examples of Irish success were those that took place inside the ethnic and working-class neighborhoods. There are hundreds of examples. A few, all from the 1900 census, will suffice. Peter O'Leary was a forty-three year old Irish-born miner. He had immigrated to the United States when he was fourteen. Margaret, his Irish-born wife of twenty-four years, had given birth to fifteen children, fourteen of whom were still living. Six of the fourteen had been born in Montana, two in Utah, four in Michigan, indicating an unsettled earlier life spent in mining towns. Neither Peter nor Margaret could read or write. But their younger children were in school and their home was owned free and clear. Bat Harrington was another Irish-born miner. He had an Irish-born wife and ten children. Like O'Leary, he was illiterate, well traveled, and a property owner.

On one street, Cora Terrace, in 1900, eleven Irish-born miners, their Irish wives, and a combined fifty-three children, most of them born in Montana, lived in homes owned without mortgages. The miners were not old men; the oldest was only forty-five and their average age was thirty-six. All were long-time residents, at least by mining-town standards; four of them had been in Montana for five years, six for between six and nine years, and one for fifteen years. Only one of the eleven had taken in a lodger; the oldest of the children was fifteen and none of the children worked. The census data indicate that only four of the men were married when they arrived in Butte. Six of them appear to have met and married after arrival; one married in 1891 and immigrated in 1893. His wife joined him in 1895; their first son was born in 1896.

Cora Terrace was in Walkerville, high on the hills north of Butte, and very near some of the Anaconda Company mines; it was a few miles in distance, a few light years in style from Butte's West Side, but the examples of these eleven, and hundreds more like them, would indicate that Butte was a good place to settle in, that the work was steady enough, wages high enough and general prospects favorable enough to justify marriage and home ownership. The home may have cost little and been worth less; these were working-class neighborhoods not far from some of the steets described so graphically by the Board of Health. At their worst, however, these homes were an improvement over what the Irish had known in Ireland or in other American industrial cities. Besides, they belonged to the families. To own a part of Butte was to be attached to the place; buying a home was a statement of intent, not an expression of some preindustrial earth hunger. It was part of finding a fair living.

The key to home ownership among the Irish miners of Butte was the same as that for the entire working class in America. They had to stay in one place long enough to accumulate a psychological and economic stake. Persistence did not come easy for any of America's workers, particularly its hard-rock miners. But those miners who did persist, though they seldom moved up in occupational class, were able to buy property. As before, and with the same caveat, the birthplace of the oldest Montana-born child, rather than document linkage, will be used to determine minimum years in Butte. Since the married Irish almost always had children, and since the unmarried were not likely to be home owners regardless of how persistent they might have been, the method seems a sound one. Certainly it yields interesting and instructive numbers. In 1900, of the Irish miners who had been in Butte four to seven years, 56 percent either owned or had a mortgage on a home. If the determinant of persistence is eight or more years in Butte, the rate of home ownership increases to 73 percent. In 1910 the four-to seven-year Irish had a home ownership rate of 45 percent, the eight-plus-year men a rate of 64 percent.[45]

A pattern is discernible. The modest achievement of home ownership required persistence, but persistence was also an end in itself, a part of the working-class definition of success. Staying put, for example, may have meant safer working conditions and better health; it certainly did mean closer ties to the ethnic, religious, and working-class community. A certain price had to be paid. Property ownership severely curtailed geographical mobility, including the possibility of repatriation. Family privacy and comfort were often sacrificed to the added income obtained from renting rooms; in both census years almost 30 percent of the Irish homeowners had between one and four boarders and/or lodgers. (Those with more than four belong under the heading of boardinghouse owner.) In Butte the money necessary to buy a home did not seem to require the employment of the younger children—in a monoindustrial town like Butte there were few jobs for them anyway—and they were able to stay in school. But it often required more than one income, at least temporarily, and it seemed always to require that fathers routinely work extra shifts and that older brothers and sisters enter the work force immediately after high school.[46]

V

The full social and economic costs of both persistence and home ownership can only be estimated. What can be argued with more confidence is that once they purchased a home, the lives of the Irish workers changed. Their ties to the community intensified. They probably either had married or were about to marry. Most important, they became separated from the more transient workers. In fact the continued presence of the latter may have produced a certain unease. Those who persisted had a sense of community; they were the core—the stable support for culture and institutions. Those who had no intention of persisting were marginal men and as such vaguely threatening. All of this may have made the persistent less likely to engage in self-proscriptive acts of labor protest or violence. These are matters to be considered under other headings. The point that must be made now is that the percentage of stable homeowners can only have increased the stability and sense of permanance in the Irish community.[47]

The Immigration Commission in 1911 assumed that the extent of home ownership was also an indicator of immigrant assimilation, but the commission raised a false standard. Buying a home was a signal of an intent to settle in, but the community to which the immigrant attached himself was itself unyieldingly immigrant. Unless the commission was prepared to argue that America had invented the idea of property (and it probably was), room must be made for the persistence of Irish cultural values and their application to America's Irishtowns. Assimilation must be judged by other standards.[48]

An obvious one was the rate of Irish marriages outside the Irish Catholic community. As was the case with most insular and self-sufficient immigrant societies, Butte's Irish-born married within the ethnic and religious community. Their endogamy was, in fact, both cause and effect of that sense of interdependence. Intermarriage between "ethnics" and natives is one of the most accurate indicators of immigrant assimilation. Marriage outside the ethnic and/or religious community was a visible sign of a breakdown of the structural integrity of the immigrant group; in the language of Milton Gordon, of "the disappearance of the ethnic group as a separate entity and the evaporation of its distinctive values." Assimilationists may have counted these marriages as small triumphs in the reduction of diverse forms. The immigrants thought them surrenders to a world they may not have liked and seldom fully understood.[49]

The Irish had little to worry about—and the assimilationists little to cheer—in Butte's marriage patterns. In spite of the fact that Irish men outnumbered Irish women by three to two, Butte's immigrant Irishmen displayed a quite remarkable preference for women of similar background and the same faith. This was owing, in part at least, to the fact that they knew only other Irish. Marriages were not arranged but encounters obviously were. Extended family ties, a common Irish background, and the strict eligibility requirements for participation in Irish life, all worked to narrow social contacts. There was even an informal Irish dating service operating out of Hibernia Hall, the Irish fraternal lodge on North Main Street in Centerville. John Leary's Dancing School and Murphy and Drummy's Dancing Club rented space in the hall for dance instruction—their hours organized around shift changes at the adjacent mines. Newly developed skills could be displayed at the weekly dances at the hall sponsored by various Irish groups with music invariably provided by John McNamara and his band. This was in addition to picnics and athletic contests, parades and celebrations. Clearly, Irishtown provided ample, if restricted, social diversion.[50]

The results were predictable. There were 3,300 immigrant Irish in Butte in 1900. Of that total, 2,100 were single. Of the nearly 1,200 who were married, fewer than 100 married before immigrating to the United States. That leaves 1,082 whose marriages took place after they had left Ireland, and of that total 1,009 (93 percent) married within the ethnic and religious group, that is, either first- or second-generation Irish. Of the 1,100 West Cork Irish who came to Butte, at least 396 married others from that same area of Ireland. Countless more married other Irish. Data from Dublin Gulch and Corktown were not collected, but a glance at the manuscript census for the wards making up those neighborhoods leaves a clear impression that the rate of intragroup marriage in those areas was even higher.[51]

Figures for 1910, though obviously describing many of the same marriages, indicate that the later immigrants were no less likely to marry first-, second-, or—based solely on surnames—third-generation Irish. By way of comparison, 74.75 percent of the Irish of New Haven, Connecticut, married "others of the same national derivation" in 1900. This percentage, however, includes the second-generation Irish, who were more likely to marry non-Irish. The rate in 1870, when there were far fewer second-generation, was 93 percent. In San Francisco in 1880, Irish of both generations married other Irish 90 percent of the time.[52]

There were cases of Irish marrying non-Irish. Bishop John Brondel noted that 291 "mixed" marriages had been recorded in the Helena diocese between 1879 and 1889. Given the scarcity of women, most of these were between non-Catholic men and Catholic women, which, though not enough to erase the hostility of the Church to mixed marriages, did allay some of its fears. Brondel explained: "When the woman is a Catholic, the promises [to raise the children as Catholics] are kept, as a rule; when the woman is a non-Catholic, which rather seldom happens, the promises are frequently disregarded." In addition, many of the non-Catholic young men "converted to win the girl." Clearly the women were the keepers of the faith. Although Brondel was not referring only to Irish marriages, the year after his report on intermarriage he went to Ireland for the express purpose of recruiting Irish priests for his "predominately" Irish congregations.[53]

There were three exceptions to the pattern of intra-Irish marriage. The earliest arriving Irishmen had few Irish women from whom to choose, and the *Manuscript Census* of 1880 lists a number of marriages between Irish and non-Irish. As more women began to immigrate, this changed. A second category of men routinely marrying outside the ethnic group were those Irish who did not live in the Dublin Gulch, Corktown, West Centerville areas. Some of these were upwardly mobile sorts who lived on the West Side. It may be instructive, for example, that Marcus Daly, Con Kelley, and John D. Ryan, three of the first four Irish presidents of the Anaconda Company, married non-Irish. The fourth, William Scallon, never married. They were not alone among the more affluent. There were also scattered throughout Butte "disaffiliates," Irishmen, many of them very poor, who chose or who were forced to deviate from the ethnoreligious world of Dublin Gulch. They married, worked, and lived their lives outside its boundaries.[54]

The third category of Irish marrying outside the community was the second generation. The percentages tell a revealing story of second-generation assimilation often, it may be assumed, in the face of first-generation hostility. In 1900, 246 sons and daughters of Irish immigrants had marriage partners selected from outside the ethnic community. This was 30 percent of the whole total of married second-generation Irish. In 1910 the figures were 269 and the same 30 percent. A look at the pattern for the Montana-born of this second generation indicates that Butte's Irishtown was also relaxing its hold. There were only thirty married Montana-born Irish—436 of them were still single adults—but of the thirty, nineteen had chosen non-Irish mates.[55]

Though only one of the criteria, intermarriage says a great deal about the degree of assimilation of Butte's Irish into non-Irish society. Arthur Mann distinguishes four types of individual response to ethnic identity and all give considerable emphasis to the selection of a marriage partner. The "total identifiers" are the nonassimilated and perhaps nonassimilable. They live their lives within a narrowly circumscribed ethnic world, having as primary associates—marriage partners obviously included—only those from that same world. Next are the "partial identifiers"—they marry Irish and regard their ethnic associations as important but not all-inclusive. Third are the "disaffiliates" for whom ethnic attachments are unimportant. Last are the "hybrids," who had no ethnic attachments to begin with and hence nothing to reject.[56]

Butte's Irish fell into all of the first three categories. The second probably claimed most of them at any given time, but that is an important point: ethnic identification changes over time. The partial identifier of 1905 becomes, to invent a fifth category between the second and the third, the potential disaffiliate of 1917. This is a central issue in the history of any immigrant working class. Men disaffiliate with an ethnic group because their identification with the working class is more important. The working Irishman, in other words, becomes the Irish worker.[57]

VI

The Irish immigrant community that emerged from all of this was a surpassingly strong one and it exercised a powerful influence on its members. Despite the transiency, the disproportionate number of men, the huge numbers of widows and single-parent children, despite even the tuberculosis, the community remained intact, the source of mutual support and assistance and the keeper of the religious and ethnic conscience. There appears to have been little social disintegration within the Butte Irish community at least until 1919. It functioned as communities, by definition, are expected to function. It imposed and enforced strict rules of eligibility and it answered the needs of those whom it admitted.

One possible consequence was that the Butte Irish, though overwhelmingly of the working class, acted out the role traditionally assigned the stable middle class. The relative prosperity of the Irish, even those of working-class background, may have had more to do with this than the strength of the Irish community, but the record is an impressive one whatever its cause. It indicates that among the remarkable aspects of the Irish experience in Butte was the relatively small percentage of Irish women in its houses of prostitution, of Irish men in its jails, of Irish children in its houses of detention.

Absolute candor does not appear to have been the rule among prostitutes but allowing even for some deceptive answers to census enumerators' questions, Butte's large red-light district contained very few of the stereotypical wayward Irish girls. *Copper Camp*, the W.P.A.-sponsored history of Butte, states that one of the largest houses "on the line" was Mae Malloy's "Irish World." That may have been true, but the *Manuscript Census* of 1910 lists only five Irish or Irish-Americans in a total of 261 women who identified themselves as prostitutes. In 1900 there were eight women out of almost 300 prostitutes who said they or their parents were born in Ireland. Among the eight was the inevitable Belle Rose.[58]

The figures from other institutional populations make the same point. It was true that of prisoners in the city jail in 1900, twenty-five of sixty-five were Irish, but by 1910, only six of sixty-three identified themselves as such. Even more revealing of the influence of an ethnic community are the 1910 figures from the children's home and the Industrial School. There were ten second-generation Irish in each—out of fifty-three in the children's home, forty-three in the Industrial School. Indeed, the only public facility in Butte in which the Irish were the predominant element was St. James Hospital. If "waywardness," "hoodlumism," and general delinquency are the consequences of a weak family or community structure, then Butte's Irishtown must be counted among the most stable ethnic communities in industrializing America.[59]

Immigrating Irish surely found it an appealing place. Brogues were heard almost everywhere. A man could get a Guinness Stout or a Dublin Porter on draft at J. H. Lynch's Nevada Saloon; Home Rule for Ireland cigars were available at Pat Driscoll's Silver Palace. At every saloon, Irish or not, a whiskey and a beer chaser was known as a Sean O'Farrell. The Irish played handball at McCarthy's gym, took Irish-language lessons from the Gaelic League. Irish games, particularly Gaelic football, were played on a regular if informal basis. In 1913, informality having lapsed into indecorum, a Gaelic Athletic Association was formed "for the purpose of carrying on games and sports in a more peaceable manner than they have been in the past in this city." From then until 1926 the association sponsored a Gaelic football league with a full season of play culminating in a final championship game. News of these and other Irish activities, both in Butte and in Ireland, was reported in all of Butte's newspapers. The *Montana Catholic* carried county-by-county news from Ireland, most of it of a society-page nature. The *Butte Independent*, bought in 1910 by the Irish immigrant James B. Mulcahy and "Devoted to the Interests of Ireland and the Advancement of True American Ideals," also carried Irish news in a section called "Where the Little Shamrock Grows." In addition to these local papers, Butte's Irish also read the *Irish World*, the *National Hibernian*, the *Rocky Mountain Celt*, the *Gaelic American*, the *Western Hibernia*, and the *Chicago Citizen*.[60]

To these sources of Irish news must be added the speakers who came to Butte. The list reads like a roster of Irish and Irish-American political and literary notables. Between 1886 and 1921 Michael Davitt, John Boyle O'Reilly, William O'Brien and John Dillon, Fathers Sheehy and McFadden—the "Patriot priests"—John Finerty, O'Brien Kennedy, John McBride, Conor O'Kelly, Bulmer Hobson, Douglas Hyde, Seamus McManus, John Rohan, Cornelius Lehane, James Larkin, James Connolly, Mary McWhorter, Hannah Sheehy-Skeffington, and Eamon de Valera, the president of the provisional Irish Republic, all made the long trip to Butte at least once, and most left with their own or their organization's treasuries richer for it.[61]

In most cases, these speakers were brought to Butte by one of the town's many Irish clubs and fraternities. As mentioned, Butte had Gaelic League and Gaelic Athletic Club affiliates but in addition there were the Parnell Guards, the Friendly Sons of St. Patrick, the Emmet Guards and Band, the Catholic Knights of Butte, the Thomas F. Meagher Guards, the Sheridan Cadets, the Daughters of Erin, the Hibernia Band, and the Hibernia Literary and Social Club. This was in addition to three divisions of the Ancient Order of Hibernians, the Robert Emmet Literary Association, and the Irish Volunteers.[62]

No immigrant community was ever fully formed in the sense that it could recreate every feature of the society and culture the immigrants had left. The transplanting of institutions is difficult at best. Add to this the presence in most American cities of an entrenched and often hostile "native" society and it is obvious why most ethnic communities were "segregant" or "subcultural." Their early arrival and the fact that Butte's was a society more in the process of becoming than fixed in place and time meant that the Irish had more relative freedom to build their world without constantly having to adjust it to external pressures. But despite these differences and advantages, there was still a defensiveness about the Irish world of Butte—a leftover, perhaps, from their experiences in other American cities—and the early dominance of the Irish in Butte did not seem to have stripped that world of any of the cohesiveness that the presence of hostile outsiders invariably produces.

In sum, though the social calculus was not quite the same in Butte as in other American Irishtowns, it was sufficiently like those others to provide the Irish workers with the necessary ingredients for an active and self-confident community.

NOTES

1. James P. Shannon, *Catholic Colonization,* pp. 14–53; Dolan, *Immigrant Church,* pp. 132–35; Funchion, *Organizations,* pp. 62–67, 72, 151–154, 156–164, 171, 173, 249–50.

2. Shannon, *Catholic Colonization,* pp. 32–53, 198. For Meagher's plans, see J. P. Carroll, "Ecclesiastical Jurisdiction," and Palladino, "Origins of the Helena Diocese," both in Brondel Papers.

3. Dolan, *Immigrant Church,* p. 134–35.

4. Howard, *Montana,* p. 85; Doig, *English Creek,* pp. 232–33. See also the statistical evidence of Butte's uniqueness in E. S. Lee et al., *Population Redistribution,* pp. 349–55.

5. See Hand, "Folklore," p. 177.

6. For Buffalo's Italians see Yans-McLaughlin, *Family and Community,* pp. 42–43. The "snowbirds" are mentioned in Ronald C. Brown, *Hard-Rock Miners,* p. 11. See the warning about climate and altitude given the young New York Irishman who asked Butte merchant P. J. Brophy about a job. Brophy to D. J. Fitzpatrick, Dec. 4 and Dec. 19, 1900, Brophy Papers. Du Maurier described snow on top of Hungry Hill (*Hungry Hill,* p. 6). It is worth noting that in early January, 1985, during the writing of this book, the low temperature in Butte was −58 degrees Fahrenheit.

7. Handlin, *Boston's Immigrants;* Thernstrom, *Other Bostonians;* George Potter, *Golden Door;* Ward, *Cities and Immigrants;* Dennis Clark, *Irish in Philadelphia;* Funchion, "Irish Chicago"; Conzen, *Immigrant Milwaukee;* Vinyard, *Irish on the Urban Frontier;* Burchell, *San Francisco Irish;* Brundage, "Making of Workingclass Radicalism."

8. Bureau of the Census, *Twelfth Census, Population,* part I, pp. clxxvi–ix, 768, 798, 875; *Thirteenth Census,* p. 592. No figure for second-generation Finns is given.

9. There are a number of studies dealing with these and related issues. Examples of the best of them would include Ralph Mann, *After the Gold Rush;* Doyle, *Social Order;* Katz, *People of Hamilton;* Dykstra, *Cattle Towns;* and Walkowitz, *Worker City.*

10. On middle-class respect for those willing to assume risks, see Frisch, " 'Gibralter of Unionism.' "

11. Thernstrom, *Poverty and Progress*, p. 204, 45–58, 102–6, 121–29.

12. Bodnar, *Workers' World*, pp. 1–2, 63–65, 177–79, 185.

13. Lyons, *Culture and Anarchy*, pp. 11–13; du Maurier, *Hungry Hill*, pp. 8, 34; Curtis, *Anglo-Saxons and Celts* and *Apes and Angels*; O'Faolain, *Story of the Irish People*, pp. 26, 57–58; Dolan, *Immigrant Church*, pp. 132–33; Davitt, *Fall of Feudalism*, p. 128.

14. The growing body of literature on American geographical and occupational mobility is nicely summarized in Ralph Mann's historiographical essay, "Frontier Opportunity." For evidence that worker mobility was greater in developing industrial communities than in stabilizing communities, see also Weber and Boardman, "Economic Growth."

15. Bureau of Census, *MS Census*, 1900 and 1910. The method used to determine persistence is based on the age and birthplace of children. As noted earlier, this does not permit a scientifically accurate analysis of the persistence of the childless. These, however, were the least likely to persist. Assuming a 3 percent persistence rate over ten years for the childless seems to yield percentages at least as accurate as the .05 + at 95 percent confidence of sampling techniques. Specifically, a count was made from the 1910 census of those Butte Irish the age of whose oldest Montana-born child indicated a residence in Montana in 1900. This particular method would work only for a city like Butte and a state like Montana where census reference to Irish children born in Montana means, almost certainly, born in Butte. There were 850 residents of Butte in 1910 the age of whose oldest Montana-born child placed them in Butte in 1900. Adding 3 percent of the remaining nondependent population of 5,956 to that figure gave a total of 1,002 who persisted. The nondependent population included only those under age 60 on the safe assumption that most of those older and many of those younger would not live to 1910. The five-year figures required a slightly different method. For these numbers, only the 1910 census was used. A count was made of those with Montana-born children the oldest of whom was five years or older. This number, 1,134, plus 3 percent of the remaining nondependent population over the age of 21 years was divided by the total nondependent population over 21 yielding the 23 percent persistence rate. The methods are not perfect, profound, or new, but they do use the whole population rather than a sample and they yield figures very close to those one would expect based on persistence rates in other American frontier towns. For these rates see Ralph Mann's very convenient table in *After the Gold Rush*, p. 266.

16. Polk, *City Directory, 1889*, pp. 461–63. David Ward argues that many of the immigrant men in eastern boarding houses intended to return to Europe (*Cities and Immigrants*, p. 118).

17. Bureau of Census, *MS Census*, 1900.

18. Daly, *Biography of Marcus Daly*, pp. 8–10, discusses the Florence Hotel. Bureau of Census, *MS Census*, 1900 and 1910; Polk, *Butte Directory*, 1905. The

3 percent figure used to determine the 10-year persistence rate of the childless is drawn from these calculations.

19. See Ralph Mann, *After the Gold Rush*, pp. 210–18, for this point.

20. Ibid., pp. 139–45, 165–66. Butte Chamber of Commerce, *Resources*, p. 9.

21. On Cornish iteneracy see Taylor, *Distant Magnet*, p. 190; Lingenfelter, *Hardrock Miners*, pp. 39–40. Thomas Meagher to Edward Boyce, Dec. 26, 1913, and Feb. 2, 1914; see also Boyce's diary entry for Oct. 20, 1900, when Boyce, then president of the Western Federation of Miners, noted that town support for miners' unions depended on miners spending their money in town. Correspondence and Diaries in Boyce Papers.

22. WPA, *Copper Camp*, p. 254. By 1908 wages were paid monthly. Polk, *City Directory*, 1908. The timing of payday and its significance to the working-class family needs more study.

23. For a discussion of the company store in the Pennsylvania anthracite region see Broehl, *Molly Maguires*, pp. 83–84, 96. For company-owned stores and boardinghouses in the West see Ronald C. Brown, *Hard-Rock Miners*, pp. 99–100, 153; Wyman, *Hardrock Epic*, pp. 65–67; Lingenfelter, *Hardrock Miners*, pp. 28–29. F. Augustus Heinze, one of Butte's copper kings, charged that D. J. Hennessy's store was owned by the Anaconda company and was being used to "bankrupt every independent businessman" in the city. See *Reveille* (Butte), Aug. 28, Sept. 4, and Sept. 10, 1902. Malone repeats the charge in the *Battle for Butte*, p. 59. Anaconda denied the accusation. See the comments of John Gillie and Con Kelley, Industrial Commission, *Mining at Butte*, 1911, pp. 4006, 4066–68.

24. Bureau of Census, *MS Census*, 1900 and 1910. For accounts of immigrant sex ratios as a function of job opportunities, see Golab, *Immigrant Destinations*, pp. 150–52. Diner, *Erin's Daughters*, pp. 72, 76, 84, 120–21, 126. The "male dominance" quote is from Kennedy, *The Irish*, p. 56. For an informative discussion of the role of women and families in establishing a sense of community see Ralph Mann, *After the Gold Rush*, pp. 42–46, 56–59, 96–99, 107–15, 119–25, 152, 161, 164–68, 210–14. For the emigration from Ireland generally see Vaughn and Fitzpatrick, *Irish Statistics*, pp. 299–303, 306–8, 318–20, 337–39; Kennedy, *The Irish*, p. 78. It is instructive to note that counties Cork and Donegal, two of the leading counties of origin for Butte's Irish, were among the very few in Ireland to send more men than women. Vaughn and Fitzpatrick, *Irish Statistics*, pp. 299–301, 319–20.

25. WPA, *Copper Camp*, p. 163; Bureau of Census, *MS Census*, 1900 and 1910. The Irish, of course, were not the only widows. For one example from hundreds, the 1910 MS census lists Sarah Telling, a thirty-nine-year-old Welsh widow with twelve children. Diner suggests that some of these census "widows" may have been deserted (*Erin's Daughters*, p. 59).

26. WPA, *Copper Camp*, pp. 145, 182–83, 291; Malone, *Battle for Butte*, pp. 73–74. The MS censuses of 1900 and 1910 record over three hundred prostitutes along West Mercury and West Galena Streets and in Venus and Pleasant Alleys. Montana, Dept. of Labor, *First Biennial Report*, pp. 232–36, 240–44,

contains statistical information on Butte's saloons and its prison and state hospital populations.

27. Silver Bow County, Mortuary Records, 1906–8; WPA, *Contagious Diseases*. The *Montana Socialist* summarized the record on contagious diseases from 1907 to 1913 in its issue of Mar. 30, 1913. On children falling down mine shafts see county *Mortuary Records*, 1902–10; Industrial Commission, *Mining at Butte*, 1911, 1915, pp. 3803, 4001, 4003. The *Butte Bystander* of June 10, 1893, had a story on the death of five-year-old Michael Lowney in a fall down a shaft.

28. Bureau of the Census, *Mortality Statistics*, 1916, pp. 42–43, 96–97.

29. Silver Bow Co. Board of Health, "Report on Sanitary Conditions." See also Industrial Commission, *Mining at Butte*, 1915, pp. 3882–91, 3893–3901, where a part of the report is reprinted, and the series of stories on public health in the *Montana Socialist*, Mar. 30, Aug. 10, 1913; Apr. 12, May 17, 1914.

30. Silver Bow Co. Board of Health, "Report on Sanitary Conditions," pp. 2–3. For evidence that working in the mines left men more susceptible to the disease see Bureau of Mines, *"Preliminary Report,"* and the comments of Doctors Murray, McCarthy, and McGinn in Industrial Commission, *Mining at Butte*, 1911, pp. 3940–45, 3960–68. The *Montana Socialist* made the same point. See issues for Apr. 12 and May 17, 1915.

31. Silver Bow Co. Board of Health, "Report on Sanitary Conditions," map following p. 4. Map reprinted in Industrial Commission, *Mining at Butte*, 1915, p. 3901.

32. Ibid., p. 5; Silver Bow Co. Board of Health, "Report Showing Results of Inspection," p. 5.

33. Roberts, "Two Montana Cities," p. 596; W. M. Bullard, State Board of Health Inspector, in *Butte Bystander*, July 29, 1893; *Butte Intermountain* (semi-weekly edition), June 7, 1891.

34. For Irish sensitivity on this issue see the *Butte Independent*, Aug. 13, 1910, and the *Butte Bystander*, Nov. 25, 1918.

35. Dubos and Dubos, *White Plague*, pp. 192, 193; Kennedy, *The Irish*, pp. 5, 49–50; Carpenter, *Immigrants*, pp. 198, 200–201; Burchell, *San Francisco Irish*, p. 33; David Ward, *Cities and Immigrants*, p. 110.

36. Polk, *City Directory*, 1889; WPA, *Copper Camp*, pp. 1, 195, 197. Quinn interview.

37. Plunkett's remarks and those of the other Anglo-Irishman are in Dennis Clark, *Irish in Philadelphia*, p. 39. The comment regarding French and Italian farming techniques was made to Fr. Sarsfield O'Sullivan while he was visiting in Ireland (interview). The *Irish World* carried a story praising the Mormon experiment in Utah and noted particularly the strong sense of community that distinguished it (Aug. 30, 1879).

38. Material from the last two paragraphs was taken from Bureau of Census, *MS Census*, 1900 and 1910; Diner, *Erin's Daughters*, pp. 20–29, 72, 120–21, 126–29.

39. This was a common pattern in industrial towns. See David Ward, *Cities and Immigrants*, pp. 6, 105; Dennis Clark, *Irish in Philadelphia*, pp. 41, 54;

Thernstrom, *Poverty and Progress*, p. 29; Handlin, *Boston's Immigrants*, p. 109. For Butte see Glasscock, *War of the Copper Kings*, p. 133. The "Irish" mines included all of Daly's properties, particularly the St. Lawrence, High Ore, Montana Consolidated, Neversweat, Michael Davitt, and Anaconda. Daly, *Biography of Marcus Daly*, p. 6.

40. Cunningham interview.

41. Walkowitz, *Worker City*, p. 117. For the tradition of Irish giving see Woodham-Smith, *Great Hunger*, p. 25; O'Sullivan interview. Father O'Sullivan also spoke of the practice of electing the handicapped to certain political offices. Both the AOH and the RELA sponsored benefits to help indigent members of the Irish community. For examples, AOH D1, MB, Dec. 15, 1886; Nov. 16, 1904; Jan. 11, 1905; RELA, MB, Jan. 27, 1896; May 7, 1903. The benefit dance for the blind miner was sponsored by the RELA and held at Hibernia Hall, Oct. 30, 1920. Tickets to this event are in the IrC. Both manuscript censuses contain the names of relatively young widows with no visible means of support who owned their homes without encumbrance. The policy of giving watchmen's jobs to old miners is mentioned by Con Kelley, vice president of the Anaconda Company, in Industrial Commission, *Mining at Butte*, 1915, pp. 3698, 3703–4. Both the *Montana Catholic* and the *Butte Independent* carried notices from Irish outside of Butte inquiring about missing friends and relatives who were reported in or bound for Butte.

42. Bureau of Census, *MS Census*, 1900 and 1910. Butte's figures correspond closely to those for the Irish in other American cities. Dennis Clark, *Irish in Philadelphia*, pp. 82–84; Handlin, *Boston's Immigrants*, pp. 54–55, 57; Burchell, *San Francisco Irish*, pp. 52–60; Thernstrom, *Other Bostonians*, pp. 186–94. On the dangers of assuming that the working class wanted to be upwardly mobile, see Rabinowitz "Race, Ethnicity," pp. 34–35; Yans-McLaughlin, *Family and Community*, pp. 34–36; Henretta, "Social Mobility"; Thernstrom, *Other Bostonians*, p. 330. On the Three Fs, see Palmer, *Land League Crisis*, pp. 117, 248, 263; Joseph Lee, *Modernisation*, pp. 65–88.

43. Miller, *Emigrants*, p. 428.

44. Glasscock, *War of the Copper Kings*, p. 97 and the *Butte Miner*, Nov. 21, 1888 give examples of early Irish success. See also Walkowitz, *Worker City*, p. 45.

45. Conzen, "The New Urban History," pp. 75–76, contains a good summary statement of this point. For specific examples see her *Immigrant Milwaukee*, pp. 74–80; Thernstrom, *Other Bostonians*, pp. 170–71; Katz, *People of Hamilton*, pp. 130–32; Doyle, *Social Order*, pp. 93–97; Ralph Mann, *After the Gold Rush*, pp. 83–86; Chudacoff, *Mobile Americans*, pp. 58–60, 126–28. Bureau of Census *MS Census*, 1900 and 1910.

46. Bureau of Census, *MS Census*, 1900 and 1910. For the sacrifice of children's education for home ownership see Thernstrom's *Poverty and Progress*, pp. 156–57 and *Other Bostonians*, pp. 170–71. On the Irish and the importance of owning property, see Thernstrom, *Poverty and Progress*, p. 117; Joseph Lee, *Modernisation*, pp. 102–3, Walkowitz, *Worker City*, p. 41; Burchell, *San Francisco*

Irish, p. 43; WPA, *Copper Camp,* p. 23; Dennis Clark, *Irish in Philadelphia,* pp. 54, 57, 127.

47. See Walkowitz, *Worker City,* p. 74; Conzen, "New Urban History," pp. 76–77; Burchell, *San Francisco Irish,* pp. 11–12.

48. Immigration Commission, *Immigrants in Industries,* 16:154, 192.

49. Gordon, *Assimilation,* pp. 80–81, 122, 155, 205–6. The quote is from p. 80. See also Kennedy, "Melting Pot?" p. 331. Kennedy states that "intermarriage is the surest means of assimilation and the most infallible index of its occurrence."

50. Hibernia Hall, Board of Trustees, Rent Ledger, July 31, 1894–Dec. 31, 1911, in AOH and RELA Financial Records. McNamara was a blind violinist and a great favorite of the Butte Irish. A member of both the AOH and the RELA, he was also an elected judge. The Irish societies sponsored a huge summer picnic in addition to a number of smaller social functions. Robert Emmet's birthday and St. Patrick's Day were always celebrated; so occasionally was Wolfe Tone's birthday and the anniversary of the Battle of Fontenoy.

51. Bureau of Census *MS Census,* 1900 and 1910. Riobard O'Dwyer, *My Ancestors,* passim.

52. Kennedy, "Melting Pot," p. 333; Burchell, *San Francisco Irish,* pp. 78–81. The pattern was similar among the Irish who emigrated to London. Lees, *Exiles of Erin,* pp. 153–54. See also Blessing, "West among Strangers," pp. 350–57.

53. Bishop John B. Brondel to Bishop Monaco, June 7, 1889; Brondel to the *Helena Independent,* Sept. 6, 1890; Brondel, "Pastoral Letter to the Priests of the Diocese," Dec. 4, 1890, Brondel Papers. See also the *Montana Catholic* of Sept. 23, 1899, which lists nine Catholic marriages for the week of September 15–21. Six were between Irish, one was Irish and non-Irish, two were between non-Irish. For Church hostility to mixed marriages see Burchell, *San Francisco Irish,* p. 86. There is impressionistic evidence from the manuscript censuses that when non-Irish men married Irish women from the Dublin Gulch area the men stayed in the Gulch. For example, Joseph Price, a Welshman, married Julia Sullivan and they lived surrounded by Irish families. Bureau of Census, *MS Census,* 1900.

54. Bureau of Census, *MS Census,* 1880, 1900, and 1910. For Kelley's and Ryan's wives and for Scallon's single status, see Marcosson, *Anaconda,* pp. 100, 103. For Daly's wife, see Toole, "Marcus Daly," p. 8–9.

55. Bureau of Census, *MS Census,* 1900 and 1910.

56. Arthur Mann, *One and Many,* in Rabinowitz, "Race, Ethnicity," p. 40.

57. On this point see Walkowitz, *Worker City,* pp. 101, 110, 128, 137–38, 157, 164–65; Cantor, "Introduction," pp. 10, 15, 20–21; Rabinowitz, "Race, Ethnicity," p. 32; Hays, "Politics," pp. 168–69.

58. WPA, *Copper Camp,* p. 183; Bureau of Census, *MS Census,* 1900 and 1910. See the condemnation of prostitution by Father Michael Moran in AOH D3, MB, Aug. 19, 1907, and by Bishop Carroll, *Anaconda Standard,* Dec. 18, 1911.

59. Bureau of Census, *MS Census,* 1900 and 1910.

60. The brogue is present even in the Minute Books of the AOH and the RELA. The recording secretaries of both were often phonetic spellers and the minutes read like a piece from Finley Peter Dunne. On the availability of Irish stout and porter, see the *Butte Mining Journal*, Oct. 19, Nov. 16, 1887; Jan. 10, 1888. The *Butte Independent* had a story about handball in the issue of Feb. 5, 1910. For the Gaelic League see AOH, D1, MB, October 25, 1905. For the Gaelic Athletic Association see RELA, MB, October 2, 1913 and July 29, 1915. WPA, *Copper Camp*, pp. 226–27, also mentions the G.A.A. The purpose of the *Butte Independent* was announced on its masthead. See also the issue of Jan. 22, 1910. Mulcahy visited both the AOH and the RELA meetings in 1910 and asked for their members' support. He later joined both organizations. AOH D3, MB, Dec. 18, 1909; RELA, MB, Dec. 23, 1909. RELA members received the *Gaelic American*; AOH members received the *National Hibernian*. RELA, MB, Sept. 24, 1903; O'Dea, *AOH*, II:1251. Reference is made to the *Rocky Mountain Celt* in AOH D1, MB, Feb. 22, 1899. The *Chicago Citizen* was mentioned by the *Butte Independent* and its editor, John Finerty, was a frequent Butte visitor. *Butte Independent*, Apr. 16, 1910; *Anaconda Standard*, July 5, 1905.

61. In addition to other newspaper sources, the following give an account of or information regarding the speeches of the men and women who visited Butte. Father Patrick Scanlon, AOH D1, MB, Mar. 17, 1885; Michael Davitt, RELA, MB, Oct. 14, 1886; John Boyle O'Reilly, RELA, MB, Apr. 3, 1890; William O'Brien and John Dillon, RELA, MB, Nov. 6, 1890; John Finerty, RELA, MB, Feb. 25, 1891; Father John Larkin, AOH D1, MB, Aug. 18, 1897; Maud Gonne, RELA, MB, Oct. 28, 1897; John McBride, RELA, MB, Jan. 17, 1901; O'Brien Kennedy, RELA, MB, Mar. 14, 1901; Conor O'Kelly, P. J. Brophy to O'Kelly, June 20, 1904, Brophy Papers; Douglas Hyde, RELA, MB, Oct. 26, 1905; Seamus McManus, RELA, MB, Oct. 25, 1906; Bulmer Hobson, RELA, MB, Feb. 14, 1907; Professor James C. Monaghan, J. R. Jackson to President, AOH, Apr. 10, 1910, "Correspondence"; Professor James Rohan, AOH D3, MB, May 27, 1911, IrC; Con Lehane, *Anaconda Standard*, Aug. 13, 1915; James Larkin, *Montana Socialist*, July 22, 1916; Hannah Sheehy-Skeffington, Ladies Auxiliary, AOH, to RELA, May 31, 1917, Correspondence; Kathleen O'Brennan, Committee of Arrangements to RELA, June 10, 1918, Correspondence; Eamon de Valera, James E. Murray to William Borah, July 30, 1919, Murray Papers; Mary McWhorter, Ladies' Auxiliary, AOH, to RELA, Apr. 3, 1921, Correspondence. See also O'Daly, *Life*, for references to the Irish men and women who spoke in Butte.

62. Since each of these organizations rented space in Hibernia Hall, mention of them is conveniently found in Hibernia Hall, Board of Trustees, Rent Ledger, July 31, 1894–Dec. 31, 1911, in AOH Financial Records. See also city directories.

CHAPTER 4

Church, Party, and Fraternity:
The Irish and Their Associations

I

As was the case in immigrant communities in every American city, the Irish world of Butte required a strong associational base. This was particularly true given the quick, almost immediate social differentiation that arose in Butte, America. If the Irish were to preserve an ethnic consciousness they would have to do it in the face of striking intra-community differences in wealth, status, and influence. This is not just a reference to the few Irish who were rich; equally important was the division within the overwhelmingly working-class Irish community between those who persisted or intended to persist and those who were still part of a transient mining work force. To this same point is the fact that the Irish in Butte faced little in the way of a hostile native community. They were not without their critics, but they could not depend on external pressure to keep their community intact.

That the Irish succeeded as well as they did is a tribute to the strength and resiliency of their organizations. That vaunted, if ultimately unprovable, Irish sociability is again at issue. But even assuming its existence, the well-defined social skills reflecting that sociability were developed in rural Ireland, where the Big House of the landlord and the county fair were among the favored places and times for social activities. The making of an Irish community in Butte would force certain adjustments in old patterns.[1]

One source of community cohesion, however, was the same regardless of where the Irish went. The parish and the Church were an inseparable part of the Irish Catholic world. In Ireland, however, this had a meaning different from that in the eastern and midwestern cities of the United States. In Boston or Chicago the Irish were reminded daily that they lived in a larger non-Irish world. The Church was among the most important of the segregant organizations that allowed them to survive it. In Butte there were fewer of those reminders and the Church, though still segregant in many of its functions, must have seemed less a besieged fortress and more the unchallenged moral and social arbiter it had always been in Ireland.[2]

The unaccustomed role of the Irish as urban pioneers was one reason. Their parishes not only had Irish names, they reflected the Irish dominance of Butte Catholicism and the Catholic dominance of Butte. St. Patrick's, founded in 1879, had 7,000 members by 1889; the Mountain View Methodists had the city's second highest membership with 145. By 1901, there were five Catholic parishes in the city. The four largest had a combined membership of over 25,000. St. Patrick's alone claimed 10,000; no Protestant denomination had more than 800. Butte, indeed, was far more overwhelmingly Catholic than it was overwhelmingly Irish.[3]

Still, particularly before 1905 when other immigrant Catholics began to arrive in significant numbers, the Irish dominated the Catholic laity of the state. As John Brondel, Bishop of Montana, noted in 1890, "America in general and our Diocese . . . in particular, have drawn a healthy, intelligent, industrious, and numerous population from Ireland." He might have added restive population for, although "we have many Irish . . . in Montana, we have not one Irish priest." Belgian, French, and Italian Jesuits had done the hard work of pioneering, but lay Irish demanded priests of like national if not county origins.[4]

The issue was not language; laity and clergy both spoke English, albeit with different and confusing accents. Certainly the larger questions of ultramontanism were not involved. The assignment of Irish priests to Irish parishes did, however, upset the assimilationist plans of the so-called Americanist clergy. That was precisely the point. Butte's Irish, like most immigrant Catholics, asked the Church to preserve the recognizable features of Irish social and sacramental life. To be assigned a non-Irish priest as a way to destroy those features was doubly insulting. With that in mind, the obviously sympathetic Brondel traveled to Ireland and the seminary at Thurles to recruit Irish priests. He wrote back that he was "pleased to say that I secured the promise of six, and three certain, who will arrive as soon as they can."[5]

But being first in Butte gave the Irish Catholics more than just numerical strength. As noted before, it meant that the emergence of an Irish Catholic middle and professional class occurred more quickly than was the case when the Irish came into a place with an established social and economic elite. Two important developments followed from this: an attendant increase in Irish patrons of the Church, and a greater diversity of wealth and position within the Irish Catholic community. Marcus Daly's generosity has already been mentioned, but John D. Ryan, D. J. Hennessy, P. J. Brophy, James Twohey, and John J. O'Meara, among many other well-placed Irishmen, were almost as openhanded.[6]

The church did not depend only on these rich, neither did it represent only their interests. Two of Butte's parishes were avowedly, almost aggressively, Irish working class. One of them, St. Lawrence O'Toole's, was located just north of Butte in Walkerville, not far from the Green Mountain and Mountain Consolidated mines. At its dedication in 1898, Bishop Brondel spoke of St. Lawrence O'Toole's as "a church of workingmen. There is not a rich man in the congregation. The church was paid for by the small contributions of the poor people." Brondell's successor, John Carroll, said the parish was "made up exclusively of working people," and its progress depended on the "generosity of Irish miners." And, both bishops might have added publicly, that of Irish mine owners; it was built on land donated by the Butte and Boston Mining Company, and Marcus Daly was among its principal benefactors. This did not affect its function, and when Brondel prayed at the dedication that "God would protect the miners in their hazardous work," he obviously knew his audience well.[7]

The official "Miners' Catholic Church," however, was not St. Lawrence O'Toole's but St. Mary's, parish headquarters for Dublin Gulch and Corktown. Built in 1902 and led from the first by Irish-born and Irish patriot priests, St. Mary's four hundred families were all Irish and all but two of those four hundred were dependent on jobs in the mines. The "rough kids," one Butte Irishman recalled, went to St. Mary's, the "fancy ones" to St. Patrick's. There can have been few parishes in the United States with so narrow an ethnic and occupational base. Its priests had to schedule mass around shift changes; 10:30 was too early for the night-shift workers, 8:00 not early enough for the day shift. During hard times, as in 1909, St. Mary's had to ask for an extension on its loans and its pastor had "to buy books for a number of children who are very poor." When the mines were at full employment, the parish paid off its debts, built a home for its priests, and renovated the home for its teaching sisters.[8]

St. Mary's, however, was also an Irish church, held together as much by the shared ethnicity of its parishioners as by their shared occupational status. In fact, it was not the loss of mine jobs that threatened the church, it was the loss of Irish miners. Some left Butte, but more seem to have moved to other and more prosperous parishes on Butte's west and south sides. They returned to St. Mary's for the marriage of their children; they returned to be buried; but they heard mass at Immaculate Conception, or St. Joseph's, or St. Patrick's. Their places in Dublin Gulch were taken by other miners' families, many of them Catholic but too few of them Irish. So serious was the exodus of Irish that the parish boundaries were extended in 1914 into "the territory of St. Patrick's." This ecclesiastical raid into the Irish sections of a neighboring parish "relieved somewhat the situation and offset for the time being the loss that was sustained." It also, however, revealed how closely the church was bound to the Irish—and they to it.[9]

It would be difficult to overstate the importance of the churches to the Irish community. Indeed, for some they were the Irish community. They baptized the babies, educated the children—over five hundred, all Irish, were enrolled at St. Mary's in 1906—married the young adults, comforted the sick, buried the dead. In the process, they provided a continuity, a sense of group solidarity that no other organization, fraternal, political, or labor, could match. Immigrant Irish belonged to the Catholic Church in much the same way that Americans of the middle or professional classes belonged to their service clubs or professional associations, and they enjoyed similar advantages.[10]

One was that, unlike Protestant denominations in which local autonomy was a functional if not definitional part of the organizational structure of the congregation, the Catholic Church transcended the limits of distended and insular villages. It permitted those who belonged to it to "transfer" parishes without loss of the sacraments and with minimal liturgical confusion. The new parish was indistinguishable from the old, made up of people of like mind and often of like origins. As such, the Church also limited the opportunities for Catholic contact with what was usually a non-Catholic majority. In a place like Butte, however, the Catholics were the clear majority and there were few chances for interdenominational contact in any event, particularly for the Irish miners. When Irish dominance of the parishes is added to Irish Catholic dominance of the largest mines, the Miners' Union, and the Democratic party, the power and influence of what was essentially a closed ethnic community is more clearly revealed.

But then it must be held in mind that this community ran the town. Their parochial schools, for example, cannot have been used as shields against the Protestant influences of the host culture; the Irish were the host culture, and they provided a sizeable percentage of the public school trustees, administrators, and teachers. In an instructive reversal of the usual pattern, Butte's Protestant minorities once protested the influence of Catholics in the public schools. This is not to say that the parochial schools were less a part of Butte's Irish community than, say, Chicago's. Enrollment figures would indicate that Butte's Irish favored a parochial education for their children. It is to say, however, that these parochial schools were not as self-consciously sectarian as they were in cities less tolerant of a Catholic and Irish presence.[11]

II

Irish influence in the public school system arose from Irish dominance of the political system. The local Democratic party governed Butte and the Irish were clearly the most powerful of its component parts. San Francisco had an Irish mayor by 1867, New York by 1880, Boston by 1884. Butte elected Edward Dugan its chief executive in 1893, less than a decade after its incorporation. It was not timing, however, but regularity that marked Butte's record. Dugan was the first of eight Irish Democratic mayors between 1893 and 1919—and each of the eight was surrounded by congenial subordinates. In 1905, to take a representative year, Mayor Patrick Mullins presided over a city council in which Irishmen held twelve of the sixteen aldermanic posts. In addition, the police judge, chief of police, building inspector, plumbing inspector, health officer, pound master, sanitary inspector, street commissioner, judge and clerk of the municipal court, two of the three city detectives, all three city jailors, thirty-six of fifty-one policemen, and twenty-one of thirty-six firemen bore unmistakably Irish names.[12]

The pattern was the same in Silver Bow County. The three county commissioners, the sheriff, undersheriff, five of seven deputies, all three jailors, both outside deputies, the clerk and recorder, four of five deputy clerks, the public administrator, surveyor, superintendent of common schools, coroner, assessor, deputy assessor, county physician, sanitary inspector, three of four health board members, the road supervisor, county attorney, and both municipal judges—all were Irishmen.[13]

This is what was meant when it was noted that the Irish were not politically circumscribed. Too much, however, should not be made of this Irish political dominance. It had little, if any, effect on class relations, except perhaps to make Irish workers think they had greater power than they did. The Irish with money knew better. Irish political dominance counted for something only when the Irish of all classes had to deal with nativist hostility directed toward all of them. There was more of that hostility than the population figures would suggest was likely.

In 1891, the leader of Butte's large Cornish population wondered aloud why, since "God had held America from the gaze of the world until . . . England was permeated by the spirit of the gospel," He could not have been as accommodating in revealing Butte. Three years later, the anti-Catholic American Protective Association seems to have been of some service to Helena's cause in that city's successful contest with Marcus Daly's Anaconda for selection as the permanent site for the state capital. Anaconda was identified in the APA newspaper as an Irish and Catholic town; Helena, it was argued, was hostile to both Irish and Catholics. It is doubtful that many votes were influenced by these charges; it is equally doubtful that the Irish forgot they were made. A year later the APA rallied enough nativist votes to replace Dugan with William Thompson, a Republican pledged to APA principles, including freeing Irish Catholics "from the tyranny of the priesthood" and freeing Butte from the "Romish hierarchy," "the henchmen . . . of that old loon," by which the APA meant the pope. Thompson was not all the association hoped he might be, but in 1896 Butte removed his "betrayal" of nativism as an issue by rejecting the APA candidate and electing another Irishman, Patrick Harrington.[14]

The APA, even before Harrington's election, offered an interesting political hypothesis regarding the source of Irish and Democratic strength. "Worthless villains" (for which read transient Irish miners) were imported "for election purposes." These "curs" were given temporary employment at Marcus Daly's mines; they stayed only long enough to return "Pope Marcus's" cronies to political office. However the Democrats did it—and the APA's novel explanation of Irish working-class mobility seems inadequate—seven of Butte's next nine mayors were Irish Democrats.[15]

The party, however, particularly before 1900, was the instrument in this relationship; ethnicity and Irish nationalism determined policy and targets. In terms of voter behavior, this meant that national and statewide questions were clearly subordinate to local and international issues. Butte and Ireland and the needs of the Irish living in each were more important than issues of state or nation, and since these "Irish issues" determined voter allegiance, the local Democratic party came to have a distinctly nonideological if not conservative cast.[16]

A perfect case in point was the election of 1888, Montana's last as a territory and either cause or occasion of Marcus Daly's famous feud with William Andrews Clark. In briefest outline, the issues were these: Clark was the Democratic candidate for territorial representative, an office thought to insure selection as Montana's first U.S. senator. Like Daly, Clark was a Butte mine and smelter owner; his election was considered a certainty in the overwhelmingly Democratic territory. His Republican opponent, Helena attorney Thomas Carter, was untested and unknown. But Carter won, in large measure because of support from Silver Bow County, including quite remarkable support from the Irish and presumably Democratic wards of Butte and Centerville. It was assumed by all, during the election and since, that Marcus Daly had instructed his remarkably pliant Irish employees to vote for Carter.[17]

Historical speculation has centered exclusively on Daly's motives. The majority verdict is that Daly thought a Republican would have greater leverage with what most observers presumed would be a Republican administration, and that this leverage could and would be used to allow Daly to continue his illegal timber-cutting practices. It was the kind of sinister act that was expected of robber barons and copper kings. It was also, obviously, one that required rather over-heated language to describe. "Behind the scenes," writes one recent historian of the Clark-Daly feud, "Marcus Daly and his allies secretly plotted Clark's defeat." "Allies" later became "cohorts" and "henchmen." The plot became a "clandestine campaign" on which Daly "put the finishing touches."[18]

The purpose of the discussion here is not to assess Daly's motives. It is at least plausible that he wanted only to continue his raids on the federal forests. More should probably be said about his ability to predict Harrison's defeat of Cleveland, an ability that borders on the miraculous given the narrowness of the final margin and Cleveland's majority of the popular vote. But Daly's alleged rascality (and powers of prophecy) aside, what of the motives of the thousands of Irish miners who were also thought safely Democratic? Did they simply do Daly's bidding or were there issues in the campaign of moment to them?

In the first place, it was possible to be an Irish Republican in Montana without losing all influence. Patrick Boland and Maurice O'Connor, both Irish and both former presidents of the Butte Miners' Union, are cases in point. This hardly constitutes a ground swell but it does indicate that Irish support for the Democratic candidate was not entirely automatic. Irish-American leaders in the East, moreover, wearying of Democratic neglect and ingratitude, suggested that 1888 might be a very good year for the Irish to swing their votes from Cleveland to Harrison. When the English ambassador to the United States publicly declared that Cleveland was a better friend of Great Britain than Harrison, a number of Anglophobic Irish-Americans responded predictably and voted for Harrison.[19]

Of related significance was the question of the tariff. Any reduction of duties meant the dumping of English goods on the American market, enriching Englishmen at the expense of American and Irish labor. An independent Ireland, moreover, would have to claim the small nation's right to protect its industries and the principle of protection became almost a litmus test of Irish nationalism. Irish-Americans did not split with their allies in Ireland over this issue and Irish-America, including Irish Butte, was strongly protectionist. So was Harrison and so were the Republicans; Clark's advocacy of tariff "reform" was consistent with the national Democratic platform—and anathema to Butte's Irish patriots.[20]

There were also compelling local issues that can explain a Butte Irishman's vote for Carter. The most obvious was that Carter was the Catholic son of Irish immigrants and a friend of the Montana hierarchy. Clark, on the other hand, was quintessentially Orange. Of Scotch-Irish descent, the son of a Presbyterian elder, a Grand Master Mason, he cannot have been the favored candidate of Irish Catholics, particularly in 1888 as they reflected on the emerging hostility of North-of-Ireland Protestants to Irish Home Rule. Clark's supporters seem to have understood as much; a Missoula newspaper, for example, identified him as a Gaelic-speaking Irish nationalist and the direct descendant of Robert Emmet.[21]

Such was not the case, but neither is there evidence to support a charge that Clark was openly anti-Irish. There is incontrovertible evidence, however, that he was either remarkably insensitive or remarkably careless. He scheduled a beef barbeque on a Friday, effectively barring Irish Catholic participation, then compounded his blunder by inviting the members of the virulently anti-Catholic Patriotic Order, Sons of America, to attend. In a speech in Missoula, Clark made slighting reference to Patrick Ford and to the protectionist policy of the *Irish World*. He then repeated what would become a favorite charge of the APA against all Irish Catholics. Clark identified Ford as "a prominent deserter from the federal army in the Civil War." Ford answered the charge, with characteristic vigor, in the columns of his newspaper, pointing out that not only was the charge untrue, it came from a man whose free-trade ideas were a calculated insult to Irishmen on both sides of the Atlantic.[22]

There was no recorded response to the Clark-Ford exchange from Marcus Daly, but immediately after the election Clark's newspaper, the *Butte Miner*, identified the "conspiracy" that defeated him as one "to influence religious prejudice against Mr. Clark." Four days later the *Miner* asked if the tactics of 1888 were to become a permanent part of Montana politics. "Will religious feeling be worked upon, and men employed in the mines be commanded to vote so and so or be dismissed?" Like all conspiracy theorists, the writer did not ask if the Irish had to be commanded to vote as they did. Nor did he consider the possibility that Clark's Friday cookout of fatted calves and his impolitic remark about Ford might themselves be interpreted as forms of religious prejudice and that the Irish needed no urging or threats from Daly to rebuke Clark for them. The possibility that Irishtown (including Marcus Daly) did not like or trust Clark and voted accordingly was not considered—at the time or later.[23]

Initially, then, the Irish supported the Democratic party because the party was usually willing to nominate candidates acceptable to them. It is unfortunate that so elementary a point needs to be made. As the Irish community became more complex and differentiated—which is to say less exclusively ethnic—it became impossible for the Democratic party to satisfy the needs of all of its Irish constituency. The party was consistent in its support for Ireland, but that became an abstract issue at best, a diversionary tactic at worst, to those Irish whose labor militancy exceeded their commitment to the Old Land. In other words, issues change, and as the enemies of the working class came to assume a more evil aspect than the enemies of the Irish, third-party reformers tried to split the Irish vote. The Democratic party was the clear choice of most of the Irish workers only when the Irish workers were the clear choice of the Democrats. But let the party grow forgetful of the terms of this arrangement and elements of the Irish working class moved into other, more congenial associations.[24]

They cannot have moved cheerfully. In Butte as elsewhere in America, the parties of reform were too often the parties of intolerance, and the Irish and their Church often found themselves the objects of reformers' scorn. The Republicans retained a stubborn streak of nativism; the national Democratic party of Bryan, Parker, and Wilson, though dependent upon immigrant votes, was not particularly sensitive to immigrant needs. The great reform movements of the nineteenth century offered the Irish no comfort. English laissez-faire had permitted them to starve; abolitionism had nearly destroyed a Union that offered them what little protection they had. Temperance was more an assault on them and their saloons than an affirmation of the advantages of sobriety; Prohibition would make sin what their Church did not make sin. Marxism attacked both their faith and their nationalism. The local Democratic party—in Butte it was called the Dalycrats—was all that was left.[25]

To a greater or lesser extent, each of these factors was at work in Butte. The APA was identified as the "chestnut raker of the Republican party"; populism was "divided" by APA "nativism." Indeed APA support for Bryan extended even to a heated denial by the APA newspaper of the "gold bug" charge that Bryan's real name was O'Brien. The Socialists were led by a Scottish Unitarian minister of distinctly evangelical tendencies; Republican progressivism was barely relevant to Irish lives. In sum, the Butte Irish miner was almost totally isolated politically. Internecine Irish struggles, as a result, occurred either within the local Democratic party or, and more commonly, outside the world of partisan politics for control of the Butte Miners' Union. It was not the party but the political process that gave definition to the Irish working class.[26]

The Dalycrats, however, were central to that process, if for no other reason than that their policies served as the point of departure for political debate. The Irishman first responded to the Democrats and aligned himself on one side or the other of its platform. Some Irish "bolted" the party, but few ever really left it. And that is the central point: political apostasy and political loyalty were both defined in the context of the local Democratic party. The emphasis, however, must be on local. State and national issues scarcely concerned these Butte Dalycrats, not because the issues were inscrutable but because they were largely irrelevant. It was the local organization that took care of the Butte Irish, got them jobs and protected them from their enemies. With the Irish community as a whole, the party's ties were strong and enduring and, though this must not be taken as witless fidelity, the local Democratic organization did become a part of the network of ethnic and working-class associations.[27]

Its function, obviously, was not just political. Like the Church with which it was closely allied, the local Democratic party had significant ceremonial and social responsibilities. And, also like the Church, it had a distinctly stabilizing and conservative influence on the Irish community which formed it. Working-class radicalism was doctrinally unacceptable to the Church, politically dangerous to the party. The radicals acknowledged the hostility of both by attacking both. But Church and party did far more than just obstruct. They provided a necessary sense of continuity, a training ground for Irish leaders, business and job contacts for Irish merchants and workers, and a measure of respectability for the Irish of whatever class.[28]

III

More important to ethnic solidarity than either Church or party, because more unequivocally and exclusively Irish than either, were the two major Irish fraternities of Butte, the Ancient Order of Hibernians

(AOH) and the Robert Emmet Literary Association (RELA). Butte's already sizeable Irish population organized an AOH division in March of 1880; in October of 1881 the Emmet Associates, later the Robert Emmet Literary Association, held its first meeting. Both groups limited their membership to the Irish-born and their sons. Both were predominantly working class, and both came to exercise considerable influence over the Irish community in Butte.[29]

The RELA was the Butte chapter—camp in the language of the organization—of the secret and revolutionary Clan-na-Gael, the American counterpart of the equally secret and revolutionary Irish Republican Brotherhood in Ireland. The purpose of the Clan from the moment of its founding in 1867 was the complete independence of Ireland from all English authority. Its methods were those of "physical force" rather than parliamentary obstruction. It was, both in object and in the means of attaining it, the linear and ideological descendant of the Fenian Brotherhood. It hoped to avoid the sillier excesses of the Fenians and hence the caricature of barroom patriot which destroyed Fenian effectiveness, but the Clan was no less frankly revolutionary. It necessarily had as its sources of inspiration a high percentage of Anglo-Irish Protestants, necessarily because Ireland during these years produced few Catholic nationalists. In Butte the Clan took its name from the Protestant Robert Emmet, celebrated the ideas of the anticlerical Wolfe Tone, and opened its own ranks to Irishmen of all faiths and no faith.[30]

The AOH was considerably less ideological. Founded in Ireland in the sixteenth century and brought to the United States in 1836, the AOH was assertively Catholic. It traced its descent not to Protestant rebels like Emmet, and never to atheistic intellectuals like Tone, but to Catholic peasants (Whiteboys as they were known) who resisted English and Protestant ownership of their lands as well as English control of their nation. Their patron was St. Patrick, not Marat or even Tom Paine, their commitment to an independent Ireland was less determined than that of the Clan-na-Gael, and their rhetorical defense of Irish rights was considerably less strident.[31]

In the older cities of Irish-America the two organizations were often rivals. The Clan traced its descent to political revolutionaries; the AOH to peasant land reformers. The Clan was thought too visionary and intellectual, too single-minded in its call for revolution, too little interested in the immediate needs of an impoverished Irish peasantry. The AOH, on the other hand, was dismissed as a priest-ridden fraternity of the ineffectual, lacking the nerve to take arms, unmoved by the mystic strains of the Gael and the legitimacy of the Irish demands for nationhood. As one Clan leader put it in 1886, the AOH "do not care a damn about our principles," and as late as 1894 the Irish Republican Brotherhood in Ireland denied membership to "Hibernians, Ribbonmen, or other non-Republican associations." As for the AOH, in 1884 it expressly proscribed membership in "the Clan-na-Gaels or any offshoot of the Clan-na-Gaels." The Butte division asked all applicants if they belonged "to any societies that the Catholic Church [was] opposed to," and, depending on the political disposition of the hierarchy, that could include the Clan-na-Gael.[32]

Some of this factional combativeness was brought to Butte. In 1883 and again in 1884 the RELA refused the AOH invitation to parade on St. Patrick's Day, insisting that the celebration of so religious a day violated their nonsectarian principles. By 1895 these principles must have seemed less important than the chance to display their Irishness, and the RELA participated enthusiastically in what by then was Butte's best-attended celebration. In 1898, however, the RELA voted not to invite the AOH to its commemoration of the execution of the Manchester Martyrs, but this appears to have been the last instance of interfraternity faction fighting until 1917. By 1890 the two organizations were co-owners of Hibernia Hall; by 1900 the national Clan-na-Gael announced that the two groups were reconciled, and by 1903 there may have been as many as two hundred men who were members of both groups, perhaps a dozen of them officers of both.[33]

This does not imply a loss of identity by either. Indeed, if two hundred men were members of both, then almost eight hundred of the associational Irish were affiliated with only one. The RELA was secret and secretive; it was never listed in the Butte city directories; its officers were known only to its members; in the minutes of its meetings members were never identified by name but only by membership number. Few priests were admitted to its ranks. Even Jeremiah Callaghan, Butte's first Irish priest and a man universally admired, was rejected for membership, though Father Michael Hannan was admitted and became one of its most active and radical members. An elaborate system of test words, hailing signs, and passwords was used to protect it from informers. Overly talkative members were expelled; potential members were rejected if thought indiscreet or if they "betrayed" the confidence of the camp. There was even a warning read at one meeting to be on the lookout for English spies. All communications from the national Clan-na-Gael were destroyed after they were read.[34]

Even its social activities, and it sponsored a good many of them, were ostensibly held to hasten the revolution. As early as 1882, the national Clan headquarters instructed the Emmets to "raise money for special arms' funds by picnics and that sort." The following year each of the camps of the Clan received word that it was their "duty to utilize every available method of raising funds for the Special Fund by picnics, balls, parties, and fairs." The RELA may have taken this responsibility seriously. It may also, however, have been only acting out the patriot game. In any event, an unidentified officer noted in 1901 that the "public can know the name of our club ... but we must not betray the Secrecy of our plans and action," while William Gallagher (#286), noted that the "mantle of charity ... [was] a cloak to cover us all in pursuit of our purpose."[35]

The AOH was less bellicose and considerably less conspiratorial. A public corporation, its members were identified in the minutes by name; its officers were acknowledged in newspapers and city directories; its meetings opened and closed with prayers by one of its many clerical members. It was closely tied to its Ladies' Auxiliary, the Daughters of Erin. Though strongly nationalistic, the AOH was less overtly revolutionary than the RELA and slower to abandon the peaceful methods of the Irish Parliamentary party. Still, the AOH was not just the Irish section of the Knights of Columbus. It too used passwords, hailing signs, and handshakes, but less, it seems, in the interests of revolutionary secrecy and more as an expression of fraternity. In Butte, the Hibernians were affiliated with the Dublin-based Board of Erin rather than the Ancient Order of Hibernians in America, headquartered in New York. The Board of Erin Hibernians were the more "Irish" of the competing branches of the order and their affiliation with it may explain the ability of the Butte Hibernians to work with the Emmets. The appeal of the AOH, quite as much as that of the RELA, was to the dispossessed if not quite radicalized Irish rebel. And neither group ever forgot its responsibilities to an independent Ireland. An English critic of both referred to the AOH as "notorious," the Clan-na-Gael as "infamous."[36]

IV

But Butte was a long way from Boston, not to say Ireland, and revolutionary objectives had to compete with other more immediate concerns. Much has been made of the Irish dominance of Butte, and the timing and numerical strength of the Irish presence did create a unique set of circumstances. Strictly speaking, the Irish clubs of Butte were not segregant in the way they were in Boston; they did not form part of a subculture the way they did in Chicago. But though the size and influence of the established Irish community must have been comforting to newly arriving Irish, it cannot have affected appreciably the obvious sense of uprootedness they felt, regardless of their last place of residence. The influence of the established Butte Irish is, then, beside the point; the Irish clubs had to perform many of the same segregant and ritualistic functions that were required of them in places where the Irish were almost entirely without influence.

The *Montana Catholic* wrote in 1899 that the AOH provided the "refuge of the exile." It gave "more comfort to sorrowing souls, dried more . . . tears forced from exiles' eyes and sent more happiness into desolate homes" than any organization in Butte, save the Church. Allowing for the melodrama, the *Montana Catholic* accurately defined the role of the AOH. In 1907, for example, a James Connolly arrived in Butte from Rostrevor, County Down. He was preceded by a letter from his local Irish AOH division which stated that those who knew him in Ireland "always fond him . . . true and faithful" and joined in "commending him to the friendship of your brotheren and . . . in wishing him success on his jurney." In the rapidly expanding Irish world this was the equivalent of a letter of marque. Father Jeremiah Callaghan undoubtedly spoke for many thousands of Irish when he thanked the AOH for the "assistance and friendship" it extended to him when he was a "stranger in Butte." The same things could have been said of the RELA. Both gave clear evidence of the associational stability of the Irish world of Butte. Irishmen roamed, particularly Irish miners, but when they arrived in Butte they discovered that an important part of their world had preceded them.[37]

The significance of this sense of continuity would be difficult to overestimate, particularly when the overwhelmingly immigrant and working-class nature of the membership of both associations is considered. As T. J. McCarthy noted, it was "the poor working people who comprise the AOH of Butte." Membership lists bear him out. During the early years, 1884–89, 104 of 108 applicants for AOH membership were immigrant miners. From 1889 until 1919, 1,239 AOH membership applications survived; 1,115 of those list occupation, and of that total 817 (73 percent) identify the applicant as a miner; another 118 were laborers or industrial tradesmen, increasing the blue-collar working class component to 84 percent. The remainder were either professionals, mining supervisors, merchants (including saloon keepers), city or county officials (including police and firemen), merchants, or clerical workers and clerks. Many of these, the police and saloonkeepers, for example, had working-class backgrounds; all had working-class sympathies. As regards origin, of those same 1,239 applications, 1,140 contain reference to place of birth; 858 (75 percent) list Ireland.[38]

It must also be pointed out, however, that Marcus Daly, William Scallon, John D. Ryan, and Cornelius F. Kelley, the first four presidents

of the Anaconda Copper Mining Company, and only Daly Irish by
birth, were also members. Other prominent Hibernians included Dan
Kelly, head of the company's legal division; Daniel Hennessy, owner
of Hennessy's Mercantile; P. J. Brophy, Butte's largest grocer; Miles
Finlen, owner of the Finlen Hotel; and the "capitalist," James A. Murray, identified in 1914 as "many times a millionaire." Of this list, only
Brophy was born in Ireland. It was an organization, in other words,
whose membership represented the entire Irish community from the
cool and aristocratic John D. Ryan to the muckers who dug the ore.[39]

RELA membership figures are comparable. The occupation listed at
the time of initiation for 804 men from 1881 until 1911 shows that
665 (83 percent) were miners or laborers. Some allowance must be
made for occupational mobility. For example, Jeremiah J. Lynch, later
a lawyer and judge and Butte's most prominent Irish nationalist, was
a miner at the time of his initiation in 1895, and a bartender in 1901.
The point, however, is clear. Butte's Clan-na-Gael membership, like
that of its Hibernians, amply confirms John Devoy's statement that
"the vast majority of our members were not men of much means."[40]

Men of means, however, did affiliate. Ryan was identified as an RELA
member, though there is no evidence in the association's records to
confirm it. P. J. Brophy was an early Clansman (#29); so was James
Murray (#13) and James Twohey (#18). Marcus Daly was proposed
for admission, suggesting at least that he was sympathetic to Clan goals,
and such Daly associates as Sam Mulville (#83), John Branagan (#28),
and Mike Carroll (#348) were all active in the RELA. William Scallon
(#129) was admitted, as was Con Kelley (#123), giving the Emmets a
claim on all of the Anaconda Company's first four presidents. Daniel
Hennessy (#38) was one of the camp's most prominent and active
members. In general, RELA membership lists support only a part of
Eric Foner's argument that the Clan was "almost entirely . . . working
class . . . [with] a sprinkling of petty entrepreneurs. By and large the
'best class of Irishmen' held aloof."[41]

These stable ethnic associations permitted the Irish worker literally
to carry his ethnicity with him as he moved through the industrializing
cities of the northern United States. The camps of the Clan-na-Gael
and the divisions of the AOH were like the parishes of the Catholic
Church or the local organizations of the Democratic party—alike in
purpose and ritual, strikingly similar in membership. And, again like
Church and party, but long before the western miners' unions federated, both permitted transfers of membership. As noted, the Hibernians
and the Clan routinely accepted the credentials of wandering Irishmen
and extended to them the full privileges of affiliation, including sick

and death benefits and informal representation by employment committees. Given the peripatetic habits of Irish hard-rock men, these were
considerable privileges. Whether these miners carried any sense of
labor solidarity with them from place to place, whether, in other words,
they constituted a floating and radicalized proletariat, cannot be known.
Transiency may have heightened their consciousness of class; it may
also have weakened it or made it irrelevant. What can be known is
that they brought their bristly Irishness with them. Mines played out;
mining camps disappeared; miners moved, died, or became merchants.
Their Church and their clubs endured.[42]

But the social and ameliorative responsibilities of the Irish clubs
extended beyond this initial welcome. New members had next to be
made to feel at home. Fortunately, the clubs were dealing with a select
audience. Merely affiliating with either of them, even by transfer, involved a certain commitment to place. The AOH had an initiation fee
of $5.00, and $.50 to $1.00 per month dues; the RELA had a $3.00
initiation fee and dues and contingency fee charges of $.50 per month.
Transfers could avoid the initiation fee, but dues and other charges
were assessed. With mine wages at $3.50 per day, this meant that a
new member of the AOH worked at least twelve hours underground
for the money necessary to join, worked another three days to pay the
routine dues and charges for a year. For the working class at least,
membership in either group cannot have been entered into casually;
a year's membership in both cost more than room and board for a
month.[43]

Despite the high costs of participation, both societies flourished. The
Hibernians counted a peak membership of over one thousand men in
1903; the RELA listed over six hundred members in 1905, making it
the second largest Clan-na Gael camp in the United States. Two things
are implied by this—other than that Butte had a lot of Irishmen prosperous enough and committed enough to join. First, most members
must at least have intended to settle in, meaning that the clubs not
only represented stability but limited their membership to those who
considered themselves to be stable. Second, the clubs must have earned
their members' support by providing services commensurate with those
dues.[44]

They discharged that latter responsibility in a variety of ways. The
employment committees and "insurance" programs are important
enough to warrant extended treatment in another section, but the clubs
did more than just get their members jobs in the mines and pay part
of the expenses for the injuries, illnesses, and deaths that too often
resulted from those jobs. Both had what can only be called a full social

schedule. Meetings routinely went into social session after the conclusion of the week's business. Some of these were given over to debates on topics ranging from immigration restriction to the relative merits of physical force and moral suasion as means to an independent Ireland. On one occasion the topic was whether the "Irish race should retain their prejudices or . . . be more broad minded and cultivate more liberal feelings." Though the entertainment value of the ensuing debate was probably considerable, the question was taken seriously.[45]

A far more common form of diversion was to turn the meeting over to "songs and recitations" of Irish rebellions or at least rebelliousness. Accompanied by ample supplies of beer, whiskey, and cigars, this re-creation of Irish shebeen society was an essential part of an immigrant worker's world. Most of the members of both organizations spent forty-eight to sixty hours a week in underground mines. Some of them went from the mines to a boardinghouse. To be able one night a week to listen, in the company of fifty to one hundred other Irishmen, to the poems and songs of the native place must have provided enormous pleasure. It was not uncommon for the clubs to vote $25.00 to $50.00 for a week's refreshments, usually three cases of beer, four boxes of cigars, and a gallon of whiskey. Members were then treated to renditions of "Sean O'Farrell," "Far from the Shores of Inishfall," "Paddies Erinmore," "There Never Was a Coward Where the Shamrocks Grow," "I Left Mother and Ireland Behind because They Were Poor," or simply unidentified songs of "the girls they left behind." When an RELA member proposed in 1884 a "rousing vote of thanks . . . to the gentlemen who furnished the refreshments for the evening," he spoke for thousands of other Irishmen over the next forty years.[46]

In addition to these near-weekly entertainments, both of the Irish societies celebrated certain national holidays. The RELA honored Emmet's and Tone's birthdays, the anniversary of the Manchester Martyrs, and the anniversary of the Battle of Fontenoy. These were "members only" affairs, accompanied by no publicity and held in the privacy of Hibernia Hall. Though hardly abstemious in tone or agenda, these yearly commemorations did have ceremonial, even ritualistic, significance. Emmet was an Irish hero; he belonged to them and they shared him with no one else. To celebrate his birthday was to reaffirm the essential separateness of the Irish world. It was an act of withdrawal, a chance to re-create in the company of men of like origin the rituals of that world.[47]

The Hibernians were less recondite. Their initiation ceremonies did involve certain ritualistic features, including a test of the new member's tolerance of pain, but generally they were more fraternal than revolutionary. They reserved their major day of celebration for St. Patrick's Day, when they sponsored a huge parade and "fancy dress" ball. But, though a public and outwardly conciliatory gesture of Irish involvement in the larger community, the parade also represented an Irish show of power, a display to the "other side" of the resourcefulness of one's own. It was, said one Hibernian, the "time honored way of showing unity and strength." The imposition of a $10.00 fine for unexcused absences from the parade indicated that the membership agreed and was determined to see that both unity and strength were fully on view.[48]

A less pugnacious but no less assertive expression of the Irish presence was the annual New Year's Ball sponsored by the RELA. The first of these galas was held in 1884, and for at least the next sixty years the Emmets hosted one of Butte's largest parties. Everyone was invited and the cable cars ran all night bringing the thousands who filled Hibernia Hall and other facilities rented for the occasion. There were rival celebrations—"all the society crowd," said one RELA member, went to the "swank" Silver Bow Club—but none to compare with the "Robert Emmet Literary Association's Gala Ball." In towns less Irish than Butte, such ethnically mixed affairs "performed a useful assimilative function, bringing newcomers into the community's social life." This was not the case here. Indeed, in many respects the RELA ball was a brazen display of Irish influence. The ball was not held on an Irish holiday and it was sponsored by a group of unabashed revolutionary conspirators.[49]

The other major event of the Irish social season was the annual summer picnic sponsored by the Associated Irish Societies of Silver Bow County. These included the Gaelic League, the Ladies' Auxiliary of the AOH, the three divisions of the AOH, the RELA, and the Irish Volunteers. Held in the mountains outside of Butte, the picnic was a fund-raiser for the cause of a free Ireland as well as a social event. It appears to have succeeded at both. Gross receipts as early as 1889 were over $4,000; by 1905 they were over $6,000. Tickets cost $.50 for individuals, $1.50 for entire families, meaning an attendance of well over 10,000 people. Expenses in 1890 included a $100.00 "prize for drilling," a $25.00 prize for "tug of war," and $20.00 for "repairs and beer glasses." There were athletic contests ranging from the Gaelic Football League championship to knife throwing. In 1902 there were four separate bars, a full lunch counter, and a dance hall. Finley Peter Dunne's Mr. Dooley cannot have had Butte in mind when he commented "Be hivens, if Ireland cud be freed be a picnic, it'd not on'y be free to-day, but an impire, begorra," but Butte's extravaganza was a case in point. Clearly, it was no ordinary summer outing.[50]

Money from the picnic and other fund-raising events went to a variety of purposes, including Irish revolutionary activity. But the two Irish societies were involved in more than financing rebellions. Their charity extended to churches, schools, and orphanages. They sent money to Galveston for flood relief and to Kansas for drought aid. The $500.00 sent by Butte's Hibernians to San Francisco earthquake victims was the fourth-largest contribution of any *state* AOH in the nation; and to it must be added the $100.00 raised by the RELA. Individuals also benefited. The Hibernians endowed a $5,000 scholarship to train for the priesthood an "Irish boy from a family who could not afford to educate him," financing it, in part, through the sale of "Douglas Hyde cigars." In the process, of course, they also insured a steady supply of parish priests drawn from the local Irish community. AOH members played Santa Claus "to the poor Irish children," paid members' debts, loaned them money, and put up their bail. When "a feeble, old respectable looking lady, giving her name as Mrs. Dougherty" asked for a railroad ticket to Deadwood, South Dakota, the AOH provided it. John McNamara, the blind violinist, was their music man; John Leary delivered the coal to Hibernia Hall; Dennis Holland was the hall's janitor; Mike Sullivan did the electrical work; John Sullivan graded the cellar and cleaned the chimney; Maurice English, attorney-at-law, was on retainer; Michael Conroy sold them insurance; Kiley and O'Leary laid the cement sidewalk. Obviously, both groups took seriously the Clan-na-Gael oath to give preference to Irishmen and fellow Clansmen in "matters of business."[51]

They may also have given them preference in matters of politics. At the very least, membership in either the AOH or the RELA gave ambitious Irishmen an effective forum as well as a ready-made and assertive constituency. The APA charged that the AOH and the RELA were quasi machines, inseparable from politics. F. Augustus Heinze, the flamboyant and determined rival of the Standard Oil-controlled Amalgamated Copper Company (the old Anaconda Company), was more specific, charging that Dan Hennessy "contrived to place himself at the head of the order of the AOH in Montana" because he "was needed [by the Amalgamated] to fool and wheedle the Irish voters." Heinze was persuaded that Hennessy could not "fool men of Irish blood and Irish brains." That he tried, however, made him a "scandal to the Church of Christ and [a] traitor to [his] race." The three divisions of the AOH reacted strongly to the charge and wrote up a denial, which Heinze agreed to publish in his paper.[52]

Doubts, though not necessarily about Hennessy, must have lingered. A member of Division 3, for example, in response to another charge that leadership in the Hibernians was a shortcut to political office, answered that the Irish were too "manly and independent . . . to use the AOH to further their interests." But even some Hibernians were unconvinced. A member of Division 1 argued that many officers "did not want the offices for the good of the order, but used the organization to elevate themselves in a business or political way." Walter Breen made the same charge about John J. O'Meara, adding that elevation in O'Meara's case meant the "accumulation of enough American coin to enable [him] to go back [to Ireland] and become an MP . . . or landlord." Whether the charges were true or not, it was obvious that associational, business, and political ties interlocked. There was nothing sinister in this. The associations appealed to the more stable elements of Butte's Irish community. Leadership in the associations went naturally to those who best represented that stability. Political and business leadership was reserved for that same element. This was not, however, an arrangement that favored political or social insurgency. Church, party, and fraternity, the alliance of priest, politician, and patriot, represented an essentially conservative coalition.[53]

A closer look at the occupations and social class of the officers of the Irish societies offers compelling evidence that it was, in fact, the middle class—merchants, some tradesmen, and professionals—that filled these positions. Whether the officers actually led, whether they gave the clubs their direction, is doubtful. They had the time and energy to serve and, obviously, the respect of the predominantly working-class membership. It was a respect easily and quickly lost, however, if they attempted to take the associations in directions contrary to those favored by that membership. Between 1885 and 1915, 272 names appear in the Butte city directories as officers of state, county, or local Hibernian organizations. Some names, of course, appear repeatedly as men were reelected. Indeed, only 107 men accounted for the total, but miners seem to have been returned to office as routinely as merchants, and there is, then, no inherent bias in the sample. Of the 272 only seventy-one were miners, and eight of those later became officers in the Butte Miners' Union; there were thirty-eight clerks, sixty-three merchants, and fifty-two professionals and local political officials. As would be expected, the percentage of miners was far higher in the earlier years, before the Irish community began to divide. Between 1885 and 1898, for example, twenty-seven of sixty-two officers were miners, another ten were employed with mining companies. As the process of social differentiation began, however, the AOH obviously turned to those who had moved out of the working class.[54]

The social status of the leadership of the RELA is somewhat more difficult to determine because of the secrecy of the organization and the use of numbers instead of names in the Minute Books. But name and number lists for certain years do exist, and there is clear evidence that the working-class members of the revolutionary RELA were as likely as those of the considerably less militant AOH to turn to shop-keepers and professionals for leadership. The names of 168 officers for twenty-three separate years between 1885 and 1914 are known. Of that total only thirty-four of those officers were miners; fifty-one were merchants, thirty-five of those, saloonkeepers. There was an even smaller core of officers than was the case with the AOH. Only sixty-seven men held those 168 offices and only fourteen of that number were miners. Nor, unlike the AOH, were miners more likely to hold office in the early years of the organization. Indeed, between 1885 and 1892, of fifty-threeoffices, saloonkeepers held twenty-three. This says nothing about working-class Irish drinking habits; it says volumes about the RELA. The saloon was the place where politics were discussed and conspiracies hatched. In that sense, it was an extension of the Clan's meeting room, and it was fitting that both the formal and the informal meetings be presided over by the same men.[55]

V

Fraternal goodwill and conspiratorial politics were not the extent of AOH and RELA responsibilities. They also took seriously their role as defenders of outraged Irish honor—and the Irish did have their de-tractors. There are scattered early references to anti-Irish prejudice, including a speech to the RELA in 1888 warning of a possible revival of "Know Nothingism," and a circular (burned after its reading) issued in 1890 by the national Clan-na-Gael with suggestions on how to "keep down the nativist element by electing men . . . favorable to us." The Minute Books of the AOH for 1891 record a committee of eight sent to "ascertain what was in the rumored threats on the lives of our priests," but there is no further record.[56]

A more formidable threat appeared two years later. The APA had formed in Butte by 1893. A number of factors explain its appearance: the election of an Irish mayor, the economic panic and attendant ethnic rivalry for jobs, the formation in Butte of the Western Federation of Miners, and the Irish nationalist movement, which by then had mo-bilized a determined resistance among the Orangemen of the North of Ireland. The election of Ed Dugan has already been discussed; the other three factors will be. At issue for the moment is the nature and tone of the APA assaults on the Irish Catholics of Butte and the associational Irishmen's response.

With an estimated membership of two thousand in 1894, including an undisclosed number of blacks in the "Colored Council," the APA was a powerful rival of the Irish and of their twin standard-bearers, the RELA and the AOH. There was little subtlety in its use of that power. In 1893 the APA attempted to take over the financially troubled St. Patrick's parochial school. A year later, on the Fourth of July, two saloons displayed APA banners, sparking a daylong riot which took two lives. The association's newspaper, the *Examiner*, openly mocked "the AOH, Clan-na-Gael, etc.," as saloon patriots; "only give them whiskey enough," said the *Examiner*, "and they will soon kill each other for the fun of it." In a section called "A Little Catechism," a writer asked why Catholics fasted during Lent, answering "that they might send the money which they would pay for food to the dago pope in Rome." A "nunnery" was a "house, or prison, of prostitution for benefit of priests." Dublin Gulch was a "concentration of shellelaghies and bad whiskey." The AOH was identified as "unpatriotic and unAmerican" while the Clan-na-Gael's "soldiers" were rumored to have demanded that a "portable distillery" be attached to each company.[57]

There was, of course, nothing strikingly original in these attacks, and the Irish societies seem to have limited their response to boycotting "sworn enemies" and forming a council of the anti-APA Young Men's Institute. The charge that Irish workers were inferior to Chinese, however, and that the United States erred in admitting the one and barring the other produced "howls from Butte's puppy papist press." Little deterred by howls, the *Examiner* insisted that "the heathen Chinee is in every way a better man than the God eating Mick and Biddy herself is well aware of the fact," as evidenced by the number of Irish women who "took up housekeeping" with Chinese.[58]

The soft-core pornography of the APA was not the only negative reference to the Irish character. The stage Irishman, that distorted portrait of Pat and Mike, created as much tension in Butte as in any other American city with a significant Irish population. The RELA and the AOH seemed particularly sensitive to these ethnic "slurs and insults." There were times when their "war" against "disrespectful caricaturing" revealed more of Irish defensiveness than of non-Irish bigotry or insensitivity. The intense racialism of the late nineteenth century was reflected in the Irish Celtic revival and, whatever the ultimate benefits of this more affirmative declaration of Irishness, it also produced easily wounded feelings. In Ireland this prickliness produced, in the words of George Bernard Shaw, the Clan-na-Gael's "brilliant idea that to satirize the follies of humanity is to insult the Irish nation." The idea made its way to the United States. The national AOH issued a violent denunciation of the works of John Millington Synge, William Butler Yeats, and Lady Gregory, referring to Synge's *Playboy of the Western World* as "the lowest type of the stage Irishman."[59]

Butte's AOH and RELA followed the lead of their national organizations. Both societies sent committees to protest everything from newspaper stories and pictures in shop windows to dramatic presentations, including one, "Finnigan's Fortune," sponsored by Father Jeremiah Callaghan's Sacred Heart parish. The AOH also formed a Committee on the Abuse of Irish Surnames to insure that Irish names not be subject to "abuse and ridicule." (Perhaps the Hibernians had in mind the Afghan rug peddler, Mohammed Akara, who changed his name to M. Murphy "for business reasons.") Whatever the explanation for its founding, the committee was only part of the generally successful AOH effort to "squelch the stage Irishman, that vile and unreal impersonation, that despicable and obnoxious creature." Unflattering reference to Dublin Gulch and Corktown was characterized by the *Butte Independent*, the city's Irish newspaper, as the work of "racial and religious bigots, . . . the decomposing brains of the Mary McLain [sic] types," a reference to the novelist Mary MacLane, whose descriptions of Butte's Irish were not uniformly favorable.[60]

But for every instance of Irish irritability there were dozens of cases where their grievances were real. The "Dreamland Burlesque," playing at the Grand Opera House, probably was a "scurrilous insult to [the Irish] people," and "Casey and LeClaire" may in fact have been "filth." Both shows were closed, the first by a visit from a joint committee of the AOH and the RELA, the second by the use of a well-tested Irish method of protest, the boycott. Both tactics were also used against a Butte newspaper that carried a story suggesting that Irish girls were often substituted for mules during spring plowing.[61]

There were a few discernible patterns to this Irish resistance to "insults . . . against our race." First, it began, at least the organized resistance to the stage Irishman, after 1900, simultaneously with a growing Gaelic self-consciousness in Ireland. That Gaelic revival required that the Irish be taken seriously, by themselves as well as their detractors, and the necessary first step in that cultural self-awareness was the elimination of mocking stereotypes. Second, it was led by Irish associations, and, as noted, the hostility of their stable and established members to the clownish Irishman may have mirrored a subtler hostility to that "clown's" actual counterpart, the newly arrived West Irish peasant. The stage Irish buffoon diminished the status of the settled Butte Irishman, but no more so than did the pardonable behavior of his less-assimilated countryman.[62]

Third, the Butte Irish saved some of their harshest strictures for those who chose as their target the Irish rebel, what Michael Davitt called that "grotesque harlequinade of saloon 'conspirator.' " This applied to labor as well as Irish nationalist "conspiracy." Specifically, critics leagued the Molly Maguires with the Fenians, and the Irish of Butte responded with considerable heat to slighting references to either. In 1912, for example, Division 3 of the AOH protested that books in the library, purporting to explain the Molly Maguires were, in fact, "printed by the Pinkerton [Detective] Agency." The books were a "slander," a "defamation" of the AOH, the Mollies, and the Irish in general. John Ferns led the protest, explaining that prejudice against the Irish had driven the Molly Maguires to "such desperate perpetrations."[63]

In combating the stage Irishman or the excesses of the APA, the Irish of Butte were, in an indirect and unconscious way, separating themselves from Ireland, or at least from Irish subordination to England. They understood—were made to understand—that they were the descendants of "slaves," that "500 years of serfdom . . . taint [their] veins." In 1880, Michael Davitt had warned that the Irish in America would never be regarded with the respect due them until the "stain of degradation" was removed from the place of their birth. Forty years later, the Irish Race Convention meeting in Philadelphia heard from a local county board that "everyone of the Irish race, whether they realize it or not, are affected by the fame or shame of Ireland, all men being affected by the position of their land of origin." Certainly the Irish of Butte realized it. In 1895 the APA referred to the Irish flag as "an anomaly, . . . the emblem of a dependency which has never been a nation." A year later it went further, denying that Ireland had any right to a flag, even an anomalous one, since "there is no Ireland."[64]

One of the most revealing, because most unconscious, expressions of the acute Irish sensitivity on this point came from Dan Sullivan in 1911. An experienced hard-rock miner and a former (and radical) officer of the Butte Miners' Union, Sullivan was testifying before a state committee formed to study and report on the hazards connected with working in Butte's mines. A committee member commented on the fact that Cuban workers were forced by law to use public health facilities and, thinking perhaps to flatter Sullivan, noted that "I take it that the civilized conditions existing among the miners in Butte is a little better than what they had down there." Sullivan's answer brushed aside the point intended: "I don't know anything about that," he said, "but I know the Cubans are free; that they got their freedom." He did not need to add that that was more than Ireland had. There was no reproach in Sullivan's reply. Ireland's independence would come; indeed as a member of the RELA and the Irish Volunteers, he doubtless believed he was hastening the day of liberation. But his answer also put some needed distance between him and Ireland. He would close with Ireland when Ireland was free.[65]

VI

Butte's nationalist associations had obviously to fight a two-front war against the enemies of the Irish. In different ways England was the more distant enemy, though it remained the ultimately responsible one. The immediate targets of the RELA and the AOH were those in the United States who taunted them with reminders that the consequences of what the Irish called English perfidy included the Irish-American's own debasement. When to this is added the intractable hostility of those who considered the Catholic Church a menace to America's free institutions, Irish-American sensitivity and pugnacity are more easily understood.

In Butte, the AOH's St. Patrick's Day parade, the RELA's New Year's Ball, the allied assaults on the stage Irishman, all represented parts of the Irish response. All were forceful displays of the Irish presence. But the most permanent and lasting monument to that presence was the AOH/RELA-sponsored memorial statue of Thomas Francis Meagher. Meagher was the perfect symbol—an active rebel in the Rising of 1848, American Civil War hero, territorial governor of Montana, a Catholic, and a Democrat, "Meagher of the Sword" confounded the charges of Butte's nativists.[66]

Butte's Irish first proposed the idea for a monument to Meagher in 1894. Initially they wanted his statue in Fort Benton, near where Meagher had died, but in 1896, not long after the bitterly contested battle over the permanent site of the state capital, they decided to put the monument on the capitol grounds in Helena. William Andrews Clark had supported Helena in the capital fight; Marcus Daly and most of Butte, including, it would appear, most of its Irish, had favored Anaconda. The decision to put the monument on the front lawn of the new capitol building cannot have been unrelated. Daly, for example, took an active role in the Meagher Memorial Association; the *Montana Catholic* even identified him, probably incorrectly, as its president. But he did serve as an officer and, more significantly, he allowed the association to "go through [his] mines and collect . . . for the monumental fund."[67]

More convincing evidence that the statue was intended as an Irish answer to its critics comes from the unpublished proceedings of the Monument Association and from the Minute Books of the RELA. In 1898 the association decided it would need $20,000 for a proper tribute and that "no subscription" would be refused, "no matter what or whence the source, with one exception." The exception was Wilbur Fiske Sanders, a vocal Helena supporter in the capital fight and one of the state's few opponents of free silver and Chinese exclusion. Sanders's first indiscretion offended their Irishness, his second and third threatened their jobs; and the Memorial Association moved that "if subscription be received from [him] it [was to] be returned . . . through the public press." Later, in 1903, RELA members learned that the Memorial Association was going to put the monument on the capitol grounds "where the APA must look in his face and salute his glorious memory for all ages." (Had Meagher not been mounted, the association would doubtless have selected another part of his anatomy for the APA to look at and salute.) In 1905 the Emmets heard that "the enemies of the Irish race . . . threatened to blow up" the statue, and in 1906 that "bigots" were criticizing Meagher and demanding that his "statue be removed from the capitol grounds."[68]

The "bigots," however, were not the only ones to threaten this memorial to an Irish-American leader. In building it, the two associations were behaving in typically segregant fashion, commemorating one of their own and defying a hostile "dominant culture." But the RELA in particular was supposed to have a more heroic purpose. In 1897 National Clan-na-Gael headquarters reminded it of that when it instructed the RELA to disassociate itself from the Memorial Association and to devote its time, energies, and money to the cause of Ireland. The Emmets "explained the situation and asked to be exempt from that order." They then behaved as if they had been exempted.[69]

The issue surfaced again nine years later, when the Memorial Fund ran out of money and the RELA membership voted to donate $300.00 from its Revolutionary Fund and loan $300.00 more from its Contingency Fund to pay the final bill on the $20,000 statue. The association's president, Timothy J. McCarthy, a grocery-store clerk and later a prominent Butte merchant, sided with headquarters, resigning his office when he could not convince the members that the donation and the loan were clear violations of the RELA's revolutionary mandate. National headquarters applauded McCarthy's loyalty and insisted that the "'R'

Fund be reimbursed and soon." The Clan was born to free Ireland, not to defy the APA and certainly not to prop up fragile Irish-American egos. The RELA responded by accepting McCarthy's resignation and replacing him with J. J. Lynch. The communications from headquarters were "read and filed" and ignored. Meagher's statue was important to Butte Irishmen; it was real and a source of immediate pride. The revolution was nothing if not abstract and distant.[70]

There would be other times when the different functions of the Irish associations conflicted with one another, or at least became confused—when William Gallagher's "cloak" became more important than the real "purposes" which it covered. There was criticism in 1899, for example, that RELA meeting attendance was high only "when some entertainment was planned." Political action in defense of "The Cause" was not enough. The Hibernians had similar problems. In 1908, Division 3 debated whether it should support a Buy-American campaign or a Buy-Irish, opting finally for the Buy-American. "This is where we make our living," explained one Hibernian, "and times here are tough." AOH Minute Books contain a number of references similar to that from 1911 when the common practice of reading "a chapter in Irish history was dispensed with," the members, it seems, "were eager to go into social session." It was never easy to take care of the Irish and Ireland at the same time. But one of the best, or at least one of the most symbolic, examples of the revolutionary giving way to the segregant occurred in 1907, when the St. Lawrence O'Toole Parish Dramatic Club asked for and got the loan of four RELA rifles for use in the Christmas play.[71]

Clearly, the Irish associations made it simpler to be and remain Irish in a non-Irish world. Even in Butte, where being Irish was not particularly burdensome, the AOH and the RELA played this ameliorative role. As such, their greatest appeal was to the first generation, who found in them a companionship that softened some of the harsher aspects of their relocation. Through these organizations, Irish immigrants met, often for the first time in their lives, Irishmen from other counties. Old-world clan and county associations, however important they may have been in Ireland, meant little in a new world heedless of both, a world where all were simply and often pejoratively "Irish," regardless of background.

It is of related significance that memberships seemed to increase in direct response to increased immigration, or increased prosperity, or—and the two were obviously associated—both. These were clubs dominated by immigrant Irish miners; when immigration was high and the mines running at full employment, membership in both rose. Events in Ireland bearing on Irish nationalist ambitions were a far less important influence, particularly for the AOH. Whatever their stated objectives, the RELA and the Hibernians had a greater appeal to homesick than to rebellious Irishmen; they met the needs of an immigrant not a revolutionary community.

Each of these organizations was a visible expression of the strength and stability of the Irish community. They served to assimilate the immigrant into Butte's Irish world first, and only when that community was well established did they begin to bring the Irish into contact with the larger world around them. Little urgency seems to have been attached to this final assimilation. Irish organizations did not negotiate with the dominant culture so much as they negotiated for it. And when the Irish finally began to integrate into the larger community, they did so from a position of strength and on terms of their own choosing.

John J. O'Meara, the wealthy Butte brewery owner whom Walter Breen accused of having parliamentary (rather than senatorial) ambitions, put the matter as clearly as it can be put when he suggested in 1908 that it was time "to mingle our entertainments with Americans and thereby show our liberality." One of his listeners disagreed, arguing that devotion to Ireland was a necessary step in developing loyalty to America. It was not just the issues, however, but the unselfconsciousness with which they were presented that makes the exchange so instructive. Only in Butte, America, was the Irish community certain enough of its place to afford to display its "liberality."[72]

NOTES

1. Dennis Clark, *Irish in Philadelphia*, pp. 94–95, 107; du Maurier, *Hungry Hill*, p. 110; Cantor, "Introduction," p. 10.

2. The Irish Catholic Church functioned much as the black churches of the American South did, both during and after slavery, as a source of ethnic and class identity. For the role of the black churches see Genovese, *Roll, Jordan, Roll*, pp. 209–13, 232–55, 280–84; Gutman, *Black Family*, pp. 70–75; Rabinowitz, *Race Relations*, pp. 206–9, 222–25.

3. Polk, *City Directory*, 1889, pp. 39–41; "Butte Parishes, 6th Diocesan Synod, July 17, 1901," in Brondel Papers; Polk, *City Directory*, 1902, pp. 82–84. Statewide in 1892 there were an estimated 27,909 Catholics and 6,209 Protestants. Montana, Board of Managers, *Montana . . . Exhibit at the World's Fair*, p. 64. In 1899 the *Montana Catholic* (Butte) claimed there were 40,000 Catholics in the state, 16,000 of those in Butte (Apr. 22, 1899).

4. Brondel to the *Helena Independent*, Sept. 6, 1890; pastoral letter, Dec. 4, 1890, both in Brondel Papers. See also Prodgers, "Callaghan."

5. Brondel to the *Helena Independent*, Sept. 6, 1890. The Irish were actively training priests for American service. Schrier, *Ireland*, p. 63. See also O'Neill, "Development of an American Priesthood."

6. Here, too, the Butte experience was nearer that of the Irish in San Francisco than in eastern cities. See Burchell, *San Francisco Irish*, pp. 88–92. Ryan was particularly generous. See Bishop John Carroll to Father J. M. Venus, Nov. 22, 1920, St. Patrick's Parish File; Father Francis X. Batens to Carroll, Jan. 29, 1921, St. Lawrence O'Toole's File; Carroll, "Remarks at Dedication of Butte Central High School," Sept. 7, 1924, Carroll Papers. For other examples of early Irish generosity see Franchi, "History of Catholic Schools of Butte"; Father Anthony de Siere, "History of St. Patrick's," St. Patrick's File; "History of St. Mary's," St. Mary's File; John J. McHatton, M. J. Burke, P. J. Brophy, John J. O'Meara, H. A. Galwey to Bishop Brondel, July 19, 1898, Brondel Papers. The *Butte Miner* had a story on the gifts of a bell and organ to St. Patrick's from William Scallon and Miles Finlen, both old Daly friends and associates (Oct. 7, 1901). One local priest complained that the "Protestants got enough of the Daly money." He wanted to make sure that Daly's sister's estate was left to the Catholics. Father Bernard Lee to Bishop John Carroll, Mar. 2, 1909, Carroll Papers. Diocese of Helena Office. See also Flaherty, *Go with Haste*, pp. 70–71.

7. Brondel's dedication remarks were printed in the *Anaconda Standard*, Jan. 17, 1898; Carroll's in his speech "On the Occasion of the Silver Jubilee," copies of both in Carroll Papers. Daly's involvement is mentioned by Father F. X. Batens in the *Anaconda Standard*, Mar. 12, 1922. The Butte and Boston Company donation is in "History of St. Lawrence O'Toole Parish."

8. Hannan, *Father English*, pp. 5, 8, 13. The Father English of the title was the Irish-born James English, the first pastor of St. Mary's. It was Father English who bought the books. See English to Bishop John Carroll, Sept. 21, 1909, St. Mary's Parish File. The "rough kids" came from Powers interview.

9. Hannan, *Father English*, p. 16.

10. "History of St. Mary's" has figures on school attendance.

11. City directories list public school trustees, administrators, and teachers. A check for the years 1889, 1893, 1898, 1905, and 1911 reveals a large Irish representation. For APA and other nativists' hostility to Catholics in public schools see Franchi, "History of Catholic Schools in Butte"; AOH D1, MB, Aug. 29, 1894; AOH D3, MB, Feb. 5, 1910; *Butte Independent*, Feb. 21, 1914, in the *Montana Socialist* (Butte), Mar. 1, 1914. The Irish organizations took an active interest in public school issues, even debating "whether public or parochial schools were better for the country." AOH D1, MB, Aug. 29, 1894; see also AOH D3, MB, Feb. 5, 1910. Funchion, "Irish Chicago," pp. 12–13, has a discussion of Catholic schools and their importance in Chicago.

12. Burchell, *San Francisco Irish*, p. 7, lists the first Irish Catholic mayors of some American cities. James, *Butte's Memory Book*, p. 288–89, lists Butte's mayors. Polk, *City Directory*, 1905, pp. 61–63.

13. Polk, *City Directory*, 1905. Butte and Silver Bow County Democratic party representatives in state government were also predominately Irish. See Waldron and Wilson, *Atlas*, passim. On the importance of politics to the Irish see

Dennis Clark, *Irish in Philadelphia*, pp. 117–20; Burchell, *San Francisco Irish*, p. 154; Green, "Irish Chicago," pp. 218–20.

14. *Butte Mining Journal*, May 27, 1891; *Butte Bystander*, Oct. 24, 1894, Nov. 17, 1894; *Examiner* (Butte), Oct. 31, 1896. The *Examiner* was the "voice" of the APA in Butte.

15. *Examiner* (Butte), May 18, June 1, 1895; Mar. 19, Sept. 3, 1896. It was reported that Marcus Daly let his mines out early so the Irish miners could vote for Harrington. WPA, *Copper Camp*, p. 47.

16. This was not an attitude unique to Butte's Irish. See Wiebe, *Search for Order*, pp. 27–37; Kleppner, *Cross of Culture*, pp. 36–69.

17. For discussions of this feud, see Malone, *Battle for Butte*, pp. 80–103, and Toole, "Genesis of the Clark-Daly Feud"; Emmons, "Orange and Green."

18. Malone, *Battle for Butte*, pp. 85–86.

19. Even Thomas Francis Meagher had once been a Republican. Montgomery, *Beyond Equality*, p. 161; Lingenfelter, *Hardrock Miners*, pp. 190–93; Devoy, *Post Bag*, II:252–54; Joseph Lee, *Modernisation*, p. 112; Campbell, *Transformation*, pp. 129–30; Cross, "The Irish," p. 190.

20. Thomas N. Brown, *Irish-American Nationalism*, p. 142; *Butte Intermountain*, Sept. 26, 1888. Malone correctly points out that eastern Montanans were high tariff men; so, however, were the Irish (*Battle for Butte*, p. 86).

21. Malone, *Battle for Butte*, pp. 13, 84–87. Clark was even a vice-president of the Butte Cricket Club. Polk, *City Directory*, 1891–92, For Carter see O'Dea, *AOH*, III:1206. *Missoula Gazette*, in *Butte Intermountain*, Sept. 26, 1888.

22. Clark's second wife was a Catholic who occasionally sang before Irish Catholic audiences. Bishop John Carroll to Father Michael Lavelle, Dec. 19, 1919, Carroll Papers; O'Daly, *Life*, [43]. The barbeque incident is from the *Butte Miner*, Oct. 17, 20, 24, 1888, and the *Butte Intermountain*, Oct. 21, 1888. Clark's Missoula speech was summarized in the *Butte Intermountain*, Oct. 7, 1888. For APA use of the same tactic see *Examiner*, Oct 5, Nov. 2, 1895; *Irish World*, Oct. 12, 1888. When finally selected a senator, Clark voted the "Irish" side of the Barry Monument and the arbitration treaties. AOH D1, MB, Mar. 16, 1904, and RELA, MB, Mar. 9, 1899; Mar. 26, 1908.

23. *Butte Miner*, Nov. 10, Nov. 14, 1888. See WPA, *Copper Camp*, p. 53 for undocumented evidence that miners were assigned more dangerous jobs for voting the "wrong" ticket.

24. The same pattern obtained in Troy, New York. The local Democrats began as the party of Irish labor because the vast majority of Irish were working class. As the Irish world became more differentiated the Democrats became just the party of the Irish. Walkowitz, *Worker City*, pp. 233–36. See also Foner, "Land League," pp. 198–200.

25. See Higham, *Strangers*, pp. 28–29, 56, 60, 79–84, 126–27, 173, 180. Bryan was given a rousing reception in Butte. See Malone, *Battle for Butte*, pp. 107–10; WPA, *Copper Camp*, pp. 5, 78; *Montana Catholic* (Butte), July 1, 1899. Cross, "The Irish," pp. 179–80; Mansergh, *Irish Question*, pp. 103–32; Thomas N. Brown, *Irish-American Nationalism*, pp. 43–44, 133–37, 148–50; Kleppner, *Cross of Culture*, pp. 73–78.

26. The "chestnut raker" quote is from the *Butte Bystander,* Jan. 19, 1895. On the Populist division see the *Butte Bystander,* Apr. 14, July 21, 1894. WPA, *Copper Camp,* p. 46. The point is not that Populists were anti-Catholic, only that some anti-Catholics were Populists. So, for that matter, were some Irish Catholics. In Butte this Irish support seems to have been the result of the Populists' support for free silver; nationally, the Populists attracted few immigrant Catholic workers. See Clinch, *Urban Populism.* Thomas N. Brown, "Political Irish," pp. 141–42. The silver issue seems to have united almost all of Butte. The Montana Free Coinage Association included among its members Marcus Daly and William Andrews Clark. See the *Butte Bystander,* July 22, 1893. For working-class Irish support of silver see the story on the Free Silver Independent Political Club of Centerville in ibid., Feb. 17, 1894. The APA was also on the side of free silver (*Examiner,* Oct. 10, 1895). The Hibernia Hall Board of Trustees even leased space for a grocery store to Absolum Bray, a prominent Butte Populist (Board of Trustees, Reports, 1895–96 and Rent Ledger, 1898). On Bray's career see the *Butte Bystander,* Aug. 27, 1892; Aug. 19, 1893; Mar. 3, 1894. Lewis Duncan, the Butte Specialist, was a two-term mayor of the city between 1911 and 1915. There is evidence that Duncan or his party was anti-Irish, and, as will be seen, few Irish were active in the Socialist party. Duncan, a Unitarian minister, more nearly fits the reformer type described by Gutman in "Protestantism and the American Labor Movement." See also the testimony of Clarence Smith, a member of Duncan's "cabinet," in Industrial Commission, *Mining at Butte,* 1915, pp. 3724–33. The Socialists were aware of the problem of attracting an overwhelmingly Catholic working class to socialism. See the *Montana Socialist* (Butte), Mar. 16, 1913; June 7, July 12, Oct. 10, 1914; Oct. 16, 1915. Montana's Progressives, Democrats like Burton K. Wheeler or Republicans like Joseph Dixon and Jeanette Rankin, were popular among the Irish miners but hardly representative of that world.

27. See Cross, "The Irish," p. 180.

28. Wiebe, *Search for Order,* p. 27. See, for example, the story in the *Montana Socialist* (Butte), Mar. 16, 1913, accusing Church leaders of "violent and abusive propaganda against socialism."

29. For the AOH see the *Montana Catholic* (Butte), June 10, 1899. The AOH D1 Minute Books do not begin until 1884. RELA (originally the Emmet Associates), MB, Oct. 25, 1881. For AOH divisions see D1, MB, Oct. 21, 1885; May 15, July 11, 1888; Aug. 11, 1897; D3, MB, June 30, 1901; AOH, Co. Board to Officers and Members, Nov. 22, 1911, Correspondence. Division 1 was founded in 1881 and remained active for the duration of this study. Division 2 was founded in 1889 and was merged with Division 1 in 1911. Division 3 was founded in 1901 and was active for the duration of this study. There are no Minute Books extant for Division 2.

30. A convenient, accurate short history of the Clan-na-Gael is in Funchion, *Organizations,* pp. 74–93. See also Devoy, *Post Bag,* I:5ff; Thomas N. Brown, *Irish-American Nationalism,* pp. 65–67, 72–73, 120–23, 155, 156, 175; Joseph Lee, *Modernisation,* p. 58; Donnelly, *Land and People,* pp. 327–30. Pollard, *Societies of Ireland,* is virulently and sometimes comically anti-Irish, but it does

reprint some primary material difficult to obtain elsewhere. On the Clan see pp. 3, 48, 99, 110. The RELA, on occasion, did ask prospective members if they believed in a "Supreme Being" (RELA, MB, June 2, 1892).

31. Funchion, *Organizations*, pp. 50–61; Davitt, *Fall of Feudalism*, pp. 42–43; O'Dea, *AOH*, II and III. See also AOH in America, Directors, "Official Statement to Officers and Members," Apr. 3, 1911 (St. Paul, 1911), Correspondence.

32. On the feud see Funchion, *Organizations*, pp. 55–56. The 1886 quote is from a remark of Luke Dillon in Devoy, *Post Bag*, II:276. See also *ibid.*, I:501–2. "Laws, Rules, and Regulations for the Government of the Irish Republican Brotherhood in 1884," in Pollard, *Societies of Ireland*, p. 279. For the AOH see O'Dea, *AOH*, III:1081; AOH, *Constitution, 1886*. See also "Application," form 1, IrC. Bishop Brondel of the Helena Diocese did condemn "secret societies" (Brondel to John Cardinal Simeoni, Sacred Congregation for the Propogation of the Faith, Jan. 8, 1884, Brondel Papers).

33. RELA, MB, Nov. 24, 1882; Feb. 16, 1883; Mar. 13, 1884; Feb. 23, 1893; Mar. 14, 1895; Oct. 27, 1898. For the decision to build and own Hibernia Hall jointly see AOH D1, MB, Sept. 5 and 19, 1888; May 5, 1889; RELA, MB, May 16, 1889. A board of trustees, with members from both groups, managed the hall. There was a single checkbook for bill paying. Hibernia Hall, Board of Trustees, MB, 1894–1925; "Rent Ledger, 1894–1911." See also Phil Murphy, Recording Secretary, AOH D1 to RELA, Officers and Members, Sept. 29, 1907, Correspondence. Notice of the 1900 reconciliation was included in RELA, MB, Sept. 13, 1900. AOH members were asked to accept the fact of reconciliation in 1902. O'Dea, *AOH*, III:1242.

34. RELA members were constantly being reminded that they must keep the workings of the club secret. See for example, MB, Sept. 17, 1882; Mar. 30, 1883; May 7, 1896; Nov. 10, 1898; Dec. 12, 1901; Sept. 3, 1903. The "black balling" of Father Callaghan is noted in RELA, "Term Report," Apr. 30, 1900. No reasons for denying him membership were ever given but in Callaghan's case they cannot have included personal unpopularity. He was one of the best-liked men in Butte. See Prodgers, "Callaghan"; WPA, *Copper Camp*, p. 190. On destroying documents see Pollard, *Societies of Ireland*, pp. 70–71, 73. For a specific example see RELA, MB, Jan. 3, 1895. For examples of RELA secrecy see MB, Sept. 10, 1882; Jan. 3, 1895; Mar. 16, 1899. For expulsions, see MB, Feb. 2, 1883, when ten men were thrown out; Apr. 4, 1889; Dec. 12, 1901. For rejections, see MB, Dec. 29, 1882; May 19, 1887; Dec. 1, 1898; July 11, 1907. There were times when the Irish-Americans wearied of the "mask and gong" rituals and the "unnecessary oaths." See Devoy, *Post Bag*, I:53; II:296. RELA, MB, Feb. 7, 1895, has an entry indicating that from that date forward the chief officer of the RELA would be known as "the president" rather than S.G. or "Senior Guardian." Copies of passwords, hailing signs, etc. are in the IrC. See also, Thomas N. Brown, *Irish-American Nationalism*, p. 175.

35. On using social occasions to raise money for revolutionary purposes see Emmet Associates (RELA), MB, July 1, 1882; Executive Body, V.C. to Camps, May 5, 1883 in Pollard, *Societies of Ireland*, p. 92. V.C. was cipher for United

Brotherhood, the other name for the Clan-na-Gael. RELA, MB, Sept. 10, 1882; Feb. 14, Sept. 26, 1901.

36. Polk, *City Directory*, 1886. For clerical participation and influence see AOH, *Ritual and Manual*, revised to 1901; AOH D1, MB, Jan. 17, 1900; Oct. 30, 1901; Sept. 8, Dec. 1, 1902; Jan. 24, Feb. 21, 1906; AOH D3, MB, June 30, 1901. For the Butte Ladies' Auxiliary see Mary McLaughlin to RELA, Nov. 17, 1922, Correspondence. *Montana Catholic*, Jan. 20, 1900. On the Juvenile Division see AOH, *Constitution, 1923*. On the Board of Erin/AOH in America split see O'Dea, *AOH*, III: 1055–58, 1067–73. The English critic was Pollard, *Societies of Ireland*, pp. 3, 48, 113, 115. Butte's AOH affiliation with the Board of Erin is mentioned in AOH D1, MB, Nov. 21, 1888; July 26, 1905. That the names of officers were sent to the *Irish World* is mentioned in AOH D1, MB, Feb. 2, 1888. The AOH incorporated in 1888 (D1, MB, Oct. 3, 1888). The RELA considered incorporating in 1891 but postponed becoming a public association until 1921 (RELA, MB, Apr. 16, Oct. 15, 1891; "Articles of Incorporation," Aug. 22, 1921).

37. *Montana Catholic*, June 10, 1899; Owen Morgan, D298, Rostrevor, Co. Down, to "Sir and Brotherss [sic]," Mar. 14, 1907, Correspondence. See also the letter written for Patrick McGuire, a transfer from Scranton, to Butte. M. J. Colman, D16, Lackawanna Co., to Officers and Members, D1, Butte, Feb. 6, 1907, Correspondence. Callaghan's remarks are in AOH D1, MB, Jan. 22, 1901. On the significance generally of Irish and other ethnic groups, see, among many other sources, Funchion, "Irish Chicago," p. 11; Cantor, "Introduction," pp. 9, 15; Dennis Clark, *Irish in Philadelphia*, pp. 110–11.

38. AOH D1, MB, Apr. 20, 1908. Similar sentiments were expressed by J. J. O'Meara in 1903, D1, MB, Apr. 15. See also AOH, Proceedings, where it was reported that the Hibernians in Havre, Montana, had disbanded because "most members were railroad workers and had to move on." AOH, Membership and Dues Ledgers, give occupations as well as names. Walkowitz makes the point that both police and saloon owners usually came from and retained a sympathy with the working class (*Worker City*, p. 110).

39. Daly's and Ryan's memberships are noted in AOH D1, MB, July 7, 1886; Nov. 28, 1900; June 1, 1904. The others' involvement with the Hibernians is found, among other places, in the Membership and Dues Ledgers. On James A. Murray's "millions," see the brief of Burton K. Wheeler in Industrial Commission, *Mining at Butte*, 1911, p. 4089.

40. RELA, Membership and Dues Ledgers. One RELA member made a slighting reference to "illiterates," saying that the organization needed "men with brains." Other members took considerable offense (MB, Aug. 28, 1890). On Lynch's occupational mobility see the obituary in the *Helena Independent Record*, Sept. 28, 1961. Devoy's comment is from *Recollections*, p. 420. The working-class origins of Troy's Fenians are noted in Walkowitz, *Worker City*, p. 93. See also Foner, "Land League," pp. 152–54.

41. Daly's nomination for membership and the favorable vote on that nomination are noted in RELA, MB, July 29, Aug. 5, 1886. There is no evidence that he was initiated. The rules of the order, however, required that a pro-

spective member be sympathetic to the purposes and policies of the Clan; Pollard, *Societies of Ireland,* pp. 307–11. For the others, see RELA, Membership and Dues Ledgers, RELA, MB, Aug. 27, 1882, mentions Brophy as a member. Foner's comment is from "Land League," p. 154. An RELA member visited San Francisco and reported that the Clan-na-Gael camp in that city included "the leading merchants" (MB, Aug. 5, 1886).

42. Consistent with the secret, revolutionary purpose of the organization, the Clan-na-Gael transfer cards were torn in two at the place left; one half was mailed to the camp in the members' new town, the other half was carried by the member. If the halves matched, the new arrival was admitted to the brotherhood. Almost one hundred of these transfer cards, still carefully taped, are in the IrC. The AOH, in addition to transfer cards, also issued traveling cards with information on height, weight, color of hair, etc. Copies in IrC. Both organizations received a significant percentage of their membership by transfer. AOH and RELA, Membership and Dues Ledgers and MB. Both organizations were also active in helping to establish camps and divisions in other towns. See RELA, MB, Aug. 30, 1888; Feb. 9, 1893; Feb. 18, 1897; Apr. 14, 1898; Apr. 2, 1903; Feb. 28, 1907; AOH D1, MB, Mar. 8, 1905; AOH *Proceedings,* 1906; AOH, "Yearly Report of Auditing Committee, 1906," Financial Records. See also the comments in Burchell, *San Francisco Irish,* p. 115. For excellent recent discussions of the issue of floating proletariat, see Stephenson, "Gathering of Strangers," and Thernstrom, "Socialism." See also Wyman, *Hardrock Epic,* pp. 252–53.

43. Dues and fees are noted in RELA, MB, Feb. 2, 1905, and AOH D1, MB, Nov. 21, 1900. Con McGee, a young Irish-born miner, paid his dues in $.25 installments; D. J. Hennessy, Butte's leading merchant, paid for the entire year on the first of every year. RELA, Membership and Dues Ledger, 1899–1903.

44. AOH, *Proceedings,* 1910; RELA, MB, May 4, 1905. In 1897 a traveling member of the Clan-na-Gael told the Helena camp that the RELA was second only to a Chicago camp in membership. The Chicago camp, at that time, had four hundred members. Sunburst Club, MB, Sept. 18, 1897.

45. Debate topics included the following: "Parnell v. the *Times*"; "Gladstone, a Friend of Ireland?"; "Grant or Sheridan?"; "The Irish Race Should Retain Their Prejudices or . . . Should be More Broad Minded and Cultivate More Liberal Feelings?"; "Direct Election of Senators?" (Direct election "won" by a vote of 15 to 12. This is the only recorded vote); "Shall Immigration be Restricted?"; "Free Silver?"; "Was Emmet or Grattan Ireland's Greatest Beneficiary?"; "Which Has Done More: Physical Force or Moral Suasion?"; "That Irishmen in General . . . Favor Expansion of the United States?"; "That Daniel O'Connell Did More Good For the Cause of Ireland Than Charles Stewart Parnell"; "Young Ireland or the Repeal Association" (RELA, MB, Dec. 27, 1888; Jan. 3, 10, 1889; Dec. 10, 1891; June 28, 1892; Feb. 16, Mar. 16, Aug. 3, 10, 17, 1893; Jan. 26, 1899; Oct. 13, 1904; June 21, 1905).

46. "Songs and recitations" were a tradition of Clan-na-Gael and Irish Republican Brotherhood meetings. See Devoy, *Recollections,* p. 286; Davitt, *Fall of Feudalism,* pp. 166–67. Examples from Butte can be found in AOH D1, MB,

Dec. 1, 1897; June 29, 1898 (an ice-cream social hosted by the Ladies' Auxiliary); Nov. 23, 1898; Mar. 28, Aug. 29, 1900; Aug. 21, 1901; Feb. 1, May 24, Oct. 23, 1905; AOH D3, MB, Oct. 24, 1904; Oct. 23, 1905; Oct. 14, 1911; Aug. 2, 1913; Feb. 12, 1916; Kane Holland to Officers and Members, AOH, July 23, 1907, T. J. Moran to Officers and Members, AOH, May 18, 1910, Correspondence; *Butte Independent,* July 9, 1910; RELA, MB, Jan. 5, 1883; Apr. 3, 1884; Dec. 13, 1888; Oct. 20, 1892; Feb. 27, 1896; Mar. 11, 1897; Nov. 23, 1899; Apr. 26, Dec. 12, 1901; June 22, Oct. 12, 26, 1905; Dec. 3, 1908; June 8, Sept. 14, 1911; May 8, 1919; Sept. 19, 1919. The drink and cigar bill for Nov. 23, 1905, was $28.50; on June 19, 1913, it was $31.00 (RELA, MB). Purchases were made from the saloon conveniently located in Hibernia Hall. The "rousing vote of thanks" was offered Mar. 6, 1884 (RELA, MB).

47. The RELA always celebrated the anniversary of the Manchester Martyrs and the birthday of Robert Emmet. Occasionally it commemorated St. Patrick's Day, Wolfe Tone's birthday, Thomas Francis Meagher's birthday, the Battle of Fontenoy, and the Fourth of July (MBs). Joseph Lee notes that the "feast of the [Manchester] martyrs superseded St. Patrick's Day as the national political feastday" (*Modernisation,* p. 58). See also Funchion, "Irish Chicago," p. 20.

48. AOH, *Ritual and Manual, 1901,* pp. 24–27, and *Ritual and Manual of the AOH in America,* pp. 40–43. The assertion that a parade was a "time honored way of showing unity and strength" was made in 1896. J. J. Lynch, Thomas McLaughlin, and Patrick Mitchell to AOH, ca. Feb. 20, 1896, Correspondence. Reference to the fines collected are in AOH D1, MB, Mar. 7, 1900; Feb. 4, 1903. On one occasion, one year after the APA/Irish riot, the AOH held its largest parade on the Fourth of July (*Butte Bystander,* June 25, 1895).

49. The first Gala Ball sponsored by the Emmets was held on Thanksgiving, 1882 (RELA, MB, Oct. 15, 1882). The rival celebration at the Silver Bow Club was noted in WPA, *Copper Camp,* p. 3. See also O'Daly, Life, [48], and *Butte Mining Journal,* Dec. 31, 1890. In 1898 the Catholic Knights planned a New Year's dance but canceled it after pressure from the RELA (AOH D1, MB, Dec. 1, 1898). The significance of these kinds of celebrations is noted in Cantor, "Introduction," pp. 9–10. See also Foner, "Land League," p. 154.

50. Information on the Irish Societies' summer picnic is in AOH D1, MB, Aug. 7, 1889; July 16, 1890; Aug. 4, 1897; Sept. 20, 1899; RELA, MB, Sept. 1, 1889; July 11, 1901; July 17, 1902; Aug. 15, 1907; Apr. 11, 1912; July 29, 1915; O'Daly, Life, [53]; Walkowitz, *Worker City,* p. 43. Mr. Dooley's remarks are from Dunne, "Freedom Picnic," p. 92.

51. For the contribution to Galveston, see RELA, MB, Nov. 8, 1900. For Kansas, see AOH D1, MB, July 29, Aug. 12, 1903. Only two county AOH organizations in the United States gave more to San Francisco earthquake relief than Silver Bow County. See AOH, *Proceedings,* 1906; AOH D3, MB, Apr. 23, 1906. O'Dea noted that Montana's total contribution was the fourth-largest among the states (*AOH,* III:1355–56). There was some grumbling about the "San Francisco assessment," though not necessarily from Butte. See AOH National President to Officers and Members, Jan. 21, 1907, Correspondence. The RELA contribution is noted in RELA, MB, Apr. 26, 1906. The scholarship for

study for the priesthood is discussed in AOH D1, MB, May 31, 1905; June 24, July 1, 1907; Mar. 27, 1912. The significance of insuring a steady supply of local (and Irish) priests is discussed in O'Neill, "Development of an American Priesthood." The custom of playing Santa Claus is in Symons Dry Goods Co. to AOH, Dec. 16, 1924, Correspondence. On the Hyde cigar see AOH D3, MB, Apr. 30, 1906; RELA, MB, July 19, 1906. Instances of AOH charity are too numerous to cite fully. Examples can be found in AOH D1, MB, Feb. 15, 1888; Feb. 6, 13, 20, 1889; Nov. 1, 1893; Mar. 25, 1896; June 9, 1897; Sept. 21, 1898; Mar. 3, 1900; Mar. 9, 1904; AOH, *Proceedings*, 1906. The RELA was less a "service" club and hence less involved in local charitable projects. Revolution, not community service, was its purpose. The "feeble, old . . . lady" was noted in AOH D1, MB, Nov. 3, 1897. The decision to use John McNamara's orchestra is in MB, Apr. 3, 1901. For the use of Irish tradesmen and professionals for the maintenance of Hibernia Hall see Hibernia Hall, Board of Directors, Report for the Year 1909; Hibernia Hall, Trustees, Report for the Year Ending December 31, 1912, IrC. The Clan-na-Gael oath to give preference "in matters of business" is in *Chicago Inter Ocean*, Dec. 16, 1893, sworn correct at Cronin trial, Chicago, reported in the *Examiner* (Butte), Dec. 21, 1895. This close association was occasionally double-edged. Knowing the Irishmen of a given location meant being able to help them; it also meant being able to find them for purposes of collecting debts. See, for example, P. J. Brophy to John Dowling, Dec. 17, 1902, and Brophy to M. F. Noon, Feb. 26, 1909, Brophy Papers.

52. The APA charge is found in the *Examiner*, May 25, 1895. See on this same point Dennis Clark, *Irish in Philadelphia*, p. 82, and Funchion, "Irish Chicago," p. 24. The charges against Hennessy were made in Heinze's newspaper, the *Reveile* (Butte), Sept. 4, 10, 20, and Oct. 8, 1902. The AOH formed a joint committee "to write up a denial" (D1, MB, Oct. 1, 1902). Hennessy was a national officer of the AOH, an officer of the RELA, and a state senator. RELA, MB, Mar. 27, 1884; O'Dea, *AOH*, III:1303; AOH D1, MB, Aug. 3 and 31, 1904; Waldron and Wilson, *Atlas*, pp. 13, 14.

53. The reference to "manly and independent" is in AOH D3, MB, June 29, 1908. Doubt was expressed in AOH, Silver Bow Co. Board, MB, Aug. 24, 1912. The charge that J. J. O'Meara and Hugh O'Daly wanted to go back to Ireland is in AOH D3, MB, Oct. 7, 1907. See also O'Daly, Life. O'Meara was very active in both Hibernian and Clan-na-Gael affairs. See AOH D1, MB, Dec. 21, 1898; O'Meara to Sunburst Club (Helena Clan-na-Gael), in Sunburst Club, MB, Oct. 9, 1899; AOH, *Proceedings*, 1906; O'Dea, *AOH*, III:1328.

54. AOH officers are conveniently listed in Polk, *City Directory*, 1885–1915. By 1919 most of the national officers were wealthy and well placed socially. "Report of John O'Dea, National Secretary, July 17, 1919," copy in IrC.

55. RELA officers' names are taken from Membership and Dues Ledgers, and MBs. Elections were held at the end of every year for the following year. The men elected were identified only by number; the numbers were checked against the number/name lists at the end of the Membership and Dues Ledgers and occupations were taken from Polk, *City Directory*, 1885–1915. See ibid. for the saloon owners as officers. Walkowitz, *Worker City*, pp. 163–64, talks

about the saloons as meeting places. This certainly was one of their important functions in Butte, particularly the Sullivan brothers' establishment located in Hibernia Hall. One of the Sullivans, Patrick J., was the longtime treasurer of both the AOH and the RELA.

56. The importance of external pressures in maintaining internal cohesion is discussed in Funchion, "Irish Chicago," pp. 25–26. Early warnings of anti-Irish and/or anti-Catholic sentiment and activity are in RELA, MB, Mar. 22, Sept. 13, 1888; Apr. 3, 1890; AOH D1, MB, June 24, 1891, IrC.

57. Malone, *Battle for Butte*, p. 66; Bishop John Carroll referred to the APA as the "malodorous offspring of Know Nothingism," in "Address on Americanism, July 4, 1917," Carroll Papers. A meeting of the "Colored Council, Number 19," is mentioned in the *Examiner*, Dec. 21, 1895. The APA's interest in taking over St. Patrick's school is noted in de Siere, "History." For the bloody fourth of July riot of 1894 see the *Butte Bystander*, July 7 and 21, 1894; WPA, *Copper Camp*, pp. 55–56; Malone, *Battle for Butte*, p. 66. The APA comments cited are in the *Examiner*, June 15, Aug. 3, Nov. 23, 1895, and Feb. 20 and 27, 1896.

58. The use of the boycott is mentioned in AOH D1, MB, Apr. 3, 1895; Feb. 19, 1896; May 25, 1904; RELA, MB, Aug. 15, 1895; Apr. 16 and 23, 1903. The Young Men's Institute was mentioned in AOH D1, MB, May 18, 1889. See also the *Examiner*, Dec. 15, 1895. The Young Men's Institute, Ravalli Council #104, was still meeting in 1901. It was listed in O'Reilly, *Butte Blue Book*, p. 38. Like all of Butte's Catholic organizations, it was overwhelmingly Irish; forty-one of fifty-one members bore unmistakably Irish names. This was the only "Blue Book" published for Butte and the Y.M.I. was the only "Irish" society listed. The "puppy papist press" charge was in the *Examiner*, Oct. 31, 1896. Not only were Butte's newspapers aggressively partisan, they also reflected, or were thought to reflect, ethnic loyalties. Marcus Daly's *Anaconda Standard*, for example, was charged by the APA with being "Rome's Montana newspaper" and the "Anaconda Papal Standard" (*Examiner*, Feb. 20, 1896). After Daly's death in 1900, however, the AOH accused the *Standard* of "a slur on [the] nationality" of a prominent Irishman (AOH D1, MB, Feb. 4, 1903). The "God eating Mick" reference is in the *Examiner*, Oct. 31, 1896.

59. See Michael Davitt's comment on the "stage Irishry" in Devoy, *Post Bag*, I:358. AOH, Silver Bow County Board, MB, Apr. 3, 1904; AOH D1, MB, Dec. 20, 1905; AOH D3, MB, Mar. 23, 1908. Lyons, *Culture and Anarchy*, pp. 63–69, contains an excellent short discussion on Irish sensitivity. The Shaw quote is on p. 69. In 1911 the Gaelic League of Philadelphia called *The Playboy of the Western World* "immoral" (Dennis Clark, *Irish in Philadelphia*, pp. 148–49). For the national AOH's condemnation of Synge's play and some of the works of Yeats and Lady Gregory, see O'Dea, *AOH*, III:1407.

60. RELA, MB, Feb. 1, 1906; AOH D3, MB, Mar. 8, 1909. The controversy over "Finnigan's Fortune" is in AOH, Silver Bow County Board, MB, Apr. 3, 1904; AOH D1, MB, Mar. 30 and Apr. 6, 1904. The Hibernians also insisted that an unnamed play by Chauncey Olcott "ridiculed our people" (AOH D3, MB, Oct. 4, 1909). On the Committee on Abuse of Irish Surnames, see AOH,

Proceedings, 1906, and AOH, *Proceedings*, 1910. The story of Mohammed Akar-a's name change is in WPA, *Copper Camp*, pp. 11, 213. The remark that the stage Irishman had been "squelched" is in AOH, *Proceedings*, 1906. *Butte Independent*, Aug. 13, 1910. Mary MacLane was a Butte "writer and authoress for newspapers and magazines," some of whose references to Dublin Gulch and the Irish were unflattering. The description of her occupation is from Bureau of Census, *MS Census*, 1910. For an example of her descriptions of the Irish see her *Story of Mary MacLane*, pp. 112–13.

61. A visitor to Butte from Seattle said he had seen more of the stage Irishman in Butte than anywhere he had ever been (AOH D3, MB, Oct. 1, 1910). The "Dreamland Burlesque" incident is in ibid., Dec. 18, 1905, and RELA, MB, Dec. 21, 1905. "Casey and LeClair" was identified as "filth" in the *Butte Independent*, Sept. 10, 1910. The joint RELA/AOH committee is noted in AOH D1, MB, June 28 and July 5, 1905. The reference to Irish women and mules was in the *Butte Miner*, Dec. 17, 1902. A five-member committee was appointed by the RELA to "call on" the paper's editor (RELA, MB, Dec. 18, 1902). For other instances of AOH hostility to "ridicule and disgrace" see D3, MB, Jan. 7, 1907, Sept. 12, 1914, and AOH, Silver Bow County Board, MB, Oct. 2, 1910.

62. For discussions of how the settled Irish attacks on the stage Irishman reflected a subtle class prejudice, see Kennedy, *The Irish*, p. 23; Miller, *Emigrants*, pp. 510–11, and "Assimilation," pp. 89–91; du Maurier, *Hungry Hill*, p. 246.

63. Davitt, *Fall of Feudalism*, p. 128. On the books dealing with the Molly Maguires and printed by the Pinkerton agency see AOH D3, MB, Jan. 20, 1912. Others in Butte, from an Irish priest to the English and Protestant Sons of St. George to the APA, also associated the AOH and/or the Catholic Church with the Molly Maguires. The priest was Father McDermott. See AOH, D3, MB, Jan. 13 and Feb. 17, 1908. The Sons of St. George blamed a Montana revival of the Mollies for the 1892 murder of the Cornishman William Penrose. See Berthoff, *British Immigrants*, p. 189; Lingenfelter, *Hardrock Miners*, p. 192. The APA asked "to what particular religious sect did the fiendish Molly Maguires . . . belong?" (*Examiner*, Feb. 13, 1896). Other references to alleged AOH ties with the Molly Maguires can be found in AOH D1, MB, Oct. 19, 1904; AOH D3, MB, Jan. 29, 1906.

64. Davitt was quoted in the *Irish World*, Nov. 13, 1880; Philadelphia County Board to Officers and Members of Philadelphia, Apr. 4, 1919, Irish Race Convention. Copy in IrC. The APA reference to the Irish flag as an anomaly is in the *Examiner*, July 20, 1895. See also ibid., Oct. 8, 1896, and Lingenfelter, *Hardrock Miners*, pp. 116, 161.

65. Industrial Commission, *Mining at Butte*, 1911, p. 3928. RELA, Membership and Dues Ledger, 1902–25.

66. On Meagher's life see Athearn, *Meagher*. There was a picture of Meagher's 69th New York Regiment from the Civil War hanging in Hibernia Hall (Hibernia Hall, Board of Trustees, MB, Jan. 18, 1903, IrC).

67. The plans for a monument at Fort Benton are mentioned in the *Butte Bystander*, Dec. 21, 1894. A year and a half later, after the capital fight, the

RELA proposed that it be built in Helena (MB, July 23, 1896). On the capital fight see the *Butte Bystander,* Oct. 24, Nov. 2, 17, 1894; Sept. 17, 1895; the *Examiner,* Aug. 20, Oct. 31, 1896. Waldron and Wilson, *Atlas,* p. 19. Marcus Daly's association with the Meagher Memorial Association is discussed in the *Montana Catholic* (Butte), July 15, 1899. Daly readily agreed to allow money to be collected in his mines. See RELA, MB, Aug. 3 and 10, 1899. Money was also collected from Bishop Brondel and Governor Joseph Toole. "Membership Certificate" for $50.00 gift in Brondel Papers. Governor Toole's $25 contribution was noted in RELA, MB, Oct. 1, 1903. Over $2,000 was collected at the picnic in 1904 (RELA, MB, Sept. 8, 1904). See also P. J. Brophy to John Fogarty, Mar. 21, 1899, Brophy Papers.

68. The reference to Sanders is in RELA and Phil Sheridan, *Proceedings, 1898.* Sanders's politics are from Malone, *Battle for Butte,* pp. 99, 106, 108. Sanders was also identified as the "chief advocate" for the Chinese in boycott cases in 1897. (*Butte Bystander,* Dec. 18, 1897). The reference to the APA's having to look in Meagher's face is from RELA, MB, Oct. 15, 1903. The possibility that the statue might be blown up "by the enemies of the Irish race" was introduced in RELA, MB, July 6, 1905. The "bigots" are mentioned in AOH D1, MB, Feb. 28, 1906. The completed monument cost $20,000. The RELA paid it off in 1906, a year after its dedication, more than a decade after the idea for it was first proposed (RELA, MB, May 12 and July 21, 1904; AOH D3, MB, Sept. 24, 1906).

69. RELA, MB, Oct. 7, 1897.

70. Ibid., Aug. 9, 23, Sept. 27, 1906.

71. Ibid., Nov. 16, 1899; Dec. 5, 1907; AOH D3, MB, May 4, 1908; Oct. 14, 1911.

72. AOH D3, MB, Nov. 30, 1908.

CHAPTER 5

Safe and Steady Work:
The Irish and the Hazards of Butte

I

Butte's Irish world was fully formed by 1900. It was a complex community consisting in almost equal parts of family, parish, ethnic associations, and occupation. Its core was the stable underground miner, the worker who had somehow passed through the transient stage of his trade and had settled in. Butte was where he would make his living. Using five years as a reasonable standard of persistence, there were approximately two thousand of these steady Irishmen by the turn of the century. In most particulars these two thousand miners fit John Bodnar's description of a worker enclave. Given their numbers, Butte's Irish were less defensive and more influential than Bodnar's mostly East European and Italian workers. For the same reason of numbers, plus the ethnic tensions between the Irish and almost everyone else, they found no cause to stretch the enclave beyond the supply of Irish Catholic miners; their enclave had as a result a more obvious ethnic base than those Bodnar discovered and named. But these are relatively minor distinctions. Ethnicity alone was not sufficient for enclave membership in any event; only stability gained one entrance.

The intent to persist was necessary for admission to the Irish miner community, but the ability to persist was fundamental to the community's survival. Steady jobs, in other words, were both source and object of the workers' world. All industrial workers feared being out of work, but the Irish, victims of a social system so disordered as to appear chaotic, feared it more than most. For many of them Ireland was the scene of remembered horrors. Their emigration was evidence of the precariousness of their hold on the place. Life in America was an improvement, but one that the Irish often had to pay for in self-esteem—dearer coin than Ireland had left them with. "No Irish Need Apply" signs closed them out of more than just jobs, and contributed to more than just economic uncertainty. Ireland made them insecure but America made them feel inferior. They took their lessons from that insecurity and inferiority, learning early, as Eugene O'Neill put it, "the value of a dollar and the fear of the poorhouse." They learned, in other words, the importance of steady work.[1]

Stable employment, however, often required workers to adopt exclusionary rules, to close employment to the unskilled, the unorganized, the unsettled, or, if necessary, those not in the ethnic and social community. The English historian, Eric Hobsbawn, argues that the power to exclude, *"never mind how,"* gave a kind of aristocratic status to workers. If the exclusion was based on skill, the result was a "natural aristocracy." If based on any other criterion—race, ethnicity, or union membership, for example—the resulting aristocracy was "contrived." For all their artificiality, however, the contrived aristocracies were no less determined than the natural to cling to the privileges of rank. In the late nineteenth century, technological changes often made craft skills obsolete, but they did not affect the importance of job exclusivity in the interests of stable employment and satisfactory wage levels. The substitution of machines for human skills changed only the criteria for exclusion, not the need to exclude. As a consequence, a growing body of contrived aristocrats was created—men who held their jobs not because they alone could do them but because they alone could get them.[2]

Like Bodnar's enclaves—perhaps like Hobsbawm's labor aristocrats—the Irish miners of Butte understood that only steady work and steady workers could guarantee the stability of the ethnic community. Irishmen worked underground because it was a way, perhaps the only way, to protect the life and values of the Irish enclave. Occasionally, as Bodnar writes, this required "cooperating with those who were more powerful," a requirement that could involve seeking job preference if not job exclusivity based on ethnicity. But however gotten, work sustained the enclave, and the Irish miners' consciousness of themselves as workers was only part of a larger awareness of themselves as participants in that enclave. In this and in their related refusal either to ape the middle class or to display the revolutionary ardor expected of a proletariat, the Butte Irish miners also behaved much as Hobsbawm's aristocrats and Bodnar's worker enclaves did.[3]

They encountered various obstacles, some that were almost unique to their trade. One was that hard-rock mining was a most unstable enterprise; few workers can have entered it because it promised steady employment. Nor was there any reason, in its early years at least, to assume that Butte's history would be any different—or any longer—than that of other western mining camps. In 1888 Bishop John Brondel referred to Butte's population as "floating" and certainly he did not except Irish Catholics from that description. The Hibernians, for example, heard the following excuses for missed meetings: "out of town," "too far away," "in Leadville," "absent from city four months," "transferred," and "dead." In addition to these casual and routine absences, mine shutdowns and failures as well as labor unrest contributed to the extraordinarily high degree of worker mobility.[4]

Butte was spared only a few of these dislocations. There were labor problems in 1878 and 1887, a corporate feud in 1891, the Panic of 1893, each of which slowed or closed operations and put men on the move. In 1903 the Anaconda Company shut down all its Montana operations in an effort—ultimately successful—to force the state to pass a fair trials act. The shutdown cost 10,000 jobs in Silver Bow County alone. That same year the company was reported to have decided that Butte and Anaconda would be better served by Republican rather than Democratic politicians. Obviously, ACM knew then what political historians have only recently discovered. Accordingly, as one Butte Irishman put it, the company brought in "Sweeds and Norway emegrants" to replace Irish workers and effect the political change. The Scandinavians, however, "did not take kindly to mining," and Butte was saved for the Democratic party. To the usual threats to enclave stability, however, now had to be added corporate caprice.[5]

The Butte Irish faced their most severe crisis, however, in 1907-8. Low prices for copper, the result of bank and stock failures as well as oversupply; an absence of railroad cars; and competition from the new mines of the Southwest were cited by the company as reasons for shutting down its mines from October, 1907, to March, 1908. Add to this the rapid inflation after 1906-7, and the suffering was considerable. Twelve thousand men were idled in Butte. An effort seems to have been made to keep the married men on by sacrificing the single ones, but as the shutdown continued through the winter more and more stable and attached miners were forced out of the city.[6]

The Irish were hard hit. St. Mary's parish in Dublin Gulch reported that "thousands of the single men and many of the married ones departed the city for almost every state in the union." AOH membership fell from 1,076 in 1904 to 666 in 1908. The three AOH divisions abandoned plans to build a new lodge "owing to the present condition in the town"; there was "just too much uncertainty" to justify the expense.

The scholarship fund was another casualty. "Too many men had left town," it was said, and those who stayed were in "straightened circumstances." The militantly revolutionary Irish Volunteers had to call off their dance and cancel their order for new uniforms. Little wonder that Dan Mahoney feared that "soon there would be no place for us in this community." That place had always been held on sufferance, not that of the non-Irish host community but of the hiring officers and their ability to provide steady work.[7]

In addition to these local disruptions, the Butte work force was further destabilized by events outside Montana. In one sense the 1887 cholera epidemic in Italy, the political upheavals in the component parts of the Austrian and Russian empires, and, as always it must have seemed, the stream of exiles from Ireland must be counted among these events. Almost anything almost anywhere in the world that put unskilled men on the road affected Butte's work force. Nearer home, strikes in Colorado, Idaho, Arizona, South Dakota, and Michigan set thousands of experienced miners to wandering. Butte was a common destination. The enclave had to try to find room for the Irish among these new men—or at least for those Irish who seemed ready to settle in. This search began, but did not end, with a job.[8]

All of these were matters of only slight concern when times were good. Indeed, the transients, the "ten day miners," were an integral part of Butte's laboring world; they added immeasureably to the excitement of the place if not to the safety of its mines. As long as hardrock mining remained a skilled and dangerous trade, the size of the work force would be limited by the supply of men who possessed the requisite ability and daring. During hard times, however, or after technological changes had stripped old skills of some of their usefulness— and Butte experienced both forms of job insecurity between 1892 and 1910—the arrival of new men willing to accept the risks of underground work created obvious tensions. The Irish community had to try to exercise some control over this volatile work force.[9]

That was never easy, but the Irish of Butte had one enormous advantage over the miners in other western mining camps. Butte was an industrial town; it produced copper ores for smelting in nearby Anaconda. It was the key component in one of the last of America's great industrial complexes. By way of obvious contrast, the gold and silver camps of the other mountain states were ephemeral things, subject not just to the routine shakes and trembles of industrial society but also and literally to running out of the resource on which they were dependent. The fluctuations in Butte's economy—particularly those occasioned by shutdowns and the arrival of new men—were the same as those felt by the workers of, say, Pittsburgh. The workers of Tombstone, Arizona, or Telluride, Colorado, would have counted themselves fortunate had their problems been so trivial. And even those camps were still operating; they were not yet ghost towns, not yet victims of terminal industrial shutdown.

Butte gave the Irish a bare chance. The town was substantial enough that the Irish could try to control the work force in the interest of steady jobs for the steady men. As previously cited persistence figures indicate, they were only partially successful. Fifteen percent of the Irish workers in Butte in 1900 were still there in 1910. Those 15 percent, however, were enough. They constituted a working-class elite, owing their status in equal measure to their skills and to the influence their persistence had earned for them. But, as with all such worker aristocracies, Butte's stable Irish miners had to reproduce themselves by recruiting new men, including their own sons, into the mines, churches, and fraternal lodges of the Irish worker community. That would have been difficult under any circumstances, but Butte, like all immigrant towns, presented the Irish with a moving target. There were disparate and shifting elements in their world. Their community was both cohesive and rapidly differentiating; part of it was fluid and transient, part was stable and settled. Irishmen at one end moved out by moving up; those at the other end moved out by moving on. The center could hold only if it could replicate itself.[10]

This capacity to replenish and remake itself was the ultimate test of a worker aristocracy's resiliency. It was, in fact, a definitional part of being an aristocracy. It was also, however, not something over which workers had much influence; general industrial prosperity and the jobs that went with it were far more important than worker control. Permanence and a sense of security came to the Irish workers' world with economic recovery and with the formation in 1899 of the Amalgamated (Anaconda) Copper Company. The creation of this corporate giant does seem to have benefited the Irish. Its strength insured steadier employment. Irishmen continued to wander into Butte and to wander out, but increasingly after 1899 they seem also to have wandered back. But the Amalgamated, for all its power, did not have Butte entirely to itself; the consolidation of 1899 was a case of corporate reorganization and recapitalization, not of the consolidation of separately owned properties. That final consolidation would also come, but not until 1906 after the "wars of the copper kings." And the "war" years, however unsettling they may have been to corporate managers, were the best the AOH and RELA would ever know. It was the consolidation which closed the conflict that brought hard times for the Irish.[11]

Membership figures reflect the pattern. Before 1899, both organizations enjoyed steady memberships, but totals grew slowly if at all, and the percentage of Irish who were affiliated with either was relatively small. The point was not that Butte and its mines were faltering; only that the prospects for steady employment were too uncertain to justify the kind of commitment required to join an Irish association. Butte was making the transition from gold and silver camp to copper town, and the full returns on the success of that experiment were not in yet. By 1898–99 with the Amalgamated and proof that copper was immune from the currency battles that destroyed silver, the Irish miner enclave, including the Hibernians and the Emmets, began its own consolidation.[12]

Both AOH and RELA memberships peaked between 1899 and the corporate consolidation and mine shutdown of 1906–8, reaching absolute highs in 1904 and 1905. The AOH, for example, enrolled thirty-seven new men in one two-week period in February of 1904. Some of these men were new to Butte but most, at least twenty-five according to incomplete records, had been in town for a year or more. A sudden burst of Irish patriotism cannot explain their interest; 1904 and 1905 were uncommonly quiet years in Irish-English affairs. The more likely explanation for this and similar membership spurts after 1900 is that peak copper production, under whatever corporate banner, provided the one thing essential to enclave growth—stable employment. Cornelius Kelley, at the time general manager of Amalgamated properties, was speaking generally when he testified that "when a man obtains a job underground it is a very steady position if he takes care of it," but his comments had particular relevance to the Irish associations and there is reason to believe Kelley knew it. Implied by his comment, of course, is that American conditions, not Ireland's needs, determined the extent of Irish-American associational involvement; but then these associations had always been more social than political, more the property of the immigrant worker than of the exiled patriot.[13]

II

Butte's Irish workers, however, were not totally dependent on the mining companies when it came to flattening out employment curves. Worker initiatives were also a part of the stabilization of the work force. Irish working-class parishes as well as the local Democratic party may have been involved in finding steady jobs; the family system clearly was. The manuscript censuses of 1900 and 1910 are filled with instances of working sons, younger brothers, and nephews living with kin and employed in the mines. The 1910 census, by asking not just what a man did for a living but where he did it, indicates how often the younger men were employed in the same mine as their older relatives. But it was the overwhelmingly working-class Irish associations, themselves extensions of church and family, that seem to have been the most active in finding work. John Commons pointed out that the AOH in America existed in part to control relations between Irish miners and non-Irish mine owners. The fact that Butte's mine owners were themselves Irish can only have made the job seem easier—whatever "control" might mean.[14]

As noted, both the Hibernians and the Emmets were required by their constitutions and bylaws to give business and, it may be presumed, job preference to fellow members, including those who had come to Butte from other camps and divisions. The AOH Manual, for example, asked under the heading of order of business if "any member knows of a brother out of employment." But even without these injunctions, the Irish clubs would obviously have played major roles in what were essentially acts of self preservation. As one Hibernian put it, there was little sense in enrolling new members unless jobs could be found for them. The responsibility for finding them fell to job committees, usually consisting of three men, who "interviewed" company officers from the president to the shift bosses in "the employment interests of the camp" or division. P. J. Kenny, a member of AOH, Division 3, called these committeemen "solicitors" whose responsibility it was "to visit the mine managers and request of them to ask their superintendents to put as many of our members to work as they can conveniently find a place for." Given the significance of the assignment, the associations selected only their "most influential brothers" to serve.[15]

How they defined influence says much about the workings of Butte's Irish world. Of thirty-seven men identified as members of job committees, only four were miners and they longtime employees whose West Side addresses suggested a certain prosperity. At least three mine company hiring officers were also involved. Eight committeemen were merchants, including Daniel J. Hennessy, whose mercantile establishment, the largest in Butte, may have been a company store. James Maher, the secretary of the Western Federation of Miners, served on both AOH and RELA job committees, as did four other local or federated union officers. Eight county officials, including Judge Jeremiah J. Lynch and County Treasurer Con Maher, brother of James, were members. There are no surprises on these committee lists. Irishmen of influence found jobs for those without influence, but, like the selection of officers, the job committees indicate the interclass nature of Irish associationalism.[16]

There were, of course, less formal methods of insuring job preference. In 1902, to cite only one example, P. J. Brophy wrote directly to Anaconda Company president William Scallon on behalf of James Casey. Casey was Brophy's "old friend"; he had "raised a family of ten children," working for twenty years as a bartender, prospector, and miner. Now he needed a job in the mines; Brophy assured Scallon that Casey could "do the work safely and acceptably." Brophy's personal intercession was undoubtedly welcome, but it may not have been necessary. One Butte Irishman counted 107 mine and smelting company hiring officers between 1880 and 1915 who were either first- or second-generation Irish. This was in addition to Irish executive officers. That he bothered to count is as important as the number. It indicates the pride all the Irish took in the success of any one of them, but it indicates as well—at least by implication—the job leverage working-class Irishmen had.[17]

Moreover, in any given year as many as two dozen mine hiring officers, foremen, and shift bosses, could be found on the membership rosters of the AOH and/or the RELA. Included were such longtime bosses as James Higgins, "Rimmer," Con, and Dan O'Neill, Mike Carroll, John Crowley, James Brennan, Ed and Patrick Kane, John J. McCarthy, Dan Holland, Mike O'Farrell, "Fat Jack" Sullivan, John Conway, P. J. Casey, and James Egan. These were "practical" miners, men who had earned their rank by their ability to mine and by their experience in selecting and handling work crews. They were also, however, strategically placed Irishmen whose positions were absolutely vital to the maintenance of Butte's Irish world. Related directly or indirectly, fraternally or familialy, to a significant percentage of the new men, they can have been expected to favor Irish job applicants in filling out their shifts. As much is implied by Ed Lawlor's comment that among the benefits of AOH membership was the chance "to know those who are in a position to give employment."[18]

In this the foremen and shift bosses may simply have been following the instructions of other and higher-placed Irishmen, particularly those four—Daly, Scallon, Ryan, and Kelley—who ran the ACM from the 1870s to the mid-1950s. Daly's successors do not seem to have been quite as devout in their support of Irish job seekers as the founder. But, with the important exception of 1906–10, the Irish were always given fair if not preferential treatment by the ACM and never, with the same exception, did it discriminate against them. As Bishop John Brondel said in 1888, "many of our richest mine owners . . . are Catholic. Our most skillful mining supts. and foremen are Catholics and Irishmen." The miners were saying the same thing when they referred to waste rock as "Protestant Ore." Indeed, one of the largest and certainly one of the most influential Irish "clubs" in Butte was the Anaconda Copper Mining Company.[19]

The Irish miner enclave understood the benefits implied by Irish-run mines. John Bodnar's argument that enclave survival occasionally required "cooperation" with the "more powerful" needs here to be recalled. How much easier that cooperation would seem if the more powerful were or had been in the enclave. One Hibernian put it succinctly. "So many of our members," said David Ryan, "are in a position to give employment." That being the case, "cooperation" could be made to seem like fraternal goodwill. As for the "few grumblers" who were not placed "through this organization [AOH]," said John J. McCarthy, a mine foreman and former union officer, "we are better off without them . . . let them join the 'Birds and Animals' organizations and see how many jobs they will secure for them." That was the point. The "birds and animals" did not enroll the hiring officers of the Anaconda mines. The Hibernians and the Emmets did. This may not have been as uncommon as the conventional interpretation, with its emphasis on native Protestant managers and immigrant Catholic workers, would have it. But neither can it have been a pattern routinely encountered.[20]

There is no record of how successful the Irish associations were in finding employment. In flush times, of course, their intervention was scarcely needed. Few job committees were formed during periods of full production; the natural tendencies of Irish hiring officers being thought adequate to the associations' needs. During hard times, as in 1907, the job committees were particularly active, though their intervention may have been more important in keeping existing jobs than in getting new ones. At all times, they could only plead, never coerce. Their appeals, however, at least until 1907, appear to have been well received. Recording secretaries included in the minutes of meetings reference to "progress" in finding jobs, or the "matter being handled," or "the bros. were assured that they would get employment."[21]

III

This last may not have been an idle boast—even though it was made during the shutdown of 1903. More was involved than just ethnocentrism or ethnic preference. The AOH and the RELA appealed to the most work-experienced, careful, and skilled members of the Irish labor force, in other words, to the most employable of the new men. Conventional historical evidence would suggest as much. The requirement that prospective members be well known to the men proposing them for membership, residency restrictions on eligibility for associational benefits, and the initiation and yearly fees were all partial checks against casual membership.[22]

Further evidence comes from the response to the crisis of 1907–8. The AOH, faced with declining membership as men left town to find work, voted to waive monthly dues and "put all members in good standing until industrial conditions improve." Good standing meant, among other things, that members would still be eligible for sick and death benefits even though absent from Butte. The assumption was that these were stable workers, that many had left their families in Butte and would return. This confidence was not misplaced. By the spring of 1908, John Conway, a shift boss, told the members of AOH Division 3 that they must do "everything in [their] power to secure work for bros. returning to town." John J. O'Meara, state president of the Hibernians, agreed; employment and membership committees should "get active, many of our race are returning to the city." A week later a Division 3 employment committee headed by Dan Lynch, a mine foreman, was told to "get its rustling clothes on; the mines were back to work." By that summer the AOH reported that its "numerical strength" was nearly "back to where it had been previous to the industrial crisis which prevailed last winter." This report was too sanguine; the Hibernians never fully recovered from 1907–8. But the number of members who persisted through a six-month industrial shutdown, or who returned when the mines reopened, is powerful testimony to the stabilizing influence of Butte's Irish enclave.[23]

A quantitative analysis of persistence rates within the two organizations offers more compelling evidence of the same point. Miners and nonminers are included in these figures, and the middle class was everywhere more likely to persist. Still, more than 80 percent of the associations' members were miners and of the minority of merchants and professionals, many began their years in Butte as miners. Of ninety-nine Hibernians in Butte in 1882, forty-six were still there in 1886, by which time the organization had grown to 149 members. By 1892 membership was down to 129 but fifty-three of those (41 percent) were among the 332 Hibernians in 1901. AOH membership ledgers for the years 1901 to 1913 are missing but of a partial membership of 136 men in 1907, fifty-five, or 40 percent, had been in Butte and on the rolls since at least 1900. The Hibernians clearly were a stabilizing force among Butte's Irish workers.[24]

So were the Emmets. Figures for the RELA are comparable and even easier to obtain. The identification of members by number and the reassignment of numbers upon the death or transfer of the previous holder, plus more complete membership information than that available for the AOH, allow a relatively precise analysis of persistence. In the nineteen years between 1903 and the "purge" of over 300 delinquent members in 1921, 977 men were enrolled in the Emmets; 436 numbers were required for identification purposes, an average of 2.2 men per number. Some of these numbers had only one holder, none had more than four. Since numbers were often left vacant for three or four years, this does not mean an average persistence of eight-plus years but it does suggest a stable membership. Turnover rates are derived from an analysis of the total number of years one man held the same number. The figures are instructive. Of the 977 RELA members, eighty-seven died in Butte five or fewer years after their initiation, leaving a total of 890 men who could have persisted. Of that sum, 344 (39 percent) were in Butte for at least five consecutive years between 1903 and 1921.[25]

It must also be emphasized that these figures apply only to a man's active, dues-paying years in the associations. Many of these men had been in Butte for years prior to their initiation; many more remained in Butte long after they had ceased to be members. These rates are, then, in even more striking contrast to the persistence rates for the whole Irish population. And those rates, 23 percent using five years as an indicator, 17 percent using ten years, are themselves "inflated" by the inclusion of these far more stable associational Irish. Clearly, the Hibernians and the Emmets attracted those Irish who wished to stay in Butte, and both organizations worked to find the jobs necessary to that persistence.

Both associations also carefully screened prospective new members. Committees of three investigated the character and habits of the men proposed for membership, and there were instances when members were rebuked for proposing those unfit, as when Pat Murray nominated the picturesque "Callahan the Bum" for AOH membership. Both clubs also had rules against gambling, both required regular meeting attendance, and the Hibernians insisted that members be "practical" Catholics and perform their Easter duties. In addition, their crusade against the stage Irishman required a certain diligence in seeing that members' behavior did not conform to the caricature. A national directive from the AOH recommended more lectures and fewer "cheap dances and smoke talks." An RELA member reminded the camp of the revolutionary goals of the organization and urged that no "illiterates" be initiated; "we need men with brains." Both organizations expelled members for fighting, for celebrating St. Patrick's Day too enthusiastically, and for engaging in noisy street debates on various issues, an action identified by a Hibernian as "unirish, unamerican, unmanly . . . and unchristian."[26]

Even more signficantly, both had strict rules against excessive drinking and public drunkenness. Again, revolutionary goals were partly responsible; "Ireland sober," it was said, "was Ireland free." That was as true in Irish-America as in Ireland itself. But, given the fact that industrialization also required a sober and dependable work force, and assuming that these rules were enforced, restrictions against drink were at least as important to the mine companies as to the patriots. In 1915, Con Kelley spoke for the industry when he complained of "grog shops" and of men drinking as they went on shift. The problem, as Kelley put it, was that "it would be looked upon as a serious interference with their American privileges if that [practice] was cut off."[27]

The RELA and the AOH did not cut the practice off but they did to a certain extent restrict it; social sessions, official and unofficial, at Crowley and Sullivan's saloon in Hibernia Hall were clearly less a threat to industrial production and safety than drinking before going on shift. What the law could not do—insure a sober and steady work force—the Irish associations might. As Father Michael Kennedy put it, the fact that so many "Hibernians held their jobs" during the hard times of 1907 "spoke well for their sobriety and ability." Kennedy offered his remarks in September, before the shutdown had taken its full toll of Irishmen, but his reference to Hibernians as men of steady habits is nonetheless important. Almost by definition, their membership, as well as that of the RELA, was limited to the most stable segment of the Irish working class, to those, according to Father Michael Hannan, who "towered above the average Irishman, morally, socially, and economically."[28]

They may also, and as a consequence, have towered above the average in job skills. Steady work over time produced those skills; associational membership, church affiliation, property, marriage, and children, honed them. Hard-rock miners did not usually carry the tag of artisan, primarily because a miner above ground was just another unskilled worker. But experienced miners were always a valued commodity, a fact known to miners and mine owners alike. It is impossible to know with absolute certainty if new Irish association members were more work-experienced than the unaffiliated Irish; the data indicate, however, that they were older and certainly they were more settled. It would be surprising indeed if they were not also more skilled.[29]

The active involvement of the associations in job placement thus served as a kind of preliminary screen, easing considerably the recruiting chores of the foremen and shift bosses. This involvement, however, was not in behalf of the entire Irish work force. Both organizations sought work only for their members; those Irish whose commitment to Catholic Ireland or to its Butte facsimile did not extend to associational membership counted for very little. Indeed, for some members they counted not at all. The employment committees, said J. J. Lynch, were instructed "to help get jobs for our idle brothers." Since enhanced job prospects were a membership lure, it made no sense to extend the services of the employment committees to the unaffiliated. Walter Breen, a shift boss himself, stated that he "would as soon get a job for a Cousin Jack as an Irishman not in the AOH." Thomas Kealy used an even more instructive analogy. "Fallen away Hibernians" were deserving of no consideration. "They were scabs," said Kealy, "worse than scabs."[30]

One consequence of this policy, as of associational membership generally, was an even greater social distance between the settled and the unsettled Irish miners, perhaps reaching the point, as Bodnar writes, "that workers with connections . . . were actually held in higher esteem than 'unattached' employees, who were presumed to be more transient." This distinction between the settled and the unsettled Irish will be of considerable importance by 1910, but for present purposes it is enough to point out the obvious: The AOH and RELA job "candidates" had an advantage over the unaffiliated Irishmen, particularly when jobs were scarce, and this preference allowed them to ride out the hard times if not intact at least in place, another signal to the Irish and non-Irish communities alike of the steadiness of this associational Irish work force.[31]

A question of significance is whether these more stable Irish miners had an advantage over the non-Irish of whatever social status. There is clear evidence that they did, particularly in Marcus Daly's Anaconda mines. A member of the Montana territorial legislature, for example, noted in 1889 that it was "a matter of common report that the laborers of [the] Anaconda were almost exclusively Irish." "Clannishness," he went on, "was characteristic of the human race," but it was unfair that "of two men equally competent to fill a position, the Irishman invariably got it." Indeed, the most significant aspect of the corporate "battle for Butte" may have been the ethnic disposition of the dominant corporation. As the Cornish miner was said to have lamented when he learned of the Anaconda takeover of the once Cornish-controlled Parrot Mine, "Good-bye, birdie, savage got thee; no more place for we."[32]

Predictably, the American Protective Association protested Anaconda's hiring practices. In 1894 the APA charged that the company's mines were Irish because, like all "soulless corporations," the Anaconda preferred "those they can control." The result was that " 'NO MAN OF ENGLISH BIRTH NEED APPLY' was virtually posted on the doors of the Anaconda syndicate of mines." English miners, in fact, were "insulted and treated with contempt by the Irish bosses," while "hundreds . . . come directly from that little island beyond the herring pond, men who know nothing about mining [sic!] . . . and are given work at these mines immediately on their arrival." The historian of Irish-American workers could not invent a better variation on the theme.[33]

It must be repeated that these charges were made within a year of both Orange-sponsored hostility to Home Rule in Ireland and the election of an Irish Catholic mayor in Butte. In addition, they came only two years after the formation—in Butte—of the potentially radical Western Federation of Miners, during a particularly severe economic depression, and immediately after violent strikes in the mining districts of Idaho and Colorado. Keir Hardy, the British labor leader, was in Butte in the summer of 1895 during the height of the APA agitation. He made the point that "religious differences have great effect in keeping laboring men apart. . . . Capital is interested in keeping up these divisions." The *Butte Bystander*, official paper of the Western Federation, agreed, accusing the APA of being "subverted to the cause of the mine owners . . . corporations delight in religious strife." These were credible charges.[34]

But so were some of those made by the APA. Nativists may have been right when they claimed that "suspicion of APA affiliation" led to immediate discharge from Anaconda mines. They almost surely were right when they claimed that Marcus Daly gave preference in hiring to Irishmen. As noted, Daly made no effort to hide his Irishness and that involved a distaste for "Orangemen and APAs." But Daly was offering Irish immigrants something few of them had ever known— steady work at decent wages in an Irish-run industry. That these Irish might have been grateful and that their gratitude might find expression in loyalty to job and place cannot have escaped his attention.[35]

Daly, in other words, had the usual manager's appreciation of the advantages to be had from hiring stable crews, many of them made up of men of tested skills, steady habits, and proven character. This latter consideration may have had more to do with Daly's earlier experience with vagabond western miners, Irish and non-Irish, than with his ethnocentrism. Daly and the Anaconda managers who followed him were aware of the usefulness of "ethnic mixing" in boosting production or combating worker solidarity. Those objects, however, required only that the work force of the district be mixed; they were not served by blending drilling teams, shift crews, or even individual mines. These could remain as ethnically homogenous as possible; in Daly's case they did.[36]

Whatever Daly's motives, and the intercessions of the AOH and the RELA may have influenced them, he employed 1,251 Irish-born—plus countless hundreds of second-generation Irish—and only 365 English-born miners among the 5,534 men working at his Anaconda mines in 1894. And these were years when the English outnumbered the Irish in Butte. As late as 1911, a decade after Daly's death, and at least five years after the first great influx of non-English-speaking miners into Butte, 47 percent of the sons of foreign-born fathers working in Anaconda Company mines were second-generation Irish; of the immigrant miners, 28 percent were from Ireland. These later figures represent a decline from those of 1894 but they still indicate a significant Irish presence. Certain mines, the Anaconda, the Neversweat, the St. Lawrence, and the Mountain Consolidated (Mountain Con)—Anaconda Company properties both before and after the consolidation of 1906—were identified as "Irish mines." The Mountain Con provided handball courts adjacent to its change rooms; jobs, if only for a couple of days, were said to be automatic for Irish immigrants; indeed, job notices were often posted in Gaelic Irish, as effective a selection device as any imaginable.[37]

IV

The Irish enclave's involvement in stabilizing the work force in the most uncertain of America's industrial trades is another example of working-class involvement in what was once thought a uniquely middle-class responsibility: the steadying of entire industrial communities. That larger contribution, however, was incidental. The enclave required steady employment; the enclave tried to insure it. Within obvious limits, it succeeded. In fact, had Butte been a steel town, had it been almost anything other than what it was, the world built by its Irish workers might have been even more durable and stable than it proved to be. But Butte was a hard-rock mining town and to job insecurities must be added the occupational hazards of underground work.

These are related issues. If job insecurity demeaned workers, so did daily exposure to injury or death; if the constant influx of new men destabilized the work force, so did it also make the work more dangerous; if job insecurity threatened the families of established miners, so did tuberculosis, the result of the ubiquitious miners' consumption; if all-Irish crews were more congenial, so too were they safer—for the deceptively simple reason that Irishmen were more considerate of the safety of other Irishmen. In sum, it was not enough for the enclave to find work for its members, it had also to assume some of the risks that that work involved.

This may have been the single most important of its responsibilities. Butte's mines were arguably the most dangerous in the world. Statistics from the years 1899–1906 show 1.14 mine accident deaths per 1,000 men working in the United Kingdom; 1.07 in Germany; .75 in Belgium; and 2.02 in France. In the period 1909–11 India's mine fatality rate was 1.18; Russia's .98; the notoriously dangerous Transvaal's 4.29. These figures are only for men working and killed underground. The practice in the United States was to count all mine related deaths, meaning that the men working in relative safety above ground were included in the computations. Mark Wyman argues that, as a result, U.S. mines appeared 40 percent safer than they were. This figure seems too high. In Butte approximately 13 percent of the miners worked on the surface. This does not include a variety of other tradesmen—hoisting engineers, carpenters, ropemen, pumpmen among them—who had topside jobs. The assumption, however, is that these were not miners and hence not counted in the fatalities per 1,000 miners employed. Since some of these surface miners died in job accidents, an 11 percent adjustment in the published statistics is appropriate.[38]

In 1896 the adjusted death rate in Montana was 9.3 deaths per 1,000 miners employed (if the adjusted figures were to be based on a 40 percent error, the rate would be 11.6); the next year it was 5.95; in 1898, 4.86. For the fourteen years from 1893 to 1906, the adjusted average fatality rate was 4.72, more than five times the rate in Russia during this same period. Using a different method of computation, in 1894 one out of every 212 Montana hard-rock miners died in a mine accident; comparable figures for the coal-mining regions are one death for every 553 men in Ohio, 487 men in Illinois, 633 men in Kentucky, 835 in Kansas. Montana's are statewide figures but there is no reason to assume that Butte's mines were safer than those of the rest of the state. In any event, in almost 90 percent of the cases, a Montana miner was a Butte miner.[39]

The Anaconda Company kept more precise figures, particularly for the years 1910–13. During that four year period, 162 men died in ACM mines, another 5,233 suffered injuries requiring medical attention. Death came, in descending order of occurrence, from falling ground; falls, usually down a shaft; blasts, most often premature detonations of dynamite; being mangled by machinery; hoisting accidents; and electro-cutions. Among the accidents were 349 fractures, including twelve bro-ken skulls and 129 broken legs; sixty-seven eye injuries resulting in twenty cases of blindness; forty-six amputations; and eighteen "scald-ings."[40]

It was almost impossible to pick up a Butte newspaper between 1880 and 1930 and not find a notice of a death or serious injury. The de-scriptions were graphic: "Skull fractured and brains scattered around," "blown to bits," "scalded to death," "torn apart" were among them. Men were not the only victims. Ed Dolan was one of six Irishmen who died in a fire in 1895 at the St. Lawrence mine; three days after his death his wife died in premature childbirth. Major disasters (more than four men killed in the same accident) occurred in 1889, 1893, 1895, 1896, 1898, 1904, 1905, 1906, 1909, 1911, 1912, 1915, 1916, 1917 (when 165 men died in a fire at the Speculator Mine), 1918, and 1919. Little wonder that there were 434 Irish widows by 1910; that of 302 parish families at St. Lawrence O'Toole, 137 were headed by widows; or that by 1940 the "population" of Butte's cemeteries was greater than that of the town.[41]

Clearly, Butte's mines were exceedingly dangerous places to work. This was known in Ireland, and not just in the mining regions of West Cork. One emigrant from County Monaghan had to promise his mother that he would never work underground; a song heard often in the West of Ireland concluded that Butte was the town "where the streets were paved with Irish bones." The same sorts of lyrics were sung in Butte. Miners' songs, seldom lighthearted, included such lines as "Don't Go Down in the Mine, Dad," as well as "God pity the miner and shield him from harm." Certain tools, particularly drills, were known as "widow makers"; loose rock was a "Larry Duggan," after Butte's Irish undertaker. Beatrice Murphy, a night nurse at Butte's Murray Hospital, kept a diary for the month of November, 1909. In that month she personally attended twenty-eight injured miners, one had a "crushed foot," another a "frontal artery cut," a third a "contused knee and eyebrow hanging completely down over left orbit." Father Brosnan exaggerated only slightly when he wrote home from Butte that "poor men [were] killed every day in one or another mine." As late as 1922 Countess Markievicz reported during a fund-raising visit to Butte that "the hospitals are full of men suffering from work in the mines. . . . They told us few men live to be old in Butte, Montana."[42]

The Countess's reference was not to mine accidents—they took only hundreds of lives—but to diseases, which took thousands. The most common and the most deadly of these diseases was tuberculosis. TB was the product of a variety of factors—genetic susceptibility and living conditions among them—but it was miners' consumption, the result of breathing the dry silicate dust of the mines, that left the lungs scarred and vulnerable. And it was in the mines that men afflicted with the con—the "Galen giggles," "rocks on the chest," as it was also known—found the bacilli that killed them. When Marcus Daly died in 1900 the attending physician commented on his earlier years in the mines, of the "unremitting labor" and the "arsenic in the air." In 1941, the Irish-born Ed Boyce, second and radical president of the WFM, died in Portland. He was in his mid-seventies but the autopsy report mentioned that "as a young man he was a miner and during the past fifty years he suffered several attacks of pneumonia."[43]

Other records give added definition to the problem. Mortuary reports for fifteen months in 1906–7 show 106 fatal mine accidents, but the reports list 277 more miners who died of respiratory illness. Of these, the average age at time of death was 42.7 years. The youngest to succumb was twenty-two; seventy-five of those who died were under forty. Clearly, working in the dry, ill- or unventilated mines and breathing silica-laden dust was to risk early death. The risk, however, was routinely assumed. From 1916 to 1919 a U.S. Bureau of Mines study found that of 1,018 Butte miners interviewed, 432 (42.5 percent) had miners' consumption, another sixty-three had tuberculosis. And once again it was not just the men who were victimized. When Bishop John Brondel at the dedication of St. Lawrence O'Toole's, prayed that God would "protect the women and children from disease," he may have spoken more than he knew. As one Butte newspaperman wrote, the miners' wives were also "unhealthy from washing clothes saturated . . . with . . . bad air and giant powder smoke, and [being] compelled to inhale the . . . deadly fumes."[44]

Some of these hazards may have been unavoidable. Butte's mines were sunk to depths of 4,500 feet; the ore-bearing rock was friable and crumbled easily; ventilation, particularly before the use of electric fans, was difficult. But whether the problems were easily corrected or not, they resulted in nightmarish working conditions. The county sanitary commission provided documentation in its 1912 report. Carbon dioxide levels in working shafts reached highs of 61.4 parts per 10,000, more than twenty times the carbon dioxide in "pure country air," ten times that in the air of Butte. In one unworked part of the St. Lawrence Mine, near where a fire was still burning after twenty years, the carbon dioxide levels were 231.2 per 10,000. The temperature and humidity often reached tropical if not unearthly highs. At the 2,300-foot level of the Original Mine, the temperature was 93 degrees, the humidity 97 percent. One observer testified that men worked full ten-hour shifts in one of these "hot boxes" without ever urinating; they sweated out the gallons of water they drank. It must also be kept in mind that there were no seasonal fluctuations in temperature and humidity, which meant that in the winter men were hoisted, in five minutes' time, from 90 degree mine shafts into outside air that routinely reached a brittle 40 degrees below zero. One longtime Butte resident remembers men emerging from the mines "covered with sweat," hitting the cold air and disappearing in balls of steam. Before the construction of change rooms, or dries, these men then walked home with their clothes frozen to them.[45]

Some occupational hazards resulted from worker neglect and/or company penury. As late as 1912, for example, of the ten mines investigated by the sanitary commission, only two provided toilet cars and only one delivered drinking water in sealed metal containers. These two, the Original and the Gagnon, happened also to be the two hottest mines investigated. In the other mines, including four recognized as "Irish," the men urinated wherever they happened to be and "answered nature's call," in the delicate phrase of the commission, in waste drifts, covering the excreta with rock. Water was sent down in open wooden kegs, a most unhygienic practice given the tendency of miners to "spitting indiscriminately." Water arrived at the 2,100-foot level of the Mountain Con, for example, with an "earthy" odor, a "decidedly yellowish brown" color, and "considerable, flocculent" sediment (flocculent: "little wooly balls or tufts"). Some of this may also have been owing to the presence on that same level of a horse barn described as "very bad, absolutely filthy . . . horse dying."[46]

These conditions provided a fertile breeding ground for a great variety of bacteria. Air samples turned up the presence of colon bacilli, Albus, Diplococcus Pneumonia, Streptococcus, Staphylococcus, Bacillus of Putrification Group, Bacillus of Vincen's Angina, Anthrax, citreus Actinomycoses, Meningococcus, Fraenkles Pneumococcus, influenza, and typhoid bacillus. This last was particularly ominous, but the commission concluded that at least forty, and more likely as many as sixty, typhoid carriers were working in the mines. This was only slightly fewer than the number of active miners with tuberculosis, prompting the commission to report that typhoid was "by no means a rare disease in Butte."[47]

Health conditions scarcely improved when the men went off shift. In fact, the commissioners believed that "the conditions under which we found many of the miners living [were] more conducive to the introduction of disease germs into the system than are the conditions

... in the mines." Specifically, they meant conditions in the miners' boardinghouses. Their descriptions were lurid. One house was described as "very unsanitary, many flies, no screens, dirty rooms never disinfected." In one small rooming house at 508 East Broadway, six men lived in one sixteen-by-nine-foot room, allowing each man twenty-five square feet of living space, 228 cubic feet of breathing space. Each resident, in other words, had room for a cot and a footlocker. The place had no windows and the outside privy was described as "filthy." Of the larger boardinghouses—and the commission limited its report to those residences found to be unsanitary—the Silver Lake Hotel had seventy-five miners in thirty-five rooms; the Hazel Block put up ninety men in forty-eight rooms; the Florence had three hundred men in fewer than one hundred rooms. Air and water samples taken from these places turned up consistently high counts of infectious bacilli, particularly for tuberculosis, completing an unrelentingly grim picture of industrial working and living conditions.[48]

But the commission, for reasons that are not clear, extended its investigation to include three unidentified working-class saloons, one of them on North Main in Dublin Gulch. The bacteriological examinations of the air in all three proved "negative"; carbon dioxide counts ranged from 6.2 to 7.4 parts per 10,000; temperature and humidity rates were 62 degrees, 69 percent; 55 degrees, 82 percent; and 57 degrees, 56 percent. That miners might stop off at a saloon between work and "home" is more easily understood in light of the conditions detailed in the commission report. That some miners might, in fact, use home only for sleeping should occasion no wonder. With an average floor space in over 1400 residences of less than 40 square feet per person, sleep was about all they could do there. As for the refreshments served at these saloons, one miner reminded the prohibitionists, "St. Monday is a thing of the past; workers don't need caretakers, they need an end to foul air and long hours."[49]

The sanitary commissioners offered a few suggestions on how to correct the problems. They wanted city and county ordinances requiring at least 600 cubic feet per person for rooming and boardinghouses. Toilet cars and covered steel water containers, together with a health check of the horses used underground, were recommended for the mines. These were matters for the companies. The commission said nothing about the companies improving ventilation by using fans or by constructing raises, though the miners thought both were feasible. The primary responsibility for improving worker health, however, rested with the workers. The commissioners held out little hope. The men, they wrote are "frequently of a very unintelligent class." Many "only work a . . . short time in one locality." But even these men, "though transient in character," could perhaps be taught. Their tutors would have to be the steady men. Fortunately, Butte had a "good percentage" of these stable types. "If this were not true," the commissioners concluded, in an interesting and early use of persistence theory, "we would not find so many owning their own homes." It was up to these steady men to convince the transients to "dispose of excreta properly lest they endanger the health and lives of the permanent residents of the locality." Thus did the sanitary commission recognize and perhaps exacerbate the existing division between the settled and the itinerant.[50]

Also of interest was the commission's discovery of what the miners had always known: that there were enormous differences in working conditions within the same mine and from one mine to another. While the temperature at the 2,300 foot level of the Original Mine, for example, was 93 degrees, at the 2,100-foot level it was only 78. At the 2,000-foot level of the Neversweat the temperature was 58; on the same level of the Anaconda it was 54. Understandably, men sought work in the cooler mines or in the cooler shafts of the same mine, meaning they sought out those hiring officers who could provide them not just with regular work but with safe and tolerable working conditions.[51]

These were related considerations. The favored assignments went to the good miners, the steady men, or—and they were not always the same—the well-connected men. The result, however, usually had to mean that the more experienced workers found and kept the coolest jobs, making those jobs, in the process, the safest as well. Since, technically, shift bosses hired new crews every day, with preference likely given to those whom they knew, a rough kind of seniority system evolved. New men worked the hottest and most dangerous parts of the mine, except when caving ground or the opening of a new drift required the services of more experienced—and better-paid—hands. The best miners refused to work in improperly ventilated mines. They found the coolest levels and returned to them every day, working them as long as possible and then moving, probably with the same shift boss, to another and equally desirable location.[52]

The 1906 consolidation of Butte's mines did not make the work steadier but it did make it easier for the stable miner to find and keep the best jobs. A man could change mines without having to change companies. In addition, as an ACM officer put it, prior to consolidation it was the practice of the corporations to build bulkheads to keep one company's "good air" from going "the other company's way." Since there was now only one company, those corporate games could cease.

It was not, however, in the boardrooms that decisions on job assignments were made. Those choices were left to the mine foreman and he became as a consequence a very important man. Shift bosses who had "pull" with the foreman were known as "meatballs" or "meat"; miners who were part of a meatball's crew were called "fine day miners"; those who managed to avoid all, or most, of the dangers were dismissed as "capons." That last reference says volumes about the world of underground miners.[53]

The pattern that emerges is clear and understandable. As important as steady work, in fact an integral part of it, was work in cool, safe drifts with congenial mates and a friendly shift boss. It may not need saying, but a broken head or miners' con had the same effect on steady work as a mine shutdown. Certainly no one could have missed the point of the sign posted on the North Butte Mine: "Don't Get Hurt. There are TEN MEN waiting for YOUR JOB."[54]

Here then was another place where "cooperation with the more powerful" might serve the interests of family and enclave, and there is evidence that that kind of cooperation was not unknown. The Irish associations had no formal committees on job assignments, though there were times when they sought safer jobs or day shifts for some of their members. The key element, however, was active participation in the Irish enclave, with or without associational membership. In other words, here as elsewhere, persistence was rewarded with a chance to persist; it meant job seniority, a chance at decent housing, and, most important, the opportunity to beat the actuarial odds of a frighteningly hazardous workplace.[55]

Those hazards and the various responses to them dominated the miners' working day. The hazards, of course, were felt by every man who went underground. The Irish response, however, was determined by the particulars of the Irish world. Milton Cantor has argued that, of all the industrial workers, miners had the greatest occupational consciousness, that their loyalties were necessarily to those others who shared the dangers of their craft and upon whose help they had to rely in case of accident. This suggests an unusually strong occupational awareness that would transcend ethnic rivalries. There are examples of such in Butte. One occurred in 1894 when Pat Gallagher and Peter Breen among many other Irish Catholics attended funeral services for John Nicholson, a Cornish Presbyterian killed in a mine accident. Since that was a year of considerable tension between the two ethnic communities, the Irish presence, as well as the wheat and sickle sheath that adorned Nicholson's casket, was an obvious signal of loyalty. Similarly, though it had nothing to do with the issue of ethnic rivalries, mention must also be made of the insistence of the Butte Miners' Union that the men who worked underground, regardless of job description or experience, be paid the same wage for assuming the same risks. This did not preclude the very skilled—or the very reckless—from negotiating individual contracts based on production or on a willingness to take uncommon risks, but it did ensure that everyone else was paid equally, and even the contract miners were paid the standard scale before drawing their contract wage.[56]

On the functional level, however, Butte's Irish miners were precisely that: Irishmen who worked in the mines, usually and always preferably with other Irishmen. In their case, occupational hazards sharpened rather than dulled ethnic awareness. When they left work they returned together to Irish neighborhoods. Their working songs had Irish themes; they combated the demons underground with Irish and Catholic incantations; they prayed to Irish saints; wore Catholic medals and scapulars; and when they died they were waked in Irish fashion, buried in an Irish cemetery following a ceremony conducted by an Irish priest reciting the ancient liturgy of an Irish church. In sum, they lived and died in an ethnic world made even more tightly knit by workplace hazards.[57]

No other of Butte's ethnic groups developed so strong an ethno-occupational awareness. And the singularity of the Irish response to occupational hazards extends beyond the ceremonial. There were peculiarities and anomolies in the Irish presence in Butte which give an added significance to the role workplace hazards played in explaining and defining their world. The Irish not only came earlier to mining, they stayed later than the other ethnic groups, and they worked the mines in disproportionate numbers. But more than just timing and occupational preference is involved. The Irish were America's diggers, in Butte as in Boston, but in Butte their digging had about it an artisanal aspect. This was true in part because a miner was a special category of worker, but it was true in greater part because a miner, even the most favorably placed, assumed great risks, not a skill perhaps, but as valued a commodity. Prestige attached to both skill and the courage to take it underground, and prestige was something few Irish workers had known.[58]

But this rare and special status did more. It enhanced the respect miners were paid by the middle class, particularly its Irish component, and slowed the division between working-class and middle-class Irish. That division was never erased but neither did it widen. In fact, the stable Irish miner probably felt a closer kinship with the Irish merchant class than with the itinerant Irish miner, and not because the stable

Irish aspired to middle-class status—indeed, greater prestige may have attached to being a hard-rock man—but because both miner and merchant sought social stability, the one for reasons of steady paychecks and safer working conditions, the other for reasons of respectability and prosperity.[59]

This shared commitment was commonly misinterpreted. Joe Shannon, for example, a frequent critic of what he saw as worker conservatism if not timidity, put the matter this way in testimony to the Commission on Industrial Relations headed by John Commons: "Fine day miners," said Shannon, ". . . got an easy place in the mine, where the air is good and they always have a good word for the company for giving them the job." There were, of course, no easy places; the air was never good. But Shannon, who ran a boardinghouse, testified further that these men were counterfeit miners; by avoiding the "heat and dust," they disqualified themselves. A commission member asked if the hard jobs "go to the men that are not inclined to be company men? "To the strong men, yes," Shannon replied, "weak in the head."[60]

Shannon implied no "Irish connection" in his attack on company favoritism. Like others among Butte's labor radicals, he was protesting the preference that arose from company loyalty, not that resulting from ethnic affiliation. Other critics, as will be seen, made the obvious connections between the old Irish, the company, and the union, and charged the last with being the handservant of the other two. Both sets of critics missed the point. Experienced miners, Irish or not, sought stable employment above all else. Theirs was a workers' world but it was not always or necessarily the world assigned them by political theorists, then or now. The prosperity and stability of the enclave was more important, because more comprehensible, than any strictly proletarian objective. This does not imply ignorance, or moral weakness, or narrowness of vision. If anything, given the complexities of the enclave and the extraordinary hazards of the workplace, it may imply their opposites.

There were, however, two inherent problems facing the enclave, and both related to workplace dangers. The first and most obvious was that the elimination of all occupational risks eliminated as well the special considerations that went with being a hard-rock man—recall the contemptuous use of "fine day miner" or the even more instructive reference to "capons." Here then were doomed aristocrats; keeping their privileged status killed them, surrendering it by becoming fine-day miners stripped them of rank.

The second problem is related to this first. The world of the Irish miner was closely knit, in no small measure because of the hazards of that world. Those hazards gave the enclave its cohesion, a cohesion that at times resembled the camaraderie of soldiers. But if dangers defined the enclave, they also and paradoxically limited its ability to reproduce itself. Butte miners were among the highest-paid workers in the United States; they were accorded a status that befitted the dangers they assumed; they understood that what they did for a living was worthy and honorable; the persistent among them enjoyed considerable job security, and three-fourths of those persisters owned their own homes. Little wonder that the immigrant Irish flocked to jobs in the mines.[61] Their sons, however, did not share their enthusiasm. The *Manuscript Census* of 1900 counted 2,192 miners out of a male immigrant population of 2,906, a percentage of 75.4. But of 2,463 men, at least one and usually both of whose parents were Irish-born, only 1,397 (56.7 percent) worked underground. In 1910 the differences were even more striking. In the first place, there were only 2,118 second-generation Irishmen in Butte, more than 300 fewer than had been there in 1900, and of those only 935 (44 percent) were employed underground. The immigrant population was down only slightly, to 2,840, and of those, 2,075 (73 percent) were miners.[62]

Given that a decent wage, status, and a chance at steady employment were a part of being a miner, this difference between the immigrants' and the second generation's choice of workplace is not reasonably explained by conventional reference to intergenerational occupational mobility. Those of the second generation did not move into white-collar or professional jobs. Neither did they move into more skilled blue-collar jobs. They only moved aboveground—horizontally in terms of occupational mobility. There was one exception. By 1911 ninety-four second-generation Irish were supervisory and/or hiring officers for selected Anaconda Company mines. This was 19 percent of the total number of second-generation Irish working in those same mines, significantly higher than the 8 percent of the immigrant Irish who held hiring positions.[63]

Thus, though fewer of the second generation worked underground, the Irish retained their controlling interest in those who did. This would indicate as well that few second-generation Irishmen can have wanted mining jobs and been unable to get them. The major factor in their not taking jobs in the mines was the knowledge of the hazards that went with those jobs. The results were the same regardless of motive. Avoidance of mining and its hazards meant that the enclave, based as surely on occupation as ethnicity, could not reproduce itself. Irish men and women would do much for the enclave but the sacrifice of their sons exceeded even their devotion. Fathers, in other words, worked in the mines so that their sons would not have to.[64]

With the exception of this fatherly advice to sons, it cannot be known how work-related deaths affected the other miners, how they reacted, to cite only two examples from thousands, to the death in 1911 of thirty-three-year-old James Sullivan from what the certificate identified as "miners' consumption." Sullivan was married, had four children, and had been a member of Butte's AOH, Division 1. What set his story apart from hundreds like it was that the death certificate was sent from Castletownbere, County Cork. Sullivan had worked Butte's mines and gone home; the exile had returned. Unfortunately, he brought too much of Butte home with him. The death in 1906, also from miners' con, of Patrick Mannix was as instructive. Mannix was Irish-born, married, a member of both the AOH and the RELA, and a twenty-five-year resident of Butte—in fact, he lived less than a block from Hibernia Hall. Ironically, he had survived the 1894 blast that took the life of the Cornishman John Nicholson. The coroner's report, under the heading "duration of disease," said that Mannix had had the con "for years." In other words, Mannix knew, as did his friends and coworkers, that his work was killing him.[65]

They may, in fact, have wondered why it had taken so long. Fifteen years was the assumed work-life expectancy of a Butte copper miner. Mannix had lived beyond his "allotted" time; the odds had caught up with James Sullivan. The survivors were also aware, however, that other mining towns were less hazardous than Butte. Dan Sullivan, for example, knew James Sullivan and Pat Mannix. Onetime president of the Butte Miners' Union as well as an RELA member, Sullivan testified before the Commons commission that in Michigan there was a "lot less con." He knew of "forty year men . . . pretty lively old chaps yet; they are trotting around with their buckets." The reward for good health, in other words, was not a comfortable retirement but the opportunity to continue work. But that was better than Butte, where Sullivan saw "my fellow workmen failing every day; they had my sympathy, they had my sympathy. I suppose if I kept on, I would be getting somebody else's sympathy." When asked, "you are a little bit afraid?" Sullivan's immediate reply was "Yes sir, I certainly am."[66]

Well he might have been. One Butte physician, Patrick McCarthy, by way of establishing his other credentials, told the commission that the rate of consumption death in Butte was "something appalling. . . . Butte is worse than any place I know of." McCarthy recommended that consumptives be "quarantined" from the mines, the practice in Michigan. Dan Sullivan dissented. He "thought it would deprive needy men of bread and butter." Besides, the air in Michigan was better than in Butte and there was less competition among the shift bosses, less, said another Irish miner, of the "constant cry for rock . . . one boss trying to beat the other."[67]

The companies, predictably, disputed this inference that their policies had anything to do with the death rate from consumption. One ACM officer told the commission that the rate was high in Butte because of the way the miners lived; another said it was because of how much and where the men drank. A third, John Gillie, offered the interesting suggestion that the rate appeared high because the "young strong men" moved to new mining districts where the mines were "shallow" and hence cooler. Older men, Gillie continued, either could not leave or "weren't hired if they did. This leaves the Butte mines with the older crew all the time." Gillie may have had a point. The hazards of Butte, plus the strong tug of its Irish community, did have obvious demographic effects. The hazards reduced the average age of the Butte Irish miner; the enclave's pull had the opposite effect.[68]

Thus the deaths of other men, particularly when "untimely," caused a variety of responses. In Butte, where it occurred with such numbing frequency, death produced feelings of fear, anger, frustration, fatalism, and despair. But, though seldom commented upon, these deaths must have given rise to more complex feelings. In the first place, industrial death in Butte was an occupational and class phenomenon. Miners died earlier than nonminers; the poor earlier than the nonpoor. This commonplace needs to be recalled, particularly when studying a town like Butte. Every work-related death reinforced the miner's understanding of the essential difference between his world and that of the middle class. Second, for all the prestige that attached to the assumption of risk, there was something about the "con" and about the deaths and injuries in the mines that was ultimately and profoundly insulting. The accidents occurred so suddenly and so randomly. But the con, too, was a sentence of death, only the length of the sentence was indeterminate. Both deeply offended the workers' sense of their own dignity.

V

Butte's Irish lived with and died from these pervasive hazards. Where and when it could—and it did have some influence—the enclave made it possible for its members to avoid some of the more obvious insecurities and dangers. The evidence cited, however, makes it clear that the Butte Irish miner, whatever his standing in his community, could not dodge all the risks. The objective hazards had to be assumed. Some of their effects, however, could be blunted. Medical bills could be paid, mortgages retired, children cared for, wakes and burials arranged. These may have been the most important of a worker enclave's responsibilities anywhere. In a place like Butte, the enclave was preoccupied with them. They were inescapable. Thus, as everywhere else in this miners' world, the largely mythical individualism of the nineteenth century gave way to associational, even communal, effort—in this instance, to minimize the full effects of the occupational risks.

Once again, the Irish associations took the lead. Both the Hibernians and the Emmets had programs to provide aid to sick and injured members and, upon a member's or a member's wife's death, to absorb funeral costs. The AOH was, if not more active in providing relief, at least more regular and systematic. All AOH members between the ages of sixteen and forty-five were eligible to receive sick benefits beginning the second week and extending for thirteen weeks, for any disabling illness or injury. The RELA offered benefits only intermittently, as the political and revolutionary demands on its money permitted. There were, of course, restrictions on AOH eligibility. The recipient had to have been a member for at least six months, his dues and fees had to be fully paid up, and the illness could not be chronic or owing to carelessness or intemperance. In addition, a weekly physician's certificate attesting to the legitimacy and lingering nature of the complaint was required, and a "sick" or "visiting" committee called on the disabled brother to confirm his complaint and verify the physician's certificates. If all these conditions were met, and they were thousands of times, the disabled received sick benefits of $8.00 per week for up to thirteen weeks, or $104.00. Since the death or funeral benefit was $100.00 ($500.00 for those willing to pay an extra "premium"), this limit possessed a certain logic.[69]

Though less than half the average wage for a Butte miner, these benefits, when added to the $8.00 to $10.00 weekly benefits paid for up to ten weeks by the unions, were sufficient to cover most of the costs of all but extended layoffs. Since Montana did not have a Workmen's Compensation Law until 1915, these benefit payments were all that was available in most cases. Fortunately for the bookkeeping departments of both the unions and the AOH, most of the injuries and illnesses that extended beyond the ten- and thirteen-week limits seem to have proven fatal before the expiration of benefits. When extended custodial health care was required, as occurred with blindings, the Hibernians and the Emmets sponsored raffles and dances to aid the stricken member.[70]

Needless to add, the demands on the AOH's sick and funeral benefit funds were unrelenting. In 1896 the AOH paid out sick benefits alone of $1,884.00; in 1899, sick benefits totaled $2,549.00; in 1903, $2,572.00; in 1911, $2,712.00. In one six month period in 1898, sick and death benefits together amounted to $1,768.00. The total for the nineteen years for which records are complete between 1885 and 1911 was $30,496.00. There were years, 1904 and 1910 for example, when almost one in every five eligible Division 1 members drew sick benefits. A typical entry in the weekly Minute Books for 1904 listed thirteen members as either "sick," "injured," or "slowly improving." It must also be kept in mind that benefits did not begin until the second week of a disabling illness or injury. Records of the sick benefits paid by Butte's two smaller AOH divisions were not found, but evidence from the Minute Books of Division 3 indicate that its sick benefits amounted to about half of those of Division 1. The funeral benefit fund of Division 1 was kept as busy, averaging almost $400.00 per year for the nineteen record years between 1885 and 1911. The five year experiment with $500.00 benefits between 1905 and 1909 increased the total appreciably, though not proportionately to the membership, suggesting that few miners could afford to pay for the increased benefits.[71]

The physicians' certificates that accompanied sick-benefit claims provide more precise evidence of the nature of member complaints. Interestingly, the forms were the same as those used by the Butte Miners' Union and in many instances the physician simply crossed out "BMU" and penciled in "AOH." Exactly 500 of these certificates survive; 474 of them from the years 1904–6. Of the 500, only 408 identify the injury or illness. Of that number, 149 were for injuries, seventy-six of them mine related; another forty-eight were almost surely mine related. The doctors were scarcely less graphic in their descriptions than the newspapermen. The list included the claims of John Gallagher, who suffered "contusions and lacerations" when struck by an ore car; Dan Harrington, whose left leg was fractured and both eyes "punctured" by a "blast"; William Brennan, who suffered a "compound fracture of the head" when struck by falling rock; Dan Shea, whose "left eye ball [was] ulcerated when burned by hot copper"; and John Murphy, who was "paralyzed from the waist down" when his back was "crushed by rock fall."[72]

The other 259 claims were for illness. It is less easy here to assume that these were the result of occupational hazards except, of course, in those cases where the doctor identified them as such. Forty-two cases of respiratory disease were so identified. Another 107 cases of respiratory distress were not attributed but may safely be assumed to have been caused by "occupation and cold," the usual explanation of cause. Certainly occupational hazards explain the letter in the AOH files from John Kennedy. It is dated April 1, 1910, and in it Kennedy wrote "i ame here . . . at tucson. . . . i came here for to see if the Climate would benfit me as i was not feeling so good in Butte. Please send benfits." Before AOH could mail sick benefits, a physician's certificate was received from Dr. H. W. Fenner. Kennedy had died of "miners' consumption" on April 11. The AOH sent his $100.00 death benefit instead.[73]

Funds to cover these benefit payments came from a variety of sources; membership dues and initiation fees covered only a part. The rest came from rental income—both the Olympia and Centennial breweries, among other commercial companies, rented space in Hibernia Hall—and fundraising events. The national AOH sponsored life-insurance programs, but copper miners were specifically excluded from benefits; the risks of insuring them were too great. Butte's AOH divisions strongly protested this exclusion but failed to have it removed. As a consequence, the sick and death benefits of Butte's Hibernians represented an entirely self-sufficient, locally financed and administered relief program, at least as it applied to that percentage of the membership that worked in the copper mines.[74]

Obviously, in an era of $3.50 per day wages, with dues set at $.50 per month, the sick and death benefit programs of the AOH required rigorous economies and stable membership totals. Benefits, for all members, were suspended in 1889 and again in 1915, the consequence of hard times and declining memberships. In 1899 and 1901 membership drives were mounted for the express purpose of replenishing badly depleted sick and death benefit funds; AOH "generosity," as one member put it, had led to "financial embarrassment." Seven years later, the county board reported that the "Order was in good shape . . . except the Death Benefit fund is a little short on account of the number of deaths during the last quarter." In 1910, Division 2 sponsored a dance "to build up the treasury . . . which has suffered badly since the first of the year on account of the death of five of our brothers. We hope you will deal generously with us." This was also Division 2's last year; in 1911 it was "amalgamated" with Division 1. The two events do not appear unrelated.[75]

What is remarkable about this record is that the men who did not mine for a living seem to have borne willingly the extra burden of providing benefits for those who did. In the RELA this occasionally required the leadership to transfer money from the "Revolutionary" or "Skirmishing" Fund to the sick benefits fund. In the AOH, the miners' demands on the benefit funds meant higher fees as well as contributions to special fund-raising events by the 25 percent of the membership that did not work in the mines. That there were no recorded protests indicates either the strength of the majority or the interclass nature of Irish associationalism. In light of the fact that non-miners provided the leadership of both organizations, the latter seems the likelier explanation.[76]

Butte's AOH divisions did mount occasional campaigns to insure strict compliance with the rules. In 1899, for example, AOH Divison 1 president John J. O'Meara, a brewing company executive, insisted that the sick or injured had to report their complaints to an AOH officer rather than to another member, as had been the case. The implication that fraudulent claims were being filed is clear. So is it in O'Meara's refusal to "recognize any Certificates from any Quaker Dr." What he meant by Quaker is unknown; probably he was simply protesting the practice of some physicians of avoiding any reference to chronic illnesses lest benefits be denied. There were other checks on abuse. Members were fined for proposing new men without first checking on the state of their health; negotiations were begun with two Butte physicians, Doctor Sullivan and Doctor Monahan, in an unsuccessful attempt to get a reduced fee for preinitiation physical exams; visiting committees were fined for "neglect"; and physicians' certificates were sometimes ignored.[77]

Generosity, however, often beyond what the rules would allow, was far more common than niggardliness. Back dues were paid by other members to insure good standing for the sick or injured, including at least one case where the RELA paid AOH dues for a member of both. Delinquent dues were paid out of sick benefits and then a new thirteen-week benefit schedule was begun; entire benefits of $104.00 were paid in advance; benefits far in excess of $104 were routinely paid, usually by permitting the member to return to work temporarily and then to reapply for another thirteen weeks. AOH members from other towns were cared for, and many of the chronically ill were paid up for life. The emphasis was on providing relief, not on strict accounting.[78]

Literally thousands of Irish men and women benefited. Thirty thousand dollars in sick benefits over nineteen years adds up to almost four thousand lost man-weeks of work for which some money was received. Pat McNichols was reported in "rather destitute circumstances" and a committee was appointed to see "that he don't need for anything." When Charles Kennedy lost his leg in a mine accident, the AOH, in addition to regular sick benefits, gave him $150.00 "from the fact that he is a cripple and unable to work" and to "assist him in buying a cork foot." Michael Francis Noon was seriously ill and stranded in Scranton, Pennsylvania. The AOH paid his medical bills, sent his wife his sick benefits, paid his way back to Butte, and deposited $50.00 with "Hennessy Mercantile for clothing for his family." Jeremiah Hurley's death in the mines left his wife without the means to support herself and her children. In addition to sick and death benefits, the AOH made her a cash donation, persuaded the mining company where Hurley worked to provide "benefits," and then hired the "widow Hurley" as a janitor's assistant for Hibernia Hall. When John Henry was killed in the Bell and Diamond Mine, a three-man AOH committee took up a collection in the mine for Henry's widow, "then in destitute circumstances." This, too, was in addition to regular sick and death benefits.[79]

The RELA, though it had no continuous program of sick benefits, provided a comparable measure of informal relief. It collected $120.00 for "the widow Curley." One hundred forty-six dollars was raised at a raffle and sent to aid Brother Ed Shields, "in distress in Ireland." The $90.00 hospital bill of Philip McLaughlin, "still sick and with no money," was ordered paid. Before James McBride died of injuries received in a "fall in the mines," the RELA secured free medical assistance and then raffled off a gold watch, raising $200.00 for his widow. When John McGrath was hurt at the Anaconda Mine, the Emmets sent a committee "to investigate the case of Mrs. McGrath and do anything possible to alleviate the suffering of John McGrath." Thomas Galena spent the last seventeen years of his life in and out of the Galen tuberculosis and the Warm Springs mental hospitals. The RELA paid all his dues and medical costs, secured his release from Warm Springs in the association's care, and brought him home.[80]

There was one other form of associational relief, one in which the RELA seems to have been the more active of the two Irish societies. The Emmets sent members to sit with and nurse "afflicted brothers" during the night. These nurses were paid the standard Butte scale of $3.50 for an eight-hour "shift," the money coming out of the RELA sick fund. It appears that only the very sick or the severely injured were assigned nurses. Obviously, providing medical attention was less the object than combating fear and loneliness. Dying away from home was a frightening prospect and the comforting presence of an old friend from Butte—often, it would seem, a man originally from the same village in Ireland—extended the definition of home and quieted some of the terrors. These vigils took place in an injured or ill member's home or in the hospital; they lasted as long as a man needed help.[81]

When a member of either organization died, resolutions of condolence were passed, sent to the nearest relative—often in Ireland—and published in local and Irish newspapers. The AOH was kept so busy with this responsibility that it composed "blank suitable resolutions of condolence . . . to suit single and married members" to speed the process. The resolutions were predictable in content. Ed Gilmore was described as an "ardent and consistent supporter of Irish independence"; Peter Harrington had been an "active and esteemed member, Company A, Irish Volunteers"; with the death of Con Murphy, the AOH "lost a faithful member, the National League of Ireland an earnest worker, and Ireland a true, devoted and patriotic son."[82]

Not all the references were to Ireland; Eugene Sullivan and James McGrath were acknowledged as Montana pioneers, both were among the "first settlers of the area." But generally these resolutions offer strong support for Kerby Miller's thesis that the Irish thought of themselves as exiled, as a people forcibly kept from home. The resolution on the death in 1911 of Anthony Shovlin is a perfect case in point. Shovlin was born in County Donegal in 1864, emigrated in 1884, came to Butte from Arizona in 1887. He had "met with the vicissitudes that are too often the lot of the Irish exile." A disciple of "Tone, Emmet, Mitchell, and Stephens, . . . the dream of his life was to see Ireland a free and independent nation."[83]

The vicissitudes of Shovlin's life and his dreams of Irish freedom were the common stuff of the Butte Irishman. But in one important way, the resolution upon his death was different from most. Shovlin was forty-seven years old, almost an old man by Butte standards. The references that appear most often are those that comment on how early death had come, on its "untimeliness." These were not thought necessary for Anthony Shovlin. More typical entries appeared in the Minute Books of the RELA for June 19, June 26, and July 10, 1902. The first noted that "number 46" (Cornelius McGee) had been "crushed in the mines and seriously injured." The next established a committee of three "to draft resolutions on the death of our Bro. Con McGee." The last was a copy of the resolutions. McGee had "been taken in the prime of his life." (He was only twenty-three.) He had been a "good and obedient son," and a "patriotic Irishman." The original of the resolution was ordered sent to McGee's mother and father in Donegal, with copies to the Butte newspapers.[84]

The associations were also in charge of wakes and burials. Death might come violently and sooner even than workers had a right to expect, but they would have no paupers' graves, no unattended wakes. In death, if not always in life, these working Irishmen would be accorded a proper respect, and no Protestant or bourgeois sensibilities figured to intrude. The wakes, particularly in the early years, were three-day and three-night affairs; bands played, the women keened, the men reminisced and grieved, celebrated and told lies—about the deceased and about themselves. It was said that more rock was broken at an Irish wake than could possibly have been loaded and taken from the mines. The wakes represented, in other words, the same mix of solemnity and hilarity as they had in Ireland. They were just as culturally determined and as culturally necessary in the new world of Butte as in the old world of West Cork or Donegal.[85]

Funerals were as carefully organized. The associations bought the flowers and wreaths, arranged the funeral mass, and provided a formal escort for the family of the deceased. The AOH had a policy of fining members for unexcused absences from another member's funeral, but there is no evidence that any fines were assessed. Full attendance at funerals was the rule, if for no other reason than that members wanted to insure full attendance at their own. The point was always to give back some of the dignity that workplace deaths had taken away. It was for this reason, too, that the RELA disinterred the remains of Miles Burke from Warm Springs and moved them to "the Catholic Cemetery where he could have a headstone." A collection was taken up for Phil Fogarty "to insure him a decent burial." The AOH sent a committee "to attend to the remains of our late brother William Hyland when taken from the mine."[86]

Both organizations also maintained plots at St. Patrick's cemetery; the RELA's was (and still is) dominated by an eighteen-foot memorial, complete with harps and shamrocks and dedicated to Ireland and the Clan-na-Gael. The Hibernians had a cemetery house, befitting the "position, strength, and dignity of the AOH in this community." The plots were carefully tended, money being appropriated for mowing, watering the flowers, and general upkeep. Celtic crosses were much in evidence.[87]

VI

Thus did this community of Irish miners attempt to deal with the insecurities and hazards, both physical and psychological, of life in the world's greatest mining city. Eric Hobsbawm has written of the importance to manual workers of safeguarding against their "primary life risks . . . namely accidents, sickness and old age, loss of time, underemployment, periodic unemployment, and competition from a labor surplus." He could have been speaking of Butte and of its Irish miner enclave. Led by its Irish associations, the enclave found steady employment for its members, then attempted to absorb and blunt some of the risks that employment entailed. In the process it freed public agencies—and to a lesser extent, the Miners' Union—from having to provide these services, and freed the Irish from having to attach themselves to non-Irish organizations to get them. Ethnic loyalties were, as a result, enhanced rather than surrendered, even to the point that Irish and miner became mutually reinforcing roles.[88]

There were countless instances of community-provided support and relief, and no Irishman, however young and healthy, can have missed the lessons taught by each. When John O'Leary, a member of the RELA, spoke of "our people" and how he "hoped the brothers [would] do all they can to help each other out"; when Patrick Kelly of the AOH urged the "brothers to stay by each other and always support a brother in distress," they were believed. There were no self-congratulatory cries of individualism from this associational working class.[89]

Nothing makes the importance of the community's assumption of risk clearer, however unconscious the lesson, than a U.S. Navy recruiting notice that appeared, curiously, in the *Montana Socialist*. The date was May 13, 1916, almost two years after the outbreak of the Great War and less than a year before America's entrance into it. No one, in other words, could have assumed that this was recruitment into a guaranteed peacetime Navy. Even war, however, was made to seem preferable to life in Butte's mines.

Mining jobs, said the Navy, were uncertain; there were strikes, layoffs, and the omnipresent threat of illness; even a mild one meant lost wages and high medical costs. The Navy promised steady work, paychecks that came whether sick or well, and free medical and hospital care. A disabling illness or injury meant economic catastrophe for the miner, no job, no prospect of a job, no income. The disabled Navy man received a "generous pension." Accidental death in the mines, "stuffy, gloomy" places at best, left "your family with only what you've saved." The Navy's death benefits were six months' pay and full pension benefits to the survivors. In the mines, promotion was slow and uncertain and marked by favoritism. In the Navy it was sure and quick and "the best man wins." Old miners were not just scarce, they were unknown. Illness and age related debilities meant their jobs went "to younger men." Navy men, on the other hand, retired after only thirty years' service, service spent, moreover, in "fresh air, sun, sea, clean, healthful, athletic life," at three-fourths their pay at the time of retirement.[90]

This was a remarkable set of comparisons. But what marks it, other than an unintentional gallows humor, was how near the AOH and the RELA came to providing the same kinds of security the Navy promised. The point is not that military service was a form of early twentieth-century welfarism—though the emphasis on security indicated not just the Navy's but the government's assumption of new responsibilities. What the recruiting notice did was provide a kind of checklist against which the "welfarism" of Irish associationalism can be measured and tested. Given the hazards and uncertainties of Butte, the associations, in fact the entire community, performed remarkably.

NOTES

1. Bodnar, *Workers' World*, pp. 1–2, 63–65, 177–79. For workers' fear of unemployment, see Keyssar, *Out of Work*. The O'Neill quote is from Miller, *Emigrants*, p. 498.

2. Hobsbawm, "Aristocracy." The "never mind how" quote is from p. 234; my emphasis. See also "Debating Labor Aristocracy" and "Artisan and Labour Aristocrats." Walkowitz discusses some of these same matters in *Worker City*, pp. 95–96, 152–53.

3. Bodnar, *Workers' World*, pp. 4–9, 65, 165–85. On this same point see Kraditor, pp. 2, 372n56; Henretta, "Social Mobility," pp. 28–41.

4. On miner mobility, see Ronald C. Brown, *Hard-Rock Miners*, pp. 10–11; Wyman, *Hardrock Epic*, pp. 58–59, 252–53; Malone, *Battle for Butte*, pp. 5–8, 57–58. The Brondel quote is from a letter to Bishop Monaco, Sept. 18, 1888, Brondel Papers. AOH, Membership and Dues Ledger, July, 1901–Feb. 1902. On receiving transfers from shut-down mines and towns see RELA, MB, May 31, 1888; June 13, July 1, July 22, 1889; Aug. 21, 1890; Feb. 11, 18, 1897; Dec. 13, 1900; Aug. 4, Sept. 1, 1904; June 8, Oct. 5, Dec. 12, 1905; Feb. 8, Sept. 20, Nov. 1, 1906. Union miners were often "deported" after unsuccessful strikes. See, for example, Western Federation of Miners (WFM), Executive Board, MB, May 25, Dec. 12, 1903; June 14, 1904; Dec. 9, 1905.

5. For the labor problems of 1878 and 1887 see Frisch, " 'Gibraltar of Unionism' "; MacPherson, "Butte Miners' Union," pp. 1–14; Smith, "Rise and Fall," pp. 3–23; Malone, *Battle for Butte*, pp. 76–77. The problems in 1891, 1893, and 1903 are discussed in WPA, *Copper Camp*, p. 288; Malone, *Battle for Butte*, pp. 40, 41, 54–56, 173–79; Clinch, *Urban Populism*, pp. 85–122. Hugh O'Daly's reference to "Sweeds and Norway emegrants" is in his Life, [30]. *Anaconda Standard*, Oct. 23, 1903; P. J. Brophy in a letter to "Miss Barclay," Jan. 28, 1903, suggested that an oversupply of copper might create problems later in the year (Brophy Papers). For the effects of the 1903 shut down on the Irish associations, see AOH D1, MB, Oct. 28, Nov. 18, 1903; AOH, Day Books, 1903, passim.

6. For the shutdown see Malone, *Battle for Butte*, pp. 193, 203, 208–9; Wyman, *Hardrock Epic*, p. 240. On another corporation's response to inventory recession see Walkowitz, *Worker City*, p. 183. There is reference in the "History of St. Mary's" to keeping married men on. See also AOH D3, MB, Sept. 23, 1907. For the increased activities of the RELA see MB, Sept. 26, Nov. 14, Dec. 12, 19, 1907.

7. "History of St. Mary's"; AOH, *Proceedings,* 1910. References to the need for a new hall and the cancellation of the plans are in AOH, Silver Bow Co. Board of Directors, MB, Dec. 23, 1907. The McCarthy quote is from AOH D1, MB, Apr. 20, 1908. McCarthy was a well-to-do grocer (Polk, *City Directory,* 1908. The scholarship fund is mentioned in AOH D1, MB, May 4, 1908. Irish Volunteers, MB, Feb. 9, 1908. Mahoney's quote is from AOH D1, MB, Dec. 1, 1907. For further evidence of hard times for the Irish see AOH D3, MB, Sept. 23, 30, Oct. 21, 1907; Jan. 6, Mar. 30, 1908.

8. Taylor, *Distant Magnet,* pp. 48–65. There were strikes in Colorado in 1880, 1896, and 1903–4; in Idaho in 1886, 1892, and 1899; in Arizona in 1906; in South Dakota in 1910; in Michigan in 1913–14. See Vernon Jensen, *Heritage of Conflict,* pp. 19–54, 72–88, 96–160, 250–55, 272–88; Lingenfelter, *Hardrock Miners,* 170–77. The Immigration Commission said union men were drawn to Butte by its reputation as a union town (*Immigrants in Industries,* part III, pp. 109, 115).

9. Hand et al. "Songs," p. 20; Hand, "Folklore," p. 1; Wyman, *Hardrock Epic,* p. 169; Gedicks, "Ethnicity," p. 147; Erickson, *American Industry,* pp. 5–8. As early as 1892 a Montana promotional pamphlet stated that "rock drills and black powder are the real miners"; no pick-and-shovel work was required (McKnight, *Mines of Montana,* p. 21).

10. Hobsbawm, "Debating Labor Aristocracy," pp. 215, 220–21.

11. On the formation of the Amalgamated, the "war of the copper kings," and the consolidation of the mines, see Malone, *Battle for Butte,* pp. 131–211. Amalgamated and Anaconda "traded" corporate names and ownership between 1899 and 1915. These corporate moves are unimportant to this study and ACM or the company will be used to mean either Anaconda or Amalgamated. Malone argues that the consolidation of 1906 was necessary to stable employment (pp. 155, 188). This was not true for the Irish. For the effects of corporate consolidation in another industrial town see Walkowitz, *Worker City,* pp. 27–29.

12. Membership figures for the AOH are in Membership and Dues Ledgers. For the RELA, the most convenient source is the Term Reports to the National Clan-na-Gael.

13. AOH, *Proceedings,* 1910; RELA, MB, May 4, 1905. On the thirty-seven new Hibernians see AOH D1, MB, Feb. 10, 17, 1904. These men were proposed for membership by Dennis O'Neill, a timekeeper at one of the mines (Polk, *City Directory,* 1904). Thirty-four men were proposed on Apr. 27 and May 4, 1904 (AOH D1, MB). Con Kelley's remark is in Industrial Commission, *Mining at Butte,* 1915, p. 3701. Kelley was an AOH member. See AOH, Membership and Dues Ledgers. He was also an ex-miner and the son of Jeremiah Kelley, Irish-born and an old and close friend of Marcus Daly. See O'Daly, *Life,* [235–37], and Marcosson, *Anaconda,* pp. 27–29. See also the remarks of Dan Madden, the Irish president of the Silver Bow County Trades and Labor Council on the significance of steady work to Butte workmen in Industrial Commission, *Mining at Butte,* 1915, p. 3831. See also Bodnar, *Workers' World,* p. 185, and Hobsbawm, "Aristocracy," pp. 227–28.

14. For evidence that family and church were involved in other towns see, for example, Dennis Clark, *Irish in Philadelphia*, p. 68; Burchell, *San Francisco Irish*, pp. 94–95; Erickson, *American Industry*, pp. 95, 98; David Ward, *Cities and Immigrants*, pp. 57–58. Bureau of Census, *MS Census*, 1900 and 1910. John Commons, who headed up the Industrial Commission that visited Butte in 1915, would write about the AOH and the mine owners in his *History of Labor*, II (1918–35), in Walkowitz, *Worker City*, pp. 168–69.

15. AOH, *Ritual and Manual, 1901*, p. 5. On the senselessness of enrolling new members and not finding jobs for them, see AOH D3, MB, Sept. 21, 1908. J. J. Lynch "interviewed John D. Ryan in the employment interests of the D (cipher for camp)" (RELA, MB, Nov. 14, 1907). See also AOH D1, MB, Aug. 2, 1905. Kenny's remarks are in AOH D3, MB, Aug. 20, 1905. The "most influential brothers" reference is from RELA, MB, Oct. 29, 1903.

16. The identification and occupation of the job committeemen come from organization MBs and city directories for given years. Union officers from 1878 to 1896–97 were given in the *Butte Bystander*, June 7, 1896, and Mar. 7, 1897. The charge that Hennessy's was a "company store" is in the *Reveille* (Butte), Sept. 10, 1902, and repeated in Malone, *Battle for Butte*, p. 59. James Maher's offices in the Butte Miner's Union and the Western Federation of Miners is noted in Vernon Jensen, *Heritage of Conflict*, p. 57, and Boyce, "Diary," Boyce Papers. For the RELA the numbers of the committeemen must be checked against the name/number list at the back of the Membership and Dues Ledgers. Job committees are mentioned in AOH D1, MB, Aug. 16, 1893; Feb. 7, July 24, 1894; Mar. 6, 1901; Sept. 23, 1903; July 13, 1904; Aug. 20, 1905; Jan. 10, 1906. For AOH D3, see MB, July 31, 1905; July 12, 1909; Jan. 8, 1910. There was a countywide, interdivisional committee in 1909. See AOH, Silver Bow County Board of Directors, MB, May 10, 1909. For the RELA, see MB, Sept. 8, 1892; June 1, 1893; May 3, 1900; Jan. 18, 1903; Nov. 14, 1907. The Irish Volunteers also had job committees. See MB, Aug. 16, 1914; Feb. 28, 1915.

17. Brophy to Scallon, Mar. 14, 1902, Brophy Papers. O'Daly counted and listed the Irish mine officers (Life, [156]).

18. Other sources for mine foremen and shift bosses include Hand, "Folklore," pp. 159, 163, 177; Hand et al., "Songs," pp. 9, 23–25, 29, 31, 33, 38, 40, 44, 46; WPA, *Copper Camp*, pp. viii, 173, 200–202, 207, 209–10; Lindsay, *Amazing Experiences*, pp. 81–82; Marcosson, *Anaconda*, pp. 22, 41; city directories occasionally listed shifters and foremen in uppercase letters; see passim. The names listed in these various sources were checked against AOH and RELA, Membership and Dues Ledgers. Lawlor's comment is from AOH D3, MB, Sept. 21, 1908.

19. For Ryan, in particular, see Malone, *Battle for Butte*, pp. 165–67, and O'Daly, Life, [235–37]. O'Daly said Ryan "belonged to all the Irish societies," [236]. Brondell to the *Catholic Sentinel*, Oct. 3, 1888, Brondel Papers. The "Protestant Ore" reference is in Hand, "Folklore," p. 167. See Marcosson's comments on the Irishness of the company (*Anaconda*, pp. 60, 76, 100–101).

20. David Ryan's comment is from AOH D3, MB, Oct. 5, 1908; John J. McCarthy's is from ibid., Apr. 19, 1913. McCarthy's job and union involvement

are noted in Polk, *City Directory*, 1908. On native owners and immigrant workers see Richard Peterson, *Bonanza Kings*, pp. 3–10; Wyman, *Hardrock Epic*, pp. 56–58.

21. RELA, MB, Nov. 5, 1903; Aug. 22, Sept. 26, Oct. 10, 1907.

22. AOH, *Constitution, 1886; Bylaws, 1887, Ritual and Manual of AOH, 1901;* AOH, *Ritual of the AOH in America;* AOH, *Constitution, 1923;* AOH, D1, Memorandum, Mar. 1, 1907, in MB; "Applications for Memberships," agenda item, in MB, passim; AOH, "Black Books," n.d., n.p., pocket-sized summary of division rules, including membership eligibility rules and nominating procedures.

23. AOH D3, MB, Feb. 24, Mar. 23, 30, July 6, 1908; AOH D1, MB, Mar. 16, 1908. On the tendency of enclave workers to return to the enclave, see Bodnar, *Workers' World*, p. 66.

24. AOH D1, Membership and Dues Ledgers. The partial list is from men proposing others for membership. Applications for Membership; Proposers and Committeemen, agenda item, MB, 1907, passim.

25. RELA, Membership and Dues Ledgers; "Vacant Numbers List, beginning 25 June, 1903," in Membership and Dues Ledger, 1899–1903. For example, in 1903 #38 was transferred from Charles McDermott, who had died, to Daniel J. Hennessy. Hennessy had been an RELA member since 1882; his previous number had been 98 and it was transferred to Jeremiah Mahoney. Hennessy died in 1908 and on Mar. 1, 1909, #38 was passed to Pat Gallagher. He died in 1910 and in 1914 the number was assigned to John J. Sullivan, who held it until he was dropped from the rolls in 1921. RELA, Membership and Dues Ledger, 1903–25.

26. For the investigating committees and blackballing, see AOH and RELA, MBs, passim. The Pat Murray/Callahan story is from AOH D1, MB, Jan. 20, 1892. See also WPA, *Copper Camp*, pp. 1, 72, 190–94, 273. Reference to the rules regarding gambling, Mass and meeting attendance, and drinking and fighting can be found in AOH, *Constitution, 1886; Bylaws, 1887;* AOH D1, MB, Apr. 20, 1892; Aug. 10, 1896; Oct. 25, 1899; Jan. 24, Feb. 21, 1906; AOH D3, MB, Feb. 5, 12, 1906; Apr. 15, 1907; Nov. 2, 1912; Mar. 13, 1913; RELA, MB, Dec. 29, 1882; Apr. 4, 1889; Dec. 12, 1901; Irish Volunteers, MB, n.d. The AOH also "demanded the relocation" of Butte's restricted (red-light) district (AOH, D3, MB, Aug. 19, 1907). Matthew Cummings, National President, AOH in America, to Officers and Members, AOH, Jan. 21, 1907, Correspondence; RELA, MB, Aug. 28, 1890; AOH D1, MB, Mar. 18, May 6, 1903; AOH D3, MB, June 15, 1912.

27. The "Ireland sober" quotation is from Lyons, *Culture and Anarchy*, pp. 79–80. See also Devoy, *Post Bag*, II:97; *Irish World*, Nov. 8, 1879. On industrialization and sobriety, see Wilentz, *Chants Democratic*, pp. 281–84, 324–25; Walters, *American Reformers*, pp. 123–43; Stivers, *Hair of the Dog*, p. 48; Gutman, "Protestantism and the American Labor Movement," pp. 19–21, 69; Rorabaugh, *Alcoholic Republic*, pp. 129–34. Kelley's remarks are in Industrial Commission, *Mining at Butte*, 1915, p. 3863.

28. Kennedy's comment is in AOH D3, MB, Sept. 23, 1907. J. J. Conway said later in the shutdown that the Hibernians were still "getting their share

of jobs" (ibid., Dec. 30, 1907). Hannan's remarks are in ibid., Dec. 21, 1908. For similar expressions of the belief that the Hibernians were the "best sort" of Irishmen see James F. Brown to "My dear Ryan [John D.?]," Feb. 13, 1907, AOH, Correspondence; AOH D3, MB, Oct. 5, 1912; P. J. Brophy to Conor O'Kelly, June 20, 1904, Brophy Papers.

29. Hobsbawm, "Aristocracy," p. 231. There was, however, a strong distinction between a miner and a mucker, between those who dug and drilled the ore and those who merely picked it up. For a discussion of the skills of the trade, including reference to drilling contests, see Ronald C. Brown, *Hardrock Miners*, pp. 54–56; 70–71; Lingenfelter, *Hardrock Miners*, p. 83; Wyman, *Hardrock Epic*, p. 14; *Butte Bystander*, June 17, July 8, 1893; June 21, 1894; Mar. 16, 1895. The U.S. Commissioner General of Immigration categorized immigrant miners as skilled workmen (*Annual Report*, 1903, p. 24). See also the reference to Irish miners as "skilled workmen at the time of their emigration" (Immigration Commission, *Immigrants in Industries*, 1911, part 25, pp. 100–101). For evidence that the miners understood that theirs was a skilled trade, see Industrial Commission, *Mining at Butte*, 1911, p. 3912. That the mine owners shared this conviction is seen in the remarks of Con Kelley in ibid., 1915, p. 3695.

30. Bodnar argues that hiring officers often let the ethnic networks fill out their crews (*Workers' World*, p. 174). See also Bodnar, Simon, and Weber, *Lives of Their Own*, p. 59. J. J. Lynch's remarks are in RELA, MB, Oct. 29, 1903; Breen's are in AOH D3, MB, Mar. 30, 1908; Kealy's in *ibid.*, July 9, 1910.

31. Bodnar, *Workers' World*, p. 174. In the middle of the shutdown of 1903, the AOH held "its grandest party ever," a clear signal of intent (D1, MB, Nov. 25. 1903).

32. *Helena Independent*, Feb. 20, 1889. See also *Butte Mining Journal*, Feb. 20, 1889. The Parrot story is from Hand, "Folklore," p. 178.

33. *Examiner* (Butte), June 15, 1895; Feb. 27, Mar. 19, Apr. 19, Oct. 31, 1896.

34. Keir Hardy's remarks are from the *Anaconda Standard*, Oct. 9, 1895. See also *Butte Bystander*, Apr. 6, June 29, July 16, 1895; May 24, 1896. See also Lingenfelter, *Hardrock Miners*, pp. 190–94.

35. *Examiner* (Butte), June 15, 1895; *Butte Bystander*, Apr. 16, July 16, 1895; AOH D1, MB, Jan. 17, 1894.

36. The advantages of an ethnically mixed work force are discussed in William Read to Walker Brothers, July 18, 1878, Alice Mining Co. Records, Letter Press Books. See also *Miners Magazine* (Denver), May, Aug., and Dec., 1900; Immigration Commission, *Immigrants in Industries*, 1911, part 25, pp. 156–57; Industrial Commission, *Mining at Butte*, 1915, p. 3747; Lingenfelter, *Hardrock Miners*, p. 225; Cantor, "Introduction," pp. 15–18. The *Montana Socialist* commented on how the "Babel of Tongues" hurt the cause of worker solidarity (Nov. 13, 1915). The AOH complained that hard-line Protestants refused "to enter into an agreement with Catholics for a strike"; O'Dea, *AOH*, III:1108.

37. The 1894 statistics are taken from Anaconda Copper Mining Company, General Office, Subject File 522, ACM Papers. On the percentage of English see Bureau of the Census, *12th Census, Population*, p. 798; Immigration Com-

mission, *Immigrants in Industries*, 1911, part 25, p. 111. As late as 1914, 19.3 percent of ACM miners were Irish. Montana, Dept. of Labor, *First Biennial Report*, p. 206. For the "Irish mines" see Hand et al., "Songs," p. 7; Hand, "Folklore," p. 177; WPA, *Copper Camp*, p. 173; Brosnan to mother, June 19, 1917, Brosnan Letters. The handball courts are shown on Sanborn's *Fire Insurance Map of Butte, Montana, 1900*. I am indebted to Brian Shovers of Butte for bringing this to my attention. The posting of job notices in Gaelic and the automatic jobs for Irish were mentioned by Father Sarsfield O'Sullivan, interview. The Irish were not alone in this practice: The Mountain View Mine was so overwhelmingly Cornish it was called the "Saffron Bun." Malone, *Battle for Butte*, p. 66.

38. The first set of figures is drawn from a report in the *Engineering and Mining Journal* and cited in Wyman, *Hardrock Epic*, p. 115; the second set is quoted without acknowledgment of source by the *Montana Socialist*, May 25, 1913. Wyman's point on the underestimation of the hazards in American mines is in *Hardrock Epic*, p. 115. The percentage of men working aboveground was obtained from data in Montana, Dept. of Labor and Industry, *Report*, 1914, pp. 293, 295. Ironically, these deaths opened up new jobs. See, for another industry, Walkowitz, *Worker City*, p. 39.

39. Montana, Dept. of Labor and Industry, *First Biennial Report*, p. 297. Figures from the coal-producing areas are from *Butte Bystander*, Feb. 17, 24, 1894.

40. ACM figures are from the Industrial Commission, *Mining at Butte*, 1915, 3874–79.

41. *Butte Mining Journal*, Nov. 2, 1887; Nov. 24, 1889; *Butte Miner*, Apr. 23, 1909; Jan. 20, 1904; July 7, 1907. The Ed Dolan story is in the *Butte Mining Journal*, Dec. 18, 1889. Butte/Silver Bow Co. Archives has a convenient index of newspaper references to accidental deaths in the mines. Major disasters are listed in the *Anaconda Standard*, June 9, 1917. See also the *Butte Bystander* of Apr. 14, 1896, for a story on the death in an explosion in the St. Lawrence Mine of Con Lowney, John Quinlan, Ed Shields, James Dwyer, John McVeigh, and Patrick O'Rourke. Obviously, all-Irish crews sometimes meant all-Irish casualty lists. Records from St. Lawrence O'Toole were from 1897 to 1922; *Anaconda Standard*, Mar. 12, 1922. The cemetery "population" figure is from WPA, *Copper Camp*, p. 163.

42. The song about paving the streets with Irish bones was related to me by Kara Kelly of New York City and Carroll College, Helena. Her Irish-born grandmother remembered hearing it. Hugh O'Daly promised his mother before leaving for America that he would not work underground in the mines (Life, [235]). Other songs are taken from Hand et al., "Songs," pp. 12–13, 15. Hand mentions the Larry Duggans in "Folklore," p. 6n15. Beatrice Murphy, "Diary of a Night Nurse." I am indebted to Teresa Jordan of Butte for giving me a copy of this diary. Brosnan to father, Feb. 18, 1917, Brosnan Letters; Gore-Booth (Countess Markievicz), *Prison Letters*, p. 289.

43. Hand, "Folklore," p. 154n2. Galen, about thirty miles northwest of Butte, was the home of the state tuberculosis hospital. That breathing the dry, silicate

dust of the mines led to TB was confirmed in Bureau of Mines, *Preliminary Report*, p. 11. The lethal effects of miners' con were often delayed. Marcus Daly's death at the age of sixty-one was partly attributable to his earlier work underground. See *Miners Magazine*, Jan. 1901; so, too, was the death, at age seventy-four, of the Irish-born president of the Western Federation of Miners, Edward Boyce. See "Autopsy on Death of Edward Boyce," Portland, Ore., 1941, Boyce Papers. In 1909, of 5,911 total deaths in Silver Bow County, a remarkable 1,148 (27.3 percent) were from tuberculosis. Montana, Dept. of Labor, *First Biennial Report*, p. 223.

44. Silver Bow County, "Mortuary Records, 1906–07," in Butte/Silver Bow Public Archives; Bureau of Mines, *Preliminary Report*, pp. 12–14; *Anaconda Standard*, Jan. 17, 1898; *Butte Mining Journal*, Sept. 21, 1887.

45. Butte Historical Society, "The Mines of Butte," (pamphlet and map, 1985). Silver Bow Co., Board of Health, "Report on Sanitary Conditions," pp. 6, 9, 10, 15, 25, 26; Joe Shannon commented on the fact that workers in the hot boxes never urinated (Industrial Commission, *Mining at Butte*, 1915, p. 3853). At that, it was reported that Butte mines were cooler than those of the Comstock (Hand, "Songs," p. 44n75). Brian Shovers of Butte said that the men were hoisted at a rate of about 500 feet per minute. Ore could be hoisted at 3,000 feet per minute. See Montana, Dept. of Labor, *First Biennial Report*, p. 314. The reference to the steam coming off the miners' bodies is from Kevin Shannon (interview); Curtin interview.

46. Silver Bow Co., Board of Health, "Report on Sanitary Conditions," pp. 1–3, 7, 15–17, 20–21, 24.

47. Ibid., pp. 1–4, 7, 9, 11–13.

48. Ibid., pp. 1, 3, 6, 12, 16–17, 19–20. See also Industrial Commission, *Mining at Butte*, 1915, p. 3837.

49. Silver Bow Co., Board of Health, "Report on Sanitary Conditions," p. 24. The remark about prohibition is from the *Miners Magazine*, July 9, 1914. "St. Monday" referred to the workers' habit of heavy drinking on Sunday followed by an unofficial "holy day" on Monday. The comment of the "reformer" Charles Loring Brace on the habits of New York's working class are worth quoting. "The liquor-shop is his picture-gallery, club, reading room and social salon. . . . His glass is the magic transmuter of drear to cheerfulness, of penury to plenty, and of a low, ignorant, worried life, to an existence for the moment buoyant, contented and hopeful." Quoted in Taylor, *Distant Magnet*, p. 213.

50. Silver Bow Co., Board of Health, "Report on Sanitary Conditions," pp. 13, 20–22. See also the testimony of Dr. C. H. Horst, city health officer, in Industrial Commission, *Mining at Butte*, 1915, p. 3845. Evidence that the miners thought that ventilation could be improved is provided by the testimony of Butte Irish labor leader Dan Holland in ibid., 1911, p. 3909. Persistence and safe or safer jobs is discussed in Walkowitz, *Worker City*, p. 74.

51. Silver Bow Co., Board of Health, "Report on Sanitary Conditions," pp. 3, 31, 34. That experienced miners sought out well-ventilated mines was noted

in Industrial Commission, *Mining at Butte*, 1911, p. 3914. See also Ronald C. Brown, *Hard-Rock Miners*, p. 69.

52. WPA, *Copper Camp*, p. 205; Bureau of Mines, *Preliminary Report*, pp. 7–9. Industrial Commission, *Mining at Butte*, 1915, pp. 3697, 3858.

53. On the ease of changing mines when most of them were owned by the same company, see Industrial Commission, *Mining at Butte*, 1911, pp. 3904–5, 3949, 3952. The reference to "fine day" miners is from ibid., 1915, p. 3857. See also ibid., 1915, p. 3865, where Con Kelley, rather heatedly, denied that he had been a "fine day" miner. On this point see Marcosson, *Anaconda*, p. 71. The "capon" label is from Hand, "Folklore," p. 164. It was said that the sons of men "with influence" got summer jobs on the surface. "Less fortunate kids" worked underground; WPA, *Copper Camp*, p. 158.

54. Frisch, " 'Gibraltar of Unionism,' " p. 22. The "Don't Get Hurt" sign is from the *Montana Socialist*, Oct. 23, 1915.

55. On the Irish associations seeking day-shift or light work see RELA, MB, Feb. 18, 1904; AOH D1, MB, July 18, 1900; AOH D3, MB, July 30, 1906; July 1, 1911; Mar. 2, 1912; Jan. 22, Apr. 8, 1916. See also J. J. Griffin to Walter Sewell, Oct. 25, 1921, and Griffin to T. F. Sullivan, Sept. 27, 1926, AOH Correspondence.

56. Cantor, "Introduction," p. 16. Nicholson's funeral was covered in the *Butte Bystander*, Oct. 24, 25, 1894. There were other instances of Irish-Cornish cooperation during the 1880s and 1890s, many of them reported in the Cornishman William Penrose's *Butte Mining Journal*. See, for example, the issues of Dec. 14, 24, 31, 1887; Jan. 7, 17, 1888; May, 10, 1891. Penrose even got the contract from the AOH for printing the organization's constitution and bylaws in 1886. For the insistence on equal pay for equal dangers see, respectively, *Labor World* (Butte), Apr. 28, 1902, and WFM, *Preamble to . . . Constitution*.

57. Hand et al., "Songs," pp. 9–14; Hand, "Folklore," pp. 13–18, 20, 24.

58. The Cornish also developed a strong enclave. However, the consolidation of the Butte mines in 1906 led many of the Cornish to leave the district; consolidation made it more difficult to secure mining leases and contract work (Immigration Commission, *Immigrants in Industries*, 1911, part 25, p. 115).

59. Frisch, " 'Gibraltar of Unionism,' " p. 22. See also the remarks of Judge J. J. Lynch in the *Montana Socialist*, Aug. 25, 1917. Elsewhere in the western mining districts, the Irish may have been unusually willing to take chances; an "Irish dividend" was the term used to describe the profits that resulted from the Irish "going deeper" (Lingenfelter, *Hardrock Miners*, p. 62).

60. Industrial Commission, *Mining at Butte*, 1915, p. 3857. See also WPA, *Copper Camp*, p. 53.

61. On the pride miners took in their work, see the remarks of John Brophy cited in Brody, *Workers in Industrial America*, pp. 3–4.

62. Bureau of Census, *MS Census*, 1900 and 1910. National statistics on Irish intergenerational mobility were noted in the *Montana Catholic*, Oct. 14, 1899. They offer indisputable evidence that second-generation Irish were leaving the

factories for better-paying jobs. The point about Butte is that there weren't any (or many) better-paying jobs than those in the mines.

63. Immigration Commission, *Immigrants in Industries*, 1911, part 18, p. 563; see also part 25, p. 115.

64. Miners' wives may also have discouraged their sons from working underground. Congresswoman Jeanette Rankin, for example, reported that she received hundreds of letters from miners' wives about the dangers of working in the mines. Rankin concluded that the women "lived in constant anxiety." *Montana Socialist*, Aug. 18, 1917. See also Hand, "Folklore," pp. 14–15.

65. For James J. Sullivan see "Death Certificate," Castletownbere, Co. Cork, Ireland, to AOH, Sept. 30, 1911, Correspondence. For Pat Mannix, see Silver Bow County, "Mortuary Records, 1906–07."

66. The fifteen-year work expectancy was mentioned by Jacob Oliver, an experienced miner, in Industrial Commission, *Mining at Butte*, 1915, p. 3839; see also 1911, p. 3916. Father Pat Brosnan was less optimistic, reporting to his parents that the men "always die after ten years"; to father, Feb. 18, 1917; "a man will die after seven years"; to father, n.d. [1917?], and the men "live no longer than five or six years"; to mother, June 19, 1917; Brosnan Letters. Dan Sullivan's comments are from Industrial Commission, *Mining at Butte*, 1911, p. 3929. AOH and RELA, Membership and Dues Ledgers.

67. Industrial Commission, *Mining at Butte*, 1911, pp. 3924–27, 3939, 3978. On shift-boss rivalries in other industries see Brody, *Workers in Industrial America*, pp. 9–11.

68. Industrial Commission, *Mining at Butte*, 1911 and 1915, pp. 3719, 3842, 3952.

69. AOH, *Constitution, 1886;* MB, Apr. 9, 1902; Memorandum, Mar. 1, 1907; "Black Book," n.d. The national AOH in America paid $24 million in sick and death benefits from its founding in 1836 to 1926; "Bulletin #2, AOH in America," 1926, in Correspondence. On RELA sick and death benefits see MB, Mar. 27, 1884; Oct. 6, 1892; July 20, 1893; Aug. 27, 1896; Nov. 22, 1906; J. J. Lynch to RELA, Nov. 2, 1899; M. J. English to RELA, Sept. 2, 1900, Correspondence. The Irish Volunteers collected money to aid "Comrade" Pat Sullivan, who had been injured (MB, Dec. 5, 1914).

70. For union sick benefits see J. C. Johnson (Butte Miners' Union) to AOH, Oct. 22, 1891, Correspondence; *Anaconda Standard*, June 13, 1896; *Butte Bystander*, Sept. 13, 1896; Dec. 18, 1897; Industrial Commission, *Mining at Butte*, 1911, pp. 3917–18; WFM, *Proceedings, 1910*, pp. 200–203; Butte Workingmen's Union, MB, Nov. 19, 1915; July 7, Nov. 14, 1916, World Museum of Mining. On Montana's Workmen's Compensation, see Dept. of Labor, National Industrial Conference Board, *Workmen's Compensation Acts*, pp. 11, 35; Wyman, *Hardrock Epic*, pp. 199–200. Raffles, dances, and other special benefits are noted in AOH D1, MB, Nov. 19, 1884; Oct. 29, 1897; Dec. 6, 1899; Feb. 28, 1900; Jan. 2, 1901; Aug. 7, 1901; Mar. 8, 1905. RELA, MB, Nov. 16, 1887; Dec. 1, 1892; Mar. 2, 9, 1893; Dec. 6, 1899; May 31, 1900; Aug. 9, 1906; Aug. 22, 1907. Both organizations also interceded with hospitals and mortuaries; see

AOH D1, MB, Sept. 29, 1897; Jan. 31, 1906; RELA, MB, Mar. 26, 1903; Nov. 16, Dec. 7, 1905; Apr. 12, 1906.

71. The figures are drawn from AOH D1, MB, 1884–1908; AOH D1, Treasurer's Reports, 1909–11; AOH D1, Nov. 2, 1898; AOH D1, Auditing Committee, "Report for the Year Ending 31 December, 1910." Reference to death benefits for members' wives is from RELA, MB, Nov. 16, 1887; AOH D1, MB, Mar. 8, 1905; AOH, Quarterly Report, June 30, 1894. The reference to thirteen men drawing benefits is from MB, Aug. 10, 1904. For D3 sick benefits see MB, passim; for an example see Dec. 21, 1907, when $72.00 was paid out in benefits. D3 once had eight pending $500.00 death benefits (MB, Feb. 3, 1908). The five-year experiment with $500.00 death benefits is found in Tim Nolan to T. J. McCarthy, Sept. 9, 1904, Correspondence; AOH D1, MB, Sept. 21, 1904; Sept. 13, 1905; AOH, Silver Bow Co. Board of Directors, MB, Oct. 6, 1909. Daniel Hennessy's widow gave the $500.00 benefit to the Helena Orphans' Home (AOH D3, MB, Apr. 13, May 18, Dec. 7, 1908). There was some criticism of the higher benefits. Father Michael Hannan, for example, thought it appealed only to the wealthy Irish and that the AOH would do better to drop it and increase sick benefits for working-class Irish (AOH, Silver Bow Co. Board of Directors, MB, Sept. 28, Oct. 10, 1908; AOH, D3, MB, Oct. 11, Nov. 9, 1909).

72. AOH, Physicians' Certificates, 1904–11.

73. Ibid.; John Kennedy to AOH, Apr. 1, 1910; Dr. H. W. Fenner to AOH, Apr. 11, 1910, Correspondence.

74. Rental income from Hibernia Hall is conveniently summarized in Hibernia Hall, Board of Trustees, Ledgers and Reports, 1885–1916. In addition to the two breweries, the hall was rented to D. J. Hennessy for the Centerville branch of his department store, to the Sullivan brothers and John Crowley for their saloon, and to Bridget Sullivan for her cigar and candy store. The building fund paid each organization a $500.00 dividend twice a year; see, for example, RELA, MB, Nov. 12, 1903. There were other sources of income. Over $1,800 was made on the summer picnics in both 1890 and 1905; AOH D1, MB, July 16, 1890; Aug. 9, 1905. In 1904, to take a year with high membership, total AOH D1 expenses were $4,119.15; receipts were $6,198.55 (MB, Jan. 8, 1905). For the protests of national AOH exclusion of copper miners see AOH, Committee on Insurance to Officers and Members, Oct. 19, 1903, Correspondence; AOH D1, MB, Nov. 11, 1902; Oct. 14, 1903; Aug. 23, 1905; AOH D3, MB, Mar. 29, Apr. 5, 1913; AOH, *Proceedings, 1906.* O'Dea, *AOH,* III:1174–81.

75. On the suspension or possible suspension of sick benefits see AOH D1, MB, July 20, Aug. 3, 1887; June 19, 1889; Feb. 27, 1901; AOH D3, Jan. 17, 1914; Jan. 2, 1915. Membership drives were discussed in AOH D1, MB, Dec. 26, 1894; April 19, 1899; Dec. 5, 1900; July 19, 1905. The reference to "generosity" and "financial embarrassment" is from ibid., Feb. 6, 1901; AOH, Silver Bow Co. Board of Directors, MB, Apr. 30, 1908. The 1910 fund-raising dance and "amalgamation" of D2 is from AOH D2 to AOH D1, June 1, 1910, Correspondence; AOH, Silver Bow Co. Board of Directors, MB, Nov. 19, 1911.

76. M. J. English to RELA, Sept. 2, 1900. The reverse was also true, i.e., money was moved from sick benefits to the revolutionary fund (MB, Nov. 7, 1901).

77. AOH D1, MB, Oct. 11, 18, 1899. Evidence that physicians routinely misrepresented certain diseases in order to insure sick benefits comes from Industrial Commission, *Mining at Butte*, 1915, p. 3837. Other checks on fraudulent claims, including fines and expulsions, are mentioned in AOH D1, MB, Aug. 31, 1898; Aug. 30, Sept. 27, 1905; AOH D3, MB, Dec. 17, 1906; AOH, Silver Bow Co. Board of Directors, MB, June 1, 1906; Oct. 10, 1908; Sept. 29, 1909; Article III, revised bylaws, AOH, Silver Bow Co., effective Jan. 1, 1910.

78. For examples of back dues being paid up see RELA, MB, Dec. 12, 1889; June 15, 1904; AOH D1, MB, Oct. 21, 1903. The RELA paid AOH dues for Ed Sheehan; RELA, MB, Dec. 19, 1907. For dues paid out of sick benefits and then another round of sick benefits begun, see AOH D1, MB, July 26, 1905; AOH D3, MB, Apr. 23, 1906. Benefits were paid in advance according to AOH D1, MB, Feb. 3, 1904, and AOH D3, MB, Feb. 24, 1908. Out-of-town Hibernians and Clan-na-Gael members were routinely aided. See, for examples, AOH D1, MB, May 5, 1889; Nov. 18, 1891; May 18, 1892; July 21, 1897; Mar. 29, Nov. 22, 1899; RELA, MB, Dec. 22, 1898. Members paid up for life are noted in AOH D1, MB, Oct. 17, 1900; RELA, MB, Dec. 10, 1903; Apr. 14, Dec. 1, 1904; Oct. 27, 1921; Membership and Dues Ledger, 1899–1903. One RELA member was paid up after he had died. Lawrence Muldoon, RELA #93, died on July 7, 1902; he was placed in "good standing," in other words his back dues were paid up, three days later. His wife thus became eligible for his death benefits. RELA, Membership and Dues Ledger, 1899–1903.

79. For Pat McNichols see AOH D1, MB, May 8, 1895. For Charles Kennedy see ibid., Apr. 5, 1905. In 1910 Kennedy was the proprietor of the Shamrock Saloon in Dublin Gulch (Polk, *City Directory*, 1910). For Noon see AOH D1, MB, Oct. 5, Nov. 2, 16, 1904; Mar. 29, 1905. For Hurley see ibid., Apr. 7, Dec. 15, 1886.

80. For Curley see RELA, MB, Nov. 16, 1887. For Shields see ibid., Jan. 2, Feb. 27, 1896. For McLaughlin see ibid., Aug. 9, 1906. For McBride see ibid., May 7, 1903. For McGrath see ibid., Oct. 17 and 31, 1901. For Galena see ibid., Apr. 5, 1899; July 10, Nov. 13, 1902; Oct. 5, 1905; Apr. 20, 1916.

81. RELA, MB, passim, but see, for examples, May 12, 1892; Dec. 12, 1895; Sept. 8, 1898; May 14, 1903; Nov. 2, 1905. The AOH, particularly in the early years, also assigned nurses. See, for example, D1, MB, Mar. 25, 1886; Nov. 6, 1889; Dec. 3, 1890.

82. References to resolutions being sent to such Irish newspapers as the *Chicago Citizen, Irish World, Gaelic American,* and *Butte Independent* are found in AOH D1, MB, Dec. 3, 1902; RELA, MB, Sept. 5, 1895; Jan. 4, 1912. The "resolution of condolence on the death of Michael Deehan," for example, was "mailed to his family in Ireland" (AOH D3, MB, Apr. 30, 1906). The AOH use of form resolutions is noted in D1, MB Oct. 14, 1903. For Ed Gilmore see RELA, MB, Nov. 26, 1914. For Peter Harrington see ibid., Jan. 16, 1914. For Con Murphy see AOH D1, MB. Nov. 17, 1886.

83. For Eugene Sullivan see AOH D1, MB, Mar. 1, 1899. For McGrath see ibid., Feb. 22, 1899. Miller, *Emigrants.* The "memorial" for Anthony Shovlin is from RELA, MB, Jan. 4, Feb. 12, 1912.

84. McGee's accident and death, with a copy of the resolution of condolence, are recounted in RELA, MB, June 19 and 26, July 10, 1902. For other reference to "untimely" deaths see (for Colman Tierney) AOH D1, MB, Aug. 1, 1898; (for Peter Hale) RELA, MB, Aug. 11, 1905; (for Pat Hanley) ibid., Sept. 21, 1905.

85. For wakes, see examples in AOH D1, MB, Nov. 16, 1898; AOH D3, MB, Mar. 11, 1907. For a fictional account of a Butte wake, complete with the Marcus Daly-like Magnus Dunn in attendance, see Murphy, *Glittering Hill*, pp. 141–67. See also Hand, "Folklore," p. 158; Duffy, *Butte*, p. 298; WPA, *Copper Camp*, pp. 186–89. For a general discussion of waking see Miller, *Emigrants*, pp. 291, 558; Wilentz, "Industrializing America," pp. 583–84; Cantor, "Introduction," p. 10. On the significance of funerals to "lower classes" see Genovese, *Roll, Jordan, Roll*, pp. 201–2.

86. AOH D1, MB, May 18, 1892; June 27, 1896; Feb. 15, 1899; AOH D3, MB, Apr. 9, 1906; RELA, "Quarterly Expenses," Apr., 1910, Cash Books. For Miles Burke see RELA, May 18, 1893. For Phil Fogarty see ibid., June 1, 1905. For William Hyland see AOH D1, MB May 18, 1892.

87. For the Emmet monument see RELA, Financial Ledger, Dec. 1, 1898, Cash Books; contract with R. A. Kitchen, July 12, 1902, noted in MB, July 17, 1902; Apr. 23, 1903. There are repeated references to cemetery plot maintenance. See, for example, RELA, MB, Dec. 1, 1898. The AOH cemetery house was described in P. J. Brophy to "Officers and Members, AOH," Apr. 28, 1903, Brophy Papers.

88. Hobsbawm, "Artisan and Labour Aristocrats," p. 259. Many of the non-Irish and/or non-Catholic organizations, though "not formally condemned by the Church," were considered to "have tendencies dangerous to Catholics"; Bishop John Brondel to C. J. Follet, Oct. 9, 1890, Brondel Papers. The Hibernians even sought a "Hibernian Wing" for Butte's St. James Hospital (AOH D1, MB, Sept. 11, 1901).

89. O'Leary's comment is from RELA, MB, Dec. 12, 1907. Kelly's is from AOH D3, MB, Apr. 9, 1906.

90. *Montana Socialist*, May 13, 1916. It may be worth noting that no Irishman listed himself as "retired" in either the 1900 or 1910 manuscript censuses.

CHAPTER 6

Irishmen and Workers: The Origins of a Western Working-Class Conservatism, 1878–1907

I

The active involvement of Butte's Irish-American societies in work-related issues reveals the dual nature of Irish associational life. However political their original purpose, the AOH and the RELA were forced by circumstances to subordinate some of their revolutionary ardor to the immediate social and economic needs of their overwhelmingly working-class constituencies. Hard-rock mining was a hazardous trade and employment opportunities were subject to wildly fluctuating cycles. The enclave associations could hardly ignore the working-class demands for safe and steady jobs. Neither could they fail to try to mitigate some of the effects of the hazards of the workplace and the unpredictabilities of the hiring process. The price, in both instances, was cooperation with the more powerful, but it was a price the associations willingly paid. The alternative was cultural dissolution.

That willingness to cooperate also made obvious the social differentiation in the Irish community. People seek favors only from those in a position to grant them. As important as this differentiation, however, was the fact that, in Butte at least, those with power and those without were more alike in values than was ordinarily the case where disparities of wealth and status were involved. This was owing in part to a shared Irishness; other immigrant enclaves, with few exceptions, lacked as clear and unifying a vision as that provided by Irish nationalism. Anglophobia, however, did not entirely mute class antagonisms anywhere else in the world; it would not entirely mute them in Butte.

To this shared hatred of England must be added the fact that all in the Irish community acknowledged a dependence upon at least part of Butte's social calculus: safe and steady work and safe and steady workers. The lives of Irish miners and the prosperity of Irish merchants—the future of the nearest thing to a permanent home many of both groups had ever known—were equally at stake. Here too Butte and its Irishtown were not entirely unique; there were other Irishmen who did dangerous work in unstable enterprises, other Irish merchants dependent upon the trade of those workers. The difference was in degree. Jobs in hard-rock mining were more dangerous and the work force more unstable than those in any other major American industry. Mining towns—even those like Butte that had progressed beyond the frontier mining camp stage—were less able to guarantee their merchants' profits than any other kind of industrial town. In both instances, the threat came from the same source: the unsettled made the workplace less safe and Main Street less prosperous.

It was the enclave's responsibility to prevent the unsettling of Butte, America. In so doing, it served the needs of the respectable Irish, particularly those of the Irish miners drawing regular paychecks. It offered nothing to the non-Irish and very little to those Irish who were part of that substantial portion of the working class that remained itinerant. In fact, regular wages—a mark of the labor aristocracy—often grew out of the labor scarcity attendant upon the itineracy of these other workers. Thus, in Butte there was a separate line dividing the stable and the unstable workers, regardless of ethnicity.[1]

This division cut through ethnic and class lines, and the result was not just a visible seam between those roles but a rough kind of social hierarchy. At the top were the settled Irish, miners and merchants, professionals and priests; next were those Irish of whatever class who gave evidence that they intended to settle in, evidence that involved expressions of interest in the enclave's associations, whether fraternal, political, or religious. The enclave recruited from these new Irishmen. Most of them were known to someone in Butte; many, in fact, were drawn to the place by ties of friendship or family. For these the enclave offered everything from job committees to dating services. Next, in no particular order, were the established non-Irish and the transient and/ or disaffiliate Irish, the men who rejected either Butte or its Irish enclave or both. Last were the truly marginal men, the non-Irish transients.

This was a working-class hierarchy. The enclave included significant numbers of middle- and upper-class Irish, but workers or those who had been workers set the rules for eligibility, and they allowed no one whose behavior or values strayed far from this working-class nexus to remain. Even this concession to interclass ethnicity exceeds what John Bodnar believes allowable. His worker enclaves consisted only of the working class. Those who moved up, moved out. This was the case in Butte, too, but there was a slight difference in the pattern of movement. Given near-total Irish dominance of Butte politics and society, there can have been few compelling reasons to want to move out—except staying alive. Otherwise, there was certainly no opprobrium attached to being an established Irish miner in Butte, and no social disgrace to associating with them.[2]

There were other expressions of this interclass cooperation. Butte's neighborhoods reflected obvious social and economic disparities. But parish lines, whether intentional or not, crossed those boundaries and all of Butte's Irish churches were, to one extent or another, working class. St. Patrick's was less so than St. Mary's or St. Lawrence O'Toole's; but the churches were too close to one another, parish boundaries, both geographical and social, were too fluid to permit significant differences of style. Add to this the fact that its Irish nationalist clubs were overwhelmingly working class, the respect paid miners for assuming extraordinary risks, the miners' pride of craft, and the shared commitment to social stability and it is clear that Irish social differentiation did not produce the usual degree of social fragmentation.[3]

The important question is not then determining if consciousness of class got in the way of ethnicity or if ethnic awareness diminished that of class. Whichever was diminished by the other would, of course, be considered the more "natural" and hence normative allegiance. But in Butte, neither simple ethnicity nor class was the norm. Steadiness, stability, settling in or at least intending to settle in, together with Irishness, were the key factors because they determined the manner in which new recruits would be integrated into the work force. It would be what Hobsbawm called a "subaltern" integration. The worker aristocracy insisted that the new men be integrated at a lower rank.[4]

The safety of the mines and the survival of the Irish community required settled workers; getting and keeping them required some enclave control of the supply, dependability, and ethnic makeup of the work force. Ethnicity was only one of the criteria. Wandering Irishmen were only slightly more welcome, because only slightly more responsible, than wandering Italians or Finns. This suspicion of transients, however, involved necessarily, if unintentionally, a suspicion of the nearest thing to an industrial proletariat that America would produce. It was, to be sure, a floating proletariat, but the consequences for worker solidarity of any working-class hostility to it are obvious, whatever the source of that hostility.[5]

This may not have been the usual pattern in Irish America. Eric Foner, David Montgomery, Daniel Walkowitz, David Brundage, and Sean Wilentz, among others, argue—often persuasively—that strong ethnic identification was not only compatible with class affiliation but actually enhanced the Irish workers' consciousness of their own and the non-Irishmen's status as workers. One result was Irish involvement in interethnic working-class radicalism, a radicalism complete with a "movement culture"; steady and skilled worker tolerance of the un-skilled and transient; well-developed habits and methods of resistance; and the sophistication, if not always the opportunity, to employ those methods to achieve radical ends. Those ends, the argument continues, ranged from industrial unionism to socialism and syndicalism and, though the ideological hegemony of capitalist and middle classes—not to mention government suppression—often diverted them, many of America's Irish workers were naturally inclined toward a class con-sciousness that was frequently radical in form and expression. This was true, moreover, in both their private (Irish) and public (worker) worlds. Indeed when the two worlds were not thought of as identical, the private was considered an instrument of and hence subordinate to the public. The worker was always a Worker even when he was acting as a member of a family, church, or ethnic association. For these historians the seams where Irish and worker were grafted were either unbreak-able, albeit visible to the discerning eye, or completely erased by the interethnic worker solidarity thought to be a natural consequence of an industrial world.[6]

II

The history of Butte's Irish workers between 1878 and 1917 fits only one half of this model. Irish ethnic identification most assuredly did enhance class and occupational awareness. It did not, however, push that awareness toward worker radicalism or toward the tolerance of transient and unskilled workers that was central to that radicalism. This is a troublesome fact because there remains the temptation to assert that Butte's Irish miners should have fit the model better than they did. But between the formation of the Butte Miners' Union (BMU) in 1878 and its destruction in 1914, the greatest mining town in the world, and the most dangerous, the town as Irish as any in the United States, was home to a union universally adjudged one of the fairest and most accommodating in the country and certainly the most con-servative in the Western mining regions.

Though born in the strike of 1878, the BMU for the remainder of its thirty-six years participated in no other work stoppages, job actions, or worker protests. During those same years, in the hard-rock mining regions alone, there were violent strikes in 1880, 1885–86, 1892–94, 1896, 1898–99, 1903–4, 1906–7, 1910, and 1912–14. This was in addition to strikes in the hard-rock industry that took place before 1878 as well as those in coal-mining towns. Since a strike is the most obvious expression of worker protest, and since most of Butte's Irish were drawn from other mining camps, hard-rock and coal, these thirty-six years of industrial harmony are of particular significance.[7]There is, of course, no reason to assume that all, or even most, of those other strikes were genuinely radical in object. Many, even those led by the Western Federation of Miners (WFM), were expressions of "pure and simple" unionism. But the federation, at least potentially, was a radical organization; radicalism is defined for these purposes as Melvyn Dubofsky defined it: "a concept of social change and a program for altering the foundations of American society and government" based ultimately on a "Marxian indictment of capitalism." Out of the WFM came the genuinely radical Western Labor Union and American Labor Union (WLU and ALU), as well as that ultimate expression of American labor radicalism, the syndicalist Industrial Workers of the World (IWW). The WFM was frightening enough. It was an industrial union, a regionally and ultimately nationally federated union, and the natural and at times bitter antagonist of the conservative, trade-union-dominated American Federation of Labor. But if the WFM begat the IWW, so it had been begotten by the BMU. The federation was formed in Butte, dominated for all its years by Butte. The BMU was local #1, with almost half the federation's membership and a proportionate influence on federation policy. The WFM was positioned midway between the radicalism of the IWW and the conservatism of its dominant local, and it remains conjectural whether sire or sired was the more troublesome for it to deal with.[8]

Neither, however, should it be assumed that the nonradicalism of Butte's miners was evidence of the embourgeoisment of the Irish or any of the other ethnic components of the mining work force. The enclave was a source of Irish working-class conservatism, but not because the interclass cooperation that sustained it dulled worker sensitivities. The conservatism of the Butte Irish miner was primarily a working-class conservatism, owing little to the hegemony of middle-class ideas and values. It is true that the Irish had certain advantages in Butte. There were more of them, and more of them with money. Their enclave had less a fortress mentality than in those areas where the Irish workers' presence was less welcome and conspicuous. As such, the enclave was not "circumscribed," not "cut off from social and political influence." But this extraordinary Irish leverage could have sustained Irish worker radicalism—if the enclave Irish worker had only been inclined to radicalism.[9]

But Butte's stable Irish miners did not act out the role of a radical proletariat and did not support the demands of the workers, Irish included, who did embrace radicalism. Thus, Con McGee's death, along with the deaths of hundreds of others, though sincerely mourned produced no audible cries for class war. The Irish, through the AOH and the RELA, waked him, buried him, and sent his $100.00 death benefits together with their resolution of condolence to his parents in County Donegal—a resolution, moreover, that assured them that their son had been a good Irishman and faithful to the nationalist cause. The BMU may have sent official representatives to the wake and the burial service, probably passed and sent a resolution of condolence—which almost surely said nothing about his being a good and committed worker—and joined its $90 death benefit to that of the AOH.[10]

There is no reason to think that these were not appropriate and satisfying responses to an industrial life and an industrial death; no reason to assume that the more natural reaction would have been a cry for both vengeance and a radical readjustment of the capitalist system—short- and long-term solutions to the death of Con McGee. The origins of Butte's Irish miners' conservatism, in other words, are not to be found by inquiring where they misspoke their assigned lines and why, but by carefully analyzing the lines they did read and the roles they did choose to play—in the full knowledge that there were alternatives.

Those roles were cause, effect, and symptom of trying to reconcile the needs of Ireland and the Irish with the needs of labor—both Irish and non-Irish; of trying to make one movement speak to the related but distinct requirements of an Irish nation, an Irish and Irish-American working-class culture, and an interethnic working class. The Irish were well practiced in the effort. In Ireland, involvement with the Land Leagues required a simultaneous commitment to both nationalism and reform—the twin objects of the New Departure. In Pennsylvania, the Molly Maguires, rough and unwelcome affiliates of the local AOH divisions, operated along a slightly different seam. Closer to Butte and to its Irishmen, the Leadville, Colorado, strike of 1880 was led by the Wolfe Tone Guards as well as the Miners' Union; in Wood River, Idaho, the strike of 1885 became particularly ugly after a St. Patrick's Day show of union and Irish solidarity. And always, of course, Patrick

Ford's newspaper reminded its Irish readers that the liberation of Ireland and the defense of the Irish-American industrial worker were intersecting movements.[11]

The importance of solidarity, whether ethnic or class or both, was the one shared lesson of these experiences. The unusually high percentage of Irishmen among the leaders of the American labor movement reflects how well that lesson was learned. As Sean Wilentz has written, "An American labor history minus a thorough account of the Irish cannot even pretend to the name." The problems arise from trying to determine how these Irish leaders defined the labor movement, why the rank and file, Irish included, elected them, and how they influenced the policies and direction of their unions.[12]

The New Departure had only partial success in Ireland. It was never able entirely to reconcile the conflicting requirements of nationalism and labor and land reform. The Irish who came from that tradition cannot be counted among the previously radicalized immigrants. The composite Irish immigrant was not an indolent and feckless Paddy; there was genuine heroism in rent wars and boycotts. But his values and belief systems had little room for the interethnic and self-conscious radicalism thought to be the natural consequence of life in industrial America.[13]

A few of those who immigrated after 1895 may have been influenced by the growing radicalism within the Irish labor movement, but it must here be recalled that even in early twentieth-century Ireland, the cause of labor radicalism was subordinated to that of an Irish nation. For example, Patrick Pearse, the author of the 1916 proclamation of the independent Irish Republic, insisted that he was no "new-fangled socialist or . . . syndicalist but an old fashioned . . . Catholic nationalist." As for James Connolly, the leader of the Irish Marxists, the English would probably have forgiven him his socialism; they executed him for sins committed in the name of Ireland. Similarly, the Molly Maguires were never certain if they were rebelling as Irishmen or as workers. The two roles were not incompatible, but neither were they synonymous. What the Irish and the immigrant experience did produce, whatever its timing, was an Irish ability to organize for purposes of agitation, an Irish awareness of the potency and the limits of that agitation, and a certain confusion as to ultimate purpose. Butte was a perfect staging area for all three legacies.[14]

Control of the Butte Miners' Union is an obvious example. As surely as the Irish ran the political party that ran the town, so did they control the affairs of the BMU. The first president of what became the Butte Miners' Union was A. C. Witter, a native of Indiana, but four of the officers who served with him were Patrick Shovlin, Edward Rooney, John Sullivan, and William Larkin. The pattern was set. From 1885 to 1914, 180 BMU officers were listed in the Butte city directories; 145 of those, a remarkable 80 percent, were Irishmen. Between 1883 and 1896, the BMU elected twenty-three Irishmen to the twenty-six highest union offices, those of president and secretary; in 1897 all fourteen of the union's offices went to Irishmen. Nothing changed in the 1900s. The president in 1901 was John J. Quinn. He was followed, successively, by Ed Hughes, William McGrath, Ed Long, Francis O'Connor, P. J. Duffy, James Shea, P. W. Flynn, Dan Holland, Dan Sullivan, George Curry, Dennis Murphy, and, in 1914, Bert Riley.[15]

As important as the Irishness of the leadership was the fact that many of the officers of the BMU were also active members of the AOH and/or the RELA. The names of the ninety-four different Irishmen who held those 145 offices were checked against the Irish associations' membership ledgers between 1882 and 1915; sixty-four of the ninety-four were members of one or both. Of the unaffiliated thirty, moreover, a few left Butte, a few were ethnic disaffiliates, but the largest percentage were participants in the enclave if not in its strictly Irish associations. The BMU may not have been a part of the enclave, but its leadership surely was.

There are dozens of examples. In 1882, Patrick Boland, president of both the BMU and the RELA, gave money to Patrick Ford's "Spread the Light" and Land League Funds. In 1893 the president of the AOH was James Maher, later president of the RELA, an officer in both the BMU and the WFM, and best man at the Butte wedding of WFM president and RELA member Edward Boyce, like Maher a native of Ireland. Two years later, in 1895, the president of both the AOH and the BMU was Miles J. Burke; his Hibernian recording secretary was Anthony Shovlin, also an RELA, BMU, and WFM officer. In 1905 the AOH hired a "solicitor," a member whose responsibility it was to bring lapsed Hibernians back to good standing. The man selected was Daniel J. McCarthy. He was the perfect choice; he worked at the Mountain Con Mine, lived in Dublin Gulch, and, most significantly, was the treasurer of the BMU.[16]

This overlapping between union officers and Irish associations was to be expected. The persistent and stable members of any community ran the community's affairs. But that only raises another and more important point. The nonradicalism of the BMU can only be understood in the context of its Irish leadership. The BMU had a total membership in 1900 of 7,000. That may have represented 80 percent of the men working in the mines. In spite of the fact that Butte's mines operated on a closed-shop basis, about 20 percent of the workers had either dodged the union walking delegate or left town prior to the thirty-day grace period for paying union dues. The union's hall, moreover, could accommodate only about 600 men, less than 10 percent of the membership. Few referenda were held, and, except for Miners' Union Day, celebrated every June 13, the rank and file did not attend union functions, weekly meetings included, in appreciable numbers. It is, in fact, reasonable to conclude that the ordinary members influenced policy only by the election of the men who would make that policy, and even here it was unusual for more than 40 percent of the membership to vote.[17]

Butte's miners were not uncommonly shy; comparable figures could probably be uncovered for any large union. In fact, comparable figures for attendance at RELA and AOH meetings have been found. But many men joined the BMU only because they had to, and the rest, like workers everywhere, did not define their world solely in terms of their jobs. The result, whatever the cause, was that a small minority, disproportionately Irish, determined union policy and if the nonradicalism of that policy is to be understood, so must the influence of this Irish dominance of the union's leadership.[18]

III

F. S. L. Lyons provides a starting place for discussing that Irish factor with his "recipe for conservatism." Lyons, of course, was describing the West Irish peasantry but his demographic criteria, late marriages, large families, and many older unmarried children living at home, may have a wider applicability. The criteria, of course, need not be interpreted as Lyons interpreted them. A case could be made that delayed marriage, or a decision not to marry, would fit more appropriately into a recipe for restiveness. Whether marriage was postponed or canceled, the result was a larger-than-ordinary pool of unattached men. In Ireland, according to the sociologist Robert Kennedy, the younger of these were the ones who either emigrated or rebelled, and late marriages were more likely a source of discontent than of political docility. This would seem to have been true of Butte as well.[19]

The numbers for Butte, however applied and interpreted, are interesting. Four hundred and forty married Irish immigrant men, selected at random from the *Manuscript Census* of 1900 and representing almost every part of the city, had an average age at marriage of 28.6 years; the median marriage age was 26.7; 150 of them (34 percent) were thirty or older before they married. For 322 second-generation Irishmen the average age at marriage was 27.1, the median was 26.2, and ninety-three (29 percent) postponed marriage until thirty or later. But these figures are only slightly higher than the U.S. median in 1900 of 25.9 years. On the other hand, they are significantly lower than the 1926 median in Ireland of 31.5, indicating that immigrants were not delaying marriage, and that the reason for postponing marriage in Ireland—uncertainty about the male's ability to find and keep steady work—was no longer a deterrent. Assuming similar motives, the men of the second generation, often the products of America's industrial towns and mining camps, were as hopeful of their futures as their fathers had been of theirs.[20]

Too much should not be made of this. Butte did not provide a sense of economic security that washed away all memories of evictions, emigrations, mine closures, and enforced idleness. If anything, it may have enhanced those fears, particularly in the early years. The Irish response, however, was neither flight nor fight, neither transiency nor labor militancy, but a firmer resolve to do whatever was necessary to prevent a recurrence of the events that had put them on the road, whether from Ireland to Michigan or from Michigan to Montana. The effect of this resolve was cautionary and conservative.

Family size contributed to the Butte recipe as surely as to the Irish. Here Lyons's reading of the data seems more appropriate to Butte—the larger the family, the steadier and more conservative the family's head. Two thousand six hundred and five children were born to the wives of a random sample of 485 immigrant Irishmen married for more than five years. Of those 2,605 children, 1,889 were still alive at the time of the 1900 census. That 27 percent death rate tells a story of its own, but the immediate issue is that of family size. Had there been no deaths at birth, the 485 working men supported for a time at least an average of 5.4 children; the median was 4.8 children. At the time of the census, the mean family size was 3.9 children, the median 3.2. In addition, for the entire Irish community of Butte in 1900, a total of 389 unmarried wage earning men and women, of the second generation alone, lived with their immigrant parents. No effort was made to calculate the number of third-generation adults living with second-generation parents. All of this would indicate that large families, working older children, and nonworking mothers were the rule in Butte as in the rest of Irish-America. These were "traditional" family arrangements; they did not involve concessions to "modernity," nor were they likely to contribute to working-class radicalism. To these figures must be added the 73 percent of the persistent Irish miners who owned their own homes and the 434 widows in 1910, with 1,117 single parent children—also not the stuff of working-class radicalism.[21]

These numbers add some needed definition to the social portrait that has already begun to emerge from nonquantitative evidence. The established Butte Irishman—married, with children, often propertied, like Lyons's peasant, figured to be "a very conservative person indeed." Settling in meant settling down. He was more industrially aware than the Irishman who stayed in Ireland, more socialized to the pace and hazards of capitalism, but his values and behavior were based on the same things: family, faith, the nature of the work he did, and, for many, the cause of Ireland. In Ireland, these values adhered to the place. They arose naturally. In Butte, they arose as naturally, and they found their most complete expression in the enclave.

The conservatism of that community cannot, of course, be fully explained demographically. Worker enclaves were too complex for that. The explanation of the conservatism of this one may well begin with a conjectural point. Butte itself had persisted. Unlike the other mining camps of the West, Butte had survived to become a major industrial city with at least the semblance of a stable industrial work force. But that work force was drawn from the itinerant miners of those other and more unstable camps. The process of "immigrant selection" may here be applied to the internal migration of the Irish. They had exercised one of their options in emigrating from Ireland; they had used and used up others in making their way to Butte. Except, then, for those who had chosen a peripatetic life, the difficulties the Irish had had in transplanting themselves bred a determination to persist, not worker radicalism. This is the significance of the shutdowns of 1903 and 1907. They called to mind earlier mine closures whether in Ireland or the United States, raising fears not only of unemployment but of forced itineracy. The Irish who settled into Butte's labor force had long memories and were, as a consequence of their previous wanderings, even more determined to find safe and steady work and attach themselves to the company of like minded men. Like-minded, particularly in the early years when social differentiation was incomplete, meant Irish. But even if this notion of immigrant selection is shown to be false, there were other and powerful reasons for Irish miners to want to settle in when they finally reached Butte.

Marcus Daly was central to all of them. By giving preferential treatment to Irish miners, joining their associations, paying for their churches, attending their wakes, and serving generally as an example of Irish enterprise, Daly blurred class distinctions and contributed to worker conservatism. His support of worker rights had the same effect. In 1878 while representing the Walker Brothers' interests in Butte, he dealt fairly with strikers dismissed by another Walker Brothers' manager as "impudent rabble, scalawags, loafers and sports." The Irish workers did not forget Daly's support. Among the three men who proposed his name for membership in the RELA in 1886 was #90, Joseph Norris; a year later Norris was elected president of the Butte Miners' Union.[22]

Daly's attitude never changed. In 1892 he paid the $10,000 bail of Peter Breen, an Irish attorney and BMU officer who had been accused of conspiracy and murder for his part in the strikes in the Couer d'Alene region of Idaho. Two years later he interceded with J. J. Hill on the side of the workers in the Great Northern Railroad strike, prompting the official newspaper of the WFM to say that Daly had "done more for labor than all the others combined. . . . [He was] a stout friend of the working man." He even "requested his workers to join unions." It cannot be known if Daly's example had any influence, but Patrick Boland, who knew Daly well and whose Irish and worker sympathies nicely reinforced one another, expressed an "intense disapproval" of labor radicalism, insisting that "those who employ have rights." Daly's "generosity," another Butte Irishman wrote in 1906, "rubbed off on Butte"; his humanity could "never be brought to consent to a reduction of the wages of his men." One result was that the BMU was "the most conservative labor organization in the West." The "radical agitators" moved on to the other mining camps "where the management was less popular with the men."[23]

Predictably, among Daly's rewards for these displays of modesty were some of the trappings of caste. He was always "Mr. Daly" or "the Honorable Marcus Daly," to the Irish associations. On his death, in a resolution signed by Irishmen of all classes, he was "fittingly described as the noblest Roman of them all." Obviously, however, they were all Romans, and if Irish miners took pleasure and satisfaction in Daly's success, they also understood that his power was available for use against the enemies of them all. As one of his contemporaries put it, Daly was the "boss Irishman."[24]

The title had more than just social meaning. By giving preference to the Irish in both supervisory and manual labor positions, he allowed them far greater control of the work force than their skills or the free operation of the labor market could have provided. There were crews in Daly's mines that were exclusively Irish, and not because the Irish were the only miners available. This was an extraordinary privilege and one with significant ideological implications. Eric Hobsbawm has argued that "any group of workers," skilled or unskilled, "which could establish the economic advantages of the artisan, notably an institutionalized scarcity on the labor market and some control over its own work was assimilated to artisan status." These were the labor aristocrats. And the labor aristocracy, Hobsbawm went on, as long as its privileged status was recognized, belonged where both friend and foe put it: on the side of conservative to moderate labor reformism. Hobsbawm, of course, was talking about English artisans. In fact, he specifically denied that a "permanent, proletarian labour aristocracy . . . would . . . need to develop if the way out of the working class was relatively open, as I think was the case for white Protestant nineteenth century Americans." But Butte's Irish miners were neither Protestant nor, except by residency, American. The "institutionalized scarcity on the labor market" arose because they—and Marcus Daly—were Irish.[25]

It is at this point that Hobsbawm's "artificial labor aristocrats" begin to reveal attitudes remarkably like those of the workers in John Bodnar's enclaves. Bodnar writes that "regular employment was the foundation of the enclave itself." The key word was "regular." It was steady work they required at a wage that permitted them to save enough to buy "the small piece of property" necessary to family security and participation in the ethno-occupational community. This was true regardless of the size or influence of that community. There were times, as shown, when this security could be insured only by playing upon ethnic ties. But this need not, in fact should not, be seen as evidence of worker victimization, or as some kind of "sweetheart" deal and hence a violation of the abstract laws of worker solidarity. It makes more sense to view it as it was viewed: an effort to control a part (one's own) of the workplace in the interests of the larger community.[26]

These are the values of a worker's enclave. They do not comport well with those of an upwardly mobile middle class, but neither are they compatible with those of a radicalized proletariat. The children of the enclave, according to Bodnar, were "socialized . . . to accept . . . steady, industrial jobs, seldom challenging the . . . system" that provided them. They learned "community rather than class-based" values and behavior, including the very important lesson that there were limits on what the bosses, even the boss Irishmen, were likely to give. Thus, among the influences that tended to moderate the protests of Butte's Irish miners must be counted the conservatism internal to their world, the result, says Bodnar, of the "meeting of the industrial with the family-based economy," or, in different language, the result of living on a seam that both divided and joined the industrial worker and the immigrant Irishman.[27]

In spite of what must to them have seemed astonishing influence, the Butte Irish miner was still an industrial worker. He had marginally more control over his working life than did other, less well situated, members of his class. But the sources of his conservatism were not appreciably different from those of other enclave workers. Daly, by guaranteeing the steady employment that was instrumental to the enclave, solidified the Irishman's world. But Daly provided more than just jobs. He was responsible for the "aristocratic" notion that the Irish could—and by rights should—have some control over the labor force. In this sense, he was their patron, and the working Irish could never be persuaded that he was an evil man. By their cultural standards, to assign evil to Daly was self-proscriptive. It damned them all.

The same could be said of other well-placed Irishmen. Historians have dismissed Daniel J. Hennessy as a Daly "henchman," and "crony," an inconsequential shopkeeper who had the undeserved good fortune of enjoying Daly's favor and whose mercantile establishment became, as a result, a company store. His Irish contemporaries were kinder. The national director of the AOH called him "one of the wealthiest men in [a] state of rich men," but he went on to add that "during the periodic depressions in the copper mines," Hennessy extended credit to "hundreds of *Irish* families who would otherwise have suffered." The day of his funeral was described as "the coldest of the winter, yet in the icy blast of that mountain city over 6,000 people with hundreds of the Ancient Order, marched" to his grave. Peter Breen argued that Hennessy was a "friend of the poor always . . . did more to help the needy . . . than any other man in Montana."[28]

Certainly he did more to help the enclave. Hugh O'Daly identified him, with unconscious irony, as "one of the best informed men in the city on Anaconda Company affairs." To some, this would have been further evidence that Hennessy's was a company store. To others, it meant only that he was in a better position than most to offer aid to the Irish community. He interceded constantly, often with Marcus Daly personally, for jobs for Irish miners. He sold provisions to the Florence Hotel, Irish-run and ACM-owned, at wholesale. Miners' paychecks were occasionally drawn on his store. This too was collusion, cried the radicals. The settled Irish miners simply thought the practice made it easier for them to get what amounted to a short-term loan. The first $500 for the construction of St. Mary's church came from Hennessy. His Centerville store was in Hibernia Hall. He was an active member of both the AOH and the RELA, a state and national officer in the Hibernians; indeed, Ireland, according to the RELA resolution on his death, "never had a truer friend, . . . he was identified with every movement" for Irish freedom. When he died in 1908, the senior and junior guardians of the RELA, Sheriff John O'Rourke and Judge Jeremiah Lynch, moved that the Emmets and the Hibernians "secure an oil painting [of Hennessy] . . . to hang in this hall."[29]

This was an uncommon honor. Workers were seldom moved to such displays of sentiment, particularly for wealthy capitalists. But the story does not end there. The portrait was to be done by John D. Ryan! His selection was as instructive a lesson in interclass ethnicity as the decision to honor Hennessy. Ryan at the time was the president of the Anaconda Copper Mining Company; a year later he would become president of the parent Amalgamated Copper Company. But Ryan, as noted earlier, was also an active Hibernian and a most generous benefactor of the Catholic Church. His selection to paint a portrait of another Butte capitalist to be hung alongside those of St. Patrick and Thomas Francis Meagher occasioned no debate. This was an Irish lodge and Hennessy had earned his place. As for Ryan, it is worth recounting the language of the AOH motion at the time of his appointment in 1904 as director and general manager of ACM's Montana properties. The division "tender[ed] to John D. Ryan, who is a member, . . . its appreciation of the fact of his election to the position of Director and general manager." Five years later, when he was made president of the Company, the RELA sent "a telegram . . . as a mark of our appreciation of his promotion to the office of president of the largest enterprise in this Country." The choice of the word "appreciation" rather than the more natural "congratulations" may have been inadvertent and careless. It may also have been quite conscious and purposeful.[30]

Obviously, it would be easy to use the Daly, Hennessy, and Ryan stories as examples of working-class toadyism. Indeed, when Con Kelley replaced Ryan as Anaconda's chief executive officer, a labor newspaper noted, without ethnic reference, that "the sycophants now fawn all over [Kelley]." This may, however, say more about William Dunn, the editor of the newspaper, than it does about the alleged sycophants. At the very least, Dunn's radicalism must be seen as a topic for research, not as a prism through which to interpret his contemporaries. In the real world of the Butte Irish miner, continued Irish control of the Anaconda Company was something to be *appreciated,* a legitimate cause for self-congratulation. Worker servility does not explain the Irish celebration of what they assumed would be its continuance.[31]

Neither does it explain the satisfaction Irish workers took in the success of Irish capitalists, particularly when, like Daly, they did not distance themselves from their Irish and worker backgrounds and wore their wealth lightly and with the proper style. The settled Irish, of whatever class, were proud of what the Irish had done for Butte. They were "the best people in the city," according to Bishop John Carroll's sister; they were the pioneers, the builders of Butte. Indeed, Hennessy and P. J. Sullivan, a miner and saloonkeeper, considered putting together a "short history of Division One" of the AOH, a hagiographic "mugbook" commemorating the members' contributions to the prosperity of the city.[32]

They never published the book, but if they had, there would have been ample space for the lives of the working Irishmen who made up the bulk of the AOH's membership. In 1897 Daly's mines marketed over 65,000 tons of copper, a third again as much as all the mines of Michigan. The Irish miners knew this, and the knowledge likely pleased them. They had dug a considerable percentage of the millions of tons of ore necessary to get it. In 1906 the AOH state convention was in Anaconda, Montana. Entertainment included a dress ball and a visit to what the AOH officers called "the greatest smelters in the world." But more was involved than industrial production. The workers' status as labor aristocrats—including the sense of *personal* superiority which was a part of that status—was also at issue. It was fitting that the visitors be favored with a walking tour of the smelter.[33]

It is likely that the working-class membership of the AOH identified Anaconda's smelters as the greatest in the world independent of any suggestion, however subtle, from the Irish middle and upper classes. There was plenty of room in the culture of work and even more in the culture of Irish immigration for pride in Irish success. Indeed, Daly's and the others' riches confirmed what Ireland's patriotic iconographers had long been arguing: that English rule alone prevented the full flowering of Irish genius, a genius for capital accumulation included. In this sense, Daly's wealth deepened the Irish workers' hatred of England and quieted to a degree any latent hostility toward capitalism.

There were, however, times when well or at least better placed Irishmen did mouth ideas commonly thought the property of a middle-class and Protestant dominant culture—recall, for example, the AOH and RELA strictures against excessive drink. In addition, on at least four separate occasions Hibernians heard speakers argue that Irishmen should "get into business for themselves and not always be working for the other fellow." Douglas Hyde cigars, named after the founder of the Gaelic League in Ireland, were also sold to finance "the higher education of Irish in [the] locality." After all, said Ed Lawlor, "nothing is too good for the Irish," and if "a Brother wanted to raise himself, he should be helped to the highest pedestal."[34]

As the occupational and social mobility figures would indicate, few Irishmen, Hibernians included, did "raise themselves." And for many of those who did, particularly those who quit the mining work force and bought a saloon, injury and illness rather than the questing spirit may have been the reason. For example, when John Hurley was injured the AOH gave him $200 in addition to his regular sick benefits and pledged "to help him in the future if he goes into any business he can make a living at." There is no record of how Hurley did but Charles Kennedy, whose severed foot was replaced with a cork model provided by the AOH, later became the proprietor of the Shamrock Saloon. James Curtin, now in his eighties, remembers that his father bought a saloon only after the miners' con left him "too crippled" to work underground. This is not to say that "upward" mobility was always or even usually an indication of an inability to work, only that in a town like Butte with well paying but hazardous industrial jobs, social mobility rates as well as the ideology of mobility must be interpreted with care.[35]

The proposed Hibernian Colonization Society teaches the same lesson. Butte's Irish learned in 1905 that the Flathead Indian reservation, located about 150 miles northwest of the city, was about to be opened to white settlement. Determined to take advantage of this opportunity, an AOH member suggested that the order's officers "secretly and earnestly establish a Hibernian Colony . . . and devise ways and means to facilitate resettlement." The Butte Hibernians may have been following the lead of their national officers, who had recommended as early as 1898 that in order to "relieve the wants of our race" land be sought for Irish industrial workers, both in Ireland and the United States. Only then would the Irish know "independence, prosperity, and usefulness, . . . as owners and tillers of the soil." Butte's AOH, as well as Bishop Carroll, added to the definition of useful the notion that in a state like Montana Irish and Catholic political influence also required that the Irish become farmers.[36]

Like the suggestion that the Irish not "work for the other fellow," claims of independence, prosperity, usefulness, and political preferment are considered the ideological property of the middle class. All but the last of them, however, also had a natural appeal to workers. They recalled strictly Irish needs and they expressed enclave as well as middle-class values. The Irish miners of Butte would have accepted them without any prodding or moralizing. In addition, the dangers in working underground must again be noted. Farming's greatest gift was not independence or prosperity but a chance, literally, to breathe. That was a working-class consideration. Second, to recall the language of Patrick Ford, "idle-owned lands with idle-starving people is murder." That was as true in Montana as in Galway and the Hibernia Colony must have seemed to some like a replay of the old Land League days.

That was an Irish consideration. Notions of middle-class hegemony are not involved.[37]

But there were powerful forces pulling against any significant Irish settlement in the Flathead. The reservation, according to one who touted the colonization idea, presented "grand opportunities . . . to all young and ambitious men." That was the problem. By 1911, when those remarks were made, Butte's Irish community was dominated not by the young and ambitious but by the old and settled, or at least ones as old and settled as the world of hard-rock mining would permit. They stayed in Butte not because the enclave needed them but because they needed it. Father Patrick Brosnan explained the matter perfectly in letters to his parents in Ireland. Some of the Irish miners made enough money to "clear out either to a ranch or to the old country. But a good many get married and don't have enough to leave." Later he wrote that "they all remained in the city where they are near their friends and where they can have weddings, wakes, etc. . . . the Irish run all the saloons and themselves and their friends are the best customers." There was, in other words, no enclave—and no likelihood of building one—on the Flathead reservation. That was the deterrent for, as Brosnan went on to relate, "the men die like gods down here in the mines."[38]

The only standard for Irish success was not, then, the upwardly striving shopkeeper or the resettled farmer. Staying alive, employed, and involved—the rewards of persistence—were enough. This was particularly true when the rewards included a chance to return to Ireland for a visit or, in far fewer instances, to stay. The evidence is incomplete, but among the members who repatriated or who reported back to either the AOH or the RELA on their trips to "the old sod" were miners like John E. Harrington, Walter Breen, Pat Kelly, John Hogan, John Ferns, Pat Breen, T. J. Kenny, Matthew Moriarity, Pat Boland, Mike Sullivan, and Jeremiah Murphy. To be sure, the hotelkeeper, Hugh O'Daly, made six trips, and Judge Jeremiah Lynch made at least three, but working Irish, obviously, did not fare badly. It is worth noting, too, that the associational Irish were far more likely to visit Ireland than to stay; this despite the fact that 17 percent of the entire West Cork immigration repatriated. The attractions of Butte and its Irish enclave, including steady work at good wages, proved difficult to resist, even for "poor exiles of Erin."[39]

Of course, few working Irish would not have traded places with Hennessy or even with merchants of less princely means, but the odds on becoming a merchant capitalist were long and the risks, both economic and cultural, were great. When (and if) Irish miners needed models, they looked for them among more recognizable sorts. As that list of 107 Irish hiring officers would indicate, they did not have far to look. Irish-born Mike Carroll, for example, a member of both the RELA and the AOH, rose from mine laborer to superintendent of the Anaconda, St. Lawrence, and Neversweat mines. The resolution on his death in 1891 noted that mining had lost "one of its ablest experts, . . . the cause of Ireland, a sincere, and fearless advocate, and the interests of labor a most faithful champion." That is an instructive list, consisting as it does of references to occupation, ethnicity, and class. Copies of the resolution were sent to Pat Ford's *Irish World*, the *Boston Pilot*, and the *Dublin Freeman*.[40]

Carroll was only one of many. James Higgins was born in Birmingham, England, most likely the son of an Irish spalpeen. He came to Butte in the 1890s and worked in many of its mines. He was a Gaelic-Irish speaker, a member of the Gaelic League, the RELA, AOH, and Knights of Columbus. When he died in 1910 he was superintendent of the Bell and Diamond Mine. Jim Brennan's was another success story. Born in County Clare, Brennan came to Butte in 1880, rustling a job as a pumpman at the Green Mountain Mine. He later became the foreman of the Mountain Con, Green Mountain, and Emma mines. Like Carroll and Higgins, he was a member of all the Irish associations. So was James P. ("Rimmer") O'Neill. A native of County Cork, O'Neill rose from a mucker to assistant general superintendent of all the Butte operations of the Anaconda Company.[41]

Clearly, occupational mobility was central to each of these stories. And the success of these Irish may have convinced others of the openness of the system or, at least, of the advantages of staying in Butte. The question, however, is not whether this was middle-class ideological hegemony but whether a "middle-class" value had Irish working-class applicability. In each of the instances just cited, mobility took place within the enclave. In fact, in each instance it involved promotion to a position that controlled the jobs necessary to the enclave's survival, not jobs which gave access to the world outside it. There is conservatism in this, but it is a workers' conservatism not an imitation of middle-class notions of the American dream.[42]

V

The key to this working-class conservatism was the control the Irish exercised over the work force. By cooperating with the more powerful, Irish workers became active partners in a collaborative effort to maintain the community. The enclave, particularly its fraternal associations, functioned as unofficial job placement centers. ACM hiring officers had only to maintain ties with the Irish community—in most instances a natural consequence of their membership in it—to insure a supply of steady workers, an arrangement which benefited the companies as surely as it did the Irish job seekers. In partial return, the foremen and shift bosses, with the approval of the mine managers, allowed AOH and RELA members free access to the mines for fund raising purposes ranging from the Boer Ambulance Corps Fund and the Thomas Francis Meagher Memorial Fund to collections taken up for the widows of members killed in the mines. They also provided day-shift work for association officers and time off for practice for the association bands. The number 2 shaft of the Mountain Con, an ACM mine run by Jim Brennan, was known as "the hospital" because the men assigned there were old and broken down; "pensions" in the form of jobs as watchmen for the "old-timers, fellows who need the money and can't work underground," were available at all the ACM mines. It could be argued that this was evidence of corporate paternalism, that of such deals are feudal relationships made, but this would have made no more sense to a settled Irish miner than the charge of worker pliancy.[43]

The most significant of this type of corporate "gift" was the Anaconda Company's willingness to close certain of its mines on such exclusively Irish holidays as St. Patrick's Day, the day of the Irish Societies' Picnic, and Robert Emmet's birthday. For example, in 1900 the RELA had "assurances that the syndicate (ACM) mines would close down . . . [picnic] day for repairs." For St. Patrick's Day that same year the AOH reported that "all the managers of the Daly mines promised that nearly all the mines would close down on that occasion." Often it was D. J. Hennessy who served as the associations' representative. In 1900 "#38 (Hennessy) waited on Mr. O'Neill" (RELA member James "Rimmer" O'Neill) regarding a day off for the picnic. Not surprisingly, O'Neill "gave leave to all who wanted to go and would . . . have the mine shut down that day." In 1907 Division 3 of the AOH called on Hennessy to negotiate a day off on St. Patrick's Day. Hennessy promised that the "matter would be satisfactory, as had been in all previous" years.[44]

But it was not the upper-class Irish alone who spoke for the enclave. In 1894 AOH and BMU president M. J. Burke approached Michael O'Farrell, Daly's nephew and the superintendent of all ACM mines, "in regard to having the Payday changed for the Picnic and Bro. O'Farrell stated he would make it alright." In 1897 the AOH sent Burke, Anthony Shovlin, and James Maher to "interview various mine superintendents . . . to secure lay offs for St. Patrick's Day." All three were—or soon would be—either BMU or WFM officers. The layoffs were granted. These were not ordinary favors. Major corporations did not routinely close down operations or change paydays because a group of workers wanted a holiday—at least not by this stage of American industrialization.[45]

The response of the non-Irish miners to the loss of a day's pay was not recorded. It may not have been too heated since most took their day off midweek, earning their "ringer," a six-day workweek, by insisting that the mines stay open on Sundays. The issues, however, and the potential for unhappiness, went beyond lost wages. The BMU was the appropriate agency to respond to these other matters. Curiously, the union gave no indication that it objected to a practice that affected it in a number of ways. In the first place, days off for Irish holidays reduced the union's chances to persuade the mine managers to close for "worker" holidays. Second, giving one element of the working class a day off at the expense, minimal though it may have been, of other elements of that class mocked the BMU's very pretensions of interethnic worker unity.[46]

Finally, the practice clearly presented the BMU with rivals to its yearly celebration of Miners' Union Day. In fact, however, even this commemoration of the founding of the BMU was an occasion for considerable Irish display. Witness the lyrics to "Miners' Union Day in Butte," with the references to "Me new green shirt I'll wear. / Six thousand miners will be marchin' / While I ride in stately ease, / Just like a Celtic warrior / As handsome as you please." In 1896 there were two grand balls on Miners' Union Day, one at Union Hall, the other at Hibernia Hall. The planning committee for the day's festivities consisted of fourteen Irishmen. There must have been times when the Irish/worker had to stop and remind himself which of his allegiances he was representing that day. As Daniel Walkowitz points out, the "non-labor social activities [of the Irish] began to compete with union-sponsored affairs and tended to be . . . inter-class, rather than intra-class." Perhaps the active involvement of the BMU leadership in the Irish-sponsored shutdowns and festivals explains the union's silence on a matter that, according to the theoretical formula, should have been of great moment to it.[47]

But the AOH celebration on March 17 was more than just an Irish holiday because the sainted Patrick was obviously more than just an Irishman. The role of the Catholic Church in neutralizing the "natural" radicalism of its working-class parishioners has been much discussed. One point not sufficiently emphasized is that Catholicism was a definitional part of Irish nationalism; the Irish wore their faith like a badge.

This did not insure greater piety but it did make more difficult Irish working-class acceptance of political theories the Church found objectionable. Socialism, for example, because it violated Catholicism, could be made to seem a violation of Irish nationalism as well. This would have required an excessively abstract reading of the formula, but Irish patriots of conservative social ideas did not hesitate on those grounds. Particularly relevant in the hard-rock districts was the Church's proscription on involvement in the Western Federation of Miners. The Montana hierarchy was less zealous, but it did conform to the pattern of Catholic anti-radicalism. Bishop John Brondel, for example, identified "secret labor societies" along with "heretics, infidels, public schools," and, according to one source, the *Irish World*, as threats to Catholicism.[48]

The avowedly Catholic Hibernians, though clearly more favorably disposed toward Patrick Ford's newspaper, were of similar mind. "Class interests," according to the Montana AOH Constitution and bylaws of 1886, "were protected by organized and exclusive institutions." Irish Catholic interests required comparable protection if, among other reasons, they were "to counteract the evil influences of secret, communistic, socialistic, and other irreligious societies." Eight years earlier the Hibernians of San Francisco, in a like mood, had vowed "to put down their feet on any semblance of communism." There is no reason to believe that individual members of the order took these warnings literally—or even seriously. Still, they reflect sentiments clearly antithetical to working-class radicalism.[49]

More significant than official condemnations was the AOH policy of paying sick and death benefits, an obvious and temporizing accommodation to capitalism, or the cooperation with the more powerful necessary to job preference. Then, too, there was the deceptively simple fact that Irish associational dues and assessments made more difficult the paying of union dues and assessments. There were almost one thousand miners on the rolls of the AOH and the RELA in 1905. More than a day's pay went for initiation fees; each man contributed nearly $24.00 yearly to causes unrelated or only peripherally related to his work. There remains, of course, the very good possibility that this conflict of allegiances was perceived differently by those who experienced it, that it was union dues that subtracted from the sum available to the Irish associations; that union meetings were the burdensome ones because union policy could be safely left to others. The likelihood that ethnic affiliation was more "natural" than class strengthens the possibility. The remark was doubtless facetious but when RELA "#22 was instructed to interview the secretary of the Miner's Union and ascertain how much he would charge for doing our janitor work," Irish miners were making a clear distinction between their Irish club and their miners' club. John Devoy, it should be remembered, had made the same distinction.[50]

As important as dual loyalties were the lessons, stated and implied, that members took away with them from AOH and RELA meetings. When future BMU president Joe Norris cosponsored Marcus Daly for RELA membership he did so at an open meeting. Walter Breen, a miner and political eccentric, proposed Con Kelley for AOH membership; this, too, at an open meeting. The discussions at these weekly gatherings were of English rather than capitalist tyranny, of Irish rather than worker solidarity. These are not mutually exclusive pairings but neither are they necessarily appositional or even compatible. As a labor newspaper lamented when the Venezuelan boundary dispute heightened tensions between England and the United States, delighting the Anglophobic Emmets, war against England "does nothing to help Irish laborers."[51]

The social mix at associational meetings and functions must also be recalled. Miners and muckers joined lawyers, merchants, and priests. They drank whiskey and beer and smoked cigars together, listened to the same speeches, rallied to the same causes. Hundreds of examples could be cited. On Emmet Day in 1889 the RELA heard a speech by D. J. Hennessy, even then a wealthy merchant, followed by a song by William Deeney, an officer of the Miners' Union. The resolution of condolence on the death of Peter Hale was written by Patrick Boland, former president of the BMU, and John J. O'Meara, a brewing company executive. O'Meara served on the Thomas Francis Meagher Memorial Committee with Marcus Daly, Anthony Shovlin, an officer of the Butte Miners' Union and James Maher, secretary of the Western Federation of Miners.[52]

Obviously, these displays of fraternal goodwill were witnessed by only a small percentage of the Irish miners of Butte. Eighty percent of them at any time were not members of the AOH or the RELA. Many of those unaffiliated were itinerants, ethnically and socially "unattached," for whom Irish associational life, though perhaps desirable, was beyond immediate reach. These men may also, however, have felt cut off from participation in strictly working-class associations. There were other nonaffiliates who had settled in but who expressed their enclave loyalties in different and less expensive and political ways. Irish church membership obviously exceeded that of Irish fraternal associations. So did attendance at association-sponsored lectures, summer picnics, and St. Patrick's Day parades. What seems clear is that the associational Irish were the leaders of the Irish enclave and that the associations' influence extended throughout it.[53]

It could also be argued that interclass exhibitions of Irish solidarity were choreographed by the middle and upper class. When Hennessy praised the RELA for avoiding most of the "jealousy" which was "the curse of the Irish race," he not only acknowledged the existence of a class division but also finessed its more threatening effects, at least for the stable, associational Irish. Con Kelley, at the time general counsel of the Anaconda Company, performed the same service to capital when he argued on St. Patrick's Day, 1910, that "all classes must unite for Ireland." Like Hennessy's remark—and Marcus Daly's hiring practices—Kelley's comment may have been cynical and manipulative, and even if it was not, many Irish workers either already believed it or took a new and important lesson from it. But what meaning attaches to the remarks of Walter Breen, who also argued that "class distinctions among the Irish impeded their progress"? Or, and more significantly, what is to be made of Maurice O'Connor's speech at an RELA celebration in November of 1892? O'Connor had been president of the Butte Miners' Union in 1889; his topic this night was "The Unity of all Irishmen."[54]

VI

All of this could be fitted neatly into what Aileen Kraditor calls a system paradigm, an analysis based on what Kraditor considers the false notion that industrial capitalism is a closed system that bears relentlessly on its working-class component. Specific reference could be made to intraethnic paternalism and the breaking down of class lines in the interests of capitalism and middle-class ideology. It is less obvious that this is how the matter was perceived in Butte, America, except perhaps by the late-arriving and transient Irish. The chances are better than even that Hennessy and Kelley were not being devious or hegemonic and that Norris and O'Connor had not been bought. They were simply expressing the values of the stable Irish of whatever class or occupation. It must again be emphasized that, whether intentionally or not, Hennessy's and Kelley's comments were of obvious service to the cause of social control. But if, in the process, they tended to reconcile labor to capital, the possibility that they reconciled capital to labor must also be considered. This last point goes beyond the interclass nature of Irish associations. It goes to the heart of Irish enclave life. The division was not just between working- and middle-class Irish but between the stable Irish of whatever class and those who were literally and figuratively unattached. The settled Irish shared a commitment to Ireland and to the world their persistence had won for them. Industrial peace in Butte forwarded the cause of both; conversely, labor radicalism jeopardized both.[55]

The common denominator at the seam—the New Departure exported to Butte—was that the enemies of Ireland and the enemies of Butte's Irish workers had both to be combated. This was acknowledged without extended comment, or complete understanding. Even when the same person served both adversarial roles—the English Unionist landlord in Ireland, for example, or the nativist mine owner or mine worker in America—there remained the important matter of determining for which of the two offenses punishment was intended. The Irish were little troubled by this abstraction. Tom Kealy, an Irish miner, gave wonderful, if totally inadvertent, expression to their confusion when he complained to the AOH of the "Englishmen in the [Montana] legislature making laws for the working man." Kealy's comment says volumes about the world of the Irish miner, but it confounds the larger historical question of Irish worker ideology.[56]

The use of the boycott, a uniquely Irish form of protest, provides a perfect case in point. As a Land League veteran then mining in Colorado put it, the boycott was learned in Ireland but "no more effective weapon . . . could possibly be used by a labor organization in bringing its enemies to time." Both scabs and hostile merchants could be "left severely alone." In Butte there were instances when labor organizations boycotted merchants, including Irish shopkeepers Martin Joyce, P. J. Brophy, and John Maguire, the last two AOH and RELA members, because they dealt unfairly with labor. On another occasion, however, the AOH voted to boycott orchestras affiliated with the Musicians' Union because the union had rejected John J. McNamara, "The Blind Boy," for membership. There were other instances when, according to the APA, the "Roman hierarcy" boycotted "Protestant merchants," presumably in the interests of Catholic sectarian dominance. And of course the associational Irish war on the stage Irishman involved RELA- and AOH-sponsored boycotts of shops and playhouses that displayed the offensive caricatures. In sum, there were instances of labor, Catholic, and ethnic boycotts, the first two overwhelmingly, the last exclusively Irish in concept and execution. The targets, however, though different in each instance, were also discreet and identifiable. There was no confusion as to the role identity of the boycotter or the purpose of the boycott.[57]

This was also the case when the boycott took place nearer the seam, when working Irish Catholics used it as an instrument of more general vengeance or, most significantly, as a way of guaranteeing the enclave.

At these times, though the boycott's targets were specific, its purposes, if not unfathomable, were at least confused. Irish control of the work force was one such instance. As the APA noted, Irish job preference necessarily involved the boycotting of non-Irish workers, a kind of ethnic closed shop that allowed one group of workers to discriminate against another group. It hardly needs to be added that this is the long road to worker solidarity. But that this form of discrimination was practiced was clearly the point of the APA's charge that "no Englishman need apply" at the Anaconda Company mines. The APA did not identify the motives of the "Irish bosses" who boycotted non-Irish workers. It assumed that they were following the lead of "Pope Marcus," who wanted complete control of his workers. To what ends, other than "Papist tyranny," was left unstated.[58]

William Andrews Clark, Daly's bitter and intractable rival, was as specific as the APA on the use of the boycott and as vague as to motive. Clark identified the boycott, along with "blacklisting, political debauchery" and the "perversion of wealth," as one of Daly's weapons in the war between the two copper kings. Daly was a "veritable dictator" (The APA had called him a "Roman Catholic dictator"); he "boycotted" all who resisted his "insolent domination." Obviously Daly was a quite-unconventional boycotter. He and his associates used it "to drive [a man] out of town;" they "boycotted all who don't vote as directed . . . they can not get a job of work." Again, the cause of labor radicalism was not well served as a consequence, but Clark hardly objected on those grounds. When asked why Daly and his associates wanted power, Clark evaded and dissembled. He did not understand—could never have understood—that Daly had set in motion a hiring system that guaranteed Irish enclave stability, that that hiring system was only partially self-sustaining and required careful maintenance, and that Daly's motives were no more (and no less) sinister than ethnic preference and the survival of Butte's Irish world.[59]

William J. Penrose was another who railed at this Irish/worker use of the boycott. His story is the most instructive of all. Penrose was an anomaly; a Cornish Methodist miner turned newspaperman, he rejected the party of 90 percent of his coreligionists and countrymen and became a strong and vocal Democrat. He explained his political conversion in a speech on Miners' Union Day in 1888. Workers were "their own worst enemies," he told the assembled miners; they must "throw away [their] prejudices concerning men of different races." Penrose certainly had. "I remember the time when I was a strict Republican and the only reason I had for it was because Irishmen were Democrats." Once awakened to the importance of "labor peace and class consciousness," he preached the "new doctrine, . . . marching arm in arm to-gether in common brotherhood."[60]

The sincerity of Penrose's conversion to worker solidarity and ethnic harmony cannot be known. Certainly he sounded like a Western labor advocate. His racial tolerance, for example, was not limitless. The Chinese, he said, were "pumpkin faced rat eaters . . . putrid with the leprosy of vice." In addition, at least until 1891, he stood with the BMU on the questions of the eight-hour day, mine safety, the closed shop, and the right to strike. Similarly, he looked the part of an en-lightened champion of Irish rights. Few Irishmen could have matched the sunburstery of Penrose's St. Patrick's Day rhetoric. He was as gush-ing in his praise of Daly and Hennessy. He denied that the Irish "pre-dominated at Anaconda properties," accusing those who charged Irish preference of being "Know Nothings." He wrote of "that wondrous religious organization, the Roman Catholic Church" and called En-gland's dominance of Ireland "a disgrace and shame." He had kind words for William Deeney upon Deeney's selection as a corporal of the Emmet Guards. When Deeney was elected treasurer of the BMU, Penrose referred to him as "one of God's noblemen." Irish workers can only have looked on in amazement. Penrose spoke to them at the seam. The genuineness of his professions, particularly on the Irish question, may be doubted—his paper was also the "offical organ of the Good Templar Lodges"—but his support was no less welcome.[61]

Then came the breach. At issue was the move of certain key Irish labor leaders from the Democratic party to a fusionist Labor/Repub-lican coalition. Among the defectors was Patrick Boland, former pres-ident of the BMU and an officer of the RELA. Another was "God's nobleman," William E. Deeney, also a BMU and RELA officer and a militant Irish nationalist. Boland became, according to Penrose, an "escapee from the insane asylum," a "blatherskate of the first water," and "a labor professional." Deeney, starting higher, fell further. He too was one of those "professional labor men, . . . who never work except to 'work' the genuine laborer." He had "never hit a drill in his life."[62]

Penrose also changed his mind on the eight-hour law. In December, 1890, he had written "that 8 hours per day [was] sufficient for any man who does manual labor." Three months later, as a member of the state legislature, he voted against an eight-hour law. As he explained the matter, a majority of the BMU rank and file was as convinced as he that legislation reducing the hours of work would force the mines to close, idling thousands of men. It was a disingenuous argument and the BMU leadership responded to Penrose's "treachery" by hanging a twelve-foot blackboard on Miners' Union Hall with a list of the names of the apostate legislators and a call to boycott, in whatever way was appropriate, each of them. Penrose's name headed the list.[63]

The full effect of the BMU boycott of Penrose's *Butte Mining Journal* cannot be known, though it is worth noting that among the advertisers who suddenly stopped using his pages was the D. J. Hennessy Mercantile Company. Penrose responded in language harsher even than that used by W. A. Clark. "The boycott," he wrote, "is a foreign importation only a little less obnoxious to decent American citizens than nihilism, communism, and kindred tenets of foreign cut throats and robbers." On another occasion he called it "the lowest, meanest, most despicable instrument of malice and revenge that was ever imported, . . . an unAmerican principle." Four years later the APA would make the same charge in much the same language. Penrose, of course, did not have to point out that the "foreign cut throats" were Irishmen, that the Irish, in fact, claimed an almost proprietary interest in the boycott as an instrument of both political and economic reform. He did, however, make clearer his intentions when he publicly urged passage of a law making it a misdemeanor to carry a foreign flag on American soil or to profess allegiance to any foreign nation or would-be nation.[64]

Penrose's attacks on Irish labor leaders continued in the spring of 1891, after his vote on the eight-hour law and the BMU boycott. In fact, Penrose added Peter Breen, Phil Hickey, and Eugene Kelly, each of them active or soon-to-be-active AOH and RELA members, to his list of labor manipulators. But far more significantly, he formed the Peace and Harmony Lodge of the Sons of St. George, an English Protestant fraternal society founded in Pennsylvania for the expressed purpose of combating the Irish Catholic Molly Maguires. Penrose had been a member of the Sons of St. George in New York City; he seemed to understand its purpose in Butte. As another Butte Englishman put it, "Penrose has brought the Englishmen of this county to the front . . . they had kept themselves in the background and were scattered broadcast over the community, . . . [now] they are banded together in one mighty body." The organization's function, however, was not political. Rather—and the lesson cannot have been lost on anyone—every Englishman was urged to join "because, if he should be unable to obtain employment, they will help him obtain it." This was Penrose's most obvious offense against the Irish community. He had challenged that community's control of the jobs necessary to its survival.[65]

Two weeks after this story appeared, Penrose was shot dead on a Butte street corner. Three Irish union leaders, William Deeney, Phil

Hickey, and Eugene Kelly, were charged with the murder. They were never convicted, although the national Sons of St. George, convinced that the Molly Maguires had resurfaced in Butte, spent $2,000 on their prosecution. Irish nationalists were as active in the defense of the three. When Deeney, Hickey, and Kelly were threatened with lynching, the Meagher Guards protected them. More remarkably, when Peter Breen, also implicated in the Penrose crime, was imprisoned for labor violence in Idaho in 1892, Marcus Daly joined the RELA in providing him and his family with financial relief. There is no certainty that Irish/workers killed Penrose. Indeed, the fact that the numbers, 3-7-77—known at the time if not later as a Masonic rather than a Montana vigilante symbol—were attached to his body is evidence either that the Irish were not involved or were clever enough to disguise it. The *Butte Mining Journal* was convinced that no labor organization had anything to do with the murder, though vague references to Molly Maguire and Mafia-type associations were frequently made. This is not, of course, the same as saying the Irish workers did not loathe Penrose.[66]

They may not, however, have known precisely the sources or the relative levels of intensity of their hostility. They may also not have cared. There was no labored effort to distinguish between Penrose the enemy of Ireland and Penrose the enemy of Butte's Irish workers. The object of the Irish workers was to guarantee safe and steady jobs, the survival of the enclave, and the social room to be Irish. These were interrelated issues and Penrose, like Clark and the APA, challenged each. Because of Daly and because of their numbers (which was the same thing), the Irish were able to protect their world from all three. However, the full effects tended toward ethnic conservativism rather than worker radicalism.

Also implied by all of this is that the older view that workers, through the BMU, exploited the War of the Copper Kings by playing corporate antagonists off against each other is only partly true. It ignores the fact that the leadership of the BMU was Irish and that the War of Copper Kings provided opportunities for ethnic as well as working-class advantage. The kingly rivals in the war were Daly, Clark, and F. Augustus Heinze. Each, like Penrose, courted the support of labor; Clark and Heinze by agreeing to the eight-hour day, Daly and the Anaconda managers by recalling their working-class backgrounds. But it is at least as significant that both Clark and Heinze, again like Penrose, tried also to match Daly's Irishness. As noted, Clark claimed to be a fluent Gaelic-Irish speaker. As for Heinze, he gave $500 to the Irish National League, claimed Norman Irish descent through his mother's family, and filled the columns of his newspaper with tales of past Irish glories and future

Irish triumphs. Obviously, Irish control of the work force gave them enormous and quite unprecedented power.[67]

This kind of power was heady stuff. Whether it was also corrupting depended on how seriously abstract notions of working-class solidarity were taken. Whatever the judgment, it seems obvious that this was not the usual formula for worker radicalism. There was no focus to Irish worker protest; no effort by the Irish leaders of the BMU to identify and mark their targets as enemies of the working class. It remains debatable, for example, which was Penrose's greater sin, opposing the eight-hour day or founding the Sons of St. George. Little wonder that both of Daly's rivals, Clark and Heinze, were uncertain if an ethnic or a class appeal would be more effective and so tried both. Since revolutionary class consciousness, however, requires as clear an understanding of antagonists as of friends, the Irish worker was an unlikely candidate for working-class radicalism.

VII

He was an equally unlikely candidate for working-class obsequiousness. Membership in an Irish enclave obviously contributed to feelings of ambivalence when it came time to define roles, but the enclave was occupational and social as well as ethnic, and an awareness of workers' rights was as basic to its purpose as an awareness of Irish rights. An Irishman did not have to be a miner to be admitted to the enclave, but he did have to acknowledge the centrality of working-class values to stay. Those values were communal. The emphasis was more on steady work and the dignity and self respect that attached to doing it well than on social mobility; on lessening the effects of job instability or occupational hazards by collective action rather than individualism; on sociability, even affability, rather than material acquisitiveness; on loyalty to friends and family rather than benign selfishness. This was a society based more on the exchange of gifts and favors than on the exchange of money. As such, though it was unlikely that the enclave would ever initiate worker protest, it was ideally situated to provide the cohesiveness and support necessary to sustain such protest should it arise. In this, and the irony is obvious, the enclave most resembled the cooperative commonwealth of the socialists' imagination. In Butte's Irish world, the community owned everything except the means of production—and enclave control of jobs came close to providing even that.[68]

All of this, however, was acted out with minimal reliance on the non-Irish. New men even learned the trade in Irish saloons or in Hibernia Hall rather than in the Union Hall. It was a world of Irish miners working Irish mines in an Irish town. Given such, the enclave displayed a strong, if not always ideologically correct, working-class bias. Even the associations' tendency to elect middle-class Irish to leadership positions may have been owing more to night shifts and willingness to serve than to social deference. Moreover, these middle-class associational leaders were usually not far removed from their own working-class origins, and in all cases were sympathetic to the legitimate needs of labor. Those sixty-four AOH and/or RELA members who held union offices are here at issue. So are the tens of thousands of dollars in sick and death benefits, the days off, and the job committees.

It follows that if Irish union leaders brought some of their Irishness to the conduct of union affairs, the reverse was also true, that worker issues played a major role in the conduct of ethnic affairs. It may even follow that, as in Bodie, California, for example, the town with the strongest Irish nationalist clubs figured to have the strongest unions. Seams function both ways; if the workers were Irish so too were the Irish workers. That was the formula of Patrick Ford. In Butte, enclave control of the work force was the most obvious expression of Irish associational involvement in work-related affairs. Ford may have questioned the propriety of what amounted to ethnic job auctions but in the real world of Butte this control permitted the needs of the Irish world and those of the American industrial worker to be simultaneously met.[69]

There were scores of examples of Irish concern with issues of general and working-class reform. When the RELA sent a delegation to Helena to help found a new Clan-na-Gael camp, the first thing the Butte Irish told the Helenans was that they had to "formulate a plan for the workers." Similarly, it was as natural that the RELA would sponsor a "resolution of mourning" on the death of Wendell Phillips as on the death of Michael Davitt. Phillips, according to the resolution, was a man who "on all occasions and under all circumstances" championed the cause of the "oppressed of all countries and creeds, especially Ireland." Davitt was "one of the greatest advocates of Irish liberty and the rights of the poor." In other words, the only difference between the two was one of emphasis.[70]

A touchier issue was that of immigration restriction. The RELA took the question—doubtless with the assumption that Asian immigration was and should be restricted—as a debate topic in 1893. Number 6 argued that immigration was "good for us and for the countries left." Number 51 was less sure; he thought it possible that "the labouring class" would benefit from restriction. Number 91 agreed but added that all deserved "the same advantages we (and our ancestors) had." No vote was taken, though the majority of the recorded remarks opposed restriction as unfair to European workers, Irish obviously included, and unnecessary to the security of American workers. Both sides in this RELA debate, however, adopted what was clearly a pro-labor position.[71]

In 1900 the AOH showed itself no less aware of workers' rights. At issue was the strike-supported demand of the Butte Clerks' Protective Union that Hennessy's Mercantile honor the early closing agreement negotiated with other Butte merchants. As will be seen, the Butte Miner's Union rescinded its initial support for the clerks and voted with Hennessy. A motion was introduced that the AOH "endorse the action of [the Clerks' Union] movement." This was followed by an important amendment from an unnamed Hibernian, who wanted to notify the "BCPU that we are a Fraternal organization and feel that we should not interfere with laborer matters." One can almost hear the seam tearing! The amended motion, however, lost to the original motion and the AOH went on record as favoring the strikers and the early closing agreement. Though hardly a return to the days of the Molly Maguires, this was a significant vote. The AOH had publicly supported a union strike against a prominent member's store in alleged violation of its exclusively "fraternal" role and despite the prevarication of the Miners' Union.[72]

These are not radical responses to worker issues. But neither are they responses that suggest the embourgeoisment of the Irish associations or of the larger enclave of which they were a part. The values of the enclave reflect its dominant working-class component, and if the middle-class leadership strayed—as when it set the price of tickets for an annual banquet at $6.00, "shutting out the common class," or when it put on the airs of "MPs and landlords"—it was quickly and firmly rebuked. Similarly, though the priests were listened to, there is no evidence that Irish miners allowed the clergy to determine their politics. Indeed, a kind of gentle anticlericalism marked the policies of both the nonsectarian RELA and the Catholic AOH. The Minute Books of both organizations contain references like that to the "domination" of the Irish peasantry by the clergy or to the "severe criticism" of Cardinal Logue of Ireland who would rather see the Irish "forever in slavery than become affiliated with the labor party," or even to charitable contributions "going into the pocket of the bishop."[73]

This was the tradition from which the BMU's Irish officers came. Obviously, it provided them with a mixed and cluttered legacy, a legacy that combined Irish nationalism and working-class conservatism with the keenest possible appreciation of workers' rights. There was a contradiction here only for those who insisted that radical class consciousness occurred naturally, almost in the biological sense of the word, in a capitalist system. Worker class consciousness was natural in a place like Butte, but radicalism was not, and neither was the subordination of other group affinities to this consciousness of class. Butte's stable Irish were the products of an ethno-occupational community; they shared its values. They were aware that there were competing value systems; they may even have listened attentively as those systems were explained to them. But in the end the only world that made sense to them was the world from which they had come and which still satisfied their needs. And, until that world failed them, they would continue to define their goals and formulate their policies according to its proscriptions.

NOTES

1. Hobsbawm, "Debating Labor Aristocracy," pp. 220–21, 223, 227–28; Bodnar, *Workers' World*, pp. 1–2.

2. See Bodnar, *Workers' World*, pp. 63–75, and *Transplanted*, pp. xviii, 85–112, 117–20.

3. For parish boundaries, see "Butte's Parish Boundaries."

4. Kraditor discusses at length the tendency of historians to assume that class allegiances were "natural" and that ethnic allegiances were "unnatural" obstacles to the full realization of class awareness (*Radical Persuasion*, pp. 1–34, 43–45, 55–85). See also Cantor, "Introduction," pp. 22–23; and Hobsbawm, "Debating Labor Aristocracy," p. 223.

5. Suggested by all of this is that the most mobile workers were potentially the most easily radicalized; or at least the most easily moved to violence. The more settled the working class, the less likely it was to embrace radical theories or radical means. See, for example, the comments in WFM, Exec. Board, MB, May 25, Dec. 12, 1903; June 14, 1904. Immigration Commission, *Immigrants in Industries*, 1911, part 25, pp. 106–8, 121–23, 142–43, 153–56. For a different interpretation, see Thernstrom, "Socialism," pp. 411–16, and *Poverty and Progress*, pp. 84–90, 167–68.

6. Foner, "Land League," pp. 150–200; Montgomery, "Irish," pp. 205–18; Walkowitz, *Worker City*, pp. 166–70, e.g.; Brundage, "Making of Workingclass Radicalism," particularly pp. 50–87; Wilentz, "Industrializing America," pp. 579–95. See also Laslett, *Labor and the Left*. It must be pointed out that each of these historians also notes that ethnic, including Irish, associations could and often did detract from class awareness on some occasions.

7. There was a relatively minor incident in 1887, when more than twenty Italian miners were forced to join the BMU. See *Butte Intermountain*, June 13, 14, 1887; Smith, "Rise and Fall," pp. 23–30; Lingenfelter, *Hardrock Miners*, pp.

188–89. On the other strikes see Vernon Jensen, *Heritage of Conflict*, passim, and Lingenfelter, *Hardrock Miners*, passim.

8. For the history of the Western Federation of Miners and the unions that were formed from it, see Wyman, *Hardrock Epic*; Vernon Jensen, *Heritage of Conflict*; Paul Brissenden, *IWW*, Dubofsky, "Origins" (the definition of radicalism is on p. 231); Dubofsky, *We Shall Be All*. On the percentage of WFM membership from the BMU see WFM, *Proceedings*, 1893–1914; Smith, "Rise and Fall," p. 5.

9. Bodnar, *Workers' World*, p. 63. Brody, *Workers in Industrial America*; p. 35; Hobsbawm, "Aristocracy," p. 224; Thomas N. Brown, *Irish-American Nationalism*, pp. 23–24; Taylor, *Distant Magnet*, p. 233. Daniel Walkowitz discusses the ways communities could sustain worker protest (*Worker City*, pp. 110–28).

10. On the BMU's resolutions, see BMU, *Constitution and Bylaws*, p. 21.

11. In 1901 copies of the *Irish World* were sent to the men imprisoned in Idaho and California for leading strikes in the mines. WFM, *Proceedings*, 1901, p. 124. On the Leadville and Wood River strikes see Vernon Jensen, *Heritage of Conflict*, p. 22, and Lingenfelter, *Hardrock Miners*, p. 173.

12. Wilentz, "Industrializing America," p. 586. For Irishmen in the American labor movement see Montgomery, "Irish." See also the Irish leaders of western mine unions in Lingenfelter, *Hardrock Miners*, passim; Burchell, *San Francisco Irish*, pp. 106, 107; Wyman, *Hardrock Epic*, pp. 46–47.

13. Kraditor argues that some immigrants, for example, the Finns, were radicalized by their European experiences (*Radical Persuasion*, pp. 12, 22, 52, 310). On this same point see Vecoli, "Comment," in *Failure of a Dream?* pp. 269–84; Gedicks, "Ethnicity," pp. 127–56. See also the comments of Frank Aaltonen in WFM, *Proceedings*, 1914, pp. 190–91.

14. The Pearse quote is from Lyons, *Culture and Anarchy*, p. 94. Broehl, *Molly Maguires*.

15. The *Butte Bystander* of June 7, 1896, listed the presidents of the union from its founding in 1878 along with the men who served with Witter. The 1897 officer list is from ibid., Mar. 7, 1897. City directories list all the officers from 1901 to 1914. AOH, Membership and Dues Ledgers; RELA, Membership and Dues Ledgers. The leadership of the BMU was far more Irish than that of the other WFM locals. See the *Butte Bystander*, Nov. 15, 1896. That was probably because Butte was more Irish than the other western mining towns. See Immigration Commission, *Immigrants in Industries*, 1911, part 18, pp. 145, 211, 547–82.

16.Information on Patrick Boland is from RELA, MB, Mar. 6, 1884; Jan. 9, 1896; the *Butte Bystander*, June 7, 1896; *Irish World*, Jan. 7, 1882. Information on James Maher is from AOH D1, MB, July 19, 1893; RELA, *Membership and Dues Ledgers*, 1894–98; the *Butte Bystander*, June 7, 1896; *Miners Magazine*, June, 1901; Edward Boyce, diary entry, May 14, 1901, "Diaries," Boyce Papers; information on M. J. Burke is from AOH D1, MB, Dec. 18, 1895; the *Butte Bystander*, June 7, 1896. Information on Anthony Shovlin is from AOH D1, MB, Dec. 18, 1895; RELA, Membership and Dues Ledgers, 1894–98; Polk, *City*

Directory, 1903; Gift and Subscription Lists, 1903, Boyce Papers. Information on McCarthy is from AOH D1, MB, Aug. 16, 1905; Polk, *City Directory*, 1906.

17. City directories give BMU memberships by year. On the 80 percent membership figures see the *Butte Bystander*, Mar. 17, 1894, and Evans, *Address*, p. 16. For a discussion of the winning of closed-shop conditions see *Butte Intermountain*, June 13, 14, 1887; Lingenfelter, *Hardrock Miners*, pp. 188–89. The thirty-day grace period is referred to in Bohn, "Butte Number One," p. 11; Haywood, "Revolt at Butte," p. 93. On the size of the Miners' Union hall see Industrial Commission, *Mining at Butte*, 1915, p. 3767; Haywood, *Bill Haywood's Book*, p. 83.

18. AOH and RELA attendance figures are from the MBs of both organizations. Generally, from sixty to one hundred men attended meetings.

19. Lyons, *Culture and Anarchy*, p. 52; Kennedy, *The Irish*, pp. 149–51, 192–94; Joseph Lee, *Modernisation*, pp. 89–106, 163–64. James Donnelly points out that once emigration became a possibility, marriage was postponed (*Land and People*, p. 222). Miller, *Emigrants*, p. 428.

20. Bureau of Census, *MS Census*, 1900; *Statistical History*, p. 15 The Irish figures for 1926 are in Bogue, *Principles of Demography*, p. 317. See also Burchell, *San Francisco Irish*, pp. 49–50; Conzen, "New Urban History," pp. 75, 76; Cantor, "Introduction," p. 15; Walkowitz, *Worker City*, pp. 106, 137–38.

21. Bureau of Census, *MS Census*, 1900 and 1910. See also Bodnar, *Transplanted*, pp. 77, 79, and Walkowitz, *Worker City*, pp. 112–14.

22. William Read to the Walker Brothers, June 21, 1878, *Alice Mining Co. Records*, Letter Press Books. RELA, MB, July 29, 1886; Polk, *City Directory*, 1888–89.

23. The Peter Breen story is from Smith, "Rise and Fall," p. 24. For Daly's early prolabor position see Malone, *Battle for Butte*, p. 55. *Butte Bystander*, Apr. 21 and Nov. 5, 1894. The Boland remarks are taken from the *Anaconda Standard*, Mar. 14, 15, 1915. Connolly, "Story of Montana," pp. 459–60. See also WPA, *Copper Camp*, p. 39; *Butte Mining Journal*, June 6, 1888.

24. For examples of reference to Daly as "Mister" or "The Honorable" see AOH D1, MB, July 7, 1886; Nov. 14, 1900; RELA, MB, Oct. 14 and 21, 1886. See also the remarks of Judge Jeremiah Lynch from AOH, *Proceedings*, 1906. The resolution is from AOH D1, MB, Nov. 28, 1900. Samuel Hauser, a very prominent Montana banker and politician, referred to Daly as "the boss Irishman." Committee on Privileges and Elections, *Report*, III:1402. See also O'Daly, *Life*, [220]; *Butte Mining Journal*, Feb. 18, 1891.

25. Hobsbawm, "Debating Labor Aristocracy," pp. 219–20, 221, 223.

26. Bodnar, *Workers' World*, pp. 1, 185.

27. Ibid., pp. 63, 165–66.

28. For a recent example of Hennessy's alleged role as Daly's crony see Malone, *Battle for Butte*, pp. 59, 88, 165. The AOH references are from O'Dea, *AOH*, III:1406–7; my emphasis. Breen was quoted in the *Anaconda Standard*, Mar. 18, 1910.

29. The reference to Hennessy as well informed on ACM affairs is from O'Daly, *Life*, [37]; see also [15, 225, 242]. Reference to Hennessy's finding jobs

for Irish association members is from AOH D1, MB, Jan. 17, 1894; RELA, MB, Aug. 7, 1907; AOH D3, MB, Sept. 9, 1907. Marcus Daly paid his employees in time checks rather than bank checks; these time checks were payable at Hennessy's store with a percentage of the wage applied to the worker's bill. Industrial Commission, *Mining at Butte*, 1911, pp. 4001, 4003, 4006, 4066–68. His $500 contribution to St. Mary's is in Franchi, "History of St. Mary's." Hennessy's store in Hibernia Hall paid $50 per month rent. Hibernia Hall, Board of Trustees, Rent Ledger, 1894–1911. There are repeated references to his addressing the RELA from 1886 to his death in 1908 in the associations MBs. References to his holding AOH offices at local, state, and national levels are in AOH, MB, Aug. 3 and 31, 1904; AOH, Membership and Dues Ledgers; O'Dea, *AOH*, III:1303, 1406. The RELA resolution at his death is from MB, n.d., [ca. Jan. 28, 1908]. The motion, made by Judge Lynch, that a portrait of Hennessy be hung in Hibernia Hall is from RELA, MB, Jan. 30, 1908.

30. Ryan was identified as the portraitist in RELA, MB, July 23, 1908. For Ryan's career see Malone, *Battle for Butte*, pp. 165–67; Marcosson, *Anaconda*, pp. 100–101; Industrial Commission, *Mining at Butte*, 1915, pp. 3683–84. The AOH resolution is from D1, MB, June 1, 1904; the RELA resolution is from MB, June 10, 1909.

31. *Butte Bulletin*, Sept. 7, 1918. Kraditor, *Radical Persuasion*, pp. 7–8, 42–46, 276–77, 297–300.

32. Cross, "The Irish," p. 180; Kraditor, *Radical Persuasion*, pp. 69–71; Mary Carroll to John Carroll, Oct. 2, 1904, Carroll Papers; AOH, MB, Apr. 24, 1901. There is no evidence the book was ever done but the idea resurfaced in 1914. AOH D3, MB, May 2, 1914. That these "mugbooks" were a way of establishing a group's social legitimacy and prominence was discussed by Milner in "Inventing Montana."

33. The 1897 production figures for Daly mines were taken from Malone, *Battle for Butte*, pp. 52–54. Hobsbawm refers to the sense of "personal superiority" in "Aristocracy," p. 236; emphasis in the original. AOH, *Proceedings*, 1906, n.p.

34. AOH D3, MB, Mar. 18, Apr. 1, 8, 29, Dec. 13, 1913; RELA, MB, July 19, 1906. Note that all of these remarks came late in the history of Butte's Irishtown.

35. The Hurley story is from AOH D1 MB, Aug. 17, Oct. 19, 1892. Kennedy is identified as the proprietor of the Shamrock Saloon in Polk, *City Directory*, 1908. James Curtin's comments are from interview.

36. RELA, MB, July 24, Aug. 3, 1905; AOH D1, MB, July 26, 1905. See also AOH D3, MB, July 24 and 31, 1905; July 7, 1908; May 13, 1911. O'Dea, *AOH*, III:1171–72; John Carroll, "Address of Bishop Carroll Pertaining to Education," n.d., ca. 1911, Carroll Papers. *Butte Independent*, Oct. 15, 1910.

37. J. J. Griffin said that after three months in the "Flat Head" his health was "very much improved." AOH D3, MB, May 13, 1911. *Irish World*, July 12, 1879.

38. AOH D3, MB, May 13, 1911; Brosnan to his mother, Apr. 11, 1917; to his father, Sept. 1, 1918, Brosnan Letters. See on this same point Kennedy, *The Irish*, pp. 71–73, 84; Dennis Clark, *Irish in Philadelphia*, p. 132.

39. There are many references to members' visiting Ireland or reporting on visits. See, e.g., RELA, MB, June 13, 1889; Jan. 19, Oct. 19, 1899; Sept. 6, 1906; June 17, Sept. 26, Oct. 7, 1909, July 18, 1912; Aug. 15, 1921. AOH D1, MB, Aug. 10, Nov. 30, 1898; Oct. 4, 1905; AOH D3, MB, Oct. 1, 1906; May 6; June 24, 1907; Oct. 28, 1911; Nov. 11, 1916. AOH, Silver Bow Co. Board, MB, May 10, 1909. RELA, Financial Records, May, 1912. In 1908 an "Irish Home-Going Movement" was begun in Chicago, founded by Francis J. Kilkenny. Its purpose was to encourage Irish-Americans to bring their money and "know how" to Ireland. *Butte Independent*, Aug. 6, 1910. On O'Daly see Life, passim.

40. For Carroll see *Butte Mining Journal*, Feb. 25, 1891.

41. For Higgins see *Butte Independent*, Feb. 12, 1910. For Brennan see the *Anaconda Standard*, Sept. 7, 1925. For O'Neill see Hand et al., "Songs," p. 29.

42. On occupation mobility as partial proof of the openness of the system see Burchell, *San Francisco Irish*, pp. 11–12; Walkowitz, *Worker City*, pp. 101, 106.

43. On the Boer Ambulance Fund see RELA, MB, Feb. 8 and 15, 1900. On the Meagher Memorial Fund see ibid., Aug. 3 and 10, 1899. On widows see ibid., Feb. 18, 1904; AOH D1, MB, Jan. 2, Aug. 7, 1901. On day-shift work see AOH D3, MB, July 26, 1909; Nov. 13, 1915; RELA, MB, Jan. 16, 1913. For watchmen see Industrial Commission, *Mining at Butte*, 1915, pp. 3698, 3703–4. For the number 2 shaft at the Mountain Con see Hand, "Folklore," p. 154.

44. RELA, MB, June 28, July 5, 1900; AOH D1, MB, Mar. 3, 1897; AOH D3, MB, Mar. 11, 1907. Tickets for the 1906 St. Patrick's Day dance were available at ACM offices. AOH, Receipts, n.d., 1906. Butte native George Oechsli commented that ACM officers were "expected" to contribute to Irish causes (interview). For other instances of mine and smelter shutdowns for Irish holidays see AOH D1, MB, July 31, 1885; Mar. 10, 1897; July 7, 1886; Mar. 13, 1889; Aug. 22, 1894; June 26, 1895; Mar. 10, 1897; Mar. 9, 1898; July 10, 1901. RELA, MB, June 13, 1889; June 29, 1899; July 18, 1901.

45. AOH D1, MB, Aug. 22, 1894; Mar. 3, 1897.

46. On working Sundays see the remarks of Con Kelley in Industrial Commission, *Mining at Butte*, 1915, p. 3712. See also Hand, "Folklore," p. 14n41.

47. Hand, "Folklore," p. 171, has the lyrics to "Miners' Union Day in Butte." On the events of June 13, 1896, see the *Butte Bystander*, June 7, 1896. On the use of Hibernia Hall for Miners' Union Day activities see, e.g., AOH D1, MB, Apr. 4, 1888; May 30, 1894; May 22, 1895; June 6, 1900. Walkowitz, *Worker City*, p. 157.

48. See, e.g., Karson, *American Labor Unions*, and "Catholic Anti-Socialism." The Church's proscription on membership in the WFM is on p. 87. On this point see also the remarks of Edward Boyce, diary entry for Apr. 7, 1902, Boyce Papers; Browne, *Church and Knights*, and "Comment"; and three excellent articles in *Labor History*: Harrington, "Catholics in the Labor Movement"; Suggs, "Religion and Labor"; and Doherty, "Thomas J. Haggerty." On Bishop Brondel see his letter to John Cardinal Simeoni, Jan. 8, 1884, Brondel Papers. Brondel's hostility to the *Irish World* was mentioned by Father Sarsfield O'Sullivan. Interview. The Democratic party was similarly useful as a moderating influence

on working-class radicalism. See, e.g., Walkowitz, *Worker City,* pp. 225, 256; Thomas N. Brown, *Irish-American Nationalism,* p. 146.

49. AOH, *Constitution, 1886.* Burchell, *San Francisco Irish,* p. 102. See also, however, the AOH's support in 1904 for striking Colorado miners and the order's condemnation in 1912 "of selfish greed and . . . intolerable industrial conditions" (*Miners Magazine,* July 28, 1904; O'Dea, *AOH,* III:1305–6). Carroll questions the influence of the Catholic clergy on labor matters in "Not Skipping the Sermon."

50. RELA, MB, Sept. 7, 1883.

51. For Breen's nomination of Con Kelley, see AOH, Membership and Dues Ledger, 1900–1901; *Butte Bystander,* Dec. 31, 1895.

52. RELA, MB, Feb. 21, 1889; AOH D1, MB, Aug. 11, 1905; RELA and Phil Sheridan Club (Anaconda, Montana, Clan-na-Gael), Proceedings of Joint Meeting, Jan. 21, 1898.

53. Total parish size in 1905 was 18,000, 8,000 at St. Patrick's, 5,000 at St. Lawrence O'Toole's, and 5,000 at St. Mary's (Polk *City Directory,* 1905). More than 10,000 people attended the summer picnic in 1907. RELA, MB, Aug. 15, 1907. St. Patrick's Day parades still (1987) attract more than 30,000.

54. Hennessy's remarks are from RELA, MB, Oct. 17, 1901. Kelley's were reprinted in the *Butte Independent,* Apr. 2, 1910. James B. Mulcahy's *Butte Independent* was an interclass Irish newspaper. That is what he had promised when he came to Butte. See RELA, MB, Dec. 23, 1909; AOH D1, MB, Dec. 18, 1909. Breen's comments are from AOH D3, MB, Sept. 24, 1910. O'Connor's are from RELA, MB, Nov. 20, 1892.

55. Kraditor, *Radical Persuasion,* pp. 55–85.

56. AOH D3, MB, Nov. 12, 1910.

57. The Colorado miner identified himself as "Kilmainham" (*Miners Magazine,* Jan., 1901). The WFM policy towards scabs was "boycott and contempt" rather than violence. They were to be "snubbed and jeered" (WFM, Exec. Board, "Report," July 14, 1910). On Maguire and Brophy see AOH and RELA, Membership and Dues Ledgers; RELA, MB, Aug. 27, 1882. The boycotts of each of these associational Irishmen, as well as that against Joyce, are from the *Butte Bystander,* Sept. 1, 1894; Nov. 29, 1896; *Butte Mining Journal,* Apr. 22, 1891. Joyce later joined the AOH. See Membership and Dues Ledgers. Catholic "boycotts are discussed in the *Examiner* (Butte), Nov. 2 and 23, 1895; Feb. 13, 1896. Boycotts against those who were guilty of showing the Irish in unflattering caricature are from RELA, MB, Dec. 21, 1905; AOH, MB, Dec. 20, 1905. The McNamara story is from AOH D1, MB, Apr. 3 and 17, 1901.

58. The *Examiner* (Butte), Apr. 19, Sept. 3, 1896.

59. Foot, "Senatorial Aspirations of Clark," pp. 34–36. *Congressional Record,* 56 Cong., 1st sess., May 15, 1900, vol. 33, pt. 6, pp. 5531, 5535–36; Committee on Privileges and Elections, *Report,* pp. 1934, 2068–71, 2147, 2167; *Examiner* (Butte), June 15, 1895; Oct. 31, 1896.

60. On Cornish Methodist voting habits see Kleppner, *Cross of Culture,* p. 70. Penrose's politics, including his "conversion," are detailed in his news-

paper, the *Butte Mining Journal*. See issues of Dec. 7, 1887; Nov. 25, 1888; specific quotes are from issues of Nov. 12, 1887, and June 16, 1888.

61. For Penrose's views on various issues see the following issues of the *Butte Mining Journal:* On Chinese, Dec. 10, 1887; Feb. 25 and May 20, 1891. On eight-hour day, Dec. 17, 1890; Mar. 15, 1891. On mine safety, June 16, 1888. On closed shop, Sept. 14, 1887; Sept. 2, 1888. On the right to strike, Feb. 18, 1891. On support for the Irish cause, Dec. 31, 1887; Jan. 25, Mar. 17 and 21, Dec. 30, 1888; Oct. 7, Nov. 16, 1890. The reference to "Know Nothings" in the legislature is from Feb. 20, 1889. The "wondrous religious organization" is from Nov. 2, 1887. England's "disgrace and shame" is revealed in Feb. 11, 1888. Deeney's qualities are mentioned in Dec. 14, 1887; Mar. 10, Sept. 5, 1888. Penrose mentions his connection with the Good Templars in Jan. 13, 1889. He had for years carried a "News from Cornwall" section much like the news from Ireland feature in the *Montana Catholic*. See, e.g., *Butte Mining Journal*, Oct. 8, Nov. 16, 1887; Oct. 28, 1888.

62. The defection of Boland and Deeney is from *Butte Mining Journal*, Sept. 7, 1890; Mar. 1, 1891. Boland was described in the issues of Sept. 7, 1890, and May 24, 1891. Deeney was criticized in the issues of Sept. 10, 1890 and Apr. 4, 1891.

63. *Butte Mining Journal*, Dec. 17, 1890. See also the issue of Feb. 25, 1891. Penrose attempted to explain his vote on Feb. 22, Mar. 1, Apr. 15 and 22, 1891. On Nov. 23, 1890, he had written on a matter unrelated to eight-hour legislation that "nothing should be done that interferes with (the mines') continued development and increase." Penrose wrote of the blackboard and boycott of his paper on Feb. 25, Mar. 1, and Apr. 29, 1891.

64. No Hennessy ads appeared after the issue of Mar. 1, 1891. The reference to boycotting as a "foreign importation" is from *Butte Mining Journal*, Apr. 19, 1891. The other quotes are from issues of May 10 and June 17, 1891. Penrose's hostility to foreign flags in Butte was in long stories in the issues of May 24, June 7 and 28, 1891.

65. The attacks on Breen, Hickey, and Kelly were from the *Butte Mining Journal*, Sept. 7, 1890; Mar. 1, Apr. 22, June 10, 1891. All three were listed as RELA and/or AOH members by 1892 (Membership and Dues Ledgers). For Penrose's involvement in the founding of the Sons of St. George, see *Butte Mining Journal*, Apr. 26, May 24, May 27, 1891. The references to England "to the front" and the promise of employment is from the issue of May 27. On the Sons of St. George in Pennsylvania, see Berthoff, *British Immigrants*, pp. 188–89. In 1892 the Butte Sons of St. George asked the RELA if the Irish organization would hang a picture of Queen Victoria in Hibernia Hall. The Emmets "threw the request away" (RELA, MB, Sept. 1, 1892).

66. The murder of Penrose is discusses in Lingenfelter, *Hardrock Miners*, pp. 190–93; Malone, *Battle for Butte*, p. 77; Berthoff, *British Immigrants*, p. 189; *Butte Mining Journal*, June 10, 1891. The rivalries between Irish and Cornish copper miners data back to Ireland and the mines of West Cork; see du Maurier, *Hungry Hill*, pp. 13–14, 23, 26. For the Meagher Guards protecting the accused Irishmen, see the obituary for William Deeney in the *Anaconda Standard*, May

17, 1924. In 1906 Deeney shot to death another Irishman, Austin O'Malley, in a quarrel. Silver Bow Co., *Mortuary Records*, 1906–7. On the help provided Peter Breen see, RELA, MB, Apr. 14 and 21, Dec. 1, 1892. Daly posted Breen's bail during Breen's problems with Idaho authorities (Smith, "Rise and Fall," p. 24). The *Butte Mining Journal* of June 24, 1891, mentioned the note with 3–7–77 attached to Penrose's body. For an account of what those numbers may have symbolized, see Myers, "Vigilante Numbers." Not long after the Penrose affair the Hibernia Hall Board rented space to Absalom Bray, a Cornishman, a Republican, later a Populist, and a member of the Sons of St. George. Hibernia Hall Board of Directors, *Rent Ledger*, 1894–1911, IrC. City directories; Waldron and Wilson, *Atlas*, pp. 13, 17.

67. The story of the BMU playing corporate rivals off against one another is told in Smith, "Rise and Fall," pp. 3–18; Malone, *Battle for Butte*, pp. 77–79, 151; Foot, "Senatorial Aspirations of Clark," p. 209. Clark's and Heinze's "gift" of the eight-hour day was publicized in the WFM's *Miners Magazine*, July and Sept., 1900. ACM, it was charged, did not immediately follow Clark's and Heinze's lead. See the comments of Joseph Shannon to the Industrial Commission, *Mining at Butte*, 1915, p. 3853. Heinze had said that eight hours would improve both the "character of the city" and "company profits." Kelley noted the strong tradition of ACM support for working men in Industrial Commission, *Mining at Butte*, 1915, p. 3715. Heinze's gift to the National Irish League is the subject of letters to him from P. J. Brophy, June 6 and June 19, 1903, Brophy Papers. Heinze claimed Irish descent from his mother in his newspaper, the *Reveille* (Butte), Oct. 11, 1902. See also the Irish stories in ibid., Sept. 20 and 23, Oct. 1 and 19, 1902.

68. For a reference to the "Cooperative Commonwealth," see the 1905 IWW document cited in Haywood, *Bill Haywood's Book*, p. 175.

69. For Bodie's contributions to Patrick Ford and the Irish Land League, see Foner, "Land League," p. 171. Bodie's union is discussed in Lingenfelter, *Hardrock Miners*, pp. 131–33. For union meetings in Irish halls see, AOH D1, MB, Feb. 18, 1891; Feb. 6, 1901; RELA, MB, June 3, 1886; Dec. 10, 1896; *Butte Bystander*, Mar. 11, 1893; Sept. 4, 1897.

70. Sunburst Club (Helena Clan-na-Gael), MB, Oct. 2, 1899; RELA, MB, Mar. 6, 1884; Aug. 10, 1899. On the Irish and Phillips see Foner, "Land League," pp. 150–51.

71. The debate over immigration restriction is from RELA, MB, Feb. 16, Mar. 16, 1893. The RELA debate mirrored the positions taken by the AFL. See Higham, *Strangers*, pp. 71–72.

72. The AOH decision to support the clerks is from D1, MB, Feb. 28, 1900. For a general discussion of the issue, including the BMU's refusal to support the BCPU, see the *Miners Magazine*, May and Dec., 1900; Smith "Rise and Fall," p. 26. The national AOH also publicly supported the strike by miners in Colorado in 1904. See O'Dea, *AOH*, III:1305–6, 1451; *Miners Magazine*, July 28, 1904.

73. Condemnation of overpriced banquet is from AOH D3, MB, Oct. 7, 1907; Feb. 15, 1909. Reference to aristocratic pretensions is from MB, Dec. 30, 1911. Gently anticlerical references are from MB, Oct. 28; Dec. 9, 1907; June 15, 1908, RELA, MB, Feb. 24, 1908; AOH, Silver Bow Co. Board, MB, Mar. 27, 1908. As early as 1889, the AOH condemned the priests' insistence on attendance at Mass as "coercive" (D1, MB, May 1, 1889).

Engine room, West Cork. Photo courtesy of Don Leary.

Anaconda, Neversweat and Mountain View Mines, Butte, Mont.

Central Butte Hill and Dublin Gulch, ca. 1905. Photo courtesy of the Montana Historical Society.

The Neversweat Mine with its famous seven stacks; Dublin Gulch in the fore-
ground. Ca. 1905. Photo courtesy of the University of Montana.

Montana Ore Purchasing Co. smelter. Photo courtesy of the University of
Montana.

Crew of the Neversweat Mine, 1902. Photo courtesy of the Montana Historical Society.

Typical physician's certificates with BMU crossed out and AOH substituted. Photos courtesy of the World Museum of Mining, Butte.

Gravestone of Con McGee,
St. Patrick's Cemetery,
Butte. Photo courtesy of
Don Leary.

The RELA monument, St.
Patrick's Cemetery, Butte.
Photo courtesy of Don
Leary.

Dedication of the statue of Thomas Francis Meagher, 1905. Photo courtesy of the Montana Historical Society.

Ancient Order of Hibernians convention outside St. Patrick's Church, Butte. Probably 1910. Photo courtesy of the University of Montana and the World Museum of Mining, Butte.

These two photos show the Miners' Union Hall in June of 1914. The top photo shows the damage done by the riot of June 13, the bottom shows the hall after it was dynamited on June 23. Photos courtesy of the University of Montana.

CHAPTER 7

Irish Worker Conservatism and the Butte Miners' Union, 1880–1910

I

Organized labor unions were only part of the associational world of the settled Irish miners, and Irish worker conservatism in Butte was reflected generally, not just in the policy of the Butte Miners' Union. Still, the ideology of any group of workers is at least partially revealed in the way its exclusively worker associations are organized, and, even more significantly, in the principles those associations embrace and the policies they pursue in defense of those principles. This was certainly the case in a city like Butte, the "Gibraltar of Unionism," with closed shops in every major industrial and commercial trade and with a dominant union for its dominant industry.[1]

As noted, the Butte mines were essentially strike-free for the thirty-six years the BMU represented the miners. As was also noted, this was not the common pattern in the western hard-rock regions. A strike, of course, was a tactic and not of itself radical, particularly when the issues were wages and working conditions. For its part, the BMU may not have gone out on strike because it had managed to win satisfactory conditions by other, less potentially violent means. Radical critics would charge that the BMU was too easily satisfied, that job security was bought with too high a price. The rights of workers required readjustments in the capitalist system, not steadier work and eight-hour days, particularly when "won" through collusive involvement with management.[2]

Whatever the radicals' fight, however—whether for socialism or syndicalism, for worker control of the shop floor, the mine shaft, or the corporate boardroom, for a share of the power of ownership or the abolition of private ownership—the unions had to be counted among the vanguard organizations of radicalism. But not all unions. Radical ends required a radical union. It had to be organized industrially rather than on the basis of trades; it had to control the work force through closed-shop agreements; it had to be of sufficient size and strength to counter the power of massed capital, meaning usually that it had to organize entire industries through federated industrial unions; it had to be "democratically" run, willing to permit the participation of all workers regardless of skill; and it had to be aware of itself and its historic mission, however that mission might be defined.

In this context, the conservatism of the Butte Miners' Union is doubly ironic. Here was an industrial union, the founding and largest local of a federation of industrial unions; one of the largest and most potent worker organizations in the United States; the guarantor of the highest wages in the industry, and the guarantor as well that those wages would be paid to all who went underground without distinction as to rank, years in service, trade, or level of skill. If this were not enough, it was all of those things by 1882, a decade at least before most of the component organizational parts of American radicalism, real or potential, were even in place. As some radical theorists might have phrased it, what happened that prevented so promising a worker organization from realizing its historic mission?[3]

The answer, of course, is that nothing happened to prevent it. The Butte Miners' Union did realize its historic mission. It was the guardian of the values of an enclave of which its leaders were a conspicuous part. It met with opposition only as the enclave began to lose strength and, simultaneously, as its constituency began to include "new" men, in the sense that significant numbers of them were non-Irish, or itinerant, or both. The BMU would not have fit the needs of a mining camp with a transient labor force. Butte was such a place prior to 1878; Leadville, Colorado, or Goldfield, Nevada, as examples, never really lost that aspect even in the twentieth century. After 1907 Butte's industrial physiognomy began again to resemble that of a mining camp more than an industrializing city. But between 1880 and about 1910 the Butte Miners' Union was perfectly suited to the needs of Butte's stable miners. The problem, then, is not with the BMU but with those, at the time and later, who assigned it a task for which it was almost totally unsuited. A closer look at its organizational structure and policies, particularly those that seemed most likely to push it toward radicalism, makes this clear.

There was, in the first place, nothing particularly radical about the industrial organization of the BMU. It is true that men of vastly different skills and trades went underground. The census marshals accepted over twenty separate occupational distinctions for underground workers. It is also true that the BMU insisted that each of these men, from the lowliest mucker to the most skilled and experienced hard-rock man, be paid the same $3.50-per-day wage. This was an uncommonly good wage, more than double that of workers in other U.S. industries. The men, however, shared the same high risks; they were deserving of the same high pay. When it is also recalled that the BMU supported the Butte Workingmen's Union in its struggle to get $3.50 for topside mine workers, the reputation of the BMU as an enlightened worker organization is further enhanced. Certainly these appear commendable steps toward social leveling and worker solidarity, particularly in light of the fact that so many worker organizations foundered on the rivalries among different crafts or the enmity of skilled workers for unskilled.[4]

There are problems, however, in applying this interpretation to the BMU's insistence on a standard wage. First, as noted, this insistence on equal pay for underground work did not arise from notions of worker unity but from a frank acknowledgment of the occupational hazards peculiar to hard-rock mining. There was an elemental fairness and humanity in this posture, but its radical implications are at least diminished by the fact that it had applicability only to equally hazardous industries—and there were none. The same point applies to the BMU's insistence that surface workers, organized in the Butte Workingmen's Union, also make $3.50. Broken-down miners, and Butte was home to many, were often forced out of the mines. Downward social and occupational mobility was less painful if old wage levels could be maintained. It could also be argued that insisting that they be paid their accustomed wage denied the mining companies a pool of potential strikebreakers, but, though farsighted, neither motive for interunion cooperation moved the BMU toward worker solidarity.[5]

Second, new drilling machines tended to even out levels of skill; a hard-rock miner could become a trammer or a topside laborer almost overnight, not because his skills had diminished but because the machines had reduced his usefulness. It was important to the union that this loss of prestige not be accompanied by a diminished wage. Third, it was assumed that a high wage, though a basic union demand, would also attract experienced miners and reduce proportionately the supply of transient tyros whose inexperience made them dangerous to themselves and those around them. In fact, union membership was initially limited to "practical" miners, and practical meant practiced. These wage agreements, moreover, did not prohibit the more-skilled miners from doing contract work and increasing—sometimes more than doubling—their pay. Thus, though nominally equal, there were clear social and craft distinctions between those who built the shafts and those who picked up the rocks—witness, if nothing else, the horror of the chambermaid at one of the Irish boardinghouses when she discovered "a mucker in a miner's bed."[6]

A fourth and related point is that the BMU's willingness to protect all underground men did not mean it was democratically run, or run as an exclusively working-class organization. Its constitution and by-laws allowed its officers, ten being a quorum, to constitute themselves the union, a provision not easily reconciled with democratic procedure. Far more significant was the BMU's violation of the substance of worker democracy. The Irish were the most numerous element in the Butte mining work force, but they were not the only element. That steady stream of Irish officers would indicate that ethnic loyalty had at least as much to do with BMU elections as working-class consciousness. Certainly it does not suggest an Irish tolerance of non-Irish candidates. Neither does the 1897 story which appeared in the *Butte Bystander*, the BMU's official newspaper, identifying southeastern Europeans as "three centuries behind northern Europeans in intelligence." These "brutish, ignorant men" would work for what no "American could live on." If they ever came to Butte, the *Bystander* concluded, the "native miners would be forced out of work." In sum, the BMU was more a trade than an industrial union, and one with strongly held ethnic and social preferences. It existed to protect the interests of the steady men. It fought unceasingly to defend their wages while they were employed underground and when age or infirmity forced them topside. There was no other issue that attracted so much of its attention.[7]

But on this issue, too, the BMU revealed its essential conservatism. Even had there been no hierarchical ordering of the work force, there is little reason to believe that an equal day's wage was particularly significant. Stable miners, like settled workers everywhere, counted their wages by the month—indeed, by 1900 they were paid monthly—or even by the year. The important part of their calculations was not the rate per working day but the number of days worked. And, to a very great extent, that was a function of job preference, of the safe and steady work that was both cause and effect of participation in a worker enclave. Of all the questions asked by the census enumerators, that regarding time off in the preceding year seems to have been taken the most casually. No valid quantitative evidence could be drawn from the answers to it. Still, a cursory look at the *Manuscript Census* for 1900 would indicate that the Irish miners living with their families in Dublin Gulch, the persisters and home owners in other words, had far less worker downtime than the unattached Irish in the boardinghouses. Cooperating with the more powerful may again be at issue, but if so, it is instructive that the BMU did nothing to interfere with the cooperation. In fact, the more powerful—the foremen and shift bosses— were themselves nonvoting, beneficiary members of the union.[8]

The federation of the western miners' unions into the WFM does not appear to have been any more radically inspired than the BMU's industrial organization. There is no question that the WFM was more powerful than any of its component locals—with the possible exception of the BMU, from which it routinely borrowed money—and that the smallest of those locals benefited from federation support. In 1896, for example, each WFM member was assessed a total of $.75 per month to provide strike relief for local unions in Colorado. In 1899 the assessment rose to $2.00 because of the strikes in Idaho. When multiplied by total WFM memberships, these assessments raised an enormous amount of money—over $200,000 in the case of Colorado strike relief funds for 1904. The founders of the WFM obviously understood that the ability to offer this kind of support was one of the advantages of federation; some may even have realized the radical uses to which this ability could be put.[9]

The conspicuously nonradical BMU, however, was often as generous as the federation. Ed Boyce, in fact, claimed that "no just appeal from sister unions was ever ignored" by the BMU. In 1892, before the WFM was formed, the BMU assessed each of its members $5.00 to support the strike in the Coeur d'Alenes; in 1904, the BMU held a "monster meeting"—the phrase is uniquely Irish—to collect money for striking miners in Cripple Creek. In addition, the initial policy of the WFM was to settle disputes through "arbitration and conciliation," not labor protest, and total assessments for the first ten years of the federation (1893–1902) were only $5.25 for each member. Providing strike relief was important, but there were other, less potentially radical motives for federation.[10]

The most obvious of these was that western hard-rock men were notoriously footloose. Constantly having to reaffiliate with a new union was burdensome and expensive for the individual miner. But of greater significance, particularly for Butte's settled miners, was the fact that this worker mobility made more difficult local union control of the size, ethnicity, and dependability of the work force. That most important principle was learned in Butte in the strike of 1878. The BMU was born in that strike, and though its leaders cannot have known the particulars of company policy, they were aware of company intent and of what it implied. The miners walked out in 1878 because the Walker Brothers attempted to cut their wages from $3.50 to $3.00 per day. William Read, with Daly a representative of the Walker Brothers' interests, supported the move because he was confident that new men could always be found to replace the strikers, that the company had only to force the old men out and wait for new ones to take their place. He "expected some kicking"; he even understood that it would "be tough getting a crew at the reduced rate," at least initially. But the strikers, the "riff-raff," as he called them, were paid off "with the hope that most of them would emigrate at once."[11]

Thus the mobility of the mining camps, the steady arrival of new men and the long-established wandering tendencies of the old, was counted on both to enlarge the labor pool and to keep it socially mixed. But Read noted another form of blending that could be turned to the company's advantage. As he put it, "the Cornish and Irish element is about equally divided and there has always been an effort to have a crew about equally mixed." Read reported that the Cornish "appeared to take quite as much interest in the strike as . . . their Hibernian brethren," but he did not waver in his belief that it was "best to have a crew of mixed origin" and he promised to "try to arrange that it will be so."[12]

Marcus Daly blocked Read's plans but the lesson was well learned. Worker mobility could be used to enlarge and diversify the labor pool, to the considerable benefit of the mining companies. The miners, to be sure, had one enormous advantage over other industrial workers: the mines could not be moved. But, like any industrial operation, they could be closed. And, like any set of workers, the hard-rock men could be replaced. Protection of jobs required that the mines stay open. It required too, as that 1897 story in the *Butte Bystander* made clear, a measure of control over the number and type of men who worked in them. The BMU learned from the shutdowns of 1893, 1903, and 1907 that it could offer no guarantees that the mines would stay open. But those shutdowns only reinforced the union's determination to exercise what control it did have—in this instance, over the size and type of the work force. Its purpose was the same as that which moved the Irish associations to a similar determination: safe and steady jobs. Butte had to become a town; it could not remain a mining camp. The miners had to become steady workers; they could not remain itinerant daredevils.

Federation was the logical response to these problems of organizing seminomadic industrial workers. And, though it would seem a secondary consideration, no one knew this better than the Irish, an appreciable number of whom were present at the federation's founding. The Clan-na-Gael was a federation; so was the AOH; so, for that matter, was the Catholic Church. Each had traveling and transfer cards, passwords, and per capita taxes—or their equivalents—long before the WFM had them. Each sought out wandering members, often on instruction from national or international organizations, and each offered a strong and important element of predictability and continuity to a people who needed both.[13]

There exists, then, the possibility that the idea to federate was borrowed from Irish nationalist clubs rather than from the literature and practice of worker protest, and that the need to federate arose from the problems occasioned by worker transiency as well as corporate arrogance. Moreover, since the industrial organization of the BMU was only partial, and that part was more a response to unique occupational hazards than an effort to unite workers of different skills, it is difficult to argue that federation and industrial organization were inherently radical. This does not mean that these two aspects of the BMU could not have been put to radical purposes; only that they were not radical, in the sense of being exclusively working-class, at their origins. They reflected enclave values and they could be used to effect radical change only if the enclave lost control of the union or was itself radicalized. The BMU may have reflected a "movement culture," but because the culture was a mix of ethnic and occupational values, so was the organizational form of the movement. Thus, on every important issue it faced, the BMU leadership took the position best calculated to enhance the security of the settled miners by stabilizing the work force and insuring steady employment.

Like the organizational structure of the union, at least one of those positions involved using "progressive" labor principles for vastly different if not strictly conservative purposes. The example is the BMU's attitude toward the eight-hour workday. "Eight hours for what we will" was a fundamental union demand throughout industrializing America. It had important social and economic implications, not the least of them being the challenge it posed to capital over the control of the workplace. Initially, the BMU was strong in its support of eight-hour legislation. Its boycott of W. J. Penrose for his defection on this issue, as well as the assumption that Molly Maguires killed Penrose, is evidence that the matter was taken seriously by Butte's miners.[14]

But not because they sought a duel with the mine owners over workplace authority. The issues for the union in the eight-hour fight were better worker health and, as a consequence of it, steadier employment over a longer period of time. As one miner put it, a man, "like a mine, does not last forever . . . and he should be able to work under conditions which . . . permit him to lay up a little money for his old age." An eight-hour day would increase by 20 percent the number of years a man could work in the mines. The ten-hour day meant a career of about fifteen years; many miners were unable to work beyond their mid-40s. The "exposure to noxious gases operates to impair their physical health and strength," said the BMU. But the eight-hour day subjected them to "poisonous fumes for a shorter period." It would also, assuming the mining companies did not go to three shifts, double from four to eight the number of hours for the silicate dust to settle. The consequences offered at least as much comfort to the mine owners as to the miners. The BMU made the point explicitly. The men, it said, "will thus be able to perform proportionately more work . . . [and] the interests of the companies will not suffer."[15]

After Penrose's death the BMU was less insistent on this issue, refusing even to support the Clerks' Union in its demand for an early closing of Hennessy's store. The Miners' Union, however, never entirely lost sight of the eight-hour day, and it was largely owing to BMU insistence and the desire of rival copper kings to win the union's favor that eight hours became first the norm and then the law in Montana's mines. But neither did the BMU forget its original reason for demanding eight-hour shifts. Guy Miller, a veteran of many mines and many miner battles, put the matter as clearly as it could be put. The eight-hour day was not part of any worker confrontation with management. It simply "lengthened the years of men's service in the mines . . . [and] multiplied the opportunity to live during their years." Thus the BMU, even as it attempted to determine the length and numbers of shifts—a progressive if not a radical idea, given the effect that the number and length of shifts had on production—mirrored an essential conservatism.[16]

On other issues the Butte Miners' Union revealed its conservatism more openly. In 1903 six of its officers accepted President Theodore Roosevelt's invitation to dine at the White House, an acceptance that was viewed variously as treasonous or, at the very least, as compromising union independence. Though strongly protesting unsafe work conditions, the BMU did little to reform them; in 1911 the state mine inspector testified that he had never received an official complaint from the BMU regarding either ventilation or sanitation. He was sufficiently fair-minded to point out that state law gave him no authority over either, but nonetheless the BMU's negligence prompted one state legislator to suggest that the hard-rock men find a coal miner of "ordinary intelligence" and have him conduct "kindergarten" classes on how to agitate for mine safety. This was more than thirty years after the union's founding.[17]

During those years, the BMU paid hundreds of thousands of dollars in sick and death benefits. It acquiesced in an employee "health plan" which offered no help at all to those suffering from miners' con and amounted to little more than a subsidy to Butte's hospitals. But it did nothing of substance to relieve working conditions in the mines, except, of course, to try to control the number of careless men allowed underground. This may have been all it could do. Agitating for mine safety would have violated the BMU constitution and bylaws, which "unqualifiedly excluded politics and all matters whatsoever relative thereto." This prohibition was not owing to any syndicalist rejection of politics as corrupt and corrupting but because politics bred what the BMU referred to as "dissension and disharmony." According to a critic in the WFM, the BMU was content with the "few crumbs" the Democratic party threw its way.[18]

This was bad enough, but compounding the BMU's sins was its alleged collusion with the Anaconda Company. It collected more than crumbs from ACM. In 1901, four years before the AOH made a similar deal, the union purchased $50,000 worth of Amalgamated Company stock; a "sound investment" for the union, said Con Kelley, and "good business" for the company. Kelley went on, in language reminiscent of that used by the union when it asked for the eight-hour day, that the stock purchase established a "community of interest between employer and employee," a point no more welcome to class-conscious unionists when applied to stock purchases than it would be when applied to time contracts. Workers, these radicals argued, make such deals only at the cost of their souls.[19]

It was this shared interest, however, that explained the company's willingness to guarantee the price of the stock. It might also explain why in 1902, 1903, and 1905 the union supported the Amalgamated in its corporate battles with F. Augustus Heinze. This was particularly the case in 1903, when Ed Long, Irish-born president of the BMU and a member of the RELA, told the union's membership that Heinze's tactics threatened mine closures and the loss of jobs. It may have been this same concert of interest that accounted for the BMU's public acknowledgment in 1903 that "for fair employers, this union will at times strain a point to be more than fair." It may even explain why in 1904 James P. Murphy, a member of the WFM executive board from Butte, threatened to take the BMU out of the federation if the WFM continued on its "socialist" course. Murphy accused federation officers, including Bill Haywood, of being "labor destroyers, living on the cream of the hard earnings of the poor members." "Haywoodism," he concluded, "is not popular in this country."[20]

Here then was a union—the largest local in the United States and potentially one of the most radical—whose leaders had unchallenged control, revealed strong craft biases, bought company stock, permitted hiring officers to retain membership, tolerated company stores and subscription "health plans," favored corporate consolidation, and declared socialism "a dead issue." And this is only a partial list of union offenses. Little wonder that business-minded contemporaries described it variously as "looking upon Mr. Daly as [its] friend and champion"; a "splendid body, many . . . were heads of families and owners of their own homes"; "orderly, cool headed, conservative, and law abiding"; "one of the most conservative bodies in the nation"; one with a "favorable attitude toward corporations"; "ever conservative in its undertakings, ever watchful of the best interests of the whole community"; even "the means of preventing serious strikes . . . by other organizations by refusing its support, cooperation, and assistance."[21]

In this context, even the BMU demand for a closed shop, a principle much applauded by labor reformers, has to be reevaluated. In the first place, the closed-shop agreement meant that every worker had to join a conservative, Irish-dominated union. More specifically, and like so much of what it did, the union's insistence on organizing every man who worked underground allowed it enormous control over who, in fact, would go underground. Moreover, the thirty-day grace period between hiring and paying union dues gave it some control over where they would be assigned. That grace period, though outwardly fair, also increased the social distance between the steady union men and the transients, a distinction shift bosses were likely to consider when assigning the more dangerous jobs. Taken together with its other policies, the BMU's insistence on the closed shop insured that when the "war on capital" came, it would begin with war against the BMU.[22]

II

Critics of BMU conservatism appeared early. Predictably, they tended to equate conservatism with corruption and company control of union policies, claiming that the companies—particularly the ACM—had bought the BMU's officers. One method was granting them lucrative lease agreements. In order to cover its flanks from stray urban reformers, the ACM was said also to offer leases to certain well-placed aldermen, but this was a favor usually reserved for the leaders of the union. In 1891 Penrose wrote that BMU officers had imposed a $5.00

fine for missing the Miners' Union Day parade, to insure a large turnout which "proved [the officers'] influence and justified the companies renewing their leases." Another favorite tactic, according to Joe Shannon, was assigning "company men" the soft jobs, both in and out of the mines. The rebels, on the other hand, were sent "where the actual work has got to be done," in the heat and dust of the deep shafts. There was also the possibility, though Shannon and the other critics did not raise it, that union officers were bought with more lucrative "gifts." John J. Quinn, for example, BMU president in 1901, was a state legislator in 1902 and sheriff of Silver Bow County in 1905. Thomas Chope, a union official in 1904 and 1906, was ACM's labor agent in 1910.[23]

There was disagreement only as to the timing of the company's domination of union affairs. Penrose and the APA figured that the union had lost what independence it had ever possessed by 1891–92. WFM president Ed Boyce, a more careful and sympathetic observer, wrote in his travel diary in 1897 that the "Butte Union was in controll of M's Daily [sic]." The Butte socialist Clarence Smith testified that the company ran union affairs by 1900 while, according to Shannon, the company "had complete control of the officers of the union, complete control" by 1907. Whatever the timing, this charge would be repeated endlessly until 1914.[24]

The company, the critics continued, used its control over union officers for a great variety of purposes. The BMU retreated on the eight-hour day because of Daly's hostility to the legislation. And, for what it may be worth, the eight-hour law was not passed until after Daly's death. According to the *Miners Magazine*, the newspaper of the WFM, it had been "Daly's tools," his "deluded slaves," who defeated a BMU resolution of support for the Clerks' Union. Indeed, the ACM used "the Miners' Union of Butte to crush the Clerks' Union." The lesson was clear—and clearly destructive of worker morale. The men must "vote as . . . told; board where told and trade at the company's store . . . or they cannot work." The stock purchase was similarly explained. The company "induced" it, according to Joe Shannon; "they rushed the hall full of some of their ardent supporters and put it over." The same tactic was used to get the contract of 1907, or to defeat socialist candidates for union office, or to destroy the smeltermen's union, or, most significantly, to break the almost filial relationship of the WFM with the BMU.[25]

Ed Boyce, the president of the WFM, was the man most affected by the enclave-inspired conservatism of the BMU. The Irish-born Boyce had strong ties to Butte and to its Irish community. He was a member of the RELA; he was married in Butte; his best man was James Maher, also an RELA, the secretary-treasurer of the WFM, president of the Butte AOH, and a former officer of the BMU. Butte was Boyce's refuge during the Coeur d'Alene strikes in 1897, when he eluded arrest by hiding out at the home of W. E. Deeney. The first offices of the federation were in Butte Miners' Union Hall. Obviously, the division between the federation he headed and its largest and founding local must have hurt.[26]

The rift began in 1897. The BMU objected to Boyce's report to the WFM convention. Boyce was sure he knew why. "The language," he wrote in his diary, "was to strong to suit Daily [sic]." Soon after this there was a motion by M. J. Burke, president of both the BMU and the AOH, "to withdraw [the BMU] from the Federation" and another requesting the "federation to move to other quarters." The motion to disaffiliate lost; the eviction notice was postponed, but two weeks later Boyce moved his offices from Union Hall. Four years later he moved WFM headquarters out of Butte. He had tried, he wrote in 1900, "to induce BMU to comply with the WFM constitution," but without success.[27]

In 1902 Boyce relocated the offices of the WFM to Denver, where Bill Haywood joined him, having replaced James Maher as WFM secretary-treasurer. Maher, for his part, remained in Butte, where he won political office as a Democrat, took over membership #1 in the RELA, and continued his hard work for both the Emmets and the AOH. Butte may have been "too Irish" for Boyce, too disarmed by Daly's power if not his charm. His status and credibility as a workers' advocate required him to find a new place where his Irishness would not force conflicting allegiances. For Maher, that Irishness was neither an embarrassment nor a constraint; it was central to his world. The evidence indicates that Maher's course was the more comprehensible to the majority of Butte's Irish miners.[28]

Boyce cannot have had Butte alone in mind when he made his diary entry for January 23, 1902, but neither can Butte's miners have been far from his thoughts. He complained of "gloomy times. . . . The WFM is without money . . . Oh! I wonder will the fool working man, especially the miners, rise in their might and have revenge upon their oppressors." In Butte, it appeared they would not. But the BMU's compliance affected federation as well as local affairs, and "life, as president of the WFM, [was] not worth living" for Boyce. "Foes within and without. Foes everywhere and no money or men with sufficient determination to banish them. It is sad indeed." As for the BMU's "company men," Boyce later that year said he wanted to send "such imps . . . to the perdition of labor's damnation."[29]

But it was not just that the ACM had bought the union leadership; it was the distinct brogue in which the negotiations for the "sale" were conducted. Given the Irishness of the BMU leadership—as well as of the Butte aldermen—it could hardly have been otherwise. Con Kelley's "community of interest" must be interpreted in this context, and his assertion that ACM had no desire to "dominate" the union and that he personally was unfamiliar with the union's leadership dismissed as disingenuous at best. At the time of the stock purchase in 1901, to cite one example, the managing director of the company was William Scallon; Kelley was the company's chief counsel; the banker who recommended the deal, and kept his bank open until midnight to facilitate it, was John D. Ryan. The president, secretary, financial secretary, and treasurer of the BMU were John J. Quinn, Frank O'Connor, Jeremiah J. Hanley, and John M. Sullivan. All involved on both sides of the transaction were members of one or both of the Irish fraternal associations.[30]

In 1906, to cite another case, the BMU delegation bolted the WFM convention over the alleged radicalism of federation policy. Critics charged that they defected on instructions from ACM. The bolters included Frank O'Connor, James O'Neill, William Malloy, Barry O'Leary, Thomas Chope, Ed Long, and Dan J. McCarthy. As in 1901, all were members of the Irish associations. McCarthy, of course, was the union treasurer hired by the AOH in 1905 to bring delinquent members back to the order. Long was the BMU president who helped to frustrate Heinze's corporate ambitions. Chope, as noted, became an ACM executive.[31]

The early critics did not ignore the Irish connection in making their accusations. Shannon claimed that Irishmen who did the company's bidding in 1907 were paid off with lease arrangements that allowed them to go over and buy "real estate in Ireland. . . . They went home." Shannon mentioned no names, but Dan Sullivan, another BMU critic, was less circumspect: "Ed Long . . . he had a lease; Dan Shea . . . he had a lease; Jerry Hanley . . . he had a lease." Sullivan would have known. Like him, each of the three was a member of the RELA as well as an officer of the BMU. Indeed, there is an interesting entry in the RELA Minute Books for 1905. "Number 204 was returning to Ireland and the camp sent good wishes." Number 204 belonged to Jeremiah Hanley, secretary of the BMU in 1900, financial secretary in 1901 when the stock deal was negotiated. As Shannon would have put it, Hanley was going home.[32]

Boyce and the WFM, though they made no specific references to the Irish connection, seemed also to understand that those imps damned to labor's special hell were made by playing upon ethnicity. Daly, according to a *Miners Magazine* story written in 1900 (probably by Boyce, and while the WFM was still in Butte), "pitted one nationality against another." Interestingly, that same year William Andrews Clark, who had nothing else in common with Boyce, made the same charge. Daly, said Clark, "had a large number of ignorant Italians, Austrians, and Sclavonians [sic] at work . . . [in his smelter]. They were led like animals to the polls." Three years later the WFM heard a disgruntled BMU delegate, himself an Irishman, charge that "if a man did not vote for a certain party or a certain ticket he [an ACM superintendant named Kelly] would not only fire him, but all the rest of his countrymen."[33]

The notion that "company control" was based on ethnicity, specifically Irish ethnicity, is further strengthened by Boyce's effort to appeal to the Irishness of the Butte work force by making a connection between conditions in Ireland and those in Butte. He noted that Daly had been chairman of the Meagher Memorial Association but that he had given no money to it. The money came from Daly's men, whom he worked "like slaves." Many, in fact, were in the "City of the dead south of Butte." More direct was Boyce's charge that this "heartless wretch, . . . forced to fly from the land of his birth on account of such persecution," was himself the "equal of the worst Irish landlord that ever lived." Indeed, according to P. A. O'Farrell, another of Daly's and the BMU's Irish critics, Daly "couldn't do in England or Ireland what he's doing in Butte." His conduct was "repugnant to [the Irish] creed and traditions." Daly, in sum, was not only an enemy of the working class, he was also a bad Irishman. But until the Irish-dominated BMU realized as much, it could never "speak its own interests."[34]

Those interests, if they were to be represented at all, had to be spoken by the WFM. This did not require the federation to demand that ethnic and religious affiliations be submerged. Its membership card stated clearly that "no matter what may be your creed or religious belief" participation in the WFM posed no conflict with "duties to country . . . religion, or fellow man." Left-wing priests like Fathers O'Grady and Hagerty were hired to give their blessings to labor radicalism; the *Miners Magazine* reprinted Finley Peter Dunne columns as well as John Boyle O'Reilly's poetic tribute to Wendell Phillips. When Michael Davitt died, the WFM's executive committee passed a resolution praising him as "a Hercules among the giants of the world . . . a great, fearless man" whose life was "one long ceaseless battle against wrong and oppression."[35]

But, though tolerant of national and religious feelings, the WFM insisted that they be subordinated to the interests of class. It was "founded on the class struggle"; its affairs were conducted "in harmony with the recognition of the irrepressible conflict between the capitalist class and the working class." Conservative priests were dismissed as "the saintly dignitaries of the church," and wars—even, presumably, those of national liberation—were "capitalist tools." Workers were routinely referred to as "wage slaves." Prior to 1907–8, the WFM was a very radical organization indeed, a strong industrial union, "of class conscious political workers, . . . the vanguard of the army that is destined to accomplish the economic freedom of the producers of all wealth," "the foundation for a universal industrial labor organization." As noted earlier, it was the intractable enemy of the pure and simple trade unionism of Samuel Gompers' AFL, the sire of the radical Western Labor Union and American Labor Union, and the source and inspiration for the Industrial Workers of the World.[36]

Conditions and events in Butte, however, had nothing to do with the radicalization of the WFM, except perhaps as negative references. The labor history of Leadville, Cripple Creek, and Telluride, Colorado; of the Coeur d'Alenes, and of Goldfield, Nevada, explains the radicalism of the WFM. It was in these places, not in Butte, that the story of western working-class radicalism was acted out. There were bitter and violent strikes, arrogant mine owners, government repression, and unstable and ethnically volatile work forces. But all of this occurred in the silver and gold mines of places that resembled itinerant work camps more than fixed industrial cities. There was no Irish enclave in Leadville. The pattern in Butte was different. Butte had about it the marks of permanence; a significant percentage of its working class consisted of men who had passed through and out of the wandering stage of hard-rock miner. Its mine owners, in part because of the corporate rivalries between them, in larger part because of Daly's and the Anaconda's Irishness, courted both worker and Irish favor.[37]

Butte, moreover, was a copper town. It dealt in rough ores, not precious metals. Copper required patience. Tons of ore yielded pounds of copper and that only after reduction and smelting processes that were themselves major industrial operations. Boyce, among others, understood fully what this meant to the culture of work in Butte. In his 1899 speech on Miners' Union Day he reminded a Butte audience that "had the mineral deposits [of the district] been composed of silver in place of copper the hum of industry would be silent; in place of a procession over one mile in length, your streets would be deserted and buildings crumbling." The gold and silver camps were as transient as the men who worked them. Butte's claim to being the "richest hill on earth" was based on its ability to sustain indefinitely the industrial equivalent of extensive agriculture, not on its flash and glitter.[38]

The town's Irish miners knew all this too, knew that they were the dominant element in a place that could provide steady jobs, and that those jobs, in their turn, provided access to an ethno-occupational enclave that met their social and spiritual needs from handball courts to sympathetic priests. The work was dangerous, but less so for the persistent, and the enclave assumed some of the financial consequences of death and disability. Daily wages were more than adequate—recall Dan Lynch's comment that only in Butte were industrial wages better in the United States than in Ireland—as long as the work was steady and the cost of living did not increase.

It is possible, of course, that Daly understood that Irish job preference was a necessary prop to the Irish enclave and that enclave values did not threaten his enterprises. It is even possible that he understood that ethnic homogeneity in his mines—the boycott of the non-Irish—would exacerbate ethnic rivalries and diminish worker solidarity. It is more likely, however, that his and his corporation's needs, as well as those of the working Irish, were best met with steady jobs, and that no collusion, no manipulation, was ever required. Heinze's schemes, for example, threatened more than ACM profits; workers' jobs were also at stake, and RELA member Ed Long's opposition to Heinze and his corporate raiders is neither mysterious nor duplicitous in view of the union's and the enclave's commitment to steady work. This was not, obviously, the unanimous perception at the time.

It is important, however, to reemphasize that the charges of BMU corruption were not brought by disinterested witnesses. There is no doubting that the BMU was a conservative union—a curious fact then as now. The simplest and most ideologically correct explanation for that conservatism was one emphasizing betrayal and corruption. Seeking out its true origins was difficult—then as now. The evidence accumulated, however, was not necessarily of collusion. Working people, as Bodnar reminds us, were not simply the objects of historical forces and processes. They were "culture bearing individuals with internally established goals." They "interacted with the society around them and helped shape a world of their own." That being the case, an assumption of shared values—of a conservatism internal to their world—is a more useful explanation of BMU and Irish attitudes than a charge of betrayal.[39]

III

Between 1906 and 1910 great chunks of that world began to crumble and fall off. The character of the mine operations was changing, and among those wounded and weakened by the changes were the Irish and their enclave. The process began with the final victory in 1906 of the Standard Oil-controlled Amalgamated Copper Company over Heinze and his corporate and judicial allies. Standard Oil had owned ACM since 1899 but, until its corporate rivals had been humbled, ACM continued to operate as the boss Irishman had always operated. That included the active courtship of both Irish and worker. As noted, the settled Irish had benefited from the boardroom and courtroom wars of the years prior to 1906.

They would not do as well under the terms of the corporate cease-fire of 1906 or the final consolidation of 1910. These corporate developments created a copper giant that on its own was the fourth-largest corporation in the United States. It is tempting to think that the strength of the Irish workers' enclave and the consolidation of Butte's mines were related, that the corporate representatives had one eye on the miners as they negotiated their mergers. As Daniel Walkowitz has written, "modest worker achievements facilitated integration of the immigrant family and community; industrial amalgamation . . . placed constraints on these achievements. Each development must be seen in the context of the other." Something like what Walkowitz describes was going on in Butte.[40]

At issue, however, is not just the greater concentration of capital the consolidation of Butte's mines permitted. The more fundamental policy change, at the working-class level, was in the immediate, day-to-day management and supervision of the mines. In 1910 Anaconda opened up large new operations in the "intermediate zone." By then it employed almost 10,000 men in its Butte mines alone another 3,000 in its smelters in Anaconda and Great Falls. Total company payrolls by 1913 exceeded $20,000,000 per year. By 1909, ACM miners detonated 4 million pounds of dynamite to extract more than 40 million tons of copper from underground workings that ran for 900 miles. It would have taken a man more than a month just to walk the length of ACM's ventilation shafts.[41]

So vast an operation required new management techniques. This was particularly the case as the eight-hour workday, passed in 1901 and fully implemented by ACM in 1906, cut into production quotas, and as competition from Arizona mines cut into ACM markets. The company had to "modernize" and make its organization more efficient. City directories by 1909 listed a dozen ACM departments where once there had been four. By 1910 the *City Directory* itself was telling its corporate clients that "for 'scientific management' of the day's work, have the latest . . . Directory within reach." That same year, ACM added an efficiency engineer to its top-level management team. Foremen were given raises to $250 a month, and assistant foremen were appointed to take over some of the administrative chores. The ACM was clearly moving away from the older, and infinitely more personal, methods of the Marcus Daly years.[42]

Among the results was that by 1906 worker control of the mine shaft had significantly diminished. For example, the companies had once offered some of their workmen individual lease and contract agreements based on tonnage. Critics charged that these leases and contracts were barely disguised bribes, but more than 10 percent of the underground men were working under them—an exorbitant number of bribes, even for the Anaconda Company. Obviously, some of those arrangements were used as incentives to skilled and productive men, not just as levers to dominate the union. Working on an individual contract was as near to a trade privilege as hard-rock mining permitted and it was estimated that upwards of a thousand "skilled and industrious" men took advantage of the privilege to make an extra $1.00 to $5.00 a day. Between 1906 and 1914 the company was less willing to continue the practice, preferring instead to use all its underground men in crews.[43]

This gave the shift bosses more authority; they became, in fact as well as name, supervisory bosses, not just hiring officers. A handsome raise to $5.00 a day and up accompanied their new responsibilities. Each shift was expected to dig and load a certain amount of ore. Meeting these production quotas was the shift boss's responsibility; his reputation, if not that of his crew, was at stake. Shift boss rivalries, it hardly needs noting, were encouraged. These changes did not represent "Taylorism" brought to the hard-rock mines (that came during the war years), nor did it represent a significant centralization of authority. This new system was no less decentralized than the one it replaced. But for the workers it meant the loss of mine shaft control; the bosses, not the workers, would run the mines.[44]

Technological changes made simpler the implementation of these organizational reforms. Single jacking—one man with hammer and drill—replaced double jacking—two men who alternated with hammer and drill. The single drills were heavier and harder for older men to use. They were also more dangerous, and their use broke up the old drill teams. Work became lonelier and, after the introduction of machine drills, less a function of honed skills and more a test of brute strength. These machine drills, "buzzies" as they were known, also worsened the ventilation problems in the deep mines, increasing the incidence of miners' con. By 1910, the two-man drill teams, many of them working on contract, had almost totally given way to gangs of singlejackers using buzzies and working under the immediate supervision of shift bosses in competition to meet production goals.[45]

In 1907, during its radical phase, the WFM officers passed a manifesto protesting that these and other technological changes had trivialized the miners' work. There is a wistfulness to this protest, as well as an awareness that the WFM was powerlessness to do anything about the new system. New drills meant enforced idleness for the skilled men too old or broken to lift them, a diminished status for those who could lift them. Indeed, there were no real miners left, only workers ranked by the machines they tended rather than the skills they had learned. "The worker," in the language of the manifesto, "wholly separated from . . . his tools, with his skill and craftsmanship rendered useless, is sunk in the uniform mass of wage slaves . . . shifted hither and thither by the demands of profit takers." Little wonder that the federation and its locals resisted all company efforts to classify and pay men on the basis of job.[46]

IV

It was said that Butte's Cornish miners, ancient enemies of the Irish, refused to make the necessary adjustments to the new system. The Immigration Commission noted that "since the consolidation . . . many of the English have left . . . because it was no longer possible for them to secure small plots which they formerly worked as cash or share tenants." For the "Cousin Jacks," more conscious of occupational roles than most, leases were an old craft privilege and they chose to leave the trade rather than continue in it stripped of the benefits and status it had always possessed for them. The Irish were less fastidious, or less able to afford to leave town. Either that or they viewed the sixteen hours a day they did not spend working as more important in defining their social status than the eight they did. Protecting those nonworking hours reqired only that the job be safe and steady and pay enough to cover the bills.[47]

The jobs were never as safe and steady as the Irish wanted. And, beginning in 1906, inflation meant they would not pay enough to take care of expenses. Some charged that the inflation that first became noticeable in that year was the natural result of consolidation. If nothing else, the company store and the company boardinghouses could charge more. That, of course, presumes a company store. By 1910 a newspaper report estimated that expenses "to live like a white man" exceeded wages at seven selected mines by more than twenty dollars per month. For working miners, with the obvious exception of being out of a job, there was nothing more demoralizing than discovering that wages could not cover routine costs. Making matters worse, the price of copper had never been higher. Whatever the cause of the inflation, it carried copper to nearly fourteen cents a pound, almost double what it had been when the companies had reached their initial wage agreement with the union in 1878.[48]

In November, 1906, the BMU asked John D. Ryan for a raise commensurate with the rise in copper prices—ACM paid record dividends in 1906 and 1907—and sufficient to recover the miners' preinflation buying power. Four dollars a day was the figure the union decided was fair. Before the union committee could present its request, however, Ryan offered a twenty-five-cent increase, then rejected the union's petition for fifty cents. The BMU was divided. Some members talked openly of a strike, but the majority (at a meeting many charged was choreographed by ACM) accepted Ryan's offer with a note of thanks. Soon after, Ryan responded by suspending his company's entire operations, citing a surplus of copper and a shortage of railroad ore cars to carry it.[49]

An angry BMU responded by amending its constitution, by a two to one referendum vote, to make $4.00 a day's pay. A committee of three—surnames, Duffy, Shannon, and Boyle—called on Ryan in March, 1907, and presented him with the union's new wage scale. Again, Ryan rejected it, although this time with a counteroffer to sit down with the union's officers and work out a mutually agreeable time contract with wages pegged to the price of copper but in no case allowed to fall below the old scale of $3.50 a day. This was an action entirely appropriate to the new age of consolidation, a written agreement between an amalgamated company and a closed-shop union. Ed O'Byrne moved that the BMU accept Ryan's offer and by the summer of 1907 a five-year contract providing for a sliding scale of wages based on the price of copper was adopted in a referendum vote. The BMU negotiators were not identified by name, but it was in connection with this contract and its ratification that Joseph Shannon commented that "those men who were instrumental in doing this, they went over and bought real estate in Ireland—the most of them, the majority of them, did." The five union officers listed in the City Directory for 1907 were P. J. Duffy,

Patrick Burns, John R. Sullivan, George Sullivan, and Patrick Harrington.[50]

The contract of 1907 was the the most significant expression of BMU conservatism, and the one that put the greatest distance between it and the federation. The WFM constitution of 1903 prohibited its locals from entering into time contracts without the prior approval of the WFM's executive board. At the 1907 WFM convention, in response to the action of the BMU, the executive board not only withheld its approval, it condemned the contract in language reserved for very special occasions. Contracts "divide the workers in their struggles with the exploiters"; they "chain . . . workers . . . destroy class instincts." This one was "null and void." By a vote of 325 to 25 the whole convention agreed. The contract, however, ran its course.[51]

Some of the WFM reaction was rhetorical excess. This was a tough year for the federation; it faced a serious challenge from the radical Industrial Workers of the World and many WFM delegates may have thought their own show of radicalism a necessity. But WFM hostility to contracts was based in larger part on the fact that a five-year contract between its largest local and the mine owners effectively eliminated the BMU from the federation for those five years; BMU miners could not strike either in defense of their own or of other miners' rights. In addition, wage agreements of this sort inhibited movement from district to district. The federation acknowledged that contracts provided steadier work but only at considerable cost to itinerant miners who found themselves all but closed out of those districts in which contractual agreements had been reached.[52]

It hardly needs saying that this is precisely what the BMU had in mind. In fact, nothing shows more clearly the different constituencies of the BMU and the WFM than this quarrel over contracts. Butte was a town, into which a substantial percentage of its mine work force was settled. Butte was their home. Most of the other WFM unions were located in temporary camps; few of the miners can have imagined themselves fixed to them. This contract, moreover, was based on sliding scales that reflected the price of copper, a provision that both stabilized the work force if prices fell and tied the workers to the long-term success of the company.[53]

Con Kelley, in defending contracts, argued that labor, as a partner in the capitalist system, should share in its rewards; this at a time the WFM was proclaiming the "irrepressible conflict between the capitalist class and the working class," the ineradicability of class differences, and the tendency of contracts to fix the working class in "the galling conditions of wage slavery." Obviously, the BMU, stockholders in the

Anaconda Company, believed Kelley, not the WFM. He had promised them steady employment. That had meaning to them; references to wage slavery did not. The contract of 1907 was thought to be one way of taking care of those steady jobs.[54]

V

The disillusionment came quickly. The Panic of 1907 drove copper prices down, but tying wages to prices did little to save jobs. By the autumn of 1907, mines were either shut down again or were operating with drastically reduced crews. By Christmas there were perhaps as many as 8,000 unemployed or partially employed in Butte. The churches and the associations, Irish and non-Irish, responded to the crisis with prayers and charity. The BMU could do nothing but watch the men leave town. Hard lessons were being relearned, specifically, that among the various threats to the maintenance of this workers' world, one was early death, another was industrial shutdown.[55]

The reasons for the shutdowns were of greater importance to historians and contemporary radicals than to the men in the mines. These last concentrated less on cause, more on consequence. Still, the workers' perception of cause had a profound effect on the lessons they took from the experience. The shutdown of 1903 is usually explained as an instance of corporate blackmail of a state. It may have been that. But it may also have been the ACM's response to Socialist victories in Butte city elections—a point also made to explain the shutdown of 1907—or to the increasingly radical language of the WFM. The stable Irish miner did not necessarily believe these latter explanations, but neither did he ignore what they implied. Similarly, the shutdowns of 1906–8 may have been part of an inventory recession or the result of a stock manipulation. But they could also have been a corporate response to the uncharacteristic and clearly unwelcome feistiness of the BMU and the growing threat of an IWW takeover of the WFM.[56]

The effect of these shutdowns was the same regardless of what prompted them. Men for whom steady work was an indispensible part of their lives suddenly had no work. Even the radicals acknowledged the force of that lesson. The enclave, consisting as it did of men with families and property, was dependent on corporate goodwill. This was not a happy development, but neither was it one for which remedies came easily to mind. Some of the settled Irish may have been radicalized by the shutdowns but all that could be known by most was that they cost jobs and weakened the enclave; abstract ideas of worker solidarity had little meaning next to that.[57]

The stories of three Butte Irish labor leaders may indicate as much. James P. Murphy was not always a conservative critic of WFM socialism. In 1903, prior to the shutdown, he was a vocal supporter of the socialist American Labor Union. In 1906 James Lowney was identified as a BMU radical; by 1910 he was a prominent BMU conservative. The shutdown of 1907 had accomplished what that of 1903 had not. This same may have been true of Charles E. Mahoney. In 1906 this Butte smelterman was a member of the executive board of the Industrial Workers of the World; by 1908 he was conspicuous opponent of IWW radicalism. The industrial shutdowns of 1903 and 1907 do not alone explain the metamorphoses of Murphy, Lowney, and Mahoney. Neither, however, is it likely that the three missed the point.[58]

The same could be said for the Irish associations. Like the BMU in the earlier shutdown in 1906, they fought to keep their members employed. The union had hoped a contractual agreement might insure steady jobs. The Irish associations relied on the unofficial agreements between Irish foremen and Irish workers. The RELA enlisted its most powerful spokesmen in the cause. Judge J. J. Lynch personally visited "president Ryan in the interests of the D." Daniel Hennessy went on a similar errand, reporting some "success" though "no progress could be expected for a week." John O'Leary, a druggist, Sheriff John O'Rourke, and Jeremiah Mahoney, an officer of the Butte Brewery, also "interviewed" Ryan in an effort "to help each other out to tide over the present dull times." As always, the AOH was as active, turning, as it often had before, to Hennessy and others of its dignitaries for help.[59]

These were proven methods, but this time it became quickly evident that the rest of the employment formula had changed. There were references as early as the shutdown of 1906 that "Hibernians got discharged to make a place for members of the compass and square and other organizations," and this in Butte, "our stronghold!" In December, 1907, it was noted that "our people were discriminated against," that "soon there would be no place for us in this community." And even after the mines reopened in March, 1908, the associational Irish continued to complain. It was a "sad condition," said Dan Lynch, a former union officer, that with so many hiring officers in the associations, "so many are out of employment." This was in October, 1908, six months after full operations had been resumed.[60]

Later that same year the AOH attempted a new tactic. It sent an employment committee to see Ryan but kept the matter "very secret so as not to get abroad and place some people in an embarrassing position." They had never been that careful—or that apologetic—before.

Eight months later another committee consisting of a shift boss, the deputy county assessor, a city fireman, and two miners had a "private meeting" with Ryan "about jobs." It is unlikely that either of these efforts to be more discreet succeeded. A little more than a year after the second visit, an interesting and instructive statement was entered into the Minute Books of Division 3. An AOH employment committee had seen Ryan. It got "a very chilly reception." Brother Ryan "thanked us for calling on him," then dismissed the committee. Perhaps, as John O'Meara thought, it was "not wise any more to be too Irish."[61]

Clearly, the old order was changing and the shutdowns of 1906–8 were both agents and objects of that change. Daniel Walkowitz has compiled a list of the options available to corporate managers as they attempted to maintain profits during the hard times of the 1870s. They could adjust hours, wages, and production quotas, introduce new machines, reduce their dependence on better-paid skilled labor, or "assert discipline on the labor process." Whatever the choice or choices, the affected industry was transformed. The newly consolidated Amalgamated Copper Company exercised each of these corporate options, plus another handy to the occasion, as it confronted the economic crisis of 1906–8. The other option—not entirely unrelated to those Walkowitz mentions—was to bring in new men, often unskilled and unattached, usually non-Irish, to work the mines. In other words, the company began to assemble a disposable work force. It drew from an enormous pool of migrant laborers—the industrial fodder of the developing Atlantic economy. These migrants were unlike immigrant workers. Usually unskilled, always unattached, they wanted only to make enough money to go home. They were literally throwaways, as interchangeable as machine-tooled parts. The companies had no stake in them or in the development of their skills. But they were cheap and available and in Butte. They met one of ACM's most immediate and pressing needs. It was this conscious shift in company hiring practice that was most destructive of the Irish miners' enclave.[62]

The decline in immigration from Ireland as well as the understandable reluctance of the second-generation Irish to enter the mines would in time have had the same results as this new hiring policy. In fact, in the other mining towns of the West, the pattern of replacing English-speaking Irish, Cornish, and native miners with migrant workers from Italy, Greece, and Finland, as well as from the various parts of the Austro-Hungarian empire, was well established by 1908. Death as well as the occupational and geographical mobility of the English-speaking miners had created vacancies in the labor force of these mining camps. The companies, according to the Immigration Commission, were thus "compelled to resort to the more recent immigrants from the south and east of Europe" to fill out their labor supplies.[63]

The ethnic composition of the new mine work force would cause trouble for the WFM. Interethnic rivalries as well as the necessity of finding organizers in the dozen or so languages of the new men were difficult problems. As an example, in 1910, in Colorado, Utah, and New Mexico, the WFM had a total membership of 8,000 men, 6,000 of whom spoke no English. Of the unorganized miners in the West, "one-third spoke the Latin tongue." WFM president Charles Moyer was determined even to visit Europe and talk to the men in the mines prior to their emigration, hoping that this preliminary briefing would make them easier to organize. The problems for the federation, however, went beyond the merely organizational. More significant, as the Immigration Commission report of 1911 put it, was the fact that the availability of these new men "has tended to prevent the advance of wages." They also tended "to prevent . . . better relations between employers and employees," and "their presence . . . has greatly hampered the formation of trade-unions." They were useful only "where mobility of labor is an advantage and where no educational qualifications obtain." According to the Immigration Commission, their presence also enabled foremen to mix their crews "to get the benefits of race competition."[64]

The social effect of these new men was equally undesirable. Employed in "gangs," the "development of a civic interest among them" was understandably hindered. They were described variously as "social outcasts," "surly," "undisciplined," "inefficient," "worthless," "bull-headed and troublesome," and, in the case of the Finns, "a race that tries to take advantage." If this were not enough, they were unsettled "as regards family life," had not adjusted to "American conditions," lived in segregated districts, and sent their wages back to their homelands rather than spending them locally.[65]

Not surprisingly, this wandering band of cutthroats had also a reputation for carelessness. They were thought hazardous to themselves and those unlucky enough to be in the shafts with them. They knew little about explosives and did not understand verbal commands given in English. These were more important issues to workers than to the companies who, in any event, had no choice but to hire them. But there was more involved than frequency of accidents. The simple fact of their availablity allowed the mining companies to change over to power drills, or widow-makers, increasing considerably the amount of silicate dust raised during drilling. Their wandering habits, moreover, allowed the companies to postpone the use of new ventilation tech-

niques. Men who intended to work in the mines for thirty days had
different expectations and made different demands than those who
counted their working lives in years.[66]

VI

Butte was aware of the reputation of these mostly non-English-speaking workmen, but until 1906–7 had had little direct experience with
them. The census of 1900 listed fewer than 1,200 "new immigrants"
in a foreign-born population of more than 10,000, a total population
of more than 33,000. According to William Andrews Clark, this good
fortune was owing partly to the fact that Montana was protected by
its isolation from "pauper" immigrants. Fritz Heinze was less certain
of the cause of Butte's English-speaking work force but no less convinced of its benefits. The United States, he said, could never have
built its present civilization with "south European immigrants." They
were lazy and (with one eye as always to the labor vote) the unions
could not organize them.[67]

The BMU may have believed him, and determined not to have to
try. As early as 1902, it pushed for and got the establishment of a
county employment bureau. Its principal allies in the city council were
Michael Dempsey and Larry Duggan, two well-established members
of the Irish community. In its first two months, the bureau had 330
men and 225 women use its services. Of the women, 201 were placed
in hotels and restaurants or as domestics; of the men, only seventy
were placed, all as "common laborers," none in the mines. Jobs in the
mines were the province of the Butte Miners' Union—and the enclave.[68]

More compelling, if not more specific, evidence of the BMU's influence was provided by the Immigration Commission report of 1911. In
a statement remarkable in its implications, the commission commented
on the fact that until recently Montana's mines had resisted the tendency, so common in the other western hard-rock districts, to employ
southern and eastern European migrants. The commissioners attributed
this to "the activity of the union, which has been largely responsible
for . . . the retention in the industry of a considerable number of the
native-born and north Europeans now employed in it." In other words,
the BMU had acted upon its earlier fears and kept the "brutish, ignorant
men" out of Butte. The consequences were what the union would have
expected them to be: The Butte wage scale was the "highest paid" in
the western mines, "considerably higher" than in Colorado; "very much
higher" than in California or Arizona. The difference was "largely due
to the dominance of the union at the Montana mines and the weakness

or absence of the union" in the other states. But on this point as well, the "native born and north Europeans" were fighting to retain a privileged status: "wage differences" between the ethnic groups, the commissioners went on, "were almost entirely due to differences in [job] distribution."[69]

The commission's conclusions indicate that, though the changes in ethnic composition were just beginning, Butte's work force was already coming to resemble those of the other mining towns in ethnic diversity and in the use of disposable migrant workers. The Irish and the BMU were obviously trying to defend traditional prerogatives. There was little chance that they would succeed. The industrial demographics were the same in Butte as elsewhere, and as irresistible: the older men in Butte died, left the mines, some left the town. For the moment, however, the "predominance in Butte of the 'American' element" had been only weakened, not "destroyed," by these developments. Butte was still more Irish and more industrial than the camps. These, of course, were the essential and related differences between Butte and the other mining districts. They meant, among other things, that its Irish miners had more to protect and more weapons to bring to the effort. The Irish-dominated BMU was principal among those weapons.[70]

But clearly, as the events of 1906–14 were to indicate, this was not the kind of union power, assuming that the union ever wielded it, that could be sustained indefinitely. The settlement of the corporate wars deprived the BMU of its previous leverage and the ACM, newly consolidated and run for the first time in its corporate life by absentees— non-Irish absentees like William Rockefeller and Henry Rodgers at that—may have decided to move against the union. The WFM was entering its most radical phase and there were murmurs that the BMU might follow or, worse, was leading, this leftward tilt. The strike rumors of 1907 can only have been perceived as further evidence that the BMU was shedding its conservatism. But even the old BMU may have been unacceptable to the new generation of corporate managers. Corporate counterattacks against strong unions were common at that time, and the BMU was the largest and one of the most powerful locals in the United States. It was an obvious target.

Also related were the occasional Socialist party victories in Butte city elections from 1903 to 1913. These, too, increased the company's fear that the principles of capitalism were not universally cherished in Butte. Hiring new men of uncertain politics was a calculated gamble, but these men were also unregistered aliens and, in municipal elections at least, no more than observers. Union elections were a different matter, but the company had, or at least thought it had, other and tested ways of controlling the union.[71]

These ideological considerations, however, seem less significant in explaining the company's new hiring policy than simple economics. ACM was running out of experienced English-speaking miners at precisely the moment it needed to expand its work force. This would have been disastrous except that machine drills made miners out of anyone strong enough to lift one and reckless enough to go underground with it. There were millions of men who fit that job description; the loss of the few thousand who knew how to mine would scarcely be felt. Second, and the irony is obvious, the anticipated passage of a state workmen's compensation law—it was adopted first in 1911—made the hiring of new men even more attractive to the companies. Compensation to survivors in cases of worker death did not have to be paid to foreign nationals, placing a premium on the hiring of unmarried transients whose families lived overseas. Workmen's compensation was expected to make the mines safer; it had precisely the opposite effect.[72]

There was a possible third motive. The company's New York-based managers may have understood that Butte's Irish enclave had been given extraordinary and, by corporate accounting, quite unacceptable privileges, and that foremost among these was the enclave's presumed right to control the work force. That control had always been held on sufferance, but an aristocratic privilege, if its origins are remote and obscure, can come to seem a proprietary right. The fact that the privilege was never used to challenge corporate authority by sustaining worker protest did not mean that it did not have that potential. It was time that the Irish enclave be disabused of the notion that its aristocratic status was held in perpetuity.

NOTES

1. William Haywood writes about Butte's Unions in *Bill Haywood's Book*, pp. 82–83. By 1897 there were thirty-six industrial and trades unions in the city, represented every one from barbers and musicians to cigar makers, bricklayers, cooks and waiters, and brewers. *Butte Bystander*, Oct. 2, 1897.

2. For an example of these charges, see the *Butte Bystander*, Sept. 18, 1897. At this time the *Bystander* was the official paper of the WFM.

3. For an example of a radical theorist who did phrase the issue that way, see Sombart, *Why Is There No Socialism in the United States*. See also Kraditor, *Radical Persuasion*, pp. 37–56, where she criticizes the a priori assumption behind the question: that there should have been a socialist tradition in the United States.

4. Bureau of Census, *MS Census*, 1900 and 1910. Among them were mucker, niper, carman, station tender, ropeman, pipeman, pumpman, carpenter, and machinist. See also the remarks of Con Kelley, who noted the long-standing insistence of the BMU on equal pay for underground work (Industrial Commission, *Mining at Butte*, 1915, pp. 3695, 3873). See also BMU, *Constitution and Bylaws*, [3]; Lingenfelter, *Hardrock Miners*, p. 227; Hobsbawm, "Aristocracy," p. 243.

5. Frisch, " 'Gibraltar of Unionism.' " Hobsbawm also points out that "a miner who left the pit was, after all, a laborer of no or little skill" ("Aristocracy," p. 231).

6. The reference to "practical" miners is from BMU, *Constitution and Bylaws*, art. I, sec. 1, 4; art. IV, 7; art. VII, 8–9. It is worth noting that the AOH was for "practical" Catholics (AOH, *Constitution, 1886*). That higher pay attracted safer workers is noted in the *Labor World* (Butte), Apr. 18, 1902. See also the BMU constitution with its reference to higher wages and "retaining skilled and experienced labor" [3]. On extra pay and contracts see Kelley's remarks in Industrial Commission, *Mining at Butte*, 1915, pp. 3873–74; Bureau of Mines, *Preliminary Report*, pp. 7–9. Evans, *Address*, p. 12. The "mucker in a miner's bed" story is from Hand, "Folklore," p. 160. James Curtin said that contract miners were assigned favored shafts (interview).

7. The rules of a quorum are from BMU, *Constitution and Bylaws*, art. 1, sec. 2, 10. See also WFM, Exec. Board, MB, June 16, 1906; *Butte Mining Journal*, Apr. 25, June 9, 1888; May 17, 1891. For BMU resistance to WFM efforts to force it to open up its membership to more workers, see WFM, Exec. Board, MB, Jan. 8, 1902; Dec. 7, 1903. The same point was made in a story on the history of the BMU in the *Montana Standard* (Butte), Aug. 11, 1940. By 1897 there were eleven separate unions representing mine workers in Butte. Only three of those, the BMU, the Brotherhood of Stationary Engineers, and the Butte Smelterman's Union, were affiliated with the WFM. The *Bystander* story was in the issue of Oct. 16, 1897.

8. City directories list the monthly paydays of the various mines. On steady work see *Butte Bystander*, Feb. 24, 1894; the remarks of Dan Madden, the Irish president of the Silver Bow Co. Trades and Labor Council, in Industrial Commission, *Mining at Butte*, 1915, p. 3831. John Gillie, an ACM officer, agreed with Madden (ibid., pp. 3742–43). Bureau of Census, *MS Census*, 1900 and 1910. BMU, *Constitution and Bylaws*, art. VII, 8–9.

9. The largest of these BMU loans to the WFM was the $30,000 interest-free loan made in 1901. WFM, *Proceedings, 1901*, pp. 33, 43–45; ibid., *1902*, p. 58. Examples of early WFM assistance to member locals can be found in WFM, Exec. Board, MB, June 29, Sept. 18, Oct. 11, 1893; Mar. 26, June 3, 1895; WFM, *Proceedings, 1904*, p. 110; ibid., *1905*, p. 188. Total WFM assessments by year from 1893 to 1914 are in the *Miners Magazine*, July 23, 1914.

10. Lingenfelter, *Hardrock Miners*, p. 204. Boyce's comment is from the *Miners Magazine*, Feb., 1900. The "monster meeting" is mentioned in *ibid.*, June 30, July 7, 1904. WFM, *Constitution and Bylaws*.

11. William Read to Walker Brothers, June 9, 17, 20, 21, 28, 30, 1878; Alice Mining Co. Records, Letter Press Books.

12. Ibid., July 18, 1878. On this same point see also Burchell, *San Francisco Irish*, p. 68.

13. Lingenfelter, *Hardrock Miners*, pp. 222–23. For passwords, per capita taxes, and transfer and traveling cards, see WFM, *Constitution and Bylaws; Butte Bystander*, May 20, 27, 1893.

14. Roy Rosenzweig discusses the conflicts between mostly immigrant workers and the middle class over how the eight hours off work should be spent in *Eight Hours*. David Montgomery emphasizes the implications of worker control over the number of hours on shift, including the obvious influence workers now had on production, in *Workers' Control*. See also Bodnar, *Workers' World*, p. 65.

15. Joseph Bracken to William Scallon, reprinted in WFM, *Proceedings, 1903*, p. 191. Life expectancies are from the remarks of Jacob Oliver in Industrial Commission, *Mining at Butte*, 1911, p. 3916. See also the remarks of M. McCusker in ibid., 1915, p. 3839. The statement from the BMU is from the *Butte Mining Journal*, Nov. 23, 1890. The policy of using a "third shift" to clear out gases was commented on by Con Kelley in Industrial Commission, *Mining at Butte*, 1915, p. 3714. See also *Miners Magazine*, July, 1900.

16. Smith, "Rise and Fall," p. 26. Guy Miller's remarks are in WFM, *Proceedings, 1914*, p. 132.

17. Wyman, *Hardrock Epic*, p. 251; *Miners Magazine*, July, 1903. The "kindergarten" remark was made by State Representative J. C. McCarthy in 1911, Industrial Commission, *Mining at Butte*, 1911, p. 3935. See also pp. 3969, 3971.

18. The BMU paid $29,000 in sick and death benefits in 1896; $64,000 in 1908. *Anaconda Standard*, June 13, 1896; WFM, *Proceedings, 1909*, p. 202. BMU members paid $1.00 per month for contract medical services. Preexisting and contagious conditions, like miners' con, were not covered. Every month Butte's two hospitals divided as many dollars as there were men in the mines—12,000 by 1912. There was considerable criticism of this policy. See, for examples, *Butte Mining Journal*, Apr. 14 and 17, 1888; *Miners Magazine*, Nov., 1901; Industrial Commission, *Mining at Butte*, 1915, pp. 3706, 3709, 3851–52. The no-politics rule is in BMU, *Constitution and Bylaws*, p. 25. The reference to the Democrat's "crumbs" is from the *Miners Magazine*, Aug., 1902.

19. Industrial Commission, *Mining at Butte*, 1915, pp. 3852–54, 3866. AOH D3, MB, Sept. 11, 1905.

20. On BMU support for ACM against Heinze, see the remarks of Clarence Smith in Industrial Commission, *Mining at Butte*, 1915, p. 3734; WFM, *Proceedings, 1914*, pp. 56–57. The expression of BMU "fairness" was reprinted in the *Miners Magazine*, Dec. 10, 1903. See also BMU, *Constitution and Bylaws*, [3]. James P. Murphy to Charles Moyer, Sept. 12, 1904, in WFM, Exec. Board, MB, Dec. 7, 1904. See also Murphy to Moyer, Sept. 11 and 17, 1904, and Murphy to Bill Haywood, Oct. 3, 1904 in ibid. Murphy, strangely, does not seem to have been a member of either the AOH or the RELA. It may be significant that by 1907 he was co-owner with Daniel F. Harrington, an active

Hibernian, of a saloon at 309 North Main—next-door to Miners' Union Hall. AOH, Membership and Dues Ledgers; Polk, *City Directory*, 1907.

21. The reference to socialism as a "dead issue" is from James P. Murphy to Charles Moyer, Sept. 11, 1904, in WFM, Exec. Board, MB, Dec. 7, 1904. The comment that the BMU looked upon Daly as their friend was made by former state representative and close Daly associate John R. Toole in Committee on Privileges and Elections, *Report*, vol. 3, p. 2167. Connolly, "Story of Montana," p. 460; *Butte Bystander*, July 21, 1894; Sept. 18, 1897; *Butte Independent*, June 18, 1910; Montana, Dept. of Labor, *First Biennial Report*, p. 25; Industrial Commission, *Mining at Butte*, 1915, p. 3757. See also Wyman, *Hardrock Epic*, pp. 251–52; Malone, *Battle for Butte*, pp. 207–9.

22. See Edward Boyce, diary entry for Jan. 15, 1901, Boyce Papers.

23. For leases to aldermen see Industrial Commission, *Mining at Butte*, 1915, pp. 3768–69. Similar penalties were imposed for missing the St. Patrick's Day parade (AOH D3, MB, Feb. 6, 1905). Shannon's comment is from Industrial Commission, *Mining at Butte*, p. 3857. For Quinn, see O'Daly, *Life*, [31]; for Chope, see Polk, *City Directory*, 1904, 1906, 1910.

24. The *Butte Mining Journal*, June 3, 1891; *Examiner*, June 15, 1895; Boyce, "Travel Diary," May 24, 1897, Boyce Papers. Clarence Smith, Industrial Commission, *Mining at Butte*, 1915, p. 3730; Joseph Shannon, ibid., p. 3854.

25. *Miners Magazine*, May, Aug., Dec., 1900; Wyman, *Hardrock Epic*, p. 211. Shannon's comments are from Industrial Commission, *Mining at Butte*, 1915, p. 3854. See also *Miners Magazine*, Aug., 1901.

26. "Introduction," Boyce Papers; RELA, Membership and Dues Ledgers. Boyce was #182. For Maher see Polk, *City Directory*, 1897–1899; RELA and AOH, Membership and Dues Ledgers. Boyce's reference to staying with Deeney is from his "Travel Diaries," May 24, 1897, Boyce Papers.

27. Boyce, "Travel Diaries," June 1, 7, and 11, 1897, Boyce Papers.

28. Boyce, "Diary," Nov. 13, 1900. Maher's later career is taken from Polk, *City Directory*, 1900–1906; AOH and RELA, Membership and Dues Ledgers, and AOH, MB, passim, esp. Aug. 8, 1899; June 17, Nov. 13, 1900; Jan. 11, 1902.

29. Boyce, "Diary," Jan. 23, 1902, Boyce Papers; *Miners Magazine*, Dec., 1902.

30. For Kelley's remarks see Industrial Commission, *Mining at Butte*, 1915, p. 3860. On Ryan's leaving the bank open see Shannon, ibid., p. 3853. See also O'Daly, *Life*, [237]. Polk, *City Directory*, 1906; AOH and RELA, Membership and Dues Ledgers.

31. On the bolters of 1906, see WFM, *Proceedings, 1906*, pp. 5, 128, 210–11. For Chope, see Polk, *City Directory*, 1912.

32. Shannon's comment is from Industrial Commission, *Mining at Butte*, 1915, p. 3854; Sullivan's is from ibid., p. 3770. RELA, Membership and Dues Ledgers; Polk, *City Directory*, 1909. On Hanley, see RELA, MB, June 29, 1905. Similar charges were brought in 1912. See WFM, *Proceedings, 1912*, p. 260. See also WPA, *Copper Camp*, p. 158.

33. *Miners Magazine*, Aug., 1900. Clark's comments are from *Congressional Record*, 56th Cong., 1st sess, vol. 33, part 6 (May 15, 1900), p. 5535. WFM, *Proceedings, 1903*, p. 193.

34. *Miners Magazine*, May, 1900; Mar., 1901; June, 1902. O'Farrell, *Butte*, p. 61.

35. Membership card in Boyce Papers. On Fathers Hagerty and O'Grady, see WFM, Exec. Board, MB, June 10, 1902; Dec. 10, 1904; WFM, *Proceedings, 1903*, pp. 66–72; *Miners Magazine*, June and July, 1900. The resolution on the death of Michael Davitt is in WFM, Exec. Board, MB, June 15, 1906. The *Butte Bystander*, the first "official organ of WFM," also carried Irish as well as labor news. WFM, *Proceedings, 1895; Butte Bystander*, Jan. 19, 1895; Sept. 11, Dec. 18, 1897.

36. On class war see WFM, "Manifesto, Dec., 1907," in Exec. Board, MB, Dec. 12, 1907. On "saintly dignitaries" and wars, see WFM, *Proceedings, 1903*, pp. 279–80. See too WFM, Exec. Board, "Resolution," in MB, Dec. 4, 1902. Suggs, "Religion and Labor," pp. 190–206. On at least one occasion the AOH objected to what it perceived as WFM anticlericism; AOH D3, MB, June 24, 1907. On WFM radicalism, see, for example, Boyce's speech of May 26, 1902, reprinted in *Proceedings, 1910*, p. 13. On Gompers (Boyce called him "Sammy"), see Exec. Board, MB, Dec. 14, 1905. See also Boyce to Gompers, Mar. 16, Apr. 7, 1897, reprinted in WFM, *Proceedings, 1897*, WFM, Exec. Board, MB, Dec. 17, 1907. There were, of course, ebbs and flows in the radicalism of the WFM. At its origins in 1893 its basic demand was modest enough. It wanted "to secure an earning fully compatible with the dangers of our employment." As late as 1902 the WFM and the Western Labor Union were both on record favoring the irrigation of the public lands as a means of "relieving congestion" and reducing the labor surplus, a goal more commonly associated with conservative unionists in the AFL. Generally, however, particularly from 1902 to 1907, the WFM embraced a quite genuine and sweeping labor radicalism based on socialist principles. WFM, *Constitution and Bylaws; Miners Magazine*, Feb., 1902; speech of Daniel McDonald (WLU) in *Labor World* (Butte), June 2, 1902; Dubofsky, "Origins."

37. Immigration Commission, *Immigrants in Industries*, 1911, part 25, pp. 91–159. These places were not as Irish as Butte either. See *ibid*, pp. 547–81; O'Dea, *AOH*, III:1263–64.

38. The speech was reprinted in the *Miners Magazine*, Mar., 1900.

39. Bodnar, *Workers' World*, pp. 5–9.

40. No dividends were paid from 1895 to 1899. From 1900 to 1904 total dividends were $9.50; from 1905 to 1909 they were $18.24. *Moody's Manual*, p. 2906. Walkowitz, *Worker City*, p. 74.

41. Industrial Commission, *Mining at Butte*, 1911 and 1915, pp. 3687, 3690, 3698, 3950; Montana, Bureau of Agriculture, Labor, and Industry, *Report . . . 1912*, pp. 275–78; Malone, *Battle for Butte*, pp. 4–5.

42. Industrial Commission, *Mining at Butte*, 1915, pp. 3693, 3873; Montana, Dept. of Labor, *Second Biannual Report*, p. 71; Malone, *Battle, for Butte*, pp. 201–7.

43. Evans, *Address*, p. 9; Industrial Commission, *Mining at Butte*, 1915, p. 3691; Curtin interview.

44. Industrial Commission, *Mining at Butte*, 1911 and 1915, pp. 3693, 3768–69, 3927, 3939, 3978; Evans, *Address*, pp. 11–12; Brody, *Workers in Industrial America*, pp. 9–12, 25–32; Hobsbawm, "Aristocracy," pp. 233; Wyman, *Hardrock Epic*, pp. 231; Montgomery, *Workers' Control*, pp. 9–27.

45. "Buzzies" were introduced in 1892 but were not in general use until around 1900. Wyman, *Hardrock Epic*, pp. 12, 84, 88–90, 169; Ronald C. Brown, *Hard-Rock Miners*, pp. 53–56, 73–74; Lingenfelter, *Hardrock Miners*, pp. 17–18; Gedicks, "Ethnicity," p. 147; Industrial Commission, *Mining at Butte*, 1915, p. 3857.

46. WFM, "Manifesto," in Exec. Board, MB, Dec. 12, 1907; Evans, *Address*, p. 11. Con Kelley wanted to pay men more for doing more. He knew, however, that any effort to depart from the standard wage for all underground work would start a "row" (Industrial Commission, *Mining at Butte*, 1915, p. 3695).

47. Immigration Commission, *Immigrants in Industries*, 1911, part 25, p. 115n. See also Samuel, *Miners*, pp. 48, 57.

48. *Butte Evening News*, July 17, 1910; Malone, *Battle, for Butte*, pp. 208–10.

49. Industrial Commission, *Mining at Butte*, 1915, pp. 3854–55; Malone, *Battle for Butte*, p. 208; Vernon Jensen, *Heritage of Conflict*, pp. 302–6.

50. Industrial Commission, *Mining at Butte*, p. 3854; Vernon Jensen, *Heritage of Conflict*, pp. 302–3; Polk, *City Directory*, 1907.

51. WFM, *Proceedings 1907*, pp. 261, 307–52; Vernon Jensen, *Heritage of Conflict*, pp. 303–4.

52. WFM, Exec. Board, Report, in MB, Dec. 17, 1907. The WFM prohibition on contracts is in article V, sec. 4 of the *Constitution and By-Laws* (rev., 1907), pp. 13–14. See also WFM, *Proceedings*, 1909, p. 381; *Proceedings 1912*, p. 307; *Proceedings 1914*, p. 261; Haywood, *Bill Hayward's Book*, p. 172; Vernon Jensen, *Heritage of Conflict*, pp. 71, 304.

53. The 1907 contract is in Kelley, Exhibit 6, Industrial Commission, *Mining at Butte*, 1915, pp. 3879–80.

54. Industrial Commission, *Mining at Butte*, 1915, pp. 3692, 3697–98; WFM, Exec. Board, "Report, Dec. 16, 1906"; "Manifesto, Dec., 1907," in MB, Dec. 14, 1907.

55. Industrial Commission, *Mining at Butte*, 1915, pp. 3853–55; Vernon Jensen, *Heritage of Conflict*, pp. 302–6; Malone, *Battle for Butte*, p. 209; Smith, "Rise and Fall," pp. 41–43.

56. For 1903 see Industrial Commission, *Mining at Butte*, 1915, p. 3854; Malone, *Battle for Butte*, pp. 173–78. On Socialist victories in Butte, see Clarence Smith's remarks in Industrial Commission, *Mining at Butte*, p. 3724; *Miners Magazine*, Feb., 1903; WFM, *Proceedings*, *1914*, p. 128; Wyman, *Hardrock Epic*, pp. 239–40, who also discusses the possibility that the shutdowns intimidated the BMU—or at least caused its leaders to rethink their position on WFM radicalism. See also Malone, *Battle for Butte*, pp. 193–94, 208–10.

57. For the radicals; acknowledgment of the effects of idleness on men used to working, see *Butte/Anaconda Joint Strike Bulletin*, Oct. 25, 1917.

58. Murphy's support of the ALU is noted in *Miners Magazine*, Oct. 1, 1903. Lowney's ideological switch is taken from WFM, *Proceedings*, *1906*, pp. 5, 128,

210–11; *Proceedings, 1914*, p. 154. Mahoney's IWW office is from IWW, Exec. Board, MB, Oct. 4, 1906, copy in WHC. For his later conservatism, see Smith, "Rise and Fall of the BMU," pp. 32–36; Vernon Jensen, *Heritage of Conflict*, pp. 170, 174, 227; Malone, *Battle for Butte*, p. 208.

59. RELA, MB, Nov. 14, Dec. 12, 19, 1907; AOH D3, MB, Oct. 21, Dec. 9, 30, 1907; Jan. 6, Mar. 30, 1908.

60. AOH D3, MB, July 16, 1906; Dec. 9, 1907; Mar. 16, Sept. 21, Oct. 5, 19, 1908; RELA, MB, Dec. 12, 1907.

61. AOH D3, MB, Nov. 16; July 6, 1908. The reference to a "chilly reception" is from Jan. 8, 1910. See, too ibid., Nov. 30, 1908; June 14, 1909; AOH, Silver Bow Co. Exec. Board, MB, May 10, 1909; RELA, MB, Apr. 28, 1910.

62. Walkowitz, *Worker City*, p. 183; Malone, *Battle for Butte*, p. 210. On the Atlantic economy and the migrant workers that were a part of it, see Golab, *Immigrant Destinations*, pp. 43–66.

63. Immigration Commission, *Immigrants in Industries*, 1911, part 25, p. 150.

64. WFM, Exec. Board, MB, 1907ff., e.g., Aug. 4, 1909; Jan. 12, Aug. 21, 22, 1911; July 15, 1913; Jan. 8, 1915. The 6,000 non-English-speaking miners is noted Exec. Board, Report, Dec. 14, 1910. Cantor, "Introduction," pp. 20–21; Taylor says that two-thirds of America's copper miners by 1910 were foreign born (*Distant Magnet*, p. 197). Moyer's remark is from WFM, *Proceedings 1914*, pp. 50–51. Immigration Commission, *Immigrants in Industries*, part 25, pp. 97, 109, 119, 151, 156–57, 211.

65. Immigration Commission, *Immigrants in Industries*, 1911, part 18, p. 341; part 25, pp. 88, 123, 151, 211; Immigration Commission, *Final Report*, 1911, p. 144; *Montana Socialist* (Butte), Mar. 6, 1915; Thomas Meagher to Boyce, Dec. 26, 1913, Boyce Papers.

66. Immigration Commission, *Immigrants in Industries*, part 25, p. 122; Silver Bow Co., Board of Health, "Report on Sanitary Conditions," p. 5; WPA, *Copper Camp*, p. 13; Ralph Brissenden, "Rustling Card," p. 765.

67. Bureau of the Census, *Twelfth Census, Population*, pp. 796–99; *Butte Miner*, Sept. 11, Oct. 3, 1888; *Reveille* (Butte), Aug. 28, 1902.

68. For Dempsey and Duggan see RELA and AOH, Membership and Dues Ledgers. The statistics are from the *Labor World* (Butte), Apr. 28, 1902.

69. Immigration Commission, *Immigrants in Industries*, part 25, pp. 119, 121, 211. See also Gedicks, "Ethnicity," pp. 133, 138, 139, 141.

70. O'Dea, *AOH*, III:1263–64 has information on the aging of the AOH membership. Immigration Commission, *Immigrants in Industries*, part 25, pp. 115, 145, 563.

71. The company acknowledged as much. See Industrial Commission, *Mining at Butte*, 1911 and 1915, pp. 3785, 4006.

72. Emmons, "Immigrant Workers," p. 54 and nn. 64–66.

CHAPTER 8

The Aristocracy Besieged: The BMU, the Enclave, and the New Immigration, 1910–14

I

The hiring of new men in Butte was part of a corporate counterattack, begun in New York by men for whom the Daly way of managing corporate affairs has to have seemed quaint at best. To Rockefeller and Henry Rodgers, the BMU had too much power, the Socialists too much potential for mischief, the Irish enclave too much of both. Daly had invested the Irish with aristocratic privilege in the 1880s and 1890s; the divestiture proceedings began about 1907. As it happened, the interests of the company would not be well served by turning to these new men; they brought an element of political as well as occupational instability to Butte, and the company eventually had to deal with both. But the decisions of corporate managers are of less concern here than the response to those decisions by the men digging the shafts and shoveling the ore.

It seems obvious now that even without these boardroom decisions to deflate the union and defuse the Socialists, there would have been noticeable ethnic changes in Butte's work force. New men were coming in; they would do the heavy work as previous immigrants had before them. It is inconceivable that the work force of a place like Butte would be forever dominated by what the Immigration Commission with unintentional irony called the "American element." Close observers would have noticed the changes. In 1906 the Balkan Saloon, "Radovich and Terkla proprietors," had opened on East Park Street. In 1908 two newspapers, the *Croatian World* and the *Servian Voice,* began publication. The *Manuscript Census* from 1910 has a number of entries like that for a boardinghouse on East Galena filled with unskilled laborers born in "Austria" and listing "Anything" under the heading for work. Of sixty-nine Montenegrins in Butte in 1911 only two had been in the U.S. more than ten years; only twenty-two could read or write English.[1]

Then, in the summer of 1910, the *Butte Evening News,* the newspaper founded by Fritz Heinze, let even the less observant know what was happening. In a series of stories, introduced with blaring headlines, the *Evening News* broke the story of "the Bohunk Invasion." Three thousand Slovaks, according to the stories, had been "imported" into Butte. They bought their jobs from complicitous foremen, lived in densely packed boardinghouses and hovels, sent most of their money back home, and, if the cartoon caricatures are to be believed, spent the rest on knives and cigarettes. These "European Chinamen," if not checked, would return Butte to an era it thought it had outlived and outgrown: a world dominated by unattached and uncaring transients. They had "destroyed Leadville and Cripple Creek," said the *Evening News,* in part by driving the Irish out; they would do the same to Butte. The place would become like those other "corporate camps where 97 percent of the miners were foreign born." This was precisely what the BMU, through the *Butte Bystander,* had warned against in 1897.[2]

The presence of these new men gave the mining companies more social and economic control over the labor force than the BMU and the rest of Butte's Irish world was prepared for. The BMU, for example, found itself strongly protesting any promotional efforts to attract new workers to Montana, even those promotions whose ostensible purpose was to fill up the state's agricultural regions. Crop failures, it seems, had the disconcertingly bad habit of making miners of farmers. But so did cholera epidemics in Italy or social and economic dislocations in Croatia. This was in addition to the arrival of the more or less experienced miners who made their way to Butte because of strikes in other western mining districts. There was no keeping up with the demand for jobs. Butte's miners had always known that a surplus of workers would strip them of considerable power. They were about to learn how and how much.[3]

The record of the BMU-sponsored Free Employment Office indicates the extent of the problem. The office had no trouble placing women, no luck placing men. In 1906 there were 2,600 more job applications than job listings and almost as many women for whom jobs were found as men. Every year from 1908 to 1913, the number of women placed exceeded the number of men as, every year, the number of male job seekers vastly exceeded the number of jobs. In 1913 there were two and one-half times as many help-wanted applications for women as for men and almost twice as many women were placed. During those same years, the cost of living continued to increase while ACM profits and dividends—if not ACM production—remained high. It required, however, no particular wisdom to know that the BMU was not in a good position to demand a renegotiation of the contract of 1907.[4]

It needed no greater wisdom to know that the special status enjoyed by the Irish would also be threatened by this new industrial calculus. John Ryan's "chilly reception" to that AOH job committee in 1910 is a pefect case in point. So too is the fact that in 1913 the AOH had to content itself with the promise that "nobody would be discharged from their employment through celebrating St. Patrick's Day," quite a change from the earlier policy of closing the mines for that same celebration. The change was as striking when it came to forming crews. John Pope of the North Butte Mining Company told the Industrial Commission in 1915 that "I don't like to see too many of one nationality put together. I would rather keep them mixed. . . . I think you get better results if you don't have all your employees belonging to one clan or nationality." Even the politics of Butte began to change. Father Brosnan wrote to his father that the Irish were "beginning to get beaten at elections partly on account of . . . Austrians, . . . Germans, and Dagos" who were coming into Butte, partly because the Irish were so divided.[5]

This was not the Marcus Daly way of doing business, but Daly had been dealing with labor shortages and corporate rivals for labor's favor and the BMU and the Irish were the beneficiaries. Now Daly was dead, ACM's rivals were bought off, and the number of workers was more than a controlled and consolidated industry could absorb. The Irish felt the effects. In 1906 the RELA investigated some trouble at the Butte Brewery. The Bottlers' Union, it seemed, "had not accepted Mr. O'Brien's application," and his job had been given to "an Italian from Dakota." In 1910, the same year that Ryan spurned its job committee, the AOH reported that it had been "hit very hard this year" and John Gavigan entertained Division 3 with a "spirited rendition" of "Looking for Any Old Kind of Job." Other songs made the same point. One asked "Oh Maggie dear, and did you hear, the news that's goin' round?" The singer could pick from three stanzas to answer: "The Irish is forbid by law," "They're firin' all the Corkies," or "They're cannin' all the savages." Another, popular at this same time, was more dirgelike. "I rustled at the Diamond," said an Irishman, "and I rustled at the Con. / The dagos are the only ones / that they are putting on. / Oh Molly,

my Irish Molly, / in Butte I stand no show, / . . . If the job don't come,
I'm on the bum, / Be-gorry, I'll be goin' some, / My Irish Molly O'."[6]

It must be remembered that these Irish laments came more than two
years after the shutdown of 1907–8. No one had jobs then. By 1910,
however, the mines were operating at peak capacity; indeed there may
have been as many as three thousand men added to the companies'
payrolls between 1905 and 1910. The combination of booming mines
and idle Irishmen bewildered the enclave. The *Evening News* offered
one explanation of what had happened. "The Bohunk," it argued, "is
welcomed where the old-time miner cannot get a job. Many white men
. . . are seeking employment." By "old-time miners" and "white men"
it would appear the *News* meant Irishmen. It called them "good old
miners of the Marcus Daly days," a reference too obvious to be missed.
Peter Breen commented simply that Daly would never have let the
"Bohunks" into Butte, a remark that says more than Breen probably
intended. Further evidence that "white" meant Irish, and that it was
Irish jobs that were being taken, came from the Slovak response. They
accused the Irish directly of inspiring the *News's* series, adding that
the Irish were losing their economic foothold because they spent too
much of their money on alcohol and Irish nationalism.[7]

It had been fifteen years since that kind of charge had been heard
in Butte. The Irish were stung by it, stung even more by the loss of
their aristocratic status. Pat McKiernan, in a neat if unwitting reversal
of previous attitudes, argued that there "was more freedom in Ireland
than in Silver Bow" and that "if we could ever free anything we ought
to free ourselves first." This sounded like Patrick Ford. Others responded in the language of outraged Irish pride. Walter Breen told the
AOH that a master mechanic on the hill had "discharged two young
Irishmen from bigotry." Martin Joyce blamed "our ever ready APAs."
John Kelly agreed: "APAism is as strong as ever in Butte, only done
more quietly and in a more secret way." According to James Murphy
there was a "strong feeling here against the Irish race." Even P. J.
Brophy, a well-placed and well-heeled Butte grocer, began to suspect
that some Anaconda Company properties were "owned, controlled,
and operated by the Masonic influence." Masonic, to Brophy, meant
"Orange."[8]

Brophy and the others were partly right; the Irish did have rivals,
but it must have been nostalgia that led them to assume they were
still Cousin Jacks, Orangemen, and APAs. The population figures for
1900, 1910, and 1920 give a truer picture. In 1900, listing only the first
generation, there were 413 "Austrians," 414 Finns, 133 Italians, and
2,474 Irish living in Butte; in 1910 figures for those same groups were

1,140 "Austrians," 1,013 Finns, 151 Italians (the Italian-born population of the county, however, was 987), and 3,196 Irish. By 1920 the population from the component parts of the old Austro-Hungarian Empire was 1,152 (with another 810 "Jugo-Slavs" living in the county), 1,003 from Finland, 192 from Italy (with 772 in the county), and 2,376 from Ireland—almost 800 fewer than had been there in 1910. By 1910 there were more than one thousand of these new immigrants, slightly fewer than one thousand Irish, in the ACM mines. The Irish population, in other words, fell partly in response and, because the company had to replace them, directly in proportion to the arrival of these new men. And, or so it most have seemed to the Irish, they came from everywhere. The Immigration Commission in 1911 counted the sons of thirty-five nations resident in Butte and working in its mines.[9]

But Butte's mines had not only become less Irish, they seem also to have become appreciably more dangerous between 1910 and 1914. The data will not permit definitive judgments on this point, and it must be kept in mind that 1896, long before the arrival of the non-English-speaking workers, may have been the most dangerous year in Butte's history. Still, the record for the later years was dreadful. In the four years from 1910 to 1913, an average of 4.68 men were killed per 1,000 men employed in the Anaconda Company mines. This is more than six times the death rate from accidents in British mines; it does not of course include deaths from respiratory diseases. Better evidence comes from the North Butte Mining Company. In 1907 the company employed 576 men underground; the number of underground accidents resulting in injury or death in that year was fifteen. In 1911, with 714 underground workers, serious accidents totaled seventy; in 1913 the company employed 769 men underground; the number of accidents had jumped to 291, almost twenty times the number in 1907 with a work force only one third larger![10]

The Miners' Union and the AOH would pay some of the bills for these injuries, illnesses, and deaths. Their records indicate a growing demand for their services. Between 1878 and 1899 the BMU averaged $7,700 per year in sick and death benefits. In 1910, with a mine work force only doubled or tripled that of the earlier years, and with no increase in benefits, it paid out more than ten times that sum. AOH expenses were comparably affected, indicating that the new men (and the new machines) were perilous to be around and that the associational Irish were less able to determine their own job assignments.[11]

II

Making these changes even more devastating to the Irish enclave was its inability to reproduce itself. The Irish may never really have known whether this failure was cause or effect of the ethnic changes in the work force. They likely did not care. What was clear was that older Irishmen were leaving the mines, but their sons were rarely entering them. Indeed, the Immigration Commission commented, with the Irish specifically in mind, that in Butte as elsewhere "the rising generation of the sons of the earlier immigrants" were not working in the mines and that this, as surely as the decline of the first generation, explained the companies' growing reliance on "Finnish, North Italians, and various Austrian races." Con Kelley spoke for the companies when he complained that "good miners are what you want," but "they are scarce." The companies would have to take what they could get. Fortunately, the unskilled were in plentifuly supply.[12]

It is possible, of course, that this failure to reproduce would have occurred in any event, that there would inevitably have been a cultural distance between the American sons and their Irish fathers. At any time and in any place, twenty-year-olds see the world differently from forty-year-olds. However explained, the second generation avoided both the mines and, except during periods of tension in Ireland, the associations. That rejection of the associations, given the ethno-occupational basis of the enclave, also had important working-class implications.[13]

Referred to as "narrowbacks" by the immigrants, the second generation did seem different and distant. Like tribal elders, Butte's associational Irish pronounced judgment on them. The old men used language that James Farrell might have used to describe his fictional Studs Lonigan—a son of immigrants, stripped of historical awareness and identity. Butte had its share of young Studs Lonigans. They "swore and blasphemed" more than their fathers. They had an "addiction to the drink habit and of hanging around saloons." They went "whoring"; they had "fallen away from religion and . . . become agnostics." They had fewer children, indicating an unbecoming this-worldliness and threatening "race suicide." Interestingly, all but the last of these judgments were offered in 1907 or 1908 as the Irish faced the crisis occasioned by the shutdown of the mines. The associations did what they could to attract and convert the second generation; meetings were made more "jocular, less sanctimonious to attract Irish-Americans." The $500 death benefit, much favored by the older Hibernians, was dropped and the savings used to keep sick benefits at a level that would continue to attract younger working Irishmen. Nothing seemed to work; the memberships remained disproportionately first-generation.[14]

The later-arriving Irish immigrants were scarcely more useful to the enclave than the second generation. They were still drawn to the mines but they came in fewer numbers than those who had come before and they brought to their work different expectations. The numbers tell an important story. In 1900, 35 percent of Butte's Irish-born had left home before 1881; by 1910, only 17 percent of the immigrant Irish had left Ireland before 1881, while 35.5 percent had emigrated after 1900. This is a significant population turnover. The work force in the mines reflected the change. Of 961 Irish-born in the ACM mines in 1911, 646 had immigrated to the United States after 1901 and 534 of those were unmarried. Like the other new men, these Irish were migrant laborers, not immigrants, disposable workers as surely as the "Bohunks." Like the other migrants, the new Irish wanted to go home—back to Ireland; they cared little about safe and steady work. The older men, the immigrant Irish, had found home in Butte's Irish enclave; they cared about little else.[15]

Ironically, the migrants knew more about industrial worlds—though considerably less about mining—than the older immigrants had. The new men were less likely to have been taken from Ireland's farms or, as O'Dwyer's genealogy indicates, from anywhere in West Cork. The emigration out of Castletownbere had not slowed in the early twentieth century, it had simply been redirected toward England and Scotland. There was another and related consideration: The later the emigration the less likely it was to be seen as coerced or tragic. Prior to 1900, the luckier Irish were thought to be those who were able to stay in Ireland; the emigrants were the unlucky ones, able to recover Ireland only by attaching themselves to one of America's social facsimiles. After 1905 that pattern had been reversed. The fortunate ones got out of Ireland. For that reason, among others, they were less interested in the enclave and its associations. They brought with them dreams and expectations different from those of the older Irish.[16]

Butte, without being fully aware of it, was witnessing an important change in its Irish immigration. The new Irish seemed more like the second generation; they may, in fact, have taken their values from those children of older Irish immigrants—young, second-generation Irish-Americans, men and women nearer their own age and products of similar social forces. The settled Irish used the same kind of language to describe the two groups. In 1917 Father Pat Brosnan reported that "some 2,000 Irish boys had come to Butte in the last month." They should not have come. "Hundreds who were raised decent now stand and beg for ten cents to get a drink." The Irishness of those 2,000 would not count for much; their effect on the work force would be no different than that of 2,000 young and transient from any other nation.[17]

Brosnan doubtless exaggerated. But even had he not, these were problems the enclave was accustomed to facing, problems it could remedy by finding the new men jobs and involving them in the enclave. Unfortunately, those who left Ireland after about 1905 showed little interest in the established Irish associations. The Cause still enlisted their energies; it was even rumored that many hundreds of intensely Anglophobic Irishmen came to Butte to escape having to fight in the British army, both before and after the passage of British conscription laws. The AOH and even the RELA, however, appear not to have been hot-blooded enough for them. Memberships spurted in 1913–14 as events heated up in Ireland but, as will be seen, this was a temporary phenomenon and the younger Irish would not continue their affiliation. The AOH and the RELA were social and fraternal organizations; they were dominated by the persisters, the old men whose memories were of an Ireland vastly different from the place these new Irish had left and whose lives reflected the social differentiation that twenty or thirty years in Butte was bound to effect. They were not likely to lend their associations to revolutionary purposes, whatever the nature of the revolution.[18]

There is the further consideration that the Butte they entered in 1906 or 1916 was not the same town it had been twenty years earlier. It was a much harsher place for an Irishman; Daly was gone and his management style, not to mention his hiring practices, had not been passed down in quite the same form. The Butte of 1912 resembled other western mining towns more than it did the Butte of 1892. The first Irish immigrants had from time to time drifted out of Butte; but they had always had the option of drifting back. The Irishman who emigrated from Ireland after about 1905 was denied that option; there was nothing to return to. Moreover, this new Butte, though it still belonged in important ways to the Irish, did not belong to young working-class Irishmen the way the old Butte had—for the simple reason that there were not many young working-class Irish left. The associations, the entire enclave, had aged appreciably. The new division was not between middle-class and working-class Irish, but between the older, settled Irish of whatever class and those, Irish included, who challenged their privileges and jeopardized their security.

As a consequence, new Irish, whether immigrant or second generation, viewed the associations as at best irrelevant, at worst untrustworthy. In 1915, in a statement with important implications, a member identified only as "new" told the AOH that the reason it could "not keep members or get them [was] . . . that they were scared of reports of what they would say at meetings being reported on the 6th floor," a reference to the Hennessy Building where the Anaconda Company had its corporate headquarters. Little wonder that, as one of its officers complained, the AOH was being "ridiculously scorned by many of our contumelious Irishmen." The reference was almost surely to younger, working-class Irish. But how else could the working class be expected to respond to an organization whose officers used words like "contumelious" and "ridiculously scorned"?[19]

III

The BMU, through its leadership, was a part of the besieged Irish aristocracy. Many of the new men who made their way to Butte, whether from Italy or Montenegro, the failed farms of eastern Montana, the mining region around Joplin, Missouri, or the "new" Ireland, were not "union men," particularly as the BMU defined union. This may simply be another way of saying that many of them were not Irish, but that aside for the moment, these unattached newcomers were as unacceptable to the BMU officers as they were to the others of Butte's steady men. They were thought instead to be the natural constituency for radical labor organizations, particularly the syndicalist Industrial Workers of the World.[20]

There is an irony in this division. The IWW, in some respects, was a lineal descendant of the Butte Miners' Union. It had arisen from the BMU-inspired Western Federation of Miners through the WFM's Western Labor Union and American Labor Union. But there were no similarities between the BMU and its indirect and, by BMU accounting, bastard offspring. The IWW, according to its own definition, was "broad enough to take in all the working class," particularly the itinerants; the most miserable of America's workers, Bill Haywood thought them. In fact, according to Tom Campbell, a leading BMU insurgent and IWW spokesman, these would, as a direct consequence of their misery, form "the advance guard of the labor movement." Campbell was prepared to "go down and out with my class regardless of creed, nationality, or color."[21]

There is very little evidence that the new men were—or ever saw themselves as—the advance guard of the labor movement. But their presence allowed those who thought they should be to challenge the established conservatism of the BMU, and, to an extent, split the union into two hostile factions. In 1910 the rebels won a temporary victory with the election of P. W. Flynn to the BMU presidency. Immediately, a "campaign of education along working class lines" was begun. Little is known about this campaign, though it almost had to have included building interethnic class consciousness, the ideological opposite of Irish aristocratic privilege.[22]

Whatever form it took, the education campaign had a divisive effect on the BMU. Guy Miller, a WFM officer, explained: As in other industrial unions, there were two types in the BMU, the conservative "who, finding things pretty fair and wages pretty fair, . . . if left alone would not exert himself to improve the conditions of others"; and the "radical" whose "duty" it was "to fight whenever there is a chance." Miller's definition of conservative fit the stable Irish miner nicely. Con Kelley, boss of the Anaconda mines, said the same thing. He acknowledged that "every advance that has been made by the wage earner has come as the result of agitation, of demand, and of successful attack." He was "raised in [that kind of] union atmosphere"; he "believed in the principle of organized labor." He did not, however, believe in the "radical tendencies" of some in organized labor "to engage constantly for [what] . . . cannot be granted."[23]

There were a number of union men who agreed. Dennis Murphy, president of the BMU in 1913, following the "conservatives' " recapture of the union's leadership, was one. Murphy insisted that conservative was not synonymous with "company man." It meant only that the BMU under his leadership would "live up to the rules of organized labor strictly" and that did not include subscribing to the anti-BMU principles of the Industrial Workers of the World. John C. Lowney, a former president of the BMU, was another union officer who understood Kelley's sense of what could not be granted. Lowney was commenting on Bill Haywood's 1910 speech in Butte, in which Haywood promised that the IWW "would nail the red flag to the mast of #1 [the Butte Miners' Union Hall] and that Amalgamated officials would climb up there every morning and get down on their knees to it." Haywood was undoubtedly inspired by Flynn's victory, though there is no reason to assume he correctly interpreted its meaning. Lowney, however, was unmoved and asked, reasonably enough, "if you can imagine the Amalgamated officials going up to kiss a red flag every morning." There was no sycophancy in Lowney's remarks. He was simply stating the obvious to men who shared his understanding of it. Among the important characteristics of any workers' enclave is its realization that "limitations existed on what was obtainable from the larger society." Kelley, Murphy, and Lowney were offering specific examples of that deceptively simple truth. Another simple truth, that all three were Irish and members of the Irish associations, should not be overlooked.[24]

The distinction, however, between those who acknowledged limits and those who did not involved more than just ethnicity. By way of obvious example, the early rebels in the BMU also included such un-mistakably Irish types as Joe Shannon, Dan Sullivan, Patrick W. Flynn, Dan Shovlin, and W. L. O'Brien. Nor were all of these men "new" Irish. O'Brien had come to Butte in 1914 after two decades of wandering the globe; but Shannon had been in and around Butte since 1890, Sullivan since 1896, Shovlin since 1899, and Flynn since at least 1903. A better case could be made that the radicalism of these five arose from their truer and more durable devotion to the principles of Patrick Ford than from their transiency.[25]

A better case perhaps, but not a convincing one; of those five only Sullivan was a member of the Irish associations, and—a miner for twenty-three years—he always tempered his rebelliousness with an awareness that only operating mines offered steady work. Shannon, on the other hand, and despite his testimony, does not appear to have been a "practical" miner. His radicalism sprang from other and mys-terious sources. In 1902 he was a BMU delegate to the WFM conven-tion; in 1905 he was organizing foreign-born lumber-mill workers near Missoula; three years later he was involved in a legal dispute with both the BMU and the WFM; from 1910 to at least 1915 he ran a Butte boardinghouse. He did not live in the Irish parts of town, had nothing to do with the Irish associations. His name appeared on no subscription lists for Irish nationalist causes, and he made a specific point of telling the Industrial Commmission that "this soul business is a kind of myth with me . . . I believe in looking after the body. . . . We have enough to do to take care of the body." This was no enclave Irishman. One-half at least of Patrick Ford's formula at the seam meant nothing to him. The new men would have to be his constituency. Whatever the source of his radical dreams, the new men alone could fulfill them.[26]

Shannon, however, and the other IWW and syndicalist-inspired rad-icals, were not the only ones to challenge the BMU for control of this constituency. The Butte Socialist party was also a rival. The theoretical socialism of the party, however, had scarcely more in common with the enclave Irish and the BMU than the strictly labor radicalism of the IWW. The party had had some success in city elections in 1903, and in 1911 it elected its chairman, Unitarian minister Lewis Duncan, to the Butte mayor's office, evidence that the hard times brought on by inflation and the corporate counterattack had pushed the city's working class, including many of its Irishmen, to break with the Democratic party.[27]

But Duncan's administration was distinguished more for its hostility to liquor, dirty streets, and houses of prostitution than for any serious assaults on the temples of capitalism. It did threaten to extend Butte's city limits to include Anaconda Company mines, a move with obvious implications for the company's tax department. What was perhaps more significant, incorporating ACM properties into the city would have ended the company's informal agreement with the county sheriff's office by which ACM security guards were automatically deputized. For these and other reasons, company managers were not pleased with Duncan and undoubtedly included his defeat, along with that of labor radicals, on its agenda.[28]

Like other American socialist parties, Butte's was run by—and to an indeterminable extent for—interests other than the working class. The 1913 membership list for the Butte Socialist party (not coincidentally, Local #1) attests to its narrow appeal. There are 498 names on the roster; occupations were found for 468 of these. Of these 468, 103 were miners and 66 were laborers. But there were 143 skilled tradesmen, 60 merchants and professionals, 52 municipal workers (this was during Duncan's tenure as mayor), and 44 housewives. Determining ethnicity on the basis of surname is tricky at best but, even extending Irish to include such frankly unlikely candidates as Coleman Allen, only 50 of the 498 appear to have been Irish. As significant, and with the same acknowledgment of risk, there are few Finnish, Italian, or eastern European names on the list. In sum, miners and unskilled laborers made up slightly more than one-third, the Irish less than one-tenth, and the enclave Irish nothing at all of the total membership. For an immigrant town, Butte's socialists were disproportionately native-born.[29]

As its election day successes would indicate, the party had more luck getting the Irish vote than it did enlisting Irish members. At that, however, there were tensions. The *Butte Independent*, James Mulcahy's Irish paper, identified Duncan as a "labor faker," and Charles Mahoney of the Butte Engineers' Union sponsored the WFM rejection of the Butte "Socialist local's" protest of the federation's treatment of Bill Haywood. More damning, and probably more representative of Irish enclave opinion, was the description of Duncan offered by James Lord, a working-class socialist and no particular friend of the WFM. Duncan, according to Lord, was "one of those freaks who has drifted into the ranks of the Socialist Party, after trying everything else, and found it profitable." Duncan did not take sides in the internal struggles of the BMU, principally because he had little in common with Joe Shannon, less even with John Lowney.[30]

If labor radicalism was ever to triumph in Butte it would have to be led by men like Shannon and the Wobblies rather than like Duncan and the Socialists, and it would have to enlist the new men. Stable Irish, in all respects more representative of working-class values than either Shannon or Duncan, would have little to do with it. The BMU, agent of that working-class conservatism, would be the radicals' immediate target. This was a BMU, however, considerably weakened by the events of 1906–12. Inflation outran wages; steady work was a casualty of the consolidation and shutdowns of 1906–8; "safe" work would not survive the hiring of new and unskilled men. As a consequence, and unlike other "aristocracies" of labor, this Irish one did not reproduce itself, either in its occupational or its strictly ethnic form.[31]

The result of all of this was that by 1907 the Irish of settled habits were losing control of the work force. A new working class was emerging in Butte, one with different perspectives and expectations. This was as true of the younger Irish as it was of the Finns or the "Bohunks." The aristocratic privileges which the settled Irish had come to think of as their due were being stripped away. Among the lessons they had learned was that their status was held on sufferance, not by the industrial equivalent of feudal writ. Their numbers had declined, their skills had become anachronisms. They were like craft weavers in an era of textile mills, relics as surely as their tools.

For almost a decade only their Irishness had sustained them, but by 1910 that, too, seemed a relic. They responded as any displaced aristocracy would. They fought to hang on to their status by attaching themselves to other forces in the community that stood for order and stability. That involved cooperating with the more powerful, but obviously the aristocracy was not unaccustomed to that form of cooperation. The resulting partnership of interests was, in fact, the source of its privileged status. The enclave was pleased to think of itself as a more nearly equal partner in the years before consolidation, with a greater influence on the terms of the alliance. But there was no reason to believe that old preconsolidation agreements could not be renegotiated and the old ways of doing business restored.

What the enclave Irish needed was a preemptive strike; a move that would restore their influence before the new men and the new rules overwhelmed them. They counted heavily on company support, hoping that the corporate madness that had cost the enclave jobs and status between 1906 and 1912 was only a temporary delusion. What they forgot—or perhaps never knew—was that the company had turned to new men because of the inadequate supply of old ones and because the new ones were cheaper. Those factors would not change. But even had the settled Irish known all this, they would still have attempted that preemptive strike. Call it a cultural habit of aristocracies. Since this was an ethno-occupational aristocracy the campaign would be a

cooperative effort. The BMU would lead it, but with considerable enclave support.

IV

The first shot was fired in 1912. In March of that year, the Anaconda
Company discharged as many as five hundred Finnish miners, all identified as socialists. Some of these Finns undoubtedly were socialists;
others were probably IWWs; most were just workers. But a delegation
representing all of them went to the BMU and demanded that the
union avenge them—*as Finns*—even to the point of calling a strike to
recover their jobs. It cannot have escaped their attention as Socialists
or Wobblies that the contract of 1907 was about to expire and that a
new time contract would close them out of the BMU for the duration
of the agreement, or that the WFM was getting ready to ally itself with
the AFL, or that a newly elected Socialist mayor was preparing his
municipal agenda. Needless to add, the BMU, the IWW, the Montana
Socialist party, and the officers of the ACM were no less alert to these
pending developments. The immediate order to fire the Finns can only
have come from Anaconda Company headquarters; the Butte Miners'
Union, Western Federation of Miners, and Socialist party would have
to respond.[32]

It fell to the BMU to respond first. Twenty-three of twenty-five members of its strike committee, holdovers from the insurgents' victories
in 1910 and 1911, favored a walkout. The two dissenters, John Lowney
and Dan Holland—both associational Irish and both moderates if not
conservatives—demanded a referendum vote of the entire membership.
Their insistence on the participation of the rank and file would earn
for them the undying enmity of the insurgents, but Lowney knew Butte
well and, as he put it, knew that had a strike been called without a
vote of the membership, "there would have been more red hell in
Butte than was ever seen in this organization before." The vote took
place over two days, the mines closing to permit full participation.[33]

The BMU had never in its thirty-four-year history called a strike. It
was not going to call one now. Approximately 60 percent of the membership went to Miners' Union Hall to cast their ballots, and, by a vote
of 4,460 to 1,121, the BMU overruled its strike committee. Lowney
estimated that more than 2,000 BMU members called themselves Socialists; at least 1,000 of these did not vote to strike. There were also
by this time almost 1,000 Finns in the mines, and assuming that half
the 500 Finns who were not Socialists voted to support their co-na-
tionals who were, this referendum would indicate that neither Finn

nor Socialist offered much support to BMU radicalism—whatever form that radicalism might take. Six weeks later, as the Socialists and IWW might have predicted, the BMU, having averted a strike, entered into a new three-year wage agreement with the ACM. Like the contract of 1907, this one both pegged wages to the price of copper and was passed without WFM approval.[34]

The ACM always insisted that the 500 men were discharged because they constituted "an undesirable class." John Gillie, superintendent of ACM mines, denied even knowing they were Socialists; it was their "method of living," he said, "the conducting of saloon matters, etc." that prompted the firings. The likelihood of that is not great. In fact, John Pope of the North Butte Mining Company admitted that he fired men solely because they were Socialists. Remarkably, the Finns and their representative, Tom Campbell, disputed only Gillie's reference to the discharged miners as socially undesirable. They agreed that ideology and politics were at most indirectly involved and then only as ethnicity determined ideology. In other words, they agreed that the firings arose because the men were Finns.[35]

In a strongly worded complaint to the WFM, the Finns accused ACM and the company-dominated BMU of "discriminating between the English-speaking people and the Finnish," the company for firing them, the union for refusing to avenge them. In every protest the dominant reference was to Finns, not Socialists, though occasionally the two were mixed as in the report that during the strike vote "throngs was yelling, 'they are all Socialists, Finlanders.' 'To hell with them.' " It was the Finns who "up to now, had been the most faithful and worthy supporters of the WFM"; it was the Finns who would "be forced to fight openly against the WFM to the bitter end" if the federation acquiesced in the BMU's refusal to strike.[36]

If Finns rather than Socialists were the victims, then Irish rather than conservatives were the miscreants. In other words, the rebels noticed, as they could hardly not have, the Irish connection. Campbell, in a reference to the strike vote, accused the BMU of "putting religion in it," not the first time that "religion" was used as a code word for ethnicity. He even called attention to a check, drawn on an ACM account and signed by John Ryan, paying for one hundred tickets to the Gaelic Football League championship, an utterly meaningless point unless he was trying to identify the ACM as an Irish club. Similarly, John Lowney can only have been answering a charge of ethnic discrimination when he insisted that the firings were for political reasons, then reminded his critics that "during the past twenty years, hundreds of men have been discharged . . . and there were as many Irish among them as any other nationality, yet there was never a strike declared by the Miners' Union to secure their reinstatement." In fact, Lowney went on, "quite a number of Irish" had lost their jobs in the 1912 firings.[37]

Lowney can not have been entirely convincing. Jacob Oliver, neither Irish nor Finnish, saw the matter more clearly. In testimony to the Industrial Commission regarding the trouble in 1912 Oliver pointed out that socialism cannot have been the issue since the Finns could not vote in city elections. He said nothing about union elections, but when asked about the charge that the union was company-dominated he replied, "Well, there was a good deal of race feeling in connection with that." As to those fired, Oliver noted that "the majority . . . were Finlanders" and that "the sentiment was opposed to going out on strike to reinstate the Finlanders." Oliver identified the Irish in particular as determined not to let the Finns " 'drive [them] out of Butte.' I heard that expressed several times."[38]

This was not, however, simply a case of ethnic rivalry and prejudice. The Finns were new men. They were young, single, and on the road. As the saying had it, they had been "looking for a job when they found this one"; they would not have minded looking again. Conservatives in the BMU and the WFM, meaning those who had settled in, put as much social distance as possible between these wanderers and the established miners. Far from constituting some kind of advance guard, the conservatives called these new workers a "foraging aggregation of transient hoodlums . . . and sweatless vagrants" for whom "direct action," including strikes and sabotage, was an acceptable method of worker protest. But strikes closed mines and cost jobs; sabotage, including "blowing up the shafts, setting fire to the mines," or putting "the pumps and machinery out of commission," obviously had a similar effect. These, according to Dan Holland and Dan Sullivan—one a BMU "conservative," the other a BMU socialist, both associational Irish— were tactics embraced by Tom Campbell and the other Wobblies as well as by the Finns. The BMU response was predictable and predictably unrestrained: "Such doctrines are extremely repugnant and absolutely abhorred by the great majority of this union."[39]

These Finns may in fact have been (as Aileen Kraditor insists most Finns were) radicalized by their experiences in Europe. One of their spokesmen, Frank Aaltonen, explained: "The labor movement and political movement in Finland are the same"; the Finns had learned from "their part in the labor movements of the Old World" the rallying cry "Injury to one is Injury to All." Significantly, that had been the motto of the Knights of Labor and was then the governing principle of both the IWW and of the Irish labor leader and IWW sympathizer James Larkin. Larkin and Aaltonen, however, never had to apply it to ethnically mixed working classes.[40]

The IWW did. Wobbly involvement in the events of 1912 was much discussed. For his part Campbell admitted to being a member of its propaganda league but he denied that the IWW had a union in Butte. Nine self-professed insurgents, most of them new to Butte, none of them Finnish, formed themselves into the Central Committee of Industrial Unionists to protest the firings of 1912, but whether these were fronting for the IWW is unknown and relatively unimportant. What is known is that the Wobblies adopted the Larkin/Finnish motto, too, and looked to the new men, those whom the conservatives had dismissed as "hobos, blanket brigades, and renegades for the emancipation of [the working] class." Charles Moyer, president of the WFM, had a different view of IWW involvement in the events of 1912. He held the Wobblies directly responsible for the 1912 rift in the BMU. That "sabotage howling coterie" had "poisoned the minds, not only of the Finnish speaking workers in our industry but others of foreign birth."[41]

Whether these new men were Wobblies or not made little difference to the leadership of the BMU—and ethnicity counted for scarcely more. What determined the BMU response was how the new men would affect the safety and dependability of working in the mines. There was little to feel encouraged about on either count. The Finns, Aaltonen told the WFM in 1914, believed in direct action—strikes and sabotage. They were born syndicalists, "which put them in a bad position" in Butte. "That is why," Aaltonen went on to charge, *the BMU "turned against them. . . . why Butte #1 eliminated those Finlanders from that organization."* This was a remarkable accusation but as remarkable was the failure of the BMU to deny it. Aaltonen, moreover, was not the only one who thought the BMU partially responsible for the firings. C. P. Connolly, a Butte Irishman, also insisted that the firings had "had the sanction of union officials." Further evidence that the company had less to do with the dismissals than the union is found in the fact that most of the Finns were offered their jobs back. ACM, it seemed, had discovered that "overzealous foremen," many of them Irish and all of them union men, had fired more Finns than the company's political situation required.[42]

By the time the company had noticed this oversight, many of the discharged Finns had left town; others, those who were rehired or never fired, were reported to have "lost all interest in the BMU," and to be withholding their "dues except where they had to pay them to keep their jobs." They cannot have been alone in this informal "boycott" of the BMU. Union membership fell from 7,000 (in a mine work force of about 11,000) in February, 1913, to fewer than 4,000 in May of 1914. By that later date there were at least 5,000 men working underground, more than half of the underground work force, who were not paid-up members of the BMU. Anyone wanting to "start trouble," according to one who did, could count on at least 4,000 of those unaffiliated workers. Here was further evidence that the old hiring system based on the ethnic community had broken down.[43]

The company's interests were no better served by this rate of delinquency than were those of the union; and 1912 was otherwise proving a very good year for the protection of the company's interests: the WFM had refused to readmit the previously expelled Haywood, signaling both the end of its brief and never very enthusiastic flirtation with IWW radicalism and the start of its affiliation with the conservative AFL. That same year, the BMU had agreed to a new three-year agreement as protective of the company's profits as of the workers' wages. There remained, however, some leftover problems: Lewis Duncan was still the mayor of Butte, the IWW was still making revolutionary noises, and the BMU and WFM were losing their hold on a significant percentage of the new and mostly transient workers. There is no evidence that the ACM held the new men directly responsible for creating these problems; considerable evidence that it believed their presence a magnet for labor radicals who had assigned the newcomers a revolutionary role and had come to Butte to help them rehearse their lines. Whether directly or indirectly, however, they had destabilized the work force. Here, clearly, was an instance where Con Kelley's concert of interest between labor and capital could be of inestimable value to both.[44]

The solution hit upon—the second shot in the conservatives' preemptive strike—was the so-called rustling card system, implemented by the Anaconda Company in December, 1912. The idea for the card came from William Daly, the superintendent of the Bell and Diamond Mines and an active member of Division 1, Butte AOH. This new hiring system required all prospective miners to secure a card allowing them to look for or "rustle" a job. The system had been used previously in the mines of the Coeur d'Alene region and, as early as 1903, in the ACM smelters in Great Falls and Anaconda. These smelters, not coincidentally, began to employ large numbers of southern and eastern European immigrants five or more years before the mines. By 1910, for example, slightly over 30 percent of the workers at the ACM smelter in Anaconda were eastern European or Italian. That was a higher percentage than for all native-born workers and more than double the percentage of Irish-born.[45]

The card system, with its implications of blacklisting, eventually became the source of enormous worker unhappiness. Even at the time of its passage a small majority (1,856 to 1,627) of those participating in a BMU referendum on the new hiring system voted to protest the use of the card. But at least 3,600 BMU members did not vote, and the union leadership took no formal action. Worker unhappiness, however, whatever its extent, cannot have arisen from the actual questions on the card. The company did want to know place of birth and citizenship status, but the only questions that outwardly addressed the issue of "sweatless vagrants" were the ones that asked "If married, where does your family reside?" and "Read and write English?" Even these can hardly be made to seem conspiratorial or discriminatory. In fact, John Commons, in Butte as chairman of the Industrial Commission, called the use of the rustling card "anarchistic, no system to it."[46]

The card did contain inquiries about former employment, including the names and addresses of foremen and shift bosses. In the case of the application used in the smelters, these previous employers could be asked to comment on the job seekers "personal character and habits." Nothing that specific appeared on the card used in the mines; only a blank section for "comments." Between December, 1912, and October, 1914, the company estimated that only "two or three" men of the approximately 20,000 who applied were denied a card. This was with 10,000 to 11,000 men underground and a monthly turnover rate of 20 to 30 percent. These figures were not seriously contested by any of the worker organizations involved at that time, but neither are they particularly to the point. Blacklisting through one devise or another was routinely used in the other mining camps; it, too, was a part of the remembered past. The "comments" section could easily have been used as the basis of blacklisting had the company wished it.[47]

In fact, however, the company did not wish it—at least not yet. Its stated motives for adopting the card suggest a very subtle prejudice against transient miners, but this was a prejudice not unique with the company. Con Kelley was once again the ACM spokesman. The old hiring system in which foremen and shift bosses simply selected their crews from the men who presented themselves at the gate every morning could be used only with a work force that was relatively stable. Butte had had that kind of work force. The majority of the miners, said Kelley, had once been "permanent residents who lived here and worked continuously." That had changed. Now there was "a very large, floating population coming in and going out at Butte." Kelley estimated that 25 percent "of the total number of men employed here [do not] permanently reside here." Some stayed a few days, others a few weeks. The result was that one-quarter of the work force was turning over every month. Little wonder that by 1913 William Daly was identified as an "Efficiency Engineer."[48]

Until Daly's rustling card system was implemented, the company had no record of its employees except that which the shift bosses carried around in their heads. Kelley pointed out to the Industrial Commission that state and federal agencies now demanded statistics on wages and injuries, and the pending legislation establishing workmen's compensation would increase that demand. But the transients also changed their names and defrauded downtown merchants who had extended them credit; "drunken and incompetent employees" went underground, jeopardizing the "welfare of the competent and sober." If fired, these "deadbeats" brought charges "against some of the foremen . . . and against representatives of men of different nationalities" who were reported to have influence over "said foremen"—a quite unintentional acknowledgment of ethnic preference.[49]

These were not motives likely to enrage the BMU. Of the rank and file, John Lowney recalled only two out of the thousands handed a card who refused to sign. Joe Shannon pointed out that with an "army of unemployed ready to take [their] places," the "company men" saw the card as a means of protecting their jobs. It should be recalled that Shannon's definition of company men was nearly all inclusive. Protest was unthinkable, Shannon noting that "it was an utter impossibility to . . . get this cosmopolitan union of ours together . . . on these things." By "these things" he meant the rustling card and blacklisting; he used "cosmopolitan" in its most literal sense. As for the union's leaders, they were no more disposed to contest this issue than they had been to contest the firing of the Finns; indeed, as in those firings, the BMU may have been actively involved in the decision to adopt the rustling card. Evidence was provided by L. O. Evans, general counsel for the company, who recalled in 1917 that "there was even a request . . . for some kind of system of identification . . . from the officials of the Butte Miners' union, as they were meeting difficulties . . . in keeping track of their members and collecting their monthly dues from them." In fact, and contrary to the earlier practice, the BMU refused to allow unemployed miners to rustle a job before joining the union and paying their dues, another instance where the closed shop, so favored by unionists generally, was used in defense of a conservative status quo. Without a job, union dues could not be paid; without a paid-up union membership, a job could not be had. A measure of union control of the work force resulted.[50]

The active involvement of the BMU in both the firings of 1912 and the implementation of the rustling card later that year could be used as further evidence that the union was corrupt, little more than a hireling of the ACM. And, depending on the definition of corrupt, a convincing case could be made. Regardless of definitions, however, it would be difficult to argue that the BMU leadership held the interests of all of Butte's miners equally central and dear to them. The BMU represented the stable men, the men for whom safe and steady work and the maintenance of the enclave had infinitely more meaning than abstract notions of worker solidarity. The new men, the reckless ones, not only for reasons of ethnicity but because they brought back unpleasant memories of the insecurities of life in mining camps, were unwelcome additions to an industrializing town.

But for Butte's radicals, whatever the source of their radicalism, it was precisely that recklessness born of "misery" that made the new men so open to radical solutions—or at least so receptive to radical rhetoric. John Lowney spoke for the steady men when he told of the limits on what workers could reasonably ask or when he called to mind the enormous social distance they and Butte had come. Joe Shannon's vision was different; his definition of worker rights was without limits and the disorder consequent upon the arrival of the new men was more the promise of a triumphant future than the reminder of an insecure past. It was this openness of industrial unions to itinerant workers and the apparently mindless radicalism of that class that made the IWW so threatening. To the settled miners, the older men who had homes as well as long memories, that type was anathema.

V

In Butte, a disproportionate number of these steady men were Irish Catholics, but they did not have to be. Their Irish Catholic backgrounds did not guarantee their conservatism, though their working-class experiences, to a certain extent, may have. These were not distinctions the critics of that conservatism were disposed to make, particularly as they contemplated the Irish connection and as other elements of the Irish world joined the BMU in its preemptive strike. The *Butte Independent*, for example, Butte's Irish newspaper edited by the Irish-born AOH and RELA activist James B. Mulcahy, spoke often and warmly of the antisocialist position of the BMU. As for the Irish associations, the AOH still preferred St. Patrick to James Larkin and the RELA was still meeting secretly and speaking in whispers. Neither group was known for its tolerance of non-Irish, whatever their class.[51]

More significant were the ideas of the Irish-American bishop of Montana, John Carroll. In 1912 Carroll, at the time national chaplain of the AOH, issued a ringing denunciation of socialism and labor radicalism, asserting, no less, that "socialism threatened every substantial institution of civilization and that the adoption of its delusive principles would wreck the nation." More specifically, and "as one in close touch with the labor situation among the miners of Montana," he spoke, inaccurately, of the IWW as "a purely Socialistic organization" and congratulated "the miners of Butte for voting them down; Irish-America has no sympathy" with socialism. A year later, in a speech to the AFL, he contrasted Butte's thirty-five years without a strike to the constant turmoil in Leadville, Colorado, then reminded the delegates that Catholic societies favored nonviolent unions. Among those societies he numbered the Ancient Order of Hibernians, praising them for that "manly Catholic resolution they passed at the . . . convention endorsing my attitude toward socialism!"[52]

It cannot be known how much attention Catholics paid to Bishop Carroll, but he must have prayed often for even a share of the total obedience non-Catholic radicals assumed greeted his every clerical word. It is unlikely that Father Michael Hannan of Butte's St. Mary's parish based any of his homilies on the bishop's pastoral letters on socialism, no more likely that Hannan's congregation would have listened to him if he had. In other words, Carroll may have had more influence among the non- or anti-Catholic rebels than he did within his own flock. The reaction to his speeches and letters from the *Montana Socialist* is a perfect case in point. The issue of March 16, 1913 (the timing cannot have been coincidental) had a story on the "virulent and abusive . . . propaganda against socialism by certain political leaders of the Catholic church." Since the paper had previously devoted a good deal of space to stories by and about socialist or at least reform-minded priests, this propaganda had to have seemed a betrayal.[53]

The *Socialist* applied these same standards to the other components of the Irish enclave. The local Democratic party was hopelessly corrupt; the BMU was led by "company tools . . . who worked to pull corporation chestnuts out of the union fire." How and to what purpose went unstated. But it was James Mulcahy who elicited the *Socialist*'s most inspired and vituperative language. He was a "company bootlicker and 'killer of socialism.' " His paper was a "sewer of Amalgamated filth," the "pet organ of the Amalgamated." He was also described as the "mud-slinging Mulcahy of the Moyer machine," a reference that linked the WFM to the BMU and thus to the company. But, given Mulcahy's strong Irish associational ties, ethnic as well as journalistic partiality was also implied.[54]

Only the IWW of the other involved organizations provoked the *Montana Socialist* to the same pitch of invective as the *Butte Independent*. The Wobblies were the "Industrial Wreckers of the World," "ultra-radical, r-r-revolutionary disciples of direct action," but for all that, "paid hirelings of the capitalist class." This completed their list. The socialists had assaulted the ACM, the Catholic Church, the Irish associations, the Democratic party, the BMU, the WFM, and the IWW. Their isolation was complete; there was no one else in town. This isolation, along with their inability to attract immigrant miners, would limit the socialists' participation in the internecine struggles of Butte's workers to that of interested spectators or hapless victims unable to get out of the way.[55]

Still, their attacks on the enclave, including the BMU, are important. They make clear that after falling into disuse for a few years, the Irish connection was again perceived as dominating hiring in Butte. Implied was that the rustling card was the instrument of that Irish recovery. This undoubtedly oversimplified the matter. The Irish miners would never recover the ground lost between 1908 and 1912; their failure to reproduce alone would have insured that. It is possible that hiring officers, if not corporate boardmen, were restoring some of the Irishmen's old privileges, that those privileges were never lost, only temporarily suspended, and that the Irish laments of 1908–12 reflected their confusion upon the arrival of new men rather than any change in company policy. However explained, by 1912 worker protest involved necessarily an attack on the Irish connection, particularly as it explained the alleged control of the BMU by the Anaconda Company. As mentioned earlier, that company control and its presumed source guaranteed that when the war on capital came it would begin with an assault against the BMU and its Irish bosses.

VI

The war began in June, 1914. On June 12, insurgents within the BMU—"progressives" as they were known by then—working at the Black Rock and Speculator mines refused to show paid-up union cards to BMU representatives. Neither mine was owned by the ACM, meaning that the men did not have to have a rustling card, and neither was known as an "Irish" mine. The next day, the progressives disrupted the Miners' Union Day parade. There was considerable violence, punctuated by an armed group of men entering the Union Hall and taking the safe and all the union's records. Money from the safe was never recovered; the records were destroyed, accompanied by cries that "we're all paid up now." Four days later, in an informal referendum boycotted by most of the loyal members of the BMU, 6,348 men identifying themselves as "miners" voted nay on the question "are you in favor of showing BMU cards to BMU officers . . . in order to work?" There were only 243 ayes. Charles Moyer, Edward Boyce's successor as president of the WFM, arrived in Butte on June 19 to resolve the conflict that was tearing the federation's founding and largest local apart. He was in attendance when the BMU held its regularly scheduled meeting on June 23, which was disrupted by progressives. Shots were fired, whether from inside the hall or out is still uncertain, killing one bystander. Moyer and the BMU officers fled; the progressives "liberated" the hall, then set off the first of twenty-six dynamite charges that reduced the hall to rubble. A new organization, the Butte Mine Workers' Union (BMWU), was formed as the rival to the now-homeless Butte Miners' Union. The BMU would never recover.[56]

There were various explanations of motive and ultimate responsibility for these events. Some progressives said that assessments in support of striking Michigan miners were too high; and, in fact, assessments for the five years from 1910 to 1914 totaled $46.50, compared to the $5.25 total for the ten years between 1893 and 1902. This might have been seen as evidence of BMU generosity, except that the progressives insisted that the money was going to Moyers and to BMU president Bert Riley who was said to be living in a style grander than he ought. There was no evidence for either charge. Other radicals spoke of the union leadership's refusal to avenge the Finns, protest the rustling card, or permit voting machines, or of "discourtesies" and slights. The best explanation may have come from Industrial Commissioner Charles Garretson, who said the progressives' unhappiness stemmed from a "great series of mosquito bites," all of them related to the charge, dating back to 1891, that the company ran the union. Blame was as casually assigned as motive. The BMU blamed the IWW; the WFM agreed but insisted that Mayor Duncan and his inept Socialists were also at fault. For his part, Duncan blamed the "foreigners," who were easily duped, and the company, adding the not-altogether-unconvincing argument that most of the Wobbly leaders were ACM spies. Eugene Debs was of similar mind on the IWW leadership; they were traitors, informers, and spies.[57]

On August 30, an explosion at the Parrot Mine destroyed the mine's hiring office, a visible symbol of the rustling card. Shortly thereafter,

Governor Samuel Stewart declared martial law and placed Butte under the authority of the National Guard. The company responded to the Parrot explosion—which even the radical BMWU denied having any part in—by shutting down some of its mines and by denying the workers any further influence over the selection of the work force by ending its closed-shop agreement with the BMU. Con Kelley said the closed shop could be restored but only if the WFM was involved; his company would make no agreement with an independent union. Such was the hold on the future of Kelley's concert of interest. Mayor Duncan, in the meantime, having survived a murderous attack by an understandably confused Finnish immigrant, was removed from office in proceedings led by Peter Breen, who had been associated at least since the Penrose affair twenty-five years earlier with both the BMU and the Irish enclave. The similarities between the two events cannot have escaped him.[58]

It is not the purpose here to attempt a full explanation for what happened in 1914—assuming always that such an explanation is possible. But even the best of the older studies of these years miss a recurring and important theme: Both sides to the conflict, the conservatives and the various and varied progressives—IWWs, socialists, Slovaks, and Finns—believed that the quarrel was between the settled and the unsettled, which to an important extent meant the Irish and the non-Irish.

Let the conservatives speak first. The rebel BMWU, according to WFM president Moyer, had "enrolled everybody—miners and nonminers, residents and those who came in for the destruction." Moyer was speaking specifically of the bogus referendum on the BMU, but his point had more generally application. Those "fellows," he went on, "will have the same power as the legitimate workers," a most instructive use of "legitimate." According to L. O. Evans, chief counsel of the ACM, "New men . . . non-workers" had been sent to Butte. These were the source of the discontent. "Our difficulty is not with the *real laboring men* of Butte, . . . the honest working men anxious to continue their labor *and support their families*." The *Miners Magazine*, official paper of the WFM, was more direct. "Every jobless IWW in the country" had been sent to Butte. It was noted at the time that it had to have been nonminers or rookies who needed twenty-six charges of dynamite to blow up the Miners' Union Hall. Any practical miner could have leveled it with three or four.[59]

The argument became a litany. The progressives were always identified as unsettled, unskilled, unsafe; they were not miners, neither were they "real workers." Dennis Murphy, a former BMU president, spoke the lines. Nonminers, he said, many of them transients called into Butte for the occasion, agitated the union issue for the political advantage of radicals who were themselves not miners. Muckie McDonald, for example, the president of the BMWU, was said by another conservative to be "unknown in Butte until a few weeks ago . . . he never worked a day in any mine." This point was disputed, but as damning was the charge that "Muck McDonald was known as a bar room fighter" who even before the troubles of the summer had said that "he didn't know whether he was going to stay in Butte or not." Obviously, it was time "for the intelligent, sober, thinking men to stand like men." James Lord of the AFL thought that they would, that the "miners who have really lived and worked in Butte would recapture the union" from what another overwrought conservative called "proletarian parasites . . . howling, fever crazed fanatics."[60]

The fairness and relevance of these charges may reasonably be disputed. They do, however, appear to have been accurate, at least for the rebel leadership. A check of the names of the thirty-three BMWU officers and runners-up against city directories turned up twenty-four who mined for a living, but only six who had been in Butte as recently as 1910. Twenty-eight of the thirty-three lived in boardinghouses; seventeen were probably of Irish descent, but none of these was a member of either the AOH or the RELA. In sum, the leadership of the radical BMWU was drawn from recently arrived miners, many of them Irish, none of them in the enclave. The ethnic and social makeup of the rank and file of the BMWU or even of those who allowed their BMU memberships to lapse cannot be known. As Dan Sullivan put it, "Well, I guess it is pretty hard to get a [BMU] record now; they were destroyed"; the BMWU apparently kept no records.[61]

The only sympathy "conservatives" felt for these "proletarian parasites" came from those who saw the radicals as childlike in their gullibility and thus not responsible for what they did. Charles Moyer, in a more charitable mood but in language not altogether becoming the president of a once-radical union, thought that the conflict would be understood by anyone who went to Butte "among the men that are not as well educated as some of us—men who are not able to grasp these things—men who are easily persuaded and whose minds are easily poisoned." The *Miners Magazine* referred to the rebels as a "disinherited class, . . . groan[ing] from the wrongs of economic slavery." The IWW heard the same groans and persuaded themselves that the disinherited would destroy capitalism. The *Miners Magazine* came to a different conclusion. "Capitalism never won a victory" without their assistance. There could be "no reign of terror" except that they "sometimes commit treason to labor." Assuming the charge had any substantive meaning at all, treason to labor can only have meant an ignorance of the importance to settled miners of safe and steady work.[62]

These were also enclave values and the new men, the rebels, were manifestly not eligible for enclave membership. No one missed this point, or failed to comment on the ethnic affiliation of the bomb throwers. The dynamite used to destroy the hall, according to the *Montana Socialist*, "was secured by Austrians and Montenegrins." A conservative said the dynamiting was done by "Austrians, Montenigrians and Finnish." Frank Aaltonen denied that charge and told the WFM convention that 75 percent of the Slavs were members of the BMWU. The Slavonians, as they called themselves, answered in a letter to their spokesman, Yanko Terzich, that this was not the case, that, as they put it, "there is not any of our men that belong to the new union—except Montenegrins."[63]

Terzich conducted his own investigation. His remarks to the WFM offer a fascinating glimpse into the ethnocentrism of these years and the effects of ethnicity on worker protest. A "man of his nationality" told Terzich that the Slavs believed that Riley and the other Irish officers of the BMU were skimming Michigan strike relief money. They had "no fact . . . only that they were [so] told by certain individuals of their nationality." "The foreigners of Butte," Terzich went on, "especially those of my nationality, are men that do not study the principles of unionism . . . they just follow leaders . . . and accept that every word is true." What else could be expected? "They cannot read the English language, they cannot write the English language, and they cannot speak the English language."[64]

The point was most emphatically not that they represented, as a consequence, a radicalized proletariat. Indeed, Terzich argued that the vast majority of Butte's "foreign" workers were "respecting and law-abiding people"—in large measure *because* they were foreign. "The foreigners are afraid of the law; I know that myself because I was raised in the country where those people come from and they . . . respect law and order." On the basis of what he had learned—and there is no reason to assume it was overly biased or distorted—Terzich blamed the bombing and the deep divisions within the union that preceded and caused it on transients brought to Butte by the IWW. It is not particulary important here if Terzich was right or wrong. It is clear that there were two factions within the BMU; equally clear that the division was largely between the settled and the still-wandering miners and that that social distinction both reflected and exacerbated ethnic differences.[65]

One incident expresses perfectly this division. In the summer of 1914, after the dynamiting of the Miners' Union Hall, the IWW sent Arturo Giovannitti, one of their publicists and an advocate of direct action, to Butte. Giovannitti was there to celebrate the new order, represented by the IWW, and to propose an epitaph for the old, represented by the BMU, an "obsolete union," as he described it. It must have been with utter amazement that veteran Butte miners heard what he said. Pointing to the rubble of what had been their hall, Giovannitti told them that "'Here Lies the Remains of 36 Years of Peace and Prosperity'; the working men of Butte," he went on, "should be ashamed of those thirty-six years." Such remarks must have seemed particularly mindless to the enclave Irish.[66]

But the conservatism of that enclave must have seemed, as one BMU critic put it as early as 1897, "only a hair's breath from cowardice." Moreover, that conservatism, as surely as the "radicalism" that challenged it, wore an obvious ethnic aspect. The BMU was not just company-controlled. It was also Irish-run. The new men may not have been "well grounded Socialists," as one of Mayor Duncan's advisers put it, but little sophistication was required to make the obvious connections between the Irish, the company, and the union. After all, by 1912 the charge of ethnic-related preference and collusion was at least twenty-five years old; it was one of the more durable legacies of Marcus Daly.[67]

The rebels were as convinced of its accuracy as the APA had been. There are many examples, and they tell an important story. In 1912 A. O. Sarell, a Michigan organizer for the WFL, wondered aloud why the BMU had not struck in defense of the discharged Finnish socialists. He was "told by all that the Union was under the control of the company." This begged the question, and when he "demanded further explanation" Sarell was told that the "great majority of the members are conservatives, that the Catholic Irish have been the leading factions among the conservatives." In 1912, according to Sarell's informants, two of those Catholic Irish, John Lowney and Dan Holland, "even told the company not to concede on the strike issue as it would be defeated on referendum."[68]

Similar arguments were made to explain the rebellion of 1914. The rebels, one of their number told Guy Miller, objected to the BMU's influence over WFM policy, but more was involved than just BMU conservatism. The federation's newspaper, the *Miners Magazine*, had been deflected from its true course. "There has never been enough [union/labor] news," Miller was told, "I go some places and they say to me, 'the magazine lies unread unless something is said in regard to the Catholic Church . . . it confines its news to every Catholic society, and every Irish saloon in the place, and then everybody points their finger at it.' "[69]

Dan Buckley, an Irishman and an IWW, explained what this Irish influence meant to anyone who dared challenge the BMU's hold on the Butte miner. The real "enemy" of radicalism in Butte, he told BMWU officer Joseph Bradley, was "religious prejudice. This may be aroused by some paid hireling of Moyer's or the copper barons in the guise of an IWW soap box orator, who may start it by killing Jesus and damning the pope. You fellows . . . want to watch for this type." Clarence Smith, a Socialist alderman during the administration of Lewis Duncan, made the same point, though in less-direct language. The division of 1914, he explained to the Industrial Commission, was "not strictly a party situation," meaning that ideological disagreements were not alone in producing unhappiness. He could not be sure the commissioners "could understand that very well," but since he "didn't wish to cast any reflection upon anyone at all," he simply presented the commissioners with a list of the names of the union leaders for the last twenty years.[70]

Finally, though it cannot be the last instance when the charge was made, the *Montana Socialist*, the paper once edited by Clarence Smith, offered its judgment on the events of 1912–14. According to the *Socialist*, the Irish enclave had given much, including its presumed radical essense, to the company. As important was the paper's judgment on what the company had given in return. At issue was the rustling card and the allegations of discrimination and blacklisting which by that time accompanied its use. The *Socialist* thought it understood the nature of that discrimination. Rustling cards were denied, said the paper, to two groups of men, those with socialist sympathies and those "antagonistic to the Knights of Columbus" and/or belonging "to the A.P.A. or the Guardians of Liberty."[71]

In other words, the rustling card had replaced RELA and AOH control of hiring. This charge had been made earlier. At the time of the rustling card in the Coeur d'Alenes, it was reported that belief "in the religion of the Catholic Church" was a prerequisite for employment. Still, the *Socialist*'s was a remarkable allegation made more so by its striking likeness to one made twenty years earlier by the APA. As remarkable is the fact that, as twenty years earlier, it may have been true. At about the same time that the *Socialist* was charging ethnic discrimination, Dan Crowley said that the time was right for the AOH to form new job committees, and Patrick Kenny told the AOH that "it was intended that we would be given the preference in Butte once more." "We" meant Hibernians, not Irishmen. In the absence of a closed-shop agreement with the BMU or some other union satisfactory to ACM, that preference was unlikely, but the more important point is that Crowley and Kenny were still thinking in those terms. They knew from long experience that the test of a labor aristocracy was still "the ability to exclude, never mind how."[72]

The leadership of the rebel Butte Mine Workers' Union cannot have known of Kenny's prediction. It is unlikely, however, that they would have argued with his assumption of associational Irish preference. Their problem was that they had to justify to other workers their destruction of the BMU, and the Irish connection was so difficult to prove. In a list of grievances they explained their revolt against the BMU and the WFM, and in the process offered more evidence of an Irish connection. "Butte Local #1," they said, "was ... in the hands of company henchmen." That much was assumed. But because of its control of the union, "the Anaconda Copper Company has been able to ... block any attempt of the miners ... to protect themselves against discrimination and corporate greed." The discrimination could have been political: the denial of jobs or preferment to socialists. But had it been only that, the BMWU would not have had to resort to the next sentence. "To explain this to those of you who have not worked in Butte will, we know, be a difficult task. But those of you who have worked here will readily understand." This was one of those grievances, said another Butte miner, that could "not be brought ... in any regular form or manner."[73]

The BMWU was more specific and more informative when it framed its constitution and bylaws. Great emphasis was placed on company hiring practices. The language of those sections was categorical: "No shift boss or foreman shall be admitted to this union under any circumstances. It shall be incumbent upon members to handle the boss on the job. Any discrimination against any group or individual by any ... corporation shall be resented by the men on the job." Three-member grievance committees were appointed for each mine; their responsibilities included dealing with any charges of discrimination in hiring or job assignment. Later, in a public announcement, the new union admonished its members to "treat the boss like a man ... and not, under any circumstances, tolerate in the future, as in the past, ... any bulldozing, browbeating, bamboozeling or abuse of any kind." This language reflected more general demands, common to syndicalist unions, for a greater measure of shop-floor—in this case mine shaft—control. But there can be little doubt that it expressed as well the barely disguised rage of those outside the enclave over the presumed and aristocratic privileges of those in it.[74]

VII

For more than thirty years the Butte Miners' Union, supported by the larger Irish miner enclave with which it was at times indistinguishable, pursued policies designed to insure a fair living, or, in Giovannitti's unintended compliment, peace and prosperity. The union had enjoyed remarkable success, bringing an important element of stability to both workplace and community. Its power derived from its source in the enclave and its affairs were often conducted in defense of that enclave. Raised in uncertainty and disorder, the Irish miners of Butte sought some measure of predictability in their lives. They were not the only beneficiaries of their success in finding it. If their values arose from the cooperative commonwealth in which they lived, the whole community benefited from the Irish defense of those values. If the enclave required permanence and stability, so did the industry and the city.

Perhaps the Irish were too successful. New men, including new Irishmen, wanted more—and less—than security, particularly as they came to understand at what cost that security was obtained. The enclave had not only moderated the labor movement, it had redefined the goals thought to inhere in that movement. The important point is that not until about 1908, and then in part because of their unwillingness to send their sons underground, did the stable Irish miners of Butte begin to lose some of the privileges of a labor aristocracy. They were convinced of the usefulness and dignity of their work, but even had they not been, they understood that only steady work permitted them to hold their place in Butte. They became, as Eric Hobsbawm writes, the "superior ins," distinguished by their respectability as much as their Irishness from the "inferior outs." This was not a status easily surrendered.[75]

The most direct challenge to this workers' world came from within the working class, from men—workers, most of them, not miners—who did not share the enclave's deep commitment to safety, stability, and industrial peace. Safe and steady work meant nothing to men who did not intend to stay; shutdowns, including those that were strike-related, affected only their decision on when to leave town, not whether they would leave. There has been considerable discussion of the effects of mobility on the mobile, less study of mobility's effects, real and potential, on the persistent. And here is where the critics of the BMU and its Irish leadership missed the point. The steady, respectable men wanted to protect the enclave by protecting their jobs, their families, and their health—goals that appeared conservative only to those for whom the enclave had no meaning.

Through its closed-shop agreement with the companies, the BMU, as surely as the AOH or the RELA, was a means of achieving those goals. Unaffiliated drifters jeopardized them—particularly as they threatened the enclave's control of the labor supply. Here it would be well to recall Tom Kealy's reference to Irishmen outside the AOH as "scabs." Thus, the usual question asked about working-class enclaves—whether in the process of serving as informal unions they usurped formal union power and deflected worker allegiance or supplemented the union's power and broadened the workers' allegiance—has little meaning in this context. In Butte, the enclave and the union were part of each other. For the steady Irishmen who ran both, breaking rock was only a small part of their world; breaking labor's chains was no part at all.

NOTES

1. Polk, *City Directory*, 1906; Murphy and Walker, *Butte, Montana*, pp. 55, 58; Bureau of Census, *MS Census*, 1910; Immigration Commission, *Immigrants in Industries*, 1911, part 25, pp. 555, 557.

2. The *Butte Evening News*, July 18, 23, 24, 1910. See also WPA, *Copper Camp*, pp. 134–37.

3. Industrial Commission, *Mining at Butte*, 1915, p. 3853; Hand, "Folklore," p. 164; Hand et al., "Songs" p. 45; *Butte Bystander*, Feb. 10, 1894; Feb. 4, 1896; Boyce to James McGrade, Mar. 12, 1901; to T. W. McGuire, May 3, 1901, in "Diaries," Boyce Papers; *Montana Socialist* (Butte), Apr. 19, 1914; Montana, Dept. of Labor, *Resources and Opportunities of Montana* (Helena, 1914). On strikes see Vernon Jensen, *Heritage of Conflict*, pp. 118–59, 219–35, 225–55, 272–88. The *Montana Socialist* wrote that the strikers were "making their last stand in Butte" (June 28, 1914).

4. Montana, Dept. of Labor, *First Biennial Report*, pp. 54–55; *Moody's Manual*, p. 2906.

5. AOH D3, MB, Mar. 8, 1913; see too RELA, MB, Apr. 10, 1913. Industrial Commission, *Mining at Butte*, p. 3747. Fr. Patrick Brosnan to his father, Feb. 18, 1917, Brosnan Letters.

6. RELA, MB, June 12, 1906; AOH D3, MB, Sept. 24, Oct. 29, 1910. The other songs are from Hand et al., "Songs," pp. 26–27.

7. *Evening News*, July 24, 1910. The paper also wrote that James Higgins, "Rimmer" O'Neill, and Jim Brennan, three prominent Irish mine foreman, would not have hired the "Bohunks" and that the Anaconda, always known as an Irish mine, was still a "white man's mine." Ibid., July 31, Aug. 1, 1910. Breen's remarks are from ibid., July 24, 1910; the Slovak response from the issues of July 23, 24, and 31, 1910. See also the AOH assurance that the *Evening News* was responsible for the stories, not the Irish, and that the Slovaks should quit blaming the wrong party (AOH D3, MB, Aug. 13, 1910).

8. AOH D3, MB, 1 Jan., 1910; Jan. 12, Mar. 13, June 7, 1913; Brophy to John Sutton, Oct. 4, 1912; to J. Hennessy Murphy, Oct. 13, 1912, Brophy Papers. Margaret Cunningham, Irish and a long-time Butte resident, recalled that anyone the Irish did not like was referred to as an APA (interview).

9. Richard Lingenfelter also assumes that the Irish/Cornish feud continued until at least 1914 and that it finally split the BMU (*Hardrock Miners*, pp. 6, 195). There is little evidence that the feud lasted that long and none at all that it had anything to do with the eventual breakup of the BMU. Bureau of the Census, *Twelfth Census, Population*, pp. 796–99; *Thirteenth Census, Statistics for Montana*, p. 594; *Fourteenth Census, Population*, p. 586; Immigration Commission, *Immigrants in Industries*, 1911, part 25, p. 555.

10. Industrial Commission, *Mining at Butte*, 1911 and 1915, pp. 3879, 3983–84; Wyman, *Hardrock Epic*, p. 115.

11. WFM, *Proceedings, 1911*, pp. 200–203; Wyman, *Hardrock Epic*, p. 182. See also the testimony of Dan Sullivan in Industrial Commission, *Mining at Butte*, 1911, p. 3931. AOH sick and death benefit payments are drawn from MB, passim. The Butte/Silver Bow Co. Archives has an index of newspaper references to fatal mine accidents from the 1880s to the 1940s.

12. Immigration Commission, *Immigrants in Industries*, part 25, p. 115; Industrial Commission, *Mining at Butte*, 1915, p. 3695.

13. See Kammen, "Introduction," p. 37, and Spitzer, "Historical Problem," p. 1364.

14. WPA, *Copper Camp*, p. 227; AOH D3, MB, June 17, 24, 1907; June 22, July 6, 1908. The "race suicide" remarks are from Bishop John Carroll, "Catholic Church and New World Democracy," Carroll Papers. Efforts to attract second-generation members are recounted in AOH D3, MB, Jan. 6, 1908; AOH, County Board, MB, Sept. 28; Oct. 6, 11, and 31, 1909. Miller, *Emigrants*, p. 511.

15. Immigration Commission, *Immigrants in Industries*, part 25, p. 113; Miller, *Emigrants*, pp. 492, 582. Blessing, "Irish Emigration," pp. 19, 21; Kennedy, *The Irish*, pp. 78, 150–56; Burchell *San Francisco Irish*, pp. 49–51; O'Dea, *AOH*, III:1390.

16. Diner, *Erin's Daughters*, p. 12; Riobard O'Dwyer, *My Ancestors*, passim; Blessing "Irish Emigration," pp. 19, 21.

17. Fr. Patrick Brosnan to his mother, Apr. 11, 1917; n.d., 1917, Brosnan Letters.

18. Vernon Jensen, *Heritage of Conflict*, p. 431; RELA and AOH D1, Membership and Dues Ledgers; RELA, Term Reports, passim.

19. AOH D3, MB, Oct. 30, 1915; John D. Sullivan to Patrick Kenny, Sept. 17, 1911, Correspondence

20. WFM, Exec. Board, MB, July 14, 1910; Immigration Commission, *Immigrants in Industries*, part 25, p. 109; Industrial Commission, *Mining at Butte*, 1915, p. 3853; *Montana Socialist*, Apr. 19, 1914. See too Brody, *Workers in Industrial America*, pp. 16–18.

21. Haywood, *Bill Haywood's Book*, pp. 174–89, esp. p. 181; Brody, *Workers in Industrial America*, pp. 37, 39; Dubofsky, *We Shall Be All*, pp. 81, 146–49;

WFM, *Proceedings, 1912,* pp. 278, 326, 346. The "advance guard" comment is from p. 278. See also WFM, *Proceedings, 1914,* p. 57.

22. WFM, *Proceedings, 1914,* p. 57. David Brody notes the adaptability of the new men in *Workers in Industrial America,* pp. 16–18.

23. WFM, Proceedings, 1914, p. 135; Industrial Commission, *Mining at Butte,* 1911 and 1915, pp. 3865, 3715, 3860.

24. Industrial Commission, *Mining at Butte,* 1915, p. 3737. Haywood's remarks and Lowney's response are in WFM, *Proceedings, 1914,* p. 154. Bodnar, *Workers' World,* p. 63.

25. Polk, *City Directory,* 1895–1914; Industrial Commission, *Mining at Butte,* 1915, pp. 3761, 3772, 3778, 3852. The conservatives generally had been in Butte even longer. Ibid., 1911 and 1915, pp. 3736, 3904, 3917–18.

26. For Sullivan see WFM, *Proceedings, 1912,* pp. 269, 354, 360; Industrial Commission, *Mining at Butte,* p. 3930. For Shannon see ibid., p. 3852; WFM, *Proceedings, 1902,* p. 4, Evans, *Address,* p. 7; WFM, Exec. Board, MB, July 7, 1908; Polk, *City Directory,* 1910–15. Shannon's "soul business" remark is from Industrial Commission, *Mining at Butte,* 1915, p. 3856. William O'Brien, another of the radicals, in testimony to the Industrial Commission was told by commission member O'Connell that O'Brien's native County Cork was "a pretty good county." O'Brien's only response was "Yes." (ibid., p. 3779).

27. On Socialist party victories see the testimony of Clarence Smith in Industrial Commission, *Mining at Butte,* pp. 3724–25. The local Democratic party was thought to be run by John Ryan and Con Kelley. See the *Butte Miner,* Sept. 4, 1910.

28. On the Socialists' program see *Montana Socialist,* Mar. 16, 1913; May 3, Dec. 5, 1914; Industrial Commission, *Mining at Butte,* 1915, p. 3728. On the Socialists' efforts to extend the city limits, see WFM, *Proceedings, 1914,* pp. 154–55. The assignment of security guards and the county's policy of deputizing them is noted in Industrial Commission, *Mining at Butte,* 1915, pp. 3704–5. Most of these guard-deputies were Irish. On Irish police and Irish workers see Walkowitz, *Worker City,* p. 213.

29. Socialist Party of Montana, Membership Record. This record is the property of Mrs. Terrence McGlynn of Butte. A duplicate copy of it, together with occupation data he compiled from city directories, was made available to me by Prof. Jerry Calvert of Montana State University. I am grateful to Professor Calvert for sharing his information with me. The Irish Socialist James Larkin frequently commented on the American Socialist party's inability to attract working-class Irish-Americans. Larkin, *James Larkin,* pp. 195–96, 222–23.

30. *Butte Independent,* Feb. 19, 26, 1910; WFM, Exec. Board, MB, Jan. 10, 1913. Lord's comments are from the *Miners Magazine,* July 9, 1914. See also Gutman, "Protestantism and the American Labor Movement." McGlynn, "Flying the Red Flag"; Calvert, " 'Making Good.' "

31. This was seldom a problem with worker aristocracies. See Hobsbawm, "Artisans and Labour Aristocrats," pp. 264–65, 271–72.

32. Industrial Commission, *Mining at Butte,* 1915, pp. 3717–18, 3725, 3729, 3744, 3764, 3785–86; WFM, *Proceedings, 1912,* pp. 20, 22, 24–25, 220–35, 254–

65, 313, 319; WFM, Exec. Board, MB, July 15, 1912; WFM, *Proceedings, 1914,* pp. 63–65, 151, 181, 190–91; Montana, Dept. of Labor, and *First Biennial Report,* p. 24. On the hostility to the pending WFM affiliation with the AFL see WFM, *Proceedings, 1912,* pp. 271–72. Vernon Jensen discusses the firings of 1912 without ever mentioning the fact that those let go were Finns (*Heritage of Conflict,* pp. 316–18).

33. WFM, *Proceedings, 1912,* pp. 20, 22, 259, 313, 319; the quote is from p. 313. Industrial Commission, *Mining at Butte,* 1915, p. 3744.

34. WFM, *Proceedings, 1912,* pp. 313, 319; *Proceedings, 1914,* pp. 190–91; Industrial Commission, *Mining at Butte,* 1915, p. 3764. A copy of the 1912 contract is on pp. 3880–82.

35. Industrial Commission, *Mining at Butte,* 1915, pp. 3717–18, 3744.

36. Butte Finnish Miners to Charles Moyer and Exec. Board, WFM, Apr. 1912, copy in WFM, *Proceedings, 1912,* p. 20; see also pp. 258, 259. WFM, Exec. Board, MB, July 15, 1912. The reference to yelling throngs is in WFM, *Proceedings, 1914,* p. 151.

37. WFM, *Proceedings, 1912,* pp. 329, 254–55, 313.

38. Industrial Commission, *Mining at Butte,* 1915, pp. 3785–86.

39. The references to "transient hoodlums" etc. is from the *Miners Magazine,* July 16, 1914. Holland's and Sullivan's comments are from WFM, *Proceedings, 1912,* pp. 269, 281–82. See also, for the notion that the radicals believed in sabotage, the *Montana Socialist,* June 15, 22, 1913.

40. Kraditor, *Radical Persuasion,* pp. 12, 22, 52, 154, 310. Aaltonen's remark is from WFM, *Proceedings, 1914,* pp. 190–91. For Larkin, see the masthead of his Chicago-based newspaper, the *Irish Worker and People's Advocate;* Dubofsky, *We Shall Be All,* p. 155; Larkin, *James Larkin,* pp. 208–9.

41. Clarence Smith said the IWW was in Butte by 1907. Industrial Commission, *Mining at Butte,* 1915, p. 3724. Tom Campbell to Officers and Members, Millers' Local #264, WFM, Aug. 7, 1912, in WFM, *Proceedings, 1912,* p. 278; see too p. 346. Moyer's comments are from his report to the WFM Exec. Board, in WFM, *Proceedings, 1912,* pp. 24–25. As for Campbell, Moyer referred to him publicly as "the lowest type of creeping reptile," ibid., p. 327. Campbell was expelled from the WFM by a 198–26 vote. Dan Sullivan was one of the 26; ibid., pp. 220–35, 359–60; Vernon Jensen, *Heritage of Conflict,* pp. 318–23.

42. Aaltonen's comments are in WFM, *Proceedings, 1914,* pp. 190–91 (my emphasis). Connolly, "Labor Fuss," p. 207. The "overzealous foremen" remark is from Industrial Commission, *Mining at Butte,* 1915, p. 3718.

43. WFM, *Proceedings, 1912,* pp. 258, 261, 265. Membership figures are from WFM, Local Unions Financial Records, 1907–32, WHC. The reference to starting trouble is from WFM, *Proceedings, 1914,* p. 170.

44. On the growing conservatism of the WFM see Wyman, *Hardrock Epic,* pp. 326–37; WFM, Exec. Board, MB, Jan. 14, 1911; Jan. 9, 1913. Guy Miller argued that the rank and file of the WFM had never been radical and that the federation's leaders had been pushed leftward by events in Colorado (WFM, *Proceedings, 1914,* p. 128).

45. O'Daly, Life, [83]; Industrial Commission, *Mining at Butte*, 1915, p. 3797; Immigration Commission, *Immigrants in Industries*, 1911, part 25, p. 601. See also Fitch, "Union Paradise"; Ralph Brissenden, "Rustling Card," pp. 755–75.

46. On the vote see WFM, *Proceedings, 1914*, p. 156; *Anaconda Standard*, Dec. 22, 1912. Copies of the card and the application for it appear in Evans, *Address*, pp. 18–19; and Industrial Commission, *Mining at Butte*, 1915, p. 3797. For the later (i.e., post-1914) protest see WFM, *Proceedings, 1914*, p. 57. Commons's comment is from Industrial Commission, *Mining at Butte*, 1915, p. 3702.

47. Immigration Commission, *Immigrants in Industries*, 1911, part 25, p. 173; Evans, *Address*, pp. 15, 16, 24; Industrial Commission, *Mining at Butte*, 1915, pp. 3700–3701, 3703. For evidence that blacklisting was used see, e.g., *Miners Magazine*, Apr., 1903; Apr. 14, 1904. There were state laws forbidding blacklisting as early as 1907; see Industrial Commission, *Mining at Butte*, 1911 pp. 3985, 4003; Ralph Brissenden, "Rustling Card," p. 762.

48. Industrial Commission, *Mining at Butte*, 1915, p. 3700. See also Evans, *Address*, pp. 13, 15–17, for a description of the old hiring practices and a discussion of how the high turnover rate had required a new system. William Daly's new title is from Polk, *City Directory*, 1913.

49. Industrial Commission, *Mining at Butte*, 1911, 1915, pp. 3700–3703, 4065; Evans, *Address*, pp. 16–17.

50. Lowney's comment is from WFM, *Proceedings, 1914*, p. 156. Shannon's are from Industrial Commission, *Mining at Butte*, 1915, p. 3855. Evans, *Address*, p. 16. On the elimination of the thirty-day grace period see Bohn, "Butte Number 1," p. 11; Haywood, "Revolt at Butte," p. 93.

51. For example, *Butte Independent*, Mar. 12, 1910.

52. O'Dea, *AOH*, III:1424, 1469; Carroll, "Address to the American Federation of Labor"; Carroll to James J. Regan, National President, AOH in America, July 16, 1914; Fr. John A. Ryan to Carroll, Sept. 27, 1910. See too the "Diocesan Resolution against French Socialists," Carroll Papers.

53. *Montana Socialist*, Mar. 16, 1913. For examples of the socialists' courtship of Catholic workers see June 1, Nov. 9, 1913.

54. Ibid., Jan. 11, Mar. 9, 1913; Mar. 1, Apr. 12, July 12, Aug. 1, 1914.

55. Ibid., July 5, Oct. 10, 1914.

56. Industrial Commission, *Mining at Butte*, 1915, pp. 3663–3866, passim; Vernon Jensen, *Heritage of Conflict*, pp. 327–35; *Montana Socialist*, June 21, 28, 1914; WFM, *Proceedings, 1914*, passim, esp. pp. 56, 100–115, 125–27, 137, 143–45, 175, 193; *Miners Magazine*, July 9, 16, 23, 1914; Montana, Dept. of Labor, *First Biennial Report*, pp. 24–34; *Anaconda Standard*, June 13ff., 1914; WFM, Exec. Board, MB, Aug. 5, 1914; Mar. 23, 1915.

57. On assessments see *Miners Magazine*, July 23, 1914; WPA, *Copper Camp*, pp. 61–66; Industrial Commission, *Mining at Butte*, 1915, pp. 3772–75; WFM, Michigan Defense Fund, Books 1 and 2; WFM, "Reports of Secretary-Treasurer, 1914." The charges against Bert Riley are noted in WFM, *Proceedings, 1914*, pp. 125, 142. The rustling card, voting machine, and discourtesies issues are from Industrial Commission, *Mining at Butte*, 1915, pp. 3735–36, 3763–68, 3773–75, 3781. Garretson's remark is from ibid., pp. 3781–82. On blame see

Vernon Jensen, *Heritage of Conflict*, pp. 325–53. Debs's comments are from *Miners Magazine*, July 16, 1914; Duncan's from WFM, *Proceedings, 1914*, pp. 124–27; Moyer's from ibid., p. 62.

58. Jensen, *Heritage*, pp. 344–53; *Anaconda Standard*, Sept. 9, 1914; *Butte Miner*, Sept. 6, 9, 19, 1914; *Montana Socialist*, Oct. 10, 1914; *Miners Magazine*, July 9, 1914.

59. For Moyer see WFM, *Proceedings, 1914*, p. 144; for Evans, *Address*, p. 10 (my emphasis); *Miners Magazine*, July 19, 1914.

60. For Murphy see Industrial Commission, *Mining at Butte*, 1915, pp. 3740–41. Muckie McDonald was characterized and the "sober men" called to arms in WFM, *Proceedings, 1914*, pp. 143–45. James Lord's remarks are from *Miners Magazine*, July 9, 16, 1914.

61. The list of the thirty-three is from *Miners Magazine*, Aug. 10, 1914. Each of the thirty-three was checked against Polk, *City Directory*, 1905–14; the seventeen Irishmen against RELA and AOH, Membership and Dues Ledgers. It must, however, be recalled that AOH ledgers for these later years were not found. Sullivan's comment is from Industrial Commission, *Mining at Butte*, 1915, p. 3767. Obviously, the destruction of these BMU records represents a significant loss for historians. They could have been used to help determine everything from persistence to ethnicity.

62. For Moyer see WFM, *Proceedings, 1914*, p. 166; *Miners Magazine*, July 16, 1914. Ironically, this is language similar to that used by the radicals to describe the same people. Kraditor, *Radical Persuasion*, passim.

63. *Montana Socialist*, June 28, 1914; WFM, *Proceedings, 1914*, p. 193.

64. WFM, *Proceedings, 1914*, pp. 125–27.

65. Ibid., p. 127.

66. Giovannitti's comments were reprinted in *Miners Magazine*, July 9, 1914.

67. *Butte Bystander*, Sept. 18, 1897. At this time the *Bystander* was the official paper of the WFM. Clarence Smith made reference to the radicals as not "well grounded Socialists" in Industrial Commission, *Mining at Butte*, 1915, p. 3726.

68. WFM, *Proceedings, 1912*, p. 260.

69. WFM, *Proceedings, 1914*, p. 137.

70. *Butte Miner*, Oct. 16, 1914. For Buckley's IWW affiliation see Haywood, *Bill Haywood's Book*, p. 367. Industrial Commission, *Mining at Butte*, 1915, pp. 3725–26.

71. *Montana Socialist*, Sept. 11, 1915.

72. The charge that the rustling card used in the Coeur d'Alene mines made specific reference to Catholicism is from WFM, *Proceedings, 1905*, pp. 308–10. There was no copy of the card included, no evidence cited, no corroboration of the charge, and no reason to assume it was true. The fact that the charge was made is interesting enough. For Crowley and Kenny, see AOH D3, MB, Jan. 21, Feb. 27, 1915.

73. BMWU, "Grievances, June 30, 1914," in WFM, *Proceedings, 1914*, p. 56; *Miners Magazine*, July 16, 1914; WFM, *Proceedings, 1914*, p. 175.

74. *Miners Magazine*, July 16, 1914; Montana, Dept. of Labor, *First Biennial Report*, 1914, p. 31.

75. Hobsbawm, "Aristocracy," p. 250.

CHAPTER 9

The Patriot Game: Butte's Irish and the Causes of Ireland

I

The Irish miners' preoccupation with finding and keeping safe and steady jobs clearly limited whatever labor radicalism might have inhered in industrializing Butte; their lives as workers did not resemble jousting matches. For some of them, however, their lives as Irishmen resembled nothing else. The Irish nationalists, and Butte had a significant number of them, retained as the most salient feature of their Irishness an enduring and relentless hatred of Great Britain. No labor radical could match the Irish patriot in ferocity of rhetoric, generosity with money and time, or size and scope of dreams. There were acknowledged limits to what workers could expect from capitalism but no apparent limits to what the Irish might exact from Great Britain. Capitalism was never denounced in language like that routinely used to describe England; the attributed evils of capitalists were nothing beside those of the English.

Every immigrant group had an associational life based on occupational and ethnic—if not national—affiliations. But no other immigrant group defined its ethnic, religious, and national allegiances as narrowly as did the Irish because no other immigrant group had so palpable an enemy. It was the English, in fact, who had forced the Irish into exile, a sin for which there could be no forgiveness. This nationalist fervor isolated the Irish-Americans from other workers, immigrant and native, not just because the Irish came from an "enslaved" nation but because, as "exiled children, . . . a banished people," in the language of Michael Davitt, they bore the responsibility of liberating the "mother country."

Their enclave was formed, then, not just of ethnocultural and occupational components but of an intensely felt Irish nationalism. There were enormous differences between the Sons of Italy, say, or the Sons of St. George, and the Clan-na-Gael, and the conclusion is inescapable that the history of American labor—as surely as that of English—would have been different had the Anglophobic Irish not been so early and dominant a component of the working classes of both nations.[1]

This does not mean that Irish-American nationalists—most of them workers—stunted the growth of what would otherwise have been a robust worker radicalism by substituting for class consciousness the diversionary interests of nation and faith. Neither does it mean, as Thomas Brown has argued, that these same workers equated a liberated Ireland with their own liberation and ascension into the middle class. Ireland and Catholicism were not diversions, and, as Eric Foner has shown, there was much in the Irish nationalist movement in the early 1880s that enhanced rather than diminished worker consciousness. This was particularly the case as hard times in America put greater social distance between working- and middle-class Irish. It is also true that during times of heightened tension in Anglo-Irish affairs, the patriot game deflected attention from other issues and produced a closing of Irish-American ranks across class lines. But at all times there were many Irish-American workers who were literally and precisely that, and who found, in Foner's terms, "no contradiction between ethnic nationalism and class consciousness."[2]

Mitigating this tendency, however, at least in Butte, was the fact that the nationalist organizations had to spend more money on sick benefits than on revolutions—of whatever sort—and had to work harder finding steady industrial jobs than facilitating social mobility. Thus Foner's contention that there were two cultures in America, one a middle class and the other a "strong, emergent, oppositional" working class, and that Irish-American nationalists divided and were assimilated along similar lines applies only conditionally to Butte. This is particularly the case if "oppositional" is to be interpreted as self-consciously ideological, an appropriate reading, it would seem, of Foner's use of the word. The cultural values of Butte's Irish, miners and sympathetic nonminers alike, were certainly working class and different from those of the middle class. They were cooperative and communal rather than competitive and individualistic. But a worker consciousness of class need not find radical expression, and in Butte there was nothing assertive about Irish working-class values, nothing inherently radical in their application. They arose naturally, almost instinctively, from the Irish background and in response to a dangerous and unstable work environment.[3]

But Brown's argument that these working-class values were only "transitional" and that bourgeois respectability was the shared goal of Irish-America is more seriously flawed. It implies that the Irish Catholic nationalists sought admission to Protestant middle-class society because that was the only option available to them. Foner's addition of a working-class alternative to the middle-class values of the dominant culture is helpful, but his worker/nationalist's world is too ideological and the presumption of its radical core too strongly held. This is partly the case because Foner, like Brown, operates on the assumption that assimilation to a segment of the dominant culture and to its ideological underpinnings was either cause or effect or both of Irish-American nationalism. For Brown the patriot game was part of the Irish assimilation with the American middle class; for Foner it was part of the Irish assimilation with the American working class. But it is more likely that Butte's Irish workers created a third and separate world, more "Irish" and pragmatic than either Brown's or Foner's, an ethno-occupational community whose values reflected neither middle-class nor self-consciously oppositional working-class values but rather came from the work most of them did and, quite literally, the company they kept.[4]

This third world, moreover, the world of the enclave, did not require meaningful assimilation to American values, whether of middle or politicized working class or both. If nothing else—and there was a great deal else—associational sick and death benefits and job committees as well as Irish job preference left little reason for the Irish to involve themselves with the non-Irish world. And, in fact, counted among the sins of Butte's Irish patriots was that they were unassimilated and unassimilable. As William Penrose put it, with the Irish clearly in mind, "all . . . must forswear allegiance to the country from which they come." It is possible, of course, that Penrose missed the extent of Irish assimilation and, as a consequence, missed the subtle interplay between Irish nationalism and American social respectability or between Irish nationalism and American labor radicalism. It is more likely, however, that for the enclave Irish—a clear majority of the settled of whatever class—an independent Ireland made them feel good not because it elevated them in social rank or gave expression to their social radicalism but because they were historically conditioned to wish it. It was the missing piece in a puzzle; it completed lives only peripherally related to those of either a striving American bougeoisie or a radicalized American proletariat. These were exiled Irish, men of "fanatical heart."[5]

It follows that there would be factionalism over both the means to secure, and the eventual form of, an independent Ireland. There was agreement only that Ireland must be "free" and that Butte's Irish must help win that freedom. As the Irish nationalists were divided so too were the patriots in Butte—as Irish in this as in everything else. It must also be recalled that the Irish nationalist and reform movements—whatever the object or level of radicalism of either—were not static, either as separate crusades or in relation to one another. They developed over a half-century and they reflected the political, social, and economic changes that occurred in Ireland and in Irish-America over those years.

In addition, there can be no definitive accounting for why some men wanted to throw bombs and use other forms of physical force while other men insisted that parliamentary tactics be used or why some Irish and Irish-Americans concerned themselves almost exclusively with Home Rule and others with the often-unrelated question of who shall rule at home. The simplest explanation, however—that if independence is won by violent and revolutionary men, the world after independence will belong to those same men—obviously provides some clues. The wealthier Irish, or those who, for whatever reason, were not sympathetic to worker goals, valued an independent Ireland in which basic social relationships were unchanged. The poorer Irish often saw that solution as merely the substitution of Irish tyrants for English. The result was considerable tension across the seam, an inner struggle between those whom Michael Davitt called the Tory nationalists and the Democratic nationalists. James Connolly would only have changed the labels.[6]

The patriot game in Butte mirrored this conflict, as it did the shifts along the seam. In fact, given the greater complexity of the American economy, the swifter pace with which it moved, and the greater social differentiation among the Irish, the divisions in Butte may have been deeper and more numerous than in Ireland. At home the Irish suffered both because Ireland was not free and because the vast majority of the Irish were poor. In Butte all knew the hurt of English policy; in an abstract way they may even have felt the pain more deeply than those in Ireland. But only some of the Butte Irish were poor. One result is that, at least until 1916, there were no Connollys in Butte, or—with the possible and temporary exception of Patrick Ford—anywhere else in Irish-America. There was no one who could combine social radicalism with Irish nationalism and provide leadership across the seam. In fact, Irishmen of radical as well as nationalist persuasion had to restrain the former lest they upset the sensibilities of those Irish-Americans who embraced only the latter.[7]

Foner is right, then, when he states that the nationalism of the wealthy Irish-Americans was of a different and generally less extreme sort than that of the poorer Irish-Americans, and that both were different from the nationalism of Ireland. Also convincing is his contention that their differences arose from their respective economic conditions and that the working-class Irish were aware that the wealthier of their countrymen, here and in Ireland, often temporized on the questions of both Irish liberty and Irish and working-class reform, particularly as the two became parts of the same cause. These wealthier Irish understood that any campaign against English capitalists and landlords was bound to raise questions regarding all capitalists and landlords. This was especially the case in a place like Ireland and "in Irish America where the center of gravity lay so solidly in the working class." In sum, the patriot game, at varying times and with varying degrees of intensity, brought to the Irishman's attention the larger issues of imperialism, ethnocentrism, clericism, and capitalist exploitation. Little wonder that Irish and Irish-American conservatives were sometimes suspicious of the game; less wonder that Irish and Irish-American social radicals believed with James Connolly that the "road to socialism lay through nationalism."[8]

Bringing these matters to their attention, however, was not the same as converting significant numbers of Irish-American workers to the radical side of each or any of them, and here Foner is less persuasive. He insists that an appreciable percentage of the Irish-American working class was radicalized by its involvement with the American Land League agitation of the 1880s and that this legacy of radicalism persisted well into the twentieth century. It could hardly have been otherwise. As Foner points out, "in the urban centers of Gilded Age America, class and ethnic differences overlapped"—the Irish were poor, the non-Irish often were not—giving Irish-American radicals a chance not only to assimilate into American society but to "transform" it. To be sure, in America at least, this transforming spirit waned after 1900, but Foner insists, without much evidence, that the lessons and the tensions of the 1880s were never lost and that the Irish-American world always contained a measurable component of working-class radicalism. It did, but not necesarily among Irish-American nationalists and, except after 1916, almost never as a part of the patriot game.[9]

Foner's arguments have a particular applicability to Butte. He mentions specifically the involvement of western mining camps, Butte included, in the reformist, Patrick Ford wing of the Land League, and he cites Edward Boyce and the Western Federation of Miners as an example of how this legacy of Irish working-class radicalism persisted.

These are important points; they make clear that the Butte Irish lined up and divided along class lines and that the charge that Irish-American workers were incorrigibly bourgeois was a false one. Whether this alignment represented an assimilation to one or another of Butte's two social worlds or was merely an adjustment to them is unimportant. The Irish were not what they had been in Ireland, and the change arose in part from Irish and Irish-American nationalist agitation. If that nationalism was either "Tory" or "Democratic," then the adjustments would be to one or the other of those sets of values.[10]

Clearly, Butte's Irish were not just divided between the settled and the unsettled; there was also a division between those who recalled and still embraced the lessons of Patrick Ford and the Land Leagues and those who rejected those lessons. Thus, being an Irish immigrant in Butte, or anywhere else in America, made it easier to understand the language of worker protest; just as being a worker, Irish or not, and familiar with the ideology of labor radicalism made it easier to understand, if not always to sympathize with, the language of Irish nationalism. The enemies of both movements were often the same: commercial and industrial capitalism, imperialism, and much that passed for "modernity."

The story of Edward Boyce provides a perfect example. Boyce was born in 1862 near Denneystown, Letterkenny, in the Ulster county of Donegal. Interestingly, the village was named after the family of William Emmet Deeney, the Butte labor leader and Irish patriot accused of the murder of William Penrose. Deeney, five years older than Boyce, emigrated in 1872. It is likely Boyce knew of him in Ireland; certainly he knew him in Butte. Boyce's parents had a small cattle and grain farm, but they never quite recovered from the hard times of the late 1870s and Edward was forced to emigrate in 1882, having witnessed, no doubt, some Land League protests, though there is no evidence that he was involved with the local chapter of the Irish Republican Brotherhood, as Deeney had been. He went first to Wisconsin, where he worked in lumber camps and on railroad section crews. In 1884 he moved to the mines of Leadville, Colorado; from there he made his way to the mines of Gold Hill, Nevada, the Coeur d'Alenes in Idaho, and Butte, Montana. He was involved in the Idaho strike of 1892, spent some time in jail—the infamous "bull pens"—and was elected in 1894 to the state legislature as a Populist. Among his antagonists in Idaho was John Hays Hammond, the man most responsible for the formation of the Mine Owners' Association, the "employers' union" which, according to Boyce, convinced the western hard-rock men of the necessity of federating their local miners' unions. In 1896 Boyce became the president of that federation, the WFM, and the principal spokesman for the radical course it finally took.[11]

This part of his career is well known. But Boyce was not just a western labor radical; as with Connolly, it is important to know that Boyce was also an Irishman. His mining claims were called the Parnell and the Emmet. While in Butte, he became a member of the RELA (#182); at one meeting, in a bitter denunciation of English policy in South Africa, he condemned England as "our Enemy, the British tyrannical Government." His personal papers for the early years contain transcribed and original poetry and prose all on the same themes: "But Saxon bonds bind me, Erin," went one of the poems, "and I must sail from thee." And so, according to another poem, "There came to the beach a poor Exile of Erine." As for Ireland, "my country" he called it, "your glory's departed; . . . tyrants and traitors have stabbed thy heart's core."[12]

But the lives of the Irish in the United States were scarcely better than they had been in Ireland. Like Pat Ford, whom he much resembled, Boyce did not believe that the U.S. was a larger version of what Ireland should try to become. Rather, he wrote, America was "the strangers' land"; here the Irish "pined in chains." Boyce was in Leadville in 1885 when a snow avalanche took several Irish miners' lives. He described the event, with an inadvertent brogue: "Crash came the thundering avalanche, lick an angry ocean wave." Men should not die that way, Boyce went on to write, or be "allowed to go without food or clothing," or be put in the "penitentiary for stealing a loaf of bread." As surely as Emmet's, in a quote attributed to him, Boyce's heart "bled in anguish for the wrongs of the poor."[13]

It is the interrelatedness of Boyce's commitments that is important. He did not make a choice between Ireland and the poor. None was required of him: the Irish were poor. There was, of course, a question of emphasis that was more than just tactical, but even here Boyce operated on the seam. Marcus Daly, after all, was not just another capitalist. He was also, according to Boyce, the worst kind of Irishman, the onetime patriot whose memory and manhood had lapsed and whose behavior as a result was as immoral as that of the worst landlord in Ireland. The mere fact that Boyce made the charge is evidence of its currency. The Irish knew that some of their enemies were clothed in green. The problem with Butte was that the Irish of the town suffered similar lapses and, like "deluded slaves [did] Daly's bidding and that of his foremen and superintendents." When John Hays Hammond emerged as one of the principal defenders of England's unjust war against the South African Boers, Boyce, this time as the president of the WFM, was quick to make an association between cruelty in Idaho and cruelty in the Transvaal. It was an association that less alert—and less Irish—observers might have missed.[14]

It is possible that had Boyce remained poor as well as Irish he would have continued to represent the interests of both and might, in fact, have become the Irish-American James Connolly. However, his marriage to Eleanor Day, the daughter of a millionaire Idaho mine owner, left him very rich and he began to resemble Thomas Brown's Irishman far more than Eric Foner's. It was not that he became acquisitive; he had acquired. He counted his wealth by the hundreds of thousands of dollars. It would, however, be too cynical to assume that that had always been his dream. He quit the WFM in 1902 and retired to Portland, Oregon, in 1905. He continued to correspond with his old allies, Eugene Debs, Clarence Darrow, John O'Neill, and Charles Moyer among them, and he continued to give—money now rather than time—to worker organizations. Interestingly, Boyce's Irish nationalism was also deflected by his new prosperity; in his case from Clan-na-Gael radicalism to AOH conservatism.[15]

Boyce's story adds an important dimension to Foner's—and Brown's—argument, if for no other reason than that Foner mentions Boyce as an example of the way an awareness of the crimes against the Irish necessarily made one sensitive to those against the worker. Boyce's early career is powerful testimony to the validity of Foner's argument; here was one working-class Irishman who did not forget the full lesson of the Land League. There were other Irishmen, in and out of Butte, whose memories were as good. The point is that there were far more of them who, though remembering the full lesson of the Land League, surrendered the social radicalism half of it to the interests of Ireland and to the safe and steady work that sustained Butte's facsimile of it.

Granted, that was not true of Ed Boyce. But Boyce led the Western Federation of Miners, not the Butte Miners' Union, which meant that he spoke more to the needs of the Irish miners in Colorado or Nevada than to their counterparts in Butte. Butte resembled a medium-sized industrial city anywhere in the U.S. far more than it did a western mining camp. It was more like a scaled-down Pittsburgh than it was a scaled-up Leadville or Gold Hill. It was also, and as a result, more typical of industrializing America than were the mining camps that Boyce's WFM represented. It is at this point that Foner's argument seems most overdrawn. Boyce's radicalism reflected the Leadvilles of the western mining regions, not Butte. Leadville, however, was not typical of industrial America. It, and the scores of WFM camps like it, would barely survive the process of industrialization. Butte, however, would survive. Using Boyce and the federation as examples of the durability of Irish-American working-class radicalism leads Foner to exaggerate the extent of that radicalism nationwide and to assume that it arose naturally from a commitment to Ireland.

The formula for a sustained protest on the seam between Irish and worker was simply not in place in Butte or—if the behavior of most Irish-American workers after the 1880s is any indication—anywhere else in America. There is little evidence that Butte's Irish labor leaders consciously sought a radical transformation of the system. Ironically, this may have been the case because of the ways Butte was *not* typical of industrializing America. Ethnic and class differences did not overlap in Butte; the Irish owned and ran the mines and were careful to support, again using Ford's words, both "the Irish world and the American industrial worker." Irish dominance made any transformation of the place something the Irish were more likely to resist than embrace.

In addition, Irish-American worker radicalism required an incongruity between the image of America as a nation of free men and the reality of America as a nation of landless and powerless industrial workers. Those who had done well, those for whom the image and the reality were congruous, did not figure to be any more attracted to socialist republics in Ireland than they were to socialist experiments in the United States. The Irish may have been landless industrial workers in Butte, but they were anything but powerless in the management of the city's affairs. There would be ample room for disagreement over the tactics of Irish nationalism, disagreement even over the related issue of whether Home Rule was enough to satisfy nationalist aspirations or whether complete independence was required. But there were few spokesmen in Butte for the nationalization of Irish lands, the withholding of rents, or the creation of a socialist republic.[16]

Finally, the extraordinary hazards and insecurities of industrial mining created a concert of interest among the stable Irish of whatever class that weakened the rivalry across class lines. As a consequence, though Butte's Irish workers understood that American industrial liberty was an issue, understood, in fact, that Ireland had to be reformed as well as freed, it was Irish political liberty for its own sake that reflected their dreams and enlisted their energies. Industrial *liberty* was an abstraction; it had less meaning for many than industrial *security*, which at least kept the enclave intact. Irish reform was remote, and, for exiled Irish, would come too late. This is evidence not of the embourgeoisment of the Butte miner but of the fact that the working class should not be defined solely as it related to capital, and Irish nationalism should neither be subordinated to nor equated with worker protest.

II

Obviously, it is important to know something of how this patriot game was played out in Butte. It began early. The Irishmen who came in the 1880s and 1890s, particularly that large percentage of them with ties to West Cork, were accustomed to the rhetoric and tactics of nationalist and reform protest, and their emigration—their forced exile—from Ireland certainly did not diminish their militancy. Neither, of course, did the pages of Patrick Ford's *Irish World and American Industrial Liberator*, the newspaper of choice for working-class Irish nationalists and one found throughout the western mining regions. There had been Fenian activity in Montana as early as 1866, complete with a promise to territorial governor and former Irish Fenian Thomas Francis Meagher to "fight for Ireland's freedom with a squadron of Irish cavalry." A Fenian Mining Company appeared in Butte in 1870, a decade before the industrialization of the city had even begun, and the first AOH division in Montana was formed in Vestal in 1877.[17]

The Irish who gathered in Butte reflected this tradition. In September of 1881 almost $500 was forwarded from the camp to the *Irish World* to aid in Land League agitation in Ireland. Technically the money went to the Irish National Land and Industrial League of the United States, as sure a description on the seam as the title of Ford's newspaper. A month later, forty-two Butte Irishmen met to form the Emmet Associates, later the RELA, camp 90 of the revolutionary Clan-na-Gael. As elsewhere in Irish-America, the Butte Clan was committed to an independent Irish republic—Home Rule was an insufficient expression of Clan nationalism—and convinced that only physical force could secure it. A year after its founding, $119, "being the amount [the RELA had] on hand to date," was sent to Ford who acknowledged it as a "handsome contribution, . . . the largest received this week." In October, 1882, the Emmets collected $5.00 from each of their 130 members, 108 of whom worked in the mines, in response to a special call from national headquarters. There were to be many more special calls; the Emmets never disappointed.[18]

In 1883 the RELA voted to confer "with the ansient order of Hibernians for the purpose of organizing an auxiliary branch of the Irish Land League in Butte City." Three years later national Clan headquarters sent a secret order to its local camps instructing them to send delegates to the Land League convention in Chicago "so that this organization can control that convention." Though more "fraternal" than the Clan—the expressed purposes of the AOH were "Friendship, Unity, and True Christian Charity"—and less convinced that violent revolution in the name of an independent republic was the proper course for Ireland, the Hibernians agreed to cooperate.[19]

From this date forward, the flow of funds from Butte began in earnest. And, according to Patrick Ford, the money attracted precisely the right kind of attention. In an editorial read at an RELA meeting, Ford warned the Emmets and other Irish-American nationalists to "beware of English spies," enforce strict discipline, and not tolerate, as one member put it, "any loud mouthed brothers." Butte was a long way from home. The conspiratorial tone can only have made the Emmets feel more important, the cause seem more urgent. They sent $104 for that cause in May, 1883; $50 more for the "Revolutionary or special arms fund" in 1884; $404.80 in 1887; $2400, through Marcus Daly's brother-in-law John O'Farrell, in 1888. One Butte Irishman recalled the Clan soliciting money to "help Holland build his first submarine so as to sink the British fleet and free Ireland." The scheme struck him as "crazey" but he gave anyway.[20]

There can have been few organizations involved in Ireland's struggle to which Butte's Clansmen did not give. John Devoy routinely received money for his newspaper, the *Gaelic American*; other contributions of from $50 to $500, to cite representative examples, went to the Patrick O'Donnell Defense Fund for the Irish-American accused of murdering the informer James Carey; to the widow of Daniel Curley, executed for his part in Dublin's Phoenix Park murders; to Irish political prisoners; to the Wolfe Tone Monument Fund for a memorial to "the founder of this grand organization"; to the Charles Parnell Monument Fund; the O'Connor Power and Patrick J. Finnigan testimonial funds; Sinn Fein; the Special Fund for Irish National Propaganda Work; and, over a period of seven years, to "that grand old Irishman, O'Donovan Rossa." All of this was in addition to routine per capita taxes, the Boer Ambulance Fund, local projects like the Meagher Memorial Fund, and special calls. These latter alone took $753.90 in 1899, $852.88 in 1901, and at least $900.00 in 1904. And this was long before the Irish resistance heated up and made even greater demands on the RELA treasury. Most of this money was drawn from either the revolutionary or contingency funds of the RELA. In 1883, two years after its founding, the RELA revolutionary fund had $139; in 1900 it contained just under $1100; in 1906, as membership increased, it grew to $2387; in 1910, after national headquarters had called on it for a variety of "revolutionary" purposes and after the shutdown of 1907–8, the fund was described as "dead broke" and contingency fund money was transferred to the cause of revolution.[21]

Whether for revolution or contingency, every member contributed equally to these funds and there is no way of knowing which of the members were particularly involved in the Cause or what these more zealous patriots did for a living; no way of knowing, in other words, if and how social differentiation affected the patriot game. Penrose, during his brief political flirtation with the Irish, said that RELA "members are among Butte's most prominent and enterprising citizens." This statement cannot be taken seriously. More informative are the officer lists and references in the Minute Books, but given the multiple roles played by the Irish associations these, too, are not altogether trustworthy guides to nationalists' feelings and the intensity with which they were held.[22]

Occasionally, however, a special fund-raiser was held and the names of participating Emmets were entered into the organization's records. These instances provide an opportunity to check members' occupations against their willingness to give beyond ordinary dues and against the radicalism of the causes to which they gave. In 1885, eighty-five members of the RELA, almost half the total membership, gave $393.50 to the Parnell Fund. This was in response to Parnell's trip to America and after his Plan of Campaign had pushed the Irish resistance, if not perilously close to radicalism, at least beyond Pope Leo XIII's tolerance. Seventy-one of the eight-five contributors were listed in the *City Directory*. An occupational breakdown of those seventy-one turned up only forty miners or mine laborers; this at a time when over 90 percent of the total membership was drawn from that class. Twenty merchants, seven of them saloonkeepers, the others grocers, hotelkeepers, and liquor and cigar dealers, contributed to the fund; so did seven skilled tradesmen, two mine foremen, the local organizer for the Knights of Labor, and a "speculator." Patrick Rooney, a miner at the Anaconda Mine, gave $.50; P. J. Brophy of Casey and Brophy Grocers, gave $20.00, as did Patrick Conlon, proprietor of the Arcade Chop House. But John Murray, a miner at the Moulton, also gave $20.00, and James C. Sullivan, a machinist in the mines, gave $10.00.[23]

It would be good to know more about these Irish-American nationalists; whether they were Irish- or American-born, for example; how old they were; their dates of immigration; their county or state of birth. Even more frustrating is that these rosters appeared so infrequently until just before and after the Irish Rising of 1916. There were, however, a couple of other lists. In 1895 fifteen RELA members were appointed a committee to "devise ways and means to organize a branch of the Irish Alliance," a new Clan-inspired revolutionary organization. The fifteen included D. J. Hennessy, even then one of the wealthiest men in Butte. But it included as well such former or present labor leaders as Patrick Boland, W. E. Deeney, and Anthony Shovlin. The man responsible for coordinating Alliance activity in Butte with former Butte miner Ed Shields, then back in Ireland, was BMU and later WFM officer James Maher. Only three members of the committee were miners and one of these, J. J. Lynch, became a prominent Butte judge.[24]

Two years later, twenty-eight Emmets formed Company A of the Irish Volunteers of America. As with the Irish Alliance, the contribution required was of time not money, but the "muster roll" is revealing nonetheless. It included BMU officers William Haggerty and Maurice Hartnett, former BMU officer Anthony Shovlin and future BMU radical Daniel D. Sullivan. Patrick Regan, the county sheriff, was a member, as was William D. Clark, chairman of the county commissioners, and James Brennan, one of the best known of Butte's Irish mine foremen. But of the remaining volunteers, seventeen were miners and two were city policemen. By 1909 the ranks of the Irish Volunteers had grown to sixty-two and forty-seven of the fifty-seven for whom occupations can be determined were miners. This may suggest that working-class Irishmen had more time than money and preferred marching to committee work. The safer argument is that although the Emmet's exclusively nationalist organizations enlisted fewer workers than the RELA itself, the patriot game was played by Irishmen of all classes.[25]

The AOH was as generous as the RELA, sometimes in the same causes. The Hibernians also gave money to Mrs. Curley; they sent $200 each to the Parnell Fund, the Irish National League, and to Patrick Finnigan; they supported the RELA-sponsored formation of the Thomas Meagher chapter of the Irish National Alliance; they even contributed to the Wolfe Tone Monument, an unlikely "charity" for a Catholic organization committed to peaceful change. There were, however, no special calls on AOH money, nor, given the amount spent on sick and death benefits, could there have been. In 1926, when the national officers summarized their organization's ninety years of service, they spoke of the $24 million spent on benefits, the $5.4 million more that went to various charities and the $50,000 for a chair in Celtic languages at Catholic University. They mentioned the organization's unceasing fight against the stage Irishman and that it had "fought for national liberty in the 'cradle land.' " But there was no reference to any direct aid to the cause of Irish independence; Michael Davitt was essentially right when he wrote that though AOH members had been of enormous value to Irish nationalism, the organization had lost its revolutionary Whiteboy origins and become "mainly a benevolent society."[26]

Mainly but not entirely benevolent—the three Butte divisions of the AOH did commit themselves in 1910 to the "complete and absolute independence" of Ireland, a position the Clan-na-Gael had taken at its founding in 1867; they heard one of their number report in 1906 that the Irish would rule Ireland and "take part in the ruling of England." But this militancy was not typical, and it was never backed by any offical AOH-sponsored fund raising. All the while, tens of thousands of dollars were distributed in sick and death benefits; $513.00 went to the San Francisco Relief Fund; John McGrath told the Butte AOH of the "suffering and panic striken people of Connaught and Northwest Ireland" and the members responded with a $500.00 contribution. In 1907 John Ferns, a Butte grocer, sought a "mere $5,000" for an AOH scholarship for Mount St. Charles College in Helena, a "small matter," as he put it "given the forty or fifty thousand raised in the last few years for many causes." Drawing from a membership no less working-class than the RELA's, the money was quickly subscribed.[27]

For the more hot-blooded, however, all of this was evidence of the Hibernians' misplaced loyalties. The problem with the AOH, said Michael Byrnes, was that it was "too much church and religion, not enough Irish nationality." The RELA rejection of Patrick Lynch was a case in point. Lynch was a longtime Hibernian. The RELA examining committee agreed that he was a "good citizen and a respectable man, but he was not a suitable man for our order," meaning, no doubt, that he was not suitably zealous in his nationalism. Thomas Kealy added to the list of AOH weaknesses the charge that AOH members had not shed their Irish parochialism and that, unlike the revolutionary Clan-na-Gael—the family of all the Irish—the Hibernians were still beset with "countyism." Generally, then, though it oversimplifies the matter, the Hibernians tended to spend their money on the Irish, wherever they might be found. The Emmets were far more single-mindedly Anglophobic; they spent their money on Ireland.[28]

The memberships of the two organizations seem to have reflected this emphasis. Unfortunately, the records do not permit precise comparisons. AOH membership and dues ledgers are missing for much of the later period. There is, in addition, the very good possibility that men who joined one organization soon after arrival in Butte, later, and for reasons that simply cannot be known, joined the other. It is difficult to track these types. Finally, there is the fact that although the associational Irish were more stable than the rest of Butte, the Irish population turned over frequently enough that unless the membership ledgers are for the same month—never mind the same year—they cannot be expected to contain the same names. Still, and with these obstacles to precise analysis in mind, it seems obvious that those whose incomes were limited would have to chose one or the other of the Irish organizations and that that choice would be based on a variety of important considerations, including many that were the legacy of Ireland or earlier stays in Irish-America. The AOH may have been "too Catholic" for some, the RELA not Catholic enough for others. The heart of the RELA may have been too fanatical, that of the AOH too conciliatory.

Whatever the explanation, of 104 members of the RELA in 1887, only 20 had been members of the AOH in April of 1886; of 322 names on the AOH membership ledger in April, 1900, only 110 also appeared on the RELA membership ledgers for 1899–1903. What is clear from these samples is that there were two separate and discrete membership lists; Butte's associational Irish consisted of AOH types and Clan-na-Gael types. Of the 110 who belonged to both at some time between 1899 and 1903, 99 were listed in the *City Directory* for 1900, a remarkably high percentage and one which provides further evidence that the associational Irish were among the more settled of Butte's population. Of those ninety-nine, fifty-six were miners or mine workers; twenty were merchants, including saloonkeepers; ten were city or county officials, including police and firemen; and two were union officers. These 110 were not necessarily the extreme nationalists. Indeed, a better case can be made that AOH membership diluted rather than enhanced the nationalism of the RELA. That may have been the purpose of AOH affiliation. As likely, however, is that where time and money permitted dual membership, the fraternal and social benefits of affiliation were more important than the chance to make a political statement. It is significant that so many working-class Irish were in this category.[29]

The greater involvement of the AOH with the Irish than with Ireland should not be interpreted to mean that the AOH operated more on the worker side of the seam, the RELA more on the Irish. Indeed, the Emmets, both individually and collectively, were more often to be found on the side of labor than were members of the AOH. There is no indication, for example, that Edward Boyce joined the Hibernians in Butte, and when William Deeney finally did, almost ten years after his affiliation with the Emmets, it was given facetious notice in the RELA minutes: Deeney, it was reported, had finally joined "the Papists." There were other labor leaders, men like Patrick Boland, Maurice Hartnett, Maurice O'Connor, Joseph Norris, and Edward Long whose names appear on the RELA rosters but not on those of the AOH. No division of loyalties is implied by, say, Patrick Boland's membership in both the BMU and the RELA. Neither does any great significance attach to his joining both. Significance is to be found in the fact that he did not join the AOH. Clearly the patriot game was played out principally by the RELA. For the many Irishmen who belonged to both organizations, the meetings of the Emmets, far more than those of the Hibernians, were the occasions for the expressions of their nationalist feelings.[30]

There is one other and related consideration. The RELA was larger relative to its national membership than was the AOH. Butte had a sizeable contingent of Hibernians; recall that Montana's AOH divisions were fourth only to those of New York, Pennsylvania, and Massachusetts in contributions to the San Francisco earthquake relief fund. At its peak in 1906 the Butte Hibernians counted almost one thousand men in three divisions. But this was at a time when the national AOH membership was over 140,000. Totals for the Clan-na-Gael, obviously, were not made public. An entry in the RELA Minute Books for 1901, however, gave 22,818 as the total membership in the Clan. Three years later, the RELA claimed 340 members. In 1897 a Chicago camp was said to have 400 members; in 1899 the San Francisco camp had about the same. Whether the RELA was actually the second-largest Clan in the United States cannot be known. But it was certainly one of the largest, and there seems to have been no exaggeration for effect in the remarks of a St. Paul Clansman who told the RELA that it was "on the highest standing in power and finance equal to all!"[31]

Arguably, then, Butte's Irish heart was more fanatical than that of any other group of American Irish. This creates two problems. One is reconciling that radical nationalism with the conservatism of the Irish-dominated Butte Miners' Union, a problem made more acute by the possibilty that the radicalism of the one produced the conservatism of the other. An answer is supplied by emphasizing not the BMU's conservatism but its power and its success in meeting working-class goals without resorting to radicalism. This does not refute Foner's association of working-class and exclusively Irish goals; it only redefines the goals and redirects the association.

The other and related problem is accounting for the radical nationalism, quite apart from its relation to working-class issues. There are no easy explanations for the uncommmon zeal of the Butte Irish patriot, but a number of points warrant mention. In the first place, the West Cork connection meant that Butte's Irish were drawn from one of the more rebellious regions of Ireland. Their familiarity with mining, moreover, reduced—if it did not entirely eliminate—the time spent in transition from preindustrial to industrial worlds, and they moved more quickly and with greater purpose into the nationalist organizations. Second, Butte's Irish, taken as a whole, were more powerful and more prosperous than any comparably sized Irish group in the United States. This permitted them the time and the resources to play the patriot game. If nothing else, it meant they did not have to take much time off to contest a hostile dominant culture. Butte may, in fact, have been what all of Irish-America would have been if only it had been able to afford it. But this uncommon prosperity and power also gave the Butte Irish a cause, or added something to an existing cause. Unless the wealthier among them were prepared to argue that they had special gifts—and some were—the Irish were left with an object lesson in what they had always suspected: that only English tyranny had prevented the fulfillment of Irish promise. As Miles Burke, a laborer in the Anaconda Mine and later a BMU officer, put it in 1891, "the Irish race was prosperous in every land but their own." From the vantage point of Butte, it might almost have seemed that way.[32]

This prosperity, however, probably convinced some of them that America did in fact resemble a larger version of what Ireland could become. Irish nationalism, in other words, was a function of satisfaction with American conditions, in which case radicalism on one side of the seam would not translate into radicalism on the other. John Branagan, a close friend of Marcus Daly and a dedicated Irish nationalist, reminded the RELA that "all in America are equal; each man has the same privileges." John Finerty, at the unveiling of the Meagher statue, was more effusive, offering the typical judgment that the Irish had learned liberty in America and that that lesson, "borne on the mountain breezes of Montana across the sea," would give to Ireland the "liberty of which England has rapaciously deprived her." Even Michael Davitt spoke of his hope that the "evils of the Irish system would not be forgotten in the freer and happier conditions of American life."[33]

There were others, however, who were less sure that conditions here were freer and happier. Patrick Ford and Edward Boyce are obvious and important examples. For them the point was not that Ireland might come to resemble America but that America so closely resembled Ireland. In other words, their Irish nationalism was in part a function of their dissatisfaction with American conditions. This leads to a third possible explanation for the strength and fervor of Butte's Irish nationalist community. For the associational Irish, the "worker" game had already been won. This might suggest a narrow definition of victory; it most certainly does suggest a self-delusion as to the real sources of power. But all of that is beside the immediate point. It was a satisfying win—in no small measure because it permitted them to concentrate on the unfinished of their two crusades.

The class consciousness of a Ford or a Boyce was too easily deflected in Butte, and class anger had almost no outlet at all among the Irish nationalist associations. Wages certainly did not figure to become a target of worker discontent, at least until 1906 when inflation shortened the list of what they would buy. Irish miners, if they had steady work, made three times as much money as, say, Irish steelworkers, and the Butte Irish knew it. Class anger could have arisen—some would argue should have arisen—in response to the fact that Butte miners died so much sooner than other industrial workers. And the Irish knew that, too. But they also knew that being Irish got them safer and steadier jobs. Irish foremen and shift bosses, AOH and RELA job committees and sick and death benefits, if anything, strengthened their sense of ethnic cohesion and hardened their nationalist resolve. The syncretic relationship of Butte and Irish and miner which has accounted for so much in the complex world of the enclave may also account for the way the patriot game was played.

III

Whatever the reasons, the RELA in particular played the game with a ferocious intensity. Their rhetoric was a match for their generosity with money. When Patrick O'Donnell was sentenced to be hanged for the murder of James Carey, the RELA responded with a formal resolution written by Daly's old friend, John Branagan. The Butte Clan condemned the "corrupt English court" that had sentenced O'Donnell "to be murdered." The informer Carey was identified as "one of the vilest and greatest villains that ever poluted the earth." Retribution was demanded: "an eye for an eye and a tooth for a tooth in whatever country or clime an English tyrant or their Irish satraps may be found." The murder of O'Donnell "would be avenged, not only in Ireland but throughout the whole English colonies." Conceivably, Branagan had a Fenian-like raid on Canada in mind. A month after the resolution was published, the RELA elected him president—technically, Senior Guardian.[34]

There was no moderation of the tone in ensuing years. In 1884 John Clark, a saloonkeeper (#9), called for the "complete destruction by any and all means of the British tyrant whenever and wherever an opportunity may offer." Thomas Murphy, a miner (#26) agreed in a "patriotic oration that was greeted with deafening applause." In 1900 England was identified as "our tyrant foe," the next year as "a powerful,

cruel and relentless foe." Such an enemy could expect no mercy. As
the RELA's secret "Ritual of Initiation" made clear "Ireland's independence can only be achieved by physical force, . . . force is the cardinal principle of our organization. . . .We will be satisfied with no half
measures."[35]

Force, moreover, no longer meant pitchforks and pikes. It was still
true, as one RELA man put it, that "5000 Irishmen can defeat 25,000
Englishmen," but technology had given the Irish new and more destructive weapons. In 1910 W. E. Deeney, still active and still angry,
shared with the RELA membership some of his theories on "the military uses to which airships could be put." If his notions were anything
like Walter Breen's, those uses included carrying Butte miners over
London. The miners, skilled in the use of dynamite, would drop explosives down the stacks of the Houses of Parliament. Pat Heaney did
not have that scheme in mind but he did suggest in 1914 "that by fair
or foul means we ought try and cripple the enemy." A year later Judge
Jeremiah Lynch argued that Germany was doing precisely that and
that the "beginning of the end of our accursed enemy is not far off."[36]

Lynch's reference to England as "accursed"—and he spoke for many
thousands of Butte Irish—may be taken literally. The Irish thought of
themselves as banished, in the language of John Finerty, a people
"driven from the shores of their native land as if they were wild beasts
by the power of England." For many Irish it was not enough merely
to fund the revolution, or provide it with ideas and direction. The exile
had to be more than a patron or an ideologue. He was one of the Wild
Geese, one of the scattered warriors. As an RELA member put it, the
Clan-na-Gael was a "revolutionary organization" and "Rebels must
be Soldiers."[37]

Certainly the military plans of the Emmets were unequivocally revolutionary. In 1886, five years after its founding, the RELA began to
consider organizing and training a rifle club. They wanted to "instruct
members in the use of arms." In 1897 the company of Irish Volunteers,
"recognizing the authority of the . . . United Brotherhood" (Clan-na-
Gael), was formed. The timing was important. The RELA was preparing
for the possibility that the Boer War, then barely begun, would require
their military presence—on the side of the Boers, of course. Befitting a
nonsectarian organization, the IVs identified one of their objectives as
"uniting the Orange and the Green in fact as well as theory." Whether
"Orange" meant the Protestants of the North of Ireland or the Boers
fighting for the Orange Free State in South Africa is unclear. In either
event, the IVs continued to drill weekly until 1901.[38]

In 1906 they began again, and not just in response to what one member referred to as "a better possibility of war in the old land." The Assistant Adjutant General, Irish Volunteers, Clan-na-Gael, had previously notified all the camps that the U.S. War Department was selling surplus rifles and ammunition to "rifle clubs . . . for the promotion of rifle practice." Status as a rifle club required only that a group "affiliate with the National Rifle Association." Once armed, national headquarters recommended that all "I.V. companies go on to practices or forced marches during the summer." In Butte, drills, though no forced marches, were resumed in the summer of 1906; a military company was formally started in July, 1907. The captain of this company, officially Company A, Irish Volunteers, was Maurice Drohan (#45). Drohan, a stonemason by trade, had recently transferred his Clan and IV memberships from New York. It is conceivable, in fact, that Drohan had not so much transferred as been transferred, that the Clan had sent him, on assignment as it were, from New York to Butte.[39]

Whatever the motives for his relocation, Drohan was a stickler for military detail. He purchased rifles, assigned books on military tactics, conducted elaborate manuevers, and ordered his men to "act like gentlemen and . . . keep out of saloons with uniforms on." Every week the volunteers practiced "firing," identified with emphasis, as the "chief element *in battle!*" There may have been some minor trouble with the local authorities; William Deeney—who would have known—informed the volunteers of the 1892 state law forbidding more than four men at a time from being on the streets of Butte with rifles. Local ordinances notwithstanding, the "glorious rifle, the . . . salvation of Ireland" was once again a part of the RELA's activities—too much a part for John Leary, the janitor of Hibernia Hall, who complained that the "banging of rifle butts was busting up the floor." The RELA appropriated money to buy rubber sockets.[40]

Predictably, this bellicose spirit did not extend to the Hibernians. The AOH formed the Hibernian Knights and the Hibernian Rifles in the early 1880s; in 1895 it put together the Parnell and Meagher Guards. But these served mostly ceremonial purposes. They led St. Patrick's Day parades and escorted visiting Irish dignitaries. Still, the number of arms and the number of men bearing them evoked old fears of Fenianism, at least in those of fearful mind. The American Protective Association was convinced that "Jesuitical interference" was behind this "arming of the AOH" and that "it [was] not Ireland they were making ready for, but America." In proper conspiratorial language, the APA noted that Catholics, counting the "92 percent Papists in the police forces," had the Protestants outgunned; "a coup de main on their part, and what could we do?" And even should England be the Irish target, the APA was properly concerned. Like the United States, England was a Protestant nation and by virtue of that "our enduring friend." Not for the only time, the APA missed the point.[41]

IV

An interesting aspect of this rhetorical and military excess is the identification of Ireland rather than the United States as home, and the insistence that the Butte Irish were no less Irish for their emigration. This, too, can only have diminished their loyalties to an interethnic, American working class. The confusion of allegiance—if such it was—marks AOH attitudes as surely as those of the RELA. The Hibernians sent money to "relieve the suffering at home." At their state convention in 1906 it was reported that "all of us are ready to go back and free Eire." And why not? As Father Michael Hannan, pastor of Butte's St. Mary's parish and a native of County Limerick, commented at the 1910 state convention, Irishmen felt "love for their country, loyalty to their adopted country." At that same 1910 meeting, John J. O'Meara reminded the Hibernians that they were members of "an Irish organization, working for our motherland." O'Meara, however, seems never to have made up his own mind on this issue. In 1896 the AOH invited "32 handsome ladies from the Daughters of Erin" to its St. Patrick's Day parade. The women represented the thirty-two counties of Ireland. O'Meara suggested instead that the AOH invite "one lady per state of the American union." His motion failed. Recall, too, that it was O'Meara in 1908 who told the Hibernians "to mingle [their] entertainments with Americans." This time it was Father Hannan who rebuked him, insisting that "a good Irishman was the best American."[42]

The Emmets did not doubt it, assuming they thought much about the prerequisites of Americanism in the first place. John Devoy, as close to a national Clan-na-Gael spokesmen as the movement would produce, even embraced the Republican party in part because its high tariff policy hurt England and aided Ireland. Such RELA (and BMU) types as Patrick Boland, Maurice O'Connor, and William Deeney also forgave the Republicans their nativist origins, if not their continuing nativism, voting for the GOP as the party of Ireland. References to the "liberty and freedom of our land," Irishmen "at home and in foreign countries," or "Russia likely to come to our aid," are everywhere in the RELA Minute Books. Meetings were opened with "patriotic songs," American anthems not among them. The "Propagation of Irish Nationalism" was an agenda item by 1890; in 1897 one meeting a month was turned over to the discussion of a "great Irishman who had the misfortune to lose his life in the cause." On the deaths of Irish leaders, many of them unknown to the vast majority of Americans, the RELA flew its Irish flag at half-mast and draped Hibernia Hall for ninety days. Such a display for, say, Charles Kickham, must have seemed passing silly in a place like Butte.[43]

This identification of Ireland as home was automatic with a people who thought of themselves as exiles; it was also a central part of the RELA image of itself as a battalion of Wild Geese awaiting only the call to return home and fight the patriots' war. Until the call came, they could only hone their skills in whatever wars were available. One such was the Spanish-American War but, as one RELA member lamented, in the struggle between the U.S. and Spain, Irishmen were fighting for the "liberty of people not bound to them by any ties of kindred or race. May God speed them and spare them to strike a blow for their own race and kindred." Another member of the RELA offered the judgment that the Irishmen in the Philippines were a "credit to the U.S. and any other country. Alas, they are not fighting for the good old Cause."[44]

This hardly dulled their enthusiasm. In fact, according to one RELA member, commitment to the Irish cause was greater in the U.S. than in Ireland and this "New Ireland" in America, as he put it, would "yet win freedom for the race." Hugh O'Daly was of similar mind. The military companies had been "formed for the purpose of taking part in any revolution that might take place against British rule in Ireland." Ireland was fortunate indeed that its emigrants were so loyal, because, according to Pat Heaney, "everything Ireland got from England she got because of the Clan-na-Gael."[45]

It is unlikely that Heaney was intentionally demeaning the Irish nationalists, but the inference that Irish-America, not Ireland, would have to win Ireland's freedom was commonly held. Irish-Americans, obviously, were not as well positioned to strike, but the unhappy fact was that the best of the Irish were no longer in Ireland. According to one RELA member, the "race was degenerating" in Ireland as "the strong ones emigrated." Father Michael Moran told the AOH that this was the Irish "donation to the U.S.: sending so many good Irish boys and girls annually." All the money sent by all the AOH divisions could not compensate; the "balance was in favor of America." Since this was a source of such considerable concern in Butte, RELA members actively discouraged further emigration from Ireland. Their efforts failed; as William Clark reported in 1901, the Irish were "coming by the boat full." Immigration figures would support Clark's contention, though the number and size of the "boats" were less than they had been. Still, it is worth calling attention to how few letters encouraging emigration can have come from the patriots.[46]

The great fear was that it might be too late for Ireland. Too many of those "men with brains" necessary to the revolution may have gotten away. That reference to brains, when applied to the RELA, caused a working-class membership to take offense. When the same principle was applied to Ireland, however, the Butte Irish were not only not offended, they required assurances. Pat Kelly, for example, returned "from the old land of his birth" and was quick to "comment with praise on the many intelligent men of our race" still in Ireland. Jeremiah D. Murphy agreed. He too had returned from the "old sod" and reported that they "had not given up hopes by no means there but hoped the day of freedom was near at hand." Still, unless emigration could at least be slowed, John Gribben feared there would not be "enough good men left . . . to do anything." Ireland's liberty would then be left almost entirely to its exiled sons.[47]

Compounding this problem was the fact that for so many of Ireland's stoutest young men the alternative to emigration was service in England's military. Emigration deprived Ireland of a patriot warrior, but the second option raised the horrible prospect of Irish-American exiles at war with Irishmen, if not in Ireland then at any of a thousand places where the Wild Geese might chose to contest the British Empire. Obviously, as one Emmet put it, a way had to be found to keep "Irish lads out of the British army." Irish involvement in the British military was a symbol of England's rule, but more significantly, it made difficult Irish-American aid to England's enemies. Another RELA member agreed and added that there were plenty of jobs in British industry; the Irish had an alternative to emigration and military service. Less than a year after these remarks were made, John Branagan returned from a trip to Ireland and informed the much-relieved RELA that "there were no real Irish in Africa fighting for England," only the "scum and tinkers of the cities . . . were fighting for the English government."[48]

There were at least two well-placed Butte Irishmen, however, whose concerns were of a different sort. Both Jeremiah Lynch and Walter Breen returned from Ireland convinced that English land reform would measureably weaken Irish nationalism. Lynch commented on the much higher percentage of land ownership in his native West Cork; Breen said conditions in his native county of Waterford were "much improved since he left thirty years ago." These reforms would undoubtedly make life easier in Ireland and slow emigration, particularly from the West. The RELA should have counted these as blessings. Unfortunately, the liberty of Ireland was thought dependent on the misery and consequent rage of the landless. The English understood this fully. The land reforms, said Lynch, were being used "to block home rule." The RELA even wrote for three hundred copies of the amended Irish land bill of 1903; if England was to kill Home Rule with kindness, the Emmets wanted at least to understand how kindness was defined.[49]

Each of these concerns implied a patriot drain. Whether from immigration or the dulling of nationalist sensibilities, Ireland was growing yearly more dependent on what the 1916 proclamation of the independent Irish Republic called "her exiled children in America." This was not a dependency that pleased the Irish in Ireland, assuming even their willingness to admit it existed. The idea that the boldest of Ireland's rebels had been forced into exile and that that exile gave to their nationalism certain special virtues denied to those luckier ones who were able to stay home was not popularly held in Ireland. It created a tension between what may be called the home guards and the emigrant nationalists, particularly those emigrants whose outward conditions were most prosperous and whose feelings of guilt were more pronounced as a consequence.

One such may have been Jeremiah Lynch. Born in Ballycrovane in County Cork in 1871, he immigrated to Fall River, Massachusetts, in 1890 and worked briefly as a deckhand. That same year he made his way to Butte. His first job was as a carman or station tender on the 300-foot level of the Anaconda mine. For a short time he tended bar. He joined the AOH in 1894, his name proposed by Quin Crowley, also a West Corkman. A year later—and it may be significant that he affiliated with the AOH first—he joined the RELA. His name flew through a process that normally took three to four weeks, and he was elected and initiated a week after he was proposed for membership. He had either made a striking impression during his time in Butte or was known before in Ireland, or both.[50]

From this point until his death in 1961, with time off for law school in Chicago and service in the Spanish-American War, Lynch was unquestionably the dominant force in the Butte Irish community. He was first elected judge of the state district court in 1906 and for the next forty-some years served as a judge in the state judicial system. He was a member of all the Irish associations, the AOH, the RELA, the Irish National Alliance, the Irish Volunteers, the Hibernian Rifles, the Gaelic League, the Gaelic Athletic Association (he was captain of the Wolfe Tones), the Irish-American Club, the Friendly Sons of St. Patrick (he was a cofounder), the Friends of Irish Freedom, and the American Association for the Recognition of the Irish Republic. Some of these associations had mostly working-class memberships; others, like the Irish-American Club, were more professional and middle class. Some, like the Friendly Sons, were strictly fraternal; others, notably the RELA and Irish Volunteers, were revolutionary. Lynch held offices in all of them, often presiding over committee meetings in his courtroom.[51]

He was described as a man of enormous charm, a Butte character of the best sort, perhaps more in love with the city and its peculiar Irish world than with Ireland itself. But his Irish nationalism, though it lacked the intensity of Maurice Drohan's, was nonetheless strongly felt. So, however, was his belief that the patriot game could be played at least as well in Butte as in Ireland. He made that point in typically vigorous style in response to a story that appeared in 1910 in the *Dublin Leader*. An unnamed correspondent had written that Montana's AOH leaders were ineffectual socialites and "deserters from their country." Lynch was among those leaders and no criticism could have stung more; it was worse by far than William A. Clark's statement that Pat Ford had deserted from the Union army.[52]

But this charge was not only cruel and unfair, it revealed a blindness and timidity Lynch believed too common among Irish nationalists. Like the "little ex-customs officer" who wrote the story in the *Leader*, most of Ireland's nationalists had "never had the enterprise to go farther east than London, or farther west than Dungarvan." Ireland's freedom would not likely be won by such as these. As for Montana's Hibernians, the men whom this "small man" in "his ignorance was pleased to call 'deserters,' they have done more during the past thirty years for Irish nationality than any equal number of men anywhere in the world." Lynch offered specifics: "They gave Parnell thousands of hard-earned dollars. . . . They raised 2,500 pounds ($10,000) to send an ambulance corps to serve with the Boers." They built the statue to Meagher, gave thousands of dollars to Douglas Hyde's Gaelic League. "In fact no Irish cause has ever failed to meet with a ready response" from Montana's Irishmen, and no "castle hack" figured to undo their reputation for "splendid generosity and practical patriotism." The Irish "at home," plagued by a "miserable intolerance and sickening factionalism," would do well to copy the example of Butte and Montana.[53]

For Lynch, then, and for thousands of others, the Irish-American was a more natural rebel than the Irishman. Unfortunately, there was an unavoidable contradiction in this position. The seam between nationalism and reform is again at issue. Land reform in Ireland, as Lynch pointed out, would both reduce emigration and dull nationalist sensibilities. Both, given the assumption that the best Irishman was an exiled Irishman, would have devastating consequences on the prospects for Ireland's independence. It meant that the number emigrating would be smaller and that the decision to leave would be prompted more by the lure of America than the treachery of England. And, in fact, the nationalism of the Irish immigrant of 1905 was of a different sort from that of the immigrant of 1875, though different in a way Lynch might not have expected. Of greater immediate significance, the decline in immigration meant that the dynamism for Irish-American nationalism—for Irish-American associational life generally—had to come from a reduced pool of immigrants and from the second generation.

V

Here is where the immigrant nationalists confronted their most unyielding problem. The second generation, as well as the later immigrants, were not as influenced by old Land League memories as the first. Those memories provided the prism through which the early immigrants saw and understood the Irish past. Making the matter worse, the English government prohibited the teaching of Irish history and culture in Ireland, leaving later immigrants, according to the national chairman of the Irish History Committee, with little knowledge of "the pathetic but inspiring story of Erin and her heroic struggle throughout the centuries." As already noted, one result was that neither group was as moved by the fraternal unity of the AOH and the RELA, indeed neither seemed to need the AOH and the RELA. P. H. Kealy was uncertain why specifically but he knew that "the new Irish immigrants were just not like they used to be twenty years ago." This unhappy reality was even clearer by 1915, but before then Irish fathers worked tirelessly to make patriots of less-caring sons and less-comprehending immigrants. Their principal weapons were compulsory Irish history in the parochial and, for a time, public schools and an active "adult education" program in Irish history, language, and culture.[54]

The RELA recognized a need for Irish history as early as 1891, but it was not until the early twentieth century that the issue became urgent. As Lynch told the 1906 AOH state convention, the children of Irish immigrants had to be taught to "revere the Faith and love Ireland . . . that they may adhere unflinchingly to the one and be ready to fight unselfishly for the independence of the other." To this end both of Montana's bishops, John Carroll in Helena and Matthias Lenihan in Great Falls, had Irish history taught "as soon as practicable." As for the later immigrant, Lynch argued that he had to be taken into the AOH "as soon as he sets foot on Montana soil." At issue was not just the love of Ireland. As Father Michael Hannan pointed out, "the day is fast approaching when emigration must necessarily cease from Ireland and when if the AOH is to . . . exist, . . . it must draw its membership from the sons of Irishmen born on American soil." But this second generation was of no value if it "knew not Ireland."[55]

Hibernians in Ireland, however, thought more was involved than just knowing Ireland. Irish-Americans, they learned to their horror, admitted young men of the second generation who had only one Irish parent. This opened up the possibility that "chinamen, negroes, and Orangemen" would be admitted to the order and the usefulness of Irish history to the conversion of those sorts was doubtful. As their previously cited criticism of the younger generation would indicate, there were older Irishmen in Butte who might have agreed, though without the reference to "hybrid Irish." A good dose of Irish history, however, was a "potent preventative for these existing evils." There is, of course, considerable irony in these and similar arguments. The full victory of Irish-American and Irish nationalism would mean a prosperous and independent Ireland which no one need ever again be compelled to leave. Unfortunately, those exiles were the foundation of Irish-American associational life.[56]

The AOH was more active than the RELA in this ultimately futile effort to make Irishmen of the second generation. The Emmets were not totally unconcerned; they acknowledged, as Lynch put it, that "the vast depopulation of our Mother Land" required that the Irish-Americans be kept Irish. Every RELA member signed a letter urging that Irish history be taught in Butte's Catholic schools (unanimity was not common in the RELA); the Emmets also raised money to buy textbooks and gave banquets and prizes for the best students. Seamus O'Moriarity (#20), even argued that the Irish language as well as Irish history ought to be taught at St. Patrick's. But the insistence that Irish history be a part of the curriculum came properly from the Hibernians, who began their agitation in 1902. For a time, the matter went well. Bishop John Brondell, a Belgian, was receptive to the idea and, at least in those parishes with strong Irish majorities, the history of Ireland was a part, usually compulsory, of the course of study. The AOH examined the Irish history students at St. Patrick's and offered a prize to the best one. Irish studies, the AOH recording secretary noted with a touch of brogue, were doing "splindedly."[57]

In late January, 1905, John Carroll was consecrated bishop of the Helena diocese. Though a second-generation Irishman and sympathetic to the Irish cause, Carroll was also an Americanist cleric who believed strongly that the Church should assist in, and force if necessary, the assimilation of its immigrant flock. By 1905, moreover, Carroll's church was far more ethnically mixed than Brondell's had been; compulsory Irish history cannot have pleased his Americanist sensibilities—or, for example, his Italian parishioners. Early in Carroll's episcopacy, the Butte AOH visited him regarding Irish history in the Catholic schools of Silver Bow County. The Hibernians sent a well-connected team, attesting to the significance they attached to the matter. D. J. Hennessy chaired a delegation made up of Anaconda Company chief executive John D. Ryan, Silver Bow County Sheriff John K. O'Rourke, Judge J. J. Lynch, Centennial Brewing Company owner John J. O'Meara, and former Butte Miners' Union president and later proprietor of the ACM-owned Florence Hotel Jeremiah D. Murphy. (Murphy, by the way, was comfortably retired; his son was employed in the ACM legal department.)[58]

This attempt at persuasion apparently failed. Later that year the three divisions of the AOH joined with the RELA and the Gaelic League in a protest that figured to move even an Americanist bishop. The organizations "demanded" that Irish history be taught in the parochial schools or "Irish parents would be requested to withdraw their children from the same." This protest succeeded where the doubtless friendlier overtures of Hennessy et alia had not. Father J. J. Callaghan, pastor at Sacred Heart and a member of Division 1, assured the AOH that Irish history was certainly being taught at Sacred Heart school, and most, if not all, of Butte's parishes seem to have adopted some program of study of Ireland's past.[59]

The problem now was whether it was the kind of history the AOH had in mind. Charles Gallagher of Division 2 reported that it "might just as well not be taught." No "reliable text" was being used, "only such things as pertained to church and religion and then only extracts selected by the sisters"; Gallagher hoped that "physical force" would not be required to persuade Bishop Carroll. There may have been times when Gallagher's facetious suggestion was considered seriously. John J. O'Meara, still not able to make up his mind whether he was Irish or American, neither or both, reminded Carroll that the Irish had built the American Catholic Church and "demanded that our children be educated in the history of our motherland." Walter Breen and Matt Canning were even more direct. Carroll, they said, had "skimmed the AOH to a fare-thee-well" for the diocese scholarship program but was now "not living up to his promise" to require the history of Ireland. Clearly, if the "sisters have time for Latin they should also have time for a few minutes of Irish History." The success of the entire parochial-school movement in the United States depended on the ability of the hierarchy to recognize the "necessity" of offering the story of Ireland's past. Should this final appeal to reason fail, the Butte Hibernians were as ready in 1911 as they had been in 1905 to pull their children from the Catholic schools. The AOH committee on Irish history, chaired for a time by Father Michael Hannan, warned Carroll that if he did not "compel Irish History to be taught, he . . . would sacrifice the patronage of the children born of Irish descent who attended the schools." They could stretch the boycott no further than that.[60]

Obviously, the Irish associations were uncomfortable with their growing reliance on the second generation and the later immigrants and with their bishop's unwillingness to turn diocesan schools into training camps for Irish nationalists. The patriots would have similar difficulties convincing the Irish, regardless of age or generation, of the importance of maintaining Irish cultural traditions. The challenge was to convince a people accustomed to defining the Irish question in terms of politics and economics that cultural considerations were also important, that there could be no Irish nation worthy of respect without the recapture of the cultural traditions which gave to the Irish a necessary self-respect. England had to be expelled but so did things English—from Irish-America as surely as from Ireland. This was not, of course, a brand new part of the patriot game but under the influence of the Gaelic League it assumed a greater urgency in the early twentieth century. The targets of this de-anglicization program were those who had allowed their Gaelicism to lapse. This included the second generation as well as the more recent immigrants, identified by one disgruntled Hibernian as "not having the same interest in the AOH."[61]

Even the earliest-arriving immigrants would benefit from a refresher course in Irish culture, particularly those early arrivals who Walter Breen said had "lost their pride" and changed their "habits and customs." Breen was speaking specifically of the tendency to drop Irish Christian names. "There was nothing to be ashamed of," he said, "to the one who knows the History of Ireland, in having an Irish Christian name." J. J. O'Meara, obviously in one of his Irish moods, agreed. He thought the priests should insist at the "baptismal font" on Irish names. At the very least, the AOH wanted "Irish names for Irish families; Irish saints for churches where the Irish people are in the majority." There was pressure, too, to hold on to Irish surnames, including their patronymic Os and Mcs. Indeed, according to Father Michael Hannan, it was a "disgrace" that the Irish would allow "their grand Celtic names to be transformed in this country."[62]

The Gaelic revival changed that pattern only slightly. Determined Gaelic Leaguers like Seamus Ó Muircheartaigh (James Moriarity) and

Seán Ó Súileabháin (John O'Sullivan) seem to have been the only Butte Irishmen to deanglicize their surnames totally, or to have taken literally the admonition to restore Irish first names: O'Sullivan's sons were Eamon de Valera and Patrick Sarsfield; Moriarity's was given the name Cuchulainn. Perhaps other Butte Irishmen were discouraged by the obvious. As Thomas Kealy pointed out, the "old names were hard to write and pronounce, like the Polander's name with 100 letters." No one should be criticized for refusing to change his surname to the Gaelic; having a name that could be easily understood was part of being a "progressive American." There is absolutely no reason to take Kealy's last comment seriously, or even to assume that he intended it seriously. He was well known for his puckish humor and his delight in provoking debate.[63]

The call for a return to Irish names was only one part of the Gaelic revival. Other Irish in Butte emphasized sports, or music and dance. But the major thrust of the cultural nationalists was to reestablish Gaelic Irish as the language of Ireland and to reacquaint Irish-America with the "language of Oisin." Thomas Concannon, of the Gaelic League in Ireland, explained: The object of the language revival was "to make Irishmen and Irishwomen of the men and women of Ireland." English would continue to be taught "but Irish first. The Irishman's head," Concannon insisted, "was large enough to know at least two languages." Immigrant Irish must have been hurt by the implications of Concannon's remarks; the cultural distance between them and "the men and women of Ireland" began to seem less easily bridged. The immigrants, however, were at least spared the antimodernist bias that marked the Gaelic revival, as well as some of the consequences of the dubious notion that the Irish had ever been anglicized to begin with.[64]

Still, the Butte Irish were predictably enthusiastic and generous in their dealings with the Gaelic League. The RELA had sponsored a series of lectures in Irish as early as 1895 and a local league was formed in 1901. When Douglas Hyde, cofounder of the movement in Ireland, visited Butte in 1906 he was well received and handsomely compensated. His fee was $600 and he collected $2,212 more from the reception committee. Hugh O'Daly wrote that he raised over $5,000 from Butte's Irish, "one-third of them Gaelic speakers." O'Daly exaggerated on both counts. Hyde also succeeded in persuading the associations to commit themselves to the long-term welfare of the Gaelic League in the home country. The RELA, AOH, and the local Gaelic League sent $600 annually, beginning in 1909 and continuing to 1914, to "defray the expenses of what is known as the Butte Organizer in Ireland." There were, in addition, occasional gifts to Hyde's league, in-

cluding one $1,617 contribution in 1908 from the AOH divisions and
the RELA. As late as 1917, the Butte League of the Connradh na Gaedh-
ilce, was still holding its twice weekly lessons in the Irish language.
Clearly, Butte's Irish community was actively involved in the Gaelic
cultural revival of the early twentieth century.[65]

VI

That involvement, however, as with the other aspects of the patriot
game, was perceived as uneven and marked by obvious class distinctions. Walter Breen—not, it must be granted, an unimpeachable source—
argued in 1906 that it was the Irish who had "acquired a little wealth"
who were quickest to drop their Irish names and assume the style of
Kealy's "progressive American." Five years earlier, in a more important
expression of this same point—Jeremiah Lynch, William Deeney, and
John Branagan—lawyer, saloonkeeper, and merchant—authored a rather
bitter RELA resolution regarding the Meagher Memorial Fund. That
monument, they wrote, "must be built by the RELA . . . as we never
did nor never may look to Millionaires and the wealthy men of our
race to do anything for . . . the glory of Ireland or of Ireland's sons."
This was an important resolution on two counts: first, it gave frank
acknowledgment to class divisions and second, it identified the RELA
as the proper repository of Irish and working-class values.[66]

As it affected the Gaelic revival, Breen's argument does not apply.
In fact, the poorer Irish, in Butte as in Ireland, were seldom moved by
abstractions like deanglicization. That was an ideological plaything of
the middle classes. Applied to the patriot game more generally, however, Breen's criticism of those with a "little wealth," together with
the RELA resolution of 1901, raises important questions. This is particularly the case in two areas of dispute in Ireland and in Irish-America.
The first is in the quarrel between the Irish Home Rulers, usually found
in the Irish Parliamentary party, and those who insisted upon an independent Irish Republic, commonly the affiliates of the Irish Republican Brotherhood or Clan-na-Gael, Sinn Fein, the Irish Volunteers, or
the Irish Citizen Army. The second is in the related disagreement between those who favored parliamentary tactics and those who insisted
that only physical force would win the patriot game. These were bitter
quarrels; in one communication to its local camps, the national Clan-
na-Gael referred to the Parliamentary party as "in the hands of our
enemies." But the disputes were not just over the tactics of Irish independence; in one very important sense, both were contested on the
seam.[67]

There were times in Butte when the disagreement assumed a strictly associational aspect, the RELA coming down on the side of physical force and an independent—though not necessarily socialist—Irish republic, the AOH wearing its nationalism more lightly, supporting parliamentary obstruction as the means to Home Rule. In 1902, for example, the RELA attempted to sever what it perceived as a link between the AOH and the Irish Parliamentary party by instructing "#38 [Daniel Hennessy]," the Butte delegate to the national AOH convention, "to vote against any AOH resolution upholding the policies of the Parliament Party." This was not, however, the usual pattern. The AOH and the RELA were too similar in their appeal to the working class to take dramatically different positions, too dissimilar in purpose to be rivals. The RELA tended to the needs of Ireland, the AOH to the needs of the Irish. Ordinarily, these were compatible objects.[68]

Factional disputes in Butte, then, were not usually between the two major Irish organizations. Rather they reflected the political divisions in Ireland and thus crossed associational lines. As in Ireland, moreover, it is difficult to predict (or assign) sides on the basis of social class. Indeed, given the 5,000 insulating miles between Butte and Dublin and the fact that Butte's Irishmen would experience the consequences of the "revolution" indirectly if at all, there was probably less predictability to the factional alignment in Butte than in Ireland. Daniel Hennessy could afford to be an RELA radical; it is unlikely he would have been as feisty had it been the IRB whose radicalism he had had to embrace or, for that matter, had he not died in 1908, before the Clanna-Gael began its own leftward tilt.

Hugh O'Daly's "radicalism" was of a somewhat different sort. He noted with pride that he had been in charge of IRB-sponsored physical force activities in South Monaghan; that he knew well-placed members of the revolutionary Invincibles as well as prominent bomb throwers— the dynamitards, as they were called; that he had met Connolly and Larkin and had spoken with Sinn Fein founder Arthur Griffith at an IRB meeting in Dublin. In fact, except for the money he had sent to finance Irish revolutions, he would have been "one of the wealthiest men in Montana," and both parts of that statement are important. At the same time, and with no apparent sense of the contradictions, he referred to Walter Breen's developing radicalism on the "Irish question" as evidence that Breen was "changing to socialism." He even insisted that "only the Irish had kept English labor unions out of the party of the Anti-Christ," that the Irish were the "balance wheel against communism."[69]

Hennessy was spared the full implications of his "radicalism"; O'Daly, rather disingenuously, denied that there were any implications to his. Patrick J. Brophy lived longer than Hennessy and was less given to self-deception than O'Daly. His story is thus more instructive. Brophy was a grocer's son, born in 1855 in County Carlow, a part of Ireland relatively untouched by Land League radicalism. He was educated and learned the grocery business in Ireland, immigrating first to Chicago (1877), then to Butte (1881), where he went into partnership in a grocery with George Casey. He quickly prospered; by 1888 he was sole proprietor of "P.J. Brophy & Co., Wholesale Grocery and Dealers in Wines and Liquors." In 1895 he moved to what would be his permananent home on Butte's fashionable West Side. By 1907 his business required a full-time secretary-treasurer—a non-Irishman named H. W. Johnson; by 1909 he was calling himself a "capitalist"; and by 1912, still a capitalist rather than a grocer, he had offices on the fourth floor of the Hennessy Building, two floors below the corporate headquarters of the Anaconda Company.[70]

Initially, Brophy was an active member of the Irish community. He was a member of the AOH and, surprisingly, the RELA as well. But Brophy was an unlikely radical, even in the cause of Ireland. He seems always to have been an antisocialist; one of his left-wing critics even referred to him as "a man of high ideals but a political and economic fanatic." Ideologically and temperamentally, he could not even sustain his youthful enthusiasm for the Irish cause. His name does not appear on the RELA Membership Ledgers after 1896 and his involvement with the AOH, judging from its Minute Books, seems to have been mostly ceremonial. John J. O'Meara was very likely talking about Brophy specifically when he complained in 1903 of "the prominent Irishmen in this Community who were at one time very popular in Irish affairs" but who, "by reason of acquiring more wealth and prosperity than the majority of our members, severed all connections with our organizations." Brophy at the time was serving as treasurer of the Meagher Memorial Fund. Three months after O'Meara made his comments Brophy angrily resigned that position, refusing even to release the money to his replacement, former BMU and WFM officer James Maher.[71]

What remaining connections he had with Butte's Irish world were limited to the respectable—he was an officer of the Irish-American Club; the religious—he was a national officer of the Knights of Columbus; the cultural—he contributed to the Gaelic League's music program; and the politically safe—he was active, or at least as active as circumstances would permit, in the United Irish League. It is this last-named affiliation that is of greatest interest, providing as it does a kind of case study of the effects of social class on ethnic consciousness and political commitment. The UIL was an arm of the politically conservative Irish Parliamentary party of John Redmond. Its policy was the same as the party's: Home Rule—that is the restoration of an Irish parliament with authority over strictly Irish matters—won through an appeal to England's sense of reason and fair play. The RELA in particular had something rather more sweeping in mind: the "complete independence of our enslaved Mother Land" won by force of Irish and Irish-American arms. That "enslavement," moreover, was not just political. Independence, according to Jeremiah Lynch, was the "only way for the Irish to get" their lands back.[72]

The UIL was thus a traitor to both Ireland and the Irish, and the RELA, despite its own condemnations of factionalism, was characteristically direct in its dealings with UIL representatives. The UIL was quite specifically "not invited" to the 1903 Irish societies' picnic, a celebration cohosted by the RELA and the AOH. The AOH relented somewhat; a year later when Conor O'Kelly visited Butte representing the UIL, the Hibernians held a reception for him, knowing their involvement would "antagonize another Irish organization." The reference can only have been to the unforgiving RELA. For example, the UIL call for the RELA to join it in a "monster mass meeting" was "thrown in the waste basket." The RELA, in fact, nearly boycotted the formal unveiling of Meagher's statue because the featured speaker, John Finerty, a founder of the UIL, was thought insufficiently committed to physical force.[73]

Brophy not only supported but, to a very great extent, represented the interests of the UIL in Butte. It was not an enviable assignment. For his part, Brophy was pleased that Ireland had come as near victory as the Land Act and Home Rule talk of 1903 seemed to indicate. The "victory . . . [would] not be as complete as we all desire," he wrote, "but it is wonderful that our race has at last compelled her tyrants to grant concessions that would have filled the heart of Emmet or O'Connell, or Parnell with joy and gladness." The Parliamentary party, he went on, must be encouraged in its good work, "not only in the settlement of the land question but also in the *greater settlement* of Home Rule which is soon to follow." It was this Land Act, of course, which had convinced J. J. Lynch of England's continuing treachery; it was Home Rule which Lynch and others had dismissed as meaningless or worse. But Brophy did not stand entirely alone. John D. Ryan gave at least $1,500 to the UIL and for a time served as the Butte league's treasurer. F. Augustus Heinze, the embattled "copper king," contributed $500 in an effort to prove he was both Irish and the friend of the working man, a tactic of doubtful value given the conservatism of the UIL.[74]

Brophy made the appropriate distinctions. The "best Irishmen in Butte," "the prominent" Irish, the "best material of our people" were Parliamentarians and Home Rulers. The "masses of Irish," however, did not approve of the Parliamentary approach. It was not because the masses were uncaring. Indeed, Butte's Irish world possessed an "abundance of good will and zeal." Nor was it because there were too few of them. Butte was an "immensely Irish community," "our people have probably a greater proportion of the population of this city than any other of the size or importance in the U.S." The problem was that their commitment found different expression. He tried to explain: The Hibernians were diverted. They were raising money for the Meagher memorial and "only too many of them are engaged in an effort to grasp some kind of political office," a nice summary of the segregant roles played by ethnic associations. As for the "other organization, known as the 'Emmetts' [sic], it would probably make it [a UIL meeting] the occasion of a demonstration of their peculiar ideas and notions." Clearly, there were "differences of opinion . . . in the matter of advancing Ireland's cause." Butte's Irish were "distressed and weakened by dissension" that might have been calmed only by strong leadership. Brophy could not assume that role and "local factional wrath" was the result. "Butte," he concluded, "has many handicaps."[75]

It still did almost ten years later. In 1912 Brophy was again collecting money for the Irish Parliamentary party. By then its conservatism was in even more glaring contrast to the policies of its Irish rivals. Brophy reported that the fund-raising had gone poorly. Butte's Irish had contributed only $1,200, "a trifling sum from so Irish a community." But he then explained that only a small percentage of that community had contributed anything at all. The money had come from personal solicitation; newspaper appeals raised "not one dollar of voluntary contribution." Moreover, "there was not a single donation less than $250 which meant that the rank and file was not represented on the list. . . . *Not a working man's dollar did we receive.* . . . our own people, the numerical strength of them, did not support . . . the policy of the Parliamentary Party." If they had, "they could pay almost the entire expense of the . . . Party without missing it." But Butte was a divided Irish town. "We have Home Rulers, Sinn Feiners, physical force fanatics, Ulstermen and Corkonians—all pulling in different directions." How much different it was twenty-five years ago when the "anti-religious movement" (the APA?) forced the Irish to unite. Now, "we have nothing whatever to fear here . . . the enemy has not much standing . . . we are so envious, so strong and so ungoverned that we have almost become lop-sided." Brophy did not exaggerate—at least as his comments pertained to the established Irish.[76]

Obviously, there were a variety of ideas in Butte on how the patriot game should be played. According to Brophy, this was the curse of power and influence. More likely it was the predictable consequence of social differentiation. The Brophys of Irish-America, the Tory nationalists, did not care as deeply about an independent Ireland, did not care at all about a socialist Ireland—or, with one eye on the working-class Irish—a socialist Butte. What is remarkable about Butte is how few Brophys there were, as Brophy himself laments. It probably is not what he had in mind when he used the word "lop-sided," but if any one group spoke for more than just its membership, it was the RELA.

The Catholic Church—and the Brophys were often self-consciously pious communicants—was another potential obstacle to a fully realized and radicalized Irish nationalist community. In Ireland and in parts of Irish-America, clerical indifference to Irish independence and hostility to Irish reform posed an enormous problem. The radicalization of the Irish required the creation of a bond between social reform and Catholicism. At the highest levels of the hierarchy this proved impossible; at the parish level, however, the younger priests, both in Ireland and in Irish-America, were far more receptive. Themselves the products of the Land League agitation, most of them drawn from the poorer classes— Irish peasant and Irish-American worker—patriot and radical priests were routinely encountered after about 1890, and Irish Catholics of radical mind, Ed Boyce for example, could attempt with some success the reconciliation of their faith and their radicalism. There were, of course, priests who clung to old notions. In 1907 a Father Carr told a "stunned" meeting of Division 3 of the AOH that Irish freedom was premature, that "if Ireland were a nation her children would not have to wander the world and spread the doctrines of Jesus Christ. When the world would be converted then Ireland would gain her independence." That was too long a time for even the most patient Irishman to wait.[77]

Carr's were not conspicuous sentiments by 1907. But the memory of clerical hostility to Irish freedom lingered, especially among the members of the nonsectarian RELA. In 1896, for example, Michael Kelly argued that the present "deplorable condition of Ireland" was owing to "Catholicity, especially English catholicity." Two years later, the Emmets refused even to meet with Father Eugene Sheehy of County Limerick and Father Michael McFadden of County Donegal on their visit to Butte, despite the fact that both priests had been imprisoned for Land League activities. Their visit, however, was to raise money for local Irish churches, a cause in which RELA patriots were not interested. Walter Breen, speaking to the AOH, made the same point. He "scorned those priests who come out to this newly settled country asking assistance to build colleges for the education of the better class in Ireland where the poor were not considered." Breen later "blasted the iron hand of the [Irish] priests for their opposition to labor unions," following that with a, for him, related attack on the Irish Parliamentary party. Little wonder that Breen was identified by Father Michael Moran as a "good Irishman but a poor Catholic."[78]

That was always part of the problem—how to be both. Breen, however, was not without clerical defenders in Butte. Indeed, one of them, Father Michael Hannan, countered Moran's remark by declaring it internally contradictory: to be one was to be the other. Hannan was the enclave's priest. Pastor at St. Mary's, the "Miners' " church, he was a self-described "Irish Exile, who has seen many dark days abroad." Hannan, as nearly as it could be done, functioned comfortably on all sides of the seams. It was said that he once punched Father Michael Barry, pastor at Immaculate Conception on Butte's West Side, because Barry had jokingly referred to his as the "lace-curtain" parish, Hannan's as the "shanty-Irish." Predictably, he was a member of the AOH. Less predictably, he was admitted without murmur of protest into the RELA (#57), joining even its military arm, the Irish Volunteers. He went on "maneuvers" with them and promised that "if anything was doing, he'd be in the firing line."[79]

VII

Clearly, being Irish in Butte provided one with a choice of possibilities. Edward Boyce, William Deeney, Maurice Drohan, D. J. Hennessy, Jeremiah Lynch, Hugh O'Daly, Patrick Brophy, and Michael Hannan were often as different as they were alike, as divided on how Ireland should be served as they were united that they must serve her. On one important point, however, this otherwise-divided Irish community was in near-unanimous agreement. Following the well-established lead of Irish patriots, Butte's Irishmen were convinced, in Parnell's phrase, that "when England is at war and beaten to her knees, the dream of the Irish nationalists may be realized" or, in shorthand version, "England's distress was Ireland's advantage."[80]

Fortunately, England was regularly distressed—or at least threatened—by foreign rivals. The Irish had a long tradition of allying with those rivals based on the defensible notion that England's enemies

were Ireland's natural friends. Since England seldom wanted for enemies, the Irish were kept busy making friends. In 1856, 1876, and 1878
the friend was Russia; in 1879, the Zulu War and the Afghanistan War
seemed promising; in 1880, a quarrel in Central America prompted
one Irishman to propose a Clan-na-Gael move against England "via
Belize and the Yucatan"; between 1881 and 1884 the English were at
war with the Mahdi in Egypt and a prominent Clansman told John
Devoy that 20,000 rifles supplied by the Clan would "turn the tide for
the rebels."[81]

These quixotic adventures took place too early for Butte's full participation. The next opportunity for Irish advantage did not. The Boer
War, in Butte as in the rest of Irish-America, was the occasion for a
great outpouring of Irish-American hope. Not only did it seem likely
to involve England in a more general war, it also revealed English
imperialism at its ugliest and gave credibility to the Irish charge that
they were victims of that same imperialism. Butte responded quickly
and with uncommon unity. William Deeney reminded the RELA in
1896 that all European countries had gained their freedom "with a gun
and a sword." Now, "through the channels of some great European
war," was Ireland's time. The Irish Volunteers, formed as English difficulties in South Africa were increasing, gave its "committee on military tactics" authority to buy twenty-four Remington rifles. The volunteers then began active drilling. That same day, somewhat
prematurely as it happened, the RELA sent a telegram to the "Transvaal
Republic congratulating the People on their absolute independence
over Great Britain." When they learned their error the Emmets went
back to their drills.[82]

The rhetoric of Irish patriotism increased after the Boer War was
officially declared in October, 1899. Again, Deeney led the verbal as-
sualts. England had been "checked . . . for the last two months, and
notwithstanding [English] bombast," the Boers were near to victory.
Now was the time for the RELA to "send its might . . . against our
arch Enemy." John Butler (#66), a miner at the Anaconda Mine, agreed,
insisting that the RELA "do something now, for our selves . . . there
is too much talk, . . . not words but action should be our Motto." Eight
months later, an unidentified Emmet repeated Butler's summon to arms.
There was still "hope for our purpose," he said. Now was the time for
"Irishmen in the [American] West to get up and do and stop talking."
From then until 1900, the volunteers practiced their arms and waited
their call to action.[83]

That call came sometime in 1899. An unknown number of RELA
members—only the names of Dan Daugherty and William D. Clark

were specifically noted—together with other Irish and Irish-Americans joined the Irish Brigade formed from among the many Irish in South Africa. Clark and Daugherty returned to Butte in December, 1899. A year later more Butte veterans of the Irish Brigade returned; they were hailed as "heroes who nobly struck a blow at our tyrant foe." The reward for their heroism was something the RELA could control: a job in the mines. A month earlier Butte was pleased to host and find jobs for nineteen touring veterans of the Irish Brigades. Like the local Irish warriors, they too were "dead broke."[84]

More common than volunteering for active duty in the Irish Brigade was the contribution of money to the Boer cause. Butte's Irish were extraordinarily generous. With the complete approval of Marcus Daly, both the AOH and the RELA sent teams of men into the mines to collect money for a Boer Ambulance Corps. The AOH committee consisted of Anthony Shovlin, a BMU officer; P. J. Sullivan, a hotelkeeper; Larry Duggan, a mortician; John J. O'Meara, a brewer; and George Dunleavy, a miner living at the Florence Hotel. Within three months, the two organizations had collected more than $4,000, making the RELA "contribution the largest received from any of the *states* on behalf of the Ambulance Corps." As for the Hibernians, the contribution of AOH, Division I, was "the highest sum in the United States." Butte's fanatical heart was seldom more prominently displayed.[85]

The associations also gave their moral support. Members of Blake's Irish Brigade made two visits to Butte, where they spoke to the RELA about the progress of the war in South Africa and the contributions of the Irish to what all hoped would be a British defeat. The RELA urged Irishmen "all over the world" to show "sympathy for the South African Republic." At a Division 1 meeting of the AOH, Recording secretary Jeremiah Lynch wrote that "several bros. made remarks on Boer War and the sympathy of the meeting with the Transvaal Republic was very apparent." Both organizations also petitioned President McKinley to deny American horses to the British troops; "thousands" of signatures were collected. After the war, they joined to fete General Joubert and Capt. O'Donnell, heroes of the Boers' unsuccessful fight for independence. Even the *Montana Catholic*, ordinarily the most politically circumspect of journals, joined in the enthusiasm with stories on the "Fighting Boers," and "New Years in the Transvaal." The *Catholic* was also careful to point out that the Boers—the Orange Free State—had once shown an unbecoming religious intolerance but that "almost all" of their proscriptive laws against Catholics had been lifted since 1896. This would not have mattered much to William Deeney. He urged the

RELA to send its support "no matter whom it was going to assist so long as it was used against England."[86]

It is conceivable that the Irish applied the lessons of the Boer War to America's policy in its nearly simulanteous conflict in the Philippines. Michael Davitt, after all, resigned his seat in Parliament in protest of English policy in South Africa. Twenty years earlier, Parnell and the Irish Parliamentary party had loudly opposed the South Africa Bill. As in so many areas of concern to them, English policy might have provided more general lessons in the assorted and related crimes of capitalism and imperialism. And, in fact, some Butte Irish did make the obvious associations. America's war with Spain to free Cuba and the Philippines was greeted by the Irish with near-unanimous approval; it indicated, they hoped, an American willingness to come to the assistance of other struggling nationalities, a point the RELA tried to bring to the attention of Irish leader John Dillon when Dillon questioned American policy toward Spain.[87]

Less well received, however, was America's refusal to acknowledge the right to independence of those same colonized people. The substitution of American for Spanish imperial control seemed both bad policy and frightening precedent. And so Edward Boyce condemned both the Philippine and the Boer conflicts as "capitalist wars," but had no comment on the Spanish-American War. Likewise, James McConnell, an Irish-born BMU officer, fought to free the Philippines from Spain but refused to support "unjust U.S. policy now that Philippine liberation had been achieved." A third representative of this position was John Fox (#209), a mason, who told the RELA that the Irish were forced to fight on England's side in the Boer War but that Irish-Americans were not compelled to fight America's equally cruel war against the Philippine people. The RELA even took for one of its debates the topic: "That Irishmen in general . . . favor expansion of the United States." The side arguing the negative won.[88]

Here, then, was another instance where a defense of Ireland necessarily involved the Irish-Americans in a defense of more general principles, in this case the right of self-determination. Irish-Americans did have a unique and radicalizing perspective on questions of land reform, the rights of workers, imperialism, nationalism, even racism. This does not mean that all, or even many, of them took the radical side on those issues. It does mean that few of them can have automatically or mindlessly rejected that radical side. Ireland was not the only victim of imperialism; the Irish were not the only victims of capitalism. Other peoples were likewise hostages to both, and as the Irish contemplated the crimes against Ireland they could hardly have ignored the effects of identical crimes against those others.

In the final analysis, however, it was not some abstract love of liberty but the patriot game that moved the Butte Irish and formed their attitudes. Their hostility to English policy in South Africa did not presage a general Irish-American anti-imperialism but rather a more determined Irish-American resolve to strike a blow for Ireland. Anti-imperialism was a tactic and one which an otherwise-divided group of patriots agreed served their larger purposes. As Pat Heaney had said, Ireland must use all means, "foul and fair," in the struggle for its freedom. And, as William Deeney made clear, they could not afford to be too scrupulous in the selection of allies. Those two would have made Faustian deals. But even the more moderate of their comrades were as determined to have their revenge against the nation that had driven them from their homes. If the Boer War was an opportunity, the developing hostility between Britain and Germany was a godsend.

NOTES

1. Davitt, *Fall of Feudalism*, p. 249; O'Dea, *AOH*, III:1060; Miller, *Emigrants*, pp. 427–92.

2. Foner, "Land League," pp. 169–70, 176, 180, 198–200; Thomas N. Brown, *Irish-American Nationalism*, pp. 24, 41, 46–49, 107–10, 118, 127–29, 133–40, 164, 166, 168–72.

3. Foner, "Land League," p. 195; Miller, *Emigrants*, p. 428.

4. "Transitional" is Foner's word ("Land League," p. 195).

5. *Butte Mining Journal*, May 24, June 7, 1891.

6. Foner, "Land League," pp. 198–200. Davitt's distinction between Tory and Democratic nationalists is from p. 192. Thomas N. Brown, *Irish-American Nationalism*, pp. 117–30; Miller, *Emigrants*, p. 426.

7. Thomas N. Brown, *Irish-American Nationalism*, pp. 127–29; Foner, "Land League," pp. 190–93; Rumpf and Hepburn, *Nationalism and Socialism*, p. 25.

8. Foner, "Land League," pp. 152–54, 168–77, 196; Dennis Clark, *Irish in Philadelphia*, p. 135; Devoy, *Post Bag*, I:455–56; Thomas N. Brown, *Irish-American Nationalism*, p. 28; Funchion, *Organizations*, p. 37; Pollard, *Societies of Ireland*, p. 75. The Connolly reference is from the *Harp*, the journal of the Irish Socialists Federation, cited in Pollard, ibid., pp. 119–20. See also the reference to Feargus O'Connor, a leader of the British Chartists and a revolutionary Irishman, ibid., p. 43. O'Brien, *Parnell*, I:168–69. Irish liberalism occasionally resembled that of the self-appointed "best men" in the United States. The Rev. George Pepper, for example, told a Butte audience in 1885 that "the landlords of Ireland are the carpetbaggers of Ireland" (*Butte Miner*, Nov. 10, 1885). See Sproat, *Best Men*, pp. 33–44.

9. Foner, "Land League," pp. 198–200.

10. Ibid., pp. 176, 199–200.

11. "Introduction," Boyce Papers. Fahey, "Ed Boyce" and *Days; Miners Magazine*, June, 1901; Lingenfelter, *Hardrock Miners*, pp. 218, 226; Vernon Jensen, *Heritage of Conflict*, pp. 57–63; Suggs, "Catalyst for Change," p. 333; Suggs, *Colorado's War*. For Deeney, see *Anaconda Standard*, May 17, 1924.

12. RELA, Membership and Dues Ledgers, 1899–1903; MB, Oct. 5, 1899. The Parnell and Emmet claims are dated June 3, 1886 for Leadville, Colo., Records and Ledgers, Boyce Papers. The poems are from Leadville, July 8, 1886, and Wardner, Idaho, Aug. 26, 1888; Jan. 31, 1890, Boyce Papers.

13. Mar. 26, 1885; July 8, 1886; Jan. 31, 1890; Sept. 8, 1896, Boyce Papers.

14. *Miners Magazine*, Feb. 1900; May, 1900; June, 1901.

15. Fahey, *Days*; Debs to Boyce, Nov. 7, 1912; Boyce to Debs, Feb. 21, 1912. Darrow was broke and asked Boyce for some money, Boyce to Darrow, Feb. 12, Apr. 2, 1912; Boyce to O'Neill, Mar. 12, 1913; Boyce to Moyer, Mar. 12, 1913. There is a 1905 AOH badge from Wardner, Idaho, and a receipt for dues from the Portland AOH, Apr. 10, 1916. On Boyce's later and more conservative Irish nationalism, see T.B. Fitzpatrick to Boyce, Jan. 17, 1913, Mar. 9, 1914; James H. Murphy to Boyce, Feb. 3, 1913; Boyce to Sen. Hanson, Feb. 8, 1913; Bishop of Oregon to Boyce, May 26, 1916; Eamon de Valera to Boyce, Sept. 20, 1919; Boyce to de Valera, Sept. 23, 1919. For money he sent to Ireland, see Ledger Books, 1918–22, Boyce Papers. Boyce's estate at his death in 1941 was $1,172,000; Fahey, "Ed Boyce," p. 30.

16. For references to the congruity between image and reality, see Thomas N. Brown, *Irish-American Nationalism*, pp. 49–53, 57–59, 90–91, 108, 122; Foner, "Land League," pp. 159–61; Davitt, *Fall of Feudalism*, p. 116; *Irish World*, Jan. 24, 1880; O'Daly, *Life*, [73]; RELA, MB, Sept. 19, 1901.

17. On West Cork, see Joseph Lee, *Modernisation*, p. 58; Donnelly, *Land and People*; Rumpf and Hepburn, *Nationalism and Socialism*, p. 44; Riobard O'Dwyer, *My Ancestors*, pp. 118, 241; Miller, *Emigrants*, pp. 427–44. *Irish World*, Nov. 22, 1879. Martin Hogan to Thomas F. Meagher, June 21, 1866; Hogan to Andrew O'Connell, Sept. 17, 1866, Hogan Papers. See, too, Andrew O'Connell Papers. Bureau of Census, *MS Census*, 1870. O'Daly, *Life*, [146–47].

18. Davitt, *Fall of Feudalism*, p. 128; O'Daly, *Life*, [34]; *Irish World*, Sept. 9, 1882; see also Jan. 7, 1882; Emmet Associates, MB, Oct. 29, 1882; Membership Ledger, 1883–85, MB, passim.

19. RELA, MB, June 8, 1883; Aug. 5, 1886; AOH in America, *Constitution*, 1886; Funchion, *Organizations*, p. 51.

20. RELA, MB, Mar. 30, June 22, 1883; Mar. 6, 1884; Apr. 7, 1887; Jan. 19, 1888. Charles O'Reilly to Andrew O'Connell, Feb. 21, 1888, O'Connell Papers; *Butte Mining Journal*, Feb. 25, 1888; O'Daly, *Life*, [38].

21. For RELA contributions to these and other causes, see RELA, MB, Dec. 15, 1882; Oct. 19, Nov. 16, 1883; Sept. 15, Dec. 28, 1892; Sept 3, 1896; Apr. 29, 1897; Mar. 16, 1899; Oct. 8, 1903; Nov. 10, 1904; Nov. 10, 1904; Jan. 26, July 13, 20, 1905; Jan. 4, 1906; June 25, 1908; Nov. 11, 1909; Jan. 27, May 26, June 23, Nov. 17, 1910; Jan. 5, 1911. For special calls see, for example, RELA, Term Reports, Dec. 31, 1899; Apr. 30, 1901; Aug. 31, 1906; MB, Feb. 11, 1904.

For money available in the revolutionary and contingency funds see MB, Dec. 31, 1883; May 26, 1910; Term Reports, Aug. 31, 1900; Aug. 31, 1906.

22. *Butte Mining Journal,* July 7, 1888.

23. On Plan of Campaign, see Miller, *Emigrants,* pp. 444–45; RELA payments to Parnell Fund, Sept. 3, 1885, in Membership and Dues Ledger, 1885–87; Polk, *City Directory,* 1885–86.

24. RELA, MB, Oct. 24, 31, Nov. 14, 1895; Polk, *City Directory,* 1895.

25. Irish Volunteers of America, Co. A, Membership Roll Call, Nov. 4, 1897; Irish Volunteers, Membership Ledger, 1909; Polk, *City Directory,* 1897, 1898, 1909, 1910.

26. AOH, MB, Sept. 21, Nov. 18, 1885; Mar. 3, 1893; Oct. 30, Nov. 13, 1895; June 16, 1897; July 13, 1905; AOH to John O'Rourke, Dec. 7, 1912, Correspondence; AOH in America, Bulletin # 2, n.d., 1926; Davitt, *Fall of Feudalism,* p. 42; see too Pollard, *Societies of Ireland,* pp. 99, 110, 115.

27. AOH, Proceedings, 1910, n.p.; Proceedings, 1906, n.p. Pollard, *Societies of Ireland,* pp. 116–17; O'Dea, *AOH,* III:1355–56, 1405, 1422, 1431. AOH D1, MB, Apr. 13, June 1, 1898; D3, MB, June 24, 1907. Ferns's occupation is listed in Polk, *City Directory,* 1907.

28. AOH D3, MB, July 15, 1907; RELA, MB, Nov. 16, 1905; July 9, 1906; AOH, Membership and Dues Ledgers, Sept. 6, 1900–Oct. 30, 1901.

29. AOH, Membership and Dues Ledgers, Apr., 1882–Mar., 1887 and 1899–92; RELA, Membership and Dues Ledgers, May, 1887–Apr. 1895 and 1899–1903. Polk, *City Directory,* 1900.

30. The reference to Deeney joining the "Papists" is from RELA, MB, Apr. 8, 1897. AOH and RELA, Membership and Dues Ledgers, passim.

31. Funchion, *Organizations,* p. 57; RELA, MB, Sept. 12, 1901; Term Report, Aug. 31, 1904; Sunburst Club, MB, Sept. 18, 1897; Apr. 6, 1899; RELA, MB, Aug. 8, 1901.

32. AOH D1, MB, Apr. 9, 1891. Polk, *City Directory,* 1901.

33. RELA, MB, June 3, 1886. Finerty's remarks are from the *Anaconda Standard,* July 5, 1905; Davitt, *Fall of Feudalism,* p. 252.

34. RELA, MB, Dec. 4, 7, 1883; Jan. 18, 1884. In 1886 John Devoy, the head of the Clan-na-Gael, interviewed Louis Riel, the leader of the Metis in Alberta, 200 miles north of Butte. Riel was in open rebellion against Canadian authorities (*Post Bag,* II:278).

35. RELA, MB, Mar. 6, 1884; Dec. 27, 1900; Apr. 19, 1901; Ritual of Initiation, n.d., n.p.; Polk, *City Directory,* 1885–86, 1900, 1901.

36. RELA, MB, Oct. 27, 1910; Sept. 15, 1910; AOH D3, MB, Apr. 6, 1908; O'Daly, Life, [38]. Heaney's remarks are from RELA, MB, Nov. 5, 1914; Lynch's from MB, June 10, 1915.

37. *Anaconda Standard,* July 5, 1905; RELA, MB, Mar. 5, 1908.

38. RELA, MB, Dec. 2, 1886; Jan. 29, 1891; Aug. 2, 1894; Irish Volunteers, *Pledge,* n.d. [ca. 1906]. The Orange and the Green remark is from RELA, MB, Feb. 11, 1897.

39. John P. Scanlon to RELA, May 1, 1906, Correspondence; RELA, MB, June 28, 1906. On Drohan, see RELA, Membership and Dues Ledgers, 1902–

25. He transferred to the RELA from Camp 40, District 4, in May, 1906. Polk, *City Directory*, 1906–12.

40. RELA, Day Book, Apr. 25, 1901–Aug. 16, 1917. For Drohan's activities see Irish Volunteers, MB, Dec. 22, 1907; May 9, Dec. 8, 1912. The battle cry, with emphasis in the original, is from MB, Aug. 29, 1907. For Deeney's warning and continued marching, see MB, Feb. 9, 1908; June 6, Sept. 5, 1907; Jan. 30, Mar. 5, Apr. 16, 1908. Leary's complaint is from RELA, MB, Dec. 5, 1907.

41. AOH, Constitution, 1886, n.p.; AOH, *Ritual and Manual, 1901*; AOH D1, MB, May 26, 1899; RELA, MB, Oct. 14, 1886; Polk, *City Directory*, 1889; *Examiner* (Butte), May 18, June 29, Oct. 5, Dec. 21, 1895; Jan. 16, 1896.

42. AOH D1, MB, July 6, 1898; AOH, Proceedings, 1906, n.p.; Proceedings, 1910, n.p. For O'Meara and the number of handsome ladies see AOH D1, MB, Feb. 19, 1896; AOH D3, MB, Nov. 30, 1908.

43. *Butte Intermountain*, semiweekly edition, Sept. 26, Oct. 3, 7, 10, 17, 1888; RELA, MB, Dec. 29, 1898; Nov. 12, 1903; Oct. 3, 1901. For patriotic songs, MB, Mar. 27, 1884; Nov. 23, 1899. The agenda changed by MB, Oct. 9, 1890; the martyrs were highlighted by MB, Feb. 25, 1897; the flag for Charles Kickham references was in MB, Oct. 22, 1882.

44. Miller, *Emigrants*, pp. 103, 143; RELA, MB, May 16, 1898; Mar. 16, 1899.

45. RELA, MB, Sept. 5, 1901; Mar. 19, 1908; O'Daly, *Life*, [130].

46. RELA, MB, Sept. 5, 1907; AOH D3, Dec. 10, 1906; RELA, MB, Aug. 1, 1901. See for evidence that the patriots did not encourage emigration, see Schrier, *Ireland*, p. 59. See also O'Daly, *Life*, [205]; *Butte Independent*, Jan. 22, Feb. 12, Oct. 1, 15, 1910.

47. RELA, MB, Aug. 28, 1890; Oct. 19, 1899; Jan. 19, 1899; Sept. 17, 1914.

48. RELA, MB, Nov. 15, 1900; Jan. 24, 1901; June 27, 1901; Joseph Lee, *Modernisation*, pp. 14–20.

49. RELA, MB, Aug. 26, 1909; Oct. 4, 1905; Apr. 23, 1903; Nov. 5, 1903. Lynch even told the RELA that the Liberal budget of 1909 would raise Irish taxes and force more Irish to emigrate (Dec. 2, 1909).

50. Material on Lynch is taken from Frank Quinn's very thorough obituary, written upon Lynch's death in 1961. *Montana Standard-Post* (Butte), Sept. 28, 1961. Polk, *City Directory*, 1895; AOH D1, MB, Feb. 28, 1894; RELA, MB, Feb. 14, 21, 1895.

51. Quinn, *Montana Standard-Post*, Sept. 28, 1961; AOH and RELA, Membership and Dues Ledgers. (Lynch was #13 in the RELA). His name and/or number appear repeatedly in both AOH and RELA Minute Books. He was a frequent speaker at meetings and held almost every office the organizations had. For examples, see Irish Volunteers, MB, Dec. 22, 1907; AOH, Proceedings, 1906; *Butte Independent*, Jan. 22, Nov. 12, 1910; Jan. 14, 1911; Riobard O'Dwyer, *My Ancestors*, p. 112; RELA, MB, Oct. 24, 1895; Apr. 16, 1908; Oct. 10, 1908; July 11, 1912; AOH D1, MB, Jan. 13, 1895, Aug. 31, 1904; Jan. 11, 1905. For meetings in his courtroom, see RELA, MB, Apr. 13, 1911; Feb. 21, 1918; Dec. 22, 1919; Committee on Sale of Irish Bonds to AOH, Nov. 26, 1919, Correspondence.

52. Quinn, *Montana Standard-Post*, Sept. 28, 1961.

53. *Butte Independent*, Nov. 12, 1910.

54. AOH D3, MB, Jan. 18, 1909; Prof. M. G. Rohan to AOH D1, Aug. 19, 1911, Correspondence; AOH D3, MB, Dec. 24, 1910; see also Nov. 29, 1910; AOH, Proceedings, 1906 and 1910, IrC; O'Dea, *AOH*, III:1390. O'Daly says that many wanted Irish history taught in those public schools with large numbers of Irish students, but generally the demand was for Irish history in the Catholic schools only (Life, [33]).

55. RELA, MB, Feb. 5, 1891; July 31, 1902; AOH, Proceedings, 1906 and 1910; AOH, Silver Bow Co. Board, MB, Nov. 16, 1910.

56. O'Dea, *AOH*, III:1055–58, 1067–73, 1079–80; Pollard, *Societies of Ireland*, p. 113; AOH D3, MB, June 17, 1907.

57. RELA, MB, July 31, 1902; Jan. 7, 1904; Sept. 14, 1905; May 9, 1907; Mar. 26, 1908; July 1, 1909; Sept. 26, 1907; AOH D1, MB, July 30, Aug. 27, 1902; D3, MB, Aug. 7, Sept. 8, 1902; AOH D1, MB, Nov. 18, 1903; Feb. 3, June 22, Sept. 21, Nov. 30, 1904.

58. On the Americanist clergy generally, see Cross, *Emergence of Liberal Catholicism*, and "The Irish," pp. 176–97; Hennessy, *American Catholics*, pp. 196–205, 216–17. Carroll was strongly identified with the Americanists. See, e.g., M. J. Kirby to Carroll, Nov. 12, 1904, Carroll Papers. AOH D1, MB, May 3, 1905; O'Daly, Life, [33]; Polk, *City Directory*, 1901 and 1905.

59. AOH D3, MB, Oct. 23, 1905; Feb. 12, 1906; June 24, Sept. 16, 1907; "Official Statement" of John Cardinal Gibbons, signed by Bishop John Carroll, Apr. 3, 1911, Correspondence; O'Dea, *AOH*, III:1434–35, 1448–50.

60. AOH D1, MB, Feb. 12, 1906; AOH D3, MB, Oct. 7, 14, 1907; June 10, 1907. O'Meara later said the demand for Irish history was "rash" (D3, MB, Oct. 14, 1907). AOH D3, MB, July 23, 1910; Nov. 4, 1911. Hannan's chairmanship of the committee is noted in O'Dea, *AOH*, III:1414.

61. AOH D1, MB, Dec. 24, 1910.

62. AOH D3, MB, Apr. 6, 1908; May 14, 1906; Nov. 4, 1907; Apr. 3, 1911; Bureau of Census, *MS Census*, 1900 and 1910. On names and their significance* see Genovese, *Roll, Jordan, Roll*, pp. 446–50. Curiously, in view of the heightened sense of cultural nationalism at this time, few Butte Irish gave their sons "Irish" forenames, whether defined politically or culturally. There were, for example, only a scattering of "Emmets" in the *Manuscript Census* and fewer still "Diarmiads" or "Tiernans." The use of *O'* and *Mc* had not always been an issue. If the records of the Irish associations are any indication, the patronymics were routinely dropped; James Neary, for example, was proposed for admission to the RELA. By the time of his initiation he was James McNeary, he was Neary again by the time his first dues were collected. The AOH was as casual; O'Leary and Leary alternated, so did Farrell and O'Farrell. The alphabetical lists of both organizations were totally unpredictable, the *O*s as often as not being listed under the letter of the root surname. AOH D3, MB, Nov. 4, 1907; RELA, MB, Mar. 15, 22, 29, 1888; AOH and RELA, Membership and Dues Ledgers. See on this last point McLysaght, *Irish Families*, pp. 14–21.

63. RELA, Membership and Dues Ledgers, 1902–25; Riobard O'Dwyer, *My Ancestors*, p. 82; O'Sullivan interview. AOH D3, MB, Nov. 4, 1907; Apr. 6, 1908; Nov. 5, 1910.

64. For other aspects of Butte's Gaelic revival, see RELA, MB, June 22, 1905; Jan. 17, July 25, Aug. 15, 1907; Apr. 29, 1909; AOH D3, MB, Dec. 23, 1907; James Connolly to AOH D1, Oct. 21, 1910, Correspondence; O'Dea, *AOH*, III:1194–96 The "language of Oisin" remark is from RELA, MB, Sept. 5, 1907; Concannon to AOH D3, in MB, Apr. 2, 1906. That the substitution of English for Gaelic Irish did not mean that the Irish were really anglicized is noted in Joseph Lee, *Modernisation*, pp. 137–39; Lyons, *Culture and Anarchy*, pp. 40, 47; Miller, *Emigrants*, pp. 426–29, 470–74.

65. RELA, MB, Oct. 31, 1895; AOH D1, MB, Sept. 25, 1901. On Hyde's visit see RELA, MB, Aug. 31, Oct. 26, 1905; Mar. 8, 15, 1906; AOH D1, MB, Oct. 25, 1905; Feb. 14, 1906; AOH D3, MB, Dec. 18, 1905; Mar. 26, 1906. The figure of $2,212 is from P. J. Brophy to J. J. O'Meara, May 31, 1906, and Brophy to John Quinn, May 24, 1906, Brophy Papers. O'Daly, *Life*, [209]. RELA, MB, May 28, 1908; Apr. 1, 8, Aug. 5, 1909; Mar. 10, 24, 1910; AOH D3, MB, Apr. 5, 1909; *Butte Independent*, July 9, 1910. The occasional contributions are from RELA, MB, Aug. 7, 21, 1908; Mar. 23, 1905; May 24, 1906; Apr. 18, Oct. 17, 1907; July 17, 1913. Hyde acknowledged Butte's generosity with personal letters of thanks—written in English. See RELA, MB, Oct. 15, 1908; Hyde to James J. McCarthy, Dec. 13, 1913; to AOH D3, Dec. 6, 1913, Correspondence. Fr. Patrick Brosnan to his mother, Nov. 20, 1917, Brosnan Letters.

66. AOH D3, MB, May 14, 1906; RELA, MB, Aug. 29, 1901.

67. RELA, MB, Nov. 16, 1890.

68. Ibid., June 19, July 3, 1902.

69. O'Daly, *Life*, [11, 100, 222]. His reference to Breen's "socialism" is from AOH D1, MB, Nov. 18, 1907.

70. Miller, *Illustrated History*, pp. 714–15; Polk, *City Directory*, 1888–1912.

71. AOH D1 and RELA, Membership and Dues Ledgers, 1882–ca. 1896, and MB, 1882–ca. 1900; *Butte Bystander*, Mar. 11, 1893; Polk, *City Directory*, 1892 lists Brophy as an AOH officer. The "economic fanatic" charge came from Lowndes Maury in testimony to the Industrial Commission, *Mining at Butte*, 1915, p. 3803. O'Meara's remarks are from AOH D1, MB, Apr. 14, 1903. Brophy's resignation from the Meagher committee is from AOH D1, MB, July 29, 1903; Brophy to J. J. Lynch, Mar. 31, 1904, Brophy Papers.

72. For the Irish-American Club, see Polk, *City Directory*, 1893; for the Knights of Columbus, see Brophy to John Helehan, May 18, 1899; for the Gaelic League, Brophy to J. J. O'Meara, May 31, 1906; for the United Irish League, Brophy to John J. Finerty, Sept. 24, 1902; to John J. O'Callaghan, National Secretary, UIL, June 20, 1903; to C. P. Connolly, Apr. 9, 1903, Brophy Papers. The UIL is discussed in Funchion, *Organizations*, pp. 272–76. RELA, "Resolution of Condolence for Dan. J. Hannifan," in MB, Mar. 24, 1904. Lynch's remark is from RELA, MB, Apr. 23, 1903.

73. RELA, MB, May 28, 1903; AOH D1, MB, June 8, 1904; RELA, MB, Apr. 23, 30, 1903; Apr. 20, May 18, 1905. For RELA attacks on disunity, see MB Aug. 8, 1889; Oct. 9, 1899; Dec. 27, 1900; Oct. 13, 1904; Sept. 23, 1908.

74. Brophy to J. J. Kelly, Apr. 1, 1903; my emphasis. Brophy to Heinze, June 6, 19, 1903; to Joseph Devlin, M.P., May 26, 1903; to C. P. Connolly, Apr. 9,

1903; to John J. O'Callaghan, June 20, 1903, Brophy Papers. See also O'Daly, Life, [209].

75. Brophy to Joseph Devlin, July 18, 1905; to John J. O'Callaghan, May 9 and 21, 1904; June 20, 1903; to Conor O'Kelly, Sept. 1, 1904; to Connolly, Apr. 9, 1903, Brophy Papers.

76. Brophy to T. B. Fitzpatrick, Dec. 12, 1912; to James Hennessy Murphy, Dec. 31, 1912, Brophy Papers; my emphasis.

77. Foner, "Land League," pp. 186–88; Rumpf and Hepburn, *Nationalism and Socialism*, pp. 9, 15–16; Joseph Lee, *Modernisation*, pp. 91, 121; Kennedy, *The Irish*, pp. 36–38; Dennis Clark, *Irish in Philadelphia*, p. 112; O'Dea, *AOH*, III:1106–8; Connell, "Catholicism and Marriage," pp. 120–22; Boyce, Scrapbooks, Boyce Papers; WFM Exec. Board, MB, June 10, 1902; Dec. 10, 1904; AOH D3, MB, Sept. 16, 1907.

78. RELA, MB, Mar. 4, July 29, 1909; Jan. 6, 1910; Aug. 29, 1912. See also *Butte Independent*, Mar. 12, 1910. Kelly's remarks are from RELA, MB, June 25, 1896. The RELA "boycott" of McFadden and Sheehy is from MB, Sept. 15, 1898. See also on this affair AOH D1, MB, Aug. 25, 1897; Sept. 7, 1898; O'Daly, Life, [130, 188–89, 207–8]. For Breen see AOH D3, MB, May 28, 1906; Oct. 28, 1911; Oct. 28, 1907.

79. AOH D3, MB, Mar. 8, 1913; "Last Will and Testament of Rev. Michael J. Hannan," n.d., 1927, M. J. Hannan File; "History of St. Mary's." Father Sarsfield O'Sullivan related the story of Hannan's fight with Barry (interview). AOH and RELA, Membership and Dues Ledgers; Irish Volunteers, MB, Mar. 29, Apr. 12, 1914; see too RELA, MB, Mar. 26, 1908.

80. Parnell's comment is from Pollard, *Societies of Ireland*, p. 77. Devoy, *Post Bag*, I:52.

81. For the Russian "alliance," see Pollard, *Societies of Ireland*, p. 47; O'Dea, *AOH*, II:914–15; Devoy, *Post Bag*, I:209–12, 358–59; Devoy, *Recollections*, p. 330. For the Zulu and Afghan wars, see Thomas N. Brown, *Irish-American Nationalism*, p. 87; Devoy, *Post Bag*, I:392, 398, 408–11; *Irish World*, Aug. 23, 1879. For Belize, the Yucatan, and the Egyptian Mahdi, see Devoy, *Post Bag*, I:352; Devoy, *Recollections*, p. 345.

82. Pollard, *Societies of Ireland*, p. 98; Devoy, *Recollections*, p. 400; Devoy, *Post Bag*, II:272, 341; Tansill, *America and the Fight*, pp. 113–20; Alan J. Ward, *Ireland*, pp. 31–38; RELA, MB, June 28, 1900. Deeney's remark is from MB, Oct. 1, 1896. The rifles were ordered and congratulations sent to the Transvaal on Aug. 27, 1897 (MB).

83. RELA, MB, Dec. 14, 1899; July 19, 1900.

84. RELA, MB, Dec. 21, 1899; Dec. 27, 1900; see too Apr. 26, 1900, when D. J. Hennessy expressed his hope that the number of Irish-Americans fighting for the Boers in South Africa would grow. *Anaconda Standard*, Nov. 23, 24, 1900; *Butte Intermountain*, Dec. 27, 1900.

85. RELA, MB, Feb. 8, 15, 1900; Apr. 12, 1900; AOH D1, MB, Mar. 21, 1900. Occupations are from Polk, *City Directory*, 1900. Totals collected and the fact that both the RELA and the Butte AOH led the nation in money collected are

from O'Dea, *AOH*, III:1224; RELA, MB, Jan. 11; Feb. 22; Mar. 15, Apr. 26, 1900; Jan. 31, 1901; AOH D1, MB, Jan. 24, Feb. 7, 1900.

86. RELA, MB, Nov. 22, 1900; Dec. 11, 1902; AOH D1, MB, Feb. 27, 1901. The RELA call for sympathy for the Boers is from MB, Sept. 28, 1899; see too MB, Jan. 9, 1899. AOH sympathy was noted in MB, Dec. 20, 1899. The petitions and the parties for Joubert and O'Donnell are from RELA, MB, Oct. 3, 1901; Jan. 2, Dec. 11, 1902; Feb. 11, 18, 1904; AOH D1, MB, Jan. 2, 1902. *Montana Catholic* (Butte), Sept. 30, 1899; Jan. 6, 1900; see too Nov. 4 and 11, 1899. The lifting of anti-Catholic laws is from Mar. 3, 1900; Deeney's comment is from RELA, MB, Dec. 14, 1899.

87. O'Daly mentions Davitt's resignation in Life, [22]. See Davitt, *Fall of Feudalism*, p. 109. Parnell's hostility is noted in O'Brien, *Parnell*, I:130–31, 133. The Dillon story is from RELA, MB, Apr. 21, 1898. See also Lyons, *John Dillon*, p. 186. The RELA did not like Dillon anyway; his conservatism angered them. See RELA, MB, Nov. 6 and 13, 1890.

88. Boyce's comments are in WFM, *Proceedings, 1902*, p. 11; see too *Miners Magazine*, July, 1902, and *Labor World* (Butte), June 2, 1902. McConnell's opposition is from *Labor World*, May 26, 1902. John Fox's remarks are from RELA, MB, Sept. 5, 1901; RELA, Membership and Dues Ledger, 1899–1903. Polk, *City Directory*, 1901. The results of the debate are in RELA, MB, Jan. 26, 1899.

CHAPTER 10

Irishtown at War: The German Alliance and Worker Protest, 1900–1918

I

Butte's Irish began their flirtation with the city's Germans in 1900. RELA member Michael McGowan told the Emmets that a "union of the Irish and the German element" should be a natural consequence of German hostility to British policy in South Africa. The alliance would also acknowledge, though McGowan probably did not know it, the active involvement of German linguists in saving the Irish language, something the Gaelic League had already noted. The courtship was begun, however, because it appeared to Irish patriots that Germany would be England's next great rival and the most formidable since France in the late 1790s. In making this judgment they were ahead of many in the U.S. Department of State, though it must be admitted that the hope, in this instance, gave birth to the prophecy.[1]

The "German element" in Butte was not particularly large. There were 901 first-generation Germans in the city in 1900, and that number actually shrank to 858 in 1910 and to 607 in 1920. Nor was it likely that Irish miners would meet them at work. In 1911, there were only sixty-four immigrant Germans and ninety-nine of the second generation working in Anaconda Company mines. But this was an active and ethnically self-conscious group of immigrants. They had a Liederkranz by 1881, an athletic Turnverein by 1886, an Order of Hermann Sohns and Sisters of Hermann Sohns by 1898.[2]

As with the anti-Catholic Boers, consorting with some of Butte's Germans did involve the abandonment of other principles to the greater cause of Ireland. Simon Hauswirth, one of the officers of the Turnverein, was also an active member of the APA and the proprietor of the Columbia Saloon, advertised as the "headquarters for APAs and all other loyal Americans." Hauswirth's indiscretions were either forgotten or thought insignificant, and in 1907 Jeremiah Lynch reported with considerable enthusiasm "on the alliance between the German societies and the . . . various Irish societies in this County."[3]

By 1908, when the national AOH sanctioned the tactic, these alliances throughout the U.S. involved "6,000 organized bodies with 1,250,000 members." By 1912, the AOH made public its approval of the "display of the Irish flag on German holidays." The alliance, the national AOH concluded, was a "master stroke in Irish affairs." The Butte AOH agreed, officially endorsing the action of its national leaders at the same convention in which it demanded the "complete and absolute independence" of Ireland. As for the Clan-na-Gael, it had begun formal and secret "diplomatic" correspondence with Germany as early as 1911.[4]

The *Butte Independent*, unofficial organ of the Irish associations, was equally enthusiastic about the Irish-German connection. The "Brits," according to Mulcahy's paper, were alarmed by the alliance and determined to break it up if they could. But the *Independent* went beyond the embrace of ad hoc political deals to suggest the intermarriage of the Irish and the Germans. After all, both peoples were of "pioneer stock"; the children of their unions would be "sturdy" and, most of them at least, Catholic. But of greater significance, since England was the "common enemy, . . . when the Kaiser is ready for the annexation of that little island, . . . the Teuton and the Celt will be joined in seeing it happen."[5]

It did not appear they would have long to wait. In 1909 Lynch informed an excited RELA that the "consensus of . . . keen observers" in Europe was that "war between England and Germany was imminent." Two years later, the judge told the Emmets to "buy rifles and drill." It was time to fight, though not necessarily on the side of the Germans. The war Lynch was then predicting would be between France and Germany and the Irish would not take sides until England "had shown her hand." But whatever side the English chose, the Irish and Irish-Americans had nothing to fear if England's navy was "as rotten as her army proved to be in South Africa."[6]

As important to Irish-America as cultivating friendly relations with the Germans was preventing the United States from negating the good work by moving toward better if not entirely amicable relations with Great Britain. Irish-Americans had benefited enormously from the rivalries between the U.S. and England; this was a feud that they could not afford to see mended. In fact, it occurred to many Irishmen that other nations—Cuba might immediately have come to mind—owed their freedom to an American war against what the AOH called "tottering empires" who "enslaved weaker people." The happy prospect of Rough Riders—most of them Irish—charging up, say, Hungry Hill would be forever crushed if England and the United States were to join in an accord of English-speaking and Protestant nations.[7]

To prevent this and keep alive the dream of U.S. aid in the liberation of Ireland, the Irish organizations consistently opposed any arbitration treaties between the U.S. and Britain. In Montana, the RELA led the effort. In the late 1890s, the Emmets petitioned the Montana congressional delegation to "vote against the arbitration treaties in the name of the Irish of Montana." They were pleased to note, without taking credit for it, that Montana's senators—William Andrews Clark was one of them—had both voted no on the proposed treaties. The question arose again in 1905. This time, the AOH joined in the protest. Division 3 "to a man" opposed any "secret treaty between America and England," and the three divisions joined the RELA in calling a "monster meeting" to urge Montana senators to vote against arbitration. In 1907 the Hibernians began what would be for the next few years an annual celebration of George Washington's birthday. Held in Miners' Union Hall, they feted Washington as the father not only of the country but of that wise and durable guide to diplomatic conduct, no entangling alliances.[8]

Four years later, when the Anglophilic administration of William Howard Taft reintroduced the idea of arbitration, the AOH's national board responded with uncharacteristic force. The board issued an "emphatic protest" against any American alliance with England "whether for 'peace' purposes" or to help England recover what the AOH presumed would be a number of lost colonies. The Butte AOH divisions, again in league with the RELA, led their own protest. A meeting, with a "delegation of Germans" in attendance, was held in Judge Lynch's courtroom to plan a "mass meeting against the Anglo-American alliance." The two Irish organizations spent $40.00 publicizing the meeting, including one well-placed advertisement in the *Montana Staats Zeitung.* [9]

As the tensions between Germany and Great Britain grew, Irish-Americans became more determined to prevent any Anglo-American rapprochement. By their accounting the only thing worse than no war between England and Germany would be a war in which the United States fought as England's ally. In February, 1914, the national headquarters of the Clan-na-Gael passed a secret resolution calling on all the local camps to form branches of what it called the American Continental League. The local branches should assume "appropriate titles"; the Clan suggested George Washington, Thomas Jefferson, U. S. Grant, Nathan Hale, and Andrew Jackson, among other conspicuous and distinctly non-Irish American patriots. Once formed, the local branches, using the "utmost care and secrecy" and enlisting as many "native Americans and Germans" as they could, were to collect signatures on the Clan resolutions and send them to their congressional delegations. The RELA chose Andrew Jackson as its "patron" and under that banner resolved to oppose anything that might compromise "strict American neturality." The resolutions went on to oppose the proposed $7,000,000 appropriation to celebrate one hundred years of peace with England, substituting instead a nationwide celebration of the Battle of New Orleans.[10]

It would have been out of character for Butte's Irish organizations, particularly the RELA, to limit their involvement to covert operations like the American Continental League. By 1913, Butte's newspapers were filled with news of approaching hostilities in Europe, and the minutes of the meetings of the RELA make clear that that news was greeted with absolute elation. The RELA had to help insure that the Irish Republican Brotherhood in Ireland and its Irish-American counterpart, the Clan-na-Gael, were prepared to take full advantage of the growing hostility between England and Germany. This meant that money had to be raised, in this instance for what the Clan called the emergency fund. The fund, John Devoy wrote the RELA in May, 1913, was making "splendid progress," owing in no small measure to "the good work your D. is doing." Six months and one more contribution later, Devoy was more effusive, thanking the Emmets "most heartily . . . for your more than generous contribution to the Emergency Fund. The generosity of the Irishmen of Butte is proverbial, and [this contribution] gives proof that the hearts of the men of our race in your city are as large as ever."[11]

But the RELA did more than just give money. Specifically—and predictably—they rearmed themselves as Irish Volunteers. Company A was back in operation as early as May, 1912. As before in 1907–8, Maurice Drohan was the company captain. He had lost none of his zeal. Members were instructed to "act like gentlemen . . . and to respect their superior officers." His "quartermaster" reported on the "guns in his care," and Drohan ordered "target practice and drill at the armory." By early 1913, he had more than sixty men under his command; marching and drilling exercises routinely attracted forty to fifty of those—all whose shift schedules permitted their attendance.[12]

Late in 1912 Drohan had good news for the men of Company A. He was "able to give a favorable report relative to the Rifles which are to be sent here from the East." Three months later, James J. McCarthy, an IV officer, heard from national Clan headquarters of "excellent prospect of getting some rifles (about 40) for the military co. attached to your D." Three weeks later two cases of repeating rifles, "billed as hardware," were sent from Boston and delivered to McCarthy's Butte address. This brought the total number of rifles to eighty-one, enough, Drohan told the RELA, to take the company "out in the hills for practice during the summer." He urged the Emmets "to acquaint themselves with military tactics and be practical soldiers of Ireland." (This completed the list: They were now "practical" Catholics, "practical" miners, "practical" patriots, and "practical" soldiers of Ireland.) A full "encampment" was held, and the target practice scores, many of them signed in Irish, were recorded in the IV Membership Ledger. Drohan took his men on maneuvers again in 1914, by which time there were two companies and Drohan needed more rifles.[13]

In November, 1913, the Irish formed their own version of the Irish Volunteers under the leadership of the moderate nationalist, Eoin MacNeill, with the not-always-welcome assistance of the rather less moderate The O'Rahilly. This Irish organization arose in response to the arming of Northern Irish Protestant opponents of Irish Home Rule. Calling themselves the Ulster Volunteers, these Protestant paramilitaries were a threat not only to the peace of Ireland but to the prospects for even a measure of Irish independence. The Butte Irish were obviously aware of the Ulster Volunteers. By 1913, however, the RELA was concentrating exclusively on the German alliance and on the war which they saw as inevitable between Germany and England. Remarkably for a people as aware as they, the Emmets made no reference to Edward Carson or any of the other Protestant opponents of Home Rule. They did offer their services to President Wilson in "any war with Mexico," an offer that appeased both nativists, suspicious of Irish-American patriotism, and the Catholic hierarchy, outraged by the anticlericalism of the Mexican Revolution. But with that exception, the IVs made no effort to conceal the fact that they were marching for Ireland and, should it come to that, for Germany.[14]

Perhaps this was owing to their growing belief that when the war came it would bring not Home Rule but a fully independent Ireland, and that the Irish Volunteers in Ireland, regardless of their motive for forming themselves, would play a significant role in that independence. Whatever their thinking—and the possibility that they were not thinking at all cannot be ruled out—the Emmets were typically generous in their support to the Irish Volunteers. In February, 1914, they voted to send $100.00 for "arming the Irish Volunteers in Ireland." This was followed by a $265.00 loan. In July of that same year they sent another $100.00, following that with a loan of $120.00 more. All of this, of course, occurred in the midst of the destruction of the BMU and the presence of the National Guard—what Drohan referred to as the "war in Butte."[15]

The O'Rahilly and MacNeill were suitably grateful, though the former, in his letter of appreciation, acknowledged a troublesome presence. In March, 1914, he wrote to James J. McCarthy and thanked the RELA for its "princely subscription." Enlisting and arming IV recruits was "prodigiously expensive." Unfortunately, "the timidity of our wealthier classes in Ireland is a great handicap. In these circumstances," he went on, "you can imagine how we welcome your communication from far away Butte." It was important that the Emmets be reminded just how far away Butte was, but more important still to be made to understand that Ireland had to fight for economic justice as well as political freedom. Many of the Irish nationalists were growing increasingly radical on this second object, accounting for what The O'Rahilly called "the apathy of a section of our countrymen," and for the fact that "not a half dozen men in Ireland . . . had spirit enough" to contribute as the RELA had in "providing our Country with an army." MacNeill was less revealing in his expression of gratitude, perhaps because he did not share The O'Rahilly's idea that the IVs were "our Country's army" or, more significantly, his idea that "our Country" had to pay some attention to social classes and the needs of the Irish poor. Still MacNeill extended his "sincere thanks to the members of the RELA . . . for their patriotism and active cooperation."[16]

Four months after the O'Rahilly letter the long-awaited war began and the Irish of Butte got a better idea of what patriotism and active cooperation might mean. A bare two days after England's declaration of war, Jeremiah Lynch told the RELA that the freedom of Ireland was "now at hand." He did not mean the Home Rule Bill of 1914, the implementation of which was suspended for the duration of the war. He was referring to a truly independent and united Irish Republic. So was Father James English, the Irish-born pastor at St. Mary's, who told a St. Patrick's Day audience in 1915 that the Irish had brought the faith to Germany and now he "hoped that the sons of imperial Germany, under the eagle of the Fatherland, will soon be in a position to help restore to Ireland that precious boon of freedom and independence."[17]

Father English was not arguing that German armies would liberate Ireland; only the Irish could win Ireland's freedom. But Germany's war with England would provide the necessary cover for an Irish rebellion. According to Hugh O'Daly, Butte Irishmen made an immediate connection between Germany's war against England and an Irish rising. He remembered that when the war began "all the Irish societies . . . collected money to buy guns for Ireland's republican army." Daly solicited money "from everyone I could approach." Some of it he sent to his "brother Father James [Daly] so as to arm the men of Clogher." RELA Minute Books tell the same story. On August 20, 1914, less than three weeks after hostilities had begun, the national Clan-na-Gael instructed the RELA to "send all the money in the treasury"; the Emmets sent $1,000.00. Two weeks later another communication from national headquarters ordered the RELA to "remit all available funds toward the cause for which this organization was established, viz. the freedom of Ireland." The RELA sent $500.00 more.[18]

As the war progressed, demands on the RELA treasury increased. In August, 1915, Clan headquarters issued a special call to which the Emmets responded with $500.00. Two weeks later, the RELA formed a twenty-one-man committee to "collect funds for to arm the men of Ireland." J. J. Lynch, probably a member of the committee, warned that "now or never is the time to contribute generously to the cause of freedom. . . . We must provide our brothers at home with the sinews of war." This was six months before the Easter Rising and the proclamation of the independent Irish Republic. That same September, the Defense of Ireland Fund was begun by the Cumann-na-mBan, an Irish women's organizaton. The money would "enable the Irish people to defend their homes, their rights, their liberties, and their persons now menaced by a foreign government"—by which the Cumann most assuredly did not mean Germany.[19]

In Butte, the Ladies Auxiliary of the AOH was involved in the fund, but the Hibernians themselves played no official part in raising money. That responsibility fell to a willing RELA. On September 8, the Emmets sent $500.00; on October 26 they sent $500.00 more. In November they sent $1,500.00. The Thirty-fifth Annual RELA New Year's Eve Gala Ball was renamed the Defense of Ireland Ball. Five hundred dollars was collected. In 1916 the pace slowed slightly; the RELA sent $750.00, all of it brought in after the Rising on April 24, for the Defense of Ireland fund. For reasons unexplained, these RELA contributions could not be publicly acknowledged in the *Gaelic American*, the official Clan newspaper, but the Emmets could take comfort in knowing that their generosity had brought Ireland "closer to its freedom."[20]

Only a victory by the Germans—"our friends across the sea," Lynch called them—could insure that freedom. It is a measure of Irish-American Anglophobia that they never seemed to have considered the possibility of Irish freedom arising from English weariness or even from an unexpected fit of English conscience. England was an "accursed" enemy, one that never tired; and certainly, as Lynch put it, one that "never showed us much leniency." Lynch was jubilant as news of German victories came in. German submarines, he told the RELA, were a dominant force, and, forgetting for the moment the Irish Catholics in the British Navy, a "few more of the English navy will see the bottom in a short time." According to an RELA recording secretary, Lynch "extolled the Kaiser and his race heavenward"; but it was not their noble character that commended the Germans to him, it was that they were "sweeping the seas." "Brittania rules the waves no more," he exulted; he was "never more confident of a German victory."[21]

But, as always, the RELA did more than just raise money and lead cheers. Less than two months after the war had begun, John Murphy (#23) pointed out that the "time may not be far distant when men as well as money would be needed." John J. Crowley (#95) answered by assuring the RELA that the Irish Volunteers were "ready to strike." Lynch agreed, as did Maurice Drohan, who urged the "boys of Company A" to be ready, "the freedom of Ireland is at hand," and soon "the boys in Ireland and in this country will get a chance to strike a blow." In fact, it was at this time and in this context that Patrick Heaney offered the interesting judgment that the RELA, "by fair or foul means . . . ought try and cripple the enemy."[22]

The RELA was not entirely alone in its radical Irish nationalism. The Hibernians devoted many meetings to discussions of the war, though J. J. Lynch, a member of both organizations, favored only the RELA with his predictions of a German victory. They considered the possibility of forming a company of Hibernian Knights—as one of their number pointed out, rifles could be had "for nothing by going as a rifle club ploy." Both AOH divisions offered "strong support" of petitions for "strict American neutrality"; both vigorously protested what they correctly perceived as the Wilson administration's pro-Allied posture. It was not, then, an entirely meaningless gesture when John O'Keefe of Minneapolis congratulated the Butte Hibernians for "helping and getting up things for the uplifting of the Motherland."[23]

More revealing was the AOH response to St. Patrick's Day in 1914 and 1915. This Irish Catholic holiday had once been the Hibernian's exclusive property. In 1914, three months before the destruction of the BMU and five months before the outbreak of the war, St. Patrick's Day had been celebrated in its usual way. The RELA was there, as were the Irish Volunteers, armed and in full uniform. Drohan's companies may have appeared vaguely comic, but they can hardly have seemed threatening. The celebration was perhaps more pious than usual, and it drew an uncommonly large number of prominent non-Irish. Generally, however, there was nothing to distinguish it from previous shows. Like modern nations parading their arms, the Irish in 1914 were simply making clear that they were still a potent force in the life of Butte.[24]

By March, 1915, matters had changed appreciably. The war had begun and there were rumors that Silver Bow County Sheriff Charles S. Henderson was going to stop the parade. In addition, an unidentified committee called on Acting Mayor Clarence Smith and demanded that the IVs be forbidden to carry arms. The AOH officers assured Smith that the parade was "not intended as a Teutonic demonstration against the allies or any one else," and added that "underground bigots" should not be allowed to interfere with an Irish holiday. They did disarm the IVs, but this hardly constituted an AOH surrender to the "underground bigots." The parade was routed through the German and Austrian sections of the city and representatives of both of those nations were invited to march with the Irish. Thousands of Irish were joined by hundreds of Germans and Austrians in this annual festival of an Irish saint! German, Irish, and American flags were carried, prompting one Butte newspaper to report—whether with alarm or surprise is uncertain—that "for the first time in the history of the world, perhaps," the flags of three nations were flown on St. Patrick's Day.[25]

This was the last time the AOH showed that kind of fervor. In fact, on the national level the German connection, the "alliance" the AOH had been so instrumental in forming, had already become an embarrassment. At the 1914 AOH national convention there was "hesitation to espouse the cause of Germany . . . despite the existing alliance with the German-Americans." It occurred to the Hibernians that it would damage "the Irish in the U.S. to be bound irrevocably to Germany should the U.S. Government declare a policy hostile to our own." Certainly the Irish-German hand-holding in March, 1915, had not been well received—in Butte or elsewhere in the United States where Hibernian divisions had decided to make graphic their alliance. Whatever their motive, for the first time since 1903 Butte's Hibernians did not parade on St. Patrick's Day, 1916. There was a march to the Catholic churches of the city but, lest it give offense to the strictly neutral or openly pro-Ally, it was led by the Rotarians! The RELA was even put on the "look out for a Scotland Yard detective who was in town" for the holiday.[26]

More troublesome for the AOH than the German "alliance" was the fact that the organization had not made up its own mind on the goals of the Irish resistance. As late as 1912, Division 3 was still "evenly split" on the question of continued support of James Redmond, his Irish Parliamentary party, and Home Rule. The next year the division telegrammed one of its members visiting in Ireland "wishing success to the Home Rule meeting in Co. Galway." As late even as 1914, with radical nationalists Roger Casement, Thomas Asch, and Diarmuid Lynch present at their convention and pleading for money for the Irish Volunteers, the Hibernians spent most of their time discussing a monument to Commodore Barry. Indeed, until James Redmond's ill-advised public support for Great Britain in the war, the official AOH position was in favor of Home Rule, which is to say, against the independent Irish Republic for which the Clan-na-Gael (and the RELA) had been fighting for thirty-five years. The Irish nationalism of the AOH was considerably more moderate than that of the RELA. This was as true in 1914 as it had been in 1882.[27]

II

By 1914 however—perhaps by 1907—radical Irish nationalism in Ireland often tended toward socialism. The two remained distinct movements, but in some quarters commitment to one was a test of commitment to the other. Conversely, the moderate nationalists were more often than not reluctant to accept radical solutions to the reform of the social system. Critics of the Irish resistance were quick to make the obvious connections. The Irish Republican Brotherhood, said one of them, was in close touch with Karl Marx. Another, after the war and the revolutionary upheavals in Russia, managed even to league Bolshevism with Sinn Fein, by then the shorthand, and inaccurate, label for Irish nationalism.[28]

Though exaggerated, there was substance to the charges, particularly when applied to the left wing of the IRB or to James Connolly and Jim Larkin. Connolly insisted that capitalist imperialism, not England, was Ireland's oppressor, and that Ireland must rid itself of its own bourgeois nationalists before its liberation could have meaning. His emphasis was on Gaelic cooperativism as much as Marxism; he found his cultural models, his alternative ideology, in old Irish legends as well as in *Kapital*. But Connolly was no primitive or unscientific Marxist. Lenin praised his writings, and his martyrdom to the cause of his nation was a severe blow to the related cause of his class. Connolly, in fact, denied that they were separate issues: "The cause of labour," as he put it, "is the cause of Ireland; the cause of Ireland is the cause of labour. They cannot be dissevered." A labor newspaper in Butte had asked in 1895 how a war against England could possibly help Irish workers. Connolly was answering that question and, in the process, linking the cause of Germany to that of radical Irish reform.[29]

Larkin, the other Irish labor leader, was more an accidental nationalist. It was the reluctance of English workers to support Irish workers that forced him to build an exclusively and self-consciously Irish union and to come to terms with the equally exclusive and self-conscious nationalist community. When that Irish union went on strike, however, in 1913, Connolly's lessons came into sharper focus. The strike was directed against William Martin Murphy, an Irish Catholic and a nationalist. It was obstructed by the Catholic hierarchy and looked on with considerable suspicion by Arthur Griffith, the founder of Sinn Fein. William Butler Yeats juxtaposed the issues exactly when he charged "the nationalist newspapers with arousing religious passion to break up the organizations of the working man."[30]

Occasionally the association of Irish radicalism with Irish nationalism, based on the assumption that the latter was subordinated to the former, produced a distorted reading of events, as in 1916 when the Socialist Walter Mills wrote of the Irish rebellion as a workers' war against capitalist tyrants. These workers, moreover, consisted of "Irish Methodists, Irish Presbyterians, Irish Catholics, and Irish agnostics" united against their bourgeois tormenters. A man who could think that could easily move, as Mills did, to the sublime assumption that Belfast Protestants were Home Rulers. These excesses aside, however, there was about one wing of the Irish nationalist movement a distinct worker radicalism. And, as surely as in the 1880s when radicalism meant land reform, there were nationalists who rejected it as diverting attention from—if not actually subverting the cause of—a free Ireland.[31]

The RELA was better able to deal with this Irish radicalism than was the AOH; by 1914 members of the RELA-sponsored Irish Volunteers were even referring to one another as "Comrade." If nothing else, Bishop Carroll's warnings against socialism had no official and little enough unofficial influence with the nonsectarian Emmets. It is revealing that Dan Sullivan, the BMU socialist, was an RELA but not a Hibernian, and that Sullivan's previously quoted reference to the Cubans having their freedom may have meant that that was more than either the Irish *or the Irish in Butte* had. It is as revealing that in working-class Butte, RELA memberships went up and AOH memberships down precisely as Connolly and Larkin began to influence the direction of Irish nationalism, and as the AOH began to advertise the fact that its officers were commonly "judges, lawyers, bankers, railroad magnates, grocery chain owners, businessmen, and Bishops." Butte's AOH routinely spoke out against left wing threats to Catholic Ireland—and Catholic Butte. The Minute Books of the RELA contain no comparable references; it was inconceivable that a working-class member of the RELA would come to the organization with the complaint brought by the young Hibernian that Irish miners feared that what they said in Hibernia Hall would be repeated in the Anaconda Company's corporate boardroom.[32]

This is not, of course, the same as saying that the RELA had been radicalized. The two associations shared many members, and the RELA had its full quota of Hugh O'Daly types—"good old Irish rebels," O'Daly once described them in the same section of his autobiography in which he dismissed Larry Duggan, an RELA leftist, as "at the head of the communists." The point is only that generally the Emmets were better able to agitate on the seam than was the AOH, not because they were more radical—though they probably were—but because they were more unequivocal in their nationalism. It must, of course, also be noted that the Butte Irish would not have to live in a socialist Irish republic. It was a free Ireland they sought. The difference is that the RELA was more determined to get it, and thus more willing to cooperate with those, Connolly and Larkin among them, who might help them.[33]

Appropriately, it was Larkin himself who revealed the weaknesses in even the RELA position. Two years after his unsuccessful 1913 strike against Murphy and one year after he had become an IWW, Larkin came to Butte. He came as the representative of Irish and international labor, and only incidentally as a spokesman of Irish freedom. On September 25 he delivered what for him was a mild speech on the near synonymity of Irish and socialist agitation; it was "a lie of the capitalists," he said, that the socialists were against religion, and none should be more aware of that than the Irish Catholics. Their cultural traditions were the antithesis of English and American commercialism, they lived for more than the ceaseless multiplication of wants. The conservative Irish nationalists were "frauds" in largest part because they wished only to substitute an Irish bourgeois capitalism for the English model. Not only would a capitalist Ireland be as exploitative of the workers as a capitalist England had been, it would be, in the deepest cultural sense, a contradiction in terms. Similarly, the destruction of the BMU in 1914 was a tragedy because it atomized the working class. The BMU was not all it could or should have been but it was at least a union, a community of miners.[34]

The day after he made these remarks, Larkin received word of the death in England of his friend and colleague, the British labor leader James Keir Hardy. Larkin determined to eulogize Hardy. Unfortunately, Acting Mayor Michael Daniel O'Connell, while agreeing to allow former Socialist mayor Lewis Duncan to speak, denied Larkin the use of the city auditorium on the grounds that his remarks would "be bad for harmony." Whether O'Connell was speaking of the war in Europe or the labor "war" in Butte is uncertain. Undeterred, Larkin reserved Carpenters' Union Hall for his speech, but Sheriff Charles Henderson forcibly interfered and the carpenters withdrew their offer. Finally, the Finnish Workers' Club opened Finlander Hall and both Larkin and Duncan had a place to speak. It was a fitting gesture given the charges of the previous summer that Irish conservatives had driven the Finns out of the BMU.[35]

In his speech—as much an attack on Irish timidity as a eulogy for Hardy—Larkin made no direct references to the bombing of the Miners' Union Hall or to the ethnocentrism that may have produced it. But by inference at least he seems to have accepted the argument that Irish Catholic conservatism had had something to do with the division within the union. Certainly his remarks, coming when they did, do nothing to diminish the credibility of that argument. He was unsparing in his contempt. "I am an Irishman," he began. "I love my native land and I love my race, but when I see some of the Irish politicians and place hunters you have in Butte, my face crimsons with shame, and I am glad they did not remain in Ireland"—a neat reversal of the idea commonly held in Butte. These traitors bore "good Irish names," so he assumed they had been taught to hate oppression. They had become, however, "the slaves of oppressors, the dirty instruments of oppression." He had come to Butte because "some sooty-faced miners who work down in these hells under this city," had asked him. These he distinguished from the "clean-faced gentlemen (with black hearts)— the so-called labor leaders." Then, in a final and obviously well-rehearsed passage, he delivered his indictment. "I tell you the Irish champions of freedom, Emmet, Mitchell, Tone . . . whose names these contemptible traders in Irish patriotism take on their lips for their own selfish purpose, would spit in the faces of these renegade shoneen Irish of Butte."[36]

Shoneen (seónini in Irish) was an interesting choice of words. Coined by D. P. Moran, an Irish cultural nationalist, it meant originally Irish Catholics who aped English ways. John Devoy was a bit more graphic, insisting that it meant "ass lickers," informers, traitors, and gentrified conservatives. Connolly and Larkin, however, used it somewhat dif-

ferently. Arguing—probably believing—that the Irish were all but con-
genital socialists, that Gaelic cooperativism was a part of the racial
memory, it was easy for them also to argue that the enemies of socialism
were, by definition, the enemies of Ireland—in a word, shoneens. Connolly, for example, wrote of taking "the control of the Irish vote out
of the hands of the slimy seonini who use it to boost their political
and business interests to the undoing of the Irish as well as the American toiler." The point was the same one Ed Boyce had tried to make
in 1901, when he referred to Daly as a bad Irishman; it was the same
point that Patrick Wallace, another Butte Irish labor radical then in
Ireland, had made in 1913 when he wrote to the *Montana Socialist* that
Irish "patriots" were too often the exploiters of Irish workers. And this,
said Wallace, was "only a repetition of what bourgeois politicians and
capitalist flag wavers do in the states." Class-conscious Irish workers,
however, would "not be put off by priest or politician."[37]

As Connolly had said, the cause of labor was the cause of Ireland.
But the cause of Ireland was becoming the cause of Germany, as those
Irish rebels in Ireland who were shouting "up the Kaiser" would indicate. Larkin was of similar mind; he could not, then, very well ignore
Irish freedom or, and more significantly, the alliance with Germany
and German-Americans that was formed to win it. In Philadelphia, on
a stage in which Irish Volunteers joined German Uhlans, he told a
Clan audience that Irish workers would "not fight for England, but for
the destruction of the British Empire and the construction of an Irish
Republic." In a speech entitled "Germany: The Friend of Small Nationalities" and reprinted in the *Montana Socialist* just before he arrived
in Butte, Larkin was quoted as saying that he hoped "that all Ireland
will not have to pay an awful price for the lying attacks of the conservatives [read shoneens] upon the noble German Nation." Seven
months later, Larkin received a letter from Connolly telling him that
the Irish conservatives were denying employment to those "who refused to enlist . . . to assist the English army."[38]

For other socialists, in this country and in Europe, the war dishonored
all the combatants; it divided the working class by nation, filled the
pockets of war profiteers, and killed the innocents. For Irish socialists,
however, one of those combatants, Germany, had the power to free
Ireland, and not just from England but from the death-dealing hand
of capitalism. Needless to add, this cannot have been a role for which
the German government felt itself particularly well suited. But by the
time Larkin reached Butte, to the related issues of Ireland and worker
radicalism had been added the even more volatile issue of a German
victory.

The problem, of course, was that few Butte Irishmen were buying all three of Larkin's ideas. That Ireland must be free was univerally accepted; there can by this time have been very few left who would be satisfied with Home Rule. That Germany could be of inestimable value in securing that freedom was less popular. There were critics— W. E. Deeney was among them—who were not impressed with Germany's potential as a liberator nation. Belgium, after all, was also a small, Catholic nation. Others remembered that Ireland had not been conspicuously well served by previous partners, whether Spain in the sixteenth and seventeenth centuries or France in the eighteenth. There were others who understood that in sinking British ships or attacking British armies, the Germans were killing Irishmen. Still, as the St. Patrick's Day parade of 1915 would indicate, Germany was the chosen instrument of Irish liberation, and what one Englishman called "Irish pro German propaganda" was commonly encountered in Butte. Where Larkin's formula truly broke down in Butte was in its insistence that the free Ireland that would arise from a Germany victory would be also a socialist Ireland, and that that socialist Irish Republic would serve as a model for working classes everywhere.[39]

There was another and perhaps related consideration that helps to explain the mixed reception accorded Larkin. The first two non-war-related raw materials put on England's contraband list were rubber and copper. Within weeks of the outbreak of hostilities, half of Butte's mines were closed, the European market for their product having disappeared. As Con Kelley put it, there was no way to deliver the copper to Germany or its allies; no way to collect for the copper delivered to England until the American debt to Great Britain was paid. Man hours worked in 1914 were down almost 30 percent from 1913 and, until June and the destruction of the BMU and August and the war, 1914 had been a very good year. ACM dividends went down proportionately. The city was filled with unemployed. Since the ACM gave preference to married men, many of those idled were young, single, and relatively new to town. J. J. Lynch complained of "the industrial depression . . . in this city"; even Crowley and Sullivan, who ran the saloon at Hibernia Hall, commented on the "dull times."[40]

It is always possible that had this latest round of mine closures continued, there would have been greater sympathy for Larkin's Irish socialism. But, and there is great irony in this, the same American loans to England that gave this nation an economic stake in an English victory also created an enormous English market for Butte copper. By the middle of March, 1915, 6,500 men were back underground; the *Anaconda Standard* confidently predicted that by May 11,000 men would be employed in Butte's mines. As the *Anaconda Standard* put it, "BUTTE BOOMS AGAIN." The "boom" was not one in which the workers shared equally, assuming they shared at all. It was based too much on the number of men working and the total payroll. But for the rest of 1915 and 1916 it served at least to divert the attention of the settled Irish miners from some of the rasher prophecies of Larkin and Connolly.[41]

III

Even more diversionary were events in Ireland. There had been constant rumors of a rising—led by whom and to what purpose were not yet known. In Butte, the RELA, as already noted, began in October, 1914, collecting thousands of dollars for the Defense of Ireland Fund. Defense from what was also left a mystery. Then in early February, 1916, J. J. Lynch told an excited RELA that he had no war news for them that night but that "in a short time there would be plenty of news." He could see "nothing ahead but success." It is tempting, and not altogether unwarranted, to claim for Lynch some advance word of the Easter Rising in Dublin. It was later reported that Clan-na-Gael president John Devoy also knew in advance of the Rising, and Lynch, as the leader of one of the largest Clan locals in the U.S., might be expected to have shared in that knowledge.[42]

By this time, however, though few in Butte knew it, the target was about to be more exclusively defined—even in Ireland—as English control of Irish affairs. Theorists who wished to associate imperialism with capitalism could continue to agree with Connolly that the cause of Ireland was the cause of labor, but with the exception of those theorists Ireland's freedom, not labor's, was now the issue—as, perhaps, it had always been. The Rising, in the words of one historian, would "devour" the labor movement. Connolly died as an Irish patriot, not as a socialist, and, according to another historian, his involvement in—and martyrdom to—what became solely a nationalist rebellion "buried Irish socialism for several decades."[43]

The associational Irish in Butte were quick to respond to the news of the Rising and of British reprisals against its leaders. They had never paid much attention to the social revolutionaries in the Irish nationalist movement; they would pay even less attention to them now. Their emphasis would be on the Irish and Kaiser Wilhelm, not the Irish and Karl Marx. The kaiser would prove troublesome enough. Many in Dublin, doubtless those who had never cheered the kaiser, thought the Rising a German plot. There were many Irish in Butte who agreed. But to acknowledge a plot is not to denounce it. It was the Clan-na-Gael that supplied the money for the rebellion, but it was Germany that supplied the arms. Thousands gathered in Hibernia Hall on April 30 to thank them. They gave $2,500 to the Cause, prompting the *Montana Socialist* to ask where all these generous Irish revolutionaries had been when Larkin was in town. They then listened to Father English say that "today we recognize Germany as an ally . . . we claim her . . . as much as Austria or Bulgaria does." This was more even than English had claimed in 1915. It was quite a remarkable comment.[44]

At that same meeting, J. J. Lynch formed the Patrick Pearse branch of the Friends of Irish Freedom (FOIF), an action he had announced to the RELA meeting of April 27. The FOIF was a Clan-inspired organization that had first been proposed in March at the Irish Race Convention. Unlike the Clan, its operations were open and public—indeed publicized. Women as well as men were eligible—of seventy-six known members from Butte, forty-one were women; members had to be Irish by birth or descent—of sixty for whom that information was given, fifty were Irish-born; all had to be convinced that Ireland should be a "free and independent Republic." It is worth noting that the Butte branch, in its bylaws, stated specifically that it would "pay no sick benefits or burial expenses from its funds." One critic charged that the FOIF "maintained close touch with the German organizations in America both before and after the rebellion." Whether true nationally or not, the Butte branch seems to have been involved in nothing more conspiratorial than the collection of money for the widows and children of the martyred rebels of 1916. In May, for example, at a meeting chaired by Father Michael Hannan, the Friends collected $2,638.30.[45]

What German contacts were maintained were probably kept by the RELA. There would be nothing again like the 1915 St. Patrick's Day "Parade of England's Enemies," but the Rising emboldened the Irish and reconfirmed the wisdom of the German alliance. The Emmets issued a "condemnation of the murder of our brothers in London," a reference to British executions. They heard from Clan headquarters that the news from Dublin was fragmentary but enough to know that "the leopard has not changed his spots. . . . We hope to live long enough to see the death of the beast." J. J. Lynch continued to insist that they would all live long enough. He freely predicted that the British fleet was the only thing "keeping her going" and that the destruction of that fleet was imminent. John Long (#188) was as sanguine. Germany, he told an RELA meeting, "will undoubtedly win the war." While they waited, the IVs continued to march and drill; some Butte residents, obviously the less-alert, thought the marchers were getting ready for the inevitable U.S. declaration of war against Germany and applauded the Irishmen's American patriotism and self-sacrifice.[46]

Even the AOH, though not as open in its advocacy of a Germany victory, was uncharacteristically pugnacious after the Rising. State president J. J. Cummings, a Butte newspaperman and also an RELA, told the Montana convention that the "Hibernians are the Irish who fight. They are the soldiers, . . . the men in the fore front." A motion to form military companies was passed; resolutions condemning "seven centuries of English misrule," as well as England's "brutal, unjust, and uncivilized manner" in dealing with the Rising, were passed unanimously. But there was also the reference, again by Cummings, to Irish divisiveness, from the faction fighters of the eighteenth and nineteenth centuries to the present divisions in Butte. "We must," Cummings insisted, "be more ready to overlook one anothers' faults." This was the traditional language of the patriot; obviously it comported poorly with that of the revolutionary, further evidence that if the Rising had not exactly devoured labor radicalism, it had at least muted its message.[47]

This unexpected though, in hindsight, predictable consequence of the rebellion was infuriating to those Irish who, like James Larkin, continued to fight on the seam. Larkin may never have been as "Irish" as Connolly; his involvement with Irish nationalists may always have been more an arrangement of convenience than an expression of a dual allegiance. But this is more a reflection of the relative importance he attached to both traditions than to the dismissal of one of them. James Pollard, no friend of either Irish nationalism or Irish radicalism, spoke of the "identity of interests between Irish-Catholic communities and extremist Labour organizations." Larkin wanted desperately for Pollard to be right. Ironically, Larkin was distrusted by many socialists—as, it would seem, he distrusted many of them. But despite these mutual suspicions, he raged against those Irish who came to the U.S. to tell the story of the Rising and spoke only the language of a free Ireland, never that of a socialist workers' republic. Particularly galling for him were the actions and speeches of Nora Connolly, who seemed able to remember that her father was *only* an Irishman.[48]

It was Larkin's self-appointed responsibility to keep alive the other half of Connolly's radicalism and preserve the dual lessons of the Rising. In July, 1916, he again brought his message to Butte. More than a thousand people, "most of them miners," according to the *Montana Socialist,* came out to hear him "talk about the Irish Rebellion." Larkin was deceiving no one in advertising his speech as being about the rebellion; the point was just that his rebellion was not always theirs.

He was at his best. Local Irish patriots "knew nothing about Ireland or Irish freedom; . . . they did nothing but talk a lot of sob stuff about Ireland in order to keep you Irish workingmen divided among yourselves." Once divided "you forget that the struggle you have here is the same you knew in Ireland—the struggle against economic and political tyranny You lose your class . . . and race solidarity . . . while you listen to these mercenary phrase mongers talk . . . about Irish freedom." At this point in Larkin's speech, James B. Mulcahy, editor of the *Butte Independent,* rose to protest. Larkin withered him. "Real Irish patriots," he screamed, "would scorn to recognize the likes of you." Then, in a final bit of advice, he told the Irish miners in the audience that if "you would . . . be true to the spirit which inspires the rebellion in Ireland, you must do your own thinking and not delegate it to any judge [Lynch?], lawyer [Breen?], editor [Mulcahy], or priest [Hannan?]." He had earlier in his remarks described the rebellion as "a working-class rising to keep Irish boys out of the British army." There is no question, however, that he included the Irish in America when he spoke of "Irish boys"; no question that he did not mean to distinguish between "the British army" and an American army allied with it. His definition was thus broader in one sense, narrower in others, than the conventional, but clearly he was calling Butte's Irish miners to new duties.[49]

Five months after Larkin's appearance, Con Lehane, another Irish socialist and a friend of both Larkin and Connolly, made more specific what those duties might be. Lehane told his Butte audience that there was no organization interested in bringing Connolly's message to the American Irish "except the Socialist movement." Obviously Nora Connolly's description of her father as a one dimensional—if not actually simple-minded—patriot was a disservice. Socialism, in fact, had always been the more urgent of Connolly's crusades. Irish workers understood that. "Socialism doesn't frighten the Irish in Ireland," Lehane said, and "the Great Irish Opportunity," was to bring this lesson to the 20,000,000 Irish in America, potentially "the unbreakable weapon" of an emerging American radicalism. As convinced as Connolly or Larkin that the Irish were uniquely drawn to socialism, and certain that Irishmen were the dominant element in the American working class, Lehane thought it required only that the Irish *be Irish* for socialism to triumph in the United States. To this end he proposed the formation of a "James Connolly reading circle in cities with sufficient numbers of Irish workers." He mentioned New York, Albany, and Boston in the East; Chicago, Cleveland, and St. Paul in the Midwest; San Francisco, Seattle, and Butte in the West.[50]

In January, 1917, Larkin made a third trip to Butte and elaborated on Lehane's remarks. There is evidence that Butte's Irish were wearying of Larkin's overheated rhetoric, but Larkin certainly cannot have thought so. He railed against the "parish pump form of patriotism" and against Irish-American capitalists, "malignant beasts in human form, . . . gombeens [exploiters] in their relations with their fellow Irish; shoneens in their slavish servility." These renegade Irishmen were guilty of "brutalizing and searing the bodies and souls of their race, over whose overworked and ill-fed, and all ill-clothed bodies," they have made their fortunes. The Irish workers remembered only the Rockefellers, Carnegies, and Morgans of American capitalism. Larkin reminded them of "the Ryans, the Walshes, the Farrells, the Crimmonses, the Dalys, who have ground out their . . . wealth from their oppressed and overworked Irish slaves."[51]

How seriously Butte's Irish took Lehane's and Larkin's comments cannot be known, but sometime late in 1916, maybe just after Lehane's visit and immediately before Larkin's third, a new Irish organization was formed. It was called the Pearse-Connolly Irish Independence Club and for the next couple of years it would speak to and for Larkin's Irish. It honored the two central heroes of 1916: Pearse, the poet and cultural nationalist; Connolly, the worker and radical nationalist. Linking the two traditions in a place like Butte was precisely what Eric Foner had in mind when he speculated on the "evolution" of the Irish-American working class and the "legacy" of the Land League.[52]

Little is known about the size or occupational make up of the club. Echoes of Patrick Ford must have been very faint by 1917, but the social differentiation and fragmentation within the Butte Irish community were more obvious by then, and it figured to have its greatest appeal among younger Irish workers, many of whom were suspicious of the conservatism of the AOH—some of the "younger Irish" thought the Hibernians a branch of the Knights of Columbus—and the one-dimensional nationalism of the RELA—the Emmets complained that some of the newer Irishmen of Butte were "discourteous" and "indifferent" to their nationalist appeals. Typical of Pearse-Connolly membership may have been Maurice Ferriter, who emigrated from his native County Kerry in 1912, spent a brief period of time in Massachusetts, then joined his two brothers in Butte's mines in 1913. By 1917 all three Ferriters were in the Pearse-Connolly Club.[53]

The principles and policies of the Pearse-Connollys were much like those of the left wing of the Irish Republican Brotherhood—or, the purely working-class of them, those of the IWW. They were products not just of the Rising but of the social changes, in Ireland and in Butte, that preceded it. The most important of these changes occurred in Butte. The place was no longer a refuge for Irish workers, in part because the Irish had lost some of their control of the work force, in larger part because of the divisions between the older and settled immigrants and the younger and transient migrants. Butte offered no promise of a fair living to these younger ones; by 1916 it was just another industrial town filled with boardinghouses, hazardous jobs, and roving gangs of unskilled disposable workers. Larkin and the Pearse-Connollys (and the Wobblies) appealed to the unsettled Irish because Butte's Irish enclave had no room for them and because their work was unsteady, unsafe, and paid too little to allow them to return to Ireland or to bring a part of Ireland to them. They were quite literally homeless. Their radicalism reflected their desperation; there was a hardness about it, an intensity and commitment equal to that of their revolutionary working-class allies of whatever nation. This was a tradition which few of the older Butte Irish, even those who counted themselves radical, can have shared or understood.[54]

Thus, except for the permanently exiled, the Pearse-Connollys can have seemed only scarcely less alien to the enclave than the Finnish Workers' Club, with which, as it happened, the Pearse-Connollys had a close association. One such permanent exile was Father Michael Hannan—he refused even to be buried in Butte, insisting, in his will, that his body be returned to Limerick. There is some evidence that Hannan was one of the founders of the Pearse-Connollys, much evidence that he allowed it to use St. Mary's Church. Certainly he sympathized with its choice of patriotic icons: Pearse, the poetic Gael, and Connolly, the revolutionary socialist. Their martyrdom by English capitalists enhanced the consanguinity of their causes. When Liam Mellows, a leader of the Irish resistance from 1915 to 1922, identified Hannan as "a tower of strength to the movement," adding that "his name . . . is a household word among us," he may have been referring to Hannan's ability, far rarer in Butte than in Ireland, to fight the battle at the seam. In the next two years, whatever their degree of sympathy for the causes, there would be ample opportunity for Irishmen to fight it.[55]

IV

In February, 1917, less than a week after Larkin left Butte, the U.S. broke off diplomatic relations with the kaiser's government. Two months later the U.S declared war against Germany, "Ireland's friends across the sea," as Lynch had called them, "our gallant allies in Europe," according to the 1916 proclamation of the Irish Republic. The American declaration of war broke the heart of Irish-America. In Butte, Lynch promised that he would be loyal to his "adopted country," but he was bitter about the prospect of American boys fighting against Ireland's allies and he grumbled about the unevenness of the Wilson administration's reponse to the outrages of England and Germany. Bishop Carroll was predictably more patriotic, exhorting Montana Catholics to buy war bonds and enlist in the army. James Mulcahy fell somewhere between Lynch and Carroll; a firm advocate of American neutrality, he now counseled the Irish to do nothing to provoke charges of disloyalty and to pray that Wilson would apply his fourteen points to Ireland.[56]

The Emmets were the most affected of the Irish organizations by America's entrance into the war. Some of them, like John Long, who six months earlier was confidently predicting a German victory, were now predicting that Ireland would get her freedom as a consequence of the inevitable German defeat. John Devoy spoke for all the Clan-na-Gael camps when he told the Congress that the organization would actively discourage any further insurrectionary activity in Ireland since such could only aid Germany, now America's declared enemy. Such rapid about-faces are bound to be dizzying. What is hard to explain is why the Clansmen—and the IRB in Ireland—were not aware in 1916 that a U.S. war with Germany was certainly possible and that, should such a war come, an Irish Rising aided by Germany would cripple Irish-Americans and make it almost impossible for the Wilson administration to help Ireland, supposing for the moment that it wanted to. Clearly, the Clan was going to have a problem reconciling the goals of an American and an Irish victory.[57]

There was a perceptible absence of enthusiasm in the RELA meetings after February, 1917. The Fourth of March committee met in Lynch's courtroom to plan the annual celebration of the Manchester Martyrs; the Emmets held bond drives and petitioned Congress to recognize the Irish Republic, whose flag they flew over Hibernia Hall. They heard speeches; attempted to counter British propaganda; continued to wear their Irish Volunteers' uniforms and to practice the manual of arms; and, of course, continued to give generously to Irish causes. Generally, however, the U.S. declaration of war on Germany denied them their platform; only treason against the United States or—and it was beginning to amount to the same thing—an RELA embrace of labor radicalism in both Ireland and Butte, would permit them to recover it. Unwilling to do either, the RELA could do nothing—except wait for the war to end. They even kept in good standing those members who had to wait it out by fighting in what the RELA had to see as an Anglo-American army.[58]

The Pearse-Connolly Club was not similarly paralyzed. St. Patrick's Day, 1917, would be its first public display of strength. The Hibernians were the traditional sponsors of St. Patrick's Day festivities; many of them remembered when the day's most sinister purpose was to show the "Cusin Jacks that the Irish aren't all dead." The Pearse-Connolly Club had a different agenda. The U.S. was about to enter a war that most internationalists and socialists had condemned, and on the side of the nation that held Ireland hostage. A simple celebration of Ireland's patron seemed out of place in 1917. There is no record of what it was the Pearse-Connollys wanted to do, what the "theme" of the parade would be. Mayor Charles Lane, however, thought he knew their purpose. He denied the Pearse-Connollys a parade permit, saying that it was an "IWW affair"—an indication that the Pearse-Connollys were seen as more than just another group of Irish merrymakers. The parade proceded in defiance of his orders. The AOH and RELA had been invited to participate and many of the Emmets and Irish Volunteers, some in uniform, seem to have done so, though the RELA accepted the invitation "only conditionally." But the Hibernians in Division 3, in a tersely worded note—the misspellings were probably unintentional—answered for thousands of conservative Irish when they "turned down the invitation of Pierce and Connelly Club to parade," announcing instead that "we are going to Mass."[59]

With the RELA in a holding action and the Hibernians at prayer, the Pearse-Connollys alone could protest. Late in March, just after St. Patrick's Day and just before the U.S. declaration of war, they scheduled a "monster parade and exercises," this time to celebrate both Easter and the Easter Rising. Again, Lane denied them a permit; again they marched anyway. At least 750 people participated; flags of the Irish Republic were prominently displayed. The established Irish leaders were not consulted. J. J. Lynch, for example, offered no advice to the Pearse-Connollys, for the simple reason that he had not been asked for any. As he put it—and every Irishmen in Butte understood the significance of his remark—"I have no influence with them." Even Father Hannan had advised against a public procession, not because he objected to its purpose—he allowed the march to begin from St. Mary's—but because he viewed it as imprudent. It permitted—it practically begged—American patriots to league Pearse and Irish nationalism, Connolly and Irish socialism, with a German victory.[60]

Six weeks later the Irish discovered what Hannan meant. On June 3, Hannah Sheehy-Skeffington, widow of an Easter Week martyr, spoke in the Butte City Auditorium. Father Hannan introduced her in a hall emblazoned with Irish Republican flags and banners. She began her remarks by saying that people had told her in the East that "she would not meet the real Irish until she came West, and that Butte was the greatest Irish town in the country." There was no missing the meaning of those remarks either. What is ironic is that Larkin had by this time dismissed Sheehy-Skeffington as he had dismissed Nora Connolly: "she never speaks of the Labour movement, nor of the Socialist Party." That may have been so, but it was not enough to spare her, or the 1,200 Irish who cheered her, the opprobrium of the American patriots. Hannah Sheehy-Skeffington, said the *Anaconda Standard*, "gave as fine a pro-German speech as has yet been heard in Butte." Butte's Irish were beginning to realize that there would be a price exacted for their fifteen years of pro-German sympathies.[61]

The established Irish shrank from paying; only the Pearse-Connollys were undeterred. On June 2, 1917, a nationwide draft registration was ordered. The Irish in Butte, faced with the prospect of bearing arms against the as-yet-unrecognized Irish Republic, were predictably upset by the order. This was especially true of younger Irishmen, already cut off from home or its Butte facsimile, whose radicalism also led them to oppose the war. From this point forward, it is impossible to determine which was the deeper well of unhappiness; it is also unimportant, since the Irish workers probably could not have deter mined it themselves. The Pearse-Connolly Club's reaction to the draft registration order may serve as the first example.

On June 3, Ed Keenen and John McDowell, identified only as two "young Irishmen, recent arrivals," were arrested for distributing anti-draft pamphlets in Butte. It is worth identifying the Irish origins of the names of these young radicals, not by way of showing where they were from—it cannot even be known if they were Irish-born—but by way of showing how few were from County Cork, Butte's traditional supplier of Irish. Keenan is associated with counties Fermanagh, Monaghan, and Louth; McDowell with County Roscommon. The pamphlets advised draft-eligible workers that registration was no less than an examination "as to our fitness to kill and murder workingmen of other countries against whom we have no grievance." A "silent strike against the war," the pamphlet continued in language that sounded like a definition of boycott, "means the greatest step ever taken by the American working class." But the appeal did not end there. This war was also being fought to aid the nation that had "riveted the chains of slavery around Ireland." Given the timing, this is a particularly important expression of the intersection between Irish nationalism and worker protest. The Pearse-Connolly Club took credit for the pamphlet, and the next day two of its officers, James Treanor and John Lennon, were also arrested. Treanor, a Dublin name, was reported to be an IWW agitator from Los Angeles and San Francisco just in town to raise money for Wobbly causes; there was considerable IWW literature found in his room. He had been in Butte, however, at least since March, when he signed the Pearse-Connolly's St. Patrick's Day invitation to the RELA. Lennon, a name associated with counties Galway and Fermanagh, was a miner at the Badger Mine and also said to be associated with the IWW.[62]

The pamphlets were preliminary to a grander Pearse-Connolly protest of the draft registration order. On June 5, certainly in association with the Finns and likely with the Wobblies as well, the Pearse-Connolly Club led a rather large and unruly antidraft protest march. The cooperation of Pearse-Connollys, Finns, and Wobblies was facilitated by the fact that by then all three organizations had moved to the same address: 318 North Wyoming—Finlander Hall! The march ended in a small-scale riot. John Korki, a Finn, and Dennis Harrington, an Irishman and former city policeman during the administration of Lewis Duncan, were arrested. Korki said he marched because he wanted "to help free Ireland." Harrington, who had Pearse-Connolly Club applications in his pocket, was quoted as saying he was "looking for Irishmen of the proper kind." It cannot be known if Harrington recalled Larkin's comments of 1916, that the Rising was of the working class "to keep Irish [and Irish-American] boys out of the British army," but clearly he entertained similar sentiments. The next day, June 6, twenty-three more men were arrested; twenty of them were Irish, but they bore names like Donlon, Gilcoyne, Clifford, Healy, McBride, Canny, and Ward, names associated with counties Galway, Sligo, Down, Clare, and Limerick. Only two of the twenty, Michael Twomey and Frank Barry, figured to have roots in County Cork. And only one of the twenty, John Coffey, a Pearse-Connolly officer from Dublin, could have been in Butte by 1915.[63]

V

Three days later, June 8, at about 11:30 P.M., a fire began in the 2,400-foot level of the Granite Mountain shaft of the Speculator Mine. Flames roared up the shaft to the surface and into the night sky. Of the 410 men who went to work on that night shift, 165 died. It was the worst catastrophe in the history of Butte mining, one of the worst in the history of hard-rock mining anywhere. On June 11, a new organization, the Metal Mine Workers' Union (MMWU, address: Finlanders' Hall!), called a strike against all the mines. Dan Shovlin, Joe Shannon, and Tom Campbell, veterans of earlier Butte labor wars, were involved in the union's formation and had major leadership roles. But non-Irish names and new Irish names also showed up on the few MMWU officer lists that were published: Frank Little, Ed Hofstede, Matt and Leon Tomisch, Pete Petaja, Scotty Robertson, and William Stoddard were joined by Joseph Kennedy, Jack Mooney, Joe McNulty, Ed Boyle, John Doran, John Grady, Jim Murphy, Tim Nolan, Tim Sullivan, Joe Mc-Bride, Irishmen who had not been in Butte long and, except for Tim Sullivan, had no apparent connection with County Cork.[64]

The timing of the strike was not propitious. The United States was two months into a war it seemed to believe could not be won without Butte's copper. Wartime strikes are never easy, strikes against vital wartime industries even less so. They create the suspicion that the enemy and its allies might be conspiring against the war effort. Add to these the charges of "German/Irish influence" as well as the conspicuous presence of both the IWW and federal troops and the situation becomes even more confused and volatile. The history of the 1917 strike and of the subsequent strikes that kept Butte in almost constant turmoil until 1920 has been told. The purpose here is not to retell it. Rather it is to insert the necessary Irish element; to show, as previous accounts have not, how inextricable were class and ethnicity.[65]

There can be little question that the Speculator fire precipitated the strike of 1917. It must be pointed out, however, and with considerable emphasis, that the Metal Mine Workers' Union was formed on June 5, before the fire and in response to the draft registration order. Michael Grace, for example, testified in the 1918 trial of William Haywood that "it was formed before the fire anyway, that is, they started to form it before the fire." "They" were almost surely the Pearse-Connollys. William Dunn, the publisher of the radical *Butte Bulletin*, the official strike newspaper, testified at the same trial that an Irish group had been denied a parade permit on June 5; the group was preparing to organize a new union on that same day. He can only have been referring to the Pearse-Connollys. John Foss, an IWW organizer from Sweden sent by the Wobblies to Butte, agreed with Dunn, stating "that the Irish had got together in the churches and had meetings in opposition to the draft" four days before the fire. But it was Charles Stevens, a reporter for the *Anaconda Standard*, who made the most direct connection between Irish and worker radicalism when he told the court that the "leaders of the P-C Club were also the leaders of the IWW in Butte."

He mentioned a McGowan, a McNulty, and a McGraw, names from the northern counties of Sligo, Donegal, and Fermanagh.[66]

Stevens was extrapolating when he identified the Pearse-Connollys with the IWW; what he knew was that the Pearse-Connolly Club had called the Metal Mine Workers' Union into being and that the MMWU was routinely associated with the Wobblies. Maybe he had heard someone sing "The Irish Scab," the strike song that concluded that "our interests are just the same / From County Cork to the State of Maine / . . . Now Erin's sons, again I say / Don't be a Slacker in the Fray." Maybe he just knew that all three organizations had the same mailing address, or that Joe Kennedy was an officer of both the IWW and the Pearse-Connollys. None of this evidence, however, gives Stevens's identification of the Irish with the IWW the ring of indisputable truth.[67]

What does ring entirely true is that the Pearse-Connollys were involved in the formation of the Metal Mine Workers' Union, that that involvement antedated the Speculator disaster by four days, and that it came about because of a draft registration order that threatened young Irish migrants with having to fight against Ireland. The fire, in other words, precipitated the strike, but even without it Butte's miners would have walked out in 1917. As Dunn testified in 1918, "evils . . . were piling up." He mentioned the abuse of the rustling card, by now a device for insuring work crews for the hot and unsafe mines; the seven- and fourteen-day layoff system, inadequate wages, inflation, and what he called the "bad tyrannies of the shift bosses and foremen." The MMWU's initial strike demands also identified long-standing grievances. Convinced that the company was now using the rustling card to blacklist all of those who wanted some kind of union representation, the MMWU made related demands for an end to the rustling card, company recognition of the union, and some union participation in hiring. Another basic demand was for six dollars a day, a wage which would barely cover the miners' escalating costs. Finally, the union wanted safer mines. Obviously, the Speculator fire was on their minds, but to suggest that it taught them something they did not already know ignores the lessons of the previous thirty years. In sum, the striking miners wanted safe and steady work at a wage that permitted them to hold their place in Butte.[68]

These demands made clear that very little had changed in the daily work routines of Butte's miners since the summer of 1914 and the destruction of the Butte Miners' Union. Indeed, if anything, the years since then had seen an exacerbation of the pressures and tensions that had led to the fall of the BMU. There was one difference. The Irish and the Finns—and not just the radicals of both groups who shared office space at Finlander Hall—seemed to be getting along better than they were in 1914. The Irish associations even invited the "Finlanders" to their all-Irish picnic in 1915 and then watched disappointedly as Finns dominated the day's athletic events. But with this not-so-minor exception, the problems of 1907–14 were still unresolved.[69]

The inability of wages to keep up with inflation was one of those problems. The companies, particularly ACM, insisted that they were paying record high wages. They made no reference to the cost of living— an understandable omission given the numbers: Yearly expenses per family for ninety-two industrial cities, including Butte, averaged $1,434 in 1918; in Butte, the figure was $1,843. As Dunn's *Butte Bulletin* noted, with some exaggeration, $7.50 in 1918 did not buy what $2.50 did "a few years ago." The United States Attorney for Montana agreed, noting that "rents and the necessities of life had gone up entirely out of proportion." Industrial wages in Montana, meaning essentially wages in Butte, Anaconda, and Great Falls, fell from first in the nation in 1900 to twentieth in 1920. All of this occurred, moreover, while the Anaconda Company was enjoying robust good health. Company profits in 1916 were fourth only to those of U.S. Steel, du Pont, and Bethlehem Steel; dividends for 1916–18 totaled $23.50 per share. During the eight years from 1909 to 1915 they had totaled only $19.75.[70]

Some of these profits may have been owing to an acceleration of the hiring practices begun before the war and to the "speed up" techniques devised to guarantee production. "Get the rock in the box," the miners' litany, had assumed a new urgency. In 1914 each job underground was occupied in the course of the year by an average of two and one-half men; in 1917, seven men held each job; by 1918 that number had jumped to a remarkable nine plus. In other words, in 1914 each employee worked an average of 137 days; in 1917 that average dipped to fifty-three days; in 1918 to thirty-eight days. When it is also recalled that the 1914 rate had occasioned comment and protest and that many hundreds of men worked steadily in the same job year after year and thus lowered the average, the full effect of this turnover can be better understood. These new men, moreover, were being worked differently. In the first decade of the twentieth century, the output per man per shift averaged between 2.5 and 3 tons. By 1914 the average stood at 1.6 tons; by June, 1919, it was 1.1 tons. Yet, despite the obvious fact that these men were less skilled and/or less hard-working, total copper production exceeded a very impressive 1.8 million tons in 1916, 1917, and 1918. The mining companies were using gang labor, and what little remained of miners' skills and pride could not survive its use.[71]

And the gangs came from everywhere—another holdover of the earlier pattern. In 1918 the nationals of thirty-eight countries, including such unlikely suppliers of American immigrants as Persia, Egypt, Bolivia, Syria, Armenia, Turkey, and Afghanistan—"black boys as they are known"—were working in the ACM mines. Company dependence on these "new immigrants" had grown steadily. In January, 1916, there were fewer than 900 of them in a work force of approximately 10,000. By August, 1918, their numbers had grown to 3,900 in a total work force of 11,000. In September, 1918, the ACM employed 10,769 men; 7,218 were foreign-born and 4,528 of these—two in every three—were southern or eastern Europeans. They were also men of distinctly unsettled habits. Of 1,575 born in "Austria-Hungary," for example, only 314 were naturalized; of 794 Finns, there were 147 citizens; of 181 Montenegrins, there were seventeen; of 194 Greeks, there were four. Just under 5,000 of these men—and their average age was almost thirty—were unmarried, and 2,325 could not read or write English.[72]

One federal official referred to this work force as "a mass of 16,000 unorganized men in a district with kaleidoscopic . . . racial characteristics." The chairman of Butte's local draft board was even more descriptive. There were "thousands of men" in Butte, he wrote, who cared "as little for the laws . . . 'as the flowers that bloom in the spring.' " They were no more assimilated "than the peasant who remained at home. We have heard . . . too much of the Melting Pot. These men simply want to escape hunger and cold and hardship." So much for huddled masses yearning to be free! But these escapees were not all from southern and eastern Europe. Among the 7,218 foreign-born miners working for ACM were 1,360 who were born in Ireland, and of that sum, 558 (42 percent) had not taken out citizenship papers. In 1910, by way of comparison, 91 percent of the Irish-born were either naturalized or had applied for their papers.[73]

In effect, the companies had succeeded in assembling a contingency work force. ACM's critics in and out of working-class organizations believed they knew why, arguing that the company was able to evade the full effects of the state's new workman's compensation law by hiring only single men with no American dependents or survivors. It was estimated, for example, that the relatives of 123 of the 165 men who died in the Speculator fire—more than 500 people—would collect no compensation at all. As one labor paper put it, "through the forethought of the companies in hiring single men, who either have no dependents or whose dependents live outside the U.S., there are no claims filed in more than one-third of the fatal accidents." The companies, on the other hand, insisted that they were compelled to hire these new men. Loans to the Allies had created a market for copper; America's entry into the war had created an irresistible demand. Even had there been industrial peace, the work force would have had to grow, and probably in the direction of an increased dependence on disposable workers. But strikes and, for a time, the draft, added to the pressures by depleting the supply of available workers and putting a premium on finding and hiring unmarried alien migrants who could not be drafted and who had no long-term stake in the town, the work force, or, indeed, their own jobs.[74]

Thus, the new men came not just to work but to take the place of those who, for whatever reason, would not. As the *Anaconda Standard* put it, in language reminiscent of that of 1878, let the veteran miners strike or leave town; there were plenty of new men to work the mines. The striking Metal Mine Workers' Union came to the same conclusion. The MMWU said that the strike breakers wanted only "a road stake big enough to hit the trail again," so the union voted $500 that it might "aid single men . . . so they can leave town." The *Strike Bulletin* reported that "most of the gunmen and scabs employed by the ACM do not even speak English." Dunn, however, had not given up hope. As the labor history of Colorado indicated, "the scab of today is the striker of tomorrow," particularly when the strikebreakers were "foreigners who needed only to be educated."[75]

The MMWU set for itself the job of education; in the process, as the *Bulletin* put it, "making Butte as 'safe for Democracy' " as the war was expected to make the world. The MMWU leaders argued, along with many others, that union membership was a necessary first step in this Americanization process. But they insisted, too, that it was a process, arduous and, more signficantly, ongoing. Thus, the MMWU spoke to the new men and printed informational bulletins in the several languages then heard in Butte. They demanded that the companies do the same when posting their safety rules—one "no smoking" sign was in fifteen languages—and when instructing new crews in how to find the exits to a shaft or how to signal the hoisting engineer. At the same time, they demanded that the companies conduct classes in English. Clearly, the MMWU believed that the companies were importing strikebreakers—and from remote and exotic climes.[76]

This was also the lesson of one of the union's recurrent appeals. In the form of a prayer, it can have meant little—except as an unwelcome reminder—to any but the new and itinerant. "Let us have some of the good things of life," the union pleaded. "Let us have homes; how many of you have that sublime thing called home?—merely a side hole in some old dreary rooming house." In addition to its obvious evocative aspect, there was an important and commonly overlooked tactical element to this appeal. In this, as, it may be presumed, in other strikes, control of worker housing, and of the lunch buckets that went with it, was vital. Strikers were evicted from company-owned boardinghouses like the Florence and the Silver Lake, their rooms taken by scabs or, when required, by the troops of the National Guard. Thus, the unions had to enlist and hold the support of the "independent" boardinghouse operators. In Butte the MMWU did. The landlady of the Clarence Hotel promised that she would not feed scabs. After hearing MMWU officers advise them to "fill the buckets of the scabs from the slobjar," the five hundred members of the Women's Protective Union voted not to put up lunch buckets unless the boarder could prove that he was not taking it below ground—hardly a credible argument in a miners' house. A few Serbo-Croatians, carrying this extended definition of home one step further, attempted even to expel from their ethnic societies all those men who continued to work during the strike. Here were boycotts— the denial of what passed for home among the single men of Butte— that improved even on the old Irish definition.[77]

Whatever the cause—though the possibility that ACM was recruiting expendable strikebreakers seems the most persuasive—new men continued to pour into Butte. Based on past experience, many might have predicted that they would also have an adverse effect on occupational safety. The companies had no reason to upgrade worker skills, including even the ability to understand warnings and instructions given in English. As the striking Metal Mine Workers put it, "the safety of mining depends on the intelligence of the miners" and "producing ore is an art. It can't be learned by the rabble now working the mines." They may be forgiven their reference to "rabble," an aristocratic label the hated Moyer might have used. The MMWU, of course, was talking about strikebreaking, not social class. The union's reference to the "art" of producing ore is rather more curious, a strange mix of nostalgia, strike-spawned desperation, and aristocratic pretension.[78]

Perhaps, however, they were simply responding to an earlier report that "there is no more room in the hospitals for the greenhorns who have been working," this despite the fact that no work was going on in the "dangerous places and hot boxes ... the hot holes where lives are snuffed out." At that, the hospital reports seem to have exaggerated only slightly. In 1916, the first year of the Workmen's Compensation Act, there were 3,084 accidents in the ACM mines alone; 41 men died in the six months between January 3, 1917, and the Speculator disaster on June 8; between May 7, 1914, and December 14, 1920, at least 239 men died in twenty-six accidents. It was in this context that the Navy ran its recruiting advertisement and that the sign reading "Be Careful! Don't Get Hurt. There are TEN MEN waiting for YOUR JOB" was posted on the door of the North Butte Mining Company. That sign may have been hyperbolic sloganeering; it may also have been the symbol of the new Butte, one that looked remarkably like the old one of 1878, when William Read stated privately that he thought the new men coming into the town would benefit the companies by providing them with a steady supply of temporary, unorganized, perhaps unorganizable, workers.[79]

Thus, as far as worker grievances were concerned, 1917 was different from 1912 only in degree; the same factors were at work: inflation, new work methods, new men, new and greater dangers. The first of those problems required only higher wages to correct; the next three were far less easily fixed, in large measure because, though the grievances had not changed, the ability of workers to contest them had. In the early years the newcomers had been recruited—forcibly if necessary—into the Butte Miners' Union. Scabs became strikers, or at least good union men. By 1917 this part of the equation was different. The BMU, of course, was gone. As late as November, 1916, there were five Irishmen claiming to be its officers, but they were likely moved more by the desire to claim BMU property than by attachment to the cause. The insurgent Butte Mine Workers' Union barely survived the 1914 rebellion it led. A new Butte Workingman's Union, Local #12985 of the AFL, had attempted for a time to fill the void, paying sick and death benefits to eligible miners, even leading a brief two-week strike in 1916. It had, however, little influence with the miners. The Western Federation of Miners was without standing in Butte, among either the old or the new men. It did place a "Slovonian organizer . . . speaking the different languages" in Butte, but the WFM was never able to overcome its reputation. It had been heavy-handed in the crisis of 1914, openly treacherous, by MMWU standards, in its dealings with the strike of 1917. Its president, Charles Moyer, was dismissed by the MMWU as the "greatest of four flushers . . . a charlatan beyond compare." The IWW was only scarcely more influential. Transient workers—the blanket men—had always been thought the IWW's natural constituency, and the Wobblies did enlist some of them in Butte, never enough for them to form what Tom Campbell had called the advance guard of the labor movement, but enough to maintain an IWW presence throughout the strikes.[80]

It was left then to the striking Metal Mine Workers to organize a work force as ethnically and socially mixed as any in America. They had considerable success, enough to close all the mines for a brief period, enough that at no time during the strike does it appear that more than 1,200 of almost 11,000 miners were working. Those 9,000 striking miners must have included some of the new men, but they may not have included as many as the union would have wished, or as IWW theorists would have predicted. For example, there were 1,287 "Austrians" working underground in June, 1917, just before the strike; 946 "Austrians" were still drawing their checks in November. These were not, of course, the same "Austrians"; there may not have been a single one from the 946 who was also counted among the 1,287. But it is as unlikely that more than half a dozen among the 1,287 were still in town when the November count was taken.[81]

In September, however, exactly twenty Austrians were counted in the mines; this out of a total "new immigrant" work force of twenty-four! The MMWU made much of this development, boasting that it had persuaded 10,000 men, including all but a tiny handful of the new men, to leave the hill. Persuasion, however, was not quite the right word—at least as it applies to miners. Far more important was the fact that on August 24 the union succeeded in convincing the smeltermen in Anaconda to walk out. The mines were closed not because the ACM could find no one to work them but because the company had no way to refine the ores and had been forced to close them. Three weeks later, the smeltermen walked back, and by December 1 figures for the Austrians were at prestrike levels.[82]

The union, in other words, had not so much enrolled new immigrants willing to strike as it had discouraged them from staying in town. The strike, if it was to be won, would have to be won by the veterans. They came remarkably close. Until September, ACM had been insisting that it had enough men to keep the mines running, some of them at up to 65 percent of capacity. This claim was never credible. One government official wrote early in the strike that work stoppages had cut copper production from 17,000 tons per day to 1,600. Even that claim was impossible to make once the company's East European work force had dwindled to two dozen men. ACM's chief counsel, Daniel Kelly, reported at that time that his company's mines were "absolutely crippled and almost shut down." What broke the union's resolve was the unwillingness of the smeltermen to stay out, and the constant flow of new men willing to work the mines. This supply of new miners was never adequate to the company's needs, but it was enough to discourage the strikers, if for no other reason than that it implied a near-inexhaustible source of men willing to work. There was no disputing the obvious: The veterans had lost the power to exclude. Winter was coming, and on December 28 the MMWU called off the strike.[83]

The union may have exaggerated slightly for effect when it said that it had 8,800 members, or when it argued that 10,000 men were honoring the strike. There seems little question, however, that at least 7,000 ACM jobs were not being filled either because unattached new men would not take them and moved on or because the well-attached old-timers refused to take them and hung on. Only the latter were truly on strike, but all of the numbers taken together indicate that there may have been as many as 5,000 of these strikers, men who did not work and did not leave. That is a significant number; not only because 5,000 is a lot of striking miners for any town, but because it included a very substantial share of the men who voted not to go out in 1912—settled men, conservatives, Irishmen.[84]

VI

The Speculator fire was not all that moved them. Father Brosnan pointed out quite specifically that the Speculator was "not an Irish mine." If the names and the ages of those killed are any indication, he could have added that it was not a mine in which many of the old-time miners of whatever origin worked. The casualty list contained a disproportionate number of eastern European, including Finnish, names. It was not even, in fact, an ACM mine; a man could be hired at the Speculator without a rustling card. Brosnan was trying to comfort his mother, not explain the subsequent Irish response; certainly he was not suggesting that settled Irish workers would be unmoved by the deaths of 165 other men, however disposable the companies may have considered them. The only point, and it is related to the one made earlier, is that the fire alone cannot explain why the old men walked out in 1917.[85]

The companies and the newspapers they controlled were also convinced that the fire was a pretense. They, however, had an alternative explanation. The strikers had purposes far more sinister than the protest of unsafe conditions, rustling cards, and wages. The ACM never quit referring to them as "cowardly agitators and non-workers" or, more specifically, as IWWs, Irish zealots, and German sympathizers, labels that soon became all but interchangeable. The fact that these company charges were self-serving does not mean they were not believed. By 1917 Irish workers, however well established, were in a difficult position. They served as the connecting link between a German victory and worker protest. They could deny ties to the IWW, but not, except for the shoneens, to some form of Larkinism. They could deny ties to Germany but not to Ireland. They could affirm their love of America but not of America's principal ally. Irish and/or worker protest had become synonymous with treason.[86]

In 1917 few bothered even to distinguish between the separate parts of the formula. L. O. Evans, chief counsel for the ACM, closed the circle by telling the Missoula, Montana, Chamber of Commerce that the MMWU was a front for the IWW, that in the IWW "the Kaiser has found one of his most effective allies," and that the IWW in its turn "found an active ally, equally imbued with the purpose of doing everything possible to hinder . . . the war [in] the members of . . . the Pearse-Connolly club." An interesting expression of that same point was sounded in 1919 when Ed Boyce, still comfortably retired in Portland, declined Eamon de Valera's invitation to chair the Oregon Commission for Irish Independence. The cause of Ireland, Boyce warned de Valera, was commonly thought "tainted with Bolshevism and IWWism." Boyce's involvement would only give credibility to those suspicions.[87]

The charge that the strikers were German sympathizers came first and easiest. This was owing only in part to the Irish-German alliance, although the St. Patrick's Day parade of 1915 with its German and Irish flags must have come to the minds of many. The more significant event, however, was the draft protest of June 5, 1917, a protest led by Irish and Finns carrying banners with messages that sounded suspiciously like the work of Wobblies. The MMWU strike came less than a week later. One hundred and sixty-five men died that week but not everyone was prepared to connect the two events. The *Butte Post* insisted that the strike was unrelated to the Speculator fire, that it was rather an extension of the draft registration protest. The *Helena Independent*, edited by Will Campbell—for whom the description "super patriot" seems inadequate—agreed. The strike, said Campbell, "appears to be of an anti-war character rather than a labor one." The *Anaconda Standard* moved this argument to its obvious conclusion when it accused the MMWU of using strike relief funds to help "slackers" evade the draft.[88]

The striking MMWU did nothing to discredit these charges when it set up its offices at 318 North Wyoming, joining earlier tenants, the IWW, the Pearse-Connollys, and the Finnish workers. America was involved in a war on the side of Russia and England. The Finns hated Russia, the Pearse-Connollys hated England, the IWWs hated the war. And the MMWU, co-tenant with these Irish and Finns, was leading a strike against the major producer of an item judged by all sides of the labor conflict to be central to the successful prosecution of that war. Copper, according to the authorities, was "an essential metal . . . in the manufacture of munitions"; copper mines were "war industry plants"; mining was "an essential industry." A strike in the copper mines was a mutiny and Irish patriots were conspicuous among the mutineers.[89]

Tightening this association was the fact that the *Strike Bulletin* and its successor, the *Butte Bulletin*, regularly carried news of the continuing Irish resistance to English rule. It would be wrong to assume that this was only a tactic, a cynical device to turn the patriot game to the interests of worker protest. It would be as wrong to assume it diverted attention from the real issues. The Irish resistance was, in considerable measure, a worker protest. The Butte strike was, in considerable measure, a rebellion of Irish miners. The inclusion of Irish news in the *Bulletin* was neither a contrivance nor a diversion; to have ignored Irish affairs would have been both. To be sure, some of those who were aware of this affinity of causes, like Brophy, took no pleasure from it; others, like Hannan or even Lynch, were in no position to argue its applicability to the situation in Butte.[90]

The Irish patriots, however, were not the only "pro-German" element in town. Other mutineers were also on board. Like the Irish, they too had been invited. The ACM, said Labor Department conciliator Hywel Davies, had made "racial changes in its employees." The draft had taken some of the established miners, the strike obviously took some more. Their places were "largely filled by Finns, Balkans, and Sinn Feiners—men whose political and industrial beliefs are too well known to need comment, but [who constitute] 50% of the working force." In case their industrial beliefs were not well enough known, Davies explained that these sorts were particularly drawn to the "unAmerican" principles of the IWW. But there was more. According to an unnamed newspaper—and the irony in these remarks is huge—prohibition increased the IWW's attraction for these workers. The prohibition of liquor meant that the "blanket men" no longer "hung out in the saloons," where they had once "found warmth and comfort and stimulants and some social pleasure." They "now have nothing to do except call meetings." The IWW hall had become their "permanent hang out, . . . an information bureau . . . and a social center." The topics of conversation had to have been no less lively for being more political.[91]

One result of the new hiring practice was that Butte, with a population of perhaps 60,000, had the fourth-largest Local Exemption Board in the United States. There were 8,677 resident aliens registered in Butte, many of them convinced either that the war was unjust or that the U.S. was fighting on the wrong side of it. Add the IWW and the Pearse-Connollys and it is easier still to understand why the Butte exemption board was not just large but had a record of "wholesale delinquency . . . unequalled, unapproached anywhere else in the U.S." This may not have been an exaggeration. Three weeks after the draft registration, three months after America's entry into the war, Butte "produced not a single enlistment from the latest call up."[92]

Hywel Davies had some advice for the mining companies and, inferentially, the draft board. They could restabilize the work force and insure its active cooperation in the war effort only by persuading the new men that the U.S. could help "to redeem and save their own countries." It would also be helpful if the workers could be persuaded that class war had to give way to the "war for civilization" against the "unrighteous Hun." Once convinced, Butte's 16,000 miners, the "inert mass," Davies called them, would "be saved from themselves." The cynicism of these remarks was almost surely unintentional, but they make clear how extremely difficult it would be for the MMWU to extricate itself from the formula for treason that was emerging.[93]

To the formula must be joined the hysteria with which it was applied. There are countless examples. The man who bore greatest reponsibility for the Speculator fire had a German-sounding name, Ernest Sallau. It followed in some quarters that the fire was started by German saboteurs. The Department of Labor mediator was told to look for "German influences"; the newspapers were filled with stories of "secret German activities," "German money," and "agents of the Kaiser." In the middle of the strike James Gerard, former U.S. ambassador to Germany and Marcus Daly's son-in-law, told a Butte audience of the special German talent for intrigue. The strikers denied any German connections. They proclaimed their "devotion and adherence to this, the land of our birth and adoption." They even demanded that the companies release the names of all their German stockholders. This counterattack did no good. In 1918 the Montana Council of Defense heard a witness testify to his "suspicion that a foreign power with whom we are at war is by a small and well trained force organizing our discontented element and using it to disrupt our industries."[94]

Since the Irish were conspicuous among the discontented elements, it was at least as difficult for them to remove themselves from the formula as it was for the MMWU. The involvement of the Pearse-Connolly Irish Independence Club in the draft resistance of June, 1917, seemed a logical extension of the Emmets' and the Hibernians' German "alliance" of 1908–15. The club's close ties to radical worker protest were no less obvious. Less than two months after protesting the draft, more than 1,000 Pearse-Connollys, resplendent in their "green sashes," marched second in line to the red-sashed IWW at the funeral of the murdered IWW radical, Frank Little. Little had given a number of Lar-kin-like speeches in his short time in Butte and the participation of the Pearse-Connollys in his funeral procession was an Irish as well as a workers' tribute.[95]

L. O. Evans understood as much when he said that the Pearse-Con-nolly Club "brought the blush of shame to the cheek of every honest Irishman." The striking MMWU drew a different conclusion. "The Connollys," said Bill Dunn in the *Strike Bulletin*, "detest tyranny and tyrants." They had a "consuming love of justice and fair play." As for shaming anyone, the only blushing Irishmen were those who knew that the Pearse-Connollys "bring the certainty of defeat home to every Irish company politician." Larkin would certainly have cheered the sentiments. They did not, however, do much to ease the fear of Irish-German complicity in the worker protests.[96]

Sinn Fein became the code word for this Irish-IWW-German con-spiracy. The organization was thought to be everywhere in Butte. Thomas Chope, commissioner of labor for the ACM and a member of the AOH, said that the strike of 1918 was led by "about 2,500 Finns, Austrians, IWWs, and Sinn Feiners, revolutionary, non-citizen Irish miners." Governor Sam Stewart believed him, attributing the strike to "Sinn Feiners, IWWs, and other undesirables." Will Campbell made the same point about the 1917 strike, blaming it on "the Sinn Feiners of Butte," while James Scherer of the National Council of Defense called Butte "more Irish than Ireland and a hot-bed of Sinn Fein ac-tivity." Even James B. Mulcahy was branded. An officer of the Amer-ican Protective League worked to block the Department of the Interior from placing land office notices in the "notorious *Butte Independent*, the only straight out Sinn Feiner sheet in western America." This news would certainly have surprised Larkin; it probably surprised Mulcahy. But the ultimate, if unintentional, expression of this legacy of the Ger-man alliance came from Colonel F. G. Knabenshue, a confused and particularly nervous intelligence officer for the War Department, who germanized even the organization's spelling. Butte, said Knabenshue, had too many "IWWs, socialists, and shin fehners."[97]

Most of this American patriotic zeal was directed toward the Pearse-Connolly club. It was the most active of the Irish associations during the war years, and the only one that wore its labor militancy openly. The Pearse-Connollys did more than just share offices with the MMWU and the IWW; they supported the strikes of 1917 and 1918 and insured that their members would be blacklisted by joining Frank Little's fu-neral cortege. The organization's files were confiscated by federal au-thorities, its officers "roughed up by company thugs." The silliest excess occurred in 1918 when the club, joined by the MMWU, asked Captain Omar Bradley, in charge of the U.S. peacekeeping force in Butte, for permission to parade on St. Patrick's Day. The RELA and the AOH were also invited to participate, not quite the equivalent of a performance bond but evidence that the Pearse-Connollys were wearying of their reputation as renegade Irishmen and that the MMWU was either well established in the Irish community or wanted to be. Bradley, who claimed both Irish descent and a "strong sympathy with the miners in their struggle for more pay and better working conditions," agreed to allow the parade as long as it was not "unpatriotic."[98]

The mayor of Butte, William H. Maloney, and the Montana Council of Defense were convinced the Pearse-Connollys could not be other than unpatriotic. Two days before St. Patrick's Day the council passed Order #1, forbidding "parades, processions, or public demonstrations" without the approval of the governor. The governor did not approve of this one, and the council instructed Bradley "to see there was no parade." Bradley revoked his permit. By then it was too late. A crowd estimated at 5,000 to 7,000 people, many of them shouting insults to "John Bull and Uncle Sam," "rioted" through Butte. Shamrocks, it was reported, were much in evidence. Of the fifty men arrested, forty-two bore unmistakably Irish names. Of the forty-two, only ten names were from Cork and only six of the Irishmen were listed in the 1915 *City Directory*.[99]

Bradley said later that there was "strong sentiment" against the parade "even by most of the Irish." He may have been right. The RELA and the AOH were reported to have approved the revocation of the permit once they learned that the parade's organizers did not intend to honor either St. Patrick or Pearse and Connolly—"our martyred patriots," the RELA called them—but rather had different purposes. How different was revealed two days later when the *Anaconda Standard* carried the story that the Pearse-Connollys were not really the sponsoring organization. Neither, for that matter, was the MMWU. Rather it was their office mates in the IWW who planned the procession and at whose feet blame for the violence and arrests would have to be placed. IWW was proving as handy a label in identifying Irish/worker protest as Sinn Fein.[100]

VII

What tantalizes about all this is the possibility that the charges may have been true; not the one that held that the Germans called the strikes, but those that hinted strongly that the Pearse-Connollys did conspire; that strikes were included when Pat Heaney told the Irish to use "fair or foul means" to cripple England; that, in other words, Larkinism lived. It was an Irishman, Diarmuid Lynch, who congratulated the *Bulletin* for being the "friend of Irish freedom," and the remark meant more than just that Dunn carried an occasional Irish story. When, for another example, the Montana Council of Defense proposed a rule prohibiting "strikes or boycotts," M. M. Donoghue of the State Federation of Labor objected, pointing out that "that word boycott would probably reach farther than the labor organizations" and that there was no reason to offer provocation where the council did not have to. Donoghue can only have been referring to Irish organizations, for whom the boycott was a featured tactic of nationalist protest. This does not prove a connection between Irish nationalism and the strikes of 1917–18; it is, however, an acknowledgment by one who would know of the seam between Irish nationalism and worker protest.[101]

The charges tantalize, but they do not convince. The IWW connection with the MMWU is almost certainly false. They were separate organizations and, although Frank Little was in Butte to try to affiliate the strikers with the IWW, there is no evidence he succeeded—or even could have. The charge of pro-German sentiment, though true of many Irish, Finn, German, and Austrian miners, cannot account for the strike unless the companies were prepared to argue that these men consciously and at some considerable cost to themselves denied the Allies copper so that their home countries might defeat the U.S., England, and Russia in the war. It is true that prior to 1917 Ireland's needs were thought better served by a peaceful Butte. After the Rising and America's alliance with England, that notion was reversed, and the possibility that Ireland—or Finland or Austria—would benefit from industrial disorder made the sacrifices occasioned by a strike easier to bear. Heaney's threat comes again to mind. But Heaney's comments were made privately and before the U.S. had become England's ally. It is a bit more difficult to dismiss the report of the Austrian who told his conationals "not to take out any copper and thus prolong the war against their country." But this was an unconfirmed rumor, though not one that requires—or would have required then—a total suspension of belief. Still, the idea that the strike was called specifically to aid Ireland or Finland or Austria is fanciful and overly conspiratorial.[102]

But the idea that the Speculator fire was the sole cause—or even that exclusively workers' issues were—is altogether too simple. That leaves the central question: Who were these 5,000 striking miners in 1917 and what motivated them? Given the timing of the strike there were no truly disinterested observers. There were, however, a few contemporaries whose judgments were relatively unclouded. The pastors of the First Presbyterian Church in Anaconda and the People's Community Church in Butte, for example, issued a formal statement ridiculing the company's contention that the strikers were Wobblies. The ministers insisted that the strikers were "honest . . . peaceful and law-abiding workers" who were fighting to preserve "those natural rights of man guaranteed in the Constitution." J. J. Lynch, in a speech given in the middle of the strike, referred to the "absolute necessity of organized labor," not for purposes the IWW would have thought important but for goals the BMU would have found familiar: a wage adequate "to keep his family in comfort and happiness and allow the miner to lay aside something for a rainy day." About the strike then in progress, Lynch said it was the "most orderly [he] had ever seen; there was less drunkeness . . . than ever before in the history of Butte."[103]

Lynch also admitted that his "sympathies" were where they had always been, "with the working man and particularly with the poor miner." There is absolutely no reason to doubt it; but it does make him more a partisan than a careful and disinterested judge. That cannot be said of Burton K. Wheeler, at the time U.S. Attorney for Montana, later a long-term Democratic senator from the state. Wheeler was no friend of the Anaconda Company but, the wails of the American patriots to the contrary notwithstanding, he was fair and impartial in his handling of the wartime strikes. In a letter to Attorney General Thomas Gregory, Wheeler wrote that the strike of 1917 was "being conducted in a manner heretofore unheard of in mining regions." There had been no violence, no lawlessness, no reckless threats of sabotage. Indeed, "among the strikers are thousands *who have been in Butte for many years.*" Later, in testimony to the Montana Council of Defense, he repeated the point, insisting that the "12,000" men who went out in 1917 were "substantial citizens" and were not "intimidated" by wandering agitators.[104]

The fact that Wheeler and Lynch felt they had to say something on this matter is as important as what they said. In spite of all the radicals thought they had learned from the lessons of 1912 and 1914, it was the established miners, the men with long and stable work histories, who went out in 1917. In different language, the aristocracy of Butte's labor—and that meant a significant percentage of its Irish—walked off the job. Their reasons must have varied, but Eric Hobsbawm, as before, supplies some important clues. The leftward tilt of the steady men—the aristocracy—was a natural extension of their favored status, the threats to it, and their determination to keep it. In 1912 and 1914 that had meant cooperating with those more powerful; in 1917 it meant defying them. In other words, *they struck in 1917 for exactly the same reasons they had not struck in 1912 or 1914.* In Hobsbawm's terms, they were "doing what they had always done: defending their rights, their wages and their now threatened conditions. . . . Only now they had to fight management . . . because management was permanently threatening to reduce them to 'labourers,' and now had the . . . means to do so." The means, for Hobsbawm, came from technological change and new techniques for managing the work force. The mining companies enjoyed those advantages in Butte, too, and before the strike used them with obvious effect. During the strike, wartime hysteria served the company's purposes—and at least as well. At that, the MMWU's demands included a return to two-man drill teams and "deliverance from Taylorism and all other so-called efficiency speeding up systems."[105]

The MMWU's emphasis on the rustling card is the surest indicator that the 1917 strike enlisted the support of the conservatives of 1912–14, Irish Catholic BMU members prominent among them. There is, of course, a double paradox in this since the rustling card had been the key weapon in the conservatives' previous efforts to hold their position. As early as February, 1915, barely eight months after the destruction of the BMU and with it the closed shop, the *Montana Socialist* reported that a list of those denied rustling cards showed that "tramps, vagrants, and IWWs" were not the only ones "blacklisted." "Married men, some thirty years in Butte," were also being denied a card. Those two Protestant ministers had said the same thing. The *Socialist* argued that "socialist leanings" were responsible for the blacklistings. A better explanation is that men were denied a card because they were pushing for an independent union, a closed shop, and the control of the work force that went with it. As much is implied by James Larkin's insistence in 1915 that the Butte miners had to restore the closed shop, even at the cost of reaffiliating with the WFM. Con Kelley made exactly that same offer to ex-BMU president J. C. Lowney in 1914. Kelley promised that ACM would restore the closed shop if the WFM could reestablish control of the workers. This had to have been one of the few times that Larkin and Kelley agreed on anything—except, of course, that Ireland must be free—and even on the issue of reaffiliation the two men had vastly different expectations. Larkin understood the deep enmity between Butte's miners and "Moyer's union," but, as he put it, "Never mind Moyer, you can take care of him afterwards." Kelley was less certain that Moyer could be brushed aside that simply, or that, assuming that Moyer were "taken care of," the miners of Butte would not build an IWW local on the remains of his WFM. The point, however, is the same: the company had used the troubles of 1914 to

destroy the union; it was now using the rustling card to destroy unionism.[106]

The Metal Mine Workers, particularly the older Irish strikers, viewed
this, with considerable justice, as a company betrayal. As a result, there
was no effort to distance the new union from the old, no repudiation
of the BMU. In fact, the MMWU admitted that it had "sprung full
grown from the ashes of the dead Miners' Union of Butte." This was
a revealing concession, indicating that the MMWs no longer held the
BMU fully responsible for 1914 and were determined to restore at least
part of what the BMU had stood for: worker control of hiring. The
betrayal of this principle came not in 1914 but later, when the company,
joined by "Moyer's union," now the International Union of Mine, Mill,
and Smelterworkers (AFL), "double crossed us" by refusing "to allow
the miners of Butte to organize." Butte had become an open-shop town.
Mr. Dooley knew what an open shop was. "Sure, tis a shop where
they kape the door open t' accomerdate the constant sthream of min
comin in t' take jobs cheaper thin t' min that has th' jobs." Butte's
miners understood completely.[107]

Control of the work force had passed entirely to the companies. But
in a place like Butte, control of the work force meant control of everything else. It was the ultimate source of privilege; to lose it was to lose
the titles and trappings of the aristocracy. The settled and steady workers had never had quite the power over the work force that they liked
to think they had. Their masters, however, had recognized their special
interests, had allowed them an uncommon measure of influence. The
use of the rustling card against them rather than for them reversed
that pattern. In Hobsbawm's words, "If the masters no longer recognized the interests of the [labor aristocracy] why should [the aristocracy]
recognize those of the masters?" This does not mean that the steady
men would embrace the cause and rhetoric of a worker radicalism
which, more often than not, sacrificed old aristocratic principles to
unknown and ultimately unknowable ends. It means only that the
settled would join the new in challenging the prerogitives of the masters of them both. There is significance enough in that.[108]

Since the rustling card was the company's means of control, it became the first target of union anger. The MMWU claimed that at least
3,500 men had been denied a card and it demanded that "the supervision of hiring [be turned over to] union committees, to prevent the
blacklisting of organized labor." Organized labor did not mean the
IWW; the blacklisted were not marginal men, they were men to be
reckoned with, men of substance. The MMWU played this theme con-

stantly. Rustling cards were denied to safety-conscious miners, veterans who had dared protest the unsafe conditions in the mines. The union commented on "our great many married members"; on the fact that its members were "bona fide unionmen." It spoke of the "many of us who have property," and of the fact that the "abuse of the rustling card drove men out of the town where they had built their homes." It even commented that the troops sent in to keep the peace were "gentlemen at all times" and thanked them for having protected "our lives and property." This was exactly the language used in 1914 to describe those whose "conservatism" had led to the destruction of the BMU.[109]

Moreover, once the strike was won, once "their communities and homes were safe" from "alien thugs" and "home guards," these "loyal employees" would return to Butte and resume their places. The Irish associations had made this same point when the shutdown of 1907–8 forced their members out of Butte. The companies were blacklisting the men who had built the city. It was this feature of its use that made the rustling card so offensive. It was not, according to the statement of the two ministers, the "necessary and harmless device" the companies said it was but a "rank injustice," a deprivation of fundamental rights. That was why the MMWU described the card system as "like slavery," a "vogue calculated to degrade the miner to the level of common chattel." It is also why the MMWU tried to distance itself from the IWW, and why it referred to this as a "legitimate" strike.[110]

There is hurt and confusion in these charges against the companies. Older men who had settled in were being stripped of rank and privilege and treated like laborers. Even their rights of "free speech and assembly" were being abridged and they determined to resolve "for all time whether or not any corporation has the right to drive men out of any district because of their views on any subject." The new hiring system had literally unmanned them, creating an "awful, paralyzing, courage-killing and coward breeding fear of loss of the Job." In the final analysis, wrote Bill Dunn, "the miners of Butte went on strike because they could no longer endure the impositions and insults heaped upon them, and because they believe that a man is entitled to decent treatment at all times." There is radicalism in that but it is nearer the spirit of 1776 than of 1917.[111]

VIII

Further confusing the issue were the increasing social differentiation in the Irish community and the related questions of Irish nationalism and worker radicalism. The patriot game had always been divisive but never more so than when it was being played out in the middle of another nation's war. The lessons of Larkin and Lehane began to assume a new immediacy as striking Irish worker "aristocrats" contemplated the events of 1917–20. The Anaconda Company was run by John Ryan and Con Kelley; its legal department was in the hands of Dan Kelly; its employment commissioner was Tom Chope; its efficiency engineer was still William Daly. The Silver Bow Council of Defense was chaired by Eugene Carroll, stoutly assisted by P. J. Brophy. The pastor at Immaculate Conception was the aristocratic and conspicuously patriotic Michael O'Donnell Barry. The sheriff of Silver Bow County was John K. O'Rourke; the mayor of Butte was William Maloney; Butte's chief of police was Jeremiah J. Murphy. All were thought to be in the pay of the ACM. The leading reactionary on the city council was John Hanratty. Senator Thomas Walsh, almost silent on the strikes and vigorous in his defense of the Wilson administration's foreign policy, sent the RELA a small statue of Robert Emmet, assuming no more was necessary to hold the organization's favor. James Mulcahy, condemned by the right as a Sinn Feiner, was blasted by Bill Dunn as a "jackal," a "professional Irishman." Ireland's cause, said Dunn, who only occasionally commented on his own Irishness, "was often betrayed by Irishmen; add the name of Mulcahy to the list."[112]

This fragmentation was a function of class and occupational differences, the inevitable consequence of the maturation of the Irish community. But if wealth divided the established Irish strikers from the shoneens, other factors isolated them from the new Irish in the Pearse-Connolly club. The new Irish were younger and usually unmarried. They came from a different Ireland, they came to a different Butte. The natural selection processes were not the same for these later immigrants. Less determined to settle in at all costs, they were unsettled and unsettling. Most of them had no prior knowledge of mining, whether in West Cork or Colorado. Most of them, in fact, were not from West Cork. Their remembered pasts were vastly different from those of the older Irish.[113]

But despite these differences, the established Irish miners joined the worker protest of 1917. This was an unexpected thing for them to do, and it can be explained only by reference to what they considered a twin betrayal. If working Irish felt betrayed by the company and the WFM, other Irishmen, workers as well as those like Father Michael Hannan, J. J. Lynch, and Larry Duggan, felt no less betrayed by the U.S. government. No involved Irishman, for example, can have failed to associate the government's attempts to suppress the *Butte Bulletin* between 1918 and 1920 with the suppression of the *Gaelic American*, the official paper of the Clan-na-Gael, and the *Irish World*. In each instance, the government's position was that these "Irish" journals were more interested in an Irish than an American victory, and that, if necessary, they would sacrifice the latter to the former. The *Bulletin* was viewed similarly. Irishmen, even those far removed ideologically from the Pearse-Connollys, had no trouble making the connection.[114]

The Metal Mine Workers' Union was the logical place to register a protest, and it appears many Irish did. But the exclusively Irish organizations were not entirely silent on the issues. The RELA, as always more militant than the AOH, publicly thanked the *Butte Bulletin* for "its strong support of the Irish cause, its refusal to be intimidated by England and the administration, and its fairness in opening its columns" to Irish news. This was less than six months after the Montana Council of Defense had demanded the suppression of the *Bulletin* as seditious. As instructive was the very brief letter sent to the Emmets by James Connolly, state secretary of the AOH. The Hibernians were protesting the action of "unknown members of the RELA" who had "removed the portrait of Daniel J. Hennessy" from Hibernia Hall. John D. Ryan had painted that portrait in 1908 to honor one of Butte's most respected (and wealthiest) Irishmen. By 1918 it, and the interclass ethnic pride it reflected, no longer seemed appropriate to at least one Emmet.[115]

There is no record of an RELA response. The thief—his crime was uniquely political—was never caught, never even identified. It is not likely, however, that the AOH pressed the issue. As surely as the Emmets, the Hibernians sat out the war and, as an organization at least, the strikes which were a part of it. This was not something they can have wished. It is true that the AOH went to Mass in 1917 rather than march with the Pearse-Connollys. But this was an act of resignation, almost of despair, not of defiance. In a remarkable story, made all the more so by the failure of anyone to comment on it, it was noted that as late as October, 1918, less than two months before the end of the war, the Hibernians had purchased a grand total of $2,500 in Liberty bonds. They could have raised that much for Ireland on a good weekend. The Benevolent and Protective Order of Elks had bought $20,900; the Greek Helenic Society had bought $16,500! A miner by the name of Pat Shea even went to a meeting of Division 3 and pointed out that "Uncle Sam had no laws" permitting the drafting of aliens into the U.S. Army. This was on June 30, 1917, three weeks after the Irish-Finn protest of draft registration. As surely as the Emmets, the AOH understood how difficult it was to be both an Irish and an American patriot in 1917–18 and how high the price would be for mixing

Irish nationalism—particularly the German alliance—and worker protest. Indeed few Irishmen—however old, of whatever class, settled or transient—likely missed that lesson.[116]

NOTES

1. RELA, MB, May 24, 1900; O'Dea, AOH, III: 1131–44, 1388.

2. Bureau of Census, *Twelfth Census, Population*, p. 797; *Thirteenth Census*, p. 594; *Fourteenth Census, Population*, p. 577. County figures, where available, indicate that most of the Germans lived in Butte, not in one of its "suburbs." Second-generation figures, where available, show a decline in their numbers as well. *Twelfth Census, Population*, pp. 768, 796–98; 878–79; *Thirteenth Census*, pp. 592–94, *Fourteenth Census*, p. 586. Immigration Commission, *Immigrants in Industries*, 1911, part 25, pp. 554, 555. Polk, *City Directory*, 1885–86, 1900; Malone, *Battle for Butte*, p. 67.

3. Polk, *City Directory*, 1890–91; *Examiner* (Butte), July 13, 1895; RELA, MB, Oct. 17, 1907.

4. O'Dea, AOH, III:1388; 1452; AOH, Proceedings, 1910, n.p.; Pollard, *Societies of Ireland*, p. 119; Alan J. Ward, *Ireland*, pp. 91–94.

5. *Butte Independent*, Dec. 3, 1910; July 16, 1910. See too Jan. 7, 1911.

6. RELA, MB, Dec. 9, 1909; Aug. 31, 1911. See too May 27, 1909; Sept. 14, 1911.

7. For a reference to Cuba, see Industrial Commission, *Mining at Butte*, 1911, p. 3928; AOH, National Board, Official Statement of Resolution, April 3, 1911, in Correspondence.

8. Clan-na-Gael, National Headquarters, to Members and Officers "On the Death of John Devoy," Oct. 11, 1928, in Correspondence. Perkins, *Great Rapprochement*, pp. 74–86, 141–44; RELA, MB, Sept. 10, 1896; May 6, 1897; Mar. 9, 1899; AOH D3, MB, Jan. 16, 1905; AOH D1, MB, Jan. 18, 1905; AOH D2, to Members and Officers, D1, Feb. 19, 1907; RELA, MB, Mar. 12, 1908.

9. AOH, Official Statement. See too AOH D3, MB, Feb. 25, 1911; RELA, MB, Apr. 13, May 4, 1911. For other references to arbitration, see RELA, MB, Apr. 6, Aug. 31, Oct. 5 and 19, 1911. Both societies also protested the Cunard Lines's refusal to sail out of the Queenstown (Cork) Harbor and demanded that the U.S. grant special concessions to the German Lloyd Line. RELA, MB, Oct. 16, 1913; "Resolution of United Irish Societies of Butte," Oct., 1913.

10. Copy of secret Clan resolution, Feb., 1914, in Correspondence. See too RELA, MB, Mar. 12, 1914; AOH D3, MB, Mar. 14, 1914.

11. John Devoy to "Sir and Brothers," May 9, 1913, Correspondence; RELA, MB, June 5 and 26, 1913.

12. *Anaconda Standard*, July 13, July 14, 1913; RELA, MB, July 24, 1913. The volunteers had begun drilling by March, 1911. RELA, MB, Mar. 9, 1911; IV, MB, May 9, Sept. 10, Oct. 7, Dec. 19, 1912; Feb. 16, Apr. 27, 1913; RELA, MB, Mar. 20, Apr. 10, July 17, Oct. 2, 1913.

13. Irish Volunteers, MB Dec. 8, 1912; EDA to Sir and Brother, RELA #322, Mar. 21, 1913, Correspondence. See also the bill of lading for "Two cases, hardware," sent via Boston and Albany RR, Apr. 10, 1913, Correspondence; EDA to James J. McCarthy, Apr. 12, 1913, Correspondence; RELA, MB, Mar. 27, 1913; Irish Volunteers, MB, May 11, 1913; Jan. 15, Mar. 1 and 29, Apr. 12, May 21, 1914; Irish Volunteers, Membership Ledger.

14. Joseph Lee, *Modernisation*, p. 144; Edwards, *Pearse*, pp. 173, 177–79. For examples of RELA awareness of the Orangemen see MB, Mar. 9, 1893; Aug. 8, 1895; Feb. 11, 1897. The offer to fight in Mexico is from Irish Volunteers, MB, Apr. 26, 1914.

15. RELA, MB, Feb. 12, June 24, July 30, 1914; RELA, Term Report for Term Ending Aug. 31, 1914.

16. U'Raithaille to James J. McCarthy, Mar. 7, 1914; MacNeill for the Oglaic na h-eireann to McCarthy, Apr. 8, 1914, Correspondence; Edwards, *Pearse*, pp. 173ff. See too the letter from Bulmer Hobson to John Devoy where Hobson complains that "The people who have the money here [Ireland] won't give it." Devoy, *Post Bag*, II:412–13. Clark argues that the wealthy Philadelphia Irish were also "found wanting" in 1914–20. *Irish in Philadelphia*, p. 152.

17. RELA, MB, Aug. 6, 1914. English's remarks are in the *Anaconda Standard*, Mar. 18, 1915.

18. O'Daly, Life, [46, 50]; RELA, MB, Aug. 20, Sept. 10, 1914. See too, Clan-na-Gael, "On the Death of John Devoy."

19. RELA, MB, Sept. 2, 9, and 16, 1915; Pollard, *Societies of Ireland*, p. 199; Defense of Ireland Fund, Receipt, Sept. 8, 1915, Financial Records. This was a gilded certificate with much Gaelic Irish script.

20. RELA, MB, Sept. 23, Nov. 11, 18, and 23, Dec. 2 and 28, 1915; Apr. 27, 1916; Receipt for $500.00, Jan. 24; Receipt for $800.00, May 2, 1916; Clan-na-Gael to RELA, Dec. 18, 1915, Correspondence. These were very large sums. Compare with figures listed in Devoy, *Recollections*, pp. 416–18.

21. RELA, MB, Sept. 24, Dec. 17, 1914; Jan. 21 and 28, Apr. 1 and 15, May 13, June 10, Aug. 19, 1915. According to one source there were 100,000 Irish Catholics in the British Army. Rumpf and Hepburn, *Nationalism and Socialism*, p. 18. See also the account in Dangerfield, *Damnable Question*, pp. 4, 130–33, 188–91.

22. RELA, MB, Oct. 1, Nov. 12, 1914; Mar. 25, 1915. See also Oct. 29, 1914. Irish Volunteers, MB, Oct. 11, 1914. Dennis Clark discusses the response to these same events in Philadelphia in his *Irish in Philadelphia*, pp. 151–53.

23. AOH D3, MB, Nov. 22, 1914; Aug. 21, Oct. 2, Nov. 20, 1915; D1, MB, May 6, July 10, 1915. See also RELA, MB, Mar. 2, 1916.

24. *Anaconda Standard*, Mar. 16, 17, 18, 1914.

25. AOH D3, MB, Mar. 13, 1915; *Anaconda Standard*, Mar. 15, 16, 17, 18, 1915.

26. O'Dea, *AOH*, III:1492. See also Devoy, *Post Bag*, II:465, 475; Pollard, *Societies of Ireland*, p. 140; AOH D3, MB, Aug. 7, 1915; Mar. 11, 1916; RELA, MB, Mar. 23, 1916; *Anaconda Standard*, Mar. 17, 1916.

27. AOH D3, MB, Apr. 13, 1912; Sept. 20 and 27, Oct. 18, 1913. O'Dea, *AOH*, III:1489–90, 1499–1500.

28. Rumpf and Hepburn, *Nationalism and Socialism*, pp. 11–13. James Connolly, by then a member of the IWW, organized the Irish Socialist Federation in 1907; he had founded the Irish Socialist Republican party in 1896. Pollard, *Societies of Ireland*, pp. 107, 119. The reference to Marx is in ibid., p. 67. The Bolshevism reference is cited in Rumpf and Hepburn, *Nationalism and Socialism*, p. 25.

29. Rumpf and Hepburn, *Nationalism and Socialism*, p. 13; Joseph Lee, *Modernisation*, pp. 150–52; Lyons, *Culture and Anarchy*, pp. 77, 95–98; Pollard, *Societies of Ireland*, pp. 119–20. Greaves, *Connolly*. The quote is from Connolly, *Workers' Republic*, Apr. 8, 1916, in Rumpf and Hepburn, ibid., p. 12. The 1895 reference is from the *Butte Bystander*, Dec. 31, 1895.

30. Rumpf and Hepburn, *Nationalism and Socialism*, pp. 11–12; *Irish Worker* (Chicago), Mar. 30, 1912; *Montana Socialist*, Nov. 9, 1913; Larkin, *James Larkin*, pp. 63–64, 221. Yeats's quote is from Lyons, *Culture and Anarchy*, p. 78. James Plunkett treats these and other events of 1907–14 in his splendid novel, *Strumpet City*.

31. Mills's remark is from the *Montana Socialist*, May 6, 1916. See also Lyons, *Culture and Anarchy*, pp. 94–98.

32. Irish Volunteers, MB, Dec. 5, 1914. For memberships see O'Dea, *AOH*, III:1090–91, 1129–30, 1380, 1413, 1489–90, 1502; Philip J. Sullivan, "Report, July, 1914," in AOH, Reports; AOH D3, MB, Jan. 5, Feb. 22, 1913; Feb. 21, 1914; AOH, Silver Bow Co., Annual Report, Dec. 31, 1916; ibid; Dec. 31, 1917, in Reports. National Clan-na-Gael memberships are unknown; RELA figures are from Term Reports, 1904–27, in Financial Records; RELA, MB, Feb. 27, Mar. 27, Apr. 10 and 24, 1914. The AOH boast is from John O'Dea, National Secretary, Report, July 17, 1919, in Reports. AOH antisocialism, in addition to examples cited earlier, is revealed in AOH D3, MB, July 7, 1912.

33. O'Daly, Life, [53, 57].

34. Dubofsky, *We Shall Be All*, p. 155. Larkin was already using "An Injury to One is the Concern of All" as his slogan. See *Irish Worker*, 1911. Haywood, "Jim Larkin's Call." The *Anaconda Standard* called Larkin a "foreign agitator" and made only passing reference to the fact that he was Irish; Oct. 3, 1915. *Montana Socialist*, Sept. 25, 1915.

35. *Montana Socialist*, Oct. 2, 1915. Duncan said the denial of the hall was not possible in England or Ireland, but only in "Autocratic Russia"—or Butte. Ibid., Oct. 9, 1915.

36. Ibid., Oct. 9, 1915.

37. Lyons, *Culture and Anarchy*, p. 59; Devoy, *Recollections*, p. 321. Connolly's quote is from the *Harp*, n.d., in Pollard, *Societies of Ireland*, pp. 119–20. Wallace's remarks are from AOH D3, MB, Sept. 21, 1913. Kate Richards O'Hare was another who preached this same lesson in Butte. See the *Montana Socialist*, May 17, 1914.

38. The "up the Kaiser" remark is noted in Rumpf and Hepburn, *Nationalism and Socialism*, p. 18. Dennis Clark, *Irish in Philadelphia*, p. 150; *Montana So-*

cialist, Sept. 18, 1915. See also Feb. 22, 1914. The Connolly letter to Larkin was cited in the issue of May 2, 1916.

39. Deeney's remarks are in RELA, MB, Dec. 17, 1914. Rumpf and Hepburn, *Nationalism and Socialism*, p. 19; Dangerfield, *Damnable Question*, pp. 127–28; Pollard, *Societies of Ireland*, p. 140.

40. Allen, *Great Britain*, pp. 660, 669; Industrial Commission, *Mining at Butte*, 1915, p. 3692; Montana, Dept. of Labor, *First Biennial Report*, pp. 30–31; Federal Trade Commission, *Report, the Copper Industry*, p. 115; *Moody's Manual*, p. 2906. Lynch from RELA, MB, Jan. 7, 1915; AOH and RELA, Board of Trustees, Hibernia Hall, MB, Jan. 11, 1915. The RELA, AOH, and Irish Volunteers all formed new employment committees during the hard times of late 1914–early 1915. RELA, MB, Dec. 24, 1914; Feb. 10 and 17, Mar. 18, Apr. 22, May 23, June 3, 1915; AOH D3, MB, Jan. 23, Feb. 27, 1915; Irish Volunteers, MB, Aug. 16, 1914; Feb. 28, 1915.

41. Allen, *Great Britain*, p. 669. Hugh O'Daly commented on this irony (Life, [46]). The point is emphatically *not* that the U.S. entered the war to protect its loans. *Anaconda Standard*, Mar. 17, 1915.

42. RELA, MB, Feb. 3, 1916; Pollard, *Societies of Ireland*, pp. 142–43. There was no indication from the Minute Books that the AOH was informed, and it is unlikely that more than a handful of the Clansmen knew of the Rising in advance. See Funchion, *Organizations*, p. 119.

43. Rumpf and Hepburn, *Nationalism and Socialism*, pp. 19–20, 21; Joseph Lee, *Modernisation*, p. 152. See too Lyons, *Culture and Anarchy*, pp. 95–98.

44. Joseph Lee, *Modernisation*, p. 155; Clan-na-Gael, "On the Death of John Devoy." English's remarks are from the *Anaconda Standard*, May 1, 1916; *Montana Socialist*, May 6, 1916; Devoy, *Recollections*, p. 477. Hugh O'Daly remembered the Clan also working with the "Hindos" (Life, [56, 57]).

45. RELA, MB, Apr. 27, 1916; Applications for Membership, Patrick H. Pearse Branch, FOIF; FOIF, *Constitution and Bylaws*, 1919; Clan-na-Gael, "On the Death of John Devoy"; The AOH was also involved with the FOIF (D3, MB, Apr. 29, May 6, 1916); Funchion, *Organizations*, pp. 119–20; Pollard, *Societies of Ireland*, pp. 142, 210–11; *Anaconda Standard*, June 12, 1916.

46. RELA, MB, May 4, Aug. 18, Sept. 21 and 28, Oct. 5 and 19, Nov. 2, 1916; EDA to J. J. McCarthy, May 6, 1916, Correspondence. Hugh O'Daly said England denied him a visa because he was a revolutionary (Life, [52]). O'Sullivan interview.

47. AOH, Proceedings, 1916; Polk, *City Directory*, 1915; RELA, Membership and Dues Ledger, 1902–25.

48. Pollard, *Societies of Ireland*, p. 237; Larkin, *James Larkin*, pp. 221–23.

49. *Montana Socialist*, July 22, 1916. Mulcahy may have thought he had something to prove. Less than a month after his encounter with Larkin he was reported to have run an Orangeman out of town. *Anaconda Standard*, Aug. 5, 1916.

50. *Montana Socialist*, Dec. 23, 1916. See too the issue of Oct. 7, 1916, and the *Anaconda Standard*, Aug. 10, 11, 12, 1915, for Lehane's earlier visits to

Butte. Connolly was reported to have spoken in Butte about 1910. *Anaconda Standard*, May 4, 1916.

51. *Montana Socialist*, Jan. 27, 1917.

52. Foner, "Land League," p. 200.

53. On the AOH and the Knights of Columbus see AOH D3, MB, Jan. 6, May 5, 1917. The AOH complained in 1916 that there were too many Irish organizations—an obvious reference to the Pearse-Connollys (Proceedings, 1916, n.p.). The RELA complaint is from MB, Oct. 12, 1916. See also MB, May 23, June 24, 1915. The story of Maurice Ferriter is from the *Butte Bulletin*, Nov. 5, 1918.

54. On this point, for an earlier group of Irish immigrants, see Lees and Modell, "Irish Countryman Urbanized."

55. O'Sullivan interview. For the Pearse-Connollys meeting at St. Mary's Church see *Anaconda Standard*, Apr. 9, 1917. "Last Will and Testament of Fr. Michael Hannan," 1927, in St. Mary's Parish File; Liam Mellows to James Murray, Sept. 21, 1920, James E. Murray Papers.

56. *Anaconda Standard*, Feb. 4, Apr. 15, June 4, 1917; Mulcahy to Senator James Walsh, Apr. 24, 1917, in *Anaconda Standard*, Apr. 25, 1917.

57. RELA, MB, May 10, 1917; John Devoy's speech, n.d., in "Clan-na-Gael Petition to Congress, 1917," in Correspondence. Pollard, *Societies of Ireland*, p. 318, argues that the Clan resolved the conflict by continuing to work for an Irish victory.

58. RELA, MB, Mar. 28 and 29, Apr. 6, Sept. 6, 1917; Feb. 21, 1918; Sen. Henry Myers to Jerry Egan, June 28, 1918; Myers to John Gribben, July 1, 1918, Correspondence; "Petition to Congress, 1917," Peter Magennis to Local Camps, Aug. 20, 1918, Correspondence; "The Irish Republic Can Pay Its Own Way," n.d., 1918, pamphlet, Correspondence. On wearing uniforms, see *Anaconda Standard*, Apr. 26, 1917. The RELA's generosity is revealed in receipts from 1917 and 1918 from the Gaelic American Defense Fund, the Irish National Fund, the Defense of Ireland Fund, and the Save St. Enda's Committee (Financial Records). The Emmets sponsored Kathleen O'Brennan's lecture in April, 1918 (MB, Apr. 25, 1918). Maurice McDonough was one of those kept in good standing while serving in the army (Membership and Dues Ledgers, 1902–25). There are no references in the Minute Books of any of the organizations to either antiwar or worker-related protests.

59. Lane's comment is quoted in *Montana Socialist*, Mar. 17, 1917. See also *Anaconda Standard*, Mar. 18, 1917. The AOH rejection of the Pearse-Connolly invitation is from D3, MB, Mar. 10, 1917. The RELA conditional acceptance is in MB, Mar. 8, 1917.

60. James Coffey and James Treanor, for the Pearse-Connolly Club, to RELA, Mar. 23, 1917, Correspondence. Lynch's remarks were quoted in the *Anaconda Standard*, Apr. 9, 1917.

61. *Anaconda Standard*, June 4, 1917. On the planning for the speech see Mamie Lenahan, State "chairlady" Ladies Auxiliary, AOH to RELA, May 31, 1917, Correspondence; Report of Hannah Sheehy Skeffington Lecture Com-

mittee of the RELA, in MB, June 3, 1917. Her fee was $250.00. Ticket sales raised $584.50.

62. *Anaconda Standard*, June 4 and 6, 1917. A copy of the typed bulletin, undated and without attribution, is included with the copies of the *Joint Strike Bulletin*, microfilm, University of Montana. See also the account in Wheeler, *Yankee*, pp. 135–38. McLysaght, *Irish Families*.

63. *Montana Socialist*, July 21, 1917; *Anaconda Standard*, June 5, 6, and 7, 1917. Polk, *City Directory*, 1910–15. It hardly needs saying that city directories are not unimpeachable sources. McLysaght, *Irish Families*.

64. For the Speculator fire see Gutfeld, *Montana's Agony*, pp. 14–22; Bureau of Mines, *Lessons from the Granite Mountain Shaft Fire*, pp. 1–98; Montana, Dept. of Labor, *Third Biennial Report*, pp. 21–22. All of Butte's newspapers covered the disaster in detail. The estimates of total casualties ranged from 163 to 165. The *Butte Miner*, June 18, 1917, contains the most complete and accurate list and it totaled 165. The names of the MMWU leaders are taken from the *Joint Strike Bulletin* and its successors, the *Strike Bulletin*, the *Butte and Anaconda Joint Strike Bulletin*, and the *Butte Bulletin*, passim. See also the names that appear in the MMWU, MB, Oscar Rohn Files, Montana Council of Defense Papers (hereafter cited as Rohn Files, MCD Papers). These Minute Books are the work of company spies, either Daniel Pohl or Warren Bennett. There are two sets of books—Bennett was checking on Pohl and Bennett's notes are more complete.

65. Vernon Jensen, *Heritage of Conflict*, pp. 432–51; Dubofsky, *We Shall Be All*, pp. 366–68; 420–21; Gutfeld, *Montana's Agony*, pp. 1–92; Rice-Fritz, "Montana Council of Defense"; Johnson, "An Editor and a War"; Wetzel, "Making of an American Radical"; Glasser, "Butte Miners' Strike." Material from the National Archives bearing on the strikes of 1917–20 is available on microfilm at the University of Montana. Hereafter, all references to this material will be cited by department and file number or record group.

66. Testimony of Michael Grace, July 12, 1918, Trial of U.S. vs. Haywood; testimony of W. F. Dunn, July 13, 1918; testimony of John M. Foss, July 11, 1918; testimony of Charles Stevens, July 11, 1918, all ibid.

67. Testimony of Joe Kennedy, July 15, 1918, ibid.; "The Irish Scab," Page Stegner, "Protest Songs from the Butte Mines," copy in ibid.

68. Testimony of W. F. Dunn, ibid. For the demands of the MMWU, see *Joint Strike Bulletin*, June 11, 1917; *Anaconda Standard*, June 14–17, 1917; MMWU to Sec. of Labor, William B. Wilson, June 23, 1917, Dept. of Labor, file 33/493.

69. RELA, MB, July 29, 1915.

70. ACM to William B. Wilson, July 25, 1917, Dept. of Labor, file 33/493; "Report of ACM," Sept. 22, 1917, ibid.; Thomas Chope, ACM Commission of Labor, to Felix Frankfurter, Sept. 18, 1918, ibid., file 20/473; Bureau of Labor Statistics, *Bulletin 357*, Dept. of Justice, Record Group 60; *Butte Bulletin*, Nov. 15, 1918; Burton K. Wheeler, U.S. Attorney, to Thomas Gregory, U.S. Attorney General, Aug. 21, 1917, Dept. of Justice, file 186701–27. There are other references to inflation in *Montana Socialist*, Jan. 11, Mar. 15, 1914; May 20, 1916;

June 23, 1917; Montana, Dept. of Labor, *First Biennial Report,* pp. 65, 87, 92, 93, 96; Lee et al., *Population Redistribution,* p. 753; see also pp. 588, 598–602, 754. ACM's ranking in the corporate world was noted in the *Montana Socialist,* Sept. 8, 1917. *Moody's Manual,* p. 2906.

71. For a discussion of new management practices during the war see Brody, *Workers in Industrial America,* p. 12; "Call for Union," June 11, 1917, in *Joint Strike Bulletin; Butte Miner,* Feb. 22, 1918; Hand et al., "Songs," p. 37; Brissenden, "Rustling Card," pp. 770, 771; Federal Trade Commission, *Report, the Copper Industry,* p. 115.

72. Statistics on ACM's work force from B. F. Swisher, National Draft Inspector, to Provost Marshall E. H. Crowder, Oct. 10, 1918, Exhibits E, F, G, H, Dept. of Justice, file 186233–61. Many men came to Butte after the strike in the Michigan copper region in 1913–14. See the letter from Charles Wirtola of the Hancock Copper Miners' Union to Ernest Mills, WFM, June 7, 1915 and the references in WFM, Exec. Board, MB, Nov. 27, 1915; Oct. 18, 1916; Sept. 13, 1917.

73. The "kaleidoscope" remark was made by Hywel Davies, Commissioner of Conciliation, Dept. of Labor, "Survey of Copper Labor Conditions in Montana," typescript, July 3, 1918, Dept. of Labor, file 33/1703. The "flowers that bloom" comment is from J. H. Rowe, chief of the Butte Selective Service office, to John Speed Smith, chief Naturalization Examiner, Jan. 31, 1918, Dept. of Justice, file 189730. Rowe was employed in ACM's tax department according to the *Montana Socialist,* Oct. 31, 1914. Statistics on the Irish rate of naturalization are from B. F. Swisher to E. H. Crowder, Oct. 10, 1918, Dept. of Justice, file 186233–61.

74. *Butte Bulletin,* Sept. 10, 1918. See too *Montana Socialist,* Jan. 8, 1916. "Call for Union," June 11, 1917, *Joint Strike Bulletin.* The labor shortage and consequent dependence on new men is noted in Evans, *Address,* pp. 10, 28; Con Kelley to C. O. Edwards, Secretary of the Montana State Metal Trades Council, July 19, 1917, Dept. of Labor, file 33/493; Hywel Davies, "Survey," Dept. of Labor, file 33/1703; Abraham Glasser, "Butte Strike," Dept. of Justice, Record Group 60; A. S. Peake to Director of Military Intelligence, May 13, 1920, War Dept., file 10110–1841; *Butte Bulletin,* Aug. 26, 1918; Burton K. Wheeler to Sen. Thomas Walsh, June 18, 1917, Dept. of Justice, file 186233–61–5; Rowe to Speed, Jan. 31, 1918, Dept. of Justice, file 186233-61. The usefulness of these new men, either because they tended to be conservative or because they could not be drafted, is noted in Brody, *Workers in Industrial America,* pp. 14–21; WPA, *Copper Camp,* pp. 294, 295; Arthur Fleming, chief of State Councils of Defense, to State Councils of Defense, Aug. 20, 1918, General Correspondence, U.S. Councils of Defense, MCD Papers. Wheeler, *Yankee,* p. 138; Edward Day, U.S. Attorney, to Thomas Gregory, Oct. 31, 1918, Dept. of Justice, file 186701–27. Very late in the war all workers in essential industries, copper mining among them, were exempt from the draft. D. M. Reynolds to Charles D. Greenfield, Aug. 29, 1918, telegram, General Correspondence, MCD Papers.

75. *Anaconda Standard*, July 8, 1917; MMWU, MB, July 31, 1917, Rohn File, MCD Papers; *Strike Bulletin #22*, July 31, 1917; *Joint Strike Bulletin #48*, Oct. 8, 1917.

76. *Joint Strike Bulletin, #59*, Nov. 6, 1917; #27, Aug. 11, 1917; #55, Oct. 25, 1917; *Montana Socialist*, Jan. 15, 1916; *Butte Bulletin*, Aug. 26, 1918; MMWU to W. B. Wilson, June 23, 1917, Dept. of Labor, file 33/493. The "no smoking" sign is a part of the permanent exhibit at the World Museum of Mining in Butte.

77. *Joint Strike Bulletin, #51*, Oct. 15, 1917. See also *Strike Bulletin, #24*, Aug. 4, 1917. *Strike Bulletin, #21*, July 27, 1917; *Joint Strike Bulletin, #54*, Oct. 22, 1917. On troops in the Florence Hotel, see A. D. Chaffin to Chief of Staff, May 15, 1920, War Dept., file 10001–1841. The *Anaconda Standard*, July 19, 1917 reported that "many" of the boardinghouses were refusing to put up lunch buckets. See also the *Butte Bulletin*, Nov. 18, 1918; MMWU, MB, July 31, 1917, Rohn File, MCD Papers; *Strike Bulletin*, 3d issue, n.d.; ibid., June 24–31, 1917.

78. *Joint Strike Bulletin #46*, Oct. 3, 1917, #52, Oct. 17, 1917.

79. Ibid., #46, Oct. 3, 1917, #60, Nov. 9, 1917; MMWU, MB, July 26, 1917, Rohn File, MCD Papers. There are general stories on mine accidents in the *Butte Bulletin*, Sept. 10 and 30, 1918; *Anaconda Standard*, June 9, 1917. See also the clipping service records at the Butte/Silver Bow Co. Public Archives. The companies responded with a well-publicized safety campaign. See, for example, *Butte Miner*, Oct. 31, 1915; Montana, Dept. of Labor, *First Biennial Report*, pp. 43–44; Butte Workingmen's Union (BWU), MB, Mar. 10, 1916. These books are in the World Museum of Mining, Butte. *Joint Strike Bulletin, #52*, Oct. 17, 1917.

80. For the BWU and WFM, see *Anaconda Standard*, June 1–14, Nov. 3, 1916; June 27, July 6, 1917; *Montana Socialist*, June 10 and 17, 1916; BWU, MB, Nov. 1915–July 1917. The BWU offered "moral and financial support to the mine workers of Butte in their efforts to organize" (MB, June 15, 1917). The WFM's continuing problems with Butte miners is discussed in Vernon Jensen, *Heritage of Conflict*, pp. 348–54. See also "Decision of the Exec. Board, WFM, in the Case of the Butte Miners' Union," Mar. 1915; WFM, Exec. Board, MB, July 30, Oct. 17, 1916; International Union of Mine, Mill, and Smelter Workers (successor to the WFM), Exec. Board, MB, Jan. 15, 18, 26, 1918. The reference to Moyer as a "four flusher" is from the *Joint Strike Bulletin, #58*, Nov. 3, 1917.

81. B. F. Swisher to E. H. Crowder, Oct. 10, 1918, Dept. of Justice, file 186233–61.

82. Swisher to Crowder, Oct. 10, 1918, Dept. of Justice, file 186233–61; *Anaconda Standard*, Aug. 25, 1917; War Industries Board to William B. Wilson, Oct. 27, 1917, Dept. of Labor, file 33/493.

83. ACM claims were noted in *Joint Strike Bulletin, #50*, Oct. 12, 1917. The government's figures are from William Fitts, Asst. Attorney General, to William B. Wilson, June 20, 1917, Dept. of Labor, file 33/493. Kelly's quote is in Charles Merz, "The Issue in Butte," *New Republic* (Sept. 22, 1917), pp. 215–17. The end of the strike is discussed in the *Anaconda Standard*, Dec. 18, 1917.

84. The membership and number of striking miners claims are from *Strike Bulletin*, #34, Aug. 30, 1917.

85. Fr. Patrick Brosnan to his mother, June 19, 1917, Brosnan Letters. There were thirty-four Irish names among the 165 listed as killed in the fire. *Butte Bulletin*, Sept. 30, 1918. On the Speculator and the rustling card, see Hywel Davies to Felix Frankfurter, July 20, 1918, Dept. of Labor, file 33/1703.

86. The quote is from the *Anaconda Standard*, June 13, 1917.

87. Evans, *Address*, pp. 2, 10; de Valera to Boyce, Sept. 20, 1919; Boyce to de Valera, Sept. 23, 1919. See also Boyce to P. H. Callahan, Oct. 4, 1919, Boyce Papers.

88. The *Butte Post* remark was cited in *Strike Bulletin*, #32, Aug. 25, 1917. *Helena Independent*, June 13, 1917; see also June 6 and 9, 1917. On Campbell's zealotry see Johnson, "An Editor and a War." The *Standard*'s charge was cited in *Strike Bulletin*, #19, July 23, 1917.

89. On copper as an essential item of war see *Montana Socialist*, Aug. 18; Oct. 13, 1917; *Butte Bulletin*, Oct. 9, 1918; William Fitts to William B. Wilson, June 20, 1917, Dept. of Labor, file 33493; Joseph Ashbridge, U.S. Marshall, to Thomas Gregory, July 12, 1917, Dept. of Justice, file 186233–61–8; Capt. J. H. Denfel to District Intelligence Officer, Aug. 26, 1918, War Dept., file 10110–753; Thomas Gregory to Newton Baker, Sec. of War, Oct. 23, 1918, Dept. of Justice, file 195397; D. M. Reynolds to Charles Greenfield, Aug. 29, 1918, General Correspondence, MCD Papers. The laws on sedition were explicit. See National Espionage Act, June 15, 1917, *Statutes at Large*, 40, part 1, p. 217; and "Espionage Act, May 16, 1918, in *Documents of American History*, II:326.

90. For examples see *Strike Bulletin*, #34, Aug. 30, 1917; *Butte Bulletin*, Aug. 20 and 29, Sept. 24, Oct. 7, Nov. 14, Dec. 4 and 30, 1918.

91. Davies, "Survey," Dept. of Labor, file 33/1703. The reference to the effects of Prohibition on worker radicalism is from an unidentified newspaper sent by Sanders Co. (Montana) Attorney Wade Parks to Thomas Gregory, Aug. 29, 1917, Dept. of Justice, file 186701–27. Montana did not go dry until Jan. 1, 1919, but the habit of meeting in union rather than beer halls was well established among many of the new men who came to Butte. See, for example, the complaint of an Anaconda, Montana, businessman to Sen. Miles Poindexter, Aug. 3, 1917, Dept. of Justice, file 186701–27.

92. J. H. Rowe to John Smith, Jan. 31, 1918, Dept. of Justice, file 186233–61. See too Burton K. Wheeler to Thomas Walsh, June 18, 1917, Dept. of Justice, file 186233–61–5; Rowe to Sen. Henry Myers, Jan. 31, 1918, Dept. of Justice, file 186233–01; *Montana Socialist*, July 22, 1917.

93. Davies, "Survey," Dept. of Labor, file 33/1703.

94. Wheeler, *Yankee*, pp. 135–38. A Scotland Yard agent in Butte told Burton Wheeler that there was more hysteria in Butte than in London (ibid., p. 149). The Silver Bow County Council of Defense was formed in April, 1917. By 1918 it had over 1,000 members. Eugene Carroll to Charles Greenfield, Apr. 23, 1917; Sept. 25, 1918, General Correspondence, MCD Papers. See MCD, MB, Nov. 25, 1918, for the council's suppression of a Butte antivivisectionist (MCD Papers). For a general discussion of the council and its activities see

Rice-Fritz, "Montana Council of Defense." See also Montana *Laws,* 1918; G. E. LaFollette to Thomas Gregory, Feb. 2, 1918, Dept. of Justice, file 189730–2. The mediator was William H. Rodgers. See his letter to William B. Wilson, July 2, 1917, Dept. of Labor, file 33/493. For newspaper stories linking the strike to Germany, see, for examples, *Helena Independent,* June 6–Dec. 19, 1917, passim; *Anaconda Standard,* June 13 and 14, 1917; *Butte Post,* Oct. 18, 1917. The *Montana Socialist* cited other examples in its issue of June 30, 1917. The Gerard story is from ibid., Sept. 8, 1917. The strikers proclaimed their loyalty on the Fourth of July (Miners and Electrical Workers, *Joint Strike Bulletin,* July 4, 1917) and demanded a list of ACM's German stockholders in *Joint Strike Bulletin,* #40, Sept. 15, 1917. Statement of Oscar Rohn, May 14, 1918, to MCD, in MCD Papers. For a general treatment of this point see H. C. Peterson and Fite, *Opponents of War,* pp. 53–56, 168–80, 235–46.

95. *Strike Bulletin,* #25, Aug. 6, 1917; #29, Aug. 17, 1917. He was buried out of Larry Duggan's funeral parlor; *Montana Socialist,* Aug. 11, 1917. The number of Pearse-Connollys in the procession was probably exaggerated. For Little see Gutfeld, *Montana's Agony,* pp. 23–36; MCD, Testimony at Hearings, II:1351–57, MCD Papers; Montana, Bureau of Labor, *Third Biennial Report,* p. 20; *Butte Miner,* July 18, 20, 21, 23, 1917; *Anaconda Standard,* Aug. 1–4, 1917; MMWU, MB, July 25, 1917, Rohn File, MCD Papers.

96. Evans, *Address,* p. 10; *Strike Bulletin,* #34, Aug. 30, 1917. By Dec., 1917, veteran Irish Socialists and revolutionary members of the Irish Progressive League were prominently identified with the Friends of the New Russia, successor organization to the Friends of the Russian Revolution. Larkin, *James Larkin,* p. 220.

97. Chope to Felix Frankfurter, Sept. 18, 1918, Dept. of Labor, file 20–473; Sam Stewart to Eugene Carroll, Oct. 9, 1918, General Correspondence, MCD Papers; Campbell to Sen. Henry Myers, Jan. 27, 1918, Dept. of Justice, file 189730; Scherer, *Nation at War,* p. 150; N. P. Walters to Victor Elting, Nov. 5, 1918, Dept. of Justice, Record Group 60; Knabenshue to Gen. Milstaff, Chief of Military Intelligence, June 4, 1918, War Dept., file 10110–103.

98. Miners and Electrical Workers, *Joint Strike Bulletin,* July 4, 1917. The raids are discussed in *Joint Strike Bulletin,* #37, Sept. 6, 1917; Burton Wheeler to Thomas Gregory, coded telegram, Sept. 16, 1918, Dept. of Justice, file 195397–1; H. C. Peterson and Fite, *Opponents of War,* p. 62. For the St. Patrick's Day, 1918, episode, see RELA, MB, Mar. 7, 1918; *Anaconda Standard,* Mar. 18, 1918. Omar Bradley is discussed in O'Daly, *Life,* [227], [233]. Gov. Sam Stewart to War Dept., Mar. 16, 1918, War Dept., file 370.6.

99. MCD, Record Series 19, Order #1, Mar. 15, 1918, MCD Papers; "Report of Capt. Omar Bradley," Mar. 19, 1918, War Dept., file 370.6; *Anaconda Standard,* Mar. 18, 1918. McLysaght, *Irish Families;* Polk, *City Directory,* 1915.

100. *Anaconda Standard,* Mar. 18 and 20, 1918.

101. Lynch to James Murray, Aug. 12, 1919, in James E. Murray Papers; Proceedings of the Joint Session, 1918, MCD Papers.

102. Little's motives are noted in MMWU, MB, July 24, 1917, Rohn File, MCD Papers. Burton Wheeler's insistence that the MMWU was not fronting for the IWW is persuasive (MCD, Testimony at Hearings, I:351–57).

103. The ministers' statement is in the *Montana Socialist*, Sept. 8, 1917; Lynch's remarks are from ibid., Aug. 25, 1918.

104. Wheeler testimony, MCD, Testimony at Hearings, pp. 351–54.

105. Hobsbawm, "Artisans and Labour Aristocrats," pp. 267–68; *Anaconda Standard*, June 14, 1917; Miners and Electrical Workers, *Joint Strike Bulletin*, June 11, 1917; *Joint Strike Bulletin*, #55, Oct. 25, 1917.

106. *Montana Socialist*, Feb. 13, 1915. A veteran Butte newspaperman also said the 1917 and 1918 strikes were different from those in 1919 and 1920 because the old-time miners, including the old Irish, went out in 1917–18 (Quinn interview). Larkin's comments regarding Moyer are from the *Montana Socialist*, Oct. 9, 1915. For Kelley's offer, see Davies, "Survey," Dept. of Labor, File 33/1703.

107. *Strike Bulletin*, #21, July 27, 1917; Miners and Electrical Workers, *Joint Strike Bulletin*, #15, July 12, 1917. See also the *Montana Socialist*, July 14, 1917. Mr. Dooley was quoted in ibid., Sept. 18, 1917.

108. Hobsbawm, "Artisans and Labour Aristocrats," p. 268. Wheeler referred to the use of the rustling card as a "weapon of political control" in a letter to Thomas Gregory, Aug. 21, 1917, Dept. of Justice, file 186701–27. See also Bernard Baruch to William B. Wilson, June 30, 1917, Dept. of Labor, file 33/493; Miners and Electrical Workers, *Joint Strike Bulletin*, June 12, 1917.

109. The "supervision of hiring" demand is from the first issue of the *Strike Bulletin*, n.d. [June 11, 1917]. The figures are from the *Joint Strike Bulletin*, #34, Aug. 30, 1917. The company disputed these figures. Evans, *Address*, p. 28; Con Kelley to C. O. Edwards, July 19, 1917, Dept. of Labor, file 33/493. The charge that cards were denied men who complained about unsafe conditions is from the *Montana Socialist*, Aug. 8, 1917. The references to stable, married, propertied, genuine union strikers are from the *Joint Strike Bulletin*, #17, July 18; #20, July 25; #31, Aug. 23; #35, Sept. 1; #42, Sept. 21, 1917.

110. *Strike Bulletin*, #22, July 31, 1917; *Joint Strike Bulletin*, #35, Sept. 1; #57, Oct. 31, 1917; Bill Dunn and Thomas Campbell, testimony, in MCD, Testimony at Hearings, II:1350–51; MMWU to William B. Wilson, June 23, 1917, Dept. of Labor, file 33/493.

111. *Joint Strike Bulletin*, #59, Nov. 6; #55, Oct. 25, 1917; Miners and Electrical Workers, *Joint Strike Bulletin*, June 11, 1917; *Strike Bulletin*, #36, Sept. 4, 1917.

112. For Carroll, Brophy, and Barry see *Montana Socialist*, July 22, 1917. For Maloney and Hanratty see Miners and Electrical Workers, *Joint Strike Bulletin*, July 10, 1917; *Strike Bulletin*, #29, Aug. 17, 1917. For Mulcahy, O'Rourke, and Murphy see *Butte Bulletin*, May 15, 1920. For Walsh see RELA, MB, Oct. 10 and 17, 1918; *Butte Bulletin*, Oct. 30, 1918.

113. Later applications to both the AOH and the RELA do not reveal quite the same West Cork connection. See MBs, ca. 1910–20; McLysaght, *Irish Families*.

114. For the government suppression of the *Irish World* and the *Gaelic American* see Dennis Clark, *Irish in Philadelphia*, pp. 151–52; Devoy, *Recollections*, pp. 469–71. On the raids on the *Butte Bulletin* see Wheeler to Gregory, Sept.

16, 1918, Dept. of Justice, file 195397–1; MCD, MB, Sept. 9, 1918, MCD Papers. For the demands that the *Bulletin* be suppressed see Asst. Attorney General R. P. Stewart to J. Merian, Dec. 3, 1919, Dept. of Justice, file 195397–28; J. Edgar Hoover to Col. A. B. Cox, Aug. 21, 1920, Dept. of Justice, file 195397– 36; Wetzel, "Making of an American Radical." Dunn became a prominent American communist. See Draper, *Roots*, pp. 316–17, 457, and *American Communism*, p. 169.

115. RELA, MB, June 12, 1919. Louis Donovan, an attorney and RELA, was a major stockholder in the *Bulletin*. Dunn testimony, in MCD, Testimony at Hearings, II:1360. J. J. Connolly to Officers and Members, RELA, Dec. 11, 1918, Correspondence.

116. *Butte Bulletin*, Oct. 4, 1918; AOH D3, MB, June 30, 1917.

Epilogue: The Postwar Years

I

Butte's Irish world survived 1917–18, but only barely and in different form. The wartime strike of 1917 was the decisive event. Played out against a backdrop of more than a decade of Irish-German cooperation, with memories of Larkin's visits still fresh, the strike resulted in charges that the strikers, the Irish, or both, were guilty of treason. That can have surprised no one, least of all the Irish strikers. Irish miners faced two different problems. Being an Irish and an American patriot had not been easy since 1900; being loyal to both Ireland and the working class had been less hard, but even that hyphenated form required some careful selection of tactics and emphasis. The war and the strike made Irish-American a contradiction in terms; Irish-worker a formula for treason. The enclave was left battered and divided.

There were more strikes in 1919 and 1920, but these appear to have been purely IWW affairs. Even with the war over, however, they retained some of their associational Irish aspects. In 1919 the strike leaders were identified as "Finnlanders, Sinn Feiners, and members of the Pearse Connolly Club and IWW." One of the military officers assigned to Butte insisted that the "situation could be solved by the prompt deportation of undesireable aliens, mostly Finns and Irish." Deportation would not be necessary in at least one instance; a headline identified one of these Irish as IWW organizer Charles Devlin (a County Tyrone name), noting that "This Boob Wishes to Go Back to Ireland."[1]

With the war over the RELA could resume its often radical advocacy of Ireland without having to worry about offending American sensibilities and opening itself up to charges of disloyalty. As a result the Pearse-Connolly Club was left with only the Connolly half of its constituency. The patriot game would again be played by the established associations. It is possible, in fact, that the IWW had by this time captured the Pearse-Connolly Club. Radical worker infiltration of "sympathetic" Irish organizations was certainly not unknown, particularly after Larkin and Lehane identified the Irish as inherently sympathetic. In San Francisco, for example, "secessionists" in the Knights of the Red Branch, the local Clan-na-Gael, were said to have driven out all the "real Republicans" and to have entered into a one-sided alliance with "IWW cranks." The Wobblies met in the Knights' hall and had their sign "in large red letters beside the Knights' own that completely overshadow[ed] it." This alleged IWW takeover was offered as part of a more elaborate explanation of how the Clan-na-Gael "split was engineered," suggesting that the seam, tighter and more nearly invisible during the war than ever before, was tearing, and that Irish-American radical nationalists would again go one way, Irish-American radical workers another. In Butte the Pearse-Connolly Club made unnecessary any IWW infiltration of the RELA, unthinkable as that might be. The Irish connection with worker protest could be kept intact by the Pearse-Connollys, but it was a loose and mostly symbolic connection.[2]

The depressed copper market also contributed to the split at the seam. John D. Ryan said in 1917 that it would be "catch as catch can after the war." He meant specifically that American copper would have to be allowed to enter foreign markets. It would enter them eventually, but not in time to save the jobs of thousands of Butte miners. In 1918 Butte's mines produced 323,000,000 pounds of copper; in 1919 barely half that. ACM dividends went from $8.00 per share in 1918 to $0 in both 1921 and 1922. In 1918 man-hours worked in American copper mines were over 150,000; in 1921 that figure was 36,000. In December, 1918, the Anaconda and Neversweat mines were closed; by January, 1919, fifteen mines were down, idling more than 7,000 men.[3]

The IWW strikes of 1919 were called to protest the treatment of California Wobbly—and Irishman—Tom Mooney, as well as wage cuts in Butte. They failed in large measure because they were strikes against closed mines. IWW and AFL recruiting efforts suffered for the same reason. The Wobblies still promised revolution; the International Union of Mine, Mill, and Smelterworkers, AFL, promised to restore the BMU to its position as the "greatest single Labor Union in the world." It even said it would not require the men to join individually but would give the BMU its old name and number back. None of the promises meant much to idle and demoralized men.[4]

Hundreds of miners left Butte every day. A significant percentage of them were Irish. For the first time since Marcus Daly began to draw them in, the number of Irish in Butte declined. In 1910 there were 4,863 Irish immigrants in Silver Bow County, 3,196 Irish immigrants in Butte. In 1920 those numbers were 3,370 and 2,376. Some of these losses were from the deaths of older immigrants and from the general drop in immigration from Ireland. But those reasons cannot explain a decline of more than 30 percent during a ten-year period when overall population figures for both the city and the county rose by almost 15 percent. Second generation numbers are unavailable for 1920, but these had declined between 1900 and 1910—reflecting, among other things, the second generation's aversion to working underground—and there is no reason to assume that this trend was reversed between 1910 and 1920.[5]

The established Irish associations were particularly hard hit by these mine shutdowns. In 1921 Ed Connolly, an AOH officer, explained to former member Alex Crossin, then in Pennsylvania, that though individual Hibernians were still prospering the order was not. Fortunately, "the people of Ireland, though deserving and in need of every assistance do not expect donations from those who cannot do justice to themselves." Connolly knew of hundreds of Irishmen in straitened circumstance owing to the "acute industrial depression" in Butte. "Conditions are very bad, . . . the mines being shut down completely, causing a tremendous amount of unemployment." By definition these unemployed had to be in Butte, indicating that the steady men still were that. But there were fewer of them and they were less able, and probably less willing, to contribute.[6]

Membership in Division 1 of the AOH stabilized at sixty by 1922, down from over 600 in 1905; it would seldom exceed sixty, and never by very much, in later years. The Emmets fared no better. In September, 1921, they "purged" more than 300 delinquent members from their rolls, men who had joined during the heady days of 1913–14 and then dropped out, either to join the Pearse-Connollys or to seek better prospects away from Butte. This reduced their roster to fewer than 100 men. Attendance at weekly meetings reflected the decline. There were eight members present at the meeting of June 10, 1920; seven at that of October 6, 1921; six on February 2, 1922; five on January 3, 1924. By 1928, the membership stood at sixty-one. William Deeney was dead by then, but the list included such other veterans as J. J. Lynch, Maurice Drohan, John Gribben, John J. McNamara—the "blind boy" and community band leader, James B. Mulcahy—still editing the *Butte Independent*, and Pat Heaney.[7]

The secretary of the Clan-na-Gael wrote in 1920 that he knew "something of the unfavorable conditions in Butte" but was still confident that the camp was doing "everything possible in the interest of the organization." He hoped they would not be discouraged; "the unsatisfactory conditions will not last." The secretary was right; they did not last. But the temporary prosperity of the mid- and late 1920s obviously did not bring restored health to the RELA or the AOH. The decline that had set in as early as 1914 would not be reversed. There is considerable irony in this, particularly as it applied to the RELA. Ireland's needs were greatest just as this revolutionary Irish-American organization was least able to meet them. Financial assistance would not suffer. As will be seen, Butte's Irish were as generous as ever. But the money came from a few wealthy, or at least solvent, Irishmen, not from the hundreds of working Irish who had supported the Land League and its successors. The source of the dollars made little difference to Eamon de Valera, president of the provisional Irish Republic, or, with Connolly's dream of a socialist Ireland gone, to anyone else of influence in Ireland. American dollars bought the same number of guns, provided the same measure of relief regardless of the social rank of the contributor.[8]

Rather the effects were felt in Irish-America. Had Ireland been ready to "strike for her freedom" in 1895 or even 1905, Irish-American support would have come from Butte's young, working-class Irish, the products of the massive immigration of 1890–1905. The support, in fact, did come from that generation of immigrants. By 1916–20, however, it was not as young and overwhelmingly working class as it had been. But Ireland was not even ready for Pearse in 1900; it certainly was not ready for Connolly or Larkin. By the time the pieces were in place in Eire, social fragmentation, a new and different crop of Irish immigrants, crises in the workplace and union hall, and the alien and allegedly seditious radicalism of the IWW had robbed Butte's Irish world of much of its cohesion and emotional energy.

The membership figures of the RELA and the AOH would indicate as much. Younger Irishmen, both first- and second-generation, were not interested in their simple version of the patriot game. Larkin guided these younger Irish—when Marx or Sorel was not. Pearse still moved them, though it is doubtful that Douglas Hyde or even de Valera could have, but Ireland's liberation was subordinate to their own and to that of the others of their class. The RELA and the AOH existed to ease the transition of immigrant Irishmen inspired by ancient hatreds, confused by industrializing worlds, offended by Pat and Mike jokes, and frightened by the consequences of occupational hazards. These were less-pressing issues to the younger Irishmen. They had less need of organizations geared to meeting them. These organizations, however, were also the traditional means through which Ireland's needs were met. They collected the money, hosted the banquets, sponsored the speakers, and petitioned the Congress. Though reduced in numbers, their members' commitment was as great as it had ever been; and, individually, their financial circumstances were often much better. Ed Connolly, for example, after explaining to Alex Crossin the severity of Butte's economic depression, then added that "we have done very well in Butte, despite the . . . depression, raising approximately $20,000."[9]

Taken together, Connolly's remarks indicate that the pattern in Butte was different from that in Ireland and, perhaps, in other parts of Irish-America. Ireland's leftward tilt between 1912 and 1916 had pushed the Brophys away; as Irish nationalism became more radical, the non-radical became less Irish. Moreover, even the provisional Irish Republic, though not the socialist showpiece that James Connolly and Larkin wanted, was capable of proclaiming the "subordination of private property to the public right and welfare," could still argue that the Irish economy had to be developed on "progressive, co-operative industrial lines." Events in Butte represented a different sort of leftward tilt; war-time hysteria and suppression, the divisive effects on the Irish community of Larkinism, perhaps even the partial failure of radicalism in Ireland, shoved a significant percentage of the younger Irish workers nearer a class-based rather than an ethnic- or ethno-occupational-based allegiance. Certainly, the Pearse-Connollys did not figure to be particularly active in raising money for the Old Sod. Thus, the RELA and the AOH would be called back to old duties, but without the breadth of support and diversity of membership they had once had. Brophy once complained that the conservative United Irish League had not raised a single workingman's dollar; the Hibernians and the Emmets were becoming as top-heavy.[10]

II

Ed Connolly's $20,000 reference was to the Irish Relief Fund. The actual money collected was $18,354, one of the highest totals in the United States. The relief fund was one of many. In 1918 one hundred and twenty-one contributors gave $482 in two days to the Irish National Fund. But of that number only fifty-one were miners or laborers, though few of the contributions exceeded $10.00 and most were for $2.00. Six weeks later the RELA collected $609 for the same fund. In 1919, sixty-nine well-placed Irish gave $4,995 through the RELA to purchase Irish Republican bonds. The association added $500 more to that total. Individual contributions were understandably larger than for the national fund, but at that a breakdown of the sixty-five bond "investors" listed in the *City Directory* indicates how narrow the RELA's social base had become. Only eight of the sixty-five were miners and they provided less than $200.00 of the total. This was not unexpected; the most frugal workingman could not afford to risk more, even for Ireland. But the fact that eight gave a little would suggest that more could have given something. Perhaps more did; the list of sixty-nine is not a complete roster of the bond purchasers. But this was an RELA list and if more miners participated in the bond drive, they did so independent of the Emmets. The list was headed by seventeen merchants, excluding saloonkeepers; fifteen mine foremen, shift bosses, and skilled tradesmen; eleven city and county employees, including police and firemen; seven professionals; and three saloonkeepers, one of whom, Charles Kennedy—probably still on the cork foot the AOH had bought him fifteen years earlier—gave $500. By May, 1920, following a grand St. Patrick's Day parade, J. J. Harrington, the local treasurer for the Butte Irish Bond Drive, had $51,700 in cash; $57,000 in pledges. Harrington was an ACM accountant; the state chairman of the bond drive was James E. Murray, a prominent Butte attorney and later U.S. senator; the two were assisted by Dan Kelly, by then ACM's chief counsel. The committee met in Judge Lynch's courtroom.[11]

The Irish Freedom Fund Drive, aided by two visits to Butte by Eamon de Valera, was as financially rewarding as the bond drive—and likely as narrowly based. By November, 1919, Butte's Irish had raised $12,061.75. The next highest total in Montana was Billings's $414.00. All of this was in addition to other, smaller fund raising efforts. The Emmets sent well over $1,000 to help save John Devoy's *Gaelic American*, the voice of the Clan-na-Gael. There were still special calls and routine assessments; the Ricard O'Sullivan Burke Memorial Fund, for example, as well as the Thomas J. Clarke Fund, to which the RELA gave $6,185.50, double its assessment. There was truth to Corkman F. J. O'Hanlon's comment to his friend in Montana that "all over Ireland every one has heard of Butte, Montana." And the truth was stretched only slightly when he added that it was a "pity that you Americans have no better use for your money than sending it here to create trouble among Irishmen, for, without your money, we would be a very quiet, contented people."[12]

As before, Butte's Irish did more than collect money. They flew the flag of the Irish Republic over Hibernia Hall four years before the U.S. government recognized the Irish Free State—and sent a Butte Irishman as America's first ambassador to it. The AOH, RELA, FOIF, and the local branches of the American Association for the Recognition of the

Irish Republic (AARIR)—one of which was appropriately named for Wendell Phillips—worked unceasingly for an American acknowledgment of the Irish Republic. Nationally, the FOIF and the AARIR were bitter rivals but little of that factional wrath interfered with Butte's support of the Irish Republicans in the Anglo-Irish war that began in 1920. Perhaps Larkin's identification of deeper and more indigenous divisions made the AARIR-FOIF quarrel seem less significant.[13]

Whatever the explanation, relative harmony prevailed among the nationalists. At one time or another, one or more of the associations demanded the collection of war debts—lest the money England owed the U.S. be used in its war against the Irish people; condemned that war as "senile bigotry" and "barbaric"—with apologies to barbarism; organized a boycott of English goods; formed and financed a bogus "Protestant Friends of Ireland"; supported the Hindus; opposed the League of Nations and American participation in the World Court; pledged to keep the Butte Irishmen returning from the war in fighting trim and ready for "the responsibilities that are in store for them." What those might have been was unstated. They toasted the "Star-Spangled Banner" and petititioned for its acceptance as the national anthem; celebrated the centenary of the Monroe Doctrine; and generally, in the language of Montana bishops Carroll and Lenihan, prayed that "the God of nations may in our day grant the fullest measure of political and civil liberty to the little green isle."[14]

If this were not sufficient to engage their time and energies, they also celebrated in their usual way, Prohibition notwithstanding, the various Irish holidays. They paraded on St. Patrick's Day and—usually with the more Irish members of the Pearse-Connolly club—on a day near the anniversary of the Easter Rising. They still paid sick and death benefits—though sick benefits fell to almost nothing and death benefits tended to pay for the burials of old men rather than the living expenses of young widows. They continued to urge the use of Irish names and protest the caricaturing of Irish habits. In sum, they did what they had been doing for more than forty years. When the Countess Markievicz visited Butte in 1922, she recalled that it was "one of the places that stand out for its reception. They met us with a band and an army." It was the Pearse-Connolly fife-and-drum band, but it may have seemed like an army. "All Sligo," she concluded, "seemed to be there!" Michael Davitt might have written similarly about his visit in 1886. But there would have been a difference in the definition of "all Sligo."[15]

By 1920 the patriot game was being played by a smaller and more socially homogenous group of Irishmen. Perhaps had the mines stayed open and employment high, the pattern of the 1890s would have been repeated: young Irish miners joining older and established hands to give a distinct occupational aspect to Irish associational life. Merchants and professionals were welcome to that world, but its soul was in the working class. That complex interplay between Irish nationalism and worker consciousness was still apparent after the war, but not in the established Irish associations. Those had gone by default to the middle and upper classes. Even Jeremiah Lynch, whose sympathies with working-class Irishmen were real and frequently expressed, seems to have surrendered his control of the Irish associations to James E. Murray, a Canadian-born attorney whose inherited wealth was counted in the millions of dollars and who had not joined the RELA until 1919, twelve years after he came to Butte. Murray was immediately elected to go to the Irish Race Convention, met with Woodrow Wilson in an effort to convince the president that his doctrine of self-determination had obvious applicability to Ireland, and rose finally to the national presidency of the AARIR.[16]

Murray was no Brophy; he was known as a "labor lawyer" and his later career in the U.S. Senate was distinguished for its liberalism. But the differences between Murray and Brophy, or, for that matter, Murray and Con Kelley or John D. Ryan, were not as great as those between Murray and Pat Boland, William Deeney, Mo Drohan, Pat Heaney, Father Michael Hannan, Dan Sullivan, or Jeremiah Lynch. And to note only that this list does not include Joe Shannon, Dan Shovlin, James Coffey, Joe Kennedy, or William Dunn indicates the extent of Irish social fragmentation and the inability of the associations to accommodate it.

III

Thomas Brown wrote of those associations that "as long as they remained close to the warming sun of Irish nationalism they thrived; but when by the very law of their being they came into contact with the divisive realities of American life they inevitably disintegrated." As previously noted, Brown pays too little attention to the "divisive realities" of Irish nationalism, to the impossibility of sustaining the fight on the seam. Still, Brown's point is more than just felicitously phrased. It is convincingly made. In 1922, however, with the beginning of the Irish civil war, Irish nationalism no longer warmed at all, even by Brown's definition, and the disintegration of Irish associational life accelerated rapidly.[17]

The civil war in Ireland was a devastating blow. America's declaration of war against Germany broke Irish hearts, but not their will or their ability to resist. The Irish declaration of war against other Irish and against Ireland stripped them even of that. The issues over which the civil war was fought were meaningful—and have been amply documented. Instead of the united and independent Republic proclaimed by Pearse and the rebels of 1916, Ireland, in the December, 1921, treaty ending its war with England, was offered a Free State, and, given the already-enacted partition of a section of northeast Ulster, a partial one at that. The exact status of a Free State was uncertain—and unimportant. By the terms of the treaty, Ireland was neither united, nor independent, nor a republic. The antitreaty forces were lead by de Valera, a favorite in Butte since his visits in 1919.

Few Irish in Butte can have been pleased with a Free State, particularly one deformed by partition, and de Valera's opposition to the treaty that gave it birth was generally applauded. The RELA formally renounced the treaty; the chairman of the AOH's Irish History Committee said the "soul" of Ireland was with de Valera and that the Free State was only a temporary—though perhaps necessary—first step toward the realization of the promised Republic. The Wendell Phillips branch of the AARIR even sent de Valera a cablegram of congratulations for reminding the world that the revolution was only half won. But opposition to the treaty became defiance, and in 1922 the defiance was met by the Free State government with military force. The civil war had begun.[18]

James Murray was surprised. He had written to de Valera that the "impending situation in Ireland filled friends in the U.S. with horror"; still, as he told another AARIR officer, he believed that civil war was "possible but not probable." When it came, "the AARIR as well as all other sympathizers were shocked and humiliated." Ireland's enemies, and there were many, were "jubilant." But "all over the country people are dropping out of this organization and holding aloof entirely from Irish agitation." AOH memberships plummeted; the "miserable and confusing development of the present form of government . . . in Ireland" made it impossible to get new members. The RELA could only "pray"—not its usual style—"that the killing of brother by brother would soon cease." Hugh O'Daly remembered thinking that "the difference between document no. one and two was not worth the life of one Irishman." That difference, however, would take the lives of many hundreds.[19]

J. J. Lynch—and his despair can be imagined—referred to Ireland only as that "distracted and unfortunate country." But he could as well have been speaking of Butte's Irish world. "Factional prejudice," said John Sullivan, had "crept into the ranks." Father Sarsfield O'Sullivan remembers his father telling him about those years in Butte. Irishtown was riven; and not, as Larkin had expected, on the basis of social class. That division remained, but this one was fought out intraclass. Men who had known and worked with one another for decades refused even to speak; the most conspicuous of these feuds undoubtedly being Father Michael Hannan's refusal even to "say hello" to J. J. Lynch because of the judge's acquiescence in the treaty. A more direct expression of this same division occurred January 1, 1923. RELA members were readying Hibernia Hall for the fortieth annual Gala Ball when six sticks of dynamite were thrown into the rear yard of the hall. The charges exploded but there were no injuries and damage was minor. The dynamiters were never identified but the evidence is persuasive that members of the newly formed and intensely antitreaty Sarsfield Club had chosen this method to show their dissatisfaction with the predominantly protreaty AOH and the hopelessly divided RELA. Adding interest to the story is Father Hannan's role as founder of the Sarsfield Club. The civil war had come to Butte. That war—both in Ireland and in Butte—made doubly hard the memories of 1917–18, when support for Ireland's cause exposed the Butte Irish to charges of sedition. The fratricide of 1922–23 made that cause seem to have been not only disloyal but slightly ridiculous.[20]

Thus, it was a tired and divided group of warriors who made up the Irish associations in the later years. They had, however, lost none of their zeal. Let Judge Lynch speak for all of them. In 1922, just before the civil war, he "predicted the early smashup of the British Empire." In 1929 he "predicted a glorious future for the old land"; in 1930 "the break up of the British empire before many years"; in 1931 the "downfall of England in this generation." These predictions are of a kind with that made by Tom Kenny in 1915, that the Irish would be given preferential treatment in the mines once more. The patriots, like the worker aristocracy, seldom produced good prophets. The Irish associations were a mix of both.[21]

IV

But the reasons for their decline explain as well the sources of their and the enclave's strength. Like immigrant working-class enclaves throughout the United States, this one had always served as a buffer against the harsher aspects of a life different from anything the Irish immigrant miners and a fair percentage of the second-generation Irish miners had ever known. As immigration declined and that life became more familiar, and as events in Ireland and Butte demoralized their membership, the organizations lost their original purpose and energy, and the enclave lost its core. In the earlier years before social differentiation had become fragmentation, and while Ireland's dreams seemed attainable, these associations buttressed the Irish world.

The enclave was both cause and consequence of the Irish response to a variety of factors. It provided jobs, comrades, and wives. It paid workers when they were sick or hurt; paid their widows when the workers died. It gave back dignity and supplied a vital sense of stability to a people often stripped of the one and tragically unfamiliar with the other. It would not be easy to split the working-class component in this cooperative commonwealth. In addition, particularly through its associations, the enclave allowed the Irish miners the enormous luxury of striking at an ancient enemy. England may have seemed more within reach from Butte than from Allihies or Deeneystown; the language of protest was probably more unrestrained in Hibernia Hall than in its West Cork or Donegal equivalent.

The pull exerted by this community was strong—at least until 1917. In 1903 and 1907 the mines were shut down and men forced out of Butte; most of the settled of those men returned—as the Irish associations assumed they would. In 1917 the steady men again left town, or were driven from it, but this time the strike was followed by the postwar shutdowns, as well as the continued presence in the work force of younger men from strange places; there was little to which the Irish could return. At that, for the older men, there is evidence that the attraction persisted. The files of the Irish associations contain numerous letters from former members, temporarily relocated. They reflect the changes, both in Butte and in the men writing.

Alex Crossin wrote in 1921 that he had a job in the Pennsylvania coal mines. "The job is, as they say in Butte, pickens . . . nice and cool and *your own boss* [his emphasis]. The mines here sure has Butte skinned for you couldn't work unless with a union button on your old cap." "Still I would much rather suffer in a hot box for less money and be back in dear old Butte, ha ha. Give my best to Con Shea and Judge Lynch." By 1923 Crossin had come back, though not to working in a hot box. Other letters came from Thomas Curtis, then logging for $3.80 a day in Oregon; he had come to Butte in 1886 and had been an officer in the AOH. Thomas Byrne wrote to the RELA from Dublin where he was the sergeant-at-arms of the Dail Eireann; A. J. Connolly also wrote from an Oregon logging camp; Mathew Moriarity from Cahircehelon, County Kerry. Both wished to be remembered to "all the boys." "The communications," wrote J. J. Lynch, the evening's recording secretary, "evoked a pleasant response from the members present." There were nine. Barney Ferry sent his RELA dues from California along with "the wish to be remembered to all his old friends." There is nothing unique about this correspondence. The files of other ethnic and occupational associations would doubtless contain similar expressions of fraternal goodwill. But those other letters would reveal what these cited also make clear: the importance of associational affiliation to the immigrant working class of the late nineteenth and early twentieth centuries.[22]

No letters make this point as well as those from J. J. Griffin. Taken together with his career they can serve as a capsule history of Irish associationalism in Butte. Irish-born, Griffin got to Butte in 1902, working first in the Moonlight Mine, then as a carpenter in the Anaconda Mine. He lived in Dublin Gulch, belonged to both the AOH and the RELA, had his first son christened Emmet Patrick. In 1907 he publicly rebuked a WFM speaker for using "degrading and uncomplimentary remarks about the Catholic priests," rebuked his "fellow Irish Catholics" for encouraging such talk "by their presence and applause." He was a strong supporter of the Hibernian Colonization Society, telling the AOH that his very temporary residence on the Flathead reservation had left him feeling better than he had in years. He left the mines in 1910 to work as a pressman in a laundry.[23]

In 1921 he wrote to AOH officer Walter Sewell from his new home in Seattle. He was, he said, "a very sick fellow; the grippe, con, or some damn thing." But he had gone to the pontifical High Mass for Irish hunger-strike victim Lord Mayor Terrence McSwiney, and he told Sewell it was "simply grand." Griffin's doctor described his ailment as "bronchitis" and the AOH sent sick benefits. By 1926 Griffin was in Pasadena, California, but he still hoped to get back to Butte. He wrote to Tom Sullivan hoping that Sullivan could persuade Con Kelley to give him a "clerical job." Even a watchman's job, the customary work for "pensioners," would "kill me off pretty quick." He reflected on "the good old times we had at the meetings," and trusted that Sullivan was "holding up the membership numerically. I guess, though," he concluded, "we all have seen better days. Regards to all the old timers." By then, old-timers were all that was left.[24]

NOTES

1. Statement of Frank Barrett, Feb. 21, 1919, in "Testimony of Witnesses on the Use of Troops," Records of the Adjutant General's Office, Record Group 94, Bulky file 370.61; Gen. J. F. Morrison to Gen. Milstaff, Feb. 14, 1919, War Dept., file 10110–903. The reference to Devlin is in an unidentified clipping in Sen. Henry Myers to Att. Gen., A. Mitchell Palmer, Jan. 16, 1920, Dept. of Justice, file 186701–27.

2. The problems in San Francisco were central to the explanation of "How the Clan 'split' was Engineered," June 6, 1926, Correspondence.

3. Ryan writing in *Nation's Business*, quoted in the *Anaconda Standard*, Oct. 18, 1917; *Butte Miner*, Dec. 12, 1918; Jan. 3, 1919; Apr. 20, 1920; *Moody's Manual*, p. 2906; Federal Trade Commission, *Report, the Copper Industry*, p. 115.

4. Dubofsky, *We Shall Be All*, p. 450; *Butte Bulletin*, Dec. 6, 20, 1918; Jan. 12, 1919; *Butte Miner*, Dec. 12, 1918; Jan. 3, 1919; AFL and IUMMSW, Exec. Board, Open Letter to the Miners of Butte, Sept. 26, 1923, WHC.

5. Bureau of Census, *Twelfth Census, Population*, pp. 878–79; *Thirteenth Census*, pp. 592, 594; *Fourteenth Census, Population*, pp. 577, 583, 586. On overall immigration from Ireland to the United States, see the *Statistical History*, p. 56.

6. Connolly to Crossin, Mauch Chunk, Pa., Mar. 21, Apr. 7, 1921, Correspondence.

7. AOH, "Quarterly Reports," passim; RELA, Membership and Dues Ledgers, 1903–25; RELA, MBs.

8. V. C. (Clan secretary) to RELA, Apr. 20, 1921. See too the secretary's letters of Sept. 14 and 21, 1921; May 15, 1922; and Jan. 23 and Mar. 10, 1924, Correspondence.

9. Connolly to Crossin, Mar. 21, 1921, Correspondence.

10. Dail Eireann (Irish Parliament), "Proclamation of 1919," in FOIF, *Ireland's Declaration of Independence and Other Official Documents*.

11. RELA, MB, May 5, 1921; Feb. 20, 1919. Bond purchasers were listed at the end of the MB for 1915; see also RELA, MB, May 20, 1920. On the bond drive, see Receipts from AOH, Misc. Financial Records; Bond Committee to AOH D1, Nov. 26, 1919, Correspondence; James Murray to Bishop John Carroll, Mar. 6, 1920—Carroll gave $200.00. Carroll to C. B. Nolan, Mar. 13, 1920, Carroll Papers. W. W. McDowell, lieut. governor of Montana and later ambassador to the Irish Free State, to Murray, Dec. 26, 1919. Murray researched the legality of the bonds. See Murray to J. J. Harrington, Feb. 24, 1920. On individual gifts and subscribers, see Murray's correspondence, 1918–21, passim, Murray Papers. O'Daly, Life, [206]. Polk, *City Directory*, 1918, 1919, 1920.

12. Irish Freedom Drive Committee of Montana, Report, Dec. 23, 1919, Misc. Financial Records, IrC. See also, RELA, MB, May 21, Oct. 30, 1919; Barry O'Leary, chairman of Audit Committee, Report, Feb. 23, 1920. For de Valera's visits, see James Murray to Thomas Walsh, Aug. 25, 1919, and Edward Phelan to James Murray, Oct. 25, 1919, Murray Papers; *Anaconda Standard*, Nov. 8, 1919. RELA and Patrick Pearse branch, FOIF, Misc. Financial Records, n.d. See too RELA, MB, Aug. 15, 22, 1918; Oct. 5, 1922; V. C. to RELA, Aug. 31, 1923; F. J. O'Hanlon, Doughmore, Co. Cork, to Henry O'Hanlon, Chinook, Mont., Mar. 29, Apr. 12, 1922, copies in Murray Papers.

13. Jos. Reidy to John Gribben, Feb. 13, 1919, Correspondence. Carroll, *American Opinion*, pp. 156–60, 187; Tansill, *America and the Fight*, pp. 393–94; Funchion, *Organizations*, pp. 9–12, 119–26. The RELA deplored the split between the AARIR and the FOIF. See MB, Jan. 29, June 24, July 1 and 8, Nov.

11, 1920. The AARIR invited the FOIF to its convention. See James Murray to Secretary Patrick Pearse branch, FOIF, Dec. 15, 1920, Correspondence. For the Phillips branch, see AARIR, Proceedings, 1921, pp. 5–6. For Wendell Phillips and the Irish, see Foner, "Land League," pp. 150–51, 162, 181, 195.

14. On war debts: AARIR, Proceedings, 1921, p. 23; RELA, MB, Sept. 29, 1921. On condemnation of the war: FOIF, "Ireland Crucified," n.d.; FOIF, "Ireland's Case for Independence," May, 1919, in FOIF, *Ireland's Declaration of Independence,* p. 10. On boycotts: RELA, MB, Oct. 7, Dec. 30, 1920. The boycott dodgers were bought from the *Butte Bulletin,* see invoice, Dec. 30, 1920. On the Protestant Friends of Ireland: Diarmuid Lynch to James Murray, Mar. 3, 1920, marked "confidential," Murray Papers. On the Hindus: Friends of India, Nov. 8, 1920, copy in Murray Papers. On the League of Nations: Sen. Thomas Walsh to Murray, Aug. 9, 1919; League for the Preservation of American Independence, Henry Watterson, pres., "Open Circular to the Citizens of Montana, 1919." Murray to Sen. William Borah, July 30, 1919, Murray Papers; RELA to J. J. Lynch, Dec. 22, 1925, Correspondence. Bishop Carroll favored the League. See "Address . . . Pertaining to Education, 1922," Carroll Papers. On "fighting trim": Joseph McDonnell to AOH D1, Dec. 20, 1918, Correspondence. On the "Star-Spangled Banner": James Deary to President, AOH D1, Aug. 21, 1922, Correspondence. On the Monroe Doctrine: RELA, MB, Dec. 13, 1923. For Carroll's and Lenihan's prayer: AOH, Proceedings, 1921, n.p.

15. For St. Patrick's Day: AOH to FOIF and RELA, Jan. 20, 1919, Correspondence. ACM gave $50.00 to AOH for St. Patrick's Day, 1921. See AOH D1, MB, Mar. 7, 1921. The Pearse-Connollys were still parading; see *Anaconda Standard,* Apr. 5, 1920. See also Pearse-Connollys to RELA, Mar. 24, 1921; James Coffey, president Pearse-Connolly Club, to AOH, Mar. 27, 1919; RELA to AOH, Apr. 24, 1919; *Butte Bulletin,* Jan. 3, 1919. The trustees of Hibernia Hall reporting facetiously that it had come to their attention that Crowley and Sullivan were still handling "licquir and such be the case." The trustees promised "to wait on" the two miscreants. Trustees, MB, Aug. 16, 1920. On sick and death benefits: AOH D1, MBs, passim. See specifically the resolutions for Con Hayes, Sept. 28, 1922; P. J. Brophy, n.d. [1928]. On the stage Irishman: William Halloway to Murray, Oct. 24, 1920, Murray Papers; RELA, MB, Dec. 11, 1919. Richard Wolfe, *Ireland's Case: An American and International Problem* (Chicago, n.d.), in Murray Papers; V. C. to John Gribben, Oct. 12, 1927, Correspondence. For the Countess Markievicz's visit see Gore-Booth, *Prison Letters,* p. 287. The IWW showed her around Butte. See also Marreco, *Rebel Countess,* p. 311.

16. RELA, MB, Jan. 2 and 16, Mar. 20, 1919; Tansill, *America and the Fight,* p. 436.

17. Thomas N. Brown, *Irish-American Nationalism,* p. 41.

18. RELA, MB, Dec. 8, 1921; AARIR, *Proceedings, National Convention, 1922,* n.p.; copy of cablegram, in AARIR, *Second Annual Convention, 1922,* n.p. See also Thomas W. Lyons to Michael Collins, Feb. 9 and 16, 1922; Lyons to Ed Doheny, Feb. 15, 1922, in AARIR, Misc. Papers, 1921–22.

19. Murray to de Valera, n.d., handwritten letter without indication it was ever sent. Murray to John J. Finerty, July 10, 1922; Murray to John J. Hearn, July 4, 1922, Murray Papers. John D. Sullivan to AOH D1, Sept. 30, Oct. 1, 1922, Correspondence. RELA, MB, Aug. 3, 1922. O'Daly, Life, [205].

20. RELA, MB, Mar. 8, 1923; John Sullivan to M. J. McDonough, AOH D1, Apr. 2, 1923. See also P. V. Cuddihy to John Gribben, Jan. 28, 1922, Correspondence. O'Sullivan interview; McCarthy interview; Anaconda Standard, Jan. 1, 2, 1923.

21. RELA, MB, Feb. 9, 1922; Sept. 12, 1929; Sept. 4, 1930; Sept. 24, 1931, IrC.

22. Crossin to Ed Connolly, Mar. 10, May 1, 1921, Correspondence; Polk, City Directory, 1922; Curtis to Charles Kennedy, June 3, 1924; Byrne to RELA, Mar. 29, 1923, Correspondence. Byrne had won a baseball pool and used his winnings to retire to Ireland. See WPA, Copper Camp, p. 7. RELA, MB, Aug. 15, 1921; Barney Ferry to RELA, Apr. 7, 1925, Correspondence, IrC.

23. Polk, City Directory, 1902ff. AOH and RELA, Membership and Dues Ledgers; AOH D3, MB, June 24, 1907; May 13, 1911.

24. Griffin to Sewell, Oct. 25, 1921; Dr. C. L. Templeton to AOH, Nov. 21, 1921; Griffin to Tom F. Sullivan, Sept. 27, 1926. Griffin died in Los Angeles in 1928. The AOH sent his widow $65 in sick benefits (the benefits had been cut from $8.00 to $5.00 a week by then) and the $100.00 death benefit, along with a copy of their resolution of condolence; E. P. Griffin to J. M. Brown, May 20, 1928; Apr. 16, 1929; Brown to Mrs. J. J. Griffin, May 24, 1929, Correspondence.

Sources Consulted

ARCHIVAL COLLECTIONS

Alice Gold and Silver Mining Company Records. Montana Historical Society, Helena.
Anaconda Company Papers. Montana Historical Society, Helena.
Edward Boyce Papers. Eastern Washington State Historical Society, Spokane.
Bishop John Brondel Papers. Diocese of Helena Office, Helena, Mont.
P. J. Brophy Papers. Montana Historical Society, Helena.
Father Patrick Brosnan Letters. In possession of Professor Kerby A. Miller, University of Missouri, Columbia.
"Butte's Parish Boundaries." Ca. 1908. Diocese of Helena Office, Helena, Mont.
Butte Workingmen's Union. Minute Books, 1915–1916. World Museum of Mining, Butte, Mont.
Bishop John Carroll Papers. Diocese of Helena Office, Helena, Mont.
Michael J. Hannan File. Diocese of Helena Office, Helena, Mont.
J. J. Hill Papers. J. J. Hill Reference Library, St. Paul, Minn.
Martin Hogan Papers. Montana Historical Society, Helena.
Industrial Workers of the World Collection. Walter P. Reuther Library of Labor and Urban Affairs, Wayne State University, Detroit, Mich.
Industrial Workers of the World. Executive Board. Minute Books, 1906. Western History Collections, University of Colorado, Boulder.
Irish Collection. K. Ross Toole Archives, University of Montana. Microfilm copy.
    Ancient Order of Hibernians
        General Correspondence: 1894–1937
        Conferences and Conventions. Proceedings of: 1898, 1906, 1910, 1916, 1921, 1923, 1927, 1948
        Financial Records: 1882–1939 (esp. Membership and Dues ledgers)
        Reports

Organization (esp. Memberships)

Minute Books: 1884–1917 (inc. Minute Books of Hibernia Hall Board of Trustees)

Robert Emmet Literary Association

Financial Records: 1883–1946

Minute Books: 1882–1925

Reports: RELA and AOH Committees (inc. Reports and Ledgers of Hibernia Hall Board of Trustees)

RELA and Phil Sheridan Club (Anaconda). Proceedings of a Joint Meeting . . . for a Monument to Thomas Francis Meagher, Butte, Jan. 1, 1898.

Irish Volunteers of America

Minute Books: 1897, 1912–15

Financial Records: 1909(?), 1912–13

Friends of Irish Freedom

Organization: 1916, 1921

American Association for the Recognition of the Irish Republic

Miscellany: 1921–1922

Sunburst Club

Minute Books: 1886–1900

Montana Council of Defense Papers. Montana Historical Society, Helena.

Metal Mine Workers' Union. Minute Books, 1917.

Montana Council of Defense. Minute Books, 1917–18.

Oscar Rohn Files.

Proceedings of the Joint Session of the State Council . . . and the County Councils . . . May 29, 1918.

Record Series 19.

Testimony at Hearings held at . . . Helena, May–June, 1918. Typescript, 2 vols.

U.S. Councils of Defense. General Correspondence.

Murphy, Beatrice. "Diary of a Night Nurse, 1 Nov.–30 Nov., 1909, Murray Hospital, Butte." Typescript in possession of Teresa Jordan.

James E. Murray Papers. University of Montana.

Andrew O'Connell Papers. Montana Historical Society, Helena.

Socialist Party of Montana. Membership Record of Butte Local No. 1. Typescript copy in possession of Mrs. Terry McGlynn, Butte.

St. Lawrence O'Toole Parish File. Diocese of Helena Office, Helena, Mont.

St. Mary's Parish File. Diocese of Helena Office, Helena, Mont.

St. Patrick's Parish File. Diocese of Helena Office, Helena, Mont.

U.S. Department of Justice. National Archives. Files 186233, 189730, and 195397. 1917–20. Microfilm copy.

U.S. Department of Justice. National Archives. Record Group 60. 1917–19. Microfilm copy.

U.S. Department of Labor. National Archives. Files 20/493, 33/493, 33/1703, 1917–18. Microfilm copy.

U.S. War Department. National Archives. Files 370.6 and 10110, 1917–19. Microfilm copy.

U.S. War Department. National Archives. Adjutant General's Office. Record Group 74, Bulky File 370.61, 1919. Microfilm copy.

Western Federation of Miners. Executive Board. "Decision . . . in the Case of the Butte Miners' Union," Mar., 1915. Western History Collections, University of Colorado, Boulder.

————. Executive Board. Minute Books. Western History Collections, University of Colorado, Boulder.

————. Local Unions' Financial Records, 1907–32. Western History Collections, University of Colorado, Boulder.

————. Michigan Defense Fund. Books 1 and 2. Western History Collections, University of Colorado, Boulder.

GOVERNMENT RECORDS AND PUBLICATIONS
Federal

Bureau of the Census. *Ninth Census of the United States: 1870, Population,* vol. 1. Washington, D.C.: GPO, 1871.

————. *Manuscript Census, Population Schedules: 1870.* Montana Territory. Microfilm copy.

————. *Tenth Census of the United States, Compendium: 1880,* vol. 2. Washington, D.C.: GPO, 1881.

————. *Manuscript Census, Population Schedules: 1880.* Montana Territory. Microfilm copy.

————. *Eleventh Census of the United States, Compendium: 1890,* vol. 2. Washington, D.C.: GPO, 1891.

————. *Twelfth Census of the United States: 1900, Population,* vol. 1, part 1. Washington, D.C.: GPO, 1900.

————. *Manuscript Census, Population Schedules: 1900.* Silver Bow County, Montana. Microfilm copy.

————. *Thirteenth Census of the United States: 1910, Abstract with Supplement for Montana.* Washington, D.C.: 1910.

————. *Manuscript Census, Population Schedules: 1910.* Silver Bow County, Montana. Microfilm copy.

————. *Mortality Statistics,* 1916. Washington, D.C.; GPO, 1918.

———— *Fourteenth Census of the United States: 1920, Population,* vol. 3. Washington, D.C.: GPO, 1921.

Bureau of Mines. *Lessons from the Granite Mountain Shaft Fire, Butte, Montana.* By David Harrington. Bulletin 188. Washington, D.C.: GPO, 1920.

————. *A Preliminary Report of an Investigation of Miners' Consumption in the Mines of Butte, Montana, Made in the Years 1916–1919.* By David Harrington and A. V. Lanza. Technical Paper 260. Washington, D.C.: GPO, 1921.

Commissioner General of Immigration. *Annual Report.* Senate Document 758. 58th Congress, 2d Session, 1903.

Committee on Privileges and Elections. *Report . . . Relative to the Right and Title of William A. Clark to a Seat as Senator . . .* Senate Report 1052. 56th Congress, 1st Session, 1900. Washington, D.C.: GPO, 1901.

Congressional Record.

Department of Labor, National Industrial Conference Board. *Workmen's Compensation Acts in the United States, The Legal Phase.* Washington, D.C.: GPO, 1917.

Federal Trade Commission. *Report, the Copper Industry.* Washington, D.C.: GPO, 1947.

Immigration Commission. *Immigrants in Industries.* Senate Document 633. 61st Congress, 2d Session, 1910.

——. *Reports: Statistical Review of Immigration.* Senate Document 756. 61st Congress, 3d Session, 1911.

Industrial Commission. *Mining Conditions and Industrial Relations at Butte, Montana.* Senate Document 415. 64th Congress, 1st Session. *Final Report and Testimony,* vol. 4, 1915.

Statutes at Large 40 (1917), part 1. Washington, D.C.: GPO, 1917.

Trial of U.S. vs. Haywood et al., 1918. Transcript in IWW Collection. Walter P. Reuther Library of Labor and Urban Affairs, Wayne State University.

Works Projects Administration. *Contagious Diseases.* Silver Bow County, 1908–12. Butte/Silver Bow Archives.

State

Montana, Board of Managers. *Montana . . . Exhibit at the World's Fair and a Description of . . . Resources.* Butte: State Publishing Co., 1892.

Montana. Bureau of Agriculture, Labor, and Industry. *Report . . . 1912.* Helena: Independent Publishing Co., 1912.

——. *First Biennial Report, 1913–1914.* Helena: Independent Publishing Co., 1914.

——. *Second Biennial Report, 1915–1916.* Helena: Independent Publishing Co., 1916.

——. *Third Biennial Report, 1917–18.* Helena: Independent Publishing Co., 1918.

Montana. Department of Labor. *The Resources and Opportunities of Montana.* Helena: Independent Publishing Co., 1914.

Montana. Joint Committee of the Twelfth Legislative Assembly to Investigate the Sanitary Conditions and the Conditions of Ventilation of the Mines . . . of Butte. *Proceedings 1911.* In U.S. Congress, Senate, Commission on Industrial Relations. *Mining Conditions and Industrial Relations at Butte, Montana.* Senate Document 415. 64th Congress, 1st Session, 1915.

Montana. *Laws . . . Passed by the Extraordinary Session of the 15th Legislative Assembly, 1918.* Helena: State Publishing Company, 1918.

Montana. Mine Inspector. *Report . . . 1889.* Helena: State Publishing Co., 1890.

Montana, World's Fair Committee. *Montana: Its Progress, Prosperity . . . .* St. Louis: Con. P. Curran Co., 1904.

Local

Silver Bow Co. Board of Health. "Report on Sanitary Conditions in the Mines and Community, Silver Bow County, December, 1908–April, 1912." Typescript. Copy in Montana Historical Society, Helena.

Silver Bow Co. Board of Health. "Report Showing Results of Inspection of Dwellings, Hotels, Rooming Houses, and Boarding Houses and Their Surroundings." 1912. Typescript. Copy in Montana Historical Society, Helena.

Silver Bow Co. Mortuary Records. Butte/Silver Bow Archives.

NEWSPAPERS AND PERIODICALS

Anaconda Standard (Anaconda, Mont).
Butte/Anaconda Joint Strike Bulletin.
Butte Bulletin.
Butte Bystander.
Butte Evening News.
Butte Independent.
Butte Intermountain.
Butte Miner.
Butte Mining Journal.
Butte Post.
Butte Strike Bulletin.
Engineering and Mining Journal (New York).
Examiner (Butte).
Helena Independent.
Helena Independent Record.
Irish Worker and People's Advocate (Chicago).
Irish World and American Industrial Liberator (New York).
Joint Strike Bulletin (Butte).
Labor World (Butte).
Miners Magazine (Butte and Denver).
Montana Catholic (Butte).
Montana Socialist (Butte).
Montana Standard (Butte).
Montana Standard-Post (Butte).
Reveille (Butte).

CONTEMPORARY PUBLISHED WORKS

American Association for the Recognition of the Irish Republic. *Proceedings . . . National Convention, Wash., D.C., Jan. 21–26, 1922.* Washington, D.C.: AARIR, 1922.

———. Butte Chapter. *Second Annual Convention, Butte, Feb. 12, 1922.* Butte: Butte Independent, 1922.

Ancient Order of Hibernians. *Constitution and By-laws, 1923.* Chicago: AOH, 1923.

—— . *Constitution and Bylaws of the AOH of America. Montana Territory . . . 1886.* Butte: Mining Journal Publishing Co., 1887. Irish Collection. University of Montana. Microfilm copy.

—— . *Ritual and Manual of the AOH in America . . . 1901.* Oshkosh, Wis.: n.p., 1901. Irish Collection. University of Montana. Microfilm copy.

—— . *Ritual and Manual of the AOH in America.* Chicago: AOH, 1906.

Atherton, Gertrude. *Perch of the Devil.* New York: A. L. Burt, 1914.

Bohn, Frank. "Butte Number One." *Masses* 5 (1914):10–14.

Brissenden, Ralph. "The Butte Miners and the Rustling Card." *American Economic Review* 10 (1920): 755–75.

Brockett, Linus. *Our Western Empire or, The West Beyond the Mississippi River.* Philadelphia: Bradley, Garretson & Company, 1882.

Butte Chamber of Commerce. *Resources of Butte: Its Mines and Smelters.* Butte: Intermountain Painters, 1895.

Butte Miners' Union. *Constitution and Bylaws . . . of the BMU.* Butte: Butte Miners' Union, rev. ed., 1902.

Connolly, C.P. "The Labor Fuss in Butte." *Everybody's Magazine* 31 (Aug., 1914), 205–8.

—— . "The Story of Montana." *McClure's Magazine* 27 (1906): 346–61, 451–65, 629–39.

The Copper Handbook: A Manual of the Copper Industry of the World. Houghton, Mich.: W. H. Weed, 1916.

Crofutt, George. *Butte City Directory.* 1885–86. Butte City: Crofutt, 1886.

Davitt, Michael. *The Fall of Feudalism in Ireland.* 1904; rpt., Dublin: Irish University Press, 1972.

Devoy, John. *Post Bag, 1871–1928.* Edited by William O'Brien and Desmond Ryan. 2 vols. Dublin: C. J. Fallon, 1948, 1953.

—— . *Recollections of an Irish Rebel.* New York: Charles Young, 1929.

Dunne, Finley Peter. "The Freedom Picnic." In *Mr. Dooley in the Hearts of His Countrymen.* Boston: Small, Maynard, 1899.

Evans, L. O. *Address to the Missoula Chamber of Commerce, 1917.* Butte: privately printed, 1917.

Fitch, John A. "A Union Paradise at Close Range." *Survey* 50 (1914): 538–39.

Friends of Irish Freedom. "Are You a Member of the FOIF for 1920?" Circular. New York: FOIF, 1920. In Irish Collection.

—— . *Constitution and Bylaws,* rev. by the Irish Race Convention, Feb. 22–23, 1919. New York: FOIF, 1919. In Irish Collection.

—— . "Ireland's Case for Independence." In FOIF. *Ireland's Declaration of Independence and Other Documents.* New York: FOIF, 1919. In Irish Collection.

—— . *Resolutions and Petitions, Second Irish Race Convention.* New York: FOIF, 1918. In Irish Collection.

George, Henry. *The Irish Land Question.* 1881; rpt., New York: R. Schallenbach Foundation, 1945.

Gore-Booth, Constance (Countess Markievicz). *Prison Letters of Countess Markievicz.* 1934; rpt., New York: Krause, 1970.

Great Northern Railway. "Harvest Excursions . . . 1888." GN Co., Advertising and Publicity Department, Magazine and Newspaper Advertisements, 1884–1970. Minnesota Historical Society, St. Paul. Microfilm copy.

Hannan, Fr. Michael J. *Father English and St. Mary's Parish. Butte, Montana: The Miners' Catholic Church and Parish.* Butte: privately printed, 1911. Copy in St. Mary's Parish File. Diocese of Helena Office, Helena, Mont.

Haywood, William. *Bill Haywood's Book: The Autobiography of William H. Haywood.* New York: International Publishers, 1929.

——. "Jim Larkin's Call for Solidarity." *International Socialist Revised* (1914): 469–74.

——. "The Revolt at Butte." *International Socialist Review* (1914): 90–94.

Johnson, Emory, and Grover Huebner. *Railroad Traffic and Rates.* 2 vols. New York: D. Appleton, 1918.

MacLane, Mary. *The Story of Mary MacLane.* Chicago: H. S. Stone & Co., 1902.

McKnight, James. *The Mines of Montana, Prepared for the National Mining Congress.* Helena: C. K. Wells Co., 1892.

Merz, Charles. "The Issue in Butte." *New Republic* (Sept. 22, 1917):215–17.

Miller, Joaquin. *Illustrated History of the State of Montana.* Chicago: Lewis Publishing Co., 1894.

O'Dea, John. *The History of the Ancient Order of Hibernians and Ladies' Auxiliary.* 4 vols. Philadelphia: Ancient Order of Hibernians, 1923.

O'Farrell, P. A. *Butte: Its Copper Mines and Copper Kings.* New York: J. A. Rogers, 1899.

O'Reilly, John B. *The Butte Blue Book, 1901: A Social and Family Directory.* Butte: The author, 1901.

Polk, R. L. *Butte City Directory.* 1887-88–1915. St. Paul and Butte: R. L. Polk Publishing Company, 1888–1916.

Pollard, H. B. C. *The Secret Societies of Ireland: Their Rise and Progress.* London: P. Allen & Co., 1922.

Roberts, Edward. "Two Montana Cities." *Harper's New Monthly Magazine* 77 (1888): 585–96.

D. A. Sanborn Fire Insurance Company. *Fire Insurance Map of Butte, Montana, 1900.* New York: Sanborn Map Company, 1900.

Scherer, James. *The Nation at War.* Garden City, N.Y.: Doran, 1918.

Sombart, Werner. *Why Is There No Socialism in the United States?* 1906; rpt., White Plains, NY: M. E. Sharpe, 1976.

Synge, John Millington. *In Wicklow, West Kerry and Connemara.* 1910; rpt. Totowa, N.J.: Rowman & Littlefield, 1980.

Thayer, William. *Marvels of the New West.* Norwich, Conn.: Henry Bill Co., 1888.

Union Pacific Railroad. *Resources of Montana . . . 1890.* St. Louis: U.P.R.R. Co., 1891.

——. *Resources of Montana . . . 1891.* St. Louis: U.P.R.R. Co., 1892.

Western Federation of Miners. *Constitution and By-laws, May 19, 1893.* Butte City: Bystander Printing Co., 1893.

——. *Constitution and By-laws. Revised, 1907.* Denver: WFM, 1907.

———. *Proceedings ... 3rd Annual Convention, Denver, 1895.* Denver: WFM, 1895.

———. *Proceedings ... 5th Annual Convention, Salt Lake City, 1897.* Salt Lake City: WFM, 1897.

———. *Proceedings ... 9th Annual Convention, Denver, 1901.* Denver: WFM, 1901.

———. *Proceedings ... 10th Annual Convention, Denver, 1902.* Denver: WFM, 1902.

———. *Proceedings ... 11th Annual Convention, Denver, 1903.* Denver: WFM, 1903.

———. *Proceedings ... 12th Annual Convention, Denver, 1904.* Denver: WFM, 1904.

———. *Proceedings ... 13th Annual Convention, Salt Lake City, 1905.* Salt Lake City: WFM, 1905.

———. *Proceedings ... 14th Annual Convention, Denver, 1906.* Denver: WFM, 1906.

———. *Proceedings ... 15th Annual Convention, Denver, 1907.* Denver: WFM, 1907.

———. *Proceedings ... 17th Annual Convention, Denver, 1909.* Denver: WFM, 1909.

———. *Proceedings ... 18th Annual Convention, Denver, 1910.* Denver: WFM, 1910.

———. *Proceedings ... 19th Annual Convention, Denver, 1911.* Denver: WFM, 1911.

———. *Proceedings ... 20th Annual Convention, Victor, Colo., 1912.* Victor: WFM, 1912.

———. *Proceedings ... 21st Convention, 1st Biennial, Denver, 1914.* Denver: WFM, 1914.

———. Executive Board. *Report, Dec. 16, 1906.* Denver: WFM, 1906.

Yeats, William B. "Remorse for Intemperate Speech." *The Winding Stair and Other Poems.* In *W. B. Yeats: The Poems,* p. 255. Edited by Richard Finneran. New York: Macmillan, 1983.

SECONDARY SOURCES
Books

Allen, H. C. *Great Britain and the United States: A History of Anglo-American Relations, 1783–1952.* New York: St. Martins, 1955.

Athearn, Robert. *Thomas Francis Meagher: Irish Revolutionary in the American West.* Boulder: University of Colorado Press, 1949.

Berthoff, Rowland. *British Immigrants in Industrial America, 1790–1950.* Cambridge: Harvard University Press, 1953.

Billington, Ray Allen. *The Protestant Crusade: A Study of the Origins of American Nativism.* Chicago: Quadrangle, 1964.

Bodnar, John. *The Transplanted: A History of Immigrants in Urban America.* Bloomington: Indiana University Press, 1985.

——— . *Workers' World: Kinship Community and Protest in an Industrial Society, 1900–1940.* Baltimore: The Johns Hopkins University Press, 1982.

Bodnar, John, Roger Simon, and Michael Weber. *Lives of Their Own: Blacks Italians, and Poles in Pittsburgh, 1900–1960.* Urbana: University of Illinois Press, 1982.

Bogue, Donald. *Principles of Demography.* New York: Wiley, 1969.

Brissenden, Paul. *The IWW: A Study of American Syndicalism.* New York: Columbia University Press, 1920.

Brody, David. *Workers in Industrial America: Essays on the 20th Century Struggle.* New York: Oxford University Press, 1980.

Broehl, Wayne. *The Molly Maguires.* Cambridge: Harvard University Press, 1964.

Brown, Ronald C. *Hard-Rock Miners: The Intermountain West, 1860–1920.* College Station: Texas A&M University Press, 1979.

Brown, Thomas N. *Irish-American Nationalism, 1870–1890.* Philadelphia: Lippencott, 1966.

Browne, Henry J. *The Catholic Church and the Knights of Labor.* Washington, D.C.: Catholic University of America Press, 1949.

Burchell, R. A. *The San Francisco Irish, 1848–1880.* Berkeley: University of California Press, 1980.

Campbell, Charles. *The Transformation of American Foreign Relations, 1865–1900.* New York: Harper and Row, 1976.

Carpenter, Niles. *Immigrants and Their Children, 1920.* Census Monographs 7. Washington, D.C.: GPO, 1927.

Carroll, Francis M. *American Opinion and the Irish Question, 1910–1923.* Dublin: Gill and Macmillan, 1978.

Chudacoff, Howard. *Mobile Americans: Residential and Social Mobility in Omaha, 1880–1920.* New York: Oxford University Press, 1972.

Clark, Dennis. *The Irish in Philadelphia: Ten Generations of Urban Experience.* Philadelphia: Temple University Press, 1973.

Clark, Samuel, and James Donnelly, eds. *Irish Peasants: Violence and Political Unrest, 1780–1914.* Madison: University of Wisconsin Press, 1983.

Clinch, Thomas. *Urban Populism and Free Silver in Montana.* Missoula: University of Montana Press, 1970.

Conzen, Kathleen Neils. *Immigrant Milwaukee, 1830–1860: Accommodation and Community in a Frontier City.* Cambridge: Harvard University Press, 1976.

Cross, Robert. *The Emergence of Liberal Catholicism in America.* Cambridge: Harvard University Press, 1958.

Curtis, Lewis Perry. *Anglo-Saxons and Celts: A Study of Anti-Irish Prejudice in Victorian England.* Bridgeport, Conn.: University of Bridgeport Press, 1969.

——— . *Apes and Angels: The Irishman in Victorian Caricature.* Washington, D.C.: Smithsonian Institution Press, 1971.

Daly, Hugh. *Biography of Marcus Daly.* Butte: The author, 1934.

Dangerfield, George. *The Damnable Question: One Hundred and Twenty Years of Anglo-Irish Conflict.* Boston: Atlantic, Little, Brown and Co., 1976.

Diner, Hasia. *Erin's Daughters in America: Irish Immigrant Women in the 19th Century.* Baltimore: The Johns Hopkins University Press, 1983.

Documents of American History. Edited by Henry Steele Commager. 2 vols. in one. New York: Appleton Century, Crofts, 1958.

Doig, Ivan. *English Creek.* New York: Atheneum, 1983.

Dolan, Jay P. *The Immigrant Church: New York's Irish and German Catholics, 1815–1865.* Baltimore: The Johns Hopkins University Press, 1975.

Donnelly, James S. *The Land and the People of 19th Century Cork: The Rural Economy and the Land Question.* London: Routledge and Kegan Paul, 1975.

Doyle, David H. *The Social Order of a Frontier Community: Jacksonville, Illinois, 1825–1870.* Urbana: University of Illinois Press, 1983.

Draper, Theodore. *American Communism and Soviet Russia.* New York: Viking Press, 1960.

——— . *The Roots of American Communism.* New York: Viking Press, 1957.

Du Maurier, Daphne. *Hungry Hill.* 1943; rpt., Cambridge: Robert Bentley, 1971.

Dubos, Rene, and Jean Dubos. *The White Plague: Tuberculosis, Man, and Society.* Boston: Little, Brown and Co., 1952.

Dubofsky, Melvyn. *We Shall Be All: A History of the Industrial Workers of the World.* 2d ed. Urbana: University of Illinois Press, 1988.

Duffy, Joseph H. *Butte Was Like That.* Butte: The author, 1941.

Dykstra, Robert. *The Cattle Towns.* New York: Knopf, 1968.

Edwards, Ruth Dudley. *Patrick Pearse: The Triumph of Failure.* New York: Gollancz, 1977.

Emmons, David M. *Garden in the Grasslands: The Boomer Literature of the Central Plains.* Lincoln: University of Nebraska Press, 1971.

Erickson, Charlotte. *American Industry and the European Immigrant, 1860–1885.* Cambridge: Cambridge University Press, 1957.

Fahey, John. *The Days of the Hercules.* Moscow: University Press of Idaho, 1978.

Finnane, Mark. *Insanity and the Insane in Post Famine Ireland.* London: Croom Helm, 1981.

Flaherty, Cornelia. *Go with Haste into the Mountains: A History of the Diocese of Helena.* Helena: Diocese Office, 1984.

Foner, Eric. *Free Soil, Free Labor, Free Men: The Ideology of the Republican Party before the Civil War.* New York: Oxford University Press, 1970.

Funchion, Michael, ed. *Irish-American Voluntary Organizations.* Westport, Conn.: Greenwood, 1983.

Gallagher, Thomas. *Paddy's Lament. Ireland, 1846–1847: Prelude to Hatred.* New York: Harcourt, Brace, Jovanovich, 1982.

Genovese, Eugene. *Roll, Jordan, Roll: The World the Slaves Made.* New York: Vintage Books, 1972.

Gitelman, Howard. *Workingmen of Waltham: Mobility in American Urban Industrial Development, 1850–1890.* Baltimore: The Johns Hopkins University Press, 1974.

Glasscock, C. B. *The War of the Copper Kings: Builders of Butte and Wolves of Wall Street.* New York: Gosset and Dunlap, 1935.

Glassie, Henry. *Passing the Time in Ballymenone: Culture and History of an Ulster Community*. Philadelphia: University of Pennsylvania Press, 1982.

Golab, Caroline. *Immigrant Destinations*. Philadelphia: Temple University Press, 1977.

Gordon, Milton. *Assimilation in American Life: The Role of Race, Religion, and National Origins*. New York: Oxford University Press, 1964.

Greaves, C. D. *The Life and Times of James Connolly*. 1916; rpt., New York: International Publishers, 1971.

Gutfeld, Arnon. *Montana's Agony: Years of War and Hysteria*. Gainesville: University of Florida Press, 1979.

Gutman, Herbert. *The Black Family in Slavery and Freedom, 1750–1925*. New York: Pantheon Books, 1976.

———. *Work, Culture, and Society in Industrializing America: Essays in American Working-class and Social History*. New York: Vintage Books, 1977.

Hachey, Thomas. *Britain and Irish Separatism from the Fenians to the Free State, 1867–1922*. Chicago: Rand, McNally, 1977.

Handlin, Oscar. *Boston's Immigrants: A Study in Acculturation, 1790–1880*. Cambridge: Harvard University Press, 1941.

———. *The Uprooted: The Epic Story of the Great Migrations That Made the American People*. Boston: Little Brown, 1952.

Hennessy, James. *American Catholics: A History of the Roman Catholic Community in the United States*. New York: Oxford University Press, 1981.

Higham, John. *Strangers in the Land: Patterns of American Nativism, 1860–1925*. New York: Atheneum, 1981.

Hirsch, Susan. *Roots of the American Working Class: The Industrialization of Crafts in Newark, 1800–1860*. Philadelphia: University of Pennsylvania Press, 1978.

Howard, Joseph K. *Montana: High, Wide, and Handsome*. New Haven: Yale University Press, 1943.

James, Don. *Butte's Memory Book*. Caldwell, Idaho: Caxton, 1980.

Jensen, Richard. *The Winning of the Midwest: Social and Political Conflict, 1888–1896*. Chicago: University of Chicago Press, 1971.

Jensen, Vernon. *Heritage of Conflict: Labor Relations in the Nonferrous Metals Industry up to 1930*. Ithaca: Cornell University Press, 1950.

Karson, Marc. *American Labor Unions and Politics, 1900–1918*. Carbondale: Southern Illinois University Press, 1958.

Katz, Michael. *The People of Hamilton, Canada West: Family and Class in a Mid-19th Century City*. Cambridge: Harvard University Press, 1979.

Kennedy, Robert E. *The Irish: Emigration, Marriage, and Fertility*. Berkeley: University of California Press, 1973.

Keyssar, Alexander. *Out of Work: The First Century of Unemployment in Massachusetts*. Cambridge: Cambridge University Press, 1986.

Kleppner, Paul. *Cross of Culture: A Social Analysis of Midwestern Politics, 1850–1890*. New York: Free Press, 1970.

Kraditor, Aileen. *The Radical Persuasion: Aspects of the Intellectual History and Historiography of Three American Radical Organizations*. Baton Rouge: Louisiana State University Press, 1981.

Larkin, Emmet. *James Larkin: Irish Labour Leader, 1876–1947*. Cambridge: MIT Press, 1965.

――――. *The Roman Catholic Church and the Creation of the Modern Irish State, 1878–1886*. Philadelphia: American Philosophical Society, 1975.

――――. *The Roman Catholic Church and the Fall of Parnell, 1888–1891*. Chapel Hill: University of North Carolina Press, 1979.

――――. *The Roman Catholic Church and the Plan of Campaign, 1886–1888*. Cork: Cork University Press, 1978.

Laslett, John H. M. *Labor and the Left: A Study of Socialist and Radical Influences in the American Labor Movement, 1881–1924*. New York: Basic Books, 1970.

Lee, E. S., A. R. Miller, C. P. Brainerd, and R. A. Easterlin. *Population Redistribution and Economic Growth, U.S., 1870–1950*. Vol. 1. *Methodological Considerations and Reference Tables*. Philadelphia: American Philosophical Society, 1957.

Lee, Joseph. *The Modernisation of Irish Society, 1848–1918*. Dublin: Gill and Macmillan, 1973.

Lees, Lynn Hollen. *Exiles of Erin: Irish Migrants in Victorian London*. Ithaca: Cornell University Press, 1979.

Lewis, Arthur. *Lament for the Molly Maguires*. New York: Harcourt, Brace and World, 1969.

Lindsay, John. *The Amazing Experiences of a Judge*. Philadelphia: Dorrance and Co., 1939.

Lingenfelter, Richard E. *The Hardrock Miners: A History of the Mining Labor Movement in the American West, 1863–1893*. Berkeley: University of California Press, 1974.

Long, Clarence. *Wages and Earnings in the United States, 1860–1890*. Princeton: Princeton University Press, 1960.

Lyons, F. S. L. *Culture and Anarchy in Ireland, 1890–1939*. Oxford: Clarendon, 1979.

――――. *Ireland since the Famine*. London: Weidenfeld and Nicholson, 1971.

――――. *John Dillon: A Biography*. Chicago: University of Chicago Press, 1968.

Malone, Michael. *The Battle for Butte: Mining and Politics on the Northern Frontier*. Seattle: University of Washington Press, 1981.

Mann, Arthur. *The One and the Many: Reflections on the American Identity*. Chicago: University of Chicago Press, 1979.

Mann, Ralph. *After the Gold Rush: Society in Grass Valley and Nevada City, California, 1849–1870*. Stanford: Stanford University Press, 1982.

Mansergh, Nicholas. *The Irish Question, 1840–1921*. Toronto: University of Toronto Press, 1975.

Marcosson, Isaac. *Anaconda*. New York: Dodd, Mead, 1957.

Marreco, Anne. *The Rebel Countess: The Life and Times of Countess Markievicz*. Philadelphia: Chilton Books, 1967.

Martin, F. X., and F. J. Byrne. *The Scholar Revolutionary: Eoin MacNeill and the Making of the New Ireland, 1867–1945*. Dublin: Irish University Press, 1973.

McCaffrey, Lawrence J. *The Irish Diaspora in America*. Bloomington: Indiana University Press, 1976.

McLysaght, Edward. *Irish Families: Their Names, Arms, and Origins.* New York: Crown Publishers, 1972.

Miller, Kerby A. *Emigrants and Exiles: Ireland and the Irish Exodus to North America.* New York: Oxford University Press, 1985.

Montgomery, David. *Beyond Equality: Labor and the Radical Republicans, 1863–1872.* New York: Oxford University Press, 1967.

———. *Workers' Control in America: Studies in the History of Work, Technology, and Labor Struggles.* Cambridge: Cambridge University Press, 1980.

Moody's Manual of Investments (Industrial Securities). Edited by John Sherman Porter. New York: Moody's Investors Service, 1948.

Murphy, Clyde. *The Glittering Hill.* Cleveland: World Publishing Co., 1944.

Murphy, Mary, and Bill Walker. *Butte, Montana: A Select Bibliography.* Butte: Butte Historical Society, n.d.

O'Brien, R. Barry. *The Life of Charles Stewart Parnell.* 2 vols. 1899; rpt., Westport: Greenwood, 1969.

O'Dwyer, Liam. *Beara in Irish History.* New York: Vantage Press, 1977.

O'Dwyer, Riobard, N.T. *Who Were My Ancestors? A Genealogy of Eyeries Parish, Castletownbere County Cork.* Astoria, Ill.: Stevens Publishing Co., 1976.

O'Faolain, Sean. *The Story of the Irish People.* 1949; rpt., New York: Avenel Books, 1982.

O'Farrell, P. J. *England's Irish Question.* New York: Oxford University Press, 1971.

Palmer, Norman. *The Irish Land League Crisis.* New Haven: Yale University Press, 1940.

Perkins, Bradford. *The Great Rapprochement: England and the United States, 1895–1914.* New York: Atheneum, 1968.

Peterson, H. C., and Gilbert Fite. *Opponents of War, 1917–1918.* Madison: University of Wisconsin Press, 1957.

Peterson, Richard. *The Bonanza Kings: The Social Origins and Business Behavior of Western Mining Entrepreneurs, 1870–1900.* Lincoln: University of Nebraska Press, 1971.

Plunkett, James. *Strumpet City.* New York: Delacorte, 1969.

Potter, David. *The Impending Crisis, 1848–1861.* New York: Harper and Row, 1976.

Potter, George. *To the Golden Door: The Story of the Irish in Ireland and American.* Boston: Little, Brown, 1960.

Rabinowitz, Howard. *Race Relations in the Urban South, 1865–1890.* New York: Oxford University Press, 1978.

Rorabaugh, W. J. *The Alcoholic Republic: An American Tradition.* New York: Oxford University Press, 1979.

Rosenzweig, Roy. *Eight Hours for What We Will: Workers and Leisure in an Industrial City, 1870–1920.* Cambridge: Cambridge University Press, 1983.

Rumpf, E., and A. C. Hepburn. *Nationalism and Socialism in 20th Century Ireland.* New York: Barnes and Noble, 1977.

Samuel, Raphael, ed. *Miners, Quarrymen and Salt Workers.* London: Routledge and K. Paul, 1977.

Scheper-Hughes, Nancy. *Saints, Scholars, and Schizophrenics: Mental Illness in Rural Ireland.* Berkeley: University of California Press, 1979.

Schrier, Arnold. *Ireland and the Irish Emigration, 1850–1900.* Minneapolis: University of Minnesota Press, 1958.

Shannon, James P. *Catholic Colonization on the Western Frontier.* New Haven: Yale University Press, 1971.

Shannon, William. *The American Irish.* New York: Macmillan, 1963.

Shaw, Douglas. *The Making of an Immigrant City: Class and Ethnicity in Jersey City, 1850–1877.* 1973; rpt., New York: Arno, 1976.

Shoebotham, H. Minar. *Anaconda: The Life of Marcus Daly, the Copper King.* Harrisburg, Pa.: Stackpole Co., 1956.

Short, K. R. M. *The Dynamite War: Irish-American Bombers in Victorian Britain.* London: Humanities Press, 1979.

Slotkin, Richard. *The Fatal Environment: The Myth of the Frontier in the Age of Industrialization, 1800–1890.* New York: Atheneum, 1985.

Sproat, John. *The Best Men: Liberal Reformers in the Gilded Age.* Chicago: University of Chicago Press, 1982.

The Statistical History of the United States from Colonial Times to the Present. Stamford: Fairfield Publishers, 1956.

Stivers, Richard. *A Hair of the Dog: Irish Drinking and American Stereotypes.* University Park: Pennsylvania State University Press, 1976.

Suggs, George. *Colorado's War on Militant Unionism: James H. Peabody and the WFM.* Detroit: Wayne State University Press, 1972.

Tansill, Charles C. *America and the Fight for Irish Freedom, 1866–1922.* New York: Devin-Adair Co., 1957.

Taylor, Phillip. *The Distant Magnet: European Emigration to the U.S.A.* New York: Harper Torchbooks, 1973.

Thernstrom, Stephan. *The Other Bostonians: Poverty and Progress in the American Metropolis, 1880–1970.* Cambridge: Harvard University Press, 1973.

———. *Poverty and Progress: Social Mobility in a Nineteenth Century City.* Cambridge: Harvard University Press, 1964.

Thompson, E. P. *The Making of the English Working Class.* New York: Oxford University Press, 1966.

Vaughn, W. E., and A. J. Fitzpatrick, eds. *Irish Historical Statistics: Population, 1821–1971.* Dublin: Irish University Press, 1978.

Vinyard, Jo Ellen. *The Irish on the Urban Frontier: 19th Century Detroit.* New York: Arno, 1976.

Waldron, Ellis, and Paul Wilson. *Atlas of Montana Elections, 1889–1976.* Missoula: University of Montana Publications in History, 1978.

Walkowitz, Daniel. *Worker City, Company Town: Iron and Cotton-Worker Protest in Troy and Cohoes, New York, 1855–1885.* Urbana: University of Illinois Press, 1981.

Walters, Ronald. *American Reformers, 1815–1860.* New York: Hill and Wang, 1978.

Ward, Alan J. *Ireland and Anglo-American Relations, 1899–1921.* Toronto: University of Toronto Press, 1969.

Ward, David. *Cities and Immigrants: A Geography of Change in 19th Century America.* New York: Oxford University Press, 1974.

Wheeler, Burton K., with Paul F. Healy. *Yankee from the West.* Garden City, N.Y.: Doubleday, 1962.

Wiebe, Robert. *The Search for Order, 1877-1920.* New York: Hill and Wang, 1967.

Wilentz, Sean. *Chants Democratic: New York City and The Rise of the American Working Class.* New York: Oxford University Press, 1984.

Woodham-Smith, Cecil. *The Great Hunger: Ireland, 1845-1849.* New York: Harper and Row, 1962.

Works Projects Administration (WPA). *Copper Camp: Stories of the World's Greatest Mining Town, Butte, Montana.* New York: Hasting House, 1943.

Wyman, Mark. *Hardrock Epic: Western Miners and The Industrial Revolution, 1860-1910.* Berkeley: University of California Press, 1979.

Yans-McLaughlin, Virginia. *Family and Community: Italian Immigrants in Buffalo 1880-1930.* 1971; rpt., Urbana: University of Illinois Press, 1982.

Articles

Blessing, Patrick J. "Irish Emigration to the United States, 1800-1920: An Overview." In *The Irish in America: Emigration, Assimilation, and Impact,* pp. 11-38. Edited by P. J. Drudy. Cambridge: Cambridge University Press, 1985.

Brody, David. "Workers and Work in America: The New Labor History." In *Ordinary People and Everyday Life: Perspectives on the New Social History,* pp. 139-60. Edited by James B. Gardner and George R. Adams. Nashville: American Association for State and Local History, 1983.

Browne, Henry J. "Comment." In *Failure of a Dream? Essays in the History of American Socialism,* pp. 103-13. Edited by John H. M. Laslett and Seymour Martin Lipset. Berkeley: University of California Press, 1984.

Butte Historical Society. "The Mines of Butte." Pamphlet and map. Butte: Butte Historical Society, 1985.

Calvert, Jerry. " 'Making Good': Socialist Government in Butte, 1911-1915." *Speculator: A Journal of Butte and Southwest Montana* 2 (1985): 23-29.

Cantor, Milton. "Introduction." In *American Workingclass Culture: Explorations in American Labor and Social History,* pp. 3-17. Edited by Milton Cantor. Westport, Conn.: Greenwood, 1979.

Carroll, James. "On Not Skipping the Sermon." *Commonweal* 3 (1984): 603-5.

Connell, K. H. "Catholicism and Marriage in the Century after the Famine." In Connell, *Irish Peasant Society,* pp. 113-61. Oxford: Clarendon, 1968.

Conzen, Kathleen Neils. "The New Urban History: Defining the Field." In *Ordinary People and Everyday Life: Perspectives on the New Social History,* pp. 67-90. Edited by James B. Gardner and George R. Adams. Nashville: American Association for State and Local History, 1983.

Cross, Robert D. "The Irish." In *Ethnic Leadership in America,* pp. 176-97. Edited by John Higham. Baltimore: The Johns Hopkins University Press, 1978.

Doherty, Robert E. "Thomas J. Haggerty, the Church, and Socialism." *Labor History* 3 (1962): 39–56.

Brown, Thomas N. "The Political Irish: Politicians and Rebels." In *America and Ireland, 1776–1976: The American Identity and the Irish Connection.* pp. 133–49. Edited by David Doyle and Owen Dudley Edwards. Westport, Conn.: Greenwood, 1980.

Doyle, David. "The Irish and American Labour, 1880–1920." *Saothar: Journal of the Irish Labour History Society* 1 (1975): 42–53.

Dubofsky, Melvyn. "The Origins of Western Working-Class Radicalism, 1880–1906." In *Labor History Reader*, pp. 230–53. Edited by Daniel Leab. Urbana: University of Illinois Press, 1985.

Emmons, David M. "The Orange and the Green in Montana: A Reconsideration of the Origins of the Clark-Daly Feud." *Arizona and the West* 28 (1986): 225–45.

———. "Immigrant Workers and Industrial Hazards: The Irish Miners of Butte, 1880–1919." *Journal of American Ethnic History* 5 (1985): 41–64.

Fahey, John. "Ed Boyce and the Western Federation of Miners." *Idaho Yesterdays* 25 (1981): 18–30.

Foner, Eric. "Class, Ethnicity, and Radicalism in the Gilded Age: The Land League and Irish America." In *Politics and Ideology in the Age of the Civil War*, pp. 150–200. New York: Oxford University Press, 1980.

Funchion, Michael. "Irish Chicago: Church, Homeland, Politics, and Class—The Shaping of an Ethnic Group, 1870–1900." In *Ethnic Chicago*, pp. 8–39. Edited by Peter d'A. Jones and Melvin Holli. Grand Rapids, Mich.: William Eerdmans, 1981.

Gedicks, Al. "Ethnicity, Class Solidarity, and Labor Radicalism among Finnish Immigrants in Michigan Copper Country." *Politics and Society* 7 (1977): 127–56.

Gordon, Michael A. "The Labor Boycott in New York City, 1880–1886." In *American Workingclass Culture: Explorations in American Labor and Social History*, pp. 287–332. Edited by Milton Cantor. Westport, Conn.: Greenwood, 1979.

Green, Paul Michael. "Irish Chicago: The Multi-ethnic Road to Machine Success." In *Ethnic Chicago*, pp. 212–59. Edited by Peter d'A. Jones and Melvin Holli. Grand Rapids, Mich.: William B. Eerdmans, 1981.

Gutman, Herbert. "Protestantism and the American Labor Movement: The Christian Spirit in the Gilded Age." In Gutman, *Work Culture and Society in Industrializing America: Essays in American Social and Workingclass History*, pp. 79–118. New York: Vintage Books, 1977.

Hand, Wayland. "The Folklore, Customs, and Traditions of the Butte Miner." *California Folklore Quarterly* 5 (1946): 1–25, 153–78.

Hand, Wyland, Charles Cutts, Robert Wylder, and Betty Wylder. "Songs of the Butte Miners." *Western Folklore* 9 (1950): 1–49.

Harrington, Michael. "Catholics in the Labor Movement: A Case History." *Labor History* 1 (1960): 231–63.

Hays, Samuel. "Politics and Social History: Toward a New Synthesis." In *Ordinary People and Everyday Life: Perspectives on the New Social History*, pp. 161–80. Edited by James B. Gardner and George R. Adams. Nashville: American Association for State and Local History, 1983.

Henretta, James. "The Study of Social Mobility: Ideological Assumptions and Cultural Bias." In *Labor History Reader*, pp. 28–41. Edited by Daniel Leab. Urbana: University of Illinois Press, 1985.

Hobsbawm, Eric. "The Aristocracy of Labour Reconsidered." In Hobsbawm, *Workers: Worlds of Labor*, pp. 227–51. New York: Pantheon, 1984.

———. "Artisans and Labour Aristocrats?" In Hobsbawm, *Workers: Worlds of Labor*, pp. 252–72. New York: Pantheon, 1984.

———. "Debating the Labor Aristocracy." In Hobsbawm, *Workers: Worlds of Labor*, pp. 214–26. New York: Pantheon, 1984.

Kammen, Michael. "Introduction: The Historian's Vocation and the State of the Discipline in the United States." In *The Past before Us: Contemporary Historical Writing in the United States*, pp. 19–46. Edited by Michael Kammen. Ithaca: Cornell University Press, 1980.

Karson, Marc. "Catholic Anti-Socialism." In *Failure of a Dream? Essays in the History of American Socialism*, pp. 82–102. Edited by John H. M. Laslett and Seymour Martin Lipset. Berkeley: University of California Press, 1984.

Kennedy, R. J. R. "Single or Triple Melting Pot?: Intermarriage Trends in New Haven, 1870–1940." *American Journal of Sociology* 49 (1944): 331–39.

Lees, Lynn, and John Modell. "The Irish Countryman Urbanized: A Comparative Perspective on the Famine Migration." *Journal of Urban History* 3 (1977): 391–407.

Mann, Ralph. "Frontier Opoportunity and the New Social History." *Pacific Historical Review* 53 (1984): 463–92.

McDonagh, Oliver. "Irish Famine Emigration to the U.S." *Perspectives in American History* 10 (1976): 357–446.

McGlynn, Terrence. "Flying the Red Flag in Butte: The Life and Times of Lewis Duncan, Butte's Socialist Mayor." Edited by David Walter. *Speculator: A Journal of Butte and Southwest Montana* 2 (1985): 3–8.

Miller, Kerby A. "Assimilation and Alienation: Irish Emigrants' Responses to Industrial America, 1871–1921." In *The Irish in America: Emigration, Assimilation, and Impact*, pp. 87–112. Edited by P. J. Drudy. Cambridge: Cambridge University Press, 1985.

Montgomery, David. "The Irish and the American Labor Movement." In *America and Ireland, 1776–1976: The American Identity and the Irish Connection*, pp. 205–18. Edited by David Doyle and Owen Dudley Edwards. Westport, Conn.: Greenwood, 1980.

Myers, Rex. "Vigilante Numbers: A Reexamination." *Montana: The Magazine of Western History* 24 (1974): 67–70.

O'Grada, Cormac. "Irish Emigration to the United States in the 19th Century." In *America and Ireland, 1776–1976: The American Identity and the Irish Connection*, pp. 93–104. Edited by David Doyle and Owen Dudley Edwards. Westport, Conn.: Greenwood, 1980.

O'Neill, Daniel P. "The Development of an American Priesthood: Archbishop John Ireland and the St. Paul Diocesan Clergy, 1884–1918." *Journal of American Ethnic History* 4 (1985): 33–53.

Prodgers, Jeanette. "Father Jeremiah J. Callahan: Butte's First Irish Priest, 1898–1906." *Montana: The Magazine of Western History* 34 (1984): 42–49.

Rabinowitz, Howard. "Race, Ethnicity and Cultural Pluralism in American History." In *Ordinary People and Everyday Life: Perspectives in the New Social History*, pp. 23–50. Edited by James B. Gardner and George R. Adams. Nashville: American Association for State and Local History, 1983.

Scheper-Hughes, Nancy. "Inheritance of the Meek: Land, Labor, and Love in Western Ireland." *Marxist Perspectives* 4 (1979): 46–76.

Spitzer, Alan. "The Historical Problem of Generations." *American Historical Review* 78 (1973): 1353–85.

Stephenson, Charles. "A Gathering of Strangers? Mobility, Social Structures, and Political Participation in the Formation of 19th Century Workingclass Culture." In *American Workingclass Culture: Explorations in American Labor and Social History*, pp. 31–60. Edited by Milton Cantor. Westport, Conn.: Greenwood, 1979.

Suggs, George. "Catalyst for Change: The Western Federation of Miners, 1893–1903." *Colorado Magazine* 45 (1968): 322–39.

———. "Religion and Labor in the Rocky Mountain West: Bishop Nicholas C. Matz and the Western Federation of Miners." *Labor History* 11 (1970): 190–206.

Thernstrom, Stephan. "Socialism and Social Mobility." In *Failure of a Dream? Essays in the History of American Socialism*, pp. 408–51. With "Comment" by Seymour Martin Lipset and "Reply" by Thernstrom. Edited by John H. M. Laslett and Seymour Martin Lipset. Berkeley: University of California Press, 1984.

———. "Working Class Mobility in Industrial America." *Society for the Study of Labor History*, Bulletin #17 (1968).

Thernstrom, Stephan, and Peter Knights. "Men in Motion: Some Data and Speculations on Urban Population Mobility in 19th Century America." *Journal of Interdisciplinary History* 1 (1970): 7–35.

Toole, K. Ross. "The Genesis of the Clark-Daly Feud." *Montana Magazine of History* 1 (1951): 21–33.

Vecoli, Rudolph. "Comment." In *Failure of a Dream? Essays in the History of American Socialism*, pp. 269–84. Edited by John H. M. Laslett and Seymour Martin Lipset. Berkeley: University of California Press, 1984.

Vedder, Richard, and Lowell E. Gallaway. "The Geographical Distribution of British and Irish Emigrants to the United States After 1800." *Scottish Journal of Political Economy* 19 (1972): 19–35.

Walsh, James. "The Irish in the New America: 'Way Out West.' " In *America and Ireland, 1776–1976: The American Identity and the Irish Connection*, pp. 165–76. Edited by David Doyle and Owen Dudley Edwards. Westport, Conn.: Greenwood, 1980.

Weber, Michael, and Anthony Boardman. "Economic Growth and Occupational Mobility in 19th Century Urban America: A Reappraisal." *Journal of Social History* 11 (1977): 52–74.

Wilentz, Sean. "Industrializing America and the Irish: Towards the New Departure." *Labor History* 20 (1979): 579–95.

INTERVIEWS

Cunningham, Margaret. Apr. 24, 1980, tape recording. Butte Oral History Project, University of Montana.

Curtin, James. Apr. 8, 1980, tape recording. Butte Oral History Project, University of Montana.

Leary, Donald. Sept. 1, 1986. Interview by David M. Emmons. Notes in possession of author.

McCarthy, Robert. June 10, 1988. Interview by David M. Emmons. Notes in possession of author.

O'Dwyer, Riobard, N.T. Aug. 26, 1986. Interview by David Taylor. Notes in possession of author.

Oechsli, George. May 14, 1985. Interview by David M. Emmons. Notes in possession of author.

O'Sullivan, Fr. Sarsfield. Nov. 19, 1984. Interview by David M. Emmons. Notes in possession of author.

Powers, Maurice. Apr. 17, 1980, tape recording. Butte Oral History Project, University of Montana.

Quinn, Frank. Nov. 20, 1984. Interview by David M. Emmons. Notes in possession of author.

Shannon, Kevin. Apr. 19, 1974, tape recording. Butte Oral History Project. University of Montana.

DISSERTATIONS, THESES, AND UNPUBLISHED PAPERS

Blessing, Patrick J. "West among Strangers: Irish Migration to California, 1800 to 1880." 1977. Ph.D. dissertation, University of California at Los Angeles.

Brundage, David. "The Making of Workingclass Radicalism in the Mountain West: Denver, Colorado, 1880–1903." 1982. Ph.D. dissertation, University of California at Los Angeles.

Carroll, Bishop John. "Address to the AF of L." n.d. [1913?]. Typescript copy in Carroll Papers. Diocese of Helena Office, Helena, Mont.

——— . "The Catholic Church and the New World Democracy." 1912. Typescript copy in Carroll Papers. Diocese of Helena Office, Helena, Mont.

——— . "Diocesan Resolution against French Socialists, 16 Janvier, 1907." Typescript copy in Carroll Papers. Diocesan of Helena Office, Helena, Mont.

——— . "On the Occasion of the Silver Jubilee of the Parish of St. Lawrence O'Toole's." Mar. 17, 1922. In Bishop John Carroll Papers. Diocese of Helena Office, Helena, Mont.

——— . "Remarks at Dedication of Butte Central High School." Sept. 7, 1924. In Bishop John Carroll Papers. Diocese of Helena Office, Helena, Mont.

Carroll, J. P. "Ecclesiastical Jurisdiction and Statistics for the Catholic Church in Montana." Feb. 17, 1910. Typescript, in Bishop John Brondel Papers. Diocese of Helena Office, Helena, Mont.

Davies, Hywel. "Survey of Copper Labor Conditions in Montana." July 3, 1918. Typescript in Department of Labor, File 33/1703.

de Siere, Fr. Anthony. "History of St. Patricks." Ca. 1908. Handwritten, in St. Patrick's File. Diocese of Helena Office, Helena, Mont.

Dowling, Catherine. "Irish-American Nationalism, 1900–1916: Butte as a Case Study." 1982. M.A. thesis, University of Montana.

Foot, Forrest. "The Senatorial Aspirations of William A. Clark." 1941. Ph.D. dissertation, University of California, Berkeley.

Franchi, Rev. James. "History of the Catholic Schools of Butte." Ca. 1910. Typescript, St. Patrick's Parish File. Diocese of Helena Office, Helena, Montana.

Frisch, Paul. " 'Gibraltar of Unionism': The Development of Butte's Labor Movement, 1878–1900." Unpublished paper, copy in Butte/Silver Bow Archives.

——— . "Gibraltar of Unionism?" Organized Labor in Butte, 1878–1896. Unpublished paper, copy in Butte/Silver Bow Archives.

Glasser, Abraham. "The Butte Miners' Strike, 1917–1920." Typescript in D. J. Glasser File, Department of Justice, Record Group 60.

"History of St. Lawrence O'Toole Parish." 1941. Typescript, St. Lawrence O'Toole Parish File, Diocese of Helena Office, Helena, Mont.

"History of St. Mary's." 1941. Typescript, St. Mary's Parish File, Diocese of Helena Office, Helena, Mont.

Johnson, Charles S. "An Editor and A War: Will A. Campbell and the *Helena Independent*, 1914–1921." 1977. M.A. thesis, University of Montana.

MacPherson, James L. "Butte Miner's Union: An Analysis of Its Development and Economic Bargaining Position." 1949. M.A. thesis, University of Montana.

Milner, Clyde. "Inventing Montana: Pioneer Memoirs as Cultural History." Nov. 8, 1985. Paper delivered at the 12th Annual Montana History Conference, Helena, Mont.

O'Daly, Hugh. Life History of Hugh O'Daly. 1945. Typescript in possession of Professor Kerby Miller, University of Missouri, Columbia.

Palladino, L. B. "Origins of the Helena Diocese, Montana." June 18, 1912. Typescript, in Bishop John Brondel Papers. Diocese of Helena Office, Helena, Mont.

Rice-Fritz, Nancy. "The Montana Council of Defense." 1966. M.A. thesis, University of Montana.

Rodechko, James P. "Patrick Ford and His Search for America: A Case Study of Irish-American Journalism, 1870–1913." 1967. Ph.D. dissertation, University of Connecticut.

Smith, Norma. "The Rise and Fall of The Butte Miners' Union, 1878–1914." 1961. M.A. thesis, Montana State University.

Stegner, Page. "The Irish Scab." In "Protest Songs from the Butte Mines." Typescript copy in IWW Collection. Walter P. Reuther Library of Labor and Urban Affairs, Wayne State University.

Toole, K. Ross. "Marcus Daly: A Study of Business in Politics." 1948. M.A. thesis, University of Montana.

Wetzel, Kurt. "The Making of an American Radical: Bill Dunn in Butte." 1970. M.A. thesis, University of Montana.

Index

A Note on the Author

David M. Emmons is on the faculty of the Department of History at the University of Montana. He holds a Ph.D. from the University of Colorado, Boulder. His research efforts have focused on the related themes of immigration, ethnicity, and the culture of work. He is the author of *Garden in the Grasslands: The Boomer Literature of the Central Plains* (1971), as well as several articles on immigration and immigrant workers in the West.